LANGUAGE ARTS ACTIVITIES

Students listen to, chorus, and make meaning with McCord's "This Is My Rock"; listen to, chorus, make meaning with, and compare Hughes' dream poems; orally interpret Turner's "Dakota Dugout" and compare it to *Sarah, Plain and Tall*; listen to Van Leeuwen's *Going West* and compare it to *Sarah, Plain and Tall*; write letters using standard form; write responses in their literature journals—especially aesthetic responses that get at feelings; select responses written in either poetry or prose to revise for inclusion in a personal showcase portfolio; dramatize episodes from the novel; meet MacLachlan through autobiographical sketches.

ART ACTIVITIES

Students make meaning with the cover art; having completed the book, they create an original cover. Students use watercolor to paint the contrasting feelings of Chapters 1 and 3; relate the use of color in the story to the mood of the story; make a finger painting of the storm in Chapter 8. Students study Van Gogh's "Sunflower" to identify the style; then use that style to paint other flowers mentioned in the novel.

MUSIC ACTIVITIES

Students listen to each seasonal component of Antonio Vivaldi's *Four Seasons:* "Winter" in conjunction with the first two chapters, "Spring" in reference to the third and fourth chapters, "Summer" in conjunction with the last chapters. They sing "Sumer Is Icumen In." (See Chapter 6 of *Communication in Action* for the full song.) They listen to, sing, and talk about the meaning of "The Impossible Dream" from *Man of La Mancha* as it relates to the core novel. They visualize the sea as they listen to Debussy's "La Mer."

COMMUNICATION IN ACTION

COMMUNICATION IN ACTION:
Teaching the Language Arts

DOROTHY GRANT HENNINGS
Kean College of New Jersey

Houghton Mifflin Company   **Boston**   **Toronto**
Geneva, Illinois   Palo Alto   Princeton, New Jersey

To George, who continues to encourage, help, and care

SENIOR SPONSORING EDITOR:	Loretta Wolozin
DEVELOPMENT EDITOR:	Susan Yanchus
SENIOR PROJECT EDITOR:	Rosemary Winfield
PRODUCTION/DESIGN COORDINATOR:	Maureen Bisso
SENIOR MANUFACTURING COORDINATOR:	Priscilla Bailey
MARKETING MANAGER:	Rebecca Dudley

Printed in the U.S.A.

Library of Congress Catalog Card Number: 93-78674

ISBN: 0-395-66856-5

Cover design: Carol Rose; cover image: Mike Mazzaschi/The Stock Market

Part opener art:

Preface	Phoebe Katz and Micki Benjamin
Part One	Chenelle Fraser and Micki Benjamin
Part Two	Ari Steinberg and Micki Benjamin
Part Three	Jacquelyn Sawyer and Micki Benjamin
Part Four	Elizabeth Kushner and Micki Benjamin
Coda	Arian Phillips and Micki Benjamin

Acknowledgment is made to the following authors and publishers for permission to reprint selections from copyrighted material:

"A Goblin" by Rose Fyleman from *Picture Rhymes from Foreign Lands,* by Rose Fyleman. Copyright © 1935. Reprinted by permission of Basil Blackwell Publisher.

Alphabet and number guide from *D'Nealian® Handwriting* by Donald Neal Thurber, Copyright © 1987 by Scott, Foresman and Company. Reprinted by permission.

"Beans, Beans, Beans," from *Hooray for Chocolate* by Lucia and James Hymes, Junior. Copyright © 1964 by Addison-Wesley Publishing Company, Inc., Reading, MA. Reprinted by permission of the publisher.

Definition of "canopy" from *Webster's II Riverside Beginning Dictionary.* Copyright © 1984 by the Riverside Publishing Company. Reprinted by permission of the publisher.

"Dreams" from *The Dream Keeper and Other Poems* by Langston Hughes. Copyright © 1932 by Alfred A. Knopf, Inc. and renewed 1960 by Langston Hughes. Reprinted by permission of the publisher. "City" from *The Langston Hughes Reader* by Langston Hughes. Copyright © 1958 by Langston Hughes. Copyright renewed 1986 by George Houston Bass. Reprinted by permission of Harold Ober Associates Incorporated.

Figure from "Sara's Story" by Anne Dyson in *Language Arts,* Vol. 58, No. 7, October 1981. Reprinted by permission of NCTE and the author.

Figures from Roger A. McCaid in Perspectives on Writing in Grades 1–8, Shirley Haley-James, ed. Reprinted by permission of NCTE.

Flip charts copyright © 1981 by Zaner-Bloser, Inc. Paper position graphics from *Creative Growth in Handwriting.* Copyright © 1975, 1978 by Zaner-Bloser, Columbus, OH. Reproduced by permission of the publisher.

Handwriting position charts from *Palmer Method, Cursive Writing, Grade 6,* teacher's edition, © 1976. Reprinted with permission of the publisher.

"Helping" from *Where the Sidewalk Ends* by Shel Silverstein. Copyright © 1974 by Evil Eye Music Inc. Reprinted by permission of HarperCollins Publishers.

"The Hippopotamus" from *Verses from 1929 On* by Ogden Nash. Copyright © 1935 by the Curtis Publishing Company. Copyright © 1959 by Ogden Nash. First appeared in the Saturday Evening Post. Reprinted by permission of Little, Brown and Company and the Curtis Publishing Company.

"How to Make a Hardcover Book" and "The Bridge They Said Couldn't Be Built" from *InConcert* by the Riverside Publishing Company. Copyright © 1989. Reprinted by permission of the publisher.

"Song of the Train" from *One at a Time* by David McCord. Copyright © 1952 by David McCord. By permission of Little, Brown and Company.

123456789-DH-96 95 94 93

Brief Contents

WRITTEN COMMUNICATION IN ACTION

Contents

APPENDICES

Charector Traits by Phoebe R. Katz

Addie

Braggert - "Chicken."

Careful - She put on a combination of shirts carfully.

caring-brave-"Wait a minute, I just want to get a good look at this horse."

artistic-"The point is to make it look like fall."

Carla Mae

afraid-"If he comes out with a gun you can forget the darn catails, I'll be running so fast you won't see me!"

bossy- "I want more bittersweet in this one."

Addie
Braggert
Carful
Caring
Brave
Artistic

Carla Mae
Afraid
Bossy

Phoebe identified the traits of two characters in her journal entry on _The Thanksgiving Treasure_.
(courtesy of Phoebe Katz and Micki Benjamin)

Preface

COMMUNICATION IN ACTION
Teaching the Language Arts

Audience and Purpose

I have written *Communication in Action: Teaching the Language Arts,* Fifth Edition, to provide teachers and prospective teachers in language arts or combined language arts and reading courses with the knowledge base and practical ideas they need to plan and implement a language arts program in which children are actively involved in thinking and communicating. Linguists explain that the purpose of human language is thought and communication: People use language to develop and share their ideas. Because language, communication, and thought are inextricably bound, I believe that language arts programs must heighten children's ability to use and interpret language, and children must be fully involved in thinking, speaking, listening, writing, and reading. I believe, too, that it is through natural and meaningful interaction with others and with written text, that young students refine their ability to use language to communicate, build their vocabulary, learn to formulate ideas, and develop understanding of the power and limitations of language.

My intent in *Communication in Action,* Fifth Edition, is to describe this kind of approach to the language arts. It is an approach that integrates the language arts—speaking, listening, reading, and writing—into the total curriculum and develops communication skills through meaning-filled interaction as children enjoy literature, are involved in cross-curricular studies, experience the world around them, and play creatively with language. In this natural, meaning-based approach, children talk and write about a myriad of thoughts read and heard. They read stories, poems, and expository pieces, including newspapers and magazines. They listen to and/or view live performances, television productions, films, audio and video tapes, recordings of fine music, and pictures, including great works of art. They use computers. They share their findings by dramatizing, telling, and showing. They contemplate and talk before writing. They collaborate as they compose, revise, and edit. They write and rewrite independently and celebrate by sharing what they have written.

In short, *Communication in Action: Teaching the Language Arts,* Fifth Edition, presents a design for the language arts that is based on my belief in the

- ✦ Integration of thinking, listening, speaking, writing, and reading into communication-centered experiences through which children learn to think and communicate naturally.
- ✦ Organization of language activities around the finest of literature, meaningful content from the social and natural sciences, direct experiences with the world around, and experiences with language itself. Within this framework, there must be sufficient attention to the development of basic communication skills and understandings.
- ✦ Development of the classroom as a community of learners who interact in large groups, teacher-guided instructional groups, and collaborative teams, and who grow in literacy through personalized reading and writing.
- ✦ Organization of learning activities into ongoing literature-based and cross-curricular units of instruction that enable young learners to think critically and creatively.

These beliefs of mine arise out of formal research and investigations by teacher-researchers who are actively involved in language experiences with children.

Revisions in the Fifth Edition

The fifth edition of *Communication in Action: Teaching the Language Arts* continues the emphasis on a natural, integrated language arts that draws heavily upon literature. In line with this emphasis, there is new material on reflecting on literature by writing in literature response journals and on teaching grammar through reading and writing.

In addition, this edition reflects the changes in the dynamic field of language arts. It provides:

- ✦ a reorganization of the parts of the book to highlight in Part Two the knowledge base that undergirds language arts instruction. This base includes knowledge about young learners and their needs, about the language and the way it is learned, and about children's literature.
- ✦ a heightened emphasis on a meaning-based language arts and on unit planning, especially the planning of literature-based units and thematic, cross-curricular units. Chapter 1 contains a description of unit planning and examples of a thematic literature unit and a unit focusing on a chapter book. Chapter 2 includes an example of a thematic, cross-curricular unit in which listening, speaking, reading, and writing are integral components. The end papers supply further examples of unit plans—examples after which readers can model units they design. Chapter 4 describes one teacher's experiences as she attempted a literature unit for the first time. The part-opening illustrations are samples of literature-based unit writing. Chapter 12 describes handwriting activity as a part of unit study. The vignettes in many chapters describe lessons within larger units of study.

◆ greater coverage of ongoing, natural assessment. Chapter 2 provides an overview of strategies for continuing assessment of student growth. Chapter 10 provides new and detailed information on portfolio assessment, and there are revised checklists in Chapters 5 and 7 for assessing listening and oral language ability.

◆ increased emphasis on collaborative learning. A detailed rationale for using collaborative team activity appears in Chapter 2, and vignettes have been revised to clarify this approach as today's teachers are using it.

◆ heightened attention to diversity and multiculturalism. Chapter 2 introduces the diversity that exists within elementary classrooms, and throughout the text the reader visits classrooms in which children from diverse language and cultural backgrounds are learning together. Chapter 2 also provides a new Forum that focuses on multiculturalism.

◆ added treatment of behavioral concerns. Chapter 2 includes a new section on children with behavioral impairments because beginning teachers must know ways to organize the classroom to minimize behavior problems if all children are to emerge as successful language users.

◆ greater attention to critical thinking. I have revised the section on critical thinking in Chapter 8 and renamed the chapter to reflect the importance of critical thinking in the language arts. I have also updated the material on critical listening in Chapter 5, on critical thinking in Chapter 7, and on critical reading in Chapter 13.

◆ highlighted two Forums as "The Teacher as Researcher"—one at the end of Chapter 4 and one at the end of Chapter 12—to reflect today's interest in the teacher as an investigator of teaching.

◆ new attention to such specific topics as individualized spelling, interactive-constructive reading, literature response groups, Readers' Theatre, puppets, Reading Recovery, discourse synthesis, and poems for two voices.

Organization

Communication in Action, Fifth Edition, has four parts. Part One develops a philosophy of teaching the language arts. It describes a dynamic language arts program in which reading and writing develop naturally through meaningful interaction. It sets forth what—based on current theory and research—I believe is important in helping children become well-spoken, literate human beings.

Part Two sets forth a knowledge base for language arts instruction. Chapter 2 describes the characteristics of elementary school children and explains how to meet the needs of children who vary greatly in behavior, language background, cultural background, ability, sensory perceptions, and speech. Chapter 3 presents basic concepts about the nature of language and language learning. Chapter 4 surveys children's literature, explaining the elements of fine literature and offering ideas for involving children in stories.

The next nine chapters form Parts Three and Four—Oral Communication in Action and Written Communication in Action. Filled with detailed anecdotal descriptions of teaching and sketches of activities and lessons, each chapter focuses on a fundamental area within the language arts: listening; creative oral expression (sharing stories and poems); functional oral expression (conversing and reporting); experiencing and critical thinking; idea making and writing; writing processes; language usage and grammar; spelling, handwriting, and dictionary use in writing; and reading. Through these chapters readers discover how to bring communication into action in elementary classrooms.

Features

Communication in Action, Fifth Edition, has pedagogical features designed to make the material as accessible and relevant as possible:

Reflecting-Before-Reading Questions

Because I believe that readers should activate what they know before reading, each chapter opens with a series of questions upon which readers reflect before beginning the chapter. The questions are set in the margin next to the opening paragraphs of the chapter. Around an anticipatory web in their learning logs, readers can respond by jotting ideas that come to mind as they think about the Reflecting-Before-Reading Questions and as they preview the chapter. Reflecting-Before-Reading Questions are a feature new to the fifth edition of *Communication in Action.*

Teaching-in-Action Vignettes

As in all editions starting in 1978, each chapter begins with a sketch of a classroom teaching episode. These sketches provide a view of what dynamic language arts teaching is like—from the teacher's vantage point. The vignettes model how successful teachers organize lessons and units so that students grow in ability to think and communicate. They demonstrate the diversity in background, ability, and interests that characterizes elementary children.

Marginal Notes

To guide and supplement reading, *Communication in Action* provides three kinds of marginal notes. *Goal notes,* the briefest of these, are in bold type next to anecdotal descriptions of lessons and state the purpose, or learning objective. *Instructional notes,* in regular type, present materials to use in designing activities similar to those described in the text: children's books, films, word lists, and examples. They also supply cautions, hints, and instructional cues. *Reference notes,* also in regular type, suggest books and articles for professional reading. These sources amplify ideas discussed at that point in the text.

Forums

In the Forums, which appear once or twice in each chapter, language arts authorities speak about goals, approaches to teaching, and the theoretical bases of language arts practices. At times, too, Forums offer a review of relevant research. At the end of a Forum are "Questions to Consider" designed to help the reader correlate the commentary in a Forum with points stressed in the chapter or an element of teaching modeled in a Teaching-in-Action Vignette.

The Teacher-as-Researcher

Twice within special Forum sections—one in Chapter 4 and one in Chapter 12—classroom teachers speak directly to the reader about action research they are conducting in their classes. They explain how they are trying new practices with their students and what they are learning from their classroom research. The purpose of these two Forums is to give readers an idea of what they can do to make their own discoveries about teaching.

Activities for Applying Ideas

To guide the reader in exploring and trying ideas, sections of *Communication in Action,* Fifth Edition, conclude with a list of activities that build and refine teaching skills. Because the teacher in action must design lessons that meet the interests and abilities of diverse groups of learners, these activities provide opportunities for teachers and prospective teachers to apply and modify suggestions from the text in their classrooms, internships, or field experiences.

Instructor's Resource Manual with Test Items and Teaching Masters

Accompanying the text is a comprehensive, updated instructor's resource manual that provides:

+ suggestions for teaching college courses in language arts and reading methodology, including questions to use in analyzing and talking about the Teaching-in-Action Vignettes and the Forums;
+ additional reading lists;
+ course syllabi;
+ chapter, midterm, and final examinations including both multiple-choice and discussion-type questions;

- ideas for portfolio compilation in language arts methods courses, including a checklist of teaching behaviors through which students can assess their development as teachers of the language arts;
- more than ninety teaching masters that can be made into transparencies for projection or can be duplicated for distribution to students.

Instructors who have not received a copy of the guide can request one from the publisher.

An Invitation to the Dance

Readers familiar with the previous editions of *Communication in Action* will recognize the continuing influence of Lewis Carroll on this edition. Although *Alice's Adventures in Wonderland* is a children's classic, Carroll has much to say to the adult, especially the adult involved in language arts instruction. Alice reminds the teacher of the importance of wonderland for children, the importance of

> *Dreaming as the days go by,*
> *Dreaming as the summers die:*
>
> *Ever drifting down the stream—*
> *Lingering in the golden gleam. . . .*

Alice reminds the teacher also of the wonderland of words that surrounds children, a wonderland where Alice can innocently ask, "Why did you call him Tortoise if he wasn't one?" and the Mock Turtle can emphatically reply, "We called him Tortoise because he taught us." The sounds and meanings of words dance through *Alice's Adventures in Wonderland*. Lewis Carroll knew all about word magic. He played with onomatopoeia, portmanteaus, the structure of language, puns, and word sounds, making the adult reader smile at the marvelously creative vehicle that language is. It is through active participation in that language and in the communication process that children grow in ability to speak, write, listen, read, and think about all manner of ideas. Welcome to that wonderland. Welcome to the dance.

Acknowledgments

I wish to express my appreciation to the colleagues and reviewers who helped me conceptualize my ideas as the manuscript evolved. I send special thanks to my friend Dr. Elizabeth Stimson of Bowling Green University. Bess provided helpful suggestions as this author began to think about directions for the fifth edition. I say "Thank you" also to my friends at Kean College who continue to support *Communication in Action:* Dr. Lillian Putnam with whom I have had many stimulating discussions about what is important in language learning and Dr. Joan Kastner who in informal discussions made me more aware of the importance of units in language arts teaching. I also thank the four educators who reviewed the fourth edition and the first draft of the fifth:

Dr. Anita Baker	Baylor University
Dr. Edward Plank	Millersville University
Dr. Mary Howard	Central State University (Ohio)
Dr. Allan Cook	Idaho State University

This edition would have been far different if these reviewers had not approached their task with the thoughtful thoroughness that they did.

In a similar vein, I would like to thank Ms. Karen Fine, a librarian in the Warren, New Jersey, Public Library who helped me locate recent children's books. Helpful too, was Tamara Avdzej of the Kean College of New Jersey Library who ordered the latest language arts and reading references and put them aside for me.

I am also indebted to the many exceptional teachers who shared ideas with me and tried activities in their classrooms. Maureen Stawasz, Deejay Schwartz, and Lorraine Wilkening are real teachers who allowed me to see them in action and to use the ideas they are developing in their classrooms as teacher-researchers. Others like Jennifer Chou are composites of real teachers. For example, Ms. Chou is really Bernice Chin—an exceptional teacher—with a little bit of another teacher added to her. Others such as Louise Patterson and Jennifer Krumm shared stories and art produced by their students. The journal entries that serve as part openers came from Micki Benjamin's third grade class in South Orange-Maplewood, New Jersey. The students made the entries during a literature unit that revolved around *The Thanksgiving Treasure* by Gail Rock (Knopf, 1974).

I wish to express my appreciation to the fine team from Houghton Mifflin Company who guided *Communication in Action,* Fifth Edition, from conception, through manuscript, and into final book form. I particularly thank Susan Yanchus, who provided positive encouragement and splendid ideas that strengthened the manuscript and the book. I also thank Lisa Mafrici, editorial assistant, who contributed ideas to the *Instructor's Resource Manual;* Rosemary Winfield, senior project editor, who skillfully guided the production of the book; and Bruce Carson, who handled the art. I send my special thanks to Loretta Wolozin, sponsoring editor at Houghton Mifflin Company, who put together this exceptional team and who has continued to support *Communication in Action* from one edition to the next. This was a group of professionals with whom it was a delight to work.

As always, I send loving thanks to my husband George, who commented on successive drafts, edited copy, checked galleys, located references, and offered both encouragement and constructive criticism. How fortunate I am to have his caring support.

Dorothy Grant Hennings
Warren, New Jersey

COMMUNICATION IN ACTION

Chenelle Fraser
Gr.3 Rm.22
Jefferson
School

Thanksgiving treasure
by Gail Rock

My Favorite Event

My best event is when Addie put mash
potados in Henry's new
jocket.

coat
hanger

Henry
Jaket

Henry

Addie

Responding in her journal to Gail Rock's *The Thanksgiving Treasure*, Chenelle drew and wrote about her favorite part (courtesy of Chenelle Fraser and Micki Benjamin).

A PHILOSOPHY FOR TEACHING THE LANGUAGE ARTS

"Cheshire Puss . . . would you tell me please, which way I ought to go from here?"
   "That depends a great deal on where you want to go to. . . . "

—Lewis Carroll, *Alice's Adventures in Wonderland*

Where do we want to go through the language arts? What do we hope children will learn? In answering these questions, we discover the answer to Alice's question—which way ought we to go from here—a question that gets at our basic beliefs about teaching the language arts.

Part One sets forth four fundamental beliefs about teaching the language arts: a belief in a natural, integrated approach, a belief in a meaning-based approach, a belief in building the classroom as a social community of learners, and a belief in planning ongoing units of instruction that require children to participate actively in listening, speaking, reading, and writing.

As you read about these beliefs, ask yourself: In what direction do I want to go in teaching the language arts? What do I believe is important? Your beliefs need not mirror those in the text. In thinking through what you believe and by perhaps writing down your beliefs, you will be building your philosophy for teaching the language arts.

CHAPTER 1

Teaching for Communication

A Natural Approach to the Language Arts

BEFORE reading the chapter, read the title, the headings, and the end-of-chapter summary. Then answer the questions in the margin on this page.

Reflecting Before Reading

What is meant by a natural, integrated approach to language arts? a meaning-based approach?

What is involved in organizing a class as a social community?

Why and how does the teacher plan units and lessons?

TEACHING IN ACTION   Walking in the Wonderland of Literature and Language

Students in Karin Topping's first grade clustered around her on the big blue rug in the communication center of the classroom. "Boys and girls," Ms. Topping began, "Today I am going to share a picture storybook with you. However, as I read, I am not going to show you the pictures as I usually do. Instead, I want you to picture in your mind, step by step, what is happening in the story. The story is *Rosie's Walk*. It is written by Pat Hutchins."

Following her introduction, Karin Topping read the simple lines of *Rosie's Walk*. When finished, she asked the first-graders to retell the story in sequence. The children found this difficult. They recalled that Rosie had gone for a walk and had returned home for supper, but they were uncertain about whether she had traveled over, around, or by the haystack and whether she had done this before or after walking past the mill.

In response to the children's uncertainty, Ms. Topping asked them to take out pencils and their literature response journals. "Let's see if we can keep track of the story action by making a picture of each event in order. Listen as I reread the story."

Listening for story sequence

Karin Topping reread the first line of the story: "Rosie the hen went for a walk. . . ." Stopping there, she asked, "What picture can we draw in our

Mapping key story happenings

response journals to show what these story words tell us and who the main character is?" One artistically talented child suggested that they draw a hen; the others agreed.

Ms. Topping pressed on, "What can we do to make our picture show that Rosie was walking?" Another child volunteered that they could draw two pictures of Rosie and connect them with a dotted line with an arrow at the end. The other students liked this idea. To help them with their drawing, Ms. Topping suggested that they place their first picture of Rosie on the left side of a page in their journals and the second one a bit to the right and slightly above the first. She demonstrated this by drawing two hens on chart paper posted on an easel and connecting the hens with a dotted line.

When the children had drawn their two pictures of Rosie, Ms. Topping returned to the book and read the next line, which tells where Rosie went first. Then she asked, "What can we draw to show this and help us remember the story action?" The first-graders decided to draw a yard with Rosie walking across it. Ms. Topping drew a yard and wrote the word *across* on her chart paper. Then she suggested that the students print that word in their journals next to their pictures of a yard.

Comprehending the meaning of relational words

After the children had drawn a picture to go with the first action of the story, Ms. Topping reread each line of the story, pausing after each reading to give them time to draw a sketch to go with it. She also asked the first-graders to choose what story words they might add to clarify the relationships described in the story. The children suggested the words *over, through,* and *past.* Ms. Topping added these words to her drawing on the easel as a model for those children who had trouble paying attention and those who had difficulty understanding because their first language was not English. When they reached the end of the story, and Rosie returned home in time for supper, the children and Ms. Topping drew a line back to the beginning to show this last action. (See Figure 1.1.)

Having completed their rough sketches, the first-graders independently refined and colored what Ms. Topping had begun to call their *storymaps.* As they polished their work, Ms. Topping circulated, stopping to ask individual children—who had diverse abilities and backgrounds—to tell her what was happening at different points in the story.

Thinking Critically and Creatively

Recalling story parts

The next day, the children shared their drawings. Using their storymaps as guides, or notes, they took turns recounting story actions. When they had retold the tale, Ms. Topping asked, "Did you like that story?" Without hesitating, the class answered with a unanimous *yes.*

Comprehending the need for conflict in a fully developed story; thinking critically

To encourage the children to think more critically, Ms. Topping replied, "You know, class, I did not really like the story as I shared it with you. There was something missing—something that good stories generally have. Think! Was anything missing in the story?" No one answered, so Ms. Topping told the youngsters to look closely as she displayed the pictures from a big book version. On the very first page, the children saw the fox hidden under the chicken coop, and they laughed as they saw all the problems the fox got into as it tried to catch

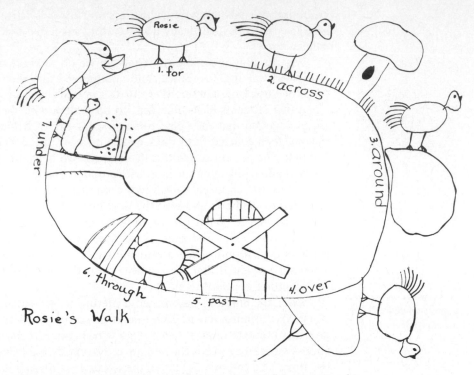

1. for
2. across
3. around
4. over
5. past
6. through
7. under

Rosie

Rosie's Walk

Figure 1.1 A Circular Storymap for *Rosie's Walk* by Pat Hutchins

Rosie. They agreed that the story was better with the fox in it. The fox added a problem and suspense—elements that many good stories have.

Then Ms. Topping guided the youngsters in creative, spontaneous role playing. "What do you think the fox was saying to himself as he looked out from under the coop at Rosie?" she asked.

The first-graders talked out as though they were the fox. "I want that chicken for supper," "She looks nice and tender," "I am really hungry," were some of the responses.

"What was Rosie saying to herself?" Ms. Topping continued.

"This is a nice day for a walk," "The sun is shining," "It isn't raining" were ideas offered for Rosie.

The children role-played each page of the story, talking out and creating "mind talk" for each character. In so doing, they were reflecting the different points of view of each character in the story as well as using language creatively. When they finished, the first-graders decided to add drawings of the fox to their storymaps; the fox was needed to add suspense to the story.

Creating Stories Orally

The next day, when Ms. Topping's first-graders gathered on the communication rug, they talked about the actions in *Rosie's Walk*. Prompted by their teacher's

Extending a story creatively

Comprehending point of view in story

Perceiving structure (circular) in a story

questions, the children analyzed the story and discovered that it ended where it began—at home—after the main character had had a series of adventures in the big world away from home. Ms. Topping explained that stories with this pattern are like circles. She drew a circle on the board, asked students to draw a circle in their literature response journals, and encouraged them to make large circles in the air with their hands to demonstrate how this story developed.

At that point, Ms. Topping introduced a puppet head of Egor the horse. She told them they were going to make up a story like *Rosie's Walk*, using Egor as the main character. To begin, she asked the children to decide whether Egor was sad or happy. They unanimously decided that Egor was sad; you could tell by the expression in his eyes.

Then she asked this series of questions: Where did Egor live? Why was he sad? If Egor were to go for a walk as Rosie did, where could he travel that would make him happy? As the children made suggestions (zoo, circus, Disney World, beach), Ms. Topping printed them on the board. Of all the suggestions, most of the children liked the idea of a story about Egor's going to a circus; there were lots of things to do there to make you happy.

Creating story sentences

Now Ms. Topping reminded the children of the first words in *Rosie's Walk* and asked them to think of a sentence about Egor to use in starting a similar circular trip-story about him. When one youngster proffered a sentence, she recorded it on large chart paper and asked for follow-up sentences to tell what Egor did at the circus and what happened at the end. She recorded the follow-up sentences in paragraph form on the chart paper and asked some students to come forward to insert periods at the ends of the sentences. The result was something like this:

Putting in punctuation to represent sentence ends

> **Egor Goes to the Circus**
>
> Egor the horse went to the circus. Egor saw clowns at the circus. Egor saw elephants. Egor saw lions. He bought a balloon. Egor came home and felt better.

Next, Ms. Topping asked the children to read the story as she moved her hand under the words. Then the children took turns reading and rereading the sentences.

Understanding story structure, or overall development

At this point, Ms. Topping noticed that some of the less mature first-graders were getting restless; the class had been talking for more than twenty minutes. She, therefore, asked the children to draw a map in their response journals to show the sequence of events in their Egor story and to connect the story events with a line to show that it—like *Rosie's Walk*—was a circular story that ended where it began.

Revising and Editing Together

The next day, Ms. Topping drew the children's attention to the story of Egor that they had written the day before. She had them read it aloud together, encouraging them to read in phrases and with rhythm.

That done, she asked the children to revise and edit their story. She did this by posing key questions:

✦ How did Egor feel at the beginning? (sad) Where can we add *sad* to our story? (before horse)

✦ Look at the sentences *Egor saw elephants* and *Egor saw lions.* How can we make one sentence from these two? (*Egor saw elephants and lions.*)

✦ What do you think Egor saw the clowns doing at the circus? (doing tricks)

✦ How can we add this idea to our second sentence? (*Egor saw some clowns doing tricks at the circus.*)

✦ From whom did Egor buy a balloon? (balloon man) What color balloon was it? (blue)

✦ How can we add these ideas to the sentence? (*Egor bought a blue balloon from the balloon man.*)

✦ What would be a good title for our story? Let's think of many possible ones. (*Egor, Egor the Horse, Egor's Walk, Egor Goes to the Circus*) Which title do we like best of all? (*Egor Goes to the Circus*)

As the children responded, Ms. Topping changed the chart so that they could see their revisions and read their combined and expanded sentences. Again she had the youngsters read the sentences aloud together, stressing the natural melody of the lines. Their revised story went like this:

Egor Goes to the Circus

Egor the (sad) horse went to the circus. He ~~Egor~~
saw clowns (doing tricks) at the circus. Egor saw elephants, (and)
~~Egor saw~~ lions. He bought a (blue) balloon, (from the balloon man) Egor
came home and felt better.

Later that day, Ms. Topping typed *Egor Goes to the Circus* into the classroom computer, using a word processing system that allows the computer to function as a typewriter with editing capabilities. She left the story on the monitor. The children could go to the monitor in pairs, with each child reading the story to his or her partner.

Listening, Role Playing, Writing, and Reading

Interpreting the structure of related stories

On successive days during communication time, Ms. Topping shared stories with a circular pattern similar to that in *Rosie's Walk: Three Ducks Went Wandering, Where the Wild Things Are, The Grey Lady and the Strawberry Snatcher,* and *The Camel Who Took a Walk.* In each case, the youngsters role-played the thoughts in the minds of the major characters and drew a storymap in their response journals to depict main events. In each case, too, they compared the story to *Rosie's Walk.*

Composing ideas on paper; see Chapter 9 for a discussion of beginning writing

In follow-up individual writing sessions, students wrote their own stories of leaving home to explore the world out there. The first-graders did the best they could with spelling and went back to add interesting details as they had done in writing together. Later, some read their original stories to a reading mate; others shared them during a class communication time; still others placed their stories in the reading corner for classmates to read.

Meeting the diverse needs of children

While the first-graders wrote their stories, Ms. Topping conferred one on one with four students. In conference, Ms. Topping listened as the youngsters told her about the stories they were drafting, helped with recording problems, and had students read aloud their favorite parts from books they were reading independently and from personal journal entries they had made that morning. At times, she also spoke quietly with the children about behavior problems that had occurred earlier in the day and about the children's personal concerns. Ms. Topping scheduled these conferences each day because in her multicultural classroom, the students had diverse language and social needs: Some were gifted learners already reading and writing with considerable facility, others were slower and needed much more support, and still others were learning English as a second language.

Evaluating stories

Similarly, in follow-up small-group sessions that Ms. Topping organized to meet special language-learning needs, students read more stories with a circular pattern of events. Again the youngsters drew storymaps depicting key actions. They drew lines to show the direction of story development. Finally, they made a critical decision: Of all the stories they had enjoyed in this literature-based unit, which was the best? The children unhesitatingly agreed that the best story was their own: *Egor Goes to the Circus!*

Developing Language Facility Through Content-Area Study

Building conceptual understanding and vocabulary

Even as Karin Topping was helping her first-graders to understand the structure of circular stories, she was also involving them in a study of melting and freezing as part of a science unit. Therefore, another afternoon found the class busily observing an ice cube balanced on a fork. This session began in the same way as the one with *Rosie's Walk*. The children described the ice cube—its shape, feel, and temperature. They talked about what it was doing—melting—and why it was melting. They drew pictures to show it melting. Later they held another

Teacher-student conferences are an integral part of an effective language arts program. Here a teacher confers with children about stories they are composing. (© 1993 Michael Zide)

Perceiving relationships between similar patterns of activity

cube in the sunshine to see whether it melted faster than one not placed in the warmth. They referred to pictures and captions in their science book to clarify their understanding. Later they filled some ice cube trays with water and put them in the freezer of the school refrigerator. They talked about what would happen to the water in the freezer. They compared putting the water in the cold freezer to putting the ice in the hot sunshine. With their teacher's guidance, they drew diagrams that showed the cycle of water turning to ice and ice melting back to water. They drew lines to connect the parts of the cycle as they had done in mapping a circular story.

Writing After Talking

Writing and editing expository prose

Because Karin Topping wanted her first-graders to learn how to write informational paragraphs as well as stories, she followed up with teacher-guided group writing. First, she asked the children to tell what they had done to the ice cube and what had happened to it. Then she asked them to reflect on why this had happened. As the children responded, Ms. Topping wrote the sentences on the chalkboard. When the students had dictated six sentences, they went back to revise, changing words and expanding ideas, guided by their teacher's probing questions. The resulting composition is shown here:

Ice and Water

We put an ice cube in the sun. It began
to drip. Then there was no ice cube. It melted.
It became water. The ice cube melted because
it got hot.

Reading for meaning

Ms. Topping entered the composition into the classroom computer and had the computer print publication copies for the youngsters. As soon as they received their copies, the children read them and put them into their science learning logs—notebooks that they kept for recording during unit study in science. As an extra project, some youngsters illustrated their reports and displayed them on the science bulletin board. The next day in the same manner, the youngsters cooperatively composed a report on melting and freezing.

Planning for and Teaching the Language Arts: Developing a Philosophy of Instruction

Why did Karin Topping organize her unit sequence as she did? What beliefs about language learning guided her approach? Following are four assumptions that are part of Karin Topping's philosophy of language arts instruction. These ideas determine in large measure how this teacher functions in planning for and teaching the language arts. You should think about these beliefs as you develop your own philosophy of instruction as it pertains to the language arts.

✦ *Belief 1.* *Children become more effective language users through natural social interaction in which they create and communicate meanings and actively use language in all its forms.* They learn through direct involvement in oral language, the thread that should run through all classroom activity from the earliest grades onward. Students should be actively involved in talking out ideas. They need to talk prior to, during, and after reading and writing. Through talk, children make connections between what they already know and what they are learning. They make connections between what they are reading and what they are writing. Speaking, listening, reading, and writing flow together as children work naturally with language and use language to anticipate and predict, raise and answer questions, sort and organize ideas, relate ideas to one another,

THE FORUM On a Whole-Language Approach to Teaching Children to Communicate

1. Stephen Kucer explains that "whole language . . . attempts to link classroom and real world activities. Because meaning generation is the focus of literacy use in the world, advocates of whole language have rightfully insisted that classrooms should reflect this fact. Thus, rather than teaching isolated skills with segmented and frequently meaning-stripped pieces of language, whole language curricula have tended to focus on the development of literacy strategies through student interaction with meaningful pieces of connected discourse" ("Authenticity as the Basis for Instruction," *Language Arts*, 68 [November 1991], 532).

2. The noted New Zealand educator Don Holdaway points out: "The most important generative idea is that of *wholeness* [in language learning]. Failure in the past has been associated with the isolation of parts by meaningless fragmentation—especially disastrous to language, which is an embodiment of whole meanings. Every linguistic process is informed by meaning. The strategies required to learn and master the 'skills' of language are dependent on the meanings which give them human sense and integrity" ("The Big Book Trend—A Discussion with Don Holdaway," *Language Arts*, 59 [November/December 1982], 821).

3. Kenneth Goodman urges teachers, "Keep language whole and involve children in using it functionally and purposefully to meet their own needs. . . . Invite pupils to use language. Get them to talk about things they need to understand. Show them it's all right to ask questions and listen to the answers, and then to react or ask more questions. Suggest that they write about what happens to them, so they can come to grips with their experiences and share them with others. Encourage them to read for information, to cope with the print that surrounds them everywhere, to enjoy a good story. This way, teachers can work with children in the natural direction of their growth" (*What's Whole in Whole Language?* [Portsmouth, N.H.: Heinemann, 1986], 7–8).

Questions to Think About

In what ways did Karin Topping—in the vignette that opens this chapter—encourage her students to use language through interaction "with meaningful pieces of connected discourse"? How did she maintain the "wholeness" of the language experience and avoid unnatural fragmentation? What do you think was her primary goal throughout the lesson series? Do you think her goal was valid? Why or why not?

evaluate ideas critically, and construct original ideas. This belief is at the core of a *natural, integrated language arts approach.* In this approach, children enjoy endless opportunities to use language to reflect on their experiences, make meaning with whole units of thought, and communicate actively.

An integrated language arts approach draws heavily on *whole-language* thinking. Whole-language advocates believe that children become literate through immersion in environments where print is everywhere. They argue that children become readers by listening to and reflecting on stories read to them, joining in the telling of stories, reading and responding critically to stories, and writing stories of their own. They believe that children become writers by actually writing and reading. In whole-language classrooms, emphasis is on children as meaning makers as they think critically and creatively together.

Read Robert Ruddell, "A Whole Language and Literature Perspective: Creating a Meaning Making Instructional Environment," *Language Arts*, 69 (December 1992), 612–620. Ruddell sets forth his beliefs and the beliefs of Brian Cambourne about how children become literate.

♦ *Belief 2.   Children become more effective language users by listening to, reading, and responding to literature; by communicating as they explore the content areas; by experiencing their world and responding verbally to it; and by playing actively with language.* This belief is at the core of a *meaning-based language arts approach.* In such an approach, children become literate through meaningful encounters with print rather than through discrete, skill-building exercises. In this approach, communication is part of every activity. Children make meaning with language as they study science, mathematics, history, music. They talk, write, listen, read, and think critically and creatively as they enjoy stories and poems. In short, in a meaning-based language arts program, communication is in action across the curriculum.

♦ *Belief 3.   Children become more effective language users when they function in classroom communities in which they interact and collaborate naturally with one another as well as think, write, and read independently.* Interaction in classrooms takes place as children function child to child, child to small group, and child to large group and collaborate with one another. It occurs as children interact in both teacher-guided and child-guided groups. Children interact as they read text, talk about it, and write in response to it. Independent activity is a natural follow-up. In classrooms, children must have opportunities to enjoy books that they have specially chosen, write down ideas that are uniquely their own, and share and celebrate what they have written. Accordingly, classrooms should be arenas for social interaction and collaboration in all its forms—large group, small group, one to one. Classrooms should foster personalized, independent activity in which children use their growing language facility to read, write, and think. This approach is especially vital in today's multicultural, mainstreamed classrooms that are home to children who are bilingual and bidialectical, who function above and below grade level, and who have social, emotional, physical, and perceptual problems that affect their learning.

A *multicultural* classroom is one in which children of diverse cultural backgrounds learn together. A *mainstreamed* classroom is one in which children with physical, visual, hearing, and speech impairments as well as gifted and slower students learn together. See Chapter 2 for more details.

♦ *Belief 4.   Children become more effective language users when their teacher has planned ongoing, cohesive blocks of instruction that enable them to function at their own level and pace, communicate actively with one another, make connections among ideas, and think critically and creatively.* To this end, a teacher must be dynamic in his or her planning, organizing ongoing literature-based, content-area, experiential, and language-focus units in which individual lessons flow into one another to meet the special needs of children with differing abilities, personalities, attention spans, and behavior patterns.

The remainder of this chapter elaborates on these beliefs: (1) the belief in a natural, integrated language arts approach that emphasizes communication; (2) the belief in a meaning-based language arts approach in which communication occurs across the curriculum; (3) the belief in organizing the classroom as a natural language-learning community that blends collaborative and personalized activity; and (4) the belief that a teacher should plan ongoing, cohesive units that encourage children to use language actively to communicate. As a whole, the next four sections present a philosophy of language arts instruction on which this book is founded. This philosophy makes communication central in the language arts. Through the language arts, children become more effective communicators—in short, more effective listeners, speakers, thinkers, writers, and readers. They do this through meaningful interaction that involves them naturally in language. *Communication in Action,* the title of this book, reflects this fundamental philosophy regarding the goal of language arts in elementary education.

An Integrated Language Arts Approach in Which Communication Is in Action

Belief 1. Children become more effective language users through natural social interaction in which they create and communicate meanings and actively use language in all its forms. To this end, classrooms should be organized so that oral language is the integrating thread within the curriculum, reading and writing blend as children read real books and communicate their ideas through writing, and children enjoy endless opportunities to use language to reflect on their experiences.

The Oral Language/Written Language Connection

Speaking and listening are channels through which most children first encounter language. Through social interaction, young children acquire the meanings assigned to word symbols, and they learn to use and interpret language for themselves.

In school, oral language involvement continues to be important as children expand and refine their communication skills and develop facility with the written language. Through talk, children learn to use language to think; through talk, they make connections between what they read and what they write. With oral language as the connecting thread, speaking, listening, reading, and writing flow into one another as children work naturally with language. Figure 1.2 depicts this natural flow among the language arts.

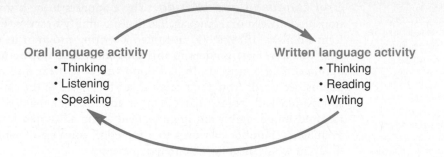

Oral language activity
- Thinking
- Listening
- Speaking

Written language activity
- Thinking
- Reading
- Writing

Figure 1.2 The Natural Flow among the Language Arts

Oral Language and Reading Researchers have investigated the relationships between oral language facility and reading. In a classic study tracing the language development of 338 kindergartners over a number of years, Walter Loban (1963, 1976) found a positive correlation among speaking, listening, reading, and writing abilities. Youngsters with low oral ability tended to have little ability to read and write. As David Dickinson (1987) explains, "Oral language provides a base required for reading to occur; that is, reading depends on oral language processing capacities." In this respect, ability to handle the written language initially is dependent on knowledge of oral language. Only later, as children develop as written language users, does their ability to use written language become less dependent on oral language facility (Flood and Lapp, 1987).

This relationship can be seen by considering aspects common to listening and reading. As Robert Shafer (1974) explains, the task of the reader is similar to that of the listener: Both must go beneath the surface of a message to interpret underlying sentence structure and assign meaning. Furthermore, both the listener and the reader must assign meaning to words. Most of the words that children understand come through listening and speaking. The more varied contacts children have with spoken words, the more meaning they bring to words as they read and write. As David Pearson and Linda Fielding (1982) explain, "language in all its facets is an integrated phenomenon. Effects in one of its sub-systems will show up in other sub-systems. There appears to be a language comprehension system, of which reading and listening are but complementary facets."

One of these complementary facets is the sound of language (Schreiber, 1980). Listeners use such features of oral language as pitch, pauses, and tone to generate meaning in reference to what they hear. Schreiber proposes that good readers read the "rhythms and melodies" of speech into texts—rhythms and melodies that are not fully communicated on paper, although punctuation marks supply some limited clues. Schreiber further proposes that one way to help children become better readers is to have them follow a written text as a teacher reads it orally. Reading in this way, children use their stronger listening skills to make meaning with print; at the same time, they learn that the rhythms of speech are characteristic of written language as well.

See also Ruth Strickland's classic study of the language growth of 575 elementary school students ("The Language of Elementary School Children," *Indiana University Bulletin of School of Education,* 38 [July 1962], 1–131). The study indicates that oral language facility bears a strong and positive relationship to overall academic achievement.

Read Russell Stauffer,
"The Language Experience
Approach to Reading Instruction for Deaf and Hearing
Impaired Children,"
The Reading Teacher, 33
(October 1979), 21–24, for a
discussion of the language
experience approach.
Language experience advo-
cates believe that children can
best learn to read by reading
content they have written or
have dictated to a teacher,
who writes it down.

Oral Language and Writing   There appears to be a similar positive relationship between oral language facility and ability to write. Russell Stauffer and
John Pikulski (1974, 1979) instituted a writing program in which oral expression was key. First-graders in this program based on the *language experience
approach* had almost unlimited opportunity to hear and dictate stories and
poems, see words from their original stories posted in the classroom, and reread
stories they had created. Later Stauffer and Pikulski analyzed the children's stories and found significant improvement along all dimensions of oral language
evaluated—number of words to a sentence, number of sentences, number of
different words, number of different pronouns.

Oral Language and Thinking   Thought and oral language are similarly
linked. According to Vygotsky (1962), thought and speech have different roots.
Up to a certain point in a child's development, thought and speech follow different lines and are essentially independent. But at a certain moment at about
age two, the lines of development meet. The child "makes the greatest discovery
of his life"—that "each thing has its name." As Vygotsky explains, "This crucial
instant, when speech begins to serve intellect and thoughts begin to be spoken,
is indicated by two unmistakable objective symptoms: (1) the child's sudden,
active curiosity about words, his question about every new thing, 'What is this?';
and (2) the resulting rapid, saccadic increases in his vocabulary." From this
point, "thought becomes verbal and speech rational."

David Olson (1983) explains the relationship between thought and language in this way: "Thought is simply speech which has linguistic form but isn't
said. In other words, a thought is an utterance which remains unspoken. That's
how thought is controlled. You engage in a dialogue with imaginary others or
with yourself. The structure of words and expressions gives thought an orderly
appearance."

Because thought is essentially verbal, not only does thinking affect language
production but, conversely, language affects thinking. Because language and
thinking are parts of the same whole, classroom oral language activity builds
both language facility and thinking ability. Specifically, as children orally sum
up, predict, hypothesize, invent, and judge, they refine their ability to think critically and creatively.

Because oral language facility is a factor in children's ability to read, write,
and think, oral interaction should occupy a significant portion of a
child's school day. By stressing oral language, elementary teachers build a foundation for other curricular experiences—for word power, reading, writing,
spelling, and study of grammar and usage patterns, as well as for study of the
content areas.

The Reading/Writing Connection

To say that oral interaction should occupy a significant portion of the school
day is not to downplay the importance of written language activity. Children

learn language through reading *and* writing. Educators today believe that children should not wait to read or write until they have strong control over oral language; they propose that children should not wait to write until they have learned to read. From their earliest years, children should be involved in reading and writing in a natural way—they should read and write because they need and want to know and communicate.

In the past, some educators have viewed reading and writing as opposite and distinctive processes: They have defined reading as receiving meaning and writing as expressing meaning. Today educators tend to view reading and writing as parts of one whole (see Squire, 1983; Kucer and Rhodes, 1986; Flood and Lapp, 1986; Harp, 1987). Readers draw on their prior knowledge of the world, of language, and of literature to construct meaning just as writers do. As Rosenblatt (1978) explains, readers create their own unique texts based on what the author has written and on what they bring to the reading. Just as with writing, reading is "meaning making" (Wells, 1986); it is active thinking that involves predicting, sorting, relating, questioning, generalizing, creating, and critically evaluating.

Robert Tierney and F. David Pearson (1983) propose that reading is actually composing. When composing text, readers plan by setting goals before reading and mobilizing the data they already have on the topic. They draft ideas as they read. They adjust their stance toward the topic and revise their understanding of the content as they proceed. They monitor their progress, rereading as the occasion demands. All of these aspects of composing while reading are aspects of composing while writing.

Bill Harp (1987) further explains the relationships between reading and writing: "The act of composing reinforces concepts important to reading comprehension." In the same way, research tells us that the act of reading leads to heightened skill in writing: Avid readers tend to be good writers. Concepts that are central to reading, such as "word, sentence, topic sentence, main idea, supporting details, sequence, and plot," are central to writing as well.

Because reading and writing are so inextricably bound, they must be viewed as one entity in language arts programs. Children read to write; they write to read. Children learn to write even as they begin to read; they learn to read even as they begin to write.

A Meaning-Based Language Arts Approach in Which Children Communicate Across the Curriculum

Belief 2. Children become more effective language users by listening to, reading, and responding to literature; by communicating as they explore the content areas; by experiencing their world and responding verbally to it; and by playing actively with language. This is a meaning-based approach to language arts in which

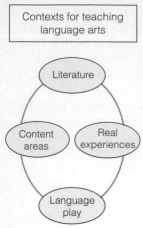

Contexts for teaching
language arts

Literature

Content
areas

Real
experiences

Language
play

children learn to listen, speak, think, read, and write through encounters with meaningful content.

A Literature-Based Language Arts

Literature is a natural base for language experiences. As Karin Topping has shown us, literature in which fine writers have handled words artfully is marvelous content for stimulating language use.

From Literature into Speaking and Listening   A teacher can structure a variety of oral language experiences around a series of literary selections. Before reading or listening, children can talk about what they already know relevant to the topic; based on an analysis of the title and the cover art, they can predict what a story is about. After reading or listening to a story, they can talk about it, interpreting feelings and motives. Reading selections in chorus, they can use their voices to signal meanings communicated through words and punctuation. Improvising after listening, they can role-play, dramatize, pantomime, and retell parts of selections heard. Thinking out loud, they can chart story happenings and in so doing better understand story development: the role of character and setting in a story, the way actions and reactions build up, the role of conflict, the use of repetition, and the simplicity of most satisfying endings.

From Literature into Writing and Revision   Writing flows naturally from talking about literature. Through group oral composition based on shared poems, stories, and dramatizations, youngsters begin to understand what goes into authoring a poem, story, or dramatization. Guided by a teacher's questions, youngsters talk out a story during oral composition. Together they dream up a main character and endow him or her with qualities that contribute to plot. They decide how their story will begin, move, and end. They try out specific story lines to find phrases that tease the ear and tickle the imagination. Similarly, children who have listened to a particular poem can create the same kind of poem together. In creating orally together, students see the pleasure inherent in writing and acquire some of the skills so important in writing.

We saw this approach in Ms. Topping's first grade as the children composed "Egor Goes to the Circus."

Individual writing flows too. Children who have composed orally together branch out to write in related styles and forms. For example, having listened to a fable and composed several fables cooperatively under teacher guidance, children compose fables of their own (see Figure 1.3). Or, as in the vignette that opens this chapter, children compose circular tales in the style of a story they have read. The term *modeling* is used today in reference to this kind of writing—writing in which the author models his or her writing after a literary selection.

Similarly, an oral encounter with literature can supply the topic and content for writing. Children who have heard several stories about cats may decide to write their own stories about cats. Children who have heard several dream poems written by Langston Hughes may decide to compose their own.

[A Fable]

Once upon a time there was a rabbit and a racoon. The rabbit was running around the racoon. The racoon got so mad he started chasing the rabbit. When the racoon got the rabbit he was going to bite him! But then the rabbit said "I'm sorry! I'm sorry"! And the racoon did not bite the rabbit.

Title: The Rabbit and the Racoon.
Moral: Always say sorry when you do some thing wrong to somebody.
By: Andrea Pereira

Figure 1.3 Fable by a Third-Grader
SOURCE: Courtesy of Andrea Pereira and Louise Patterson.

See Chapter 10 for an in-depth discussion of writing processes. Aspects of writing processes are rehearsal, drafting, revising and editing, and sharing.

Revision and editing also become natural aspects of writing when children compose together based on a shared literary experience. Guided by teacher questions of the kinds Ms. Topping asked in reference to "Egor Goes to the Circus," children restructure sentences, substitute more exciting words, add ideas, and change punctuation and capitalization. Such cooperative revision lays the foundation for the revising children do when they compose independently and later confer with their teacher and classmates.

Content Area Study and Language Learning

See the back end papers for an example of such a cross-curricular unit on Appalachia.

Many of the same language activities can occur as part of integrated units of study in the content areas. Children learn science and mathematics, social studies and art, health and music as teachers share short passages from encyclopedias, almanacs, dictionaries, and other informational books. They learn by viewing films, filmstrips, and videotapes and by reading on their own. They pursue firsthand investigations that require interviewing, cooperative laboratory activity, and small-group interaction. They respond by talking through ideas and making notes in their learning logs, as in Figure 1.4.

These pursuits involve youngsters actively in reporting, sharing, listening, questioning, and reading to find out. They also lead into discussions in which youngsters brainstorm ideas and facts they have gathered. In brainstorming, students call out all manner of points that come to mind on a topic; these serve as data to be analyzed and organized into logical patterns and categories.

Writing follows. In teacher-guided groups, students can compose together, compiling informational paragraphs that summarize important data they have discovered and adding sentences that communicate significant generalizations and conclusions. Writing together during subject matter study, children identify the main ideas they want to express and points needed to support the main ideas. Then, guided by questions from their teacher, they cooperatively draft sentences and paragraphs. At this stage, they record their sentences and paragraphs on a board, chart, or word processing computer. Having drafted their thoughts roughly, they return to revise and edit.

It is important that youngsters have the opportunity to write as part of unit study in the content areas. Today theorists talk of the need for children to understand the structure of stories if they are to comprehend and write stories. They talk too of the need for children to understand the structure of informational material if they are to comprehend such material and write logically developed papers and reports of their own. Given this point of view, teachers must reserve some subject matter study time for oral experiences with writing.

As in literature-based sequences, teacher-guided group writing leads naturally into collaborative and independent writing activities in which youngsters apply language skills acquired through teacher-guided oral composition. It leads as well into independent reading through which students add to their understanding of a topic. Groups and individuals share their findings with the class. Sharing can take many forms: expressive oral reading, choral speaking, dramatizations, or preparation of a clean copy for others to read.

Clearly, no arbitrary separation exists between the language arts and the content areas in meaning-based language units. Children refine their communication skills as they use them to learn across the curriculum. In the same way, there is no arbitrary separation of time blocks for reading, listening, speaking, writing, or thinking. One language activity flows naturally into another in the classroom as it does in real life. Figure 1.5 depicts this flow.

Everyday Experiences and Language Learning

What is true of literature and the content areas of the curriculum is true of children's everyday experiences: Teachers can use children's experiences with people, things, and ideas around them as content for language activity.

Children are easily prompted to talk about events they have experienced

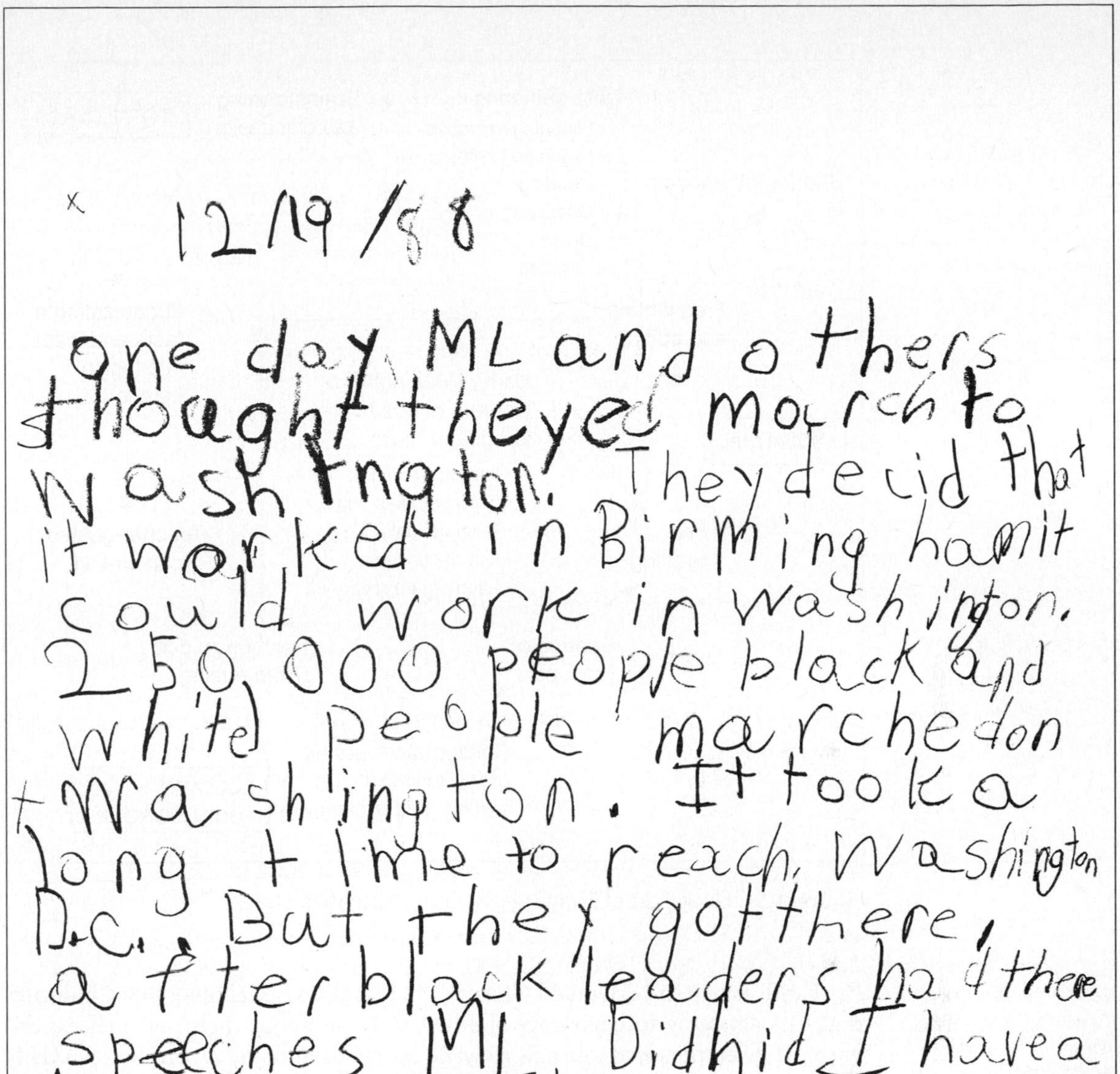

x   12/19/88

one day ML and o thers thought theyed morch to washington. They decid that it worked in Birming hamit could work in wash inton. 250,000 people black and white people marche d on Washington. It took a long time to reach Washington D.C. But they got there, after black leaders had there speeches ML Didhid I have a dream speeche

Figure 1.4 A Third-Grader's Entry in His Social Studies Learning Log
SOURCE: Courtesy of Mark Burness and Louise Patterson.

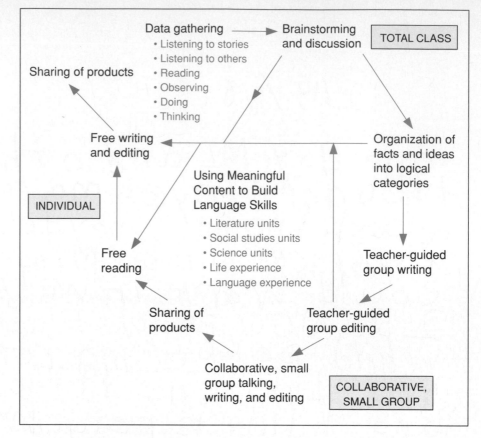

Figure 1.5 Flowchart of Language-Building Activities

Donald Graves and Lucy Calkins have done extensive research on the development of writing skills as part of the University of New Hampshire Writing Project and the Teachers College Project.

firsthand. Research by Donald Graves (1983) and Lucy Calkins (1986) indicates that it is also easy to encourage children to write about their personal experiences. If given personal journals to write in, children enjoy recording on a daily basis, describing things that happened to them and their feelings and reactions. Functioning as authors, they like to share orally what they have written, getting feedback from their audience to improve their writing. And they particularly like to select from their personal writings pieces to publish. *Publication* here means organizing a piece, perhaps as an illustrated book, for sharing with others.

Capitalizing on children's eagerness to talk and write about things they know directly, teachers can also plan language experiences around a class trip, a community event, or a happening in the life of one or more children. Children can talk about, role-play, interview, brainstorm possibilities, write and edit in groups and on their own, share their products, and read to find out more. The flow of classroom events in Figure 1.5 relates to these kinds of experiences as well as to those with literature and the content areas.

Language Play and Language Learning

In Karin Topping's first grade, much language learning occurs as children react in oral and written form to people, ideas, and things met in literature, subject study, and everyday experiences. At times, however, this master teacher encourages active play with language. Our complex language system presents endless avenues for creative exploration through which students gain understanding of how their language works and learn to handle spoken and written forms. "Languaging together," children can play with the way we

- ◆ Represent speech sounds on paper,
- ◆ Build words from roots, affixes, and other words,
- ◆ Change words through use,
- ◆ Put words together in sentences,
- ◆ Expand and transform sentences,
- ◆ Use punctuation marks, pauses, tone, and pitch of voice to communicate meaning.

All these aspects of language are open to oral exploration, which leads to individual reading and writing.

What Research Says about Skill Development   Research supports the contention that oral "play" with language has an effect on children's ability to communicate. James Martin (Porter, 1972) has reported growth in the sentence-writing skills of third-, fourth-, and fifth-graders through a program that stressed understanding of sentence features reflected in children's own oral sentence making and involved children in "inductive, open-ended investigations of aspects of English sentences." Children in the Martin study played actively with the pauses and changes in intonation that signal sentence endings and major sentence units. They related these features to written ones, specifically punctuation marks. The researcher found that children in the experimental program showed significantly superior growth in sentence writing compared to children in a traditional grammar program. Martin explained his findings in this way: "Two aspects of oral language performance apparently contribute much to written communication: (1) an awareness of the relationship between intonation patterns of oral language and punctuation signals of the written facsimile, and (2) 'sentence-sense'—the ability to differentiate between sentence units and non-sentence units."

Language Study as Play   Through language play, children can refine their ability to use language effectively and their understanding of how their language works. As part of language explorations, children can expand and reduce sentences, play orally with word order, invent tongue-twisting sentences, and disassemble lengthy sentences to get at their core meaning. Children can fatten and reduce words by adding and removing affixes. Almost every aspect of language is open to these kinds of explorations.

The word *play* is used to describe this approach to language exploration. The activity has literally become a game with children performing gamelike operations: guessing, searching, solving puzzles, pantomiming, and inventing. The setting for word play is generally a group in which language explorers interact orally, with a resulting gain in listening and speaking skills.

One of the most difficult tasks teachers have is to sustain the gamelike quality of language study. In the past, unfortunately, children have not reacted enthusiastically to study of how their language functions. Language exploration, however, can be exciting if the teacher organizes it orally and uses creative approaches through which students can become actively involved in their language. Chapter 11 explores these approaches in depth.

The Classroom as a Social Community

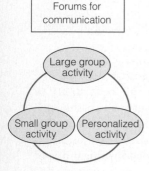

Belief 3.   Children become more effective language users when they function in classroom communities—especially multicultural communities—in which they interact and collaborate naturally with one another as well as think, write, and read independently. To this end, teachers should structure whole-class, collaborative-group, and one-on-one interaction. They should provide opportunities for personalized, independent study during which children use their growing language facility to read, write, and think. This section describes ways to organize the classroom as a social community in which children learn language naturally through interacting and doing.

Whole-Class Activity

As we saw in Karin Topping's classroom, whole-class activity—in which almost all students participate—serves a unifying function and develops the multicultural classroom as a community of learners (Berghoff and Egawa, 1991). It provides time for children to listen to informational content and stories; talk out ideas met through listening and reading; brainstorm, compose, and improvise as a class; dramatize and chorus together; and refine basic skills through language play. It also provides time for direct instruction. In 1985, a Commission on Reading of the National Institute of Education suggested a need for more whole-class activity, especially as children build reading facility.

Preplanning is essential for whole-class activity to succeed. Teachers must know what they hope to achieve through instruction and have a clear idea of the sequence of activities and the kinds of questions they plan to use. Perhaps the single most important factor in determining the effectiveness of whole-class instruction is the teacher's skill as questioner and responder. Does the teacher ask questions that relate primarily to factual content? Or does the teacher ask questions that get children to compare, critically evaluate, decide, and generalize? Does the teacher respond to children's remarks by evaluating and criticizing? Or does he or she respond by celebrating children's contributions and asking them to expand on what they have said? These are the kinds of things a teacher must consider in reviewing the effectiveness of whole-class activity.

Small-Group Collaboration and Instruction

For specific ideas on how to organize literature study groups, read Suzi Keegan and Karen Shrake, "Literature Study Groups: An Alternative to Ability Grouping," *The Reading Teacher*, 44 (April 1991), 542–547. For a rationale for team collaboration, read William Glasser, *Control Theory in the Classroom* (New York, HarperCollins, 1986) and Robert Slavin, *Student Team Learning*, rev. ed. (Washington, D.C.: National Education Association, 1988).

Independent small-group activity generally emerges from whole-class instruction. During writing workshops, interacting in two- or three-person teams, youngsters can be involved in oral and written composing, including both prewriting and rewriting tasks. During reading workshops, children can pair off to read to each other. Or in study teams, children can discuss literary selections and prepare them for telling, dramatizing, or taping. They can research a topic cooperatively and prepare their findings for reporting to the class. In collaborating, a group or a pair of youngsters draws on one another's strengths (Berghoff and Egawa, 1991). They gain a sense of belonging and develop the esprit de corps that is found within sports teams and that builds self-esteem (Glasser, 1986).

A teacher can also organize children into groups for direct instruction, especially when he or she finds several youngsters with similar needs. This is often the case in reading and spelling and with children who have special problems because they are learning English as a second language or have vision or hearing impairments. Through small-group instruction, a teacher can respond to the psychological, intellectual, and cultural differences of children in the class.

A major advantage of collaborative and teacher-guided group activity is that there is a social component—a component lacking when children work continuously on individualized activity. In some classrooms, children spend hours completing dittos; with the advent of computers, they are spending hours entering answers. In these classrooms, children may spend a half hour or so functioning as part of a teacher-guided reading group; however, since much of this time is occupied in silent reading, there is little opportunity for normal social interaction. Peer-group activity is one way to avoid neglect of oral communication: As the teacher interacts with one group of youngsters, others can collaborate with their peers, teaching and learning from one another.

Personalized Activity

See Figure 3.1 for an example of a personalized study guide, or contract.

Group oral language experiences provide a fine base on which to build worthwhile personalized study, geared to individual interests, needs, and abilities. From a period of intensive oral activity in class-size or small, collaborative groups, children move in directions determined by their diverse interests and needs. Working individually, they reflect on what they have experienced, read, and talked about; working individually, they set goals and apply and practice strategies learned (Pardo and Raphael, 1991). For example, students who require more time to master a spelling pattern can use individual study time for additional practice. Others who have quickly mastered that pattern but enjoy play with the sounds of words can create sound effect poems in which the sound just encountered recurs. Others who have been refining their reportorial skills can work together preparing information and ideas for eventual presentation to the class. Still others can curl up with a book chosen for recreational reading or go to a quiet corner to write in a private diary.

The Learning Station   Learning stations are used to personalize language study. A *learning station* is a place where children pursue a task on their own or in small groups, completing an activity outlined there. At the station are the materials needed to complete the task and, in some instances, a correcting guide so that children who have completed a task can identify areas requiring further attention.

Learning stations are generally set up in classroom corners, in alcoves created by placing bookshelves perpendicular to the wall, or along walls so that children face a bulletin or chalkboard. Tasks organized at a station include work with filmstrips and filmstrip viewers, audiotapes and tape recorders, videocassettes and players, computers and computer-assisted programs (CAI), flat pic-

Children collaborate as they read together during a reading workshop. (©1993 Jean-Claude Lejeune)

tures, realia, scissors, paste, and books. In some instances, several tasks can be set in one alcove or on one bulletin board, in which case we call that classroom area a *learning center*.

Language Centers   Possible centers that have special roles in language learning include the following:

✦ An Interest Reading Nook where there are books to read for pleasure. In the nook is a comfortable chair or two.
✦ An Interest Talk Corner, where two or three youngsters can discuss points raised in class sessions or share pressing concerns.
✦ A Language Production Center, where children think, write, and illustrate. Here youngsters collaborate on writing and illustrating a literary magazine, parents' newsletter, or picture storybook using the production facilities available, such as a laminating machine and a desktop, computer-based publishing setup.
✦ A Language Skills Center, where children refine spelling, handwriting, reading, listening, and writing skills. In this center are word and sentence cards, spelling and reading games, handwriting practice materials, and tapes and a tape recorder for use in focused listening.

As noted earlier, language center experiences generally are outgrowths of group activity. Through group interaction, children learn what they will be doing and how to manipulate the hardware—the viewers, projectors, computers—that is a part of the activities they will pursue.

Organizing for Effective Classroom Management

Classroom management is a factor to consider in selecting from among organizational patterns, especially in choosing formats in which verbal interaction is a key element and self-expression is valued, but the noise level is reasonable. This is especially true in situations where many children come to school with behavior problems. Experienced teachers like Karin Topping generally keep the following points in mind to ensure a smoothly functioning community of learners:

✦ Establish guidelines for acceptable patterns of interaction early on. (For example, we do not talk while someone else "has the floor."; We wait our turn; we do not "pump our hand" to get the teacher's attention.)
✦ Involve students in the formulation of classroom communication "rules." (For example, teacher and students cooperatively develop behavior contracts, which participants sign.)
✦ Establish procedures for classroom operation. (For example, at the sound of the drum, all must attend to the teacher; completed papers are placed in the "in" basket; pencils are not sharpened during class discussion, only during work periods.)
✦ Make sure that students know the tasks they are to do at times when the teacher is conferring with an individual or small group. Make sure materials

are available for completion of independent tasks. (For example, students work from chalkboard or duplicated lists of required and/or recommended tasks.)

✦ Be aware of children's special needs before problems arise, and plan activity based on a clear understanding of students' attention span. (For example, check for signs of restlessness and inattention during discussions and, when noted, switch tasks or means of instruction.)

✦ Maintain eye contact during discussions, move about the classroom, and bring as many students into the discussion as possible.

✦ Never use language activity or the withdrawal of it as punishment. (For example, do not assign compositions on why I should pay attention. Written communication should never be punishment.)

Instructional Planning for Communication in Action

Belief 4. Children become more effective language users when their teacher has planned ongoing, cohesive blocks of instruction that enable them to learn at their own level and pace, communicate actively with one another, make connections among ideas, and think critically and creatively. To this end, a teacher must organize units in which individual lessons flow into one another to meet the diverse needs of children with differing abilities, personalities, attention spans, and behavioral patterns.

Units are integrated, cohesive, flowing blocks of experiences that provide students with many natural opportunities to listen, speak, write, read, and think. Units can be literature based, with language experiences evolving out of interaction with a series of related stories, poems, and expository selections. Or units can be content-area based, with language, music, and art experiences being part of the exploration. A unit organization lends continuity to children's reading and provides an overarching framework for planning daily lessons.

One kind of literature-based unit is *thematic*: Language experiences grow out of a series of pieces that relate to a common message, or theme. Examples of themes include "Recognizing and Overcoming Our Fears," "Making Things Happen," "I Am Somebody," "Differences Are Good," "Surviving in the Natural World." Figure 1.6 shows a map and a linear management plan for a brief unit of this type. The unit includes literature that students read together or alone and from which the theme arises (the *integrative dimension*) and additional literature that relates to the theme from which students choose books, articles, and poems to read on their own (the *independent dimension*). Often teachers derive the theme of a unit like this from the social studies and/or sciences, with the goal being growth in content-area learning as well as in oracy and literacy.

A second kind of literature unit—one that can be superficial in the primary grades—is topical. In a *topical* unit, experiences are organized around a series of literary selections that relate to a topic such as chocolate, dragons, bears, or monsters—common topics in use today in primary classrooms.

In "Technology and Thematic Units: An Elementary Example," *The Reading Teacher*, 46 (February 1993), 442–445, Shelley Wepner says, "Thematic units offer elementary teachers endless opportunities to use literature for extending and enriching learning across disciplines." Wepner provides an example of a unit organized around two books (*The Big Wave* and *Sadako and the Thousand Cranes*) that help expand children's understanding of the geography, history, and culture of Japan.

For material on one type of genre unit, the unit on biography, read Myra Zarnowski, *Learning about Biographies: A Reading-Writing Approach* (Urbana, Ill: National Council of Teachers of English, 1990).

Read M. Jean Greenlaw et al., "A Literature Approach to Teaching about the Middle Ages," *Language Arts*, 69 (March 1992), 200–204, for a description of a social studies unit that draws heavily from literature. See also *Book Links*, a bimonthly periodical from the American Library Association, 50 East Huron Street, Chicago, Illinois, 60611-9969, for lists of children's books organized around such topics as settling the West, colors, Scandinavia, tropical rain forests, and letters in the classroom useful in unit planning.

"Reading aloud" means that the teacher orally shares a piece of text with the class. "Reading along" means that the teacher shares as the students follow in their texts. "Reading alone" means that students read to themselves after a preliminary discussion that establishes a purpose for reading. "Reading with a mate" means that students pair off to take turns reading aloud to one another.

A third kind of literature unit is *author based:* Students read selections by one author to learn something about style in writing and more particularly about the style of that author. Examples include focus units on the poems and stories of Judith Viorst or the stories of Arnold Lobel.

A fourth kind of literature unit is *genre based.* For example, in a unit, students may read several folktales, coming away from their study with a heightened understanding of that genre.

A fifth kind of literature unit is organized around a *chapter book.* The chapter book is a full-length novel in its original (not an abstracted or excerpted) form. Listening, speaking, and writing activities flow out of reading the core novel. At appropriate points in the unit, children read poems and articles that relate to the novel's theme, setting, and author. Extended novel units are becoming popular, starting as early as second grade. Many teachers are "doing" several novels a year with their students (Au and Scheu, 1989; Zarrillo, 1989).

This section discusses ways to plan literature-based units and the lessons that comprise them. For an example of an integrated thematic unit that starts with an organizing idea from science and in which children collaborate as they read, write, and think critically, see Figure 2.1 and the vignette that opens Chapter 2.

Designing Units

The first step in planning literature-based units is to identify the objectives sought. Curriculum specialists recommend that teachers think in terms of specific language learnings students will acquire or refine. Statements of specific learnings are called *objectives.* Examples of objectives, stated in terms of something the student is able to do by the end of a literature unit, are: "The student is able to give at least two points to support his or her judgment that a story is an effective one"; "The student is able to relate events in a story to real-life events"; "The student is able to compose a series of paragraphs that describe the characters in a story."

The second step is to identify the literature and the theme that will serve as foci of the unit and lead to the achievement of the objectives. In a few cases, teachers are free agents empowered to make decisions about what children will read. In most cases, however, teachers make decisions in collaboration with peers based on the school curriculum, which lists specific novels and other literature for each grade level or provides possibilities from which teachers—with input from their students—choose. At this stage, in developing a unit around a chapter book, teachers themselves must think deeply about the meaning of the book to be read, because the meaning the author communicates provides the theme of the story and of the unit. At the same time, they must decide how they intend to handle each chapter (as a read-aloud, a read-along, a read-alone, or a read-with-a-mate) and what activities they will use in relation to each chapter of the core book (the *focal dimension*). Again with input from their students, teachers must identify related literature that they will share orally with the class

The Map of the Unit: Overcoming Fear

FOCAL DIMENSION

Theme of the Unit: We all have fears. The more we recognize what we fear the more we are able to overcome our fears and appreciate the joys of living.

Unit Objectives: Through interaction with literature and one another, children are able to:

✦ identify and overcome their fears, particularly of the dark and of the night;
✦ predict what a story or poem is about based on title, cover, and other clues;
✦ orally join in to the chorusing of a poem and the reading of a story;
✦ bring their feelings to bear on the interpretation of a poem or story;
✦ express their feelings during talk time and in writing;
✦ use context clues to predict the meaning of unfamiliar words;
✦ perceive similarities and differences within several pieces of writing;
✦ collaborate in the writing of a group poem or story.

INTEGRATIVE DIMENSION

Selections from which the theme arises and that all students will listen to or read and talk about

✦ "Whenever I feel afraid . . ." from *The Sound of Music*—music connection;
✦ "A Goblin" by Rose Fyleman;
✦ "Someone Came Knocking" by Walter de la Mare;
✦ "Strange Bumps" from *Owl at Home* by Arnold Lobel (Harper, 1975);
✦ *Owl Moon* by Jane Yolen (Philomel, 1987);
✦ *Where the Wild Things Are* by Maurice Sendak (Harper, 1963).

INDEPENDENT DIMENSION

Additional selections that relate to the theme that students may read on their own

✦ *Ira Sleeps Over* by Bernard Waber (Houghton Mifflin, 1972);
✦ *In the Night Kitchen* by Maurice Sendak (Harper & Row, 1970);
✦ *Eugene the Brave* by Ellen Conford (Little, Brown, 1978);
✦ *There's a Nightmare in My Closet* by Mercer Mayer (Dial, 1968);
✦ *What's Under the Bed?* by James Stevenson (Greenwillow, 1983);
✦ *That Terrible Halloween Night* by James Stevenson (Greenwillow, 1980);
✦ Other stories from *Owl at Home* by Arnold Lobel (Harper, 1975);
✦ *The Adventures of Isabel* by Ogden Nash (Joy Street/Little Brown, 1991);
✦ *Henry and Mudge and the Bedtime Thumps* by Cynthia Rylant (Bradbury, 1991).

Figure 1.6 A Map and Linear Management Plan of an Early-Primary Literature-Based Thematic Unit

Linear Management Plan for Learning and Assessment: Overcoming Fear

INTEGRATIVE DIMENSION

Opening Celebration: sing "Whenever I feel afraid" from *The Sound of Music;* share times when we have been afraid; brainstorm things that scare us; make a finger painting.

"A Goblin" by Rose Fyleman: predict what the poem is about based on the title and first line; listen for what the author feels; discuss our fears; read along while listening; chorus the poem together; dramatize scary things; draw a picture of the feelings expressed in the poem; write collaborative poems about our own fears; as a class, write poems with short lines in the style of Fyleman; write about times we were afraid.

"Someone Came Knocking" by Walter de la Mare: predict what the poem is about based on the title; listen for what the author feels; draw a picture that depicts the feelings in the poem; hypothesize who came knocking; talk about when we have felt the same way; talk about when we are afraid; talk about why we are afraid; write about our fears; chorus the poem on several occasions; chorus "A Goblin"; decide how this poem is similar to "A Goblin" and how it is different.

"Strange Bumps" from *Owl at Home* by Arnold Lobel (Harper, 1975): predict what the story is about based on the pictures; listen for how the main character feels; read along while listening; talk about why the character feels that way; tell when we have felt the same way; think about the multiple meanings of the word *bump;* dramatize the story; write about what makes us afraid; decide how this story is similar to "A Goblin" and "Someone Came Knocking" and how it is different.

***Owl Moon* by Jane Yolen (Philomel, 1987):** predict what the story is about based on the title and cover; listen for how the main character feels; talk about why she is not afraid; talk about similar times when pleasure took the place of fear; use context to figure out word meanings; reread the story to a partner; dramatize the story; write about times when we were unafraid; decide how this story is similar to "Strange Bumps" and how it is different.

***Where the Wild Things Are* by Maurice Sendak (Harper, 1963):** predict what the story is about based on the title and cover; listen for how the main character feels at the beginning of the story, in the middle, at the end; decide how these feelings are similar to or different from those of the character in *Owl Moon;* talk about when we feel afraid, when we feel brave; write about our fears and our pleasures using either poetry or story format; share our writings; dramatize our writings.

Climactic Celebration: Sing "Whenever I feel afraid. . . ." Share times when we have been brave. Share stories and poems we have written in this literature unit.

Ongoing Assessment Activities:

These activities will be a continuing aspect of the unit—

✦ Informal observations of children's reactions as they listen to poems and stories, their contribution to discussions held before and after they listen to a poem or story, and their contribution to choral speaking, singing and dramatic activities; ✦ Analysis of student's written responses that they have revised, edited, published, and showcased in their writing portfolios; ✦ Checklists based on stated objectives and completed after individual conferences with students (e.g., in conference, ask students to predict based on the title and cover of an unfamiliar book; ask them to read along as you reread "A Goblin" and ask them to tell their feelings and the meaning the poet was trying to communicate); ✦ Anecdotal records that describe student behavior.

or that all students will read—poems that enrich the theme, content-area selections that provide background information, and articles about or by the author of the core book (the *integrative dimension*). In the same way, teachers must identify stories, poems, and articles available in the classroom that children can choose to read on their own (the *independent dimension*).

The third step in planning a literature-based unit is to determine how to celebrate the beginning of a class's journey into a book and its arrival at the end. Experienced language arts teachers build anticipation days before students embark on a book journey. They display book clues in the room—objects that relate to the book and/or maps that show the story location. They share a poem or story that strikes at the theme, and they involve students in related artistic, musical, physical, or conversational activity. For example, one fourth-grade teacher celebrated an upcoming journey into *Charlotte's Web* by having children join hands and then raise their arms into the air to form a human spider web. Children also made colored-twine webs, attached a word of their own choosing to their webs, and hung the webs around the room. A fifth-grade teacher celebrated *Number the Stars* with a trip to a planetarium, a discussion of what a star means, and a reading of the poem from which Lois Lowry derived the title of her book. A sixth-grade teacher celebrated the beginning of Avi's *Nothing But the Truth* with a singing of the United States national anthem and a discussion of what it means to be a patriot and how truth can be distorted.

Similarly, experienced language arts teachers heighten children's final feelings about a book through a celebration of literature. For example, one second-grade teacher culminated students' journey into *Nate the Great* with a treasure hunt and a pancake feast—accompanied, of course, by talking and writing. In a fifth-grade classroom, the final celebration of *Shiloh* was the dramatization of story scenes and a critical debate of justice in the story and in real life.

The fourth step in planning a literature-based unit is to decide on the listening, speaking, reading, writing, science, social studies, art, music, and physical activities that are part of the unit. Obviously, the objectives determine in great measure the things the teacher and the students do with the literature they read or hear. Less obvious is the fact that students contribute to the planning. For example, as children read poems, novels, short stories, and expository pieces, they brainstorm writing options—things they would enjoy writing about in response to the literature. They also contribute by locating related pieces for class and independent reading.

Still another important aspect of planning a literature unit is deciding on the means of evaluating students' progress toward the stated objectives. Today emphasis is on informal means of assessment: observation of student behaviors, anecdotal records, checklists, portfolios. Emphasis is also on children as participants in the assessment process. You will read more about these approaches later in this book.

Figure 1.7 shows a map and a linear management plan that delineate the focal, integrative, and independent dimensions, the sequence of instructional activities, and the assessment activities of a unit based on Patricia MacLachlan's *Sarah, Plain and Tall* and that a teacher could use to plan ongo-

Read Natalie Babbitt's "Protecting Children's Literature," *The Horn Book*, 66 (November/December 1990), 696–703, for a caution about making a good story "bear too much weight" by taking it apart to examine it critically. As Babbitt warns, "Fiction is a fragile medium."

For a comprehensive discussion of units, read Marjorie Lipson, et al., "Integration and Thematic Teaching," *Language Arts*, 70 (April 1993), 252–263.

ing lessons. The chart on the front end papers clarifies cross-curricular connections.

Adapting a Basal Unit

In some school districts, teachers are required to organize children's reading/writing activities around a basal reading series containing literary selections grouped as units. When this is the case, teachers must still function as the primary planners; they organize children's language experiences by drawing creatively and discriminately on the ideas and selections in the series.

Teachers adapting a basal unit may begin a unit by having students read the original, full-length, paperback version of a novel rather than the excerpted version in the reading series and use that novel as the focal dimension of the unit. Or teachers may begin with a series of poems or a novel of their own choosing that relates to the theme of a unit in the reading series. In working creatively with a mandated basal reading series in these ways, teachers do not have children read all the selections in the basal; rather, they select those that meet the needs and interests of the children in the class and add others that relate. They skip selections, suggesting skipped pieces as independent reading options, and they decide on the order in which they will use the pieces given in the text. Creative teachers, who view basals as anthologies, sometimes skip entire units in the basal as they build alternate units with their students.

Designing Lessons Within a Unit

Just as teachers build units by identifying their objectives, the literary content, and the activities used to realize their objectives, so do they plan the lessons within a unit by considering the learnings they hope to achieve, the activities they will use, and the materials needed.

What are the attributes of an effective lesson? Madeline Hunter (1982) proposes that the opening is especially important in that it sets the focus and motivates students; she calls that opening an *anticipatory set*. Hunter states that the teacher "should take advantage of the beginning of the class time to create an anticipatory set in students which will take their minds off other things and focus their attention. . . . An anticipatory set also can hook into students' past knowledge and trigger memory or some practice which will facilitate today's learning." The latter is especially true of the anticipatory set of a lesson that is part of an ongoing unit; the anticipatory set helps students recall and review the previous lesson in the unit and make the connection with what is to come. In addition, students' responses to the anticipatory set provide diagnostic information about the knowledge and skills students already possess. Obviously, any lesson that begins with the teacher telling students to turn to page 35 in their text, read it, and write an answer to the question at the end of the page fails to establish a motivating anticipatory set.

A Lesson Plan Format
Topic
Objectives
Sequence of activities
Anticipatory set
Instruction and modeling
Guided practice
Independent activity
Closing set
Materials
Evaluation

The Map: *Sarah, Plain and Tall* by Patricia MacLachlan

FOCAL DIMENSION

Theme of the Unit   We all have a need to belong. Our dreams for a life in which we love and are loved motivate what we do and encourage us to take risks.

Unit Objectives   Through interaction with *Sarah, Plain and Tall* (MacLachlan, Harper & Row, 1985) and related literature, children will be able to

+ Predict (who, when, where, and what will happen) based on their analysis of the title and the cover of a novel and predict continuously as they read
+ Visualize story scenes
+ Infer character traits based on character actions
+ Compare events, characters, and places found in a novel
+ Infer time and place
+ Hypothesize reasons and relationships
+ Relate their own feelings to those of a story character and create a personal meaning out of the reading of a book
+ Use context to figure out the meanings of unfamiliar story words and the way those words function in a sentence (e.g., as noun, verb, and so forth)
+ Use story words new to them in talking and writing about the story
+ Create writing topics based on the reading of a book, rehearse and draft in response to reading, and edit and revise what they have written in preparation for sharing
+ Keep a literature response log and highlight their writing in a portfolio
+ Work in collaborative groups and contribute to a whole-class discussion
+ Orally read favorite lines from a story using the voice to heighten meaning
+ Find pleasure in reading a chapter book and responding to it by talking and writing

INTEGRATIVE DIMENSION

All students will read these selections either alone or together.

"This Is My Rock" by David McCord (poetry); "Dream Dust" by Langston Hughes (poetry); "Dreams" by Langston Hughes (poetry); "The Impossible Dream" from *Man of La Mancha* (music); "Sumer Is Icumen In" (poetry); *The Four Seasons* by Antonio Vivaldi (music); "Dakota Dugout" by Ann Turner (poetry); *Going West* by Jean Van Leeuwen (Dial, 1992).

Segments from the encyclopedia about sod houses, the plains, and the development of the railroad in the United States; segments from the social studies book about life on the Great Plains; large wall map of the United States (history and geography); videos.

Material from Patricia MacLachlan's Newbery Medal acceptance speech, *Horn Book* (July/August 1986), which describes elements of her life (nonfiction).

INDEPENDENT DIMENSION

These selections relate to the theme or the author of the focal book. Students will select from them to read on their own.

Other books about prairie life: Harvey's *My Prairie Year: Based on the Diary of Elenore Plaisted* (Holiday House, 1986); Wilder's *Little House on the Prairie* (Harper, 1935) and *Little Town on the Prairie* (Harper, 1941); Anderson's *Christmas on the Prairie* (Clarion, 1988); Conrad's *Prairie Songs* (Harper, 1985), *My Daniel* (Harper, 1989), and *Prairie Vision: The Life and Times of Solomon Butcher* (Harper, 1991); Freedman's *Buffalo Hunt* (Holiday House, 1988).

Other dream poems by Langston Hughes: "A Dream Deferred," "Dream Keeper."

Other books about the need to belong: Spinelli's *Maniac Magee* (Little, Brown, 1990).

Other books by Patricia MacLachlan, especially *Three Names* (HarperCollins, 1991); other articles by MacLachlan about her view of writing.

Figure 1.7   A Map and Linear Management Plan for a Fifth-Grade, Literature-Based Novel Unit

The Management Plan: *Sarah, Plain and Tall* by Patricia MacLachlan

FOCAL DIMENSION

Opening celebration: Tap prior ideas about the words *plain* and *tall*; predict characters, time, place, and plot based on cover clues.

Chapter 1 (aloud—class): Listen to infer character traits based on what people say and do and to hypothesize time and place; make character wheels; chart unfamiliar and interesting words; write to Sarah from the point of view of characters met in the first chapter.

Chapter 2 (alone): Share letters to Sarah before reading; read to check predictions in letters to Sarah; expand ideas about character and setting; add to character wheels; as Jacob, write to Sarah to tell her to come.

Chapter 3 (reading mate): Retell events from Chapter 2 before reading and tell how the characters felt during the events; read to make an events/feeling chart; after reading, list all the color words in Chapters 3 and 1 and decide why there is a difference: chart unfamiliar words based on context clues: write about your response to Sarah.

Chapter 4 (aloud—class): Review the kind of character Sarah is before reading by expanding on a Sarah character wheel; read to find evidence that Sarah will stay, that Sarah will go; write what you think will happen next.

Chapter 5 (alone): Review the kind of character Caleb is by expanding his character wheel; read to propose a title to the chapter; chart unfamiliar words based on context clues; write about your response to Caleb.

Chapter 6 (reading mate): Review the kind of character Anna is; read to compare this chapter to the first chapter; how are they different? how are they the same? why? Write your response to Anna or your response to the way this author writes. Identify similes.

Chapter 7 (alone or reading mate): Review the story by proposing titles for prior chapters; read (1) to decide what the author is trying to tell us about life and what is important to happiness and (2) to create a title for this chapter; write your reaction to the author's main story meaning; chart unfamiliar words.

Chapter 8 (alone or reading mate): Review the kind of man Papa is; read to pick the high point of the chapter; be ready to say why you picked it; write your response to Papa or to any of the chapter events.

INTEGRATIVE DIMENSION

Listen to and chorus "This Is My Rock" by David McCord; talk about our own "rocks."

Chorus again "This Is My Rock" by David McCord; reflect: Who is Caleb's rock? Anna's? Papa's? Listen to "Winter" from *The Four Seasons*.

In collaborative teams, read about life on the Great Plains from the social studies text. Compile a lifestyle map.

Listen to, chorus, and reflect on "Dream Dust" by Langston Hughes. Think about what Sarah's dream was, Anna's, Caleb's. Chorus together "Sumer Is Icumen In." Listen to "Spring" from *The Four Seasons*.

In collaborative groups, prepare "Dreams" by Langston Hughes for oral sharing.

Listen to a recording of "The Impossible Dream" from *Man of La Mancha*. Reflect: Was Anna's dream impossible? Sarah's? Caleb's?

In research teams, read segments from the encyclopedia about sod houses, the development of the railroad in the United States; share findings.

In poetry interpretation teams, prepare "Dakota Dugout" by Ann Turner for oral expression. Sing along with "Mail Order Annie."

Listen to material from Patricia MacLachlan's Newbery Medal acceptance speech, *Horn Book* (July/August 1986); relate it to the novel.

Continued

The Management Plan *Continued*

FOCAL DIMENSION	INTEGRATIVE DIMENSION
Chapter 9 (aloud—class): Review story by the teacher dressing up and playing the role of Sarah or Jacob; decide what Sarah brought with her (stress things like courage, hope, fear as well as Seal, the sea stones, and the shells): listen to enjoy, paint pictures in the mind, and grow feelings in the heart; write your response—was Sarah really plain? Write sequels.	Use a large wall map of the United States to plot Sarah's travel route from Maine to the Great Plains. Listen to *Going West;* compare it to time, place, and feelings of *Sarah.* View video on Nebraska and Maine—*The Land, the Sea, and the Children.*
Climactic celebration: In teams, talk about favorite parts; dramatize them; share dramatizations and sequels during a session where everyone dresses up as a character from the novel.	Make a mobile containing things from the story that are key in its development; tell why you included what you did.

Ongoing Assessment Activities

Students will keep a literature response journal in which they record their ongoing responses to what they are reading. They will compile a portfolio of writings and drawings they have made to showcase their response to the novel. While students are reading alone or with a mate, the teacher conducts individual conferences in which each student talks about personal responses to the novel and to his or her independent reading and discusses his or her literature journal entries. The following assessment activities will be a continuing aspect of the unit:

✦ Informal observations of children's contribution to discussions held before and after reading or listening to a chapter of the book ✦ Informal observations of children's interaction with other students in literature groups and as they read to themselves ✦ Analysis of students' written responses in their literature logs and written responses that they have revised, edited, published, and showcased in their writing portfolios ✦ Checklists based on stated objectives and completed after individual conferences with students ✦ Anecdotal records that describe student behavior

See the lesson in Figure 1.8 for an example of an anticipatory set that includes brainstorming, webbing, and predicting.

The main segment of a lesson includes *instruction* and *modeling* of processes that students will later have to perform on their own. Instruction can include the oral sharing of a story, poem, or informational selection; a discussion of key ideas; or the viewing of a film or filmstrip. Modeling, in this context, means talking and/or doing together to demonstrate to students how to proceed as they study and learn. For example, students and teacher cooperatively create a poem following a pattern students may use later for independent writing. Or the teacher shares a paragraph similar to those children will later read, indicating aloud the thoughts that come to his or her mind while making meaning with the paragraph. Or the teacher models how to form a web of ideas as a way to get ready to write.

According to Mark Aulls (1986), a primary benefit of verbal modeling is that it makes otherwise "covert processes observable to the student." Aulls writes, "You cannot get some students to internalize a process by simply telling or even explaining what the steps are. . . . Verbal modeling provides the opportunity to show how to do something."

As part of the instructional and modeling phase of a lesson, the teacher should check students' understanding. In checking for understanding, the teacher can ask students to respond with a nonverbal signal (e.g., holding up a question mark card if a sentence being displayed is a question), respond with choral responses, answer individually, or write a brief response. There should be time too for *guided and independent activity*, wherein students try out what they have been learning (Hunter, 1982).

At some point in the lesson sequence—either before or after guided or independent activity—the teacher must pull the threads of the lesson together and seek closure. During the *closing set*, students identify main ideas, summarize what they have learned, and generalize. If they have drawn or written, they share what they have done.

When students and teacher are involved in doing and talking together, learning/teaching becomes an *action process*. Lesson planning for action-process teaching includes these elements:

1. Setting objectives—what it is children will learn through the lesson;
2. Planning an anticipatory set that involves students cognitively and emotionally;
3. Designing a plan for instructing and for modeling the mental acts children are to perform;
4. Designing a plan for guided and independent activity;
5. Planning for closure.

Qualities of Action-Process Language Arts Lessons

Lessons in the language arts are varied; no one lesson design is functional in all situations. Nevertheless, we can generalize about successful lessons:

✦ Successful lessons are based on meaningful content. This content is derived from literature, the subject areas, everyday experiences, or the nature of language itself.
✦ Lessons have an oral language component, such as brainstorming, discussion, or dramatization. Students and teacher are actively, verbally involved in communicating together.
✦ Reading and writing parallel the oral experiences. Students who are talking

about or acting out ideas are often eager to write down their cooperative productions, write independently, and/or read more on the topic.

✦ Children share what they have learned and produced. Oral sharing flows naturally from individual and group writing.

✦ One lesson interrelates with others in a unit. Small-group interaction flows out of periods of whole-class oral involvement; personalized study is based on small-group and whole-class work.

Figure 1.8 depicts a plan that one teacher designed as part of the novel unit outlined in Figure 1.7. It details proposed activities to introduce the book and the first chapter, not those that actually transpired. Rarely in teaching can lesson plans be implemented exactly. Children contribute suggestions. Unscheduled events or behavior problems interrupt plans. Activities that appear ideal in pre-planning misfire. Modifications are to be expected given the variables functioning in elementary classrooms. Realizing this, one experienced teacher, Anita Baker, always has a backup plan ready. If her Plan A misfires, she shifts to her Plan B.

Then, too, the plan in Figure 1.8 represents the thinking of an experienced teacher rather than the outline recorded in a plan book. Typically, experienced teachers do not write full sentences but use summary phrases that call to mind the objectives and activities they have previously thought out. They jot reminders on Post-it ™ notes, which they stick directly on the page of a book they are sharing. Viewed from this perspective, lesson planning is more a process of thinking and notemaking rather than one of detailed writing.

The lesson in Figure 1.8 follows Russell Stauffer's Directed Reading-Thinking Activity format, in which readers predict before reading, read to test predictions, and repeat the predict-read-test sequence as they continue to read. With listening, this is called the Directed Listening-Thinking Activity. See Chapter 5 for more on DLTA.

Trade Books, Textbooks, Materials, and Technology in the Language Arts

Books are primary resources in language arts. Clearly, a wide variety of books must be housed in dynamic classrooms—books galore to tease the senses, tantalize the imagination, and provide information; books that teachers read aloud to children; and books that children read because they want to.

Many classrooms house a variety of graded textbooks as well. How are teachers to use these? The temptation is to open the language arts book and begin there. Some inexperienced teachers do just that. They introduce a lesson with "Everyone turn to page 8. Keith, read the opening paragraph. Good. Pam, take the next. Are there any questions?" When none appear, such teachers continue, "Okay, complete the ten sentences beneath the two paragraphs." Used this way, the language arts text is a dead-end road resulting in minimal language use and no active involvement.

Language arts texts should play a reinforcing role. First, they can be used to back up understandings gleaned from oral encounters. For example, youngsters who together have played with a component of language go to the text to read about concepts with which they have already been orally involved. Second, language arts texts can provide word and sentence materials. If children are making

TOPIC OF LESSON: Characterization in Stories

GRADE LEVEL: Fifth

CONTEXT: Story Listening—*Sarah, Plain and Tall*
by Patricia MacLachlan

OBJECTIVES: Through the lesson, students will refine their ability to predict what characters will do in a story; infer the kind of person a character in a story is by what he or she says and does; and visualize a story scene.

PROPOSED SEQUENCE OF ACTIVITIES:

1. Anticipatory Set: Introduce *Sarah, Plain and Tall* by showing the cover and by asking students to brainstorm the thoughts brought to mind by the words *plain* and *tall*. On this prelistening web, record thoughts attached to the appropriate word:

Have children predict what they think the story is about, based on the title and the cover art. Ask listeners to study the cover art and predict who the characters are going to be.

2. Instruction and Modeling: Read the first two pages aloud to the students. Ask them to listen to verify their predictions about who the characters are and to visualize the scene in their minds. Stop at the lines "Mama died the next morning. That was the worst thing about Caleb." Ask: "Who are the main characters so far? What kind of person is Anna? How do you know? What kind of person is Caleb? How do you know?" As students respond, develop this chart with them:

	Kind of Person	Evidence from Story That Supports Our Inference
Caleb Anna		

Describe for children the picture that the scene makes in your mind. Tell students that as you read the story aloud you visualize that scene in your mind. Then ask students to predict again who Sarah is going to be and what is going to happen next. Ask students to listen to predict and to visualize the next scene in their minds.

3. Guided Practice: In the same fashion, keep reading sections of the first chapter aloud to the group, having them predict and visualize. Add Papa to the character analysis chart and encourage children to give words that tell the kind of person he is and evidence to support their inferences. Encourage children to add more words and supporting evidence to the chart regarding Caleb and Anna. Add Sarah to the chart, and based on her letter, have children predict the kind of person she is. Stop reading just before Caleb tells his father what he wants him to ask Sarah. Ask the students to predict (based on what they have heard so far) what Caleb wants his father to ask.

Figure 1.8   A Lesson Plan for Upper Elementary Grades

4. Guided Practice: Tell the students that Caleb, Anna, and Papa write letters to Sarah. Ask students to predict what each will write in his or her letter and record students' predictions on a chart like this one:

The Character	Things That the Character Will Tell or Ask Sarah
Caleb Anna Papa	

5. Closing Set: Ask students to review with you what they have been doing orally and together as they listened to the story. After students have verbalized some of the things they did as they listened, tell them that when you listen or read, you generally do the same things in your head they have been doing orally together—predicting what characters will do, inferring the kind of person a character is based on what he or she does and says, and picturing in the mind the scene in the story. Tell them that you generally start anticipating a story even before you begin it based on information on the cover.

6. Following-up Independent Activity
a. Suggest as a writing option that students write a letter to Sarah as one of the three characters would have done. Tell them that tomorrow they will read the next chapter of *Sarah, Plain and Tall,* but before they do, students who have chosen this writing option may read their letters aloud so that the class can compare them with what the story characters actually wrote to Sarah.

b. Suggest that students make similar character charts for books they are reading during Sustained Silent Reading. Tell students that they will have time to share their charts during small-group literature sharing time.

MATERIALS: *Sarah, Plain and Tall* (New York: Harper & Row, 1985); large chart paper.

EVALUATION: Children share the predictive letters they have written and the charts they have made about characters from books they are reading. Children continue to predict, visualize, and infer during future listening sessions with *Sarah, Plain and Tall.*

Figure 1.8 *Continued*

sentence strips to cut into subject and predicate parts, expand into longer sentences, reorder, or transform into related patterns, the book gives examples. Third, some newer series offer poems and stories that children can prepare for choral speaking and individual oral interpretation. Some provide maps showing the origins of English, language trees, and selections from Old, Middle, and Modern English. These materials serve as content to be interpreted during a class discussion. Finally, language text series provide a framework for instruction—a kind of scope and sequence guide. Even experienced teachers find texts beneficial as references, for they tell what skills and topics are important for children of this age and provide ideas that can be adapted.

Teachers will want to draw on other print materials: teacher-made classroom labels in early childhood classrooms, charts, word cards, samples of environmental print that serve diverse purposes, bulletin boards with a verbal component, magazines, newspapers. They will also want to tap into technology. Films and filmstrips, especially those relevant to content-area study, supply background information. Films also provide a visual rendition of novels, which can be viewed after students have read a book and are ready to make comparisons. Audio- and videotapes and disks can similarly provide content for discussions and composition. Today videocassette recorders (VCRs) allow teachers to store documentary and news programs for later retrieval. Camcorders enable students and teacher to produce films of their own.

Today microcomputers are being used for a variety of purposes within the language arts. One is the delivery of instruction. Commercially produced, computer-assisted instructional software packages (CAI) are available to teach vocabulary, content, and skills. Some of these programs are simulations that require the user to make decisions based on information supplied. Some are games with an educational intent. Others are drills—nothing more than workbook pages on a screen.

A second purpose of microcomputers is the management of instruction. Programs are available that allow the teacher to monitor student progress, compute grades, and keep numeric and anecdotal records. Given the nature of some computer-managed instructional packages (CMI), the user must beware of the pitfall: overreliance on quantifiable data. Although the language arts teacher must maintain records, recordkeeping is not the goal of instruction; as the old saying goes, it should not be "the tail that wags the dog."

A third purpose is word processing and desktop publishing. With the addition of a word processing program and a printer, a microcomputer functions as a typewriter with built-in editing capabilities. Used as a word processor, the computer becomes a powerful tool in teaching writing and reading and in the development of vocabulary. As we saw in Karin Topping's classroom, when children interact orally and create compositions together, the teacher or a student can type the texts directly into the computer; the children can immediately read on the monitor what they have written and shortly have a paper copy in hand. In the same way, young people can use microcomputers for individual writing. As part of a literature-based unit, students can use desktop publishing programs to generate flyers, brochures, literary magazines, and books. Many educators believe that word processing and desktop publishing are among the most significant and creative educational applications of the microcomputer for language arts programs. Using such systems, the student is a producer of ideas, not just a responder to a set of directions. In short, he or she becomes an active communicator—a meaning maker.

See, for example, videos like *The Land, the Sea, and the Children* from Films for the Humanities and Sciences that integrate well into literature-based units. See also a video like *Skylark*, a sequel to *Sarah, Plain and Tall*.

- ✦ Design a literature-based thematic unit for primary-grade youngsters. Perhaps use "Making Good Things Happen" as the theme of your unit. Follow the pattern in Figure 1.6, and identify the objectives and literature that make up the integrative and independent dimensions. Propose activities to use with the literary selections. Include an art, music, or physical activity.
- ✦ Design a chapter book unit for intermediate-grade students. Follow the pattern in Figure 1.7, and identify activities to go with each chapter of your novel. Include content-area activities such as the geography map investigation and the study of life on the Great Plains from the *Sarah, Plain and Tall* unit. Identify the objectives and literature in the integrative and independent dimensions of the unit.
- ✦ Design a lesson based on a chapter of a novel. Perhaps use a chapter from *Charlotte's Web*. Follow the lesson format in Figure 1.8: topic, primary and secondary objectives, sequence of activities (including an anticipatory set, instruction and modeling, guided and independent activity, and a closing set), materials, and evaluation.
- ✦ Read *Language Arts*, the journal of the National Council of Teachers of English. Each issue focuses on one or two language or literature concerns. Also, check *The New Advocate*, a journal that addresses the importance of literature in a whole-language program and *Primary Voices K-6*, NCTE's newest journal by teachers for teachers.

·········· A Summary Thought or Two

TEACHING FOR COMMUNICATION

The purpose of this chapter was to set forth a philosophy, or point of view, about teaching language arts. The chapter proposed that children become more effective language users by

- ✦ Interacting naturally as they create and actively communicate meanings within classrooms where listening, speaking, reading, and writing flow together;
- ✦ Responding to literature, communicating as they explore the content areas, experiencing their world and responding verbally to it, and playing actively with language;
- ✦ Functioning in classroom communities in which they interact as members of

small and large groups as well as study independently in ways that meet their own needs;

✦ Functioning in classrooms where teachers plan ongoing literature-based and content-area units that involve children in all of the language arts: listening, speaking, reading, and writing.

If teachers begin in these ways, a blending of the traditional language arts results. Listening and reading, the processes through which people build an ever increasing repertoire of language meanings and garner input from others, have pivotal places in a language arts program. Speaking and writing, the processes through which people draw on their repertoire of meanings and skills to transmit messages to others, flow parallel to listening and reading. At the same time, youngsters are actively involved in thinking critically about ideas they receive and produce. The result is integrated, meaning-based language experiences in which reading, listening, speaking, writing, and thinking are part of a larger whole: *communication in action*.

RELATED READINGS

Busching, Beverly, and Judith Schwartz, eds. *Integrating the Language Arts in the Elementary School*. Urbana, Ill.: National Council of Teachers of English, 1991.

Butler, Francella. *Sharing Literature with Children: A Thematic Approach*. Prospect Heights, Ill.: Waveland Press, 1991.

Goodman, Kenneth, Yetta Goodman, and Wendy Hood, eds. *Organizing for Whole Language*. Portsmouth, N.H.: Heinemann Educational Books, 1991.

Hydrick, Janie, ed. *Whole Language: Empowerment at the Chalk Face*. Urbana, Ill.: National Council of Teachers of English, 1991.

Kiefer, Barbara, ed. *Toward a Whole Language Classroom*. Urbana, Ill.: National Council of Teachers of English, 1990.

Neumann, Susan, and Kathleen Roskos. *Language and Literacy Learning in the Early Years: An Integrated Approach*. Fort Worth, Tex.: Harcourt Brace, 1993.

Noyce, Ruth, and James Christie. *Integrating Reading and Writing Instruction in Grades K–8*. Boston: Allyn and Bacon, 1989.

Pappas, Christine, Barbara Kiefer, and Linda Levstik. *An Integrated Language Perspective in the Elementary School*. New York: Longman, 1990.

Schwartz, Susan, and Mindy Pollishuke. *Creating the Child-Centered Classroom*. Kantonah, N.Y.: Richard Owens, 1991.

Shanahan, Timothy, ed. *Reading and Writing Together: New Perspectives for the Classroom*. Norwood, Mass.: Christopher-Gordon Publishers, 1990.

Slavin, Robert. *Student Team Learning*. Rev. ed. Washington, D.C.: National Education Association, 1988.

Vacca, Richard, and Timothy Rasinski. *Case Studies in Whole Language*. Fort Worth, Tex.: Harcourt Brace Jovanovich, 1992.

Winograd, Peter, ed. *Exemplary Practices in Literacy Development and Instruction*. Newark, Del.: International Reading Association, 1992.

11/11/91   Feelings About Mr. Rehnquist
    I think Mr. Rehnquist is grouchy, because he was accusing Addie's dad of crashing into him. He was also mean, because he came out with a shotgun yelling at Addie and Carla Mae. But on the other hand, the only reason he is mean, Is because he lives alone and is sad all the time. If you were a hermit, wouldn't you be mad?

        Ari Steinberg

11/26/91   Chapter 9
    I think Mr. Rehnquist is nice to people he knows. He also tries to hide it. I feel just a little like I did before, because when he thinks of memories ✻ he is nice and he has been thinking of lots of memories in the past chapter. I think he's also a little unreasonable because he's making Addie pay him for taking care of his horse. ✻
    ✻ I'd only like him as a grandfather at certain times.

Ari responded in his journal by reacting critically to a character in *The Thanksgiving Treasure* (courtesy of Ari Steinberg and Micki Benjamin).

A KNOWLEDGE BASE FOR TEACHING THE LANGUAGE ARTS

"We had the best of educations—in fact we went to school everyday—"
"I've been to a day-school, too," said Alice. "You needn't be so proud as all that."
"With extras?" asked the Mock Turtle, a little anxiously.
"Yes," said Alice.

—Lewis Carroll, *Alice's Adventures in Wonderland*

What does it take to provide children with the best of educations—with extras? In answering this question, we must tap into the knowledge base that supports and gives direction to our instruction: knowledge about the children whom we teach, of the way children develop as language users, and of the fine literature that is out there to entice children into reading and writing.

Part Two focuses on this three-pronged knowledge base that undergirds the language arts. It describes elementary children as diverse with emotional, linguistic, cultural, perceptual, and expressive characteristics that affect their language learning. It explains how children learn to think and interact socially, describes how children learn to handle the components of their language, and discusses ways children can learn about their language. It presents an overview of children's literature and provides a framework for analyzing and responding to books. The thesis that unites Part Two is that the language arts teacher must "own" a base of knowledge about learners, language, and literature to function successfully in today's multicultural, mainstreamed classrooms.

As you read the chapters in this part, keep asking yourself: How does this knowledge base relate to my teaching of the language arts? What are the implications of these ideas for me as a classroom teacher?

CHAPTER 2

Diversity in the Multicultural, Mainstreamed Classroom

Meeting the Social and Language Needs of All Children

BEFORE reading the chapter, read the title, the headings, and the end-of-chapter summary. Then answer the questions in the margin on this page.

Reflecting Before Reading

How does the teacher meet the needs of all children—children with behavior impairments, from diverse language backgrounds, with varying abilities, with sensory impairments, and with speech problems?

_____

_____

How does the teacher assess children's growth as language users?

_____

_____

_____

Learning to take notes based on direct experiences

See Figure 2.1 for a schematic of the unit, Preserving Nature's Habitats.

TEACHING IN ACTION   Preserving Habitats: A Thematic Unit

As part of a thematic, content-area unit, Beth Venezia and her third-graders were visiting the Fanwood Nature Center. The class had planned the trip based on the suggestion of two class investigative teams that were focusing their study on plants and animals in the environment. Earlier these students had written a letter to the center to set a time for a class visit and had made a follow-up telephone call. In preparation, the two teams had shown the class a map of the layout of the nature center and explained what they would see there. The teams had obtained their information from an explanatory folder from the center.

Now, as the third-graders walked along, the members of the Plants-in-Our-Environment Investigative Team stopped by each labeled tree to record its name in their learning logs. Chandra checked unfamiliar trees in the pocket-size Golden Nature Guide _Trees: A Guide to Familiar American Trees_, which she had borrowed from the library. Walking and talking, the students described what they were seeing, reflecting aloud on relationships among the living things and identifying familiar plants like maples and ferns. Along on the trip was Lina Moreira, a signer, and two parent volunteers. Ms. Moreira translated what was being said into sign language for RuthAnne, a child with limited hearing, and translated the child's signs into speech. Each parent walked along with a hyperactive child, who might have wandered if not watched closely.

Shortly the class came to a thicket, where the youngsters sat down to watch for birds. When the children sighted an unfamiliar bird, Janice and José, members of the Animals-in-Our-Environment team, looked it up in Peterson's *Field Guide to the Birds* by comparing key features with illustrations in the guide. Reading the entry to herself, Janice summarized the information for the class. Ms. Venezia mentioned that several birds were nesting in the thicket. Mark, the word keeper for the week, recorded *thicket* in his learning log as the class talked about why the word was a good describer of what they saw.

Building concepts through direct experience

Learning in Collaborative Teams

Learning to cooperate with others of diverse backgrounds and abilities

Back in the classroom, the third-graders talked briefly as a whole class, reflecting on what they had seen at the Fanwood Nature Center. Then they disbanded to work collaboratively in their investigative teams. On this afternoon, the Plants-in-Our-Environment Team and the Animals-in-Our-Environment Team merged to write a summary of their visit. The merged teams included Chandra from the Plants Team and Janice from the Animals Team, both of whom were gifted learners and facile readers with substantial vocabularies. Referring to their learning logs, team members talked about the trees they had noted—sassafras, sweet gum, tulip—checking the tree guide and trade books they had previously taken from the library for more information. As they proposed sentences, Lamal, a stutterer who was already turning into a computer hacker, entered them in the classroom computer.

When the six children from the two teams had drafted a paragraph, they checked punctuation, juxtaposed sentences to achieve a more logical order, and decided on a title. At that point, Ms. Venezia conferred with them, asking questions to guide their revisions and reminding them to run the computer spelling checker before Lamal printed a final publication copy to share with the class the next day.

Working on individual needs

Having prepared their next day's presentation, the six students turned to other cooperative or individual activities. Lamal printed publication copies on the computer and then viewed a filmstrip about reptiles to get information for his report on reptiles; as he viewed the strip, he entered the information into a computer database. José, who was gifted in art and was learning English as a second language, worked with Janice, a linguistically gifted child, on their bird book. José drew labeled sketches of birds based on illustrations in the Peterson guide, while Janice read in the guide for information to describe the birds. Later, chorusing together, they read a poem from Paul Fleischman's *I Am Phoenix*, which they were preparing to share with their classmates. Alone at a table, Chandra wrote vigorously; she had completed her research on trees and was well into a revised draft of her research report. When she had reached her saturation point and no longer felt like writing, she took out the book she had chosen for pleasure reading and settled back to enjoy. Frank was writing too, but slowly, a first draft on flowering plants, which he would later edit with Chandra, his writing mate. Shortly he left for the resource room to work with a teacher on his literacy problems.

Developing productive work habits

And then there was Bruce—a member of the Plants Team. Bruce walked about the classroom, pushed his desk around, and started to bother Chandra. At that point Ms. Venezia came over to him. She reviewed the rules of behavior the class had agreed on, emphasizing that in this class students did not disturb

PRESERVING NATURE'S HABITATS

Theme. We must preserve nature's habitats.

Objectives. By the end of the unit, the student is able to ✦ explain how organisms interact with the habitat in which they live and how human beings affect nature's habitats ✦ take personal actions that show respect for the environment ✦ read selectively for relevant material for a report ✦ organize information in a data synthesis chart ✦ organize facts and ideas for presenting to the class ✦ develop a first draft of a report and then edit and revise it for publication ✦ write a letter asking for information or stating a concern ✦ work cooperatively with others.

Focusing questions. How are plants and animals dependent on their environment? How do plants and animals affect their environment? What is a food chain? What impact do human beings have on natural food chains? What is an endangered species? What can humans do to lessen their negative impact on nature's food chains?

Integrative literature that ties the unit together (used in whole-class instruction). Baylor, Byrd, *The Other Way to Listen*; Fleischman, Paul, *Joyful Noises*; Kalman, Benjamin, *Animals in Danger*; Lewis, Patrick, *Earth Verses and Water Rhymes*; Newton, James, *Forest Log*; Tresselt, Alvin, *The Beaver Pond* and *The Dead Tree*.

Integrative activities for whole-class involvement. Take a trip to a nature preserve. Observe a miniature environment in the classroom: ant colony, fishbowl. Listen to literature read aloud. Discuss read aloud content, especially on food chains. Chorus poems for two voices from *Joyful Noises* and *Earth Verses*. Write poems together and alone modeled after *Joyful Noises* and *Earth Verses*. Chart together a model letter requesting information, another expressing concern. Create a model data synthesis chart on endangered species based on a survey of *Animals in Danger*.

Possible activities for small groups and individuals. Arrange a trip to a nature preserve. Look at organisms under a microscope; draw and label. Collect and label leaves, seeds, cones, etc. Use a field guide to identify organisms. Grow a common plant from seed; observe development. Listen as others in a team read aloud in a relevant reference; organize data as a web. Write a letter requesting information. Locate a video on subtopic. Write a summary of the video. Read for information on a subtopic. Make a data synthesis chart to organize information. Share information with the class. Prepare a brief written report; revise and edit it. Develop reports as an illustrated booklet. Locate information about food chains. Draw a food chain. Make a mural that shows life in a particular habitat. Listen to nature music to set a mood; write poems for two voices and earth verses that reflect the mood. Write a letter to the editor of a local paper expressing concern about the environment.

Animals in Our Environment

Focusing questions. What kinds of plants live in our environment? How do plants contribute to the natural environment? How do they fit into food chains? How do they contribute to the welfare of human beings? How can we preserve plants?

Literature. Baker, Jeff, *Patterns of Nature*; Christini, Ermanno, *In the Pond*; Coldrey, Jennifer, *The World of Frogs*; Daly, Kathleen, *A Child's Book of Snakes, Lizards, and Other Reptiles*; Fleischman, Paul, *I Am Phoenix: Poems for Two Voices*; Hirschi, Ron, *What Is a Bird*; Peterson, Roger, *A Field Guide to the Birds*; Pluckrose, Henry, *Reptiles*; Saint-Saens, Camille, *Carnival of the Animals**.

Plants in Our Environment

Focusing questions. What kinds of animals live in our environment? How are animals dependent on their environment? How do birds and reptiles fit into food chains? What are the carnivores and herbivores in our environment?

Literature. Darby, Gene, *What is a Plant?* and *A Tree Is a Plant*; Hogan, Paula, *The Dandelion*; Jennings, Terry, *Seeds*; Kirkpatrick, Rena, *Seeds and Weeds, Leaves,* and *Flowers;* Lewis, Naomi, *Leaves;* Selberg, Ingrid, *Nature's Hidden World;* Selsam, Millicent, *A First Look at the World of Plants;* Vivaldi, Antonio, *The Four Seasons* and "The Goldfinch"*.

Figure 2.1 Map of a Thematic Unit, Grade 3: Preserving Nature's Habitats *Indicates musical selections.

Rivers, Brooks, and Ponds

Focusing questions. What plants and animals live in brooks, rivers, and ponds? How do these organisms fit together in food chains? How does human activity affect food chain relationships in brooks and ponds? What can we do to preserve these habitats?

Literature. Bartlett, Margaret, *The Clean Brook* and *Where the Brook Began*; Belemary, David, *The River*; Brown, Mary, *Wings Along the Waterway*; Carrick, Carol, *The Brook*; Clegg, John, *Pond Life*; Holling, Holling C., *Paddle to the Sea*; Kirkpatrick, Rena, *Pond Life*; Locker, Thomas, *Where the River Begins*; Michle, Reinhard, *A Day on the River*; "Row, Row, Row Your Boat"*.

Forest Habitats

Focusing questions. What plants and animals live in the forest? How do the plants and animals fit together into forest food chains? What happens when humans destroy part of a forest food chain? What is a giant sequoia? What is a rain forest? What can we do to save the sequoia and the rain forests?

Literature. Adler, David, *Redwoods are the Tallest Trees in the World*; Armer, Laura, *The Forest Pool*; Baker, Jeannie, *Where the Forest Meets the Sea*; Bellamy, David, *The Forest*; Hirschi, Ron, *Who Lives in . . . the Forest?*; Lerner, Carol, *Flowers of a Woodland Spring*; Newton, James, *A Forest Is Reborn*; Yolen, Jane, *All in the Woodland Early*; Copland, Aaron, *Appalachian Spring*; MacDowell, Edward, *Woodland Sketches**.

Desert Habitats

Focusing questions. What plants and animals live in a desert? How do desert plants and animals fit together into desert food chains? What happens when humans destroy part of a desert chain? What causes a desert? Why do deserts spread? What can we do to prevent the spread of deserts?

Literature. Baylor, Byrd, *The Desert Is Theirs* and *Desert Voices*; Bash, Barbara, *Desert Giant: The Saguaro Cactus*; Busch, Phyllis, *Cactus in the Desert*; Catchpole, Clive, *Deserts*; John, Naomi, *Roadrunner*; Siebert, Diane, *Mojave*; Grofé, Ferde, *Grand Canyon Suite**.

The Seashore and the Ocean

Focusing questions. What plants and animals inhabit the seashore and the oceans? How do the plants and animals fit together in ocean and seashore food chains? How do humans affect the oceans and shore? What are the effects of an oil spill? What can we do to protect Earth's oceans and seashores?

Literature. Carrick, Carol, *Beach Bird*; Blashfield, Jean, *Oil Spills*; Booth, Eugene, *Under the Ocean*; Gordon, Sharon, *Dolphins and Porpoises*; Holling, Holling C., *Pagoo*; Kirkpatrick, Rena, *Shore Life*; Lilly, Kenneth, *Animals of the Ocean*; Seymour, Peter, *What Lives in the Sea? What's at the Beach?*; Debussy, Claude, *La Mer**.

others. Then she reviewed with him the tasks that were his contribution to the unit, gave him samples of leaves, needles, and cones that the nature center had provided, and looked over his shoulder as he began to make sketches of them to illustrate the encyclopedia of plants he was writing. Later in the week, Ms. Venezia conferred with Bruce's grandmother, his primary caregiver. She suggested that the grandmother talk with Bruce each day about his accomplishments and read aloud with him each evening.

Functioning within a community of learners

While the two teams were viewing, reading, writing, and sketching, the other students pursued individual or collaborative tasks intended to meet their needs. Behind the bookcase, in the viewing corner, the members of the team investigating forest habitats were viewing a videotape on rain forests. The members of the team working on the seashore and oceans were in the library, where the librarian was helping them locate information for their booklike report on water pollution. The members of the Desert Habitat Team were taking turns reading aloud to one another from a book on desert cacti. The members of the team investigating rivers, brooks, and ponds were discussing the organization of the book they were cooperatively writing, with each third-grader (especially Stuart, who generally wanted things done his way) insisting that his or her chapter be the first in the book. When Stuart stood up and shouted out that his chapter had to go first, Ms. Venezia went to the team, told Stuart to sit down, and helped the students use reason to resolve the problem: "What topic logically belongs first?" she asked.

Managing Diversity in the Classroom

While the students worked in teams and on their own, Ms. Venezia used some of her time to troubleshoot. She visited with individual students and groups that had problems in learning, socializing, and/or behaving. She kept alert to what the teams were doing and moved quickly to solve problems before they developed into unmanageable situations.

Learning English as a second language

In addition, Ms. Venezia conferred more formally with students who had special needs and with the investigative teams. That afternoon she conferred with José and Erica, who were learning English as a second language. In conference, she had them orally generate sentences modeled after sentences she proposed with words from the outing (e.g., "I saw a maple tree"; "I saw a cardinal in the maple tree"). To clarify meanings, she displayed pictures of trees and samples of objects as she and the students generated sentences. She also reminded the students about the English sentence-making program in the computer that they could run.

Learning to abide by the social amenities of language

Ms. Venezia also conferred with the Desert Habitat Team. She helped them organize a web of ideas based on the material they were reading aloud. During the group conference, Ms. Venezia accepted variant language patterns; children who spoke a variant form of English (e.g., Black English) used their own dialect to express ideas. On the other hand, Ms. Venezia did not accept a "four-letter word" used by one youngster. She stopped, made eye contact with the child, and explained in no uncertain terms that this language was inappropriate in classroom discussion.

Language Arts for All Children

The range of abilities and disabilities, interests and disinterests, previous experiences, and language backgrounds in most elementary classrooms is generally as broad or broader than that in Ms. Venezia's third grade. This is especially so since the advent of the Education for All Handicapped Children Act, or Public Law 92-142, which guarantees to every child the right to learn in the least restrictive environment (Congress of the United States, 1975). The term *least restrictive* relates to provision of instruction that meets individual needs; however, the term often implies assimilation of children with significant auditory, visual, speech, and/or physical disabilities into regular classrooms—what today is called *mainstreaming*. In the words of Kirk, Gallagher, and Anastasiow (1993), "Placement in integrated environments better prepares [exceptional] students to become well-adjusted contributing members of society."

At the same time, the range of differences within a classroom is broadened by the presence of youngsters from diverse cultures whose first language is not English and of others who speak variant forms, or dialects, of English. Learning side by side in multicultural classrooms with these children are youngsters who have severe learning problems, others who are extremely gifted, and still others who are attention deficit, hyperactive, and/or simply turned off to learning.

How does one busy teacher meet the needs of thirty or more children in an inclusive elementary classroom? In this chapter, we will examine possible answers to this tough question, keeping in mind what we observed in Ms. Venezia's third grade:

◆ The importance of providing a language-rich environment,
◆ The value of collaborative activities in enabling learners to read and write at their own levels and contribute based on their strengths,
◆ The value of ongoing literature- and content-area–based units in meeting diversity,
◆ The importance of maintaining a positive attitude toward all children and a close relationship with the home,
◆ The need for the teacher to cooperate with resource room teachers, specialists in the education of exceptional children, guidance counselors, psychologists, and school nurses.

Because space limitations prevent thorough coverage here, readers are urged to investigate topics in greater detail by studying texts on behavior impairments, multiculturalism, English as a second language, dialects, reading disabilities, and exceptional children.

Children with Behavior Impairments

In today's elementary schools are children who have a variety of emotional and social disorders. Some children are hyperaggressive; they hit, push, kick, swear, and want their own way. Some are hyperactive; they can't sit still, constantly get out of line, and fiddle around. Some have an attention-deficit disorder and can pay attention for only short periods, if at all. Others are withdrawn and make few contacts with others. And still others are completely turned off, for whatever reason, to school or are bored with school and just "act up." Because behavior disorders are so diverse, it is hard to generalize about ways to handle them. Yet teachers must deal with those youngsters who have behavior impairments if the classroom is to be an environment where all children can learn language happily together. In this section, we will discuss three approaches to working with students with behavior impairments: the team model of instruction, literature-based and thematic unit learning, and behavior modification.

The Team Model of Instruction

In *Control Theory in the Classroom* (1986), William Glasser explains the importance of the need for power in learning to read and write. By *power* Glasser means believing in oneself. Successful achievement, attention, and applause satisfy this need.

Glasser theorizes that the need for power affects children's learning to read and write. In their heads, people store pictures of activities that satisfy their needs. Initially, youngsters enter school with a positive picture of learning; they perceive reading and writing as exciting. But because of the way reading and writing are taught, they fail. Failing, they "take the picture of reading [and writing] as a need-satisfying activity out of their heads." In its place they put a picture of themselves as nonreaders and nonwriters and as disrupters whose misbehavior entertains other students.

How should teachers function so that students do not develop negative pictures of reading and writing and of themselves as learners? Glasser counsels patience in teaching young children to read and write. He suggests providing them with much opportunity to experience, make, view, listen, and speak. He advises that teachers read aloud to children, encourage them to join in the telling of stories, talk about literature with them, and expand vocabulary naturally through oral interaction. Teachers should stress ideas rather than letter-perfect renditions as children begin to read and emphasize ideas over correct spelling as children begin to write. They should keep the fun in early learning. What Glasser essentially proposes is a whole-language approach, which Constance Weaver (1991) suggests is the best way to work with attention-deficit children.

The same is true in upper grades. Often upper-grade teachers rely on individual assignments rather than on activities that require group interaction and cooperation: They assign students to read selections and write compositions without preliminary discussion. They assign homework and allocate class time to going over it. Glasser contends that this assignment model of instruction applied in the upper grades reinforces some students' view of themselves as nonreaders and nonwriters.

Read also Susan Hill and Tim Hill, *The Collaborative Classroom: A Guide to Co-operative Learning* (Portsmouth, N.H.: Heinemann, 1990), and Faye Brownlie, Susan Close, and Linda Wingren, *Tomorrow's Classroom Today: Strategies for Creating Active Readers, Writers, and Thinkers* (Portsmouth, N.H.: Heinemann, 1990).

In place of an assignment model, Glasser proposes a learning-team model. Rather than reading and writing by themselves, behavior-impaired upper-graders may be better off reading and writing in teams. According to Glasser, "we are all social animals; we need the support and interest of others" to make reading and writing interesting. Collaborating on a learning team to complete a project, older students gain a sense of belonging, which builds a perception of self-worth. "Belonging provides the initial motivation for students to work, and as they achieve academic success, students who have not worked previously begin to sense that knowledge is power and then want to work harder." The better students fulfill their needs for power and friendship by helping those who are weaker (as Janice helped José in the opening vignette). The weaker students fulfill their needs by contributing to a successful group endeavor; working alone, they rarely experience success. Students begin to rely on themselves rather than totally on their teacher to guide their learning (Glasser, 1986).

Collaborating to complete a science experiment as part of a cross-curricular unit, students gain a sense of accomplishment and build a positive self-concept. (© 1990 Joel Gordon)

Literature-Based and Thematic Unit Learning

Read the article on which this section is based: Marilyn D'Alessandro, "Accommodating Emotionally Handicapped Children Through a Literature-Based Reading Program," *The Reading Teacher*, 44 (December 1990), 288–293. Read also the following article, which gives ideas for integrating music with literature: Linda Lamme, "Exploring the World of Music Through Picture Books," *The Reading Teacher*, 44 (December 1990), 294–300.

Marilyn D'Alessandro (1990) teaches severely emotionally handicapped eight- and nine-year-old children in a multiethnic, special education setting in Brooklyn, New York. Some of her students are neurologically impaired, some come from chaotic homes, and some are foster children who have lived in many different homes. For this reason, she establishes an atmosphere that is "calm, regular, and above all, fair," with some rules that are nonnegotiable and apply equally to everyone.

While teaching these children, D'Alessandro found that when she changed from a basal-bound to a literature-based reading program, students' interest level went up and their attention and behavior improved. Students in her program read aloud in a teacher-guided group and discussed novels that appealed emotionally to them, such as *Charlotte's Web, Tales of a Fourth Grade Nothing*, the *Polk Street School* series, and *Journey to Jo'Burg*. They participated in numerous activities based on what they were reading, such as viewing videos, constructing papier-mâché animals, cooking, and visiting the zoo. D'Alessandro discovered that through this approach, the children "learned to control their emotions so that they did not interfere with comprehension while reading." Children whose normal behavior included shifting, pushing their desks, screaming, and fighting would "sit at a round [reading] table, crowded between other children, without panicking" and listen to a story that became an "avenue of escape" from their own problems. Most important, students came to view themselves as readers. They would choose to read, were proud of their reading ability, and asked other teachers to read with them in the same way.

See Figure 2.2 for an example of the kind of activity that works well as part of a unit.

Like Marilyn D'Alessandro, many teachers are building literature-based units into their language arts programs. They are also building thematic, content-area units as we saw earlier in Beth Venezia's classroom. Teachers are moving in these directions because the projects and investigations that are part of these units provide opportunity for individualizing instruction. These activities enable the teacher to meet the diverse learning needs of students and prevent some discipline problems from occurring.

Behavior Modification

But as anyone who has taught in an elementary classroom knows, discipline problems do occur, and they occur daily. One of the most productive approaches to discipline problems in the classroom is behavior modification, which uses positive reinforcement of acceptable behavior to decrease occurrences of unacceptable behavior. In one study, a preschooler withdrew from peer interaction, seeking adult attention by whining and complaining of illness. Observers in the classroom noticed that when the child exhibited the undesirable behaviors, the teacher attended to her. When the child finally joined into the class interaction, the teacher attended to the other children. Using behavior

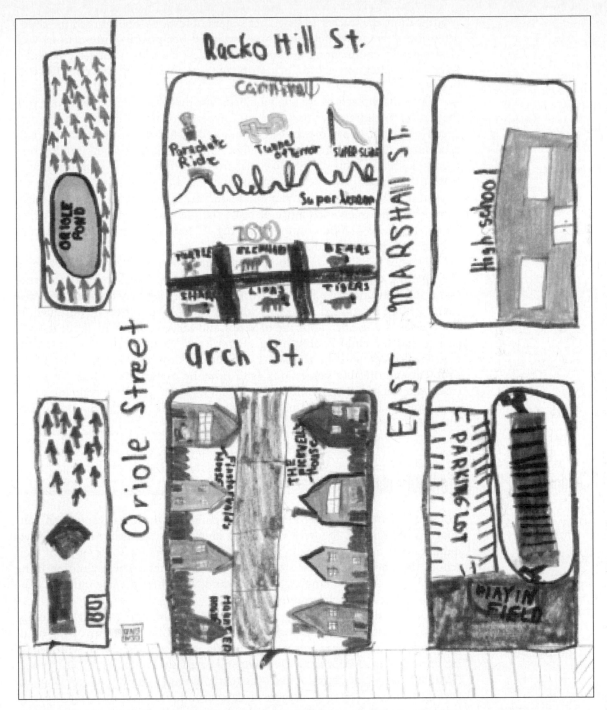

Figure 2.2 A Map Based on *Maniac Magee* by a Fifth Grader Who Is Growing Up in a Polish-American Home and Who Read the Book During a Class Novel Unit

SOURCE: Courtesy of Derek Jamiolkowski and Dena Underwood.

modification, the teacher reversed her system of rewards. She ignored the child's attention-demanding behaviors and rewarded her positive interactions with classmates by commenting favorably. After a few days, the youngster exhibited fewer adult-attention-getting behaviors and was interacting more readily with peers.

Elementary teachers are applying behavior modification in their work with inattentive, withdrawn, hyperactive, and hyperaggressive children. They ignore specific deviant behaviors, but as soon as the child does something socially acceptable, they reinforce that behavior. Thus, primary teachers might comment, "Let's all sit up straight like Richard." Watching children collaborate in teams, they might say, "Let's keep our voices at a conversational level like the boys and girls on the Forest Habitat Team." In upper grades, teachers might commend a normally inattentive or restless student after a discussion in which he or she made a good comment, saying, "That was a great idea you contributed, Michael. You did a good job today."

Behavior modification techniques are harder to apply than to describe, as the opening vignette indicates. Remember that Ms. Venezia spoke to Bruce about his disruption of Chandra's work. Sometimes a behavior is so disruptive that it cannot be ignored, especially when it could harm others if continued. In these cases, the teacher stops the behavior and talks to the child about it, indicating that the child is preventing others from learning. In some cases, the teacher also contacts the primary caregiver, making him or her aware of the problem and offering suggestions as to how the caregiver can help. In severe cases, the teacher consults the school psychologist or guidance counselor, who may provide additional information on ways to handle the problem or talk with the child to get at underlying causes.

Children with Diverse Language and Cultural Backgrounds

See Elizabeth Quinero and Ana Huerta-Macias, "All in the Family: Bilingualism and Biliteracy," *The Reading Teacher*, 44 (December 1990), 306–312. Also see Hwa-Ja Lee Lim and Dorothy Watson, "Whole Language Content Classes for Second-Language Learners," *The Reading Teacher*, 46 (February 1993), 384–393, for an exciting description of an ESL program in which language is naturally and functionally learned.

In today's elementary classrooms are also children whose native, or first, language is not English. Students whose first language is Spanish, Arabic, or Vietnamese learn and interact with native English speakers for some or all of their school day and are instructed by monolingual teachers. These children bring not only their diverse language backgrounds but their diverse cultures. The result is multicultural classrooms.

Collaborative team activity and ongoing literature and content-area units, approaches discussed in the previous section, are as helpful in involving bilingual children in language learning as they are in engaging children with behavior impairments. As Elizabeth Quintero and Ana Huerta-Macias (1990) explain, "Whole language activities both in the native language and the target language are appropriate." Having already discussed collaborative and ongoing unit learning, we will focus in this section on ways to help children learn English as a second language and ways to help all children develop an appreciation of cultural diversity.

English as a Second Language (ESL)

The language arts teacher plays three roles in helping children learn English as a second language. First, the teacher serves as a speech model. Often those who are becoming bilingual—who are learning English even as they maintain proficiency in their native language—converse at home and in their communities in their native language. As a result, their inability to communicate in English cuts them off from neighborhood English-speaking children. Their major contact with English is at school, and their beginning attempts at English mimic the pronunciation, intonation patterns, and sentence patterns heard at school. The need for teachers who speak English well cannot be overemphasized.

Second, the teacher must be aware that the child's native language differs from English not only in vocabulary but in the speech sounds that make up words, in basic sentence patterns, in intonation patterns, and even in nonverbal behavior. For example, Spanish speakers who have already learned their alphabet pronounce the vowels as /ah/, /ey/, /ee/, /o/, /oo/, not as /a/, /e/, /i/, /o/, /u/; thus, they have difficulty distinguishing among words such as *cut, cat,* and *cot.* There are structural differences, too. The descriptive adjective usually follows the noun in Spanish. Other basic structural differences include no *s* for the third-person singular verb; no use of the auxiliaries *do, does, did,* and *will;* and substitution of the verb *to be* for the verb *to have.* Spanish speakers may also have difficulty adjusting to some of the conventions of written English. The manner of indicating questions and exclamations differs in the two languages; so does the use of direct quotations.

Once aware of such differences, the teacher can design oral sequences that focus on them. Much of this work occurs in small groups as the teacher gathers together children learning English as a second language and provides practice with basic sentence and sound patterns. During sessions, conversations grow out of firsthand contact with objects and pictures, role playing serves as a context for using language, and pantomime takes the place of verbal language when communication breaks down.

Some specific strategies for building language facility that are described in Chapter 11 are especially helpful:

1. *Expansions:* adding words at key spots in a sentence;
2. *Transformations:* transforming kernel sentences into questions, exclamations, and negative sentences;
3. *Sentence building:* creating sentences from subject and predicate parts;
4. *Sentence combining:* Building one sentence from two short sentences.

Rhythmic interpretation of sentences using typical English rhythm patterns, discussed in Chapters 6 and 13, is also helpful.

A third role of the teacher in language arts for children whose first language is not English is to communicate sincere appreciation for the culture of speakers of other languages. The goal of instruction is not only the acquisition of a

Bilingual expresses the assumption that children will become proficient in a target as well as in their native language.

Read Christine Sutton, "Helping the Nonnative English Speaker with Reading," *The Reading Teacher,* 42 (May 1989), 684–688, and Pauline Gibbons, *Learning to Learn in a Second Language* (Portsmouth, N.H.: Heinemann Educational Books, 1993).

These activities should be oral so that children gain control over sentence patterns.

THE FORUM   On Promoting Cultural Awareness

1. The sociologist James Fallows writes, "America is unusual because of its fundamental idea of how a society holds itself together. American society is not made of people who all happened to be living in a certain region or who have some mystic tribal tie. It's made of people who came or were brought here from somewhere else. . . . One of the things that make America most unusual is its assumption that race should not matter, that a society can be built of individuals with no particular historic or racial bond to link them together. This is a noble belief: it makes America better than most societies. . . . The force that motivates the country is a vision of people always in motion, able to make something different of themselves, ready for second chances until the day they die. . . . The vision starts with the act of immigration—choosing to become an American—and continues through the choices and changes that make American life so different from Japanese or Italian life" ("The Importance of Being Abnormal," *More Like Us* [Boston: Houghton Mifflin, 1989]).

2. Doris Walker-Dalhouse proposes, "The multicultural and multiethnic composition of our society today necessitates instruction that addresses the literacy needs of all of its people. Instruction must promote cultural awareness and a valuing of parallel cultures. . . . Multiethnic literature can be used as an important tool in helping all students develop a healthy self-concept, one that depends upon a knowledge of and a sense of pride in family and educational background. The use of multiethnic literature can also extend the knowledge base of individuals in parallel cultures by exposing them to the differences and similarities between their culture and that of other groups" ("Using African-American Literature to Increase Ethnic Understanding," *The Reading Teacher*, 45 [February 1992], 416–422). To these ends, Walker-Dalhouse develops literature-focus units in which students listen to or read such books as Hamilton's *Zeely*; Greene's *Philip Hall Likes Me, I Reckon Maybe* and *Get On Out of Here, Philip Hall*; Lester's *To Be a Slave*; and Taylor's *Let the Circle Be Unbroken*. See Lee Galda's "Exploring Cultural Diversity," *The Reading Teacher*, 45 (February 1992), 452–460, for a bibliography of children's books that reveal the "cultural wonders of our world." For an example of a multicultural literature unit, see Howard Miller and Karen Dumey, "Weaving a Spell with African Folktales," *Journal of Reading*, 36 (February 1993), 404–406.

Questions to Consider

Do you agree with Fallows' view of the uniqueness of America? Why or why not? Why is it important to build social sensitivity to the needs of others? How can reading literature contribute to that sensitivity? What could Ms. Venezia have done to develop such sensitivity in her class?

Read Catherine Walsh, "Language, Meaning, and Voice," *Language Arts*, 64 (February 1987), 196–206, and Dorothy King, "Assessment and Evaluation in Bilingual and Multicultural Classrooms," in *Assessment and Evaluation in Whole Language Programs*, ed. Bill Harp (Norwood, Mass: Christopher-Gordon, 1991), 159–175.

second language with parallel development in the first (bilingualism) but also the ability to function within both the American and the native cultures (biculturalism). To achieve biculturalism, the teacher can allot time for sharing ideas about the customs that are part of the life of different peoples. Holidays celebrated by children who come from other parts of the world can be observed in classrooms, just as Halloween and Thanksgiving are celebrated there. Appreciating diversity, the teacher can encourage native English speakers to learn words introduced by Spanish, Vietnamese, or German speakers. In this way, native English speakers begin to appreciate diverse languages and cultures, and newcomers feel that the language and culture they bring are of value.

Language Arts for Migrant Children

The United States and Canada have a relatively large population of migrants—seasonal workers employed in agriculture who follow jobs from place to place. Although not all migrant workers are bilingual and bicultural, many of those in the Southwest are among the language different. In the classroom, migrant children pose an additional problem: They stay only a short time in school and then move on or even miss schooling altogether.

In most programs geared to meet the needs of the migratory population, teachers must emphasize the development of a healthy self-concept. Children who move have less opportunity to develop close friends. Because they are often poor, speak a different native language, and have different cultural backgrounds, they may be the target of other children's taunts. However, these children have strengths. They may be more knowledgeable about geographical differences, having traveled more widely; they may be capable painters, vocalists, storytellers. Teachers must help these children display their talents, for success is necessary in the development of a positive self-concept. Teachers must also help children interact naturally with classmates, placing them in collaborative groups where they can learn, contribute, and feel good about themselves.

In the same way, teachers must emphasize target-language development for those whose native language is not English. They should supply extensive first-hand experience as a base for oral interaction and design lessons that involve considerable oral work to develop a functional speaking-listening English vocabulary. Experience charting (as described in the opening vignette in Chapter 1) is an important tool for making the transition between oral and written language. Students can dictate charts in both their native and target languages, going on to read what they have composed. In addition, teachers should share stories from the children's own cultures, using them as a base for informal conversations.

Finally, teachers and schools must assume responsibility for children's health problems, assuming that if children are poorly fed or in ill health, they will be less likely to acquire language facility. Many districts employ a home-school liaison to keep communication lines open and refer needy families to agencies supplying food, clothing, and other help. Educational service centers in some districts provide consultants and workshops to assist teachers in meeting the special language needs of migratory children.

Dialectically Different Children

Most languages comprise a number of variant forms, or dialects, that differ in vocabulary, syntactic structure, and/or pronunciation. This diversity should be expected, because language is always changing and words and expressions mean different things to different people.

Linguists remind us that no dialect of a language is inherently superior and none is deficient. Variations of languages are different because they have changed in response to the needs of the people using them. In discussing dialects, the words *correct* and *incorrect* are inappropriate. The appropriate question is whether the language variant communicates clearly to listeners.

Read Jo Ann Taylor, "Teaching Children Who Speak a Nonstandard Dialect to Read," *Reading Improvement,* 24 (Fall 1987), 160–162.

Yet feelings about the desirability of certain forms do exist. "I be goin'" communicates clearly, but the usage strikes a negative chord in some people. The same is true of such expressions as "I ain't got none" and "I done it." These expressions, which are socially unacceptable to large numbers of speakers, have been termed *nonstandard.*

Unfortunately, some expressions that are part of some dialects are nonstandard. This poses a problem for youngsters who come to school speaking a nonstandard variant. These children often test lower on standardized tests of verbal facility than their classmates, for their ability is being measured in a dialect other than their own.

Regional and Social Group Dialects

One kind of dialect that poses only minor problems to educators has regional origins. Contrast the varieties of English spoken in New England, the Midwest, and the Southeast. Words like *grease, root, car, creek,* and *metal* have decidedly different pronunciations. Words like *tonic* and *soda, hoagie* and *submarine* convey different meanings in different parts of the country.

A second kind of dialect is based on social group. In the United States, some groups have developed dialects identifiable in terms of vocabulary, sentence structure, and pronunciation. These dialects include Black, Cajun, Appalachian, and Hawaiian English—dialects that to some are socially unacceptable, or nonstandard. According to Joan Baratz (1969), these dialects are "well-ordered, highly structured, highly developed language systems" with extensive vocabularies and consistent rules for sentence making. Speakers of these variants apply sentence-making rules just as automatically and consistently as speakers of other dialects. Because some of the structures of these dialects are considered nonstandard by many teachers, however, their speakers are at risk of falling behind in school.

Educational Approaches to the Dialectally Different

For a discussion of problems associated with the term *at-risk children*, read Barbara Flores et al., "Transforming Deficit Myths about Learning, Language, and Culture," *Language Arts*, 68 (September 1991), 369–379.

How to approach the education of those speaking nonstandard dialects is a question of continuing concern. Logically, three approaches exist: to replace, to keep, and to add.

To Replace   The replace approach attempts to replace the nonstandard dialect with the dialect standard for the region. As they speak, children are "corrected" to bring their language in line with the standard. The problems with this approach are numerous. Children who are made to believe there is something wrong with their speech may stop speaking in school, which is counterproductive. Then, too, language is a social phenomenon, a part of culture; in requiring a complete dialect change, schools are destroying culture.

To Keep   The keep approach takes an opposite tack: Every dialect has equal communication potential, and no child should be forced to speak or write a dialect other than the one the child has acquired within his or her social group or region. The dialect children bring to school should be accepted as a structurally consistent means of communication, fully capable of carrying messages to others. This dialect should be used as the medium of instruction, say advocates of the keep approach. Children should be encouraged to express themselves in their own dialect rather than in the standard one.

There are numerous problems with the keep approach. First, few books have been written with nonstandard sentence patterns and vocabulary. Speakers who wish to read must know how to interpret the syntax and vocabulary of the standard form. Second, nonstandard dialects are not used in a vast range of business and social situations. Nonstandard speakers are less likely to find high-paying managerial and professional employment.

Note that Ms. Venezia used this approach in her classroom.

To Add   The add approach is a middle-of-the-road position. Advocates urge full acceptance of the language diversity children bring to school. Children should be encouraged to communicate in their dialect, sharing ideas and enjoying verbal interaction. Advocates suggest, however, that it would be unfair not to introduce the standard dialect to children who speak a nonstandard one, because this might hinder their economic advancement. For that reason, teachers are urged to provide opportunities for children to learn standard English as a second dialect so that they can function in situations that call for the standard. Meanwhile, they continue to speak their own dialect in social situations calling for the first dialect. In effect, the add approach helps children become bidialectal.

As with the other approaches, achievement of bidialectal skill poses problems. Even as children are learning to read, they must learn to handle the standard dialect in its oral form, which is not required of children who grow up speaking standard English.

Despite its weaknesses, the bidialectal position remains the most popular

Read Jean Gillet and J. Richard Gentry, "Bridges Between Nonstandard and Standard English with Extensions of Dictated Stories," *The Reading Teacher*, 36 (January 1983), 360–366. The article describes a four-step language experience approach to teaching standard English forms.

approach. To teach standard English as a second dialect, elementary teachers can rely on the same strategies highlighted in the section on bilingual children: lots of oral activity in which children build, transform, expand, combine, and orally interpret standard English sentence patterns; much opportunity to participate in experience charting and oral reading of the charts; and collaborative and unit learning.

Teacher attitude is important. Everyone who teaches should be familiar with the nature of dialectal differences and understand that no dialect is better than others. Teachers should be aware of any tendency they may have to judge forms of speech and to react to the form rather than to the content of a message. They need to take care not to interrupt children to correct sentence or word structure. Constant interruption and correction can easily turn a pleasurable sharing time into a period of discomfort that children dread. Communication, after all, means sharing, and successful sharing of meanings is a major goal of classroom oral interaction.

Children Who Are Learning Disadvantaged or Learning Disabled

A "must-read" article is Laura Robb, "A Cause for Celebration: Reading and Writing for At-Risk Students," *The New Advocate*, 6 (Winter 1993), 25–40. It describes Laura Robb's literature-based activities with at-risk seventh and eighth graders.

Another group that is the concern of the elementary school teacher consists of children whose academic achievement is below their peers'. Some children are poor achievers because of low IQs. Studies indicate that about 20 percent of the population have IQs between 70 and 90 and that these youngsters are usually placed in regular classrooms for most of the school day. Other children are poor achievers because they lack motivation or interest in school activities or have had limited experiences with language and books before coming to school. In a sense, these children are *learning disadvantaged*.

Other students are *learning disabled*; they have, in the words of the Education for All Handicapped Children Act of 1975, a disorder "in one or more of the basic psychological processes involved in understanding or in using language, spoken or written, which disorder may manifest itself in imperfect ability to listen, think, speak, read, write, spell, or to do mathematical calculations."

Children Who Are Learning Disadvantaged

Read Katherine Maria, "Developing Disadvantaged Children's Background Knowledge Interactively," *The Reading Teacher*, 42 (January 1989), 296–300, for a description of a way of handling reading with children of limited experiential background.

How does the teacher work with children who are learning disadvantaged? Katherine Maria (1989) proposes that the teacher focus on what children know rather than on what they do not know. She recommends having children brainstorm before reading to activate their prior knowledge, focusing children's attention before reading on the concepts central in a selection, and using a variety of before-reading strategies.

Along similar lines, Michael Ford and Marilyn Ohlhausen (1988) suggest that the teacher

- Focus on real, meaningful learning through the use of thematic units;
- Emphasize use of whole-language activities that capitalize on children's oral language skills;
- Implement whole-class activities (such as personalized reading and journal writing) that have built-in individualization;
- Use open-ended projects (such as the publication of a team booklet or class newspaper, or the production of a drama);
- Plan writing activities that allow individual students to respond at their own levels and provide structure for writing;
- Use group incentives and internal competition (such as award of a bronze medal for 800 minutes of independent reading—a goal within the reach of most readers, a silver medal for 900 minutes, and a gold medal for 1,000 minutes) to motivate children to read;
- Implement a cross-grade sharing arrangement with a group of younger students in which slower upper-grade children read easy stories to a younger, receptive audience.

Also important are helping children to appreciate their own styles of reading and writing and helping them to "expand upon personal images of themselves as literate learners" (Taylor and Dorsey-Gaines, 1988).

In many schools today, resource room teachers (or Chapter 1 teachers) give special instruction to children who are below grade level in reading and writing. These teachers typically handle a limited number of children at any one time and work in resource rooms equipped with materials to help children with learning problems. Often the classroom teacher must tell the resource room teacher learnings to emphasize with a child and, in some cases, provide ideas as to the instruction required. The classroom teacher called upon to set up a learning plan for the child with reading and writing problems must remember that giving drill exercises to a child who does not like to read will probably make that child dislike reading even more. The classroom teacher must encourage the resource room teacher to engage children creatively in whole-language activities that involve story listening, discussion, and group writing and to use interesting content from science, history, and geography.

Children Who Are Learning Disabled

Learning disabilities have a variety of causes. Brain dysfunction, genetics, lack of early environmental stimulation, severe malnutrition in the early years, and biochemical factors are among causes identified by Kirk, Gallagher, and Anastasiow (1993).

One form that learning disability can take is alexia. The term *alexia* applies to a reading disability that may be related to a central nervous system impairment, such as a lesion in the brain. Some people with alexia cannot grasp a whole word; they put even the simplest words together letter by letter. Others

Read about Reading Recovery, an early intervention program to help low-achieving six-year-olds become readers. It grows out of the work of Marie Clay (1985). In Reading Recovery, "reading and writing abilities are developed within lessons that use natural language and predictable texts rather than isolated skill drills" (Lola Hill and Mary Hale, "Reading Recovery," *The Reading Teacher*, 44 [March 1991], 480–483). See also Diane DeFord, Carol Lyons, and Gay Su Pinnell, *Bridges to Literacy: Learning from Reading Recovery* (Portsmouth, N.H.: Heinemann, 1991).

For a discussion of problems with the term *learning disability*, read Joyce Salvage and Phyllis Brazee, "Risk Taking, Bit by Bit," *Language Arts*, 68 (September 1991), 356–366. See also Carol Fuhler, "Let's Move Toward Literature-Based Reading Instruction," *The Reading Teacher*, 43 (January 1990), 312–315, for a discussion of reading literature with learning-disabled students.

THE FORUM On Literature in Resource Room Programs

1. Hilary Sumner explains the importance of resource room instruction that goes beyond drill on skills: "The program in a resource room must be adapted to each individual. It should encourage literacy through the constant interaction of the student's listening, speaking, reading, and writing experiences. Thematic units are particularly successful ways to create this interaction. . . . A literacy approach is profoundly more appropriate for learning disabled students than the typically controlled remedial approaches used in the past" ("Whole Language Assessment and Evaluation," in *Assessment and Evaluation in Whole Language Programs*, ed. Bill Harp [Norwood, Mass.: Christopher-Gordon, 1991], 145).

2. Marjorie and Ronald Shumaker report a study in which sixth-grade remedial students made remarkable reading progress through a literature-based approach in which children discussed a book they were reading (*Sadako and the Thousand Paper Cranes* [Dell, 1977]), wrote responses, read related books, and pursued a variety of creative activities. Shumaker and Shumaker conclude: "In remedial reading programs, literature supplies multiple benefits. . . . It suggests strategies for enduring and overcoming painful life situations and transitions. It enhances the child's self concept and reduces the isolation of the struggling student. It has the look, sound, and rhythm of language as used by masters. Unlike the artificial language constructs of workbooks, unlike the anonymous voices of textbooks, this is real language, the potent medium of writing and reading. . . . The experience of reading in school should be active, pleasurable, and motivational. To accomplish all of these goals, literature written for children should be at the center of any remedial reading program" ("3000 Paper Cranes: Children's Literature for Remedial Readers," *The Reading Teacher*, 41 [February 1988], 544–549).

Questions to Consider

What advantages does an integrated language arts approach to the teaching of remedial reading offer over a workbook approach? Why do some resource room teachers rely on fill-in-the-blanks activity rather than involving children in reading, writing, and oral language? How can literature be used to help children become bidialectal or bilingual?

with alexia can recognize the meanings of words but cannot read them aloud (Holowinsky, 1983).

Neurological problems that affect writing go under the name of *agraphia*. Some students with this condition manifest problems in writing from dictation. Others are able to write letters dictated one by one but cannot write syllables or words.

Considerable controversy exists as to how to work with children who have neurological impairments. The teacher who is uncertain about a child with a severe problem in reading or writing should consult a learning disability specialist, if there is one in the school district, for it is important to distinguish between problems caused by poor motivation and those caused by a disability such as alexia.

Gifted and Talented Children

In most elementary schools, slow and gifted learners learn together in the same classroom. Lewis Terman (Terman and Merrill, 1960), the "pioneer" of intelligence testing, identifies three categories of giftedness: the high average (IQs ranging from 110 to 120), the superior (IQs between 120 and 140), and the very superior (IQs between 140 and 170). Children in these categories generally exhibit rapid language development, since most IQ tests are verbally based.

Yale psychologist Robert Sternberg (1984) questions heavy reliance on IQ tests in determining children's potential for learning. He notes that high IQ neither ensures intelligent performance in real-life situations nor correlates positively with success in life. In Sternberg's words, "intelligent performance in the real world centers on the ability to capitalize on one's strengths and to compensate for one's weaknesses and on the ability to modify the environment so that it will better fit one's adaptive skills." Sternberg also questions whether tests given under time pressure are true indicators of intelligence and proposes that such tests fail to identify the potential of children who have grown up in environments characterized by some type of deprivation. Clearly, too, giftedness can be expressed in diverse ways. Children can have musical, artistic, technical, and/or social talents.

Characteristics of Gifted Children

To identify youngsters with exceptional mental abilities, teachers should ask these questions:

+ How rapidly does this child learn? How clearly does he or she perceive relationships?
+ How probing are the child's questions? How curious is he or she?

- How extensive is the child's oral vocabulary?
- How easily does the child pick up and retain information?
- How divergent are the child's answers? How creative and novel are his or her approaches to problems?
- What level of questions does the child answer? Does the child respond well mainly at the factual level, or is he or she able to hypothesize, predict, and generalize?

A factor that confuses some teachers trying to identify gifted children is that this category includes youngsters who are disabled in speech, hearing, vision, or social adjustment. A noteworthy example is Helen Keller, who was both deaf and blind. A gifted child can be shy, restless, and inattentive; he or she can be a stutterer or exhibit articulation problems. Particular care must be taken in working with children who speak a different native language or dialect. Although these youngsters may do poorly on traditional tests, some within the group have the sharpness of mind that characterizes giftedness.

Programs for Gifted Children

For an annotated bibliography of materials on reading for gifted children, see Ann Lukasevich, "Three Dozen Useful Information Sources on Reading for the Gifted," *The Reading Teacher*, 36 (February 1983), 542–548. For teaching ideas, see Honre Gitelman, "Motivating Accelerated Learners to Read," *The Reading Teacher*, 37 (March 1984), 678–679.

Gifted children tend to be rapid language learners. They read at an early age and may enter school as self-taught readers and writers. They have vocabularies that astound the average adult and perform higher-level cognitive tasks with ease. As a result, they require little drill with the basics, for they grasp ideas quickly. Instead of drilling, the teacher must open doors that encourage youngsters to discover, reflect, and think critically. The teacher should

- Provide a large array of books that will fascinate students who are already intrigued by words (the *Guinness Book of World Records*, an atlas, a world almanac, encyclopedias, a giant dictionary, field guides, an adult thesaurus);
- Schedule trips to the library to select books that will stimulate curiosity and satisfy children's hunger to learn;
- Schedule small-group discussions that treat subjects in greater depth than is possible in an inclusive class;
- Ask questions that lead readers to interpret, apply, analyze, synthesize, and evaluate;
- Encourage children to interrelate aspects of a particular experience and go beyond repetitive tasks to solve related problems;
- Suggest sophisticated assignments such as interviewing; researching; keeping notes for the entire class; making tapes, filmstrips, or slides; creating language games; and compiling a computer data base;
- Encourage leadership by asking youngsters to lead a discussion, explain, or help others;
- Encourage children to participate in special events such as young authors' conferences and science fairs.

Personalized reading is a means through which accelerated learners can expand their knowledge and interests beyond the regular curriculum. (© 1993 Jean-Claude Lejeune)

Ask gifted readers to compare two different versions of the same story; several books by the same author and/or illustrator; books by two different authors and/or illustrators. Then have students develop original versions or write in the style of a writer analyzed.

For language-gifted children, writing must be welded with reading as they develop the ability to handle diverse literary forms and styles. Writing original versions modeled after published story structures and styles, writing and sending letters to magazine and newspaper editors, writing critical reviews of stories, writing abbreviated encyclopedias, almanacs, atlases after researching a topic are all writing activities that flow naturally out of reading that language-gifted children can pursue independently or in teams.

As with dialectally different children, teacher attitude is important. James Gallagher (1975) reports that research studies "present us with a portrait of hostile feelings of teachers toward the gifted student." He suggests that these feelings are a reaction to the threat gifted youngsters pose to teachers. A description of one gifted youngster's manner of interacting with adults (Hildreth, 1966) hints at how a youngster may unknowingly intimidate a teacher:

> One day a visitor strolled over to the shelf of new books in a school library, picked out a book, and leafed through it. An alert ten-year-old stepped right up. "Here's a better book on horses than that one," he commented. "It has beautiful pictures." He exclaimed over details in the book, then picked out several others rapidly. "My favorite picture—lions in the jungle," and he sketched the story rapidly. The visitor turned the page, commenting on the next picture, "Leopards, no, wildcats." "Oh, no," said the boy, "those are cheetahs." "Have you read all these books?" inquired the visitor, indicating a row of 200 or 300 volumes. "Well, not quite all of them (modestly), but I know what most of them are about" (Hildreth, 1966).

Children with Sensory Impairments

In the past, children with severe sensory impairments spent most of their school years in special classrooms instructed by teachers trained in educating students with disabilities. Today, as a result of Public Law 94-142, the regular elementary teacher must deal with hearing and visually impaired youngsters, who spend some or all of their day in inclusive classrooms.

Children with a Hearing Impairment

Read Joanne Carlsen, "Between the Deaf Child and Reading," The Reading Teacher, 38 (January 1985), 424–426. See also Elizabeth Fielding, "Dealing with Auditory Processing Problems in the Classroom," Reading Today, 10 (June/July 1993), 28.

Although deaf children are generally not placed in regular classrooms, children whose hearing is impaired to an extent that interferes with normal language learning and oral participation may spend some or all of their day in an elementary class. The teacher has a twofold responsibility to these youngsters: to identify those who have an impairment and to aid them in language development despite their disability.

Behaviors that may be clues to some loss of hearing include speaking in a very loud voice, repeating answers already given, an inability to distinguish certain language sounds and make those sounds clearly, and playing a tape recorder at a high volume. Children who a teacher suspects have an impairment should be referred to the school health services for diagnostic testing.

Authorities advocate the use of specific procedures when working with hearing-impaired children in regular classrooms:

✦ Seating children where they can see the teacher's lip movements; not standing before a strong light source that may prevent children from observing moving lips; forming children's chairs into circles during talk times; and refraining from talking while a child's back is turned;
✦ Talking clearly and naturally in full sentences; writing important directions on the board;
✦ Allowing children to move around the room to be where they can hear best;
✦ Encouraging children to participate in oral interaction;
✦ Using a computer that substitutes a blinking menu bar for the audible, attention-getting beep.

For a comprehensive treatment of deafness in children, see D. Moores, *Educating the Deaf: Psychology, Principles, and Practices* (Boston: Houghton Mifflin, 1987).

Learning to speak, read, and spell poses problems for children who are hard of hearing. Phonics, which relies on perception of differences in sounds, may be physically impossible for some, requiring greater reliance on contextual clues, sight words, and structural analysis. Tactile, kinesthetic, and visual techniques for learning to spell gain in significance over approaches that stress sound-symbol relationships. For some children, speaking is a parallel problem; distortions of speech sounds occur because youngsters cannot hear the sounds.

In most, if not all, cases, children with a hearing impairment who are integrated into regular classes have some hearing, which can be amplified with hearing aids and used to facilitate interpretation and production of speech. Individualization is necessary, with the child being guided through an instructional sequence beginning with recognition of gross sounds and leading to the ability to discriminate speech sounds that look alike when formed on the lips. To assist children in producing difficult speech sounds, many schools make available a speech therapist, who can also help the teacher by providing suggestions, materials, and information on how to adjust the program.

Children with a Visual Impairment

Like a hearing impairment, a loss of visual acuity can affect a child's ability to interpret and produce language. Often the elementary school teacher first recognizes a possible impairment by observing that a child bends the head down to the desk or holds a book up near the eyes when reading, squints at the board, covers one eye, blinks excessively, and/or thrusts the body forward to see. A youngster may say that he or she cannot see board writing or complain of blurriness while reading. A teacher should refer a child who exhibits a combination of these symptoms to the child's caregiver and to the school health service for eye examination.

Children with some vision loss, especially a loss that cannot be corrected with glasses, can be helped by

- ✦ Placement near the board;
- ✦ Instruction in small groups, clustered around an easel where words are written clearly in large print;
- ✦ Use of a reader-mate, who reads directions printed on the board;
- ✦ Use of paper on which the lines have been darkened; use of darkened handwriting models; use of raised-letter models;
- ✦ Use of hearing, feeling, and touching rather than low-intensity pictures as a stimulus for speaking and writing;
- ✦ Preparation of special materials such as tests in large print; dictation of test questions;
- ✦ Provision of large-print versions of written materials and of computer technology that allows print magnification on the computer screen;
- ✦ Provision of chart paper on which to write down individual stories in large print.

Children with visual impairments may find computer use difficult. Other solutions include screen reading programs, speech synthesizers, and the option to view on-screen images in white on black ("The Macintosh and Disability Access," *Syllabus*, No. 23 [Summer 1992], 6–11).

Children with Speech Problems

There are four major kinds of speech problems: articulation disorders, stuttering, phonation problems, and delayed or limited speech development. In most school systems, a speech therapist has direct responsibility for helping children with speech problems. The teacher's responsibility lies in identifying youngsters with impairments and providing a relaxed environment that encourages children to speak.

Articulation Disorders

Articulation disorders are the most frequent communication problems in children. Some youngsters substitute one sound for another, as in using the /w/ for the /r/ to produce *wed wose*; or the /t/ for the /k/ to produce a *tite* rather than a *kite*; or the /d/ for the /t/ or /th/ to produce *drain* for *train* and *dat* for *that*. Some youngsters omit sounds, especially those they find too difficult to produce and/or those they do not hear. Final-consonant sounds are commonly omitted in speaking, and a few youngsters produce no final-consonant sounds at all. A third form of articulation disorder is distortion. The /s/ is commonly distorted, accompanied by extraneous hissing or whistling sounds.

Speech specialists suggest two causes of articulation disorders: faulty learning of the English sound system and physical problems that prevent the production of language sounds. In the first case, therapists provide instruction on exactly how each sound is produced and are rather successful in remediating the problem. Speech disorders related to physical functioning, as would be the case with cerebral palsy, cleft palate, or severe hearing loss, are less easily corrected; these require treatment by trained specialists.

Stuttering

For a discussion of the theory and treatment of stuttering, see A. Bloodstein, *A Handbook of Stuttering*, 3rd ed. (Chicago: National Easter Seal Society, 1987).

Stuttering is a speech disorder that in its most severe state is accompanied by exaggerated physical behavior—gasping for air, contortions of the face, blinking of the eyes, tensing of the body. Many children between three and five years of age typically repeat speech sounds, and adults often repeat in speaking. This is normal speaking behavior. Somehow, from normal speaking behavior severe stuttering develops with the physical manifestations associated with what specialists call *secondary stuttering*. Although it is not entirely clear why and how secondary stuttering develops, it is considered a learned behavior. Attempts to avoid stuttering may be responsible to some extent for the development of accompanying physical behaviors.

Phonation Problems

Phonation disorders include problems related to intensity, pitch, quality, and rhythm of the voice. The husky, the monotone, the shrill, the nasal, and the too-soft voice are all phonation problems. Some are organic, resulting from a faulty mouth, nose, or vocal fold structure. Some are learned through associations with parents who speak similarly. Some may relate to psychological functioning.

Delayed or Limited Speech Development

A few children in early primary grades exhibit almost no speech at all. By twelve months, they are not speaking the two or three words typical of most young children; by twenty-four months, they have not yet begun to put together very simple sentences. Children generally are considered to have delayed speech development if they fall about twelve months behind these norms. Delayed development can result from overall mental retardation, hearing impairment, lack of speech stimulation in the home, and severe emotional shock.

Teaching Children with Speech Problems

Remediating a severe speech disorder requires specialized training that most elementary language arts teachers lack. For this reason, the need for highly qualified speech therapists cannot be overstressed. In school districts with insufficient personnel, teachers should work to see that the staff is expanded so that every speech-impaired child has access to specialized attention during the week.

The classroom teacher can provide more generalized attention, especially in the lower grades. The teacher can involve children continually with the sounds of language. Informal conversations between teacher and students help youngsters see how pleasant speaking can be. Listening to stories and poems, chorusing and singing songs and rhymes, playing games that require differentiation among sounds heighten children's sensitivity to language sounds. Greater sensitivity can be built through specific language exercises that focus on particular speech sounds. Youngsters who have an articulation problem can practice producing different sounds as part of a teacher-guided play with sounds. The child works on a particular sound or problem, with the teacher *not* correcting or pointing out speech errors during general oral conversation activities. Continual correction makes speaking unpleasant and can worsen the problem.

Some attempt can be made to remediate phonation problems during oral interpretation of selections. Working within a group, children can vary pitch and loudness and experiment with different ways to project the voice. Choral speaking is an excellent way to develop vocal control as children interpret lines of poetry and prose, using pitch, loudness, and tone to communicate meanings.

Stuttering is a more difficult problem. Teachers of young children must realize that repeating sounds is typical behavior at this stage. Labeling a child a stutterer and drawing this "condition" to parents' attention may well produce a stutterer from a normal child. Kindergarten teachers in particular should help parents to accept the normal repetitions of youthful speech, encouraging the child to talk and listening easily to him or her.

Perhaps the major contribution a teacher can make to an older child who has already acquired the physical characteristics associated with secondary stuttering is to be patient, giving the youngster sufficient time to contribute, and to encourage other children to be patient and considerate. Teachers may be prone to urge children to speak more quickly or slowly, to stop and start over, to take a deep breath. Instructions such as these aggravate the situation, however, and may cause a young person with secondary stuttering characteristics to stop contributing. They also may result in aggravated physical mannerisms.

Other productive activities include creative dramatics, puppet plays, role playing, reading along while listening, and audiotaping.

Continuous Assessment of Children as Language Users

To provide children with experiences in line with their individual needs, teachers must assess children's strengths and weaknesses on a continuing basis. This applies to all children—those who are disabled in some way, those who are "average," and those who excel. In this section, we turn our attention to assessing children's growth as language users.

Assessment Through Ongoing Observation

Peter Winograd and his colleagues (1991) propose that viable assessment techniques are those that help students gain ownership of their learning. Students keep track of which books they find easy to read and which they enjoy most.

They decide what writing they will edit and how they will edit it. They identify their own reading and writing goals. To this end, Winograd concludes that "teachers' informal observations and intuitions about children's needs are far more useful than are scores from formal tests: and that especially useful are observations of students' behaviors and responses while engaged in meaningful reading and writing tasks." Informal observations provide data for making instructional decisions and helping parents understand their children's progress. To systematize their observations, teachers record segments of behavior on checklists and study work samples created over a period of time. They schedule conferences or interviews in which they encourage students to assess their own progress. They use the results of standardized tests sparingly to support their own observations.

Parents (or other caregivers) must be involved in literacy assessment. Caregivers "provide the multicultural link to the classroom both in terms of social and emotional support and in terms of providing teachers with important factual information about language and culture" and about their children (Quintero and Huerta-Macias, 1990).

For a discussion of checklists and matrixes, see Edward Paradis et al., "Accountability: Assessing Comprehension During Literature Discussion," *The Reading Teacher*, 45 (September 1991), 8–17.

Checklists   As teachers increasingly recognize assessment as an ongoing activity on which they base curriculum decisions, checklists are growing in popularity. An observational checklist itemizes literacy traits to be rated with some type of scale. The child

1. Chooses reading (or writing) as a free-time activity,
2. Revises and edits after writing a first draft that the child has chosen for publication,
3. Uses guide words systematically to locate dictionary entries during editing,
4. Contributes ideas to literature study group discussions.

Rating scales include such evaluative terms as *always, generally, never, poorly, adequately,* and *exceptionally.*

Some teachers develop a comprehensive checklist of traits, use the list to assess each child's growth several times a year, and share the checklist with parents. Other teachers develop a master list of traits related to a specific skill area, such as language facility in small-group discussions. Each child's name appears on the checklist, and the classroom teacher observes each child during group discussions over a period of several weeks and assesses his or her progress relative to the traits. Examples of checklists are shown in Figures 5.9, 7.8, and 10.13.

Sometimes home caregivers are asked to evaluate their children's attitude toward reading and writing and their children's reading/writing behaviors via a checklist. Anthony Fredericks and Timothy Rasinski (1990) propose an attitudinal scale for parents to complete periodically with the following items. The child

✦ Understands more of what he or she reads,
✦ Enjoys being read to by family members,

- ✦ Finds time for quiet reading at home,
- ✦ Sometimes guesses at words, but the guesses usually make sense,
- ✦ Can provide a summary of stories read,
- ✦ Has a good attitude about reading,
- ✦ Enjoys reading to family members,
- ✦ Would like to get more books,
- ✦ Chooses to write about stories read,
- ✦ Is able to complete homework assignments.

Caregivers respond by indicating whether they strongly agree, agree, disagree, or strongly disagree with the proposition. They also report what strengths they see, areas that need improvement, and concerns they have. In responding, caregivers get ideas for activities they can pursue with their children.

Anecdotal Records   Another aid to ongoing assessment is the anecdotal record, which describes a student's behavior. For example, during show-and-tell, Mattie brings in rocks she has collected and tells about each specimen, including the scientific name. During storytelling, Keith—who generally is unenthusiastic about most things—tells the story of Paul Bunyan with great skill. During collaborative study, Maria fools around. These tidbits are the stuff of anecdotal records. At the end of the school day, the teacher jots a few key points in the folders of one or two children, making sure to accent the positive as well as record incidents that suggest weaknesses.

For an in-depth analysis of portfolios, read Robert Tierney et al., *Portfolio Assessment in the Reading-Writing Classroom* (Norwood, Mass.: Christopher-Gordon, 1991); Bill Harp, ed., *Assessment and Evaluation in Whole Language Programs* (Norwood, Mass.: Christopher-Gordon, 1993, abridged); and Donald Graves and Bonnie Sunstein, eds., *Portfolio Portraits* (Portsmouth, N.H.: Heinemann Educational Books, 1992).

Portfolios of Children's Work   Especially in the area of written expression, work samples supply evidence of progress. Some teachers encourage each child to keep an active writing portfolio, or folder, as well as a showcase portfolio of specially chosen pieces (described in more detail in Chapter 10). These teachers compare a child's pieces for signs of progress and areas in which instruction is needed. Some teachers involve children in the analysis of the dated pieces in their portfolios, encouraging them to identify their strengths and weaknesses. Teacher and child use a checklist of specific traits to compare dated papers written over several months and compiled in the portfolio. The child also assesses his or her own growth as a writer in selecting pieces that will comprise a showcase portfolio to share with parents.

Individual Conferences   The personalized conference is the ideal setting for assessing pupil progress. Listening to a child read in a one-to-one conference, listening to the child talk about a composition, or going through a portfolio with a child, a teacher can observe a variety of language behaviors. Observations can be recorded as anecdotal records and on checklists. Youngsters can participate by suggesting areas where they have made the greatest progress and areas that require attention.

Strengths and weaknesses noted in a conference determine both the kinds of group and individual tasks to be undertaken and the content of those tasks. A teacher can also note problems to refer to learning specialists—the psychologist, reading specialist, speech therapist, and resource room teacher. These specialists can help the teacher design lessons to meet unique needs and can contact parents, educating them on how best to help their children at home.

Standardized Tests

Some understanding of children's growth in language skills can come from the standardized tests administered in most school districts. The typical battery of achievement tests, such as the Iowa Tests of Basic Skills and the Metropolitan Achievement Tests, contains subtests that measure vocabulary, reading comprehension and speed, understanding of the mechanics of writing, spelling, and so forth. However, these tests measure skills out of context; children who can handle spelling on tests or tell how the language is used do not necessarily apply these tools in writing. But used in conjunction with ongoing assessment of literacy, the tests supply specific diagnostic information (Cooter, 1989).

Besides the test batteries, school districts sometimes use tests of specific skills. For example, the Durrell Listening-Reading Series, the Sequential Tests of Educational Progress Listening Test, and the listening test that is part of the Cooperative Primary Tests are available to assess listening. Again, such tests should not be the sole measure but be used in conjunction with more informal ongoing assessments.

✎ Building and Refining Your Teaching Skills

✦ Map a thematic, content-area unit in which children collaborate in teams as in Figure 2.1. Identify books you could use to facilitate learning of children with diverse backgrounds, abilities, and learning problems.

✦ In a special education class or resource room, observe children who are learning through the literature-based unit approach. Identify the specific instructional strategies the teacher is using. Consider how the same strategies could be used in a multicultural, mainstreamed classroom.

✦ Some specialists advocate a calm and unstimulating environment for highly excitable, emotionally disturbed children. What problems does this pose for the elementary teacher trying to provide a language-rich, stimulating environment for the majority of children? How can the teacher resolve this dilemma?

..........A Summary Thought or Two

DIVERSITY IN THE MULTICULTURAL, MAINSTREAMED CLASSROOM

Who are the children who are learning in today's elementary schools and whose needs the teacher must meet? Today's elementary students are youngsters with diverse emotional, linguistic, cultural, perceptual, and expressive characteristics that affect their language learning. This chapter has described these children and detailed ways teachers can involve them in language and learning.

Two ideas were developed in the chapter. First, the teacher's role is to employ strategies that involve children actively and naturally in language and literature: collaborative team learning and literature-based and content-area–based units that involve talking together, reading aloud, oral composition, dictation to the teacher, use of concrete materials, and oral play with language. These strategies allow students to work at their own level within a multicultural, mainstreamed classroom.

Second, the teacher has a role in early identification of language-learning problems. For this purpose, the teacher relies on such ongoing assessment tools as checklists, anecdotal records, portfolios, and individual conferences as well as more objective, standardized measures. The teacher uses information gleaned through informal and formal assessments as a basis for planning personalized and group instruction, requesting assistance from learning specialists, and soliciting assistance from the home.

RELATED READINGS

Allen, JoBeth et al. *Engaging Children: Community and Chaos in the Lives of Young Literacy Learners.* Portsmouth, N.H.: Heinemann Educational Books, 1993.

Collis, Mark, and Joan Dalton. *Becoming Responsible Learners: Strategies for Positive Classroom Management*. Portsmouth, N.H.: Heinemann Educational Books, 1991.

Five, Cora Lee. *Special Voices*. Portsmouth, N.H.: Heinemann Educational Books, 1991.

Freeman, Yvonne, and David Freeman. *Whole Language for Second Language Learners*. Portsmouth, N.H.: Heinemann Educational Books, 1992.

Glazer, Susan, and Carol Brown. *Portfolios and Beyond: Collaborative Assessment in Reading and Writing*. Norwood, Mass.: Christopher-Gordon, 1993.

Harp, Bill, ed. *Assessment and Evaluation in Whole Language Programs,* abridged ed. Norwood, Mass.: Christopher-Gordon, 1993.

Harris, Violet. *Teaching Multicultural Literature in Grades K–8*. Norwood, Mass.: Christopher-Gordon, 1992.

Hayes, Curtis, Robert Bahruth, and Carolyn Kessler. *Literacy Con Carino: A Story of Migrant Children's Successes*. Portsmouth, N.H.: Heinemann Educational Books, 1991.

Kirk, Samuel, James Gallagher, and Nicholas Anastasiow. *Educating Exceptional Children*. 7th ed. Boston: Houghton Mifflin, 1993.

Labuda, Michael, ed. *Creative Reading for Gifted Learners: A Design for Excellence*, 2nd ed. Newark, Del.: International Reading Association, 1985.

Richard-Amato, Patricia, and Marguerite Snow. *The Multicultural Classroom*. White Plains, N.Y.: Longman, 1992.

Roderick, Jessie. *Context-Responsive Approaches to Assessing Children's Language*. Urbana, Ill.: National Council of Teachers of English, 1991.

Stires, Susan, ed. *With Promise: Redefining Reading and Writing Needs for Special Students*. Portsmouth, N.H.: Heinemann Educational Books, 1991.

Swallow, R., and K. Huebner, eds. *How to Thrive, Not Just Survive*. New York: American Foundation for the Blind, 1987.

Tierney, Robert, Mark Carter, and Laura Desai. *Portfolio Assessment in the Reading-Writing Classroom*. Norwood, Mass.: Christopher-Gordon, 1991.

CHAPTER 3

Language and Children's Language Development

Where Communication Is in Action

BEFORE reading the chapter, read the title, the headings, and the end-of-chapter summary. Then answer the questions in the margin on this page.

How do children learn to think and to interact with others?

_____

_____

_____

How do they learn to use language to communicate?

_____

_____

_____

How can children learn about their language?

_____

_____

_____

These oral activities can also be organized as teacher-guided small-group sessions, especially where extreme discipline problems make it difficult to teach a large group.

TEACHING IN ACTION   *A Yellow Ball Afternoon*

Eileen Morris and her fourth-graders were gathered for a Yellow Ball Afternoon: a period of intensive communication in which youngsters manipulated and played directly with sounds, words, and sentences; composed orally; listened to and dramatized stories; interpreted poems through choral speaking; and/or shared their reports, written compositions, and ideas. Through languaging together—using and manipulating language—these fourth-graders were acquiring skills of communication as well as an understanding of the way their language works. Here is a reconstruction of their afternoon.

On a Yellow Ball Afternoon

A yellow ball was hanging by the doorway as the fourth-graders arrived after lunch. This was a signal that they would start the afternoon with a languaging-together time. Interpreting the yellow ball, the youngsters pushed back their desks and placed their chairs in a Communication Circle. As each child added his or her chair to the circle, Ms. Morris placed a piece of construction paper, a crayon, a lap board, and a rhythm band instrument in front of it.

Playing with the Sounds of Language

When everyone was ready, the teacher suggested: "Let's begin with some rhythm making. Listen as I repeat a rhyme that you may know."

Striking the drum placed on the floor before her chair, Ms. Morris kept a steady beat as she recited the familiar rhyme

Pease porridge hot.	*Some like it hot.*
Pease porridge cold.	*Some like it cold.*
Pease porridge in the pot	*Some like it in the pot*
Nine days old	*Nine days old.*

After just one recitation by the teacher, the fourth-graders joined the voice chorus and simultaneously maintained the beat by striking or shaking their rhythm instruments.

Upon completion, Ms. Morris turned to the youngsters on her left: "Will you be the ones who like pease porridge very hot? As we repeat the rhyme, keep chanting 'very hot, very hot, very hot.'" At that point the Hot Team discussed what body action they could perform to communicate some meaning of the poem. The youngsters decided that stirring would be appropriate; as the class spoke the lines of the rhyme and maintained the beat with the rhythm instruments, the Hot Team chanted "very hot" and stirred with their arms.

Then the teacher turned to the youngsters on her right. They became the Cold Team and decided to mime a tasting motion as they chanted "very cold, very cold, very cold."

Now the whole chorus was ready. As the left group stirred and chanted "very hot," the right group tasted and chanted "very cold." The remainder chorused the words of the rhyme and maintained the beat with the rhythm band instruments.

After the children had repeated the rhyme several times, they thought about how porridge left in a pot for nine days would taste. Students offered words like *smelly, rotten, gummy, sticky, gooey, buggy,* and *foul.* With the aid of a classroom thesaurus, the children added *distasteful, unappetizing,* and *unpalatable* to a chart entitled "Nine-Day-Old Words." Then they talked briefly about why people in the past might have had to eat nine-day-old porridge. They played with the meaning of *pease,* which defied dictionary solution but could be figured out from the context. They decided that the word might be a lengthened form of *peas,* which was in the dictionary and fit the meaning of the verse. In talking together, the youngsters used *unappetizing* and *distasteful* to describe the experience of eating old porridge.

Manipulating Homophones

Relaxed from the initial choral speaking, talking, and vocabulary-building activity, the fourth-graders picked up their lap boards, crayons, and construction paper. Slowly Eileen Morris reached into her straw mystery bag to pull forth a pear. "What is this?" she asked. "Write its name on your paper and draw a sketch of it." The children worked quickly and then displayed their papers to compare their spellings. A dictionary check by the class word sleuth verified *pear* as the spelling of the fat fruit set before them. Ms. Morris next reached down into the mystery bag, pulled out a paring knife, and began to pare the

1. In *The Ape That Spoke*, John McCrone writes: "The voice inside our heads seems to well up like a spring of water that cannot be capped. It bubbles on and on in an endless stream of thoughts and suggestions, and no matter how hard we try, we cannot shake it off. If you attempt right now to empty your head of all thoughts and sit quietly with a blank mind, you will probably last barely a second" ("Strange Voices in the Head" [New York: William Morrow, 1991], 178).

2. David Corson makes an interesting point about "mind talk": "There is every reason to believe that we speak inside and to ourselves far more than we speak outwardly to others" (*Oral Language Across the Curriculum* [Cleveland, England, and Philadelphia: Multilingual Matters, 1987], 8).

3. James Moffett contends that in reading and writing we modify inner speech and in so doing enlarge how we think: "Reading and writing temporarily change how we talk to ourselves. Eventually this may change how we feel and think. . . . When we read, we introject the text into our inner life and at the same time project our inner life into the text. This is heady interaction" ("Reading and Writing as Meditation," *Language Arts*, 60 [March 1983], 315–317).

Questions to Consider

How do you use inner speech during conversation? During reading? During writing? In what other situations do you use inner speech? How much do you use it? For what purposes? Is your mind ever blank? If so, when? How can a teacher help children use inner speech more effectively, especially during reading and writing?

on to the learner their modes of thinking; rather, according to Vygotsky, they pass on words and word patterns that already have common meaning within the human community. These words and patterns are employed in egocentric, socialized, and interiorized speech.

How School Programs Contribute to Language Power

If we base school language programs on the ideas of Piaget and Vygotsky, talking becomes the bridge to continued cognitive and language growth. Clearly, children must have opportunities to use inner and socialized speech, and teachers must model out loud how they talk to themselves as they read, write, and listen. Although little research evidence exists that suggests how to assist children, we can hypothesize some strategies.

pear. Now the assignment was "Write down what I'm doing and draw an illustrative sketch." Again the children wrote, drew, displayed their words, and checked the dictionary. At this point, Ms. Morris reached into the bag and pulled out a pair of scissors, a pair of tongs, and a pair of rolled-up trousers. "How are these objects similar wordwise?" she queried. "Write the word common to all these objects." When the children did not respond, the teacher revised her instructions, asking the youngsters to call out relationships until they hit on the word *pair*. Again the children tried spelling the word on their papers and the sleuth verified it in the dictionary.

A *homophone* is a word that sounds the same as another but carries a different meaning.

Next, Ms. Morris spread word cards showing *pair, pare,* and *pear* on the floor, and the youngsters matched the cards with the associated objects. Then she picked up a card at random and asked a student to use it in a sentence. She repeated this procedure several times. Finally, Ms. Morris posed a task: "Compose a single sentence containing all three of our homophones in a funny, yet meaningful, way." The fourth-graders wrote and then shared their word plays with the group, displaying their sentences as the class decided whether the spelling of each homophone was correct.

A Language Game

Because Ms. Morris had detected some restlessness in the group, she now shifted mood and direction. "Let's play the adjective and adverb game that we learned during our last Yellow Ball Afternoon," she proposed. The youngsters smiled their approval, so she printed a sentence on chart paper posted on a nearby easel: "A _____ horse ran _____ ." The children recalled that any word that would fit in the first slot between the determiner and the noun was an adjective, and on construction paper they listed words that logically could fill the slot. After a minute of rapid writing, they placed their cue card papers on the floor directly in front of them. Then the game began.

Developing a sense of adjective position in a sentence

One child started a rhythm by slapping the left hand on the left leg, then the right hand on the right leg, then snapping the left fingers, and finally snapping the right fingers. At the snap of the left fingers, a player suggested an adjective to fit in the slot; then, at the snap of the right fingers, the player said the word *horse*, without breaking the rhythm. In the order in which they sat, each youngster took a turn, and the rhythm of slapping and snapping got faster and faster. The rule was: Don't repeat a word already given, and maintain the rhythm or you're out. When the rhythm had passed around the Communication Circle several times with only a few misses, the group turned to adverb play. Now they prepared cue cards containing words that could fill the adverb slot of the sentence and played the game by saying the word *ran* on the snap of the left fingers and an adverb on the snap of the right. Once more the action got fast and furious as youngsters added adverbs: *ran here, ran wildly, ran away.*

Developing the concept of adverb-ness

And Now the News!

Sharing and discussing information

Next, Ms. Morris sequenced in a quieter activity. Each week two students would volunteer to be news reporters. The reporting job consisted of keeping abreast

Gathering in the Communication Circles, children share their projects; in the process they develop as language users. (© 1993 Jean-Claude Lejeune)

of local and world news and sharing it with the class. Now the reporters from their spots on the Communication Circle told of a recent airline disaster. Other youngsters who had seen film of the incident on TV added information; some commented on the causes of the disasters.

Building functional vocabulary

As students and teacher talked, the words *disaster, incident, control tower,* and even *aeronautics* surfaced. Ms. Morris reinforced them by using the terms herself. In summing up the news report, students identified the key words they had been using and added them to the alphabet charts of words that were posted side by side beneath the chalkboard; that is, they added *aeronautics* to the *Aa* chart, *disaster* to the *Dd* chart, and so on. As they did so, several students proffered sentences using the particular word in a meaningful way.

Branching Out

Working independently

Now the class was ready to disperse for individual study. Some students would work in collaborative teams, readying a dramatization for presentation or writing silly homophone stories. Others would confer with Ms. Morris, editing stories they had written. Still others would pursue the individual tasks indicated on their personal study guides, sheets they used to guide their independent language activities. Before the fourth-graders dispersed, the teacher reviewed the options on the children's guides, or learning contracts. Each guide differed slightly, but some specific activities were common to all. The common activities related to whole-class instruction and had been designed to increase fundamental skills and understandings. The other items met individual learning needs. Juan, a Mexican American for whom English is a second language, included activities that gave him an opportunity to develop his facility with English as well as to read a book to which he could relate. Juan's contract is shown in Figure 3.1.

Name: _Juan Agillo_   Week of: _February 4_

                                                    Date   Date
                                                    Started   Completed

Independent Reading: _And Now Miguel_

Independent Writing: _Compose a series of silly homophone sentences based on the list of homophones on the board._

Writing Station Activity: _With Bruce, write a "Nine Day Old Story" filled with powerful words._

Recording Corner: _Read a paragraph from And Now Miguel on the tape. Choose an exciting one that others would enjoy._

Computer Center: _Complete "Homophones" program._

Other Station Activities: _____
Word Activity 2: Meet More Homonyms. Work on your Spanish dictionary for English speakers with your dictionary writing team.

Other Independent Activities at Your Desk: _____
_____

Figure 3.1 A Personalized Study Guide, or Contract

How Children Learn to Think and Interact with Others

Through meaningful experiences with language—such as those that occur as young children interact with their families and friends and those that take place in school during a Yellow Ball Afternoon—children (1) grow in general cognitive facility and (2) begin to use language to think and interact with others. In this section, we will consider these two important aspects of language development.

Children's Cognitive Development

To communicate effectively, a person must possess a storehouse of facts and points to share with others. Even more important, he or she must be able to operate intellectually on those facts and to compare, categorize, generalize, and think critically. Jean Piaget (1965) provides a framework for understanding how children of different ages are likely to think about material and events. According to Piaget, there are four stages in children's cognitive development:

Stage 1: Sensorimotor (birth to age 2)	A period of visual and manipulative exploration of the physical environment
Stage 2: Preoperational (age 2 to age 7)	A period of rapid language development when the child begins to think with words, imitates adult behavior, and judges objects in concrete terms
Stage 3: Concrete operations (age 7 to age 11/12)	A period when, through manipulation of objects, the child mentally transforms concrete data into generalizations about reality and concepts based on similarities and differences
Stage 4: Formal operations (ages 11/12 and up)	A period when the child can go beyond the concrete to use language in an abstract way

In sum, as children mature, they learn to think in abstract rather than concrete terms and become less dependent on firsthand experience as a basis for thought.

Today theorists prefer a less rigid interpretation of children's cognitive development. Nonetheless, if applied flexibly, Piaget's stages are useful tools in looking at overall patterns in child development. Knowledge of the stages through which children develop cognitively is important as the teacher asks students to think and talk about all kinds of ideas. For example, considerable research has been done on how children think about and respond to stories. In extended studies, Alan Purves (1975) has found that the way children respond to stories varies with age, as suggested by Piaget's framework. Third-graders think literally, making such comments as "It's about a rock" and "He got a whole bunch of cats." Their evaluative statements express their feelings about a

THE FORUM   On an Interactive View of Language Development

1. In *Children's Language and Learning*, Judith Lindfors talks about how the young child acquires language: "We know that the most important people in the young child's language environment, his family members and care givers, do not provide him with a rigorous language learning 'curriculum.' Rather, they engage with him and with each other (in his presence) in real communication in a wide range of contexts and situations. These typically involve linguistic structure far more complex than the child controls. . . . Virtually every child, without special training, exposed to surface structures of language in many interaction contexts, builds for himself—in a short period of time and at an early stage in his cognitive development—a deep-level, abstract, and highly complex system of linguistic structure" (Englewood Cliffs, N.J.: Prentice-Hall, 1987, 93, 97).

2. Glenda Bissex explains the kind of interaction that leads to language growth: "Children learn language among people who respond to their meanings before their forms. We are eager to attach meanings to babies' first speech sounds. We do not immediately correct a beginning speaker's misarticulations; in fact we sometimes imitate them. We do not insist that beginning speakers talk in complete sentences, but may expand their one or two word sentences to check if we have understood their unverbalized meanings" ("Growing Writers in Classrooms," *Language Arts*, 58 [October 1981], 787).

Questions to Consider

Lindfors and Bissex tell us that social interaction is important in language acquisition. What does this statement imply about what we should do with children in elementary language arts programs? In what specific ways is social interaction a part of the language-learning environment of Eileen Morris's Yellow Ball Afternoon?

story and omit reasons for their judgments. They make comments such as "It sounds good" and "It's funny."

According to Purves, fourth-graders make similar responses except that the older children comment more about personal relations and attempt comparisons between story characters and themselves. Thinking more critically, they may cite reasons: "The reason I liked that was because I like curious people" and "I like it because it sounds true." In contrast, fifth-graders begin to comment on literary aspects: "Because it rhymes and I like the words," "the feeling of the words," "the way he said it."

Research demonstrates similar results when children are asked to think critically about story acts. According to Myra Weiger (1976), second-graders judge acts in terms of clear-cut categories of right and wrong set down by adults. Justice is administered by authority figures, as shown by such comments as "My mother don't like us to tell lies. She'd keep us in the house"; "That's what my father does to me"; "I don't like fighting 'cause I know it makes God mad." Weiger finds that many fourth-graders still judge by referring to adult authority. Some, however, function at higher levels, as shown in this comment: "They kept bothering her and she couldn't take it no more so she just moved away and they learned a lesson."

A fine book for a values discussion is Phyllis Reynolds Naylor, *Shiloh* (New York: Atheneum, 1991). Ask upper-graders to judge the rightness of Marty's actions. Use Naylor's Newbery acceptance speech (in *The Horn Book*, 68, July/August 1992, 404–411) in conjunction with the novel.

By sixth grade, many students respond in terms of a concept of equity. A typical sixth-grader's response to Pinocchio is: "Since he was just a puppet, he wouldn't know better." This response considers extenuating circumstances. Based on her findings, Weiger proposes that children need more opportunity to react to moral dilemmas so that they develop a mature sense of justice. She concludes that "children's literature provides an effective method of developing moral judgment in children because it deals with moral experience at every age." In language arts, children should have numerous opportunities to think critically and talk about a variety of topics. In this way, they develop their ability to operate intellectually on facts and points they receive and to communicate their own ideas to others.

Development of Communication and Thinking Power

Piaget (1965) also supplies teachers with a framework for studying children's growth in language use. According to his theory, young children go through two developmental stages in their progress toward a mature use of language to communicate and think: the *egocentric* and the *socialized* (see Figure 3.2). Young children's speech is egocentric in that they talk aloud without reference to an audience. Piaget describes three categories of egocentric speech, none of which involves interaction with others:

- ✦ *Repetition:* Youngsters repeat sounds for the sheer pleasure of hearing them. These sounds may be words, but little meaning exists in the repetitive stream.
- ✦ *Monologue:* Youngsters talk aloud to themselves without addressing a listener.
- ✦ *Dual or collective monologue:* Youngsters talk aloud in the presence of another person, but that person may not be attending and does not respond.

With maturity comes the ability to address others—the key to social communication. Socialized speech communicates these kinds of content:

- ✦ *Information:* Youngsters exchange thoughts with another person, saying things that might interest the listener.
- ✦ *Criticism:* Youngsters comment on the activity of others, addressing their remarks to others as part of interaction.

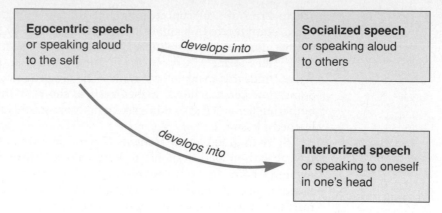

Figure 3.2 Forms of Speech

+ *Commands, requests, and threats:* Youngsters tell or ask others to do things, addressing these remarks to others.
+ *Questions:* Youngsters ask questions and expect answers.
+ *Answers:* Youngsters answer questions and respond to the requests of others. To be able to do this, they must have listened to and thought about what was heard.

According to Piaget, children's early speech is mainly egocentric. As late as ages six and seven, some spontaneous speech still exists in the form of the monologue; children simply talk aloud to themselves. Youngsters in kindergarten, for example, can be heard talking in monologue or dual monologue as they pursue tasks independently.

See Chapter 10 for a discussion of the role of inner speech, or mind talk, in skillful writing. See Chapter 13 for a discussion of inner speech and reading.

Talking aloud to oneself is key in the development of thinking and language abilities. Lev Vygotsky (1962, 1986) believes that in older children thought is related to *interiorized* (or inner) *speech*—talking to oneself within one's head. As children mature, egocentric speech diminishes and becomes interiorized. Interiorized speech is a mechanism on which the adult relies when thinking through a difficult problem. It is the basis of complex thought and is especially important when composing words on paper.

As the title of his book *Thought and Language* suggests, Vygotsky emphasizes the relationships between thought and language. In teaching language, we are essentially teaching thought. Vygotsky writes:

> Thought *and* language, which reflect reality in a way different from that of perception, are the key to the nature of human consciousness. Words play a central part not only in the development of thought but in the historical growth of consciousness as a whole. A word is a microcosm of human consciousness.

As children develop the ability to use words to think and to communicate, verbal interactions with adults are essential. Adults supply "the ready-made meaning of a word, around which the child forms" an idea cluster. Adults do not pass

Facilitating Inner Speech To encourage growth in the art of talking to the self, teachers can do the following:

Use *Iktomi and the Boulder* by Paul Goble (New York: Orchard, 1988) to introduce children to the idea of mind talk. In Goble's book, smaller print is used to give the thoughts in Iktomi's mind.

1. Supply "let's pretend" telephones and microphones in preschool, kindergarten, and first grade. Children go to the Talking-to-the-Self Center to explain something into a telephone or microphone.
2. Establish an Explaining-Aloud Center in second and third grades. Children go there to explain something studied—a process, idea, topic—into a tape recorder or to another student.
3. Give children tasks composed of a series of steps. Suggest that they tell themselves how to perform each step as they do it.
4. Encourage rather than discourage talking to the self "whisper-style" when a job gets tough. When youngsters find a job hard to do, suggest that they speak to themselves. Children can do this as they form letters in writing; cut, paste, and draw; and read and write.
5. Do group talking out loud as part of reading, writing, and problem solving. Ask children to say what they are thinking during these activities.
6. Encourage children to tell themselves stories read or heard. Have them create stories of their own first by talking out loud to themselves and then by talking to themselves in their heads.
7. Divide children into talking-out-idea pairs. Children tell their classmates a story they have invented before writing it down.

Facilitating Socialized Speech In primary grades, children learn to socialize. This means not only that youngsters learn to cooperate with others; they also learn to exchange information, ask, answer, and request.

Elsewhere the Communication Circle is called First Circle or Magic Circle.

Many teachers use the Communication Circle (a variation of the Yellow Ball Afternoon) to assist young children in their growth toward socialized speech. Upon entering the classroom, children gather together, clustering around a central rug to socialize. Here *socialization* means exchanging thoughts, commenting, questioning, answering, and thinking critically.

Examples of Communication Circle activities include

1. Sharing completed work, such as compositions and drawings, with listeners saying what they liked.
2. Sharing objects from home on a topic being studied. For example, when studying community helpers, children bring in magazine pictures or objects they associate with a particular helper. They explain what they have brought in, and listeners comment on things shared.
3. Repeating story material in sequence. Children take turns telling parts of a story they know. Each child tells a bit. Another child takes up the story where the previous one stopped. Here children function as "socialized listeners" to continue the story.
4. Sharing thoughts by whispering in two-person groups. After a talk or story time, each child whispers a favorite part to an echo-mate. Then each child

shares with the total group the words whispered while the echo-mate listens to check that the idea is communicated correctly.

These activities require the socialized, or two-way, speech that characterizes mature adult interaction. They are essential in early grades.

How Children Learn to Use Language

The word *communicate* comes from the Latin *commūnicāre,* which means "make common or make known"; *commūnicāre* derives from *commūnis,* which means "common." This suggests that communication is a social process whose ultimate purpose is a common understanding—a unity within the social group. Through social interaction in a variety of situations—interaction that begins at birth or even before—children acquire language facility. In communicating with others, they learn to use the (1) words and sounds, (2) syntax or sentence structure, (3) intonation patterns, and (4) nonverbal language and social conventions that are inherent aspects of their language. We will now look at these four aspects of language that children acquire in their development as language users.

Words and Sounds

Language—the arbitrary symbol system humankind has devised to represent things, events, and ideas in the world around them—is the bedrock of communication. The words of language are the repositories of humankind's collective and individual experience. Through words, humans think with a degree of clarity and precision superior to that of organisms lacking verbal speech. The ability to use words to speak thoughts has enabled Homo sapiens to escape the present. John McCrone (1991) explains,

> Mammals, like dogs and apes, live only in the present. Chimps may often look as if they are thinking even when simply sitting in the shade of a tree, yet they are still being driven by the changing world around them rather than responding to chains of internal thoughts. . . . Their wordless minds can react only to the events that surround them at a particular moment. Human minds, however, have broken free. We can think about the past, make plans for the future, and fantasize about imaginary events. . . . Language is the key.

W. N. and L. A. Kellogg's (1933) classic study of the child and infant chimpanzee reared in the same home for a year attests to the primacy of verbal language in human thought. The Kelloggs found that the chimp kept up with the child in its intellectual development until the child began to talk. After that the chimp dropped behind, limited by its inability to use words.

At ten to thirteen months, children utter their first word—a naming word such as *mama* or *dada,* which they apply to any person who supplies food, a smile, or a change of diaper. In a few months' time, many children control about ten words, which are likely to include nouns like *ball* and *doggy*, specific names like *Mommy*, and action words like *give* and *bye-bye*. By twenty-four months children's vocabulary averages 150 words, and by three to four years about 1,000 words. Words acquired early tend to be nouns and verbs, with a very few prepositions used to show relationships. Of course, these parameters are general. Philip Dale (1976) cautions, "age is not a good indicator of language development. Children vary greatly in their rates of development."

Concept Formation and Word Power Children gain control over words by gradually attaching symbolic labels to things they encounter in their world. These are the same labels they hear members of their family use in interaction with them and others in their immediate environment. The wagonlike vehicle in the family garage is called *car*; so are those shorter and lower models seen on the highway. As youngsters attach the label *car* to numerous models that differ in many respects but share a number of characteristics, they build a concept of *car*. They learn to recognize a car so that any new car is quickly assigned to that category.

According to Robert Howard (1987), "A *category* is a class that stimuli are placed in according to some similarities. A *concept* is something in a person's head that allows him to place stimuli in or out of the category."

Concepts differ in their level of abstraction. *Car* represents a relatively concrete concept, for a person can point to this sample and to that one. In contrast, concepts such as *honesty, pleasure,* and *thoughtfulness* are more abstract. They represent traits to which one cannot point directly.

According to Hilda Taba (1964), concept formation begins with recognition of the essential qualities of things. A simple example will clarify this process of differentiation, which is at the heart of all conceptualizing. A youngster looking at a cat and hearing an adult apply the label *cat* to it may repeat in telegraphic form the sentence the adult has spoken. If Mommy has said, "Look at the cat there in the tree," the child may reduce and repeat, "Cat there." Later, seeing another animal with four legs that is meowing and has a coat of fur, the child may point and say, "Cat," meaning "There is the cat." Still later, spotting another four-legged, furry animal (holding an acorn in its paws), the child repeats and says, "Cat come," meaning "I want the cat to come here."

At this point, in conversational style the adult may say, "That's a squirrel." At still another point, as parent and child look at pictures in a storybook and interact verbally, the child may apply the word *cat* to lions and tigers as well as to the familiar neighborhood tabby.

Piaget (1964) uses the terms *assimilation* and *accommodation* to describe the processes through which children "fatten up" their concepts. He explains that as youngsters interact in and experience new situations, they assimilate new data into their conceptual understanding. At the same time, they must change—or accommodate—the concepts they build as they meet new data that do not fit into their existing conceptual schemes. In this way, youngsters fine-tune their use of the word labels they apply to phenomena in the world around them. Viewed from this perspective, concept formation is an active, fluid process of exploration and discovery; it requires numerous encounters and interactions that allow youngsters to assimilate more details and refine their growing understanding.

Robert Howard (1987) defines a *schema* as "a mental representation of a set of related categories." He suggests that students may not comprehend what they read because they cannot assimilate the details within their existing schemata.

Individual concepts do not function in isolation; rather, they are related to other concepts in a hierarchical framework that theorists term *schema* (plural *schemata*). A person's concept of "cat," for example, is part of a more comprehensive concept, "pet," which in turn is part of a larger concept, "animal." The network of these interrelated concepts—a schema—is stored in the brain such that it can be modified as children encounter new but related examples. From this perspective, what children already "know" (or what schemata children already possess) determines to a great extent what they learn in new situations. From this perspective, what teachers do before children listen, read, and experience is extremely important. Teachers should organize lessons so that children can relate their past experiences to what they are about to do or read. In this way, they heighten children's learning in the new situation.

Word-Building Blocks: Phonemes and Graphemes

Phonemes are indicated in this way: /ey/, /d/, /m/, and so forth

The words of a language are made up of speech sounds, or *phonemes*. Roger Brown (1958) defines a phoneme as "the smallest unit of speech that makes a difference to a listener or a speaker." For example, say *bat, hat, fat, sat* aloud. The change of the consonant sound at the beginning of each word makes a difference in the meaning sent to a listener. Each word starts with a different phoneme. Now substitute a different vowel sound in each word: *bit, hit, fit, sit*. An English speaker hears a difference in the middle sound of a pair like *bat* and *bit*. Again the speaker is dealing with two different phonemes: the short *a* and short *i* sounds. Linguists have identified about forty phonemes that make up the English sound system.

English writing is an alphabetic system in which the printed form attempts to represent the sounds of the language. The written language provides one or more graphic symbols, or *graphemes*, for each of the sounds that comprise words. Although there is no one-to-one correspondence between speech sounds (phonemes) and their graphic symbols (graphemes), there is a strong correspondence in the English language.

For a summary of Kuhl's research, read Marcia Barinaga, "Priming the Brain's Language Pump," *Science*, January 31, 1992, 535.

How do children learn to communicate with the phonemes and graphemes of their language? According to Patricia Kuhl and her associates (1992), human babies show a similar pattern of phonetic perception regardless of where they are born: "They discern differences between the phonetic units of many different languages, including languages they have never heard, indicating that the perception of human speech is strongly influenced by innate factors." Early experiences within a particular language community, however, reduce infants' ability to perceive differences among speech sounds that do not make a difference in their native language. As Kuhl explains, "Adults exhibit a pattern of phonetic perception that is specific to their native language, whereas infants initially demonstrate a pattern of phonetic perception that is universal." Her research suggests that infants' phonetic perception is altered very early by their exposure to the particular language in which they are reared. Working with American and Swedish babies, Kuhl and her colleagues discovered that as early as six months of age, an infant's ability to discern phonemes has begun to be limited to those sounds that make a difference in his or her native language. This is much earlier than the age at which infants acquire word meanings.

Children begin to develop as language users as they interact naturally with family and friends. (© 1993 James Carroll)

Although children discern phonemes at an early age, they do not learn language by segmenting words into phonemes or generating meaning in reference to discrete phonemes. Research suggests that children cannot separate words into phonemic segments with any degree of accuracy until the end of first grade. After analyzing many studies in this area, Maryanne Wolf and David Dickinson (1985) report that separation of words into phonemic segments is "virtually impossible" until the end of first grade, when 70 percent of children can segment. However, these researchers posit a "strong relationship between early segmentation skills and later reading and spelling: *the more aware the child is of the sound system, the easier it is to learn to read.*"

For ways to increase children's phonemic awareness, see Hallie Yopp, "Developing Phonemic Awareness in Young Children," *The Reading Teacher*, 45 (May 1992), 696–703.

Children learn to speak their language by interacting with people and gradually building and refining their conceptual understanding and the related word symbols. The same is true in reading. David Olson (1983) reminds us that as children learn to read, larger units of meaning are actually more significant than discrete phonemes. In generating meaning in reading, children should use the "context of larger structures first," focusing on story, conversation, and sentence meanings before words and on words before phonemes and graphemes. The strong correspondence between the English speech sounds and their graphic symbols supplies some assistance for students learning to read and write, but only as an aid to meaning-based clues. This is the theory behind the whole-language philosophy.

Word Building Blocks: Morphemes   A *morpheme* is the smallest meaning-bearing unit of language, a meaningful sequence of phonemes that cannot be subdivided without destroying the meaning of the unit. Consider the word *boys*. Its meaning can be analyzed: *boy* means "young man" and cannot be subdivided without losing that meaning; *-s*, in this instance, means "more than one." *Boy* and *-s* are morphemes—true building blocks—for words are constructed systematically with them. Some morphemes stand alone as words; *boy, cat, sing, two, five, of* are free morphemes. On the other hand, bound morphemes cannot function alone. English prefixes and suffixes like *-ness, -y, dis-, pre-*, and *mini-* are bound morphemes, as are inflectional endings like *-ed, -ing, -s*, and *-er*.

Children learn early how to handle the word-building characteristics of English. Jean Berko (1958) studied the word-building skills of four- to seven-year-olds to determine whether young children could generate the plural and possessive forms of nouns, the present tense, third-person singular and past tense forms of verbs, and the comparative and superlative forms of adjectives. Berko found that children of that age were already beginning to function according to the systematic word-building rules of English.

Because the oral language of elementary students reflects with a high degree of consistency the systematic ways words are constructed in English, children's language can provide firsthand material through which they develop a heightened awareness and appreciation of how their language operates. Students with mature understanding of the ways words are built from free and bound morphemes can unlock new words by bringing their understanding to bear on words they read and hear. Understanding can also be brought to bear in spelling, as will be pointed out in greater detail in Chapter 12. Furthermore, there is pleasure to be had from working actively and orally at putting pieces of word puzzles together.

Syntax, or Sentence Structure

To learn a language is not only to acquire meaning-filled word symbols; it is also to acquire the syntax of that language. *Syntax* refers to the arrangement of words into meaningful and grammatical sentences. Just as people use words to send messages, so do they use the ordering of words to communicate thought. There is a world of difference in the messages sent by these two sentences, a difference achieved by a shift in word order:

> As dusk fell, John saw the tiger.
> As dusk fell, the tiger saw John.

All languages share certain syntactic features, even though they differ in vocabulary and rely on different means to achieve similar ends.

1. Languages have rules for converting statements into questions, negatives, and imperatives.
2. Languages rely on noun and verb phrases as the basis for sentence construction.
3. Languages have words used to modify nouns and verbs.
4. Languages contain built-in ways to transform one kind of phrase form into other phrase forms, for example, "the bird flew off" into "that the bird flew off" or into "the bird that flew off."
5. Languages have ways to combine equivalent grammatical units: "John saw me" + "Jack saw me" = "John and Jack saw me" (Martin, 1964).

Theories Regarding Acquisition of Syntax Today we look to *transformational-generative grammarians* to explain the way language works. Transformational-generative grammarians describe the way language users build (generate) sentences and change (transform) them. These linguists emphasize similarities in syntax among the languages of the world. They postulate that languages, though similar in surface characteristics, differ in deep, or underlying, structure.

The difference between surface features and deep structure becomes clear by thinking about two sentences that on quick examination appear similar:

John is easy to please.   John is eager to please.

Noam Chomsky (1968) points out that these sentences are far from similar. In the first, someone else is pleasing John; in the second, John is the pleaser. Furthermore, a different underlying structure is suggested by the fact that the first sentence can be changed, or transformed, into a completely sensible sentence: "It is easy to please John." The same transformation performed on the second sentence results in "It is eager to please John," which does not make sense.

The ability to use and interpret the deep structure of their language is what children develop as they acquire language facility. They learn to speak in the noun phrase/verb phrase pattern that typifies language; they learn to handle question making, command making, negation, and modification by trying out these patterns. In so doing, they produce original utterances that adhere to the recurring patterns of their language. By the time children enter school, they generally can do all of these things with language. In this respect, although youngsters coming to school do not know the vocabulary used to describe their language—do not know how to label and talk about nouns, verbs, and so forth—they have a relatively good command of its grammar.

Chomsky explains children's ability to generate original sentences by suggesting that what children are doing is grasping the underlying "rules" governing sentence production. Children do not consciously think out, verbalize, and apply these linguistic rules but gradually develop an intuitive sense of how to put words together in meaningful units. This generative theory of language development explains a speaker's capacity to create sentences he or she has never heard or read. The speaker functions in terms of the rules for sentence building that he or she has internalized through hearing spoken sentences. Such functioning is possible because of the human being's innate predisposition for language.

David Rumelhart and James McClelland (1987) question the theory that children learn language by intuitively learning "rules." Based on their work with computer models, they propose that children learn language by learning analogies, by reasoning that "this word sounds like that word," by making associations. To support their view, Rumelhart and McClelland cite the reasoning of a five-year-old boy. Asked what grade comes before the seventh grade, the boy replied, "Sixth." Asked what grade comes before the sixth grade, he replied, "Fifth." Before fifth, the boy answered, "Fourth." Before fourth, the boy said, "Thirdth," before third, "Secondth," and before second, "Firsth." Interestingly, when Rumelhart asked the five-year-old the grades starting with kindergarten, the boy stated all the words correctly. Rumelhart and McClelland posit that the boy was reasoning by analogy rather than functioning on a "rule" that he had internalized.

Pinker and Prince (1987) debate the meaning of Rumelhart and McClelland's work: They contend that children do internalize language-making rules when they learn language. Kolata (1987) sums up the current view of language acquisition: "There is still no consensus on how children learn" to put words together to form sentences. Are they working with internalized "rules" or reasoning by analogy? The question is wide open.

Research on Syntax Acquisition

Researchers have studied how young children gradually learn to form grammatically correct sentences. Roger Brown and Ursula Bellugi (1966) report that imitation of parental statements plays a part; a very young child may repeat a sentence produced by a parent, in the process reducing it to the essential elements while retaining the original word order, or syntax. Where the parent says, "The dog was barking," the child reduces the sentence to a two-word utterance: "Dog barking." At other times, the child produces original utterances that are reductions of typical English sentences. A parent conversing with a young child, according to Brown and Bellugi, tends to repeat and expand the child's utterances, adding auxiliaries, determiners, and prepositions to the basic words. When the child says, "Mommy glasses," the parent expands to "Yes, Mommy has her glasses" (See Figure 3.3).

Read Glenda Bissex, *GNYS AT WRK: A Child Learns to Write and Read* (Cambridge, Mass.: Harvard University Press, 1980); also Bissex, "Growing Writers in Classrooms," *Language Arts*, 58 (October 1981).

Glenda Bissex (1981), whose book *GNYS AT WRK* (1980) describes the literacy development of her young son Paul, summarizes an interesting point about children's early speech. Children do not start speaking in single words or sounds but in one- and then two-word sentences. In a child-parent conversation, "Car" may really mean "I hear a car"; "Sweater chair" may really mean "My sweater is on that chair." Within the context of the social interaction between parent and child, the telegraphic sentence of the child takes on extended meaning—a meaning that the parent expands in responding.

Bissex writes, "Children learn to talk by interacting with an environment

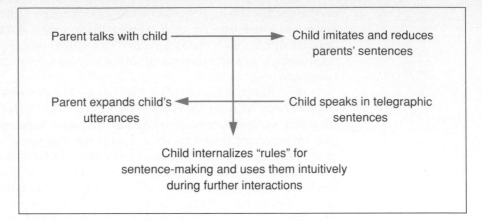

Figure 3.3 An Interactive Model of Early Language Development

that provides rich information about language: they learn by speaking, being spoken to, asking questions, and listening to speech. From models of older speakers they learn the values and functions of speech; they receive feedback, support, and encouragement. . . . Children learn to talk by talking in an environment that is full of talk." In that environment, the parent functions as a conversation "coach." According to Gordon Wells (1979), a relationship exists between the extent to which parents support and expand their children's contributions to a conversation and the youngsters' linguistic level when they enter school. Parental support and expansion of children's conversations also have a positive effect on children's later reading achievement.

Social Interaction and Literacy   Social interaction is also a key influence in children's literacy development. In the words of William Teale (1982), "natural literacy development hinges upon the experience the child has in reading or writing activities which are mediated by literate adults, older siblings, or events in the child's everyday life." Teale contends that interactive literacy events are essential in children's development of reading and writing ability. To learn to read and write, youngsters must participate fully in story reading or writing, conversing actively as part of their encounter with print.

   This suggests why reading and talking about stories with children matters so much, both at home and at school, and why school programs that require much filling in the blanks are unproductive. Solitary fill-in-the-blanks activity fails to provide the social interaction between child and adult so important in continued language development—an interaction that does occur during a shared literary experience of which natural conversation is a part. The same is true of language programs that put greater stress on individual letters and sounds than on meaningful sentence and story units.

   It also suggests why writing must occur within a social context and mean more to young children than an exercise in letter formation. According to

R. Kay Moss and John Stansell (1983), young children generally do home writing because they like it; its language reflects more completely children's full range of language resources. In contrast, early school writing tends to be less creative, reflecting children's belief that this writing is done not to communicate or to enjoy but to practice letter forms, spelling, and page arrangement. Then, too, school writing generally is done without social interaction. Children must be quiet. Yet, as Anne Dyson (1981) points out, "Talk is an integral part of beginning to write"; it provides both meaning and the systematic means for getting that meaning down on paper. Writing, as well as reading, is an interactive process.

Vocal Intonation

Even as some linguists provide ideas on how people learn to generate meaningful sentences, others—the *structural linguists*—describe the structures through which speakers communicate meaning. One element of communication that structural linguists have been investigating is intonation. Intonation is an integral and distinctive part of any language system. It is the rhythmic pattern, the melody of speech; it plays a significant role in the overall sound of English and other languages as they are spoken and read orally or ultimately written down and read silently. Through natural social interaction in which the child reduces adult utterances and the adult (or older sibling) expands a child's words using the melody patterns of the language, the child gradually acquires that melody.

The features of intonation include

✦ *Stress:* the emphasis given to sounds, words, or phrases; the word *accent* is sometimes used synonymously with *stress*;
✦ *Pitch:* the highness/lowness level of the voice; scientists use the word *frequency* to refer to pitch;
✦ *Pause:* the juncture that separates units of speech.

Carl Lefevre (1973) sees wide and varied applications of understandings about stress, pitch, and pause to language arts instruction, applications ranging from basic rhythms in primary instruction to acting and artistic interpretations of poetry. The applications extend to translating speech into written form and oral interpretation of the written word.

Stress Through changes in stress, a speaker alters the meaning of his or her words. Take, for example, these parallel sentences:

Have you ever seen a house fly?
Have you ever seen a housefly?

Other examples to enjoy: Did you see the horse stall? shoe box? umbrella stand? stocking run? mouse trap? lamp shade?

Orally, the difference in meaning is communicated through differences in stress. In the first sentence the speaker puts stress on *fly*, and in the second on *house*. By creating similar sets of sentences, children see how accent affects meaning. In a similar way, youngsters can generate pairs of sentences based on phrases like *kitchen sink, short cut, diamond ring, wind chime.* In each case, students must first use the phrase with the typical pattern in which the second word of the pair is a noun and then use it to produce a humorous meaning by making the second word into a verb.

Pitch   Pitch refers to the highness or lowness of the voice, or its rise and fall. Although in English there are four pitch levels—low, normal, high, and extra high—in conversation people tend to restrict themselves to low, normal, and high. Pitch changes can convert utterances from declarative into interrogative and exclamatory sentences, for there is a relationship between the vocal lift and fall and a speaker's intent to state, question, or exclaim. Try this sentence: "The water is boiling." By shifting the pitch pattern, you will be able to convert the statement into a question or an exclamation.

The ability to perceive pitch patterns in speech helps the writer edit ideas on paper. A writer who hears the sound of an exclamation can punctuate it. One who recognizes differences in the sounds of declarative and interrogative sentences is able to tell when to end a sentence with a period and when to end it with a question mark.

Pause   Pause, or juncture, refers to the ways speakers terminate their speech flow. At times speakers make quick breaks in their speech to distinguish between expressions like *a name* and *an aim, I scream* and *ice cream, illegal* and *ill eagle* (Lefevre, 1973). Speakers pause slightly longer at the comma stops in *Margaret, my friend, is at Central School.* Pausing at the comma stops in this sentence or ones containing parenthetical expressions or series constructions, the voice does not go up or down but stays level. A similar pause is used at the comma stop in the sentence *Our grass needs cutting, but our mower is broken* and at the semicolon break in *The star performer arrived; then the program began.*

Slightly longer pauses occur at the ends of sentences and generally are accompanied by upward or downward movements of the voice. A fade-fall juncture typically is used at the end of a statement as the flow of speech fades before the speaker begins another utterance. A fade-rise juncture is used at the ends of some questions as the flow of speech fades and the voice rises to a higher level.

Clearly, these pauses in speech bear a relationship to punctuation in written communication. Without conscious thought, a speaker relies on fade-fall and fade-rise junctures to divide speech into oral sentence units to sharpen meaning for listeners. The upward fade-out at sentence ends communicates "I'm asking"; only in sentences that begin with question-signaling words like *how, when,* and *why* is the upward rise unnecessary. In writing, terminal punctuation serves the same purpose, but to punctuate effectively a writer must be able to distinguish the sounds of a sentence and translate them into sentence signalers—commas, periods, question marks, and exclamation marks.

Interpretive Intonation   Most people are aware that the way they speak communicates how they feel—fearful, bored, excited. Linguists distinguish

Robert Frost writes, "A sentence is a sound in itself on which other sounds called words may be strung. You may string words together without a sentence-sound to string them on, just as you may tie clothes together by the sleeves and stretch them without a clothes line between two trees, but—it is bad for the clothes."

among these emotional aspects of vocal expressiveness and grammatical aspects such as pitch, stress, and pause, which are dictated by the structure of the language system. Emotions expressed vocally are an "over story," placed on top of the sentence structure of the utterance. In no way, however, does this fact downgrade the significance of tone of voice.

Nonverbal Language and Social Conventions

To communicate, one must be able to use and interpret the very pronounced gestures and more subtle posturings and eye movements that accompany speech. Albert Scheflen (1972) notes the purposes body language serves as an adjunct to verbal language. Some moves speakers make frame and punctuate verbal interaction. A nonverbal expression may say, "I am finishing my statement" or "I am beginning a different idea." Some movements instruct, suggesting "Sit there," or "I am in charge." Others warn of consequences: "That's wrong," "Don't do that," "Be careful!" In such instances, body language is regulatory and may be used purposefully for social control. Still other body movements communicate bits of information: "Yes," "No," "Maybe." Some movements, such as shaking hands, taking someone's arm in walking, or opening a door, are part of the rituals society uses to maintain the social order and make that order agreeable. Other movements communicate feelings: fear, pleasure, excitement, anger. According to Stephen Norwicki and Marshall Duke (1992), in face-to-face interaction only 7 percent of emotional meanings are sent through words; 55 percent are sent through facial expressions and 38 percent through tone of voice, posture, and gestures.

Listeners use body language to communicate without speech. They sometimes regulate who is next to speak by turning and focusing attention on the person chosen. Listeners indicate their lack of understanding or disagreement by frowning, their agreement by nodding, their interest by leaning forward. They indicate desire to speak verbally by a variety of gestures. Such cues make verbal pronouncements of who is to speak next unnecessary; they also tell a speaker how clearly he or she is getting the message across, whether the person is talking too quickly, or perhaps whether he or she is boring a listener.

Like verbal behavior, nonverbal behavior is learned through social interaction. For example, children learn turn taking in conversation at an early age through interaction with their parents (Snow, 1977). Also like verbal behavior, nonverbal behavior does not have a single universal meaning. To English speakers a smile generally is a sign of joy, excitement, friendship; but at times English speakers smile not because they are happy but because smiling is expected of them. Moreover, people from diverse cultural backgrounds do not draw on an identical nonverbal vocabulary. Persons from some cultures use touch more than do persons from others; they may stand more closely in communicating and use more gestures. In this respect, "silent languages" are as numerous as the languages differentiated by the linguists.

Read Roger Arles, *You Are the Message: Secrets of Master Communicators* (New York: Dow Jones–Irwin, 1988), for more on nonverbal communication. See also Norwicki and Duke (1992). These authors have found that 10 percent of children have one or more problems in sending or receiving nonverbal signals—a condition they term *dyssemia*.

Instructional Implications

In this section, we have considered what is important in language learning. From the ideas presented, three generalizations about language instruction emerge:

✦ Social interaction—communication—should be central in language arts programs and in all of elementary education, because through interaction, children learn to use both spoken and written language.

✦ In a language program, students should be actively involved with words, sentence and intonation patterns, and the kinesic behaviors and social conventions of their language. This social involvement occurs in natural situations and is a necessary part of reading and writing, as well as of oral activity.

✦ Because language is speech and writing is the representation of speech sounds, students should have numerous opportunities to participate in oral language activity and to play with the relationships between speech sounds and graphic symbols and between intonation patterns and punctuation signals.

✎ BUILDING AND REFINING YOUR TEACHING SKILLS

✦ Observe a group of preschoolers at play. List specific language behaviors you see. Note evidences of monologue, dual monologue, and nonverbal language.

✦ Locate a story to share with a group of preschoolers. Decide how you can involve the children in social interaction as part of an experience with the story. Next, share the story and encourage interaction before, during, and after story reading.

✦ Analyze a language arts series and ask: In what ways does the series help children use the sentence patterns of their language, the intonation patterns, body language? How does it help children expand their vocabularies? What literary experiences does it provide?

How Children Learn About Language

To know a language is to know how to use that language—its words, syntax, intonational patterns, and nonverbal signals. Accordingly, to teach language arts is first to develop children's ability to communicate. This is the primary thrust of this chapter. But there is another way to know a language—to know *about* it.

Learning About the Symbolic Nature of Language

The human mind has devised arbitrary systems as vehicles for communication and for thinking. Words are actually symbols without meaning in and of themselves. Over the years, people have attached meanings to the combinations of articulated sounds of which words are composed and to the arrangement of these words in phrases and sentences. They have attached meanings to the intonations of voice and to the kinesic behaviors that are part of language. Over time these words, patterns, and behaviors have changed and grown into languages. Some knowledge about language is essential as a background for communicating with others, especially in a pluralistic society.

Take, for example, the fact that language is an arbitrary system. The linguist Robert Hall (1960) explains that there is no inherent relationship between an object and the word symbol created to represent it. The meaning of the symbol is derived from the situations with respect to which it tends to be used. The words *dog, chien, Hund,* and *sobaka* all refer to the familiar canine friend, depending, of course, on where the speaker lives. No one of these words is inherently better than any other. This is an important understanding to acquire, for one should not view another person as superior or inferior because of the particular language or dialect he or she speaks.

Activities that further children's appreciation of the symbolic nature of language can be fascinating. Here are a few ways to involve children with this fundamental characteristic of language:

- *Symbols around us.* Children make a collection of the visual symbols that surround them—symbols such as those for peace, danger, and good luck; the signs used to represent professional groups; the logos adopted by industries to represent their products. Young language investigators analyze the symbols to see whether they perceive a relationship between the symbol and the meaning being communicated.
- *My sign.* Young people who have studied visual symbols that are part of their culture enjoy creating symbols for a product of their own invention, a family crest, a school logo, or a class symbol.
- *Pictographs.* Ancient peoples wrote down thoughts in picture form; they might have drawn a horse, for instance, to represent that animal. Students use a modification of picture writing by creating rebus stories in which they use pictures to represent words.
- *Hieroglyphics.* Upper-graders can study samples of highly stylized pictures recorded by the ancient Egyptians. For example, ⋀⋀⋀ was the stylized picture, or *hieroglyph*, that represented water. In the case of a hieroglyph, it is relatively difficult to determine from the picture what is being represented; thus, the picture is called an *ideograph* rather than a pictograph. Young people can invent original ideographs that they introduce into their own writing.
- *Chinese characters.* Some Chinese characters are compound ideographs, a combination of stylized pictures that, taken as a whole, communicate the

Use Vladimir Vagin and Frank Asch, *Here Comes the Cat!* (New York: Scholastic, 1989) to help children appreciate language diversity. Use Ann and Paul Rand, *Sparkle and Spin: A Book about Words*, reissued ed. (Abrams, 1991), for a playful look at language.

Use words like

eye

nose

hand

mouth
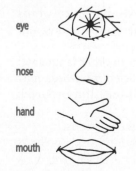

desired meaning. For example, ⊟ represents the sun, while ⸻ represents horizon. The symbol for dawn combines the two signs ⊟, while three suns ⊞ represent the idea of clear or crystal. Moon is represented ⊟ while bright is communicated through the symbol ⊟⊟ . Can you figure out why? Many books provide information like this. The preceding examples came from Morris Sawdesh's *The Origin and Diversification of Language*, in which a page of Chinese characters is clearly depicted. Using pen and ink, upper-graders can reproduce Chinese characters they find in books and encyclopedia articles about writing systems. Their sketches can perhaps explain how ideographs are combined to communicate complex meanings.

Use Morris Sawdesh, *The Origin and Diversification of Language* (Hawthorne, N.Y.: Aldine, 1971), for examples.

Learning About Language Origins and Change

Another kind of knowledge about the English language centers on its origins and evolution. During the late nineteenth century, *historical linguists* began to study the development of the English language. They identified English as belonging to the Indo-European language family and recognized it as a Germanic language more akin to Dutch, German, Icelandic, Norwegian, Danish, and Swedish than to Latin and the Romance languages (see Figure 3.4). The historical linguists developed generalizations about English language origins and changes based on a comparative study of the vocabulary, syntax, sounds, and spellings of the various languages. Today, generalizations commonly encountered in language arts texts include the following:

Language is constantly changing
Supporting Ideas:

1. New words are constantly being added to a language to meet the demands of a changing lifestyle and environment.
2. Word-making mechanisms include compounding, development of words that are analogies of existing words, incorporation of slang expressions, and merger of parts of other words.
3. New words come into a language through borrowing from other languages; this occurs when language groups meet and interact. Scientific words may result through conscious construction of words based on Latin or Greek roots and affixes.
4. Some words drop from common usage as the need for them lessens.
5. Existing words may acquire new meanings, pronunciations, and spellings over time.
6. What is considered acceptable usage may become unacceptable, and vice versa.

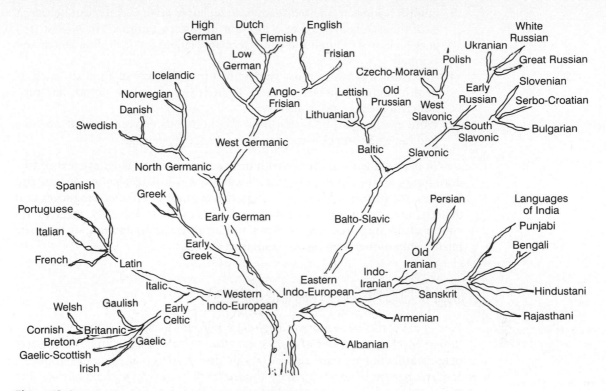

Figure 3.4 The Family of Indo-European Languages

7. As dialectal groups within a language interact, some language cross-fertilization occurs.
8. Dictionaries are records of word spellings, meanings, and pronunciations; dictionaries change to reflect changes in the language.

Some forces exist to stabilize language
Supporting Ideas:

1. Books about language, such as dictionaries, style manuals, and grammars, have a stabilizing effect on language, holding back changes in written expression that appear in everyday oral expression.
2. Rapid means of transportation and of oral communication—telephone, television, radio—tend to unify language.

Some languages are related through common ancestry
Supporting Ideas:

1. Generally, there are more similarities among languages related through common ancestry than among those not so related.
2. Major language groups are called *families*; families trace their origins to a common ancestor.

3. English belongs to the *Indo-European language family*, which can be traced back thousands of years to a location in eastern Europe. The closest language relatives to English are the Germanic languages, including Dutch and German.
4. American English is most similar to other dialects of English, such as British English; however, major differences in vocabulary, syntax, and pronunciation exist among dialects.
5. Word changes can be traced back for thousands of years so that one can find out when and how most words entered the language.

To place students in contact with these generalizations, language texts introduce topics on the development of alphabet systems, language borrowings and families, the history of English, comparisons among different languages and dialects, and the history of specific words and names. Typically, these topics appear at the upper elementary level and heighten understanding of language relationships rather than increase language facility.

Ways to Handle Historical Language Materials

See Robert McCrum, William Cran, and Robert MacNeil, *The Story of English* (New York: Viking, 1986), and *Word Mysteries and Histories* (Boston: Houghton Mifflin, 1986).

References such as *The Story of English* by Robert McCrum, William Cran, and Robert MacNeil and *Word Mysteries and Histories* offer background on language origins and change. Having read about the way language has developed, a teacher may be tempted to share the material by telling and explaining; the material *is* fascinating and storylike. On the other hand, it is possible for children to discover some of the relationships for themselves. By studying samples of different languages, youngsters gain appreciation not only of language as a changing medium of communication but of the way linguists operate.

Language Comparison Studies One form that language investigation can take is the comparison study. Youngsters use English—foreign language dictionaries to discover equivalent words in other languages for common English words. For this activity, stack on a table translation dictionaries for some of the Germanic and Romance languages, as well as for a language not belonging to the Indo-European language family, such as Japanese, Hungarian, Hebrew, or Finnish. During free time students look up a chosen word in each dictionary and record data on a bulletin board chart. Later, students analyze the chart to see whether they can generalize about the languages that are most closely related.

See Figure 3.5 for a time line charting linguistic events in the history of English.

Word Searches Where did a particular word come from? Students can attempt some answers based on searches in which they systematically track word origins and hazard an educated guess. An impressive beginning is consideration of idioms, where figurative meaning differs from literal. Children can think about how expressions such as *a bee in his bonnet, flipped his lid,* and *walking on thin ice* came into being.

A TIME LINE OF IMPORTANT LINGUISTIC EVENTS
IN THE HISTORY OF ENGLISH

	Angles, Saxons, and Jutes wandered in northern Europe.	Ancient English borrowed words from Latin.
A.D. 449	Angles, Saxons, and Jutes moved into Britain, pushing the Celts into Wales and portions of Ireland and Scotland.	English borrowed words from Celtic.
A.D. 597	Anglo-Saxons were converted to Christianity by Latin-speaking missionaries and learned the Latin alphabet.	English borrowed words from Latin.
Old English **A.D. 866**	Anglo-Saxons opposed the invading Vikings from the North.	English borrowed words from Vikings.
1066	Normans (French) invaded, conquered, ruled Britain, and gradually became English.	English borrowed words from Old French.
Middle English	English people began to make contact with peoples speaking other languages.	English began to borrow words from a multitude of languages.
1500	English people rediscovered the classical languages, Latin and Greek.	English borrowed words from Latin and Greek.
	English people brought their language to North America (as well as to India, Australia, New Zealand, South Africa).	English borrowed heavily from other languages: American Indian, Dutch, German, French, Portuguese, Spanish, Japanese, Chinese, Hebrew, Malay, and so forth.
Modern English **1700**		

Figure 3.5 A Time Line Showing the Development of English

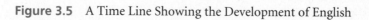

An interesting reference is Isaac Asimov, *Words on the Map* (Boston: Houghton Mifflin, 1962). Invite older students to browse through Asimov's *Words of Science* (Boston: Houghton Mifflin, 1962). His *Words from History* (Boston: Houghton Mifflin, 1968) is equally inviting.

Students enjoy tracing the origins of words to discover the manner and time of their introduction into English. Since English has borrowed words from all the languages of the world, the investigation takes on geographical overtones as students search dictionaries to find words with Chinese, Arabic, Russian, Hebrew, and other origins. Some interesting words to pursue are *coffee, sauna, tea, banana, koala bear, babushka, succotash, apostrophe,* and *batik.* Working in teams with dictionaries that indicate etymology, investigators scan the pages to find the country of origin of these present-day English words. As they discover them, they tape word cards on a globe to show origins. Other interesting words are *hamburger, turkey, danish,* and *frankfurter*—words that quite literally come off the globe. Later, pairs collaborate in a word-search station to think of other words to add to the globe.

A next step is for children to trace the origin and meaning of their own first and last names. Children plot last names on a map to show place of origin. They use suffixes like *-s, -son, -ssen,* and *-ski* and prefixes like *Ben, Mc,* and *O'* to figure out meaning. Some dictionaries supply the meaning of first names as well as the origins.

Language Investigation and Social Study

Word study fits easily into social science units, for the development of language parallels the development of people. Language change reflects migration, conquest, and trade patterns. Similarly, language tells much about the social relationships and values of people past and present. It reports scientific, technological, and industrial progress as well as geographic and economic factors overcome in an attempt to build and maintain a way of life. In this respect, the surfacing of new words in a language and the falling into disuse of others serve as a barometer on which investigators can read changes in human activity.

In terms of classroom study, as students trace the development of their country, they consider not only how their nation changed but how their language changed in response. One way to correlate language and social study is through map investigations. In thinking about the early settling of New England, children search maps for town, city, and state names that reflect the origins, values, and ways of life of the colonists, as well as the geography of the new land. Looking at the settlement of the middle colonies, children compare the names they find on maps of New Jersey and New York with place names in England, Holland, and Germany. As they trace the westward movement, they search maps for names that indicate who the pioneers were, what their interests and religions were, what perils they encountered, and even what the first industrial, agricultural, or mining ventures were.

A search of one state map—Idaho—produced these names: Moscow, Salmon Creek, Sun Valley, Lewiston, Silver City, Twin Falls, Butte, Bonner's Ferry, Yellow Pine, and Coeur d'Alene.

In sum, much of what children learn about the history of language can be accomplished in the context of social investigations. In so doing, children perceive language as part of human activity and as a changing medium of communication that reflects events in the world.

..........A Summary Thought or Two

LANGUAGE AND CHILDREN'S LANGUAGE DEVELOPMENT

This chapter stressed the following themes:

1. Children acquire language by interacting with others. As children meet and use language in a variety of social situations, they grow in their ability to handle the ideas for which words are symbols. Talking to themselves and to others, they also grow in their ability to think abstractly and use the words, sentence structures, intonation patterns, nonverbal language, and social conventions that characterize their language.

2. Because language is primarily an oral system devised by the human mind as a vehicle for communication, oral interaction must occupy a considerable portion of students' time in elementary schools. Through talk, children build skill in using both oral and written language and come to understand how their language functions and how it has developed.

RELATED READINGS

Barinaga, Marcia. "Priming the Brain's Language Pump." *Science*, January 31, 1992, 535.

Begley, Sharon, et al. "Mapping the Brain." *Newsweek*, April 20, 1992, 66–70.

Berko-Gleason, Jean. *The Development of Language*. Columbus, Ohio: Merrill, 1985.

Brown, Roger. *A First Language: The Early Stages*. Cambridge, Mass.: Harvard University Press, 1973.

Dyson, Anne, and Celia Genishi. "Research Currents: Children's Language for Learning." *Language Arts*, 60 (September 1983), 751–757.

Fox, Sharon. "Research Update: Oral Language Development, Past Studies and Current Directions." *Language Arts*, 60 (February 1983), 234–243.

Harste, Jerome, Virginia Woodward, and Carolyn Burke. *Language Stories and Literacy Lessons*. Portsmouth, N.H.: Heinemann Educational Books, 1984.

Just, Marcel, and Patricia Carpenter. *The Psychology of Reading and Language Comprehension*. Boston: Allyn and Bacon, 1987.

Lindfors, Judith. *Children's Language and Learning*. 2nd ed. Englewood Cliffs, N.J.: Prentice-Hall, 1987.

Menyuk, Paula. *Language Development: Knowledge and Use*. Glenview, Ill.: Scott, Foresman, 1988.

Smith, Michael, and John Locke. *The Emergent Lexicon: The Child's Development of a Linguistic Vocabulary*. San Diego: Academic Press, 1988.

Taylor, Denny, and Dorothy Strickland. *Family Storybook Reading*. Portsmouth, N.H.: Heinemann Educational Books, 1986.

Vygotsky, Lev. *Mind in Society: The Development of Higher Psychological Processes*. Cambridge, Mass.: Harvard University Press, 1978.

Wells, Gordon. *The Meaning Makers: Children Learning Language and Using Language to Learn*. Portsmouth, N.H.: Heinemann Educational Books, 1986.

Wood, David. *How Children Think and Learn*. Oxford, England: Basil Blackwell, 1988.

CHAPTER 4

Literature in the Language Arts

Where Childhood's Dreams Are Twined

Reflecting Before
Reading

What are the qualities
that make literature fine?

_____

_____

How does the teacher
bring children and
literature together?

_____

_____

How can the teacher
teach content with
literature?

_____

_____

_____

_____

_____

_____

Gaining ownership of a
story through repeated
readings

BEFORE reading the chapter, read the title, the headings, and the end-of-chapter summary. Then answer the questions in the margin on this page.

TEACHING IN ACTION   Through the Caterpillar Hole

Amy, a four-year-old with a year of nursery school to her credit, sorted through a stack of picture storybooks. She quickly chose Eric Carle's *The Very Hungry Caterpillar.* "Why did you pick that?" a teacher-friend asked Amy. Amy answered as quickly as she had made her choice: "I like it. We read it in nursery school, and I can poke my fingers in the holes."

Though Amy knew the story of how the hungry caterpillar ate its way through oranges, strawberries, and cupcakes to emerge a beautiful butterfly, she settled down to enjoy the story and pictures again. She also enjoyed a follow-up experience. In a piece of construction paper, her teacher-friend cut a hole like those in the pictures depicting the caterpillar's feast. Amy selected red to color around the hole to show something that the caterpillar either ate or might eat its way through. She turned the paper over to color purple around the opposite side of the hole. She explained, "This is an apple he ate" and "This is a plum he ate." The teacher penciled Amy's statements in extra large print next to the drawings and read them aloud to Amy, who read them back. For Amy *The Very Hungry Caterpillar* proved a response-filled excursion into storyland. Clearly, this book by Eric Carle had the potential to involve Amy with language. Carle has written many books that very young children enjoy. They are particularly appealing to children like Amy who have some loss of vision.

Ways to Analyze Children's Stories: Qualities That Trigger Responses

Fine literature is the red blood of a language arts program. It carries the content—the oxygen, so to speak—for language experiences. But more important, literature sustains life by transfusing it with rhyme and reason, escape and enchantment, joy and sorrow. Consequently, selecting books with literary qualities that evoke a deep response is crucial in language arts teaching. Teachers face an abundance of stories from which to choose, an abundance so varied that understanding what makes a book fine is essential for making wise choices.

Charlotte Huck (1993) defines literature as "the imaginative shaping of life and thought into the forms and structures of language" and defines the subject of literature as "the human condition; life with all its feelings, thoughts, and insights." The reader responds to this aesthetic ordering of life's experiences in great stories and is transported beyond immediate perceptions to feel deeply—to care, to want, to cry, to laugh, to love, to hate, and perhaps to understand for the first time. Some writers can weave so complete a spell with words that the story becomes reality and for a moment the real world ceases to exist.

A reader's response grows from his or her prior experiences with life, literature, and language; yet the author's skill in telling a story is an equally significant determinant of the reader's response (see Figure 4.1). To catch a reader in the web of a story, an author must create believable characters, interweave elements of plot, establish a setting in which the characters can function with integrity, develop a theme that pulls story threads together, and make words sing in the mind. In books for the younger reader, the illustrator must contribute pictures that tell the story as forcefully as the words and stimulate equally strong responses. *Character, plot, setting, theme, words,* and *illustrations:* these are the major elements of a story.

Key Story Elements

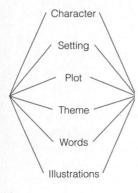

Character

Setting

Plot

Theme

Words

Illustrations

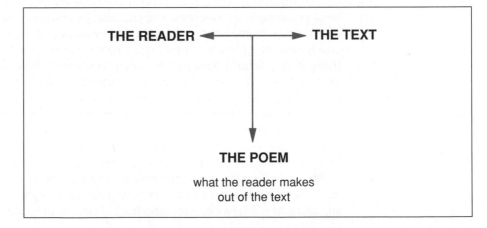

Figure 4.1 A Transactional Theory of Literary Response

THE FORUM   On What Happens When Reader and Text Come Together

1. In explaining her theory of literary transaction in *The Reader, the Text, the Poem*, Louise Rosenblatt uses the term *poem* to describe the "two-way process" that occurs when a reader and a text come together: The reader creates "the poem" as he or she reads a literary work, or "text." The poem is "an event in time. It is not an object or an ideal entity. It happens during a coming-together . . . of a reader and a text. The reader brings to the text his past experience and present personality. Under the magnetism of the ordered symbols of the text, he marshals his resources and crystallizes out from the stuff of memory, thought, and feeling a new order, a new experience, which he sees as the poem. This becomes part of the ongoing stream of his life experience, to be reflected on from any angle important to him as a human being" ([Carbondale and Edwardsville, Ill.: Southern Illinois University Press, 1978], 120; see also Rosenblatt, "The Transactional Theory of Literary Work, in *Researching Response to Literature and the Teaching of Literature*, ed. C. R. Cooper [Norwood, N.J.: Ablex, 1985], 33–53).

2. In a similar vein, Lee Galda explains readers' differing responses to literature: "Response to literature is both personal and social. Personal style, reading preferences, cognitive development and other factors contribute to a reader's response to a text. At the same time the style and structure of a text influence how a reader responds. Finally, the context in which the response occurs is of vital importance. Students' responses to literature can be limited by teachers who insist upon one particular mode" ("Readers, Texts, and Contexts," *The New Advocate*, 1 [Spring 1988], 99–100. For more on differing responses based on "the kind of social and historical individuals we are," see Joel Taxel, "Notes from the Editor," *The New Advocate*, 5 [Summer 1992], v–xv, and W. Nikola-Lisa, "Read Aloud, Play a Lot: Children's Spontaneous Responses to Literature," *The New Advocate*, 5 [Summer 1992], 199–213).

3. Carole Cox and Joyce Many expand on the meaning of an aesthetic response to literature: "Children who read aesthetically repeatedly make associations with their own life experiences and the experiences of others . . . . This appears to be quite simply a component of a fully lived-through evocation of a literary work. . . . The signs of the aesthetic response may include: picturing and imagining while reading or viewing; describing a strongly felt sense of the verisimilitude of the evocation, the reality of being there, imagining themselves in a character's place or in story events; questioning or hypothesizing about a story; extending a story or creating new stories; making associations with other stories and

their own life experiences; and mentioning feelings" ("Toward an Under-standing of the Aesthetic Response to Literature," *Language Arts*, 69 [January 1992], 28–33).

Questions to Consider

Rosenblatt, Galda, Cox, and Many emphasize the reader's personal response to literature. How can the teacher help ensure that the literary transaction between reader and text is worthwhile and that the reader responds aesthetically?

Character

Jerry Spinelli, *Maniac Magee* (Boston: Little, Brown, 1990). Read also Pamela Travers, *Mary Poppins* (New York: Harcourt, Brace, 1934), and E. B. White, *Charlotte's Web* (New York: Harper & Row, 1952), for fine examples of characterization.

Some characters remain in the mind for many days. Readers remember Maniac Magee because that special young man becomes real to them. Maniac is a full-blown character. Even in their first meeting, readers see Maniac Magee as "one part fact, two parts legend, and three parts snowball." They see him as a persistent kid who keeps at Amanda until she loans him a book. They see him as a fleet runner and an "ace" punter who snatches a football right out of the hands of James "Hands" Down. They see him as a brave rescuer of the weak who saves Arnold Jones from the torments of older boys and from a case of the "finster-wallies." Throughout, they know that Maniac really cares about people.

See Figure 4.2 for a character web that highlights the multi-dimensionality of Maniac Magee. Use it as a model for constructing a web that connects descriptive infer-ences to character actions. For other ideas to help children understand characterization, read M. Jean Greenlaw, "Books in the Classroom," *The Horn Book*, 64 (November/December 1988), 820–822.

The Multidimensionality of Characters Writers of fiction are concerned first and foremost with character. According to Donald Graves (1991), almost without exception professional writers "cite the preeminence of character over plot; that is, events occur because of the nature of the characters involved." The power of *Maniac Magee* lies in its central character. Maniac has qualities that all of us possess, for who has not longed for a place where he or she belongs? But Maniac goes beyond the ordinary. Spinelli paints Maniac larger than life so that the reader cannot help but turn the page to find out what this tall-tale hero of today will do next. Yet in some ways the reader already knows, for Maniac per-forms with a certain consistency. He rarely steps out of character to become other than his independent, tough, fearless, open, and essentially caring self. Because Maniac is multidimensional, human but larger than life, consistent in his actions, and has an underlying caring streak, Maniac Magee becomes a friend the reader remembers.

Strong characterization is essential in books for upper-elementary readers. For example, thirteen-year-old Brian Robeson is the whole story in Gary Paulsen's *Hatchet*. Brian quickly learns that the only way he will survive alone in the rugged Canadian wilderness is to draw on his inner resources. It is Brian who must overcome his fears to land the small plane in which he is traveling. It is Brian who conquers not only his environment but himself as he overcomes the mosquitoes that attack him, teaches himself to make fire and to catch fish and later game, and endures excruciating physical and emotional pain. And it is a stronger, wiser, more mature Brian who returns home with a greater understanding of the problems he faced before being forced to fight for his own survival.

How Character Is Developed Through *descriptions*, authors fill out the bare flesh and bones of characters with human feelings. In *Jennifer, Hecate, Macbeth, William McKinley, and Me, Elizabeth*, for example, E. L. Konigsburg introduces Jennifer through the eyes of Elizabeth, the narrator, who sees Jennifer feet first. Elizabeth thinks, "They were just about the boniest feet I had ever seen. Swinging right in front of my eyes as if I were sitting in the first row at Cinerama."

But description takes the reader only to Jennifer's surface. Her *words* and *actions* take the reader inside to see her whole self. Jennifer says things like

> Witches convince, they never argue. But I'll tell you this much. Real witches are Pilgrims, and just because I don't have on a silly black costume and carry a silly broom and wear a silly black hat, doesn't mean that I'm not a witch. I'm a witch all the time and not just on Halloween.

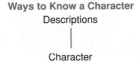

Ways to Know a Character
Descriptions
Character
Dialogue   Deeds

Jennifer does unique things, too, like writing notes in a strange script and operating masterfully on trick-or-treat night. Through the descriptions, dialog, and deeds, the reader sees Jennifer as a "really sharp cookie."

Characters are less fully developed in books for early-primary-grade youngsters. Still, in picture storybooks the reader generally finds a group of characters or one character who is the focus. Take as an example Marjorie Sharmat's *Frizzy the Fearful*, in which the reader meets Frizzy Tiger. Frizzy, the reader quickly learns, is afraid of everything, which is something no self-respecting tiger should ever be. He tries to hide his cowardice from his friends because he is especially scared that they will find out he is a "fraidy cat." But they do! Despite his embarrassment at being found out, Frizzy cannot overcome his fears until the day he musters all his courage to rescue Nova Cat, who is stuck up a tree—just six inches. Although communicating a fundamental message about overcoming one's weaknesses little by little, the story is short, and nearly all a reader knows about Frizzy is his fearfulness. This is the single dimension of personality that the reader sees; yet it is enough for the young child, who still can identify with the tiger.

Identifying with the Character The reader's ability to identify with story characters is a major test of the effectiveness of characterizations. The stories that enmesh the reader in their events are those in which the reader can almost completely identify with a character. What the reader brings to the story

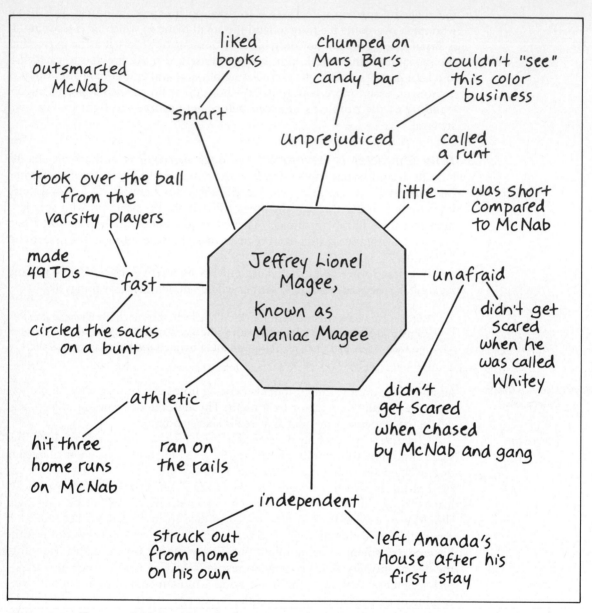

Figure 4.2 Character Web Based on the First Sixteen Chapters of *Maniac Magee*

determines to a great extent whether such identification occurs. This suggests that not all good books are good for all children. With the young child, it does not matter whether the main character is male or female; the young child is able to identify with Frizzy Tiger because feelings of fear and embarrassment are part of childhood. With older children this is not so true, for the problems of growing up male and those of growing up female differ. As a result, boys can identify more easily with some characters and girls with others.

Despite these differences, some characters attract a wide readership. Usually these characters do things that children wish they could do or feel emotions that lie at the heart of growing up. Astrid Lindgren's *Pippi Longstocking* continues to appeal because every youngster has imagined how it would be to do exactly as she or he wants. What youngster has not dreamed of being the hero of the moment? Likewise, even though Mildred Taylor's *Roll of Thunder, Hear My Cry*; *Let the Circle Be Unbroken*; and *The Friendship* tell what it is like to grow up black in a place where being black means being poor and harassed, they have almost universal appeal because of the intense emotions they engender. The reader feels with Cassie and her brothers and in the process is changed even as the characters are changed by the unfolding events.

Plot

Huck (1993) discusses the importance of plot in fiction: "Children ask . . . , 'Does the book tell a good story?' The plot is the plan of action; it tells what the characters do and what happens to them. It is the thread that holds the fabric of the story together."

Plot in Picture Storybooks In picture storybooks, the plot is relatively simple. There tends to be one main sequence of events, with few or no subplots to deflect attention from the main character, and one central problem, or conflict, to be resolved. Generally, each action flows from earlier ones; as a result, the reader can anticipate to some extent what will occur and what the final outcome will be. Take, for example, Paul Goble's *The Girl Who Loved Wild Horses*. The story is simple. The native American girl has a special understanding for horses and spends her free moments with them. Then one day a thunder squall drives the horses and the girl into a far-off valley, where she meets a beautiful wild stallion. She lives there with the wild horses until her people find her. Home again, she is discontent and explains to her family, "I love to run with the wild horses. They are my relatives. If you let me go back to them, I shall be happy for evermore." The reader knows then that the girl who loves wild horses will someday have the joy of running free among the Horse People. In this as in many other picture storybooks, the plot develops step by step, coming to a simple yet satisfying end that the reader can almost anticipate.

Often that end is the place where the action began, which gives the story a circular structure. An example is Chris Van Allsburg's *The Garden of Abdul Gasazi*. The tale begins with Alan and Miss Hester's dog Fritz standing on the porch watching Miss Hester leave for a visit with her cousin. After an active morning, Alan and Fritz take a nap on the couch and then go for a walk that brings them to the garden of Abdul Gasazi. Alan loses Fritz in the garden, only to have the mysterious Gasazi say that he has turned Fritz into a duck, for he hates little dogs. Heartbroken, Alan heads home with Fritz the duck under his arm, but the duck flies off with Alan's hat and Alan returns to Miss Hester dogless and duckless. There he finds Miss Hester and Fritz; Alan feels silly for believing that Abdul Gasazi could turn the dog into a duck. But after Alan

See also Van Allsburg's *Jumanji* (Boston: Houghton Mifflin, 1983) and *Two Bad Ants* (Boston: Houghton Mifflin, 1988).

leaves, Miss Hester finds Fritz on the porch with Alan's hat in his mouth, leaving readers to figure out what really happened. Stories such as this are "turn-about" tales, because the ending takes a twist the reader does not anticipate.

In some stories, especially folktales that have been retold over the ages, plot develops through repetition of the action. An example is the classic tale of the father and son who leave their village in the Nigerian bush country to seek wisdom in the world beyond. When they start out, the man and the boy ride the family camel, but, meeting criticism, the man has his son climb down and walk. Again meeting criticism as they continue, they change places: The boy rides and the father walks. Once more they are criticized, and they decide that both will walk. This, of course, brings more criticism. What does the man decide to do? What has he learned about the wisdom of the world? The reader knows before the third repetition of the action where the story—as well as the man, the boy, and the camel—is going. He or she begins to tell the tale before the writer does, actively joining in the storymaking. This is a "just imagine story" because the reader can just imagine what is to happen before it comes to pass. Figure 4.3 summarizes the repetitive and other plot patterns commonly found in children's stories.

Plot in Longer Books   Books for middle-graders are more complex. Some are episodic, with each chapter telling another adventure and with a major character whose presence in each chapter ties the book together. Episodic books are ideal for children who are beginning to develop the attention span to stay with longer stories. Each chapter can be read separately, providing shorter units for a single reading or listening session. Two episodic books with continuing appeal are Lindgren's *Pippi Longstocking* and Robert McCloskey's *Homer Price*.

Upper-grade students are eager for the greater complexity supplied by books like Ellen Raskin's *The Westing Game* and Katherine Paterson's *Jacob Have I Loved*. Both these books differ from those previously described. They do not develop linearly, with each event centering on a main character or a group of closely related characters functioning as one; rather, the development of these books is more like a river than a line. *The Westing Game* has an involved cast of characters; their actions interweave to form a mystery that even the adult reader has trouble unraveling before the end. In *Jacob Have I Loved*, a conflict between twin sisters binds the story together. This conflict has a powerful impact on the older twin and on the reader's perception of the situation. The complex design of such books tantalizes the maturing reader to read to the end.

Believability of Plot   The author's effectiveness in weaving plot can be judged by how believable the story appears, regardless of whether events in the real world occur as they do in the book. The reader who slips down the rabbit hole with Alice quickly accepts the strange things in this wonderland. Lewis Carroll paints it with a brushstroke so vivid that the reader never rebels and says, "That couldn't happen." To the reader, it *is* happening.

This reaction is particularly true of stories that blend fantasy with reality. An old favorite is Leo Lionni's *Swimmy*, the tale of a little black fish who inhab-

See Harold Courlander, "How Ologbon-Ori Sought Wisdom," in *Olode the Hunter and Other Tales of Nigeria* (San Diego: Harcourt Brace Jovanovich, 1968).

A variation of the episodic book is the diary composed of separate daily entries. See Beverly Cleary's *Dear Mr. Henshaw* (New York: William Morrow, 1983), which consists of a series of letters to an author and diary entries.

This Alice, of course, is in Lewis Carroll's *Alice's Adventures in Wonderland*.

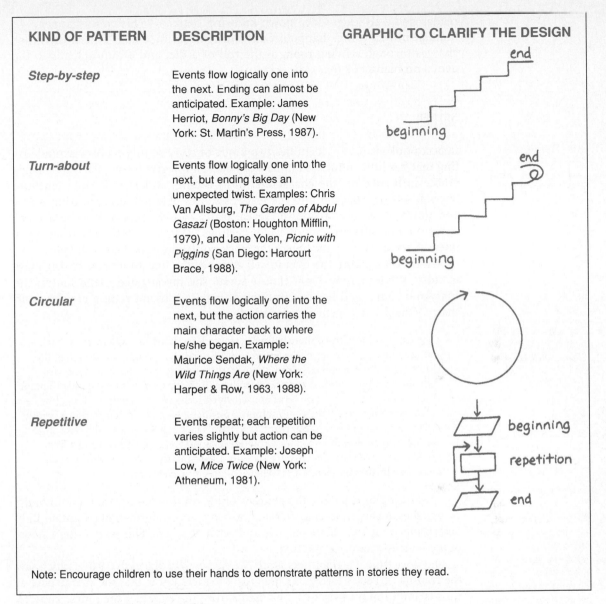

KIND OF PATTERN	DESCRIPTION	GRAPHIC TO CLARIFY THE DESIGN
Step-by-step	Events flow logically one into the next. Ending can almost be anticipated. Example: James Herriot, *Bonny's Big Day* (New York: St. Martin's Press, 1987).	
Turn-about	Events flow logically one into the next, but ending takes an unexpected twist. Examples: Chris Van Allsburg, *The Garden of Abdul Gasazi* (Boston: Houghton Mifflin, 1979), and Jane Yolen, *Picnic with Piggins* (San Diego: Harcourt Brace, 1988).	
Circular	Events flow logically one into the next, but the action carries the main character back to where he/she began. Example: Maurice Sendak, *Where the Wild Things Are* (New York: Harper & Row, 1963, 1988).	
Repetitive	Events repeat; each repetition varies slightly but action can be anticipated. Example: Joseph Low, *Mice Twice* (New York: Atheneum, 1981).	

Note: Encourage children to use their hands to demonstrate patterns in stories they read.

Figure 4.3 Plot Patterns in Stories

To trigger a discussion of believability with older students, share Washington Irving's *Rip Van Winkle*, ill. by Thomas Locker (New York: Dial, 1988).

its the underwater realm of medusas, lobsters, and seaweed. Nowhere in this realm are the red fish who are Swimmy's friends, for they have been gobbled up by the large tuna. When Swimmy, lonely and friendless, meets a new school of red fish, he takes action. He teaches them to swim as one big fish, with Swimmy serving as the eye. In this book, events move inexorably toward the point where the little fish will find a way to survive. This ending is tremendously satisfying, for who has not felt the need for friends to return? In accepting the end, the reader says—although deep down knowing better—"This could happen." In fantasy, unreal things happen! Cats and church mice talk, a herd of rhinos charges through a living room at the roll of a die, and a mouse tends to the dental problems of a fox.

Setting

Read Jeffrey Garrett's "Virginia Hamilton: 1992 Andersen Winner," *Book Links*, 2 (January 1993), 22–25, for a discussion of how one author handles place.

Rebecca Lukens (1991) identifies two kinds of story settings: a background setting that has little influence on the story and an integral setting that has considerable influence on the characters, plot, theme, and mood. Some authors develop settings that tap into the reader's senses of smell, taste, hearing, sight, and touch. They use setting to "reveal traits and changes in the characters," move the plot forward, and heighten feelings (Watson, 1991). When setting is integral, it can serve as the hub of the story, controlling characters and plot.

Author Katherine Paterson is well aware of the important role setting plays in story. While writing *Jacob Have I Loved*, she investigated island life off the Maryland shore, and her descriptions of her Rass Island setting are clear and sharp. Visualize this scene in your mind's eye:

From Katherine Paterson, *Jacob Have I Loved* (New York: Crowell, 1980), 1–2.

> The ferry will be almost there before I can see Rass, lying low as a terrapin back on the faded olive water of the Chesapeake. Suddenly, though, the steeple of the Methodist Church will leap from the Bay, dragging up a cluster of white board houses. And then, almost at once, we will be in the harbor, tying up beside Captain Billy's unpainted two-story ferry house, which leans wearily against a long, low shed used for the captain's crab shipping business. Next door, but standing primly aloof in a coat of fierce green paint, is Kellam's General Store with the post office inside, and behind them, on a narrow spine of fast land, the houses and white picket fences of the village. There are only a few spindly trees. It is the excess of snowball bushes that lends a semblance of green to every yard.

According to Paterson, the patterns of life on this remote island dominated by marshes, a church steeple, ferries, crabbing, and watermen like Captain Billy determine what the characters are and what they do. The place—the Chesapeake—melds character and plot.

Another good book for clarifying the relationship between setting and plot is Lois Lowry, *Number the Stars* (Boston: Houghton Mifflin, 1989). See Figure 4.4 for a way to show the importance of an integral setting to story development.

So does time. Paterson sets *Jacob Have I Loved* in the early 1940s, which saw the trauma of Pearl Harbor. As they read, readers know that the remoteness of Rass Island cannot protect its inhabitants from the events of the times. Time, as well as place, affects story.

Theme, or Central Meaning

In Judith Viorst's *Alexander and the Terrible, Horrible, No Good, Very Bad Day*, the reader learns that everyone has days when everything goes wrong. It was that way for Alexander, who on his terrible, horrible, no good, very bad day counted wrong, sang wrong, lost his best friend, and discovered he needed a

SETTING CHAIN

Place: Denmark   Time: World War II

Characteristics of that   Reflections in the story:
time and place:

Denmark was   The Nazis are occupying
occupied by the Nazis.   Denmark when the story
                               begins.

Armed soldiers   Nazi soldiers stop Annemarie,
patrolled the streets   Ellen, and Kristi as they come
of Copenhagen.   from school as the story
                               opens.

Nazis attempted to   Nazis close Mrs. Hirsch's button
round up the Jewish   shop. The Rosens leave
people of Denmark.   suddenly. Ellen stays with the
                               Johansens, pretending to be Lise,
                               Annemarie's dead sister. The
                               Nazis come looking for the
                               Rosens.

Danish Resistance   Peter is a member of the
smuggled out the   Resistance. He helps to
Danish Jews.   smuggle out the Rosens.
                               Annemarie helps by
                               delivering the important
                               packet.

In the process, Danes   Peter is captured and
were caught and   executed. Annemarie's parents
killed.   tell her that Lise died as a
                               result of her resistance
                               activities.

Figure 4.4 Setting Chain Based on Lois Lowry's *Number the Stars*
Note: Read Lois Lowry's "*Number the Stars:* Lois Lowry's Journey to the Newbery Award," *The Reading Teacher,* 44 (October 1990), 98–101, for an explanation by the author of how her own feelings for Denmark were important in her writing of the book.

return visit to the dentist. Through Evaline Ness's *Sam, Bangs, and Moonshine*, the slightly older reader learns that telling lies can be dangerous.

As Lukens (1991) points out, theme is the underlying meaning, or idea, that unifies the story. Generally speaking, the successful writer communicates theme through events and characters rather than through an overt statement as in a fable. Byrd Baylor never tells readers of *Hawk, I'm Your Brother* that enslaving another being is wrong, but that message comes through. The Indian boy frees his beloved hawk, who reaches its glory soaring high above the Santos Mountains.

Sometimes meanings are hidden deeply below the surface. This is true of *allegory*, which can be interpreted on three levels:

See Kathryn Au, "Constructing the Theme of a Story," *Language Arts*, 69 (February 1992), 106–111, for a discussion of how to involve children in story themes.

1. On the surface, with readers reacting to story events that excite;
2. In terms of central meaning, or theme;
3. In symbolic terms, with consideration of what the characters or events represent in the real world.

A number of books read by children in the upper grades are allegories. Upper-graders have appreciated Richard Bach's *Jonathan Livingston Seagull* since its appearance twenty-five years ago. They realize that Jonathan symbolizes the creative nonconformist who explores uncharted ways. Similarly, in Kenneth Grahame's classic *Wind in the Willows*, Rat, Mole, Badger, and Toad symbolize qualities associated with people, like generosity and vanity.

There are, of course, less sophisticated allegories. Leo Lionni's *Tico and the Golden Wings* is an allegory. Tico at first stands for society's outcast and later represents the person who discovers that material things do not necessarily make one happy. The golden feathers symbolize possessions. One teacher, Rona Zandell, introduced her fifth-graders to allegory through *Tico*. Her students let their imaginations spin as they brainstormed all sorts of allegoric relationships between story and real-life events. Then they went on to compose original allegories.

Clearly, children react more in terms of concrete story events and underlying themes than of allegoric meanings. As youngsters from ages ten to eleven begin to think in the abstract, however, they sometimes can explore below the surface. As Ms. Zandell discovered, some picture books are allegories with hidden meanings that upper-graders can interpret. These kinds of literary experiences contribute to children's cognitive growth, for symbolic literature has the power to move youngsters into abstract thinking.

Verbal Style

According to William Anderson and Patrick Groff (1972), "The foremost determinant of literary effectiveness is language. Only through language can literature communicate; whether written or spoken, the essence of literature is always verbal."

Through language the author communicates plot, character, and theme. Descriptive passages clarify a character's appearance and aspects of the setting.

Dialogue propels the plot, while specific words set the mood. Repeated words also forward the plot, establish the tone, and provide sounds pleasant to the ear. Words are the paint of the writer, who must dip into his or her pot to find the combinations of sounds and meanings needed to create a harmonious verbal picture.

Word Sounds Word sounds play a major part in books for younger children. Theodore Geisel, better known as Dr. Seuss, was a master of sounds. Dr. Seuss wrote with a rhythmic rhyming so natural that an oral reader feels the words must always have belonged in that order. Dr. Seuss played with alliteration and rhyme to achieve special effects; it is Horton who hatches the egg and lazy Mazy who claims it in the end in *Horton Hatches the Egg*. Humor too comes through repetition, simple at times, as in "My goodness! My gracious! My word!", and more involved at other times, as in the recurring line "An elephant's faithful one hundred percent!" Dr. Seuss also played with onomatopoeic words like *whizz, thumping, bumping,* and *squeak.* Many of the same effects splashed in large scale by Dr. Seuss are found in other stories children enjoy, albeit painted with a more muted stroke.

Word Meanings Through his or her choice and patterning of words, an author sets the stage for the story. Listen to the pictures of Maine that Robert McCloskey paints beautifully with words in *Time of Wonder* and *One Morning in Maine.* Listen to Berta and Elmer Hader's *The Big Snow* to see winter created through the magic of word pictures. Search for an owl with Jane Yolen during the time of the *Owl Moon,* feel the cold, and listen to the quiet of the night. Masters of complete and realistic description, McCloskey, the Haders, and Yolen help the reader perceive the world through fresh eyes.

Through artful word choice and patterning, an author also adds humor. Read the comic description of Jennifer trick-or-treating in Konigsburg's *Jennifer, Hecate, Macbeth, William McKinley, and Me, Elizabeth.* Short, staccato sentences juxtaposed in rapid succession communicate the efficient technique that Jennifer uses to ensure a bounty of treats. Konigsburg proves a master of the art of tongue-in-cheek humor. So does Eric Kimmel when he plays entertainingly with language and human motivation in *Four Dollars and Fifty Cents.* Originally published as a short story in *Cricket, Four Dollars and Fifty Cents* won the Paul A. Witty Short Story Award in 1990. Although elementary children are tickled by Kimmel's tall tale of Shorty Long's attempts to avoid paying his $4.50 debt, the humor in the story is such that it makes for equally good reading aloud in junior and senior high schools.

The Paul A. Witty Short Story Award is given each year by the International Reading Association to the author of the best short story published in a children's periodical. *Cricket* magazine (Peru, Illinois) published the winning story from 1988 to 1992 and is a fine source of read-aloud stories.

Pictorial Style

See Appendix B for a list of recent Caldecott and Newbery Medal winners.

Readers of *Time of Wonder, The Big Snow,* and *Owl Moon* find their experience with literature heightened by the illustrations. Books for the younger child tend to be picture stories in which meaning is communicated through words and pictures and pictures at times dominate. The importance of pictures in these

THE FORUM On the Elements of Story

Speaking at the 37th Annual Convention of the International Reading Association (May 7, Orlando, Florida), Paul Zindel, author of the novels *The Pigman* and *My Darling, My Hamburger* identified five elements in a successful novel:

1. The theme—the meaning the author is trying to convey (according to Zindel, "theme is most important in story");
2. The catalytic grabber—the way the author gets the action going;
3. The need—the purpose for which the main character strives (in Zindel's words, "the need drives the characters");
4. The central question—the question in a reader's mind that must be answered by story's end;
5. The turning point(s)—one or two events that turn the story in a new direction;
6. The subplot—the plot underlying the main action that often carries the theme.

A reader can ask questions about a novel based on these elements: How does the theme relate to my life? How and why does the catalyst affect me? How does the need apply to me?

Zindel explains that the same elements are part of a reader's life. Thus, a reader can ask: What is the theme of my life at this stage? What catalysts exist in my life? What needs drive me?

Questions to Consider

Read a young-adult novel, and use Zindel's elements to analyze it. Respond by writing in your personal literature journal where you keep notes about books you are reading. Organize a literature study circle of fellow students or teachers. Share your notes with your study circle so that you come to a heightened appreciation of story. Use Aldo Cardarelli, "Teachers Under Cover: Promoting the Personal Reading of Teachers," *The Reading Teacher*, 45 (May 1992), 664–668, as a guide for forming your own literature study circle.

books is indicated by the fact that each has been recognized for artistic excellence by being awarded the Caldecott Medal, presented yearly by the American Library Association to the artist of the most distinguished American picture book for children. This is in contrast to the Newbery Medal, awarded each year to the author who has made the most distinguished contribution to American literature for children.

Harmonizing Words and Pictures Through Color Successful storybooks illustrate the verbal story line with pictures that harmonize with the words. Illustrators achieve this harmony in a number of ways. One is to use color, or

For a similar use of color to highlight story elements, see Susan Seligson and Howie Schneider, *Amos: The Story of an Old Dog and His Couch* (Boston: Little, Brown, 1987), and Peter Parnall, *Apple Tree* (New York: Macmillan, 1988).

the absence of it, to enhance story meanings. For example, in the Caldecott winner *The Funny Little Woman* by Arlene Mosel, Blair Lent's illustrations washed in soft greens, yellows, and browns show where the action is occurring. When the funny little woman is tucked cozily in her little house, it is filled with color; but when she falls down the hole after her dumpling, the underworld blooms with color and the little house appears as a black-and-white sketch, probably as it remained in the woman's memory while she lived in the realm of the oni. Later, when the woman escapes to the upper, real world, the lower one fades into black and white while color again lights up the little house.

Harmonizing Words and Pictures Through Size In Dr. Seuss's *And to Think That I Saw It on Mulberry Street*, the pictures get larger and larger as Marco's imagination takes over and return to normal size only when Marco tells his father what he actually saw on Mulberry Street. Similarly, in Maurice Sendak's *Where the Wild Things Are*, the pictures occupy more and more of the page as Max travels farther and farther from his very own room into the land of the wild things. Changes in picture size can thus be an effective way to communicate meaning.

Harmonizing Words and Pictures Through Detail When Max becomes king of the wild things, Sendak shows him wearing a crown. When Peter in *The Snowy Day* walks with his feet pointing out like "this" and pointing in like "that," Ezra Jack Keats shows tracks in the snow doing just "this" and "that." And when Squire Lovel of Trove in *Duffy and the Devil* loses all the clothes that his wife has contracted with the devil to make for him, Margot Zemach shows a squire clothed only in shoes, clutching his hat in front of him. In each case, words and pictures are in harmony.

Use Mitsumasa Anno et al., *All in a Day* (New York: Philomel, 1986), to help children understand differences in art styles. The book, which touches on the theme of cultural diversity, has art by nine distinguished illustrators.

At times, too, illustrations supply additional detail. In Ann Grifalconi's *The Village of Round and Square Houses*, the softly muted drawings provide a picture of life as it is lived in the village of Tos. In the same way, the muted drawings in Judith Hendershot's *In Coal Country* provide the details of setting for that story.

In books for upper-graders, pictures play a lesser but still significant role. In most cases, the pictures are pen-and-ink sketches scattered sparingly through the book. The effect, however, can be powerful, as in Paula Fox's, *The Slave Dancer*; here Eros Keith's illustrations are stark, communicating a sense of overwhelming horror.

Books for Children and Youth

In language arts, children should read stories in which character, plot, setting, and theme—the key structural elements of story—are finely crafted. They should read stories in which words dance across the page and illustrations add to the aesthetic and emotional experience. In addition, children should be introduced to a variety of literary forms: picture books, poetry, traditional tales, modern fantasy, contemporary realism, historical fiction, biography, and informational books. Carl Smith (1991) explains "Each type of literature presented to a young reader serves two functions: to develop a schema for that literary genre and to encourage the application of thinking skills in a variety of literary engagements. . . . Reading a variety of literary genres has a related positive effect on writing."

Little has been said in this chapter about the qualities of fine poetry and nonfiction. Especially important in poetry is the uniqueness of the images. In informational literature, authenticity and accuracy are foremost. But verbal style is significant in all literature. After all, words form the core of the aesthetic experience. Writers are ultimately judged by the way they handle words.

See Chapter 9 for a discussion of poetry and Chapter 6 for details on poetry and choral speaking. See also Beatrice Schenk de Regniers et al., *Sing a Song of Popcorn* (New York: Scholastic, 1988) for an anthology of poetry illustrated by eight Caldecott Medal–winning artists.

✎ Building and Refining Your Teaching Skills

 ✦ Select three Newbery-winning books to analyze in terms of the criteria discussed in the chapter. See Figure 4.5 for a web with points to consider.
 ✦ Study five Caldecott-winning books to see how pictures and words combine to tell the story.

Bringing Children and Books Together

Read Carole Urzua, "Faith in Learners Through Literature Studies," *Language Arts*, 69 (November 1992), 492–501, for a description of how one teacher uses literature with junior high/middle grade students. Read also Robert Ruddell, "A Whole Language and Literature Perspective," *Language Arts*, 69 (December 1992), 612–620, for an excellent discussion of readers' motivation as they connect with a story.

A major goal of the language arts is to foster a love of literature in children who, as they read, "make associations with their own life experiences and the experiences of others" (Cox and Many, 1992). How do teachers bring children and books together to engender this kind of response?

Today many educators answer this question in terms of ongoing literature-based units that give students opportunities to read several related books or a chapter book and make connections as they read. (See Chapter 1 for a discussion of this approach and the Teacher-as-Researcher Forum in this chapter for an example.) Educators talk, too, of having students respond by drawing or writing their ideas in literature response journals and later sharing their responses with other students in literature-discussion circles. In their response journals, students react to the designs of stories they have read, create stories modeled after stories read, and reflect on relationships within stories. In this section, we will consider ways to encourage such active and personal responses.

Reacting to the Design of a Story

As you know, stories have a design: step-by-step, turn-about, circular, or repetitive. A literature-based unit can help students achieve an understanding of story

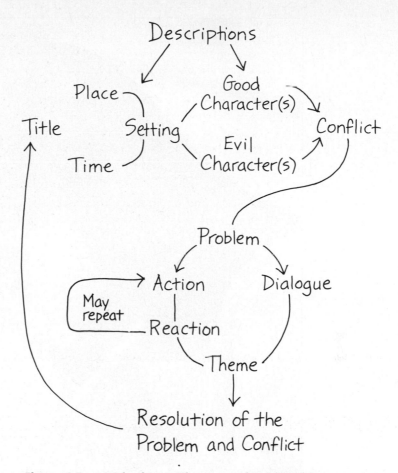

Figure 4.5 A Web of Story Elements and Relationships

Enjoy Charlotte Huck, "Literacy and Literature," *Language Arts*, 69 (November 1992), 520–526, in which Huck describes a comprehensive literature program with the goal being "to produce children who not only know how to read but who also become readers." Huck's article is a "must-read" for teachers building literature-based programs.

design through active story listening and follow-up discussion. Children join in the telling of a story, anticipating, predicting, and helping to make the story. In talking about it, they use hand motions to clarify the pattern. They climb their hands upward in ladder fashion as they retell the events of a step-by-step story. They climb their hands upward and make a final twist as they retell a turn-about tale. They make a circle in the air as they talk about a circular tale and a series of circles in talking about a repetitive story. Having physically interpreted story designs, they can draw pictures in their response journals that depict the designs of other stories they hear or read.

Another activity that fits easily into unit study is mapping the flow of happiness and sadness in a story. Many stories for young children are essentially growl/grin stories that start with a problem and finish with a resolution of it. This is the pattern of comedy, which children can perceive as early as preschool. Children can make sad and happy paper plate faces. As they retell a story after a listening time, they hold up the face that expresses the emotion conveyed in the story. In so doing, they see the structure of the story—from a growl (sad face) to

Students can respond to stories they have read by drawing or writing in their literature response journals. (© 1993 Jean-Claude Lejeune)

a grin (happy face). They also begin to understand at a simple level the roles of conflict and resolution of conflict in story. Again, physical involvement leads into a drawing response, with young children drawing sad and happy faces in their literature journals as they reflect on other stories they hear or read.

Upper-graders can use the same framework for interpreting story structure, going beyond the simple growl/grin story to grin/growl/grin stories and growl/growl/growl stories as part of a unit on the short story. Growl/growl/growl, of course, is the pattern of tragedy. At this level, students use their hands to graph in the air the rise and fall of feelings in a story. Having reacted physically, they make mood graphs in their literature response journals as they respond to other stories.

Creating Stories with Design

Use the big-book version of Kalan's story with primary youngsters. Check with Scholastic in New York City.

Perhaps the best way for both primary- and intermediate-level children to respond to stories and books is through storymaking. Children can respond by creating stories that incorporate elements of stories heard or read. Take, for example, Robert Kalan's *Jump, Frog, Jump*. The book begins simply, "This is the fly that climbed out of the water." The second line adds and repeats, "This is the frog that was under the fly that climbed out of the water." Successive lines add on to the second line and repeat the whole. Kalan also repeats the title words, *Jump, Frog, Jump*. After listening to and joining in the telling of the Kalan piece, youngsters can orally compose a similar sequence, guided by the teacher. Later they can write stories with similar repetitive elements in their literature response journals, working on their own or in collaboration with a writing mate.

Share *Hey, Al* in tandem with Sendak's *Where the Wild Things Are*. Young children can see the similarities in design. Comparing stories with similar designs helps children understand the nature of story structure.

In the same way, children can create growl/grin stories after listening to one such as Arthur Yorinks's *Hey, Al*. The story begins with Al being unhappy about the "dump" in which he lives. When a large bird suggests, "Hey, Al . . . Have I got a place for you," Al takes him up on his offer and goes to birdland in the sky. For a time Al's growls turn into grins, but paradise quickly palls. Al flies home, losing Eddie, his dog, in the process. But growls turn into grins when Eddie makes it home safely. The last line, "Paradise lost is sometimes Heaven found," is the ultimate grin ending. After hearing this story and together orally making a growl/grin story, youngsters can compose similar stories of their own—and doing so is easy, for the young authors know the design.

Some books are perfect for involving children in writing original descriptions and even chants. Barbara Cooney's *Chanticleer and the Fox* contains a marvelous description of that proud rooster. Cooney tells us that Chanticleer's crowing was more "trustworthy than a clock," his comb was "redder than fine coral," and his bill "shone like jet." Youngsters who have met this mighty bird can together compose a description of the fox, who appears later in the story. Similarly, youngsters who have read Byrd Baylor's *The Way to Start a Day* can brainstorm descriptions of the sunrise and incorporate them into chants they compose in response to the book's directive: "Go outside and face the east and greet the sun with some kind of blessing or chant or song you made yourself and keep for early morning."

Other books lend themselves to word play. For example, young children who have listened to Robert McCloskey's *Make Way for Ducklings* can play with the repeating *-ack* sounds—*Jack, Kack, Lack, Mack, Nack*—by chorusing them together and creating their own repeating-sound stories. In much the same way, upper-graders who have read Verna Aardema's *Why Mosquitoes Buzz in People's Ears* can borrow the Ashanti-style, repetitive-word effect that Aardema uses as they respond by writing stories of their own. Later they can listen to Gail Haley's *A Story, A Story*, in which repetition serves the same function, and compare it with the Aardema tale.

Thinking Cognitively and Aesthetically About Story Relationships

Obviously, higher-order thinking should be part of children's response to literature. Students should be encouraged to predict, compare, think critically, feel deeply, and relate what they read to their own lives. Figure 4.6 shows a response guide for predicting during listening and reading. Students pause to ask: What is going to happen next? What clues support my prediction? They answer by writing in their literature response journals. Students can also respond by drawing, if they prefer. In their journals they draw what happened first, then, and after that. Then they draw their prediction—what will happen next—as Joseph did in the series shown in Figure 4.7.

Students can also compare and critically evaluate stories within a literature-based unit. After hearing or reading stories with a similar theme, characters, set-

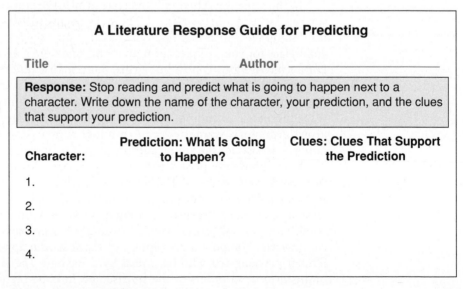

A Literature Response Guide for Predicting

Title _____ Author _____

Response: Stop reading and predict what is going to happen next to a character. Write down the name of the character, your prediction, and the clues that support your prediction.

Character:	Prediction: What Is Going to Happen?	Clues: Clues That Support the Prediction
1.		
2.		
3.		
4.		

Figure 4.6   A Prediction Guide

Also use a nonfictional account of ducks with this book to help children begin to understand the difference between fiction and nonfiction.

Read James Flood et al., "Am I Allowed to Group? Using Flexible Patterns for Effective Instruction," *The Reading Teacher*, 45 (April 1992), 608–616, for a description of one third-grade class that created stories based on the model supplied by Aardema (*Why Mosquitoes Buzz in People's Ears* [New York: Scribner, 1975]).

Figure 4.7 A Student's Prediction While Reading *Maniac Magee*
SOURCE: Courtesy of Joseph Abadin and Jennifer Kramm.

For a discussion of ways to use charts to record children's responses to literature, read Nancy Rosen and James Hoffman, "Language Charts: A Record of Story Time Talk," *Language Arts*, 69 (January 1992), 44–52.

Study the children's writings that serve as part openers in this text. Each is a child's response to a novel the class was reading together.

ting, and/or problem, students can ask: How are these stories the same? How are they different? In their response journals, students make a three-column chart. In the first column, they list words such as *author, setting, principal character, major problem in the story, and how the story was resolved*. In the two other columns, they enter data about two stories they have heard or read. Beneath the table, they write a critical response: which story they preferred, which was more believable, which was more realistic—with reasons to support their judgments.

Another way students can respond to stories is to put themselves in the place of a character. Key questions here are: What kind of character is this? How am I like this character? How am I different? Related questions are: How does this character feel? How do I feel as I read? When have I felt the way the character does? The response guide in Figure 4.8 can help students tap into their thoughts and feelings as they read. In responding to a guide, mounted as a bulletin board chart, students write notes in their literature response journals to share later with their response group. Emphasis is on getting ideas down, not in writing "perfect" English.

Responding to the Content of Books

Not all books tell a story. Some provide information useful in content-area unit studies. Rather than simply reading about a topic in a textbook, students can investigate it by reading in a variety of informational books that relate to the topic, recording their findings in their learning logs, and sharing their findings with classmates.

Books as Sources of Information

Another upper-grade science-related book you may enjoy sharing is David Macaulay, *The Way Things Work* (Boston: Houghton Mifflin, 1988).

Informational books are especially valuable in thematic science and social studies units. They can be used in a variety of ways. An example is Mitsumasa Anno's *Sundial*. Upper-graders can use this informational book, which contains elaborate pop-up displays, to find out how sundials work. Based on it, they can construct sundials as they study what causes day and night. Consider also *Anno's U.S.A.* Upper-graders can read it at the culmination of a study of American history. In talking about each page of this wordless trip across the United States by a great Japanese artist, students can use their understanding of history to make a companion text.

More typical of the informational books available is Marcia Sewall's *The Pilgrims of Plimoth*, which one fifth-grade teacher used as integrative literature in a thematic unit on the beginnings of America. She read the book to the class, stopping occasionally to ask the children to record events on a time line. Students also made a web that summed up basic data about the colony. To do this,

A Literature Response Guide for Character and Feeling Analysis

Title _____ Author _____

Response: Stop reading, select a character, and write down his or her name. Decide: What kind of person is this character? Write down words that describe the character. Decide: How is this character like you? different from you? Repeat for other characters in the book. Make a chart like this in your response journal.

Character	Qualities of the Character	How the Character Is Like You; Is Different from You
1.		
2.		
3.		

Response: Stop reading. Describe what is happening in the story. Decide: How does the character feel at this moment? Write down some feeling words. Decide: How do I feel at this moment? Write down some feeling words. Decide: When have I ever felt the way the character feels? Make a chart like this in your journal.

Description of the Event	How the Character Feels	How I Feel	When I Have Felt Like the Character Feels
1.			
2.			
3.			

Figure 4.8   A Character and Feeling Analysis Guide

they used the major headings within the book as subheadings on their web. Figure 4.9 is the outcome.

Peter Spier's *We the People: The Constitution of the United States of America* can be used in a similar way. The teacher can orally share the explanation of how the Constitution came into being. While listening, students plot the events of 1787–1790 on a time line (see Figure 4.10). Later they can make a web based on Spier's drawings that accompany each key phrase of the preamble: "We the people of the United States," "in Order to form a more perfect Union," "establish Justice . . . ."

Informational books written in story form, such as Alice and Martin Provensen's Caldecott Medal–winning book *The Glorious Flight Across the Channel with Louis Bleriot*, also have a place in content-area studies. The Provensens tell how Bleriot experimented with flying machines until he

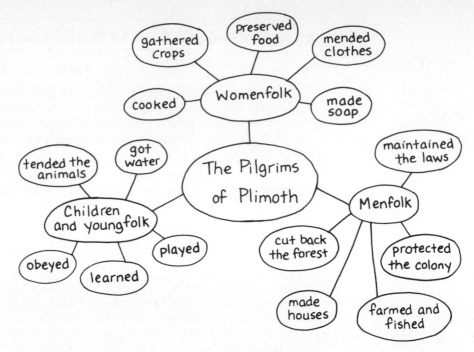

Using selection headings from the book (menfolk, women-folk, children, and youngfolk), students record related data on a web as they read. They also discuss role expectations of the past. Later they write paragraphs based on the web.

Figure 4.9 A Data Web for *The Pilgrims of Plimoth*

Use in this context Russell Freedman. *The Wright Brothers: How They Invented the Airplane* (New York: Holiday House, 1991).

developed a plane that could fly, and how he became the first person to fly across the English Channel. Listening to this story as part of a unit on transportation can help children learn about the development of the airplane.

In the lower primary grades, informational books may provide the basic content for a discussion. One significant example is Riki Levinson's *Watch the Stars Come Out*, the story of two immigrant children who make the trip to America on their own. Children can talk about why people leave their own country and move to another, what the Statue of Liberty (shown in the story) means, and what it must feel like to travel on one's own. Often it is useful to develop as a unit two or three books that relate to the same concept—in this case, immigration. Here the teacher might also share Nancy Levinson's *I Lift My Lamp: Emma Lazarus and the Statue of Liberty* and Betsy Maestro's *The Statue of Liberty*.

One warning is in order before moving on. Teachers generally accept the idea that they should read aloud to young children. Often, however, this oral sharing is restricted to stories read to children in the lower grades. Equal attention should be paid to sharing informational content during science and social studies; such sharing enhances youngsters' basic listening, reading, writing, and speaking skills while building their understanding of fundamental concepts. Oral sharing is as important at the intermediate level as it is in the primary grades.

A TIME LINE FOR RECORDING STORY EVENTS

Think about the events. Record on a time line when each event occurred.

Date	Event
Date	*Event*
May 14, 1787	First delegates assembled in Philadelphia.
September 17, 1787	The delegates adopted the Constitution.
by January 1788	Connecticut, Delaware, Georgia, New Jersey, and Pennsylvania had ratified the Constitution.
February 1788	Massachusetts ratified the Constitution.
April 1788	Maryland ratified the Constitution.
July 1788	South Carolina and New Hampshire ratified the Constitution, making it the law of the land. Later, Virginia and New York ratified the Constitution.
1789	North Carolina ratified the Constitution.
1790	Rhode Island ratified the Constitution.

Figure 4.10 A Vertical Time Line Based on Peter Spier's *We the People*

Books and Significant Issues

Read Laura Robb, "Books in the Classroom: Controversial Novels," *The Horn Book*, 68 (May/June 1992), 374–376, for an account of the use of controversial novels with at-risk students.

Sibling relations, divorce, old age, death, sex, minorities, terrorism, female roles, and drugs are just a few issues popular with authors writing for today's youth. Because books deal with such a wide spectrum of issues, they can stimulate discussion.

A case in point is Katherine Paterson's Newbery Medal–winning *Bridge to Terabithia*. In it death breaks up a friendship between a young boy and girl. How overwhelming death is comes clearly across to the reader as Paterson writes: *"God—dead—you—Leslie—dead—you.* He ran until he was stumbling but he kept on, afraid to stop. Knowing somehow that running was the only thing that could keep Leslie from being dead." In the same vein is Carol Carrick's *The Accident*, which is about the death of a beloved dog. The first is for the upper elementary reader, the latter for the primary child. Both can spark discussions that will help children better accept their own feelings about death.

Similarly, a number of books vividly describe the treatment of minorities. *Behind Barbed Wire* by Daniel Davis tells, in striking terms, the story of the internment of Japanese Americans during World War II. Milton Meltzer's *Never to Forget: The Jews of the Holocaust* focuses on the Jewish experience during that war. Russell Freedman's *Indian Chiefs* depicts the problems Native Americans faced as they were systematically pushed from their land. If portions of these books are read aloud as part of a history unit, students begin to comprehend the extent of the crimes human beings have committed against one another and assess their own attitudes toward others.

Read also Russell Freedman, *Lincoln: A Photobiography* (Boston: Houghton Mifflin, 1987), for a discussion of Lincoln's view of slavery.

The books just described are not really controversial; their use brings little adverse reaction in most communities. However, books that treat sex and drugs in explicit terms do upset some parents. Parents have objected to such books as Beatrice Sparks's *Go Ask Alice*, the diary of a fifteen-year-old who turns to drugs and sex and finally dies of an overdose, and Norma Klein's *Mom, the Wolf Man, and Me*, the story of a youngster who lives in an unconventional family arrangement with her never-married mother and her mother's boyfriend. The same is true of a book like Judy Blume's *Forever*, which is sexually explicit. Whereas Blume's *Blubber* is widely acclaimed for its clear, honest, and humorous treatment of the problems of growing up, *Forever* is controversial. Similar books to which parents may object belong in libraries for young people to select, read, and judge critically. It is difficult, however, to make this more explicit fiction an integral part of the elementary school language arts curriculum.

Sex Role Stereotyping in Books

A major thesis of this chapter is that children can broaden their conceptual understanding through books. One problem with this idea, however, is that some books are flawed. They present a stereotypical view of people and of the roles people play in society. Specifically, in some children's books, women are depicted engaged primarily in passive pursuits. They follow, never lead, their male counterparts. Their concern is primarily with clothes, jewelry, beauty, food, and finding Prince Charming. In contrast, men are depicted in more active pursuits—participating in sports, going to work, solving problems, doing many jobs.

In the past twenty years or so, some progress has been made, and today many books portray women in more active and varied roles. Today more books depict girls as well as boys as clever, capable, and athletic. However, since children continue to read the older stories, they still come in contact with the old stereotypes—stereotypes that affect how they feel about themselves and their role in society.

Before leaving the topic of sexism in literature, let us consider the effect of stereotyping on males. If males in stories are generally depicted as strong and forceful and if such signs of emotion as weeping are portrayed as "unmanly," the young boy who feels far from strong and expresses his feelings through tears may come to believe that there is something "wrong" with him. Likewise, the roles in which males are depicted in stories can be limiting. Today more and more men are assuming homemaking tasks and opting for careers in nursing, secretarial work, and preschool education. Books should depict males performing all these roles if today's boys are to get a complete picture of the occupational possibilities open to them.

Ethnic Stereotyping in Books

Some books are flawed not only by sexual stereotyping but by limited and distorted views of diverse ethnic groups. Until recently, few books for children included main characters who are members of racial or religious minorities, and few showed adult members of minority groups operating within the full range of available occupations. Even today the number of books featuring Native Americans, African Americans, Mexican Americans, and Asian Americans remains relatively small, and few depict adults in these groups pursuing careers in the most respected professions. Recent books that feature minority characters have generally been folktales, with retelling of African, Mexican, and Native American stories becoming popular. Examples are Marcia Brown's Caldecott Medal–winning picture book *Shadow* and Margot Zemach's *Jake and Honeybunch Go to Heaven*, neither of which does much to overcome the stereotyping that was typical of children's books of the past. It fact, they may actually reinforce some stereotypes.

One of the first books to treat blacks in a completely natural way was Lorraine and Jerold Beim's *Two Is a Team*. A picture storybook of the 1940s, it describes a friendship between two little boys, Ted and Paul, one of whom is black and the other white. Another landmark was Ezra Jack Keats's *The Snowy Day*, which tells of the delight of Peter, a little black boy, in the snow. Since then, Keats has written other books about Peter, and other authors have contributed books that incorporate interracial friendships, depict the horrors of slavery and discrimination, and describe how members of a wide range of ethnic groups handle day-to-day problems of living. But these books have only scratched the

Read Robert Lipsyte, "Listening for the Footsteps: Books and Boys," *Horn Book*, 68 (May/June 1992), 290–296. Lipsyte writes, "Boys have to learn what girls already know, that a book is something you can make into a cave, and that you can crawl into the cave, roll around in it, explore it, find out what's in it, and what's in you."

See also the more recent Jerry Spinelli, *Maniac Magee* (Boston: Little, Brown, 1990).

surface. If children are to acquire a meaningful view of life within a pluralistic society, they will need many more books that depict diverse ethnic groups interacting in a variety of situations.

Implications for Teaching

In selecting books to share and recommend, teachers must be aware of the covert and sometimes overt messages books send to readers. Sometimes teachers are so accustomed to hearing stereotypes that they fail to see evidence in classroom books and in their own behavior. The teacher's first step in overcoming stereotyped views is to keep alert for instances in which any group of individuals is treated differently from other groups or in a discriminatory manner.

Once a teacher is alert to possible stereotypes in literature, he or she will note many instances, since most of the folktales and fairy tales of the past give a stereotyped view of people. Should schools discard such pieces in favor of more relevant stories? Should they rewrite the stories of the past? Huck (1987) takes an appealing middle-of-the-road position on this issue:

> There is no point in denouncing fairytales for their sexist portrayal of beautiful young girls waiting for the arrival of their princes, for evil stepmothers or nagging wives. Such stories reflected the longings and beliefs of a society long past. To change the folktales would be to destroy our traditional heritage. . . . But today's books must reflect a more liberated point of view.

Accordingly, teachers must help children see folk literature as a reflection of a different time and place. They can ask children to consider how a particular tale might be different had it been written today. Simultaneously, teachers must help children make contact with literature that reflects a less stereotypical view.

✎ Building and Refining Your Teaching Skills

- ✦ Identify books that (1) develop children's interest in words, (2) expand youngsters' perception of an issue important today, (3) build understanding of a science or social studies concept, and (4) counteract a sexual stereotype students have developed.
- ✦ Read several issues of *The Horn Book*, which provides reviews of children's books. For reviews, see also recent issues of the *Bulletin of the Center for Children's Books*, newly associated with the University of Illinois at Champaign–Urbana's Graduate School of Library and Information Science. Read also recent issues of *The New Advocate* for articles on children's literature in whole-language classrooms.

For a discussion of the teacher as researcher, read Eleanor Kutz, "Teacher Research: Myths and Realities," *Language Arts*, 69 (March 1992), 193–197. For an account of another teacher's journey into literature with a group of nine- to twelve-year-old students, read Judith Rosenfeld, "Books in the Classroom," *The Horn Book*, 68 (July/August, 1992), 501–503.

THE FORUM   The Teacher as Researcher

Dorothy Strickland reflects on the changing character of the educational researcher. Whereas in the past Strickland went into classrooms to do research, today she collaborates "on research teams where classroom teachers are involved in every aspect of the investigations. Indeed, it is frequently the teachers themselves who initiate much of the research." . . . These teachers "are encouraged by a need to construct their own knowledge about things that are important to them" ("The Teacher as Researcher: Toward the Extended Professional," *Language Arts*, 65 [December 1988], 754–764).

Maureen Stawasz is such a teacher-researcher. Having taught reading with a basal text to students grouped according to ability, Ms. Stawasz decided to experiment with a class reading of a chapter book by taking her sixteen sixth-graders on a journey into Doris Buchanan Smith's *A Taste of Blackberries*—a journey that would involve the children in listening, speaking, reading, and writing. She explained, "Through my unit, I hoped that the students—my travelers—would share the lives of the characters and the painful, yet healing, plot of the story. I hoped that my travelers would freely express themselves both in discussion and writing, relating their personal experiences and feelings to the story events. Students' written responses throughout the unit would comprise a literary magazine, a memento of their journey with *A Taste of Blackberries*." Here is Maureen Stawasz's description of that literary journey:

The Travelers

My sixteen travelers were sixth graders with varying levels of reading skills and interest. Most read on or above grade level. One youngster had received Resource Room services for reading until this year. Another child had arrived from Poland four months before and had just started to pick up English. Two or three others were passive readers; they would read, but usually needed considerable motivation. All the students responded well to teacher read-alouds.

Most of the students in the class had experienced death in some form—the death of a grandparent, a parent, a friend, a pet. This was important background, for *A Taste of Blackberries* is based on the sudden, incomprehensible death of a young boy and the feelings experienced by a friend left behind.

Ms. Stawasz suggests that to develop the integrative dimension of the unit, orally share "Secret Talk," a poem by Eve Merriam; "Poem" and "Youth" by Langston Hughes; and Carol Carrick's story *The Accident*. Weave in a musical thread—Rimsky-Korsakov's "The Flight of the Bumblebee" and Claude Debussy's "Nuage" (Cloud). Ask students to look through a book of art masterpieces to locate a painting that creates the same mood as *A Taste of Blackberries*.

The Journey

An aura of suspense surrounded the start of *A Taste of Blackberries*. It took us two days before we were prepared with the necessary "supplies" for the trip. To start, I publicized the trip: "Wednesday is the day we start our whole book, *A Taste of Blackberries!* Get ready for Wednesday!" This aroused the students' curiosity; students knew that this was going to be something different from their weekly skip through the basal reader stories.

It was important for the children to become familiar with our "destination." What do blackberries taste like? Each child received two blackberries because blackberries were out of season and very costly. Since each had only two berries, they could not gobble them up. Instead, they savored each berry. Together, we inhaled the sweet smell. We placed a single berry on our tongues to feel the softness and the bubbly sacs of juice. Slowly we pressed the berry to the roof of our mouth to let the juice inside run over our taste buds and slip down our throats. We let our teeth take over to finish off the berry. On charts in our response logs, as well as on a master chalkboard chart, we described the LOOK, FEEL, TASTE, and SMELL of our berry. We ate the second berry at our leisure with eyes closed.

In a section of our response logs, we wrote the title and author of the book. Then we looked at the cover. The cover shows two boys picking blackberries on the outskirts of a small town. On the cover is the quote, "We planned to have fun all summer. . . ." We talked about the title, predicting the setting, the characters, the traits of the characters, and the kind of fun two boys could have in the summer.

The next day, I read aloud the first chapter of the book. Students listened to identify the characters and their traits. Having listened, students worked in pairs to make a character web for each of the main characters introduced in the chapter. We came back together to share our webs and talk about Jamie and the narrator. Our journey had begun.

With the exception of the last chapter, students read the following chapters—one a day—to themselves. Generally we used the pictures in the chapter to get ready to read so that the weaker readers were able to handle the text on their own. We made responses in our journals and shared our thoughts after reading. The children initiated these discussions; they were eager to ask questions about things they didn't understand and to tell about similar experiences that had happened to them and how they had felt. We identified "power" words in the chapter and used the context to figure out meanings. We suggested a title for the chapter since chapters are untitled in the novel. We proposed writing options based on the chapter that we could try during writing workshop.

It was slow going at first. The children were getting used to the characters and the build-up of the plot. More advanced readers were quick—too quick—with their responses during follow-up discussions;

For a discussion of ways to encourage children to spend time reading to themselves, see Linda Fielding and Cathy Roller, "Making Difficult Books Accessible and Easy Books Acceptable," *The Reading Teacher*, 45 (May 1992), 678–685.

more reluctant readers sat further down in their seats, happy to let the others take over.

The "travelers" were hooked after Chapter Three when tragedy strikes Jamie, a major character. Everyone was eager to read Chapter Four, only to have their worst fears confirmed; the character they were getting to know was dead. Their question was, "What will happen next?" The sixth graders predicted events to come.

The travelers journeyed on; this trail of death was familiar. Could we use our own experiences with death to get us through this unexpected turn? This we did; we shared our experiences, our confusion, and hurt with honest openness. We began to compile our deeper understandings in our class literary magazine, dedicating it to loved ones we had lost.

At the suggestion of a student who at the start was content to let the others do the talking, we read the last chapter aloud. It seemed as though the travelers, who were responding emotionally at this point, wanted to come together and celebrate the final leg of the journey. Every traveler applauded spontaneously as I read the last word. We had become a community that had shared the specialness of the book, our thoughts, and our writings. We had created the literary magazine, *Tasting Blackberries*, as a showcase portfolio of our experiences with the book. In groups, we had researched, formulated ideas, composed, edited. At the end of the unit, each one of us had a copy of our class magazine.

The Destination

Assessment of a literary journey of this type must be in terms of individual reading attitudes as well as skills. I gave no worksheets, I distributed no vocabulary lists, I gave no tests, and I did not ask children to write answers to comprehension questions at the end of each chapter. How could I determine changes in reading behavior?

Obviously, I had to use informal assessment through observation and work products. For example, as we read, the children debated who the two characters on the cover were. We knew one was Jamie, the boy who died, and the other was the narrator. We studied the traits of each character and debated as to which character was which on the cover. Kristy, one of my sink-in-the-chair readers, made a clever discovery that excited us all. In Chapter Five, Smith mentions that the narrator needed help parting his hair. Kristy pointed out that only one of the characters on the cover had a part in his hair; he must be the narrator. I was elated for Kristy and noted in my anecdotal records for the day that Kristy was showing evidence of being able to read for details and to draw conclusions.

Maureen recommends that for independent reading during the unit, suggest Katherine Paterson's *Bridge to Terabithia*, which touches on the loss of a friend. Suggest, also, books that get at the meaning of friendship: Betsy Byars' *The Cybil War*, Jean Little's *Look Through My Window*, and Zlipha Snyder's *The Egypt Game*.

Dana took awhile to come around. She generally didn't participate unless asked directly. But she was the one who announced she didn't want to wait another day to find out how the story would end, and "Couldn't we *please* read this last chapter out loud together today?"

Jarrett, a tough little guy, cried softly to himself in class. Was he identifying with the characters and plot? Of course. Monique wrote me a letter saying she tried to open up but it was hard because she almost started to cry. Michelle, Diana, and Jackie had great ideas for sequels and asked if they could have more time to write their ideas down. Everyone wanted to know other books by Doris Buchanan Smith, so one day we headed to the library to check the card catalog.

Through their journals and the magazine, the children were involved in different writing. They wrote personal narratives, messages from the point of view of one of the characters, letters of sympathy to the deceased boy's mother, and poetry. One writing option at the end of Chapter Seven was to write a eulogy for Jamie. Only one child attempted it initially. When Monique shared her eulogy with the class, five others decided to write eulogies for the literary magazine. Others edited paragraphs they had written in their journals and wanted to include in the magazine. They rewrote them so they would sound exactly as they wanted them. Were they writing to a specific audience? Were they claiming the writing as their own? Were they revising to communicate their ideas? Most certainly.

The sixth graders were very positive about both the reading and the writing. They volunteered to take on extra assignments to add to the magazine. They referred to the story at times other than when they were reading *A Taste of Blackberries* or writing in response. For example, the word *environment* came up in science discussion one afternoon. "Yeah, you know," said Jackie, "Like Mrs. Mullins's garden had a peaceful environment. That's why the kid went in there after Jamie died."

Reflecting Back

When I was a high school freshman, I had an English teacher named Miss Rice. As a child, I had devoured any books I could get my hands on. That is why my mother and I could not understand how it was that I could never pass one of Miss Rice's book reports. I could tell everything that happened in the book, but I could not satisfy Miss Rice. I realize now that my teacher wanted me to respond to the meaning of the book. I read the book *A Separate Peace* three times before my oral book report conference with Miss Rice. Before the conference I said to her, "The only thing I don't understand is what was the separate peace?"

Writing options the children tried: People Who Are Gone But Not Forgotten; A Character Speaks; Poetry for Jamie; A Eulogy for Jamie; A Letter to Jamie's Mom; Stages of "Good Grief"; Blackberry Recipes; An Interview with a Character; What to Do When Stung by a Bee; A Report on Bees; A Report on Allergies; A Biography of D. B. Smith.

"That, Maureen, is the whole question of this book," she answered.

Through my experiences reading *A Taste of Blackberries* with my sixth graders, I am convinced that children need more quality experiences getting at the underlying meaning of a book—at the personal meaning a book has for them. I am not referring to decoding skills. I am not referring to retelling skills. I am referring to helping children to relate to the characters, feel with them, and develop even as the characters are developing. I am referring to involving children in an aesthetic experience that is so intense that students want to continue reading and cry and clap in response. Students need to grasp the pleasure of a book. They need to explore beyond the words and relate the plot to their own lives.

Reading *A Taste of Blackberries* with my students has convinced me that teachers need to demonstrate the pleasure and the emotional pull of reading. This cannot be done through lectures, through worksheets, through assigning book reports. The way to make children want to read is to travel with them through a few books, creatively expanding their literary journey through writing whenever possible. In time students will get hooked; they will select reading as a way to fill their time and writing as a way of responding. This feeling for reading and writing cannot be drilled into students; the change is subtle, bit by bit.

My experiment with *A Taste of Blackberries* has also convinced me that reading chapter books from beginning to end is particularly effective with slower readers. When chapter books are read over a period of days, these readers have time to get to know the characters and are grabbed up by the dynamics of the plot. They begin to look forward to reading. They anticipate what will happen next to the characters. I can honestly say that reading a chapter book made a difference for my slower readers.

My sixth graders now "own" *A Taste of Blackberries*. They own it because it became a part of them and they became a part of it. It's a good feeling "owning" a book.

I teach at the elementary school in the same town where I went to high school. In about three years, many of my students will be sitting in Miss Rice's English class. I have faith that their book conferences with Miss Rice will be better than mine.

Questions to Consider

What qualities characterize a teacher-researcher? In what ways did Maureen Stawasz change the way she approached reading and literature with her sixth-graders? How did she change the way she assessed their learning?

.........A Summary Thought or Two

LITERATURE IN THE LANGUAGE ARTS

The underlying theme of this chapter is that fine literature is an essential component of elementary school programs and that children should be encouraged to read widely in a variety of good books. The fundamental goal of continuing contact with literature is that children learn to love books and to respond actively while reading. To achieve this goal, teachers must bring to literature study a joy in life: an interest in little things like mushrooms, measuring worms, and minnows that occupy such an important place in children's stories; a delight in the sounds of language; an intense desire to find out; a commitment to understand people and living; and ultimately a love of books that reflect the things, the people, and the sounds of life and language. Without a love of books, teachers find it hard to instill such a love in children.

A second theme of the chapter is that through contacts with fine books, children can acquire a host of other learnings. Specifically, they can learn to

> Teachers can use these behaviors as items on an assessment checklist.

- ✦ Appreciate excellence in the writing and illustrations they find in books;
- ✦ Select books that meet their particular needs and interests;
- ✦ Interpret and evaluate stories, poems, and selections of nonfiction;
- ✦ Write in many different forms (picture, picture story, fable, realistic story, and so forth);
- ✦ Communicate through vocabulary and sentence patterns expanded by contact with diverse patterns and varied content;
- ✦ View the world and living from an expanded horizon stripped of traditional stereotypes.

Such learnings are possible if teachers introduce children to books in which character, plot, setting, theme, words, and illustrations are skillfully interwoven and build language experiences with children that tap the word, sentence, story, picture, and content power of books.

RELATED READINGS

Anderson, Philip, and Gregory Rubano. *Enhancing Aesthetic Reading and Response*. Urbana, Ill.: National Council of Teachers of English, 1991.

Benedict, Susan, and Lenore Carlisle, eds. *Beyond Words: Picture Books for Older Readers and Writers*. Portsmouth, N.H.: Heinemann Educational Books, 1992.

Brown, Carol, and Carl Tomlinson. *Essentials of Children's Literature*. Boston: Allyn and Bacon, 1993.

Cianciolo, Patricia. *Picture Books for Children*. 3rd ed. Chicago: American Library Association, 1990.

Cullinan, Bernice. *Children's Literature in the Reading Program*. Newark, Del.: International Reading Association, 1987.

Cullinan, Bernice, ed. *Invitation to Read: More Children's Literature in the Reading Program*. Newark, Del.: International Reading Association, 1992.

Farrell, Edmund, and James Squire, eds. *Transactions with Literature*. Urbana, Ill.: National Council of Teachers of English, 1990.

Fox, Paula. "To Write Simply." *The Horn Book*, 67 (September/October 1991). 552–555.

Freeman, Evelyn, and Diane Goetz Person, eds. *Using Nonfiction Trade Books in the Elementary Classroom: From Ants to Zeppelins*. Urbana, Ill.: National Council of Teachers of English, 1992.

Greenlaw, M. Jean. "Books in the Classroom." *The Horn Book*, 67 (September/October 1991), 636–639.

Huck, Charlotte, et al. *Children's Literature in the Elementary School*. 5th ed. New York: Holt, Rinehart and Winston, 1993.

Johnson, Terry, and Daphne Louis. *Literacy Through Literature*. Portsmouth, N.H.: Heinemann Educational Books, 1987.

Karolides, Nicholas. *Reader Response in the Classroom: Evoking and Interpreting Meaning in Literature*. White Plains, N.Y.: Longman, 1992.

Kiefer, Barbara, ed. *Getting to Know You: Profiles of Children's Authors*. Urbana, Ill.: National Council of Teachers of English, 1992.

Langer, Judith. *Literature Instruction: A Focus on Student Response*. Urbana, Ill.: National Council of Teachers of English, 1992.

Language Arts, 69 (November 1992). The focus of this issue is literature-based language arts programs.

Nugent, Susan, ed. *Literature for Children and Young Adults*. Urbana, Ill.: National Council of Teachers of English, 1985.

Phelan, Patricia, ed. *Literature and Life: Making Connections in the Classroom*. Urbana, Ill.: National Council of Teachers of English, 1990.

Schwarcz, Joseph, and Chava Schwarcz. *The Picture Book Comes of Age: Looking at Childhood Through the Art of Illustration*. Chicago: American Library Association, 1991.

Sutherland, Zena, and May Hill Arbuthnot. *Children and Books*. 8th ed. New York: HarperCollins, 1990.

Temple, Charles, and Patrick Collins, eds. *Stories and Readers: New Perspectives on Literature in the Elementary Classroom*. Norwood, Mass.: Christopher-Gordon, 1992.

Wason-Elliam, Linda. *Start with a Story: Literature and Learning in Your Classroom*. Portsmouth, N.H.: Heinemann Educational Books, 1991.

Wood, Karen, ed. *Exploring Literature in the Elementary Classroom: Contents and Methods*. Norwood, Mass.: Christopher-Gordon, 1992.

The
Thanksgiving Treasure
Setting

Gr3 Rm22
Jacquelyn
Sawyer
Jefferson
~~Sx~~ ~~S~~ School

Addie-and her house

It takes place in Nebraska in 1947 around thanksgiving time. Addie lives in Nebraska Clar River town.

Jacquelyn responded to *The Thanksgiving Treasure* by identifying the setting of the novel (courtesy of Jacquelyn Sawyer and Micki Benjamin).

ORAL COMMUNICATION IN ACTION

*"The time has come," the Walrus said,
"To talk of many things:
Of shoes—and ships—and sealing wax—
Of cabbages and kings—"*

—Lewis Carroll, "The Walrus and the Carpenter"

How do we encourage children to talk of many things—significant things such as shoes (industry), ships (commerce), and sealing wax (human communication), everyday things such as cabbages, and things that are at the heart of stories, such as kings, knights, and faraway places? In answering this question, we must look at ways to involve children in listening, in speaking, and in critical thinking.

The chapters in Part Three focus on oral communication within an integrated language arts program. The basic thesis of the chapters is that children become effective users of their language through natural, meaningful interaction in classrooms where they talk, listen, and think as they encounter the tasks of everyday living; as they listen to, read, and respond to stories and informational content; and as they write about all manner of ideas from the world of books and the world of action and ideas all around them.

As you read Part Three, keep asking: How can I make meaningful talk a natural part of my classroom so that children develop their ability to listen, speak, and think critically? As you read, visualize yourself interacting in the kind of learning environment being described.

CHAPTER 5

Listening for Meaning
Learning to Listen and Listening to Learn

Reflecting Before Reading

BEFORE reading the chapter, read the title, the headings, and the end-of-chapter summary. Then answer the questions in the margin on this page.

How does the teacher help students listen to learn?

_____

_____

Learn to listen?

_____

_____

What are the purposes for which people listen? How do teachers include these purposes in the curriculum?

_____

_____

Activating prior knowledge; using metacognitive awareness to enhance comprehension

For a discussion of interdisciplinary lessons such as this, read Heidi Jacobs, *Interdisciplinary Curriculum: Design and Implementation* (Alexandria, Va.: Association for Supervision and Curriculum Development, 1989). The book also talks about learning logs.

TEACHING IN ACTION   Getting at the Root of Conflict

It was social studies time in Ann Arnold's sixth-grade class. Youngsters of varying abilities and backgrounds sat with learning logs open as Ms. Arnold introduced the topic of the lesson by displaying a page of the social studies text and pointing to and reading aloud the main heading: "How People Resolve Conflict." She told the class that when she reads a main heading, she thinks for a moment about what the heading brings to mind. She asked the class to predict what they thought the passage would be about. A student scribe recorded points on the chalkboard in a weblike arrangement to show relationships (see the upper half of Figure 5.1).

Instruction and Modeling of Processes

Having activated what the students already knew, Ms. Arnold read aloud the introductory section of the text, indicating as she went along the thoughts that came to mind as she read. Then she held up the text to show the first minor heading in the section: "Trial by Battle." She explained, "I always look at all the subheadings before reading to get an overview. I use them to predict what the subsections will be about and to propose questions to ask myself while reading. What do you think this section will be about? What questions would you keep in mind as you read?"

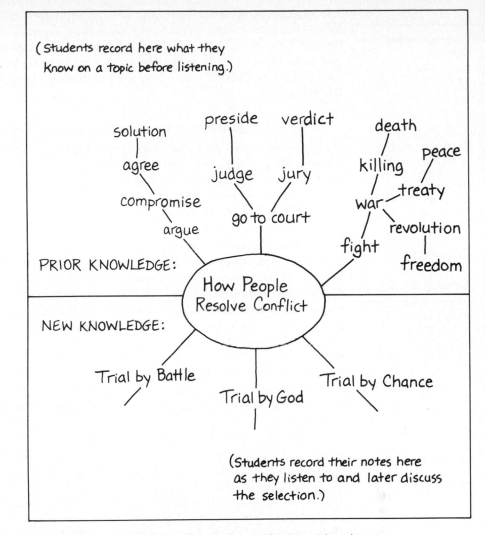

(Students record here what they know on a topic before listening.)

solution

agree

compromise

argue

preside   verdict

judge   jury

go to court

death

killing   peace

war   treaty

revolution

fight   freedom

PRIOR KNOWLEDGE:

How People
Resolve Conflict

NEW KNOWLEDGE:

Trial by Battle

Trial by God

Trial by Chance

(Students record their notes here
as they listen to and later discuss
the selection.)

Figure 5.1   A Web for Recording Before and During Listening

**Surveying and
predicting as a basis for
listening**

This lesson is a modification of
a Directed Listening-Thinking
Activity; students predict
before listening just as they
make predictions before
reading in a Directed Reading-
Thinking Activity.

Next, she pointed to the other subheadings in the section ("Trial by God" and "Trial by Chance") and asked the children to predict what those subsections were about and to propose questions to keep in mind while reading or listening to them.

At that point, Ms. Arnold broke her class into three listening teams with specific tasks to perform while she shared the selection. Students in Team One were to listen to take notes on the content of the first segment of the selection, "Trial by Battle," using their proposed questions as a listening guide and writing notes in their learning logs on the lower half of the conflict idea web as in Figure

5.1. Students on the other two teams were to write down at least two questions to ask the note-taking team. In the same way, Team Two students were to become note takers as the teacher shared the second segment, "Trial by God," and Team Three students were to become note takers as she shared the last segment, "Trial by Chance." The others were to think up questions to ask the note takers later on.

Learning to Listen and Listening to Learn

For a discussion of the importance of reading to children, see Jim Trelease, *The New Read-Aloud Handbook* (New York: Penguin, 1989), and Jim Trelease, "Jim Trelease Speaks on Reading Aloud to Children," *The Reading Teacher*, 43 (December 1989), 200–206.

When the directions were clear, Ms. Arnold read each section aloud, modeling fluent reading to the group. From time to time, she would stop in midsentence to tell the class a thought that occurred to her.

Discussion followed, with the youngsters who had written questions based on what they had heard directing those questions to the note takers. The students tended to ask factual questions like "What is a duel?" To encourage analytical and critical thinking and to model question asking, the teacher interjected a few questions: "Do you believe that few people were killed? Why? What were the advantages and disadvantages of this way of settling conflict?" As the students considered the second and third segments of the selection, they began to ask these kinds of questions of their peers, and a general discussion developed in which students considered examples of when those ways of settling conflict were used in their country. They talked of the duel between Aaron Burr and Alexander Hamilton (which they had studied in fifth grade) and the way trial by the will of God was used during the Salem witch trials (examples not in the text). They recalled Frank Stockton's short story "The Lady, or the Tiger?" which they had read previously, and categorized it as an example of trial by chance.

Finally, Ms. Arnold asked, "If you were living then and you had to settle a conflict, which of these three ways would you prefer? You must pick one." Students thought, picked, and shared their choices and reasons.

Again a discussion—at times rather intense—ensued. Students began to say, "None of these ways is right," and the teacher suggested that they think of an alternative. The students suggested trial by jury based on the facts of a case. The teacher asked the students to write a paragraph in their learning logs telling why trial by jury would be a fairer way to settle conflict than any of the other ways. She told them they would begin the next social studies lesson by sharing their paragraphs while others listened to think critically about the question: What is the fairest way to resolve conflict?

Seeking Closure

As the lesson came to an end, Ms. Arnold sought closure. She asked the students to review the steps they had taken in preparing to listen and in actually listening. The students explained that they had begun by reading the main heading and thinking about what they already knew about that topic. They recalled that they had then listened to the teacher read the introductory section and that she had commented as she read. Next, they had focused on the subheadings, predicting what content would be included and raising questions to answer. They noted too that while they listened they recorded important content in their learning logs and thought of questions to ask and answer. They recalled that they had talked about what they had heard after listening to the teacher's oral reading of the selection.

Learning How We Learn

People's understanding of how they learn and know is called *metacognition*. The final section of this teaching-in-action vignette is geared to develop metacognitive understanding. See Chapter 13 for a discussion of metacognition.

Ms. Arnold explained to the class that what they had done in working with this selection as a group was what they should do as they listen and read independently. In listening, they should identify the main topic and identify what they already know on that topic. In listening, they should talk to themselves in their heads, listen for major changes in subtopics (as indicated in print by subheadings), raise and answer questions in their heads, review what they have heard, and perhaps write down main points.

Ms. Arnold also explained that what they had done before, during, and after listening was similar to what they should do before, during, and after reading. In reading, they should think about what they already know, survey headings, and raise questions before reading; comment to themselves as they read; raise and answer more questions during reading; and review after reading. She told them that they would shortly read about trial by jury and would apply this strategy to their reading.

Listening and Learning: Adding Action and Purpose

As Ann Arnold shared the selection about ways to resolve conflict, her sixth-graders listened intently. They made predictions before listening. They listened to test their predictions and to write down key points and questions. Later they willingly entered into the give-and-take of discussion, listening to the comments of others and responding analytically and critically to them. For them, the social studies lesson was pleasurable and meaningful. It was also a natural bridge into writing and reading and a time to fine-tune auding skills through active, purpose-filled participation. By *auding*, we mean listening that involves a higher order of comprehension and appreciation.

Listening Actively

In classrooms listening should be an active process, with students reacting rather than passively receiving. Active listening goes beyond reception or even retention of ideas. It requires listeners to generate thoughts and express them in some way. Active listening is demonstrated both verbally and nonverbally. According to Thomas Faix (1975), signs of active listening are (1) physical or vocal expressions of feeling, (2) cooperation with others in a group,

(3) expressions of acceptance toward others in a group, and (4) expressions of desire to keep an open mind. Other signs are asking clarifying questions and sticking to the topic.

In classrooms, responses to listening may be more overt. Children may respond physically by choosing, manipulating, or organizing materials; by purposefully using their bodies to respond; or by moving spontaneously in reaction. They may respond by telling, retelling, writing, dramatizing, drawing, and/or reading.

Franklin Ernst (1968) indicates that listeners' responses are almost continuous if the listeners are fully attending. He states: "Listening is an activity evidenced by movement on the part of the not-now-talking person. It is manifested in the behavior by the physical, visible motion of the listener's body. . . . To listen is to move, to be in motion for the words of the talker." Motion includes changes in position, movement of muscles in rhythm with a speaker's sentences, and changes in facial expressions. The truly involved listener is mentally active, with activity reflected physically.

A number of factors influence how actively youngsters listen. Faix mentions class size, design of classroom space, and time of day. Understandably, large class size can limit active listening. A physical barrier that cuts down eye contact has a similar potential for interfering with interaction. Then, too, children are more alert during morning hours and less alert after play periods. The teacher is also a factor. Whether she or he is a thoughtful listener, is open to differences, and is a person to be trusted with intimate thoughts are determinants of how freely children respond. The structure of a lesson is another factor. A strong anticipatory set at the beginning of a lesson can motivate attentive listening; so can a lesson design that requires children to be critical.

Other factors relate to the age of participants and their level of self-control. Young children have more limited attention spans and are less able to handle abstract content than older children.

Working for active response is essential if schools are to overcome the passivity to oral communication that teachers have observed. A 1992 study by the National Assessment of Educational Progress (NAEP) reports that 62 percent of fourth-graders, 64 percent of eighth-graders, and 40 percent of twelfth-graders say they watch at least three hours of television a day. A quarter of the fourth-graders say they watch more than six hours of TV daily (Stout, 1992). This diet of televiewing has made some children into passive receivers, for televiewing is a simple receptive process. Teachers must help children become more critical listeners as well as more actively involved ones.

Listening with a Purpose

Classroom listening should be purpose filled (Funk and Funk, 1989). One way to give listening a purpose is to ask students to (1) predict the content of a passage before listening, (2) listen to test their predictions, and (3) summarize and retell after listening. This procedure is known as the Directed Listening-Thinking Activity, or DLTA (Stauffer, 1980). Ms. Arnold's lesson that opens this chapter is this type of activity. More recently, Choate and Rakes (1987) have proposed a variation of Stauffer's Directed Listening-Thinking Activity. In the Choate and Rakes procedure, called the Structured Listening Activity, or SLA, the teacher introduces a passage by relating the content to the students' experiences and discussing special vocabulary. The teacher then directs the students to listen for important points. Next she or he shares the passage, using visual aids such as pictures or transparencies to focus attention and stopping to intersperse prediction cues such as "What do you think will happen next? Why?" After reading the passage aloud, the teacher asks questions, especially questions that require higher-order thinking. He or she seeks closure by guiding students to summarize, retell, and elaborate on ideas. Both the DLTA and the SLA are useful in that students listen with a purpose.

A second way to make listening purposeful is to use listening as a method of instruction across the curriculum. Some experiences with social studies, science, and the humanities should be oral, with students listening to articles, stories, and poems. If these experiences are structured carefully, children refine listening skills as they listen for detail, build relationships among ideas, and formulate opinions relative to content. At the same time, they learn content.

See Dorothy Hennings, "A Read Aloud with Nonfiction: Reflective Listening in Fourth Grade," in *Beyond the Read Aloud* (Bloomington, Ind.: Phi Delta Kappa, 1992), for an example with science content.

Listening to learn must become an integral part of the elementary curriculum—part of mapping activities in social studies; graphing and measuring in mathematics; investigations in science; and study of music, art, and literature. To complete a map, graph, or investigation, youngsters must listen for detail, a sequence of steps to follow, and key words. During music, youngsters must listen to the lyrics, looking for words that paint a clear picture. During art, they must listen as the teacher describes how to mix paints and hold a brush. And during story time, they must listen for words that send a happy message and words that send a sad one.

Similarly, listening blends naturally with the other language arts. For example, writing can be part of an oral language experience, as in the vignette that opens this chapter. Through listening, students gather data and develop relationships among those data; during follow-up writing, they organize the data for future sharing.

In the same way, listening and reading go together. Obviously, reading can develop out of listening. Children can independently read on a topic introduced through a listening sequence. Ms. Arnold organized activity in that way: She used listening to get students ready to read.

But Ms. Arnold used listening in another way as she built the listening/reading connection. She modeled what she does as she engages in listening, a teaching procedure that "can enhance a student's repertoire of listening skills" (Winn, 1988). She showed students how to activate what they already knew before listening; how to use transitional signals—in this case, subheadings—to think before listening; how to formulate questions based on

THE FORUM On Listening Comprehension and Reading Aloud to Children

1. Jim Trelease advocates reading aloud to students. He proposes that reading aloud exposes "the student listener to a positive reading role model; new information, the pleasures of reading, rich vocabulary, good sentence and story grammar; a book he or she might not otherwise be exposed to; fully textured lives outside the student's own experience; and the English language spoken in a manner distinctly different from that in a television show. Simultaneously the student listener's imagination is being stimulated, attention span stretched, listening comprehension improved, emotional development nurtured, the reading-writing connection established, and, where they exist, negative reading attitudes reshaped to positive. Is there a textbook or workbook that will accomplish all that in a 15 minute period or even an hour?" ("Jim Trelease Speaks on Reading Aloud to Children," *The Reading Teacher*, 43 [December 1989], 200–206). Find and read this reference as well as Trelease's popular *The New Read-Aloud Handbook*.

2. Deanna Winn writes about the need for listening instruction: "Children need to learn how to think about and react to what they hear. They need to participate in structured experiences that cause them to question, to sort, to organize, to evaluate, and to choose. They need to learn skills that will enable them to become connoisseurs and rational consumers of auditory input" ("Develop Listening Skills as a Part of the Curriculum." *The Reading Teacher*, 42 [November 1988], 144).

3. Hal and Gary Funk write, "Listening instruction should permeate the school day and not be restricted to the language arts program. Don't separate instructional periods with artificial listening situations. . . . The appropriate time to develop children's listening skills and habits is anytime they are expected to listen. Some of the best opportunities occur during art, music, physical education, social studies and science activities" ("Guidelines for Developing Listening Skills," *The Reading Teacher*, 42 [May 1989], 660–663).

Questions to Consider

How did Ann Arnold involve students in active listening? What other strategies could she have used to achieve other listening goals? What did she achieve by reading aloud to her students? What kinds of materials should a teacher read aloud to his or her students? How often should a teacher read aloud? At what age levels is reading aloud appropriate? How can you make your own sharing of stories more effective?

Literature-based read alouds encourage active listening and make the reading connection. (© 1993 Michael Zide)

the headings; how to talk to themselves in their heads while listening; how to review after listening. These strategies are as important in reading as they are in listening.

Listening and speaking connect as well. There are two basic kinds of listening/speaking situations. First is conversational listening/speaking, where an immediate give-and-take results in a cross-flow of ideas. Face-to-face discussions of the kind seen in Ann Arnold's class are typically conversational, with one person and then another assuming the talking role and others functioning as "not-now-talking" persons. In contrast, in presentational, or reportorial, listening, a major presenter or presenters maintain the primary speaking role, with listeners contributing through nonverbal feedback and occasional verbal input.

If children are to learn to function as listeners in both conversational and presentational situations, classrooms should reflect the ways listening occurs in everyday living. Andrew Wilkinson (1970) advocates spending more classroom time in conversational and discussion circles "in which two or three or half-a-dozen are sitting around, and ideas get discussed and pushed around." He proposes "splitting children up into groups and working in that way." Bob Lange (1981) concurs. He sees the need for variety in class organization (for example, occasionally breaking into small groups of different sizes and personalities) to

The National Assessment of Educational Progress (Stout, 1992) reports that a quarter of fourth-graders and a fifth of eighth-graders say they never discuss what they read in class. Without discussion time, children lack opportunity to hone their conversational listening/speaking abilities in a natural way.

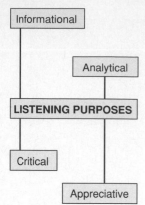

Informational

Analytical

LISTENING PURPOSES

Critical

Appreciative

ensure that students' language experiences run the gamut from informal to formal. Children can then learn to vary their listening approach depending on the situation.

By participating in presentational situations, children learn to use their bodies to express their understanding. They learn to raise questions, ask for clarification, and take simple notes. Since high school and college instruction tends to be presentational, these skills are essential.

As this section implies, children and adults listen for a variety of purposes. These purposes fall into four categories: (1) to gather information, (2) to analyze information received, (3) to judge critically, and (4) to appreciate, or enjoy. Let us turn next to these purposes, keeping in mind that they blend in natural listening situations.

Listening for Information

At some point as they listen, people are concerned with gathering information, or getting the facts straight. In doing this, they may have to

◆ React to details;
◆ Recall and respond to the content of a message;
◆ Respond to the sequence and organization of a message;
◆ Follow a set of oral directions;
◆ Identify the topic, main idea, and supporting details of a message;
◆ Construct a set of notes containing the key points (main ideas and supporting details) of a message;
◆ Summarize a message;
◆ Take action based on a message.

This section outlines ways to help children refine these skills naturally during content-area and literature encounters.

Reacting to Details

Listening to stories can sharpen children's perception of details. A favorite strategy of preschool and primary teachers is to ask students to participate in a storytelling by contributing sounds, words, and/or actions. An easy beginning is the sound story, one to which many sounds can be added to make the sharing more active.

Ms. Somer, a primary teacher, uses Marjorie Flack's *Ask Mister Bear* as a sound story. In it a little boy asks a series of animals what he should give his mother for her birthday. Before telling the story, Ms. Somer introduces each animal to her listeners, who try out sounds associated with each one. Then she divides her class into sound groups; each group becomes an animal in the story and makes that animal's sound whenever its name occurs. Many other talking-animal stories can be used as sound stories; well-known examples are *Henny Penny, The Three Little Pigs*, and *The Bremen Town Musicians*.

Listeners join in the telling of some selections by contributing words. A perfect story for this activity is the repetitive *The Little Red Hen*. Groups can become the hen, the pig, and the goose to contribute: "'Not I,' said the pig. 'Not I,' said the goose. 'Very well,' said the little red hen, 'I will do it myself.' And she did." Here children also acquire a basic reading skill: using the ongoing story line to anticipate words that will come next. Other stories useful for predicting and joining in while listening include Nonny Hogrogian's *One Fine Day* and Dr. Seuss's *Horton Hatches the Egg*.

Recalling and Responding to the Content of a Message

Children must progress beyond the elemental activity just described and listen to recall and respond logically to the content of a message. Purpose-filled listening for detail occurs as children cooperatively pursue learning tasks, talk informally, and participate in structured discussions after an oral presentation.

Pursuing Cooperative Work Tasks The tasks that several youngsters complete together are natural contexts for developing skill in detailed listening. Working cooperatively, children must listen closely to make a verbal response

Listening skills can develop as students work together on a purposeful task, such as the editing of one child's writing. (© Jean-Claude Lejeune)

that maintains the logical flow of ideas and ultimately gets the job done. Collaborative tasks that require considerable give-and-take and careful listening for detail include

- Composing poems, stories, letters, and written reports in groups;
- Deciding how to lay out a final draft of material written in teams;
- Editing one another's writing on a face-to-face basis;
- Deciding how to organize and present a group report;
- Preparing for puppet shows, dramatizations, and pantomimes;
- Planning for parties, trips, or speakers;
- Investigating a science problem in pairs or teams.

Conversing Informally   Another natural situation for building detailed listening skills is the informal talk group consisting of two or three youngsters. After a school holiday, assembly, or individual reading period, youngsters meet with conversation mates to talk about things done, enjoyed, or read. Faix (1975) suggests that in small groups children can also share descriptions of a favorite friend, an exciting school subject, a hobby, or a highly admired adult.

Informal conversations between two youngsters who meet in a classroom Conversation Nook to talk briefly about a matter of mutual concern hold a similar potential for growth in conversational listening skills. Because voices are kept low, a youngster must listen closely to respond to the stated detail. Some teachers schedule time for informal conversations in which the topic is wide open and participants decide what they will discuss.

Responding to Group Presentations and Shared Material   Especially in the upper grades, oral reporting in the content areas can be structured to facilitate recall of detail. The teacher can propose that reporting teams announce the three or four topics they will explain. Listeners divide into three or four groups, each taking reponsibility for raising questions and recalling details on one of the topics. After the reporting time, listeners review details on their topics while presenters determine whether others have picked up essential points. The listeners ask questions about material presented and summarize what they have heard.

Ms. Arnold used a variation of this approach in her lesson.

In much the same way, the teacher can handle informational films and books, newspaper articles, and magazine clippings shared orally. For example, before sharing a book on rivers with second-graders, the teacher might suggest that children sitting on one side of the room listen to find out where and how rivers start. Those in the middle listen to find out how rivers get bigger. Those on the remaining side listen to find out how rivers end. All listen to find out where the rain comes from. Or before sharing a news clipping on strip mining with sixth-graders, the teacher can urge them to identify problems associated with strip mining and how the proposed law explained in the article deals with those problems. Guidance of this kind helps youngsters focus their attention on significant detail.

Similarly, science, social studies, and current events discussions structured

See Figure 7.1 for an example of a listening-discussion guide.

around a listening-recording guide can lead to increased skill in listening for detail. The guide lists three or four questions, with space for recording information. As students share information, listeners record points in their guides. Later they use their notes to summarize points made by the reporting team.

Responding to Sequence and Organization

Another informational listening skill is the ability to respond to sequences in material heard. This material can be a story or subject matter content.

Story Sequences   Because many stories have a step-by-step sequence, literary selections provide fine content for sequential listening. A time line is one way to record events from stories. This is simply a line on which one plots events in order of occurrence. A story such as Marie Hall Ets's *Play with Me* lends itself to this kind of interpretation in the lower grades. The child in *Play with Me* meets a series of animals, each of which he frightens away. Finally, as the child sits quietly, the animals return and one nuzzles his cheek. Listeners can sketch each animal on a time line or write the animals' names there in the order mentioned in the story. Later they use their time lines to retell the story. Stories that translate easily into time lines are those in which events follow in orderly succession.

Middle-graders to whom the teacher reads a portion of a longer story on successive days find time line construction equally challenging. Older groups can develop a wall-size story line that extends across one side of their classroom, as in Figure 5.2. Each day students use the line to recall events heard during previous listening sessions and mount additional cards that summarize events encountered in the story that day.

Science and Social Studies Sequences   Whenever content in social and natural science incorporates a series of events, listening for sequence is possible. The teacher introduces material with the suggestion "Let's listen to find out the sequence in which events take (or took) place." This introduction is appropriate with books and films that describe natural science cycles: the egg-tadpole-frog-egg cycle, the egg-caterpillar-cocoon-moth-egg cycle, the water cycle, the rock cycle. It is appropriate with material that relates a series of historical events.

During or after listening, students can record events on a straight time line, or on a circular one in the case of natural science cycles. Or after listening, children can review events in a sequence by ordering labeled cards on a flannel board or clipping them to the classroom story line. At times the teacher prepares in advance the cards to be sequenced, and students order them based on information from a film or informational book. At other times youngsters form teams, make sequence cards, order them, and then compare their orderings with those of other groups. This approach is one way to handle biographies. Having viewed a strip or listened to a passage describing the life of a historical

Use also Ann Jonas, *Round Trip* (New York: Greenwillow, 1983), and Mwenye Hadithi and Adrienne Kennaway, *Hot Hippo* (Boston: Little, Brown, 1986).

Children's magazines are also a fine source of stories and articles to read to middle-graders. Check *Boys' Life, Cobblestones, Cricket,* and *Monkeyshines* for stories to share.

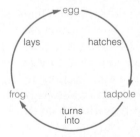

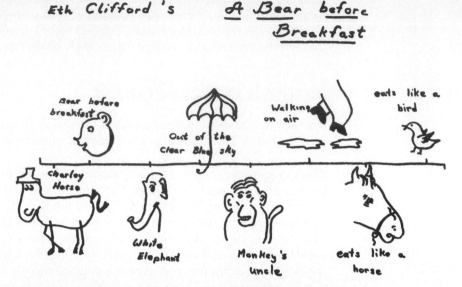

Figure 5.2 A Story Line of *A Bear Before Breakfast* by Eth Clifford

figure, upper-graders record key events from the person's life on cards and order their cards chronologically.

Following Directions

Often people must go beyond recall to perform tasks based on information heard. The normal tasks of a classroom provide opportunities to develop children's ability to follow directions. Each day, a teacher tells children how to line up for a special purpose; how to position, fold, and cut paper; how to complete a series of personalized learning tasks. At these times, he or she must use precise transitional words (*first, then, finally, when*) and demonstrate how to use those words to keep track of what to do. Children repeat segments of the directions to ensure that they know what they are to do. In repeating, they practice a strategy that skillful listeners use when faced with oral directions: repeating them in shortened form.

Tasks associated with all areas of study provide good contexts for listening to directions. Let us look at a few examples to clarify the varied contexts in which skill can develop naturally.

Measuring and Graphing in Mathematics A second-grade teacher was introducing his students to the ruler. He began with a simple counting direction: "Count the number of spaces marked off on the ruler." Children counted first in unison and then individually, concluding that there were thirty spaces. The teacher told the second-graders that each line on the ruler marked off an equal distance called a *centimeter*. Together they pointed to the 1-centimeter mark, the 5 mark, the 9 mark as the teacher called out numbers. Next, the teacher divided the class into work-checking pairs. As he continued to call out directions like "Point to the 22-centimeter mark," the children pointed and checked with their work assistants to see if both were pointing to the same spot. During a follow-up session, children drew lines with their rulers, making each a centimeter length announced by the teacher. In this oral work with numbers, children had to listen to know where to point.

A teacher working with older youngsters used graphing to refine listening skills. These youngsters knew the names of the axes (x and y). Using these names, the teacher announced points to be plotted on a graph. When the students had plotted a number of points, they connected them to discover a picture hidden there. Again, youngsters were developing listening skill in a purpose-filled context.

Today the availability of a multitude of concrete manipulatives through which to develop mathematical understanding provides the opportunity to develop listening skills through mathematics. In developing a concept, the teacher demonstrates the thinking necessary to solve a problem and then announces directions for setting up cubes, organizing rods, lining up pegs—directions children perform on the spot. Moving among the students, he or she sees whether participants have understood the concept and followed the directions.

Following Computer Directions   The same type of listening occurs as children learn to handle a computer. The teacher first demonstrates and then orally gives directions for loading disks, keyboarding, and programming, perhaps referring in the process to a chart of basic directions he or she displays. Whether children have listened closely is immediately evident: Does the computer do what was expected, or does it flash an error message? Given an error message or two, children learn they must attend more closely to directions to get their computer functioning. Sometimes two children who are having trouble following directions can work together at a computer so that they can talk out the sequence of steps to follow.

Getting the Gist of a Message

Getting the gist of a message—grasping its main idea—is the heart of informational listening. How can teachers help children build this skill?

Topic Finding   Most educators recommend that teachers first help children identify the topic of a communication (see Aulls, 1986), for the gist of a message is the main point being made about that topic. To get at the main idea, one must know the topic.

One way to help children is to model the process of topic finding. During a social studies lesson, for example, a teacher might say: "When I listen, I start by asking myself, 'What is the author talking about?' In answering this question, I identify the topic. For example, suppose I hear this:

From "Using a Thermometer,"
Our Country's Communities
(Morristown, N.J.: Silver
Burdett and Ginn, 1988).

> Rain, snow, wind, heat, and cold are all part of weather. Weather is the way the air is at a certain time. The weather may change from day to day or even from hour to hour. It might be sunny this morning and cloudy this afternoon. Or it might be dry today and wet tomorrow.

As I listen, I keep asking myself: 'What is this about?' I listen for key words that keep repeating. I do not wait until the end. I keep talking to myself in my head, trying to get at the topic. In this case, the word *weather* keeps repeating. Everything in the message relates to the weather, so I know that weather is the topic."

Main-Idea Making   Keeping the topic in mind, a listener identifies the main idea. Again the teacher should model the process—in this case, the process of main-idea making. He or she may say, "When I listen, I keep sifting through the points being given, and I keep asking myself, 'What point is the speaker making about the topic?' Again, I keep talking to myself in my head, gradually putting the main idea together. In this case, the main idea is that weather is the way the air is at a particular time—sunny, rainy, snowy. All the details relate to that point."

Having modeled the process of main-idea making, the teacher should encourage students to use the process to learn. The teacher might read aloud passages from content-area texts and ask children to identify topics and main ideas, telling how they arrived at both. For example, a teacher might share this paragraph from a social studies text during unit study:

From "Using a Thermometer,"
Our Country's Communities
(Morristown, N.J.: Silver
Burdett and Ginn, 1988).

> A useful tool that tells us something about the weather is called a thermometer. Thermometers are used to measure the temperature of the air. Another way of saying this is that a thermometer tells us how hot or cold the air is. If you had a thermometer hanging outside your window, you would be able to tell if it was cold enough to need a coat outdoors or if the weather was warm enough for you to wear shorts.

Then the teacher initiates a question-answer sequence such as this:

"What is the topic?"

"Thermometers."

"How do you know?"

"The word *thermometer* keeps repeating; the whole thing is about thermometers."

In this case, children are being asked to identify the topic and tell how they arrived at it. In the same way, they can tell how they arrived at the main idea. They must keep asking themselves: "What's the big idea about thermometers that this passage is getting at?"

Children can practice their strategies for topic finding and main-idea making as they listen to a host of oral communications. While viewing a film, students ask themselves, "What's the topic? What is this film saying about the topic? How do I know?" They ask the same questions as they listen to a panel discussion, an oral report by other students, or a radio news report. Teachers should design many opportunities for children to think in terms of topics and main ideas, especially during unit study. Through continued work in a variety of contexts, children refine their listening strategies. Reading comprehension also improves, since the strategies for finding topics and making main ideas in listening apply to reading.

Relating Main Ideas and Supporting Details In content-area study, listening for main ideas flows naturally into working with significant details. For example, during unit study a teacher can read a passage aloud from a children's science text and stop at key points to encourage them to talk about how they found the topic and made a main idea. The teacher can then reread the passage, asking youngsters to give key details that support the main idea. The strategy students use in listening for detail is to ask themselves as they listen: "Does this detail help support the main idea?"

Taking Notes That Include Main Ideas and Supporting Details

A listening guide for an outline:

I. _____
   A. _____
   B. _____
   C. _____
II. _____
   A. _____
   B. _____

A helpful set of notes includes main ideas and supporting details. Outlining is one strategy for highlighting the relationship between main and supporting details that may be useful as students take notes during a presentation or discussion. Children record the main idea of a section as a main heading in an outline (for example, *I*). They indicate subordinate points beneath the main idea (*A, B, C*). By outlining in this way, students develop the ability to devise a set of organized notes related to fundamental concepts in a content area. This ability develops only with practice, however, so the teacher must walk and talk children through the outlining process step by step and review it often.

Drawing a graphic that depicts relationships among ideas is a second note-taking strategy. The teacher can model how to use a graphic organizer, or visualization, to record main and subordinate ideas during listening by saying, "Sometimes it helps me to visualize the relationship between a main idea and the supporting details. I record the main idea in a box and hang the supporting details from that box. I use a similar strategy when I read. I write the main idea in a box. Then I turn my sheet and write down supporting details connected to the main idea." (See Figure 5.3.) After listening to a short message or hearing a paragraph read to them, students can cooperatively create similar graphic organizers that clarify relationships among ideas.

Summarizing a Message

Another way to process messages is to summarize important points. The teacher can model how to do this by saying, "We have been discussing the relationships between weather and climate. After I have been involved in a discussion, I often review in my head the important points. The points I see as important are. . . ."

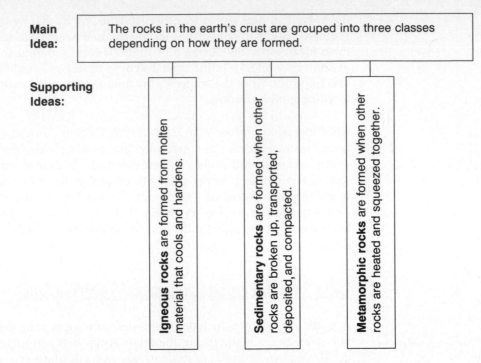

Figure 5.3 A Graphic Organizer for Relating Main and Subordinate Ideas

As a way to seek closure in a lesson, on successive days after class discussions the teacher can ask children to sum up important points and note them on the chalkboard. On other occasions, she or he can ask students to sum up by talking to themselves in their heads and then sharing their thoughts with others in small talk-out groups. The groups produce a list of key discussion points. In upper grades, students write down summary points on their own after participating in a discussion. Again, this activity models summarizing after reading as well as summarizing after listening.

Taking Action Based on a Message: More Activities for Informational Listening

The day-by-day tasks of the classroom—specifically, encounters with literature and the subject areas—are natural contexts for developing children's ability to listen, respond to, and take action based on the informational content of messages. Here are some ideas for organizing those encounters:

✦ *Introduce your partner.* On the first day of school, pair off the students. Student pairs chat, telling each other key facts about themselves: name, address, birthday, hobbies, favorite subjects, favorite movie or book. Youngsters introduce their friends to the class and relate facts learned through listening.

- *Carry the message.* Where young people are allowed to leave the classroom to carry messages to other classes or to school personnel, make some messages oral ones. Give the student a brief oral message and ask him or her to ask for, listen to, and remember the return communication.
- *Take the message home.* At the end of the afternoon, encourage primary-grade children to summarize the things they did during the day. Ask several listeners to repeat the points. Suggest that upon arrival home they tell a caregiver what they did in school.
- *Story outlines.* Read a story to a literature-listening group. Ask children to draw three pictures, the first telling what happened in the beginning, the second detailing what happened in the middle, and the third showing the end. Students retell the story to a partner using their pictures as notes.
- *Ordering a story.* Before storytelling, prepare a series of cards, each one outlining a key story event. After listening, children order the story cards.

✏️ BUILDING AND REFINING YOUR TEACHING SKILLS

- Think about a content-area topic that you will be teaching. Design a lesson in which you develop an informational listening skill as you teach the topic. If you are currently teaching, try your lesson in the classroom.
- Design a listening/recording guide to use as part of an ongoing literature experience in primary grades. Design a more sophisticated guide to develop systematic note-taking skills in upper grades. If possible, try the guides in a classroom.
- Make an audiotape for use during a science or social studies unit. Set the tape in an individual listening station, and have children listen to identify the main idea. Be sure to select a topic appropriate for the children's age level. Ask students to react to your tape: Did they enjoy it? Did they find it boring? Did they appreciate the quality of your voice?

Listening Analytically

The purpose of *informational listening* is to grasp the facts and respond to them. *Analytical listening*, in contrast, occurs as people go beyond the facts to think about the verbal and nonverbal components of a message. People listen analytically when they

- Infer relationships among ideas by contrasting and comparing points, categorizing ideas, generalizing based on examples, proposing reasons and causes, hypothesizing effects, predicting outcomes, applying ideas to other problems, and citing related examples;

✦ Distinguish between fact and opinion;

✦ Infer a speaker's feelings and point of view based on the verbal components of the message;

✦ Infer meanings from a speaker's gestures, vocal intonations, and facial expressions.

As this list indicates, analytical listening is an inferential thinking process in which people get at underlying meanings. It relates to informational listening because inferring requires an information base.

Inferring Relationships Among Ideas

A major strategy for helping children develop skill as analytical listeners is to share a selection, model ways to think about it, and then suggest activities that encourage children to identify similarities and differences, categorize, propose reasons and causes, predict, and generalize. Summing up the research on teachers' questions, however, Lange (1982) concludes that teachers usually ask questions that call for simple facts. They need to ask more questions that elicit analytical thinking.

To prepare youngsters for higher-level listening, teachers can rely on a Directed Listening-Thinking strategy and pose analytical tasks or questions before sharing a passage. In introducing an informational passage, for example, a teacher can pose one of these tasks or questions that can be readily modified for introducing a story:

✦ *Comparing and contrasting.* How does this procedure compare with the way we do it today? How is it different? How does the method of farming in Japan compare with the way we farm in our country? How is the daffodil similar to the tulip? How is it different?

✦ *Categorizing.* Let's listen to find out if this was a period of increasing or decreasing population. Let's listen to decide whether this was a period of general content or discontent.

✦ *Giving reasons.* In those days, why did they make their schools out of sod or logs? Why did the colonists work together rather than alone to make their birchbark canoes?

✦ *Predicting outcomes.* Let's listen to decide what may happen if people continue to use gasoline at the rate they do today.

✦ *Generalizing.* Let's listen to figure out where most of the early settlements were located. Let's listen to figure out how most gases behave when heated.

✦ *Giving examples.* Let's listen to see if we can think of other countries where they would most likely have very cold winters.

✦ *Hypothesizing.* Let's listen to see if we can hypothesize ways that Americans can cut back on their oil consumption.

Teachers can ask these questions as part of content-area studies, realizing that they must proceed cautiously with primary-graders, who have trouble with abstractions. Instead of always having children read their texts to themselves, teachers can read aloud as children listen and then follow with a discussion of the points heard. In leading a follow-up discussion, teachers may want to start by asking children to identify the topic and make the main idea. But this is only a beginning; teachers must lead children up the cognitive ladder to analyze ideas.

Work with analytical listening can model and lead naturally into work with analytical reading. The same thinking tasks are appropriate in reference to passages read. Thus, as youngsters contrast, compare, generalize, predict, and give reasons as part of listening, they learn skills applicable to reading.

Distinguishing Fact from Opinion

A second facet of analytical listening is distinguishing between fact and opinion. This is a difficult task, and before attempting it in oral contexts, even sharp upper-graders require preparation. They start by discussing pairs of statements taken from texts they are reading:

+ Oranges are grown in California and Florida. (fact)
  Apple juice tastes better than orange juice. (opinion)
+ The temperature reading at noon today was 26° C. (fact)
  That water is too cold for swimming. (opinion)

Based on the examples, students generalize about the nature of fact and opinion:

+ The truth or falsity of a factual statement can be proved by pointing to specific instances.
+ Different opinions can be stated on the same question.
+ Opinions cannot be proved definitively.
+ Opinions contain elements of "should," "must," "best," "too much."
+ Opinions represent people's personal preferences or feelings.

Having generalized about the nature of fact and of opinion, students working in groups can identify examples of fact and of opinion in material they have just read or heard or in statements they have made themselves. On two pieces of oak tag—one labeled *fact*, the other *opinion*—students record examples. The examples should be discussed, for this is not an easy task. Later the students ask: Are all the statements listed appropriately? In some cases, students may debate a statement's factualness and record it on both sheets. In so doing, they recognize that the line between fact and opinion is not always clearly drawn.

Inferring Point of View and Feelings

In *Language in Thought and Action*, S. I. Hayakawa (1964) distinguishes among the emotional meanings of words that determine a speaker's impact on listeners. He calls words like *louse* and *slob* "snarls," for they carry negative connotations, and more positive words like *sweetheart* and *home* "purrs." Nonverbal and vocal expressions similarly carry negative or positive messages. This means that as children listen, teachers must stress the way meanings are being expressed.

Comprehending Implied Meanings   Primary-graders can learn about the emotional impact of words through a search in which they identify "happy" and "sad" words. To begin, children in two-person teams cut two large clown faces from light-colored construction paper. One face is happy, the other sad. Instead of drawing the facial expressions with lines, however, children print "happy-meaning" words in the shape of eyes, mouth, hat, and so forth. In the same fashion, they draw the features of the sad clown with "sad-meaning" words.

Once children have identified words with happy and sad connotations, they listen for very pleasant, sad, angry, ugly, bored, and/or excited words in stories. They pencil these on other faces and add words found in the dictionary and thesaurus that communicate a similar feeling.

Upper-graders can handle connotation in greater depth. They can identify purrs and snarls in films, especially films on controversial issues. After viewing a selection, students think about those narration words that sent a positive or negative message.

Inferring Underlying Feelings   While listening to poetry, elementary children can pinpoint the feelings the poet is conveying. Some of the haunting pieces by Langston Hughes are useful for oral sharing; listeners can reflect on the feelings conveyed by a piece such as the following:

For other poems by Langston Hughes, see *Don't You Turn Back* (New York: Knopf, 1969).

> ### Dreams
>
> Hold fast to dreams
> For if dreams die
> Life is a broken-winged bird
> That cannot fly.
>
> Hold fast to dreams
> For when dreams go
> Life is a barren field
> Frozen with snow.

Check your local film library for *Hailstones and Halibut Bones* and *Attic in the Wind* from Miller Brody (New York) in their filmed versions. Use them for listening for feelings.

While listening, youngsters visualize meanings and then sketch or paint the feeling communicated by the poem. Later, they convert their pictures into a word collage by adding key feeling words from the poem.

Listening to analyze the feelings of story characters is also a productive experience. Teacher Barbara Woods has devised a simple listening guide to stimulate youngsters to analyze the feelings of characters. Across the top of a duplicated sheet, she draws a row of smiling faces and across the bottom, a row of frowning faces. Under each face she draws a line. As children listen to stories, they decide which characters are generally happy and which are unhappy, and they write the names of the characters under the appropriate listening-guide faces. Since changes occur in a story and unhappy characters become happy, students may write the name of a character beneath both a happy and an unhappy face and draw an arrow from one to the other to show the direction of change.

In the same way, intermediate students can graph the emotional swings of a story. On the vertical axis of a graph, they plot words that describe emotional extremes, such as *very happy, very sad*. On the horizontal axis, they plot *story beginning, story middle, story end*. Then, as they listen to a particular story, they construct a graph line starting on the far left at *story beginning*. The graph line flows up and down to reflect changes in emotion in the story.

Upper-graders can plot several graphs for one story or poem. Each graph is from the point of view of a different character or group of characters. For example, students can plot emotional highs and lows first for Mudville and then for the opposing team as they listen to "Casey at the Bat." Figure 5.4 is a sample graph based on the story *May I Bring a Friend?* by Beatrice Schenk de Regniers; it contains words suggesting story happenings.

Inferring from Nonverbal and Vocal Expressions

Words and sentences are vehicles through which people communicate orally. In addition, people use nonverbal and vocal expressions to get their feelings and ideas across. Often what Sara Lundsteen (1979) calls the "person-context" actually determines a listener's response. By *person-context*, Lundsteen means a speaker's facial expression, eye focus, gestures, stance, gross body motions, tone of voice, inflections of voice, pauses, loudness, and pitch, as well as changes in these characteristics.

Because nonverbal and vocal expressions can engender strong feelings in a listener and even cause him or her to tune out, a listener should know how a speaker is using those expressions and what effect they have on his or her reactions. This is especially true in situations where conversationalists purposefully manipulate their nonverbal and vocal expressions to achieve a desired effect.

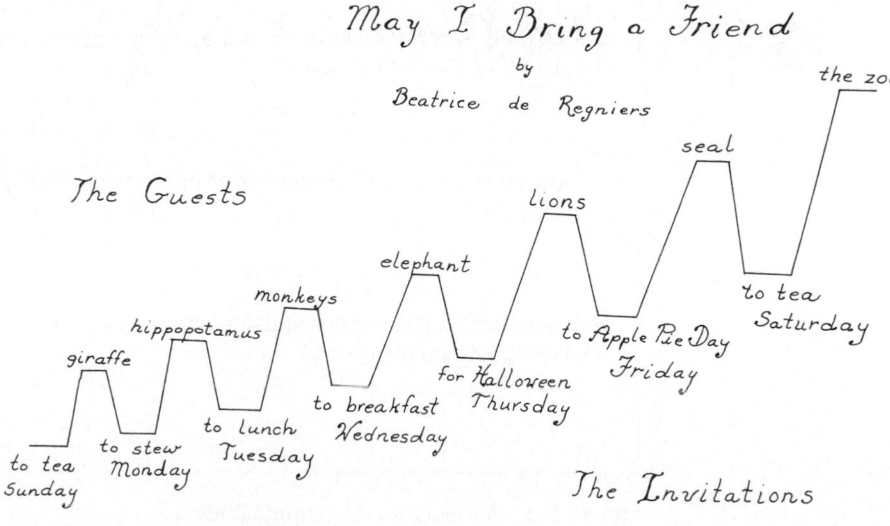

Figure 5.4 A Story Graph

Use picture reading also to introduce a storybook to be shared; ask listeners to study the cover picture and predict what might happen in the story.

Picture Reading   Picture reading offers an easy introduction to meanings sent nonverbally. Mrs. Jaye, a kindergarten teacher, snipped from magazines pictures showing people in different interactive situations. She mounted each picture on construction paper and drew comic-strip balloons from each mouth. In a talk session, her children brainstormed what the people were thinking. She asked: Do the people like one another? How do we know? How do the people feel? How do we know?

The children produced amazingly perceptive inferences. One picture showed a woman holding a potato masher. The children inferred that the woman was angry; the expression on her face and the way she held the masher told them that. The thoughts they gave her were: "My husband is not home yet, and this food will go bad. I'm mad."

Media Interpretation   In the upper grades, a more sophisticated study of impression management as employed on TV commercials and political telecasts is possible. Students in one sixth grade watched TV commercials and studied how performers manipulated vocal and nonverbal language. They used a TV listening guide as shown in Figure 5.5.

INTERPRETING NONVERBAL AND VOCAL MESSAGES ON TELEVISION

1. How does the performer use gestures as part of the message?

2. How does the performer stand, sit, and position his or her head?

3. Does the performer use facial and eye expressions as part of his or her communication? If so, how?

4. How does the performer vary his or her tone of voice, pitch, and loudness of speech?

5. Evaluation: Is this performer using nonverbal and vocal means of communication effectively?

Figure 5.5   A Television Listening Guide

These sixth-graders had a great time with some of the commercials in which businesspeople advertise their own products. Using the understandings they had built up in interpreting commercials, they went on to analyze videotaped speeches of politicians to see if they could detect instances of impression management. Later they analyzed messages sent by people they knew: parents, siblings, teachers. To this end, they constructed guides for recording aspects of body and vocal language. Through their study, these youngsters became more aware of the impact of vocal and nonverbal messages.

More Activities for Analytical Listening

Here are some additional activities a teacher can use to promote analytical listening:

+ *Are they the same?* As children consider a community or national issue, share with them two articles, reports, editorials, or letters to the editor. Ask: Are both articles saying the same thing? If they differ, what is the difference?
+ *Snarls and Purrs.* Read related letters to the editor to students who are studying an issue. Ask children to identify the snarls and purrs.
+ *Adjective play.* As children learn about adjectives, ask them to identify adjectives that describe characters they meet in stories they hear. Children must give reasons for their choice of adjectives.
+ *Story variations.* Different versions of the familiar fairy tales exist. Read two or more versions of a tale such as *Cinderella*, and ask youngsters to listen for ways they vary.

BUILDING AND REFINING YOUR TEACHING SKILLS

+ Locate an article and prepare questions that will lead children to compare, contrast, categorize, identify reasons or implications, hypothesize, or predict. Share the article with a group, and try out your questions.
+ Work on your own ability to distinguish fact from opinion. As you listen, at times think: Is that a statement of fact? Of opinion?
+ Identify statements you believe to be facts and others you believe to be opinions. Share them with a group of fellow teachers or teachers-to-be, and discuss the reasons for categorizing the statements as you did.

Listening Critically

Listening can also be a judgmental process with listeners deciding about the rightness, goodness, or harmfulness of ideas and the way those ideas have been presented. People engage in critical listening when they

◆ Formulate opinions, preferences, and judgments and support them with reasons;
◆ Evaluate stories heard by assessing characters, plot, and style;
◆ Weigh the quality of a TV show, movie, tape recording, or sound filmstrip;
◆ Identify some messages as "propaganda" and evaluate them as harmless or harmful.

See Chapter 8 for a discussion of critical thinking.

The processes of formulating opinions, supporting judgments with reasons, and evaluating, assessing, and weighing are all critical-thinking operations.

Lundsteen (1979) contends that in the past schools have failed to emphasize listening in which judgments are a part. She warns that if this continues, schools will fall short in their responsibility to prepare students to function fully. Today young and old alike are assimilators of ideas emitted by the mass media, particularly television. Are people selective and critical in choosing programs? Are they selective and critical of ideas they encounter? Do they know the bases of decisions they make? Or are they nondiscriminating and gullible? Following are some ways to build judgmental listening into the curriculum so that youngsters become discriminating consumers of oral messages.

Formulating Opinions, Preferences, and Judgments

Children who have analyzed information heard can take the next step and express opinions, preferences, and judgments about it. This is especially true as children listen and respond to material in the content areas and in current events. For this purpose, the obvious question is: Given a choice among these possibilities, which would you choose? Why would you choose that one? For example, first-graders who have studied pictures of winter and summer during a discussion of climate can think about which scene they would prefer to be in and tell why.

A classic study by Hilda Taba supports a question sequence that starts with lower-order questions and moves to higher-order ones (*Thinking in Elementary School Children, Cooperative Research Project 1575* [Washington, D.C.: U.S. Department of Health, Education, and Welfare, 1964]).

In designing questioning sequences that help children formulate opinions and judgments, teachers usually find that some work with informational listening is necessary. Thus, Ms. Arnold, who planned the lesson on forms of justice, divided her listeners into three teams, each to focus on one form of justice being described. In follow-up discussion, listeners from each team elaborated on the form of justice on which they had concentrated during listening. Only after youngsters had a clear concept of what was involved in each form did they express opinions.

Judging Story Characters and Actions

Similar sequences can be part of story listening: Children listen to comprehend what is happening and to make judgments about characters and actions. In this context, Barbara Woods's guide for analyzing happy and unhappy characters described earlier can serve as a guide for judging good and evil characters, particularly in fairy tales, where the line between the two is clearly drawn. The format of the guide remains the same: two rows of faces, one with pleasant expressions, the other with evil grins. Youngsters who have listened to a story print the names of good characters under the pleasant faces and those of evil ones beneath the leering faces. For example, when judging characters in *Hansel and Gretel*, young children might list Hansel and Gretel on the top row and the witch and the stepmother on the bottom. Supporting their judgments with specifics, they print the deeds performed by the characters on the faces. See Figure 5.6 for a variation of this type of guide.

Children can progress to multifaceted judgments to make a second sheet for a story, this time considering whether characters are shrewd or gullible. Shrewd ones are labeled across the top and gullible ones across the bottom. By doing this, evaluators become aware that good characters sometimes are gullible while evil ones may be shrewd. Students in upper grades are able to identify other contrasting qualities, such as quick versus slow or wise versus foolish, and can make similar judgments as they respond in their literature journals to stories they have read.

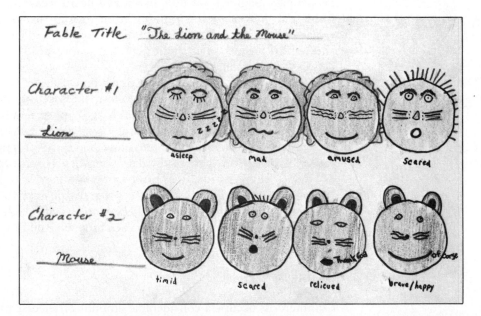

Figure 5.6 A Character Study
SOURCE: Courtesy of Maxine Owens and Cindy Davis.

In the same way, older students can judge story actions rather than characters. They begin by sequentially recording story actions on a time line. Having plotted the major happenings, they decide which acts were morally right and which were morally wrong, and they indicate their judgments on the time line by circling items with different-colored flo-pens. If a work group consists of several children and each child evaluates right and wrong independently, there will be differences of opinion—differences that stimulate discussion. Youngsters will be eager to justify their opinions.

With youngsters who have had little experience with critical listening, first attempts should be group ones that model how to do it. Before sharing a story in which an essentially good character does something wrong but for a good purpose, such as Patricia Coombs's *The Magic Pot*, the teacher draws a line on chart paper. As each event in the story occurs, a volunteer writes a summary phrase on the line. Then children and teacher go back to judge each act, circling good acts in red and wrong ones in blue. Older students can talk about extenuating circumstances.

Students who have joined in teacher-guided critical listening can form groups to plot other stories. First, they listen to a story as a class; afterward, they form three-person teams. Each team summarizes story events and then judges them. Later teams compare their evaluations and orally support them with reasons.

Judging a Performance

People pass judgment on things seen and heard. Leaving a movie, they say, "I liked that. It was good." Flipping from one TV program to another, they remark, "I can't stand any more of that!" People often judge quality informally and fail to consider what specifically they like or dislike. Is it the content, the delivery, or a combination of both?

Because young people spend so much time televiewing, they need to be able to assess the quality of performances to make wise use of their viewing time. One way to get children to look critically at TV programs is to have them name favorite programs, with names recorded on the board. As follow-up, they vote to determine their five favorite programs as a class—programs that deserve the rating "excellent." As part of the discussion that occurs, upper-graders should ask themselves: What qualities must a program possess to be judged excellent? In contrast, what qualities must a program possess to be judged average or poor? Later youngsters form their own lists of excellent, good, and poor programs, indicating one reason for each program listed.

For a description of one group's study of commercials, read Jane Wright and Lester Laminak, "First Graders Can Be Critical Listeners and Readers," *Language Arts*, 59 (February 1982), 133–136.

Identifying Propaganda

Commercials occupy a considerable amount of telecast time and may distort facts to create particular impressions. For these reasons, students need to be able to judge how valid an advertising appeal is.

An article that aids in identifying instances of hard sell is Daniel Tutolo, "Critical Listening/Reading of Advertisements," *Language Arts*, 58 (September 1981), 679–683. It includes persuasive words (e.g., *new, sensational, revolutionary, last chance*) and weasel words (e.g., *help, virtual, comforts*) used by advertisers.

Commercials distort facts in a number of ways. One way is through use of glittering generalities—claims so general they could not possibly be true. A statement such as "Product X outperformed the other leading competitor on absolutely every test" is an example of a glittering generality. A second form distortion can take is the bandwagon effect: The advertisement claims that everyone is turning to the product, especially people "in the know." It plays on people's desire not to be different or left out. Commercials may also include personal endorsements or testimonials by celebrities—celebrities who may not even use the product and are being paid merely for the use of their names. A fourth sales strategy is to stack the deck, citing only the good points and

DEVICES FOR MANIPULATING FACTS IN ADVERTISING

Purpose: to discover examples of fact manipulation in commercials and advertisements

Task: Listen to TV commercials and study magazine ads. Find statements that fit each of the categories:

Type	Definition	Examples
1. Glittering generality	A statement so general that it could not possibly be true	
2. Bandwagon effect	A statement suggesting that everyone is turning to the product	
3. Testimonial	A statement by a celebrity or company representative attesting to the merits of the product	
4. Deck stacking	A statement giving only the good points and ignoring the obvious weak ones	
5. Positive association	An attempt to associate the product with pleasurable things	

Figure 5.7 A Guide for Categorizing Commercials and Advertisements

omitting the weak ones. When this occurs, a commercial contains half-truths. Finally, ads attempt to associate their product with things that carry a positive connotation. For example, cigarette ads show smokers amid sparkling clear brooks, green grass, fresh air—the antithesis of the dirty air smokers create.

Upper-graders find it challenging to listen and read for examples of these selling devices. They may start with newspaper and magazine advertisements and analyze how facts have been distorted. Working from an outline such as the one in Figure 5.7, students categorize statements they have identified. Later they turn to TV commercials to identify other examples that fit into each category.

More Activities for Critical Listening

Here are additional activities to foster critical listening:

+ *Doublespeak.* Students look for examples of "doublespeak" in telecasts and broadcasts. Some examples of doublespeak are calling a shovel a "combat implacement evacuator," calling slums "inner cities," calling the bombing of a country "air support." The National Council of Teachers of English considers doublespeak dangerous, for language is being used purposefully to hide important facts.
+ *Putting on a positive light.* Students look for examples of euphemistic language: substituting words with more pleasant associations for words that carry a negative connotation. Examples are calling a road a "parkway," a factory district an "industrial park," a lavatory a "powder room." Mount a piece of oak tag on a bulletin board so that students can list examples as they find them.
+ *Clarifying values.* Some of the techniques of values clarification developed by Sidney Simon (1976) and Louis Raths (1978) are helpful in critical listening that involves a judgment. Chapter 8 amplifies these techniques and provides specific examples.

✎ *BUILDING AND REFINING YOUR TEACHING SKILLS*

+ Find a book in which a character commits a "naughty" act. Share the book with children, and follow up with small-group discussions in which they tell why they consider the act naughty. At this point, you might want to reread the section of Chapter 3 that describes Weiger's study on children's reactions to naughty acts in stories.
+ Study the story *Pinocchio.* Devise a sequence of questions to use with upper-graders to help them formulate judgments about story acts, consider the reasons behind the acts, and think about the nature of punishment. Try your sequence with a child.

Listening Appreciatively

Pleasure is the key feature of appreciative listening. People listen appreciatively when they take pleasure in the

✦ Content of stories, poems, dramatizations, and music;
✦ Sounds of language—its rhythm, repetitions, rhymes, alliterations;
✦ Moods expressed and mental pictures conjured up through striking language usage.

Clearly, appreciative listening has shades of informational and analytical listening. Often the reason people enjoy a story is that they like the way ideas build one upon the next. Often too pleasure comes from information extracted from words and sounds. Because appreciative listening blends naturally into other forms, in engaging children in appreciative listening the teacher engages them in other forms as well. In actual teaching it would be impossible, as well as impractical, to separate one from the other.

Enjoying Stories

It is a delight to teach appreciative listening with story content, for there are so many ways to make listening pleasurable. One technique students enjoy is the *drawing story*, in which the teller draws a picture while sharing the words of the story. Here is a story with directions for visual sharing indicated on the picture in Figure 5.8; the teller completes that part of the drawing as he or she shares the words written on the lines. This story was written cooperatively by a group that had enjoyed Don Freeman's *Tillie Witch* and decided to write their own witch story.

Molly and Holly
It was Halloween day and Molly Witch was upset. She could not find her best friend Holly. Where was Holly? Molly did not know, and because Molly and Holly always went out haunting on Halloween night, Molly set out to find Holly. The first thing Molly did was to climb down the well at the end of the yard. "Holly," she called, "are you down here?" But Holly was not down in the well.

At the bottom of the well was a long, dark tunnel that snaked its way under the yard and into the woods on the other side. Molly crept through the tunnel until she came to the other end. She and Holly kept a ladder there to climb out. Up the ladder went Molly calling, "Holly! Holly! Are you here?" But Holly did not answer.

Molly took the last step up the ladder and called again. But just as she put her foot on the last step, she tripped and went falling back. Carefully she pulled herself up and out. "Holly, are you here?" Molly screeched again. But all Molly heard was silence.

So Molly boarded her magic surfboard, which she used instead of a broom, and swooped out toward the coast.

She spun across the Atlantic, came low over Europe, swooped down across Africa, shrieked her way over Asia, hurtled across Japan, and began the long trip back across the Pacific, stopping only for a moment in Hawaii to catch her breath.

Then Molly was off again, calling out: "Holly, are you here? Don't you remember that tonight is our big night for haunting?" But as Molly crossed the last stretch of Pacific Ocean and struck out across North America toward home, she didn't see Holly and she didn't hear Holly.

As Molly flew close to home and was nearing her own home yard, a thought struck her. Maybe Holly was hiding under one of the two rocks that Molly and Holly used to jump out at passers-by. Molly lifted up first one rock and then the other, but no Holly. Then she looked atop the high TV tower where Holly often liked to perch, but no Holly. She looked in the hole in the old oak tree.

"Well," thought Molly to herself, "I guess I will have to go out haunting by myself." So she flew down the road, steering directly for the house she intended to haunt first. She was just getting ready to screech down the chimney when she heard a noise behind her. The noise cackled:

It's Halloween night—
Holly's night, Molly's night.
Beware of fright and witches that bite.

Molly turned around and looked behind. And do you know what? There was Holly right behind her all the time, riding on a magic broomstick and all ready for Halloween haunting.

Children are held spellbound as they listen to a drawing story and see the related picture take form on chalkboard or easel. Partway through, the teller will recognize the gleam that comes into students' eyes as one by one they see what the final drawing will be. Children enjoy inventing similar stories to share with listening classmates. To trigger story invention, teachers can supply a few shapes (two examples appear in the margin). Children build stories to accompany the shapes.

Another mood-setting technique is reading a story or poem to music as children visualize setting and/or action. The musical composition selected should blend in rhythm, pace, and mood with the story or poem to be shared. As the teacher reads, the composition serves as background music. With lower-grade children, for example, the reading of Jane Yolen's *Owl Moon* can be combined with a recording of classical music. With upper-graders, a potpourri of lines from Richard Bach's *Jonathan Livingston Seagull* stimulates appreciative listening when read to the accompanying sounds of "Ebb Tide."

Enjoying Language Sounds

There is also pleasure to be had in listening to the sounds of language. In this vein, a teacher may share a passage filled with repeated words that add a natural rhythm to the story. Listening to Arlene Mosel's *The Funny Little Woman*, children identify phrases that tease their ears like the dumpling "rolled and rolled," the woman "tumbled and tumbled," and "her feet stuck in the mud, her hands stuck in the mud, and she fell into the mud." To get children thinking in these terms, a prelistening directive may be "Let's all

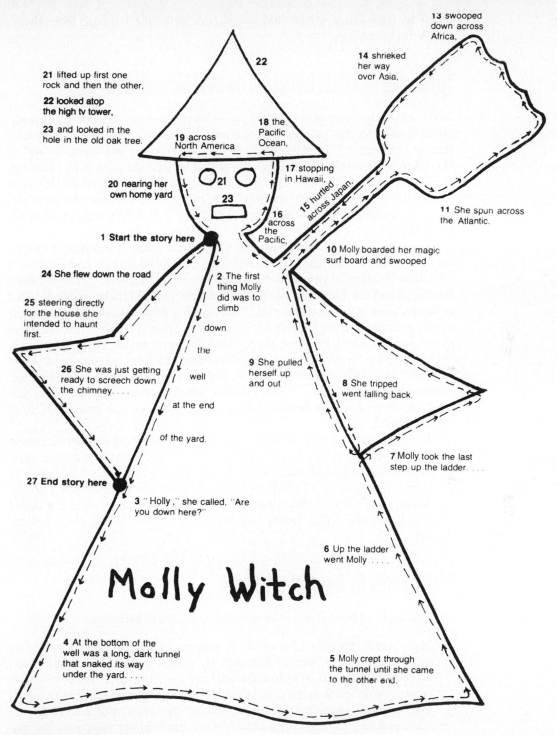

Figure 5.8 Molly Witch

listen to find some words that we particularly like because they sound delightful to our ears."

Appreciating the Images Painted and the Mood Set with Words

In the same way—and at the same time—a teacher can build children's appreciation of the pictures painted and the mood set with words. On occasion, a teacher can suggest, "Let's listen for words that make us feel warm inside" or "Let's listen for words that paint pictures that we can see even if we close our eyes." Given this task as they listen to Ezra Keats's *Apt. 3*, children identify such word patterns as "loud juicy snoring," "the man played purples and grays and rain and smoke and the sounds of the night," and "sad, lonely feelings—like the rain outside."

Even primary children can work toward appreciation of mood and images. One first-grade teacher chose Paul Galdone's *The Horse, the Fox, and the Lion* to introduce children to mood in story. She began by focusing on the pictures. Having shared the story, she asked, "How do the pictures make you feel? What in the pictures makes you feel sad?" The children spoke of the sad look in the horse's eyes and the way he held his head down. From there they listened again to the words, looking for those that created the same mood. When the teacher read, "The horse, feeling very sad, wandered away till he came to a forest where he might find shelter under the trees in bad weather," the children interrupted. Those words were as good as the pictures in telling them that the horse was unhappy. Later, as a class they composed a story with a similar mood: a story of a sad billy goat.

In upper grades, a fine choice for appreciative listening is the ballad. Listening to a recording, youngsters visualize in their mind's eye and then express with watercolor and brush some of the images painted so vividly with words in the ballad. Listening to a ballad, they identify particularly expressive phrases. Here is the ideal time to ask: What words make us see exactly what the ballad writer is describing? What feelings are being expressed? How are these feelings shared?

More Activities for Appreciative Listening

Here are some additional activities to foster appreciative listening:

✦ *Noisy words.* Provide a list of noise makers: jet planes, pneumatic drills, motorcycles, trucks, electric dishwashers, electric drills, clocks, gulls, monkeys, ducks. Students write sound words they associate with each object, such as *roar, rattle, clank* in the case of a dishwasher. They add descriptive adjectives to words originally listed: *steady roar, ear-shattering rattle, loud clank.*

✦ *More noisy words.* Conduct a sound-word search in the thesaurus for synonyms of words like *whine, purr, squawk, holler, whistle.* Students will be amazed at the number of words they will find.

BUILDING AND REFINING YOUR TEACHING SKILLS

✦ Find a story to share. Read and study it. Practice telling the story in a creative way; then share it with a group.
✦ Tell a drawing story to a group of listeners. Carl Withers's *The Tale of a Black Cat* is an easy tale for the beginning storyteller.

..........A Summary Thought or Two

LISTENING FOR MEANING

This chapter developed these major points:

1. Listening in classrooms should be active, with students generating ideas in relation to a message rather than passively receiving.
2. Classroom listening should be purpose filled: Children generate meaning as they listen to stories, poems, and material from the content areas of the curriculum and take part in natural listening/speaking activities that include both conversational and presentational situations. Listening activities prepare children for both reading and writing and model underlying thinking processes.
3. In classrooms, children should be given the opportunity to listen to (a) gather information, (b) analyze, (c) judge, and (d) appreciate so that they acquire a full range of listening skills. Figure 5.9 provides a checklist teachers can use to assess students' growth in specific listening skills and older students can use to identify their strengths and weaknesses. It outlines the key informational, analytical, critical, and appreciative skills this chapter stressed.

RELATED READINGS

Boodt, Gloria. "Critical Listeners Become Critical Readers in Remedial Reading Class." *The Reading Teacher*, 37 (January 1984), 390–394.

Choate, Joyce, and Thomas Rakes. "The Structured Listening Activity: A Model for Improving Listening Comprehension." *The Reading Teacher*, 41 (November 1988), 194–200.

Devine, Thomas. *Listening Skills Schoolwide: Activities and Programs*. Urbana, Ill.: National Council of Teachers of English, 1982.

Greenlaw, M. Jean. "Books in the Classroom." *The Horn Book*, 63 (September/October 1987), 647–649.

Hennings, Dorothy Grant. *Beyond the Read-Aloud: Learning to Read by Listening to and Reflecting on Literature*. Bloomington, Ind.: Phi Delta Kappa, 1992.

A SELF-ASSESSMENT LISTENING CHECKLIST

	I am able to:	Always	Most of the time	Some-times	Never
A. INFORMATIONAL	1. React to details				
	2. Recall and respond to the content of a message				
	3. Respond to the sequence and organization of a message				
	4. Follow a set of oral directions				
	5. Identify and relate the topic, main idea, and supporting details of a message				
	6. Take notes on a message				
	7. Summarize a message				
	8. Take action based on a message				
B. ANALYTICAL	9. Infer relationships among ideas; specifically:				
	a. Contrast and compare points				
	b. Categorize ideas				
	c. Generalize				
	d. Propose reasons and causes				
	e. Predict outcomes				
	f. Apply ideas				
	10. Distinguish fact from opinion				
	11. Infer a speaker's point of view and feelings				
	12. Infer meaning from the nonverbal and vocal expressions a speaker uses				
C. CRITICAL	13. Formulate opinions and judgments; support judgments with reasons				
	14. Evaluate stories heard				
	15. Weigh the quality of an oral message or performance				
	16. Identify some messages as propaganda and evaluate these as harmless or harmful				
D. APPRECIATIVE	17. Take pleasure in the content of stories, poems, and dramatizations when heard				
	18. Enjoy the sounds of language				
	19. Enjoy the moods expressed and the pictures conjured up through striking language use				

Name of student _____ Date _____

Figure 5.9 A Checklist for Assessing Listening Development

Pearson, P. David, and Linda Fielding. "Research Update: Listening Comprehension." *Language Arts*, 59 (September 1982), 617–629.

Shoop, Mary. "InQuest: A Listening and Reading Comprehension Strategy." *The Reading Teacher*, 39 (March 1986), 670–675.

Trelease, Jim. *The New Read-Aloud Handbook*. New York: Penguin, 1989.

———. "Jim Trelease Speaks on Reading Aloud to Children." *The Reading Teacher*, 43 (December 1989), 200–207.

Winn, Deanna. "Develop Listening Skills as a Part of the Curriculum." *The Reading Teacher*, 42 (November 1988), 144–146.

CHAPTER 6

Creative Oral Communication

Expressing Stories and Poems

Reflecting Before Reading

BEFORE reading the chapter, read the title, the headings, and the end-of-chapter summary. Then answer the questions in the margin on this page.

In what ways can the teacher involve children in creative oral communication?

Why is this involvement important?

TEACHING IN ACTION   Dramatizing "The Three Billy Goats Gruff"

Everyone was ready. The flannelboard was propped on the easel of Karin Topping's first grade. The children's eyes were alert, watching as Ms. Topping began to tell "The Three Billy Goats Gruff."

Creative Storytelling

"Trip, trap, trip, trap," the children echoed softly as the littlest billy goat Gruff went over the bridge. "Trip, trap, trip, trap," they chorused more loudly as the middle goat Gruff went over. "It is I, the middle billy goat Gruff, going over the bridge," they contributed based on what had happened to the littlest goat. "Why don't you wait for my big brother Gruff," they suggested, again based on what had happened to the littlest goat. "Oh, no, you're not!" they roared for the troll, using their meanest voices. Because "The Three Billy Goats Gruff" is a repetitive tale, the children were able to predict what the characters would say; they could readily contribute repeated words even as their teacher demonstrated story action by placing and moving pieces on the flannelboard.

Responding to story patterns by predicting

Having heard the story once, the first-graders were eager to "do" it again. This time some became little Gruffs, some middle Gruffs, some big Gruffs, and others mean trolls. Now as their teacher narrated the story, youngsters from the role-playing groups contributed the speaking words, improvising as they went along to add to what the characters said. Standing up, they used their bodies to express movements to go along with the "Trip, trap, trip, trap." They shook their heads and stamped their feet to simulate goat or troll actions—at times encouraged by their teacher, who asked, "What else do you think the goat said? How do you think the troll moved his eyes and face as he spoke? Tell me. Show me."

The result was an impromptu retelling of the story that bordered on creative drama. Later that day, the children made paper bag puppets to go along with "The Three Billy Goats Gruff." Some made trolls, some goats, depending on their personal preferences.

Creating a Drama Together

The next day, when the children gathered on the communication rug, they brought their troll and goat puppets with them and gathered in groups according to the characters they had chosen.

Creating original story
ideas through sponta-
neous drama

"Let's go on with our story, children," Ms. Topping proposed. "Goats, you are now in the field on the other side of the bridge. What are you doing? Feeling? Saying to one another?" The children responded in terms of the delicious grass they were eating and how glad they were to get rid of the mean troll.

"Stand up, trolls! Move like trolls!" directed the teacher. "Look, billy goats, here comes a band of other trolls. Why do you think they are coming? What can you say? What do you do? Trolls, what do you say? How do you move your bodies? Your face? Your eyes? Goats, how do you feel as the trolls get nearer?"

Guided by their teacher's organizing questions, the goats and the trolls spontaneously created and acted out a drama in which the trolls came after the goats and the goats outwitted the trolls, this time by hiding under the bridge.

At this level, a natural follow-
up activity is the reading of
"The Three Billy Goats Gruff"
in its big-book version. See
Chapter 13.

That sequence played out, Ms. Topping asked, "But suppose you trolls were not bad ones after all. How could you have moved your bodies and faces to show this? What could you have said to the goats? What would you goats have said to the trolls?" The children responded by doing, speaking, and adding sounds like *clump, clump, clump* as they moved their puppet heads and took the parts of the characters represented by those puppets.

Role Playing to Understand Content

The children in Ms. Topping's first grade really enjoyed dramatizing "The Three Billy Goats Gruff." They asked if they could play out a story again. So another afternoon found them in the communication center, listening to another picture book: *Ox-Cart Man* by Donald Hall.

This time, the teacher began by reading the book and sharing the pictures. After an initial reading, the children went back to interpret the pictures, reading into each the thoughts and words of the man and the other people depicted. They spoke out as though they were the characters in the story, different children contributing different lines, prompted by their teacher's probing questions: "How do you think the man felt as he said good-bye to his family? What did he say? What else? What did they answer? What expressions did he have on his face?"

Because *Ox-Cart Man* tells the story of the cycle of the seasons and the way one family in early nineteenth-century New England reacts to those changes, the drama the children produced was a serious one. In proposing what characters were thinking, saying, and doing, the children encountered a lot of content. They had to talk about the seasons and what each member of the family did. They had to consider the differences between life in early nineteenth-century America and life today.

The children most enjoyed dramatizing the part where the man sold the wool and the shawl, the candles and the shingles. They called out, like the man, "Come and buy. See what I've got." To do this, they selected objects from the classroom to hold up and "sell," describing their goods much more fully than in the story. The result was a marketplace of activity through which the children handled major concepts from the social studies—goods, trade, production—as they created orally and spontaneously together.

Creative Oral Expression in the Classroom

Elementary-school youngsters should have numerous opportunities to hear stories and poems and to react orally and creatively, as we saw happening in Ms. Topping's classroom. Ways to achieve this goal are through participatory story listening and storytelling, spontaneous drama, Readers' Theatre, pantomime, more formal drama festival times, and choral speaking. Through these experiences, children learn to

- ✦ Put words together to express ideas in mind,
- ✦ Use their voices and/or bodies to highlight ideas,
- ✦ Use visuals to add clarity to a message,
- ✦ Express themselves orally with some degree of confidence and poise,
- ✦ Think creatively, extending a story to predict, imagine, and propose.

Read Olga Nelson, "Story Telling: Language Experience for Meaning Making," *The Reading Teacher*, 42(February 1989) 386–390; R. Craig Roney, "Back to Basics with Storytelling," *The Reading Teacher*, 42 (March 1989), 520–523; and Karen Gallas, "When the Children Take the Chair: A Study of Sharing Time in a Primary Classroom," *Language Arts*, 69 (March 1992), 172–182.

Participatory Storytelling

In *Look What Happened to Frog,* Pamela Cooper and Rives Collins (1991) speak of the importance of storytelling. They suggest that the sharing of a story is like the giving of a gift: It enriches the lives of those who receive it. Storytelling is an integral part of teaching. Telling stories while they teach, teachers clarify and illustrate points; at the same time, they model storytelling strategies for children who themselves are becoming tellers of stories.

Participatory storytelling as part of story listening is a fine beginning for developing children's ability to express themselves orally. Stories have a straightforward sequence that provides a ready introduction to sequencing and pacing of ideas. They have an inherent appeal for children; youngsters love to hear stories and can easily develop interest in sharing similar tales. Also, stories for children are action filled. In telling them, youngsters must vary intonation, express meanings through face and body, use props where appropriate, and

See Denny Taylor and Dorothy Strickland, *Family Storybook Reading* (Portsmouth, N.H.: Heinemann Educational Books, 1986), for a treatment of the importance of story listening in young children's language development. For a discussion of language play and dramatic play as responses to literature, read W. Nikola-Lisa, "Read Aloud, Play a Lot," *The New Advocate*, 5 (Summer 1992), 199–213.

select the most expressive words. These abilities are what story sharing is all about.

Research shows that oral activity related to stories increases children's ability to use language effectively. In a study by Dorothy Strickland (1973), youngsters in an experimental group were exposed to a literature-based oral language program. They enjoyed a daily story, which was followed by a period of storytelling, puppetry, creative dramatics, role playing, choral speaking, and/or discussion. Children in a control group listened to stories but did not participate in oral activities. Strickland found that both groups showed increases in language facility, but those involved in active oral follow-ups made significantly greater gains.

A more recent study by Maryellen Cosgrove (1987) showed similar gains in reading as a result of story listening. In Cosgrove's study, fourth- and sixth-graders listened to stories three times a week for twelve weeks. The students evidenced significant improvement in reading attitudes, independent reading, and comprehension when compared to a control group that was not read to. Similarly, Patricia Kelly (1990) reported heightened student interest in literature when third-graders were involved in story listening, Readers' Theatre activities, role playing, and choral speaking.

Researchers have been investigating the effect of having children retell stories after listening to or reading them (Morrow, 1985, 1986; Gambrell, Pfeiffer, and Wilson, 1985; Gambrell, Koskinen, and Kapinus, 1985; Brown and Cambourne, 1989). Using retelling in classrooms, teacher-researchers share a story, model retelling of that story, provide opportunities for children to retell stories after hearing and reading them, and encourage children to create original stories. This interesting research indicates that oral retelling significantly improves children's comprehension, their sense of story structure, and the language complexity of original stories they dictate (Morrow, 1986; Koskinen, Gambrell, Kapinus, and Heathington, 1988).

Oral sharing of stories belongs in the upper as well as primary grades. Jim Trelease (1989) describes one remedial sixth-grade class where the teacher, Mrs. Hallahan, simply read each day from the book *Where the Red Fern Grows*. Trelease explains:

> A hardened, street-wise, proud group (mostly boys), they were insulted when she began reading to them. "How come you're reading to us? You think we're babies or something?" they wanted to know. After explaining that she didn't think anything of the kind but only wanted to share a favorite story with them, she continued reading *Where the Red Fern Grows*. Each day she opened the class with the next portion of the story and each day she was greeted with groans. "Not again today! How come nobody else ever made us listen like this?"
>
> But [Mrs. Hallahan] persevered, and after a few weeks (the book contained 212 pages), the tone of the class's morning remarks began to change. "You're going to read to us today, aren't you?" Or, "Don't forget the book, Mrs. Hallahan."
>
> "I knew I had a winner," she confess[ed], "when on Friday, just when we were nearing the end of the book, one of the slowest boys in the class went home after school, got himself a library card, took out *Where the Red Fern Grows*, finished it himself, and came to school on Monday and told everyone how it ended."

In this case, story sharing by the teacher led naturally into storytelling by a student and could easily have developed into dramatic retelling.

Similarly, Richard Rodriguez (1981) explains how he was affected by a teacher's reading aloud to him as part of remedial instruction:

> Most of the time we took turns [reading]. I began with my elementary text. Sentences of astonishing simplicity seemed to me lifeless and drab. . . . Then the old nun would read from her favorite books, usually biographies of early American presidents. Playfully she ran through complex sentences, calling the words alive with her voice, making it seem that the author somehow was speaking directly to me. I smiled just to listen to her. I sat there and sensed for the first time some possibility of fellowship between a reader and a writer, a communication, never *intimate* like that I heard spoken words at home convey, but one nonetheless *personal*.

Creative oral story sharing, storytelling, and story retelling are not frills of the elementary language arts; they are integral components that lead to a heightened ability to use both oral and written language.

Spontaneous Drama

Read also Steve Hoffman and Linda Lamme, *Learning from the Inside Out: The Expressive Arts* (Wheaton, MD: Association for Childhood Education International, 1989).

Informal classroom drama also has a major place in the oral language curriculum. The Joint Committee of the National Council of Teachers of English and the Children's Theatre Association (1983) explains, "Informal classroom drama is an activity in which students invent and enact dramatic situations for themselves, rather than for an outside audience. This activity, perhaps most widely known as creative drama, . . . is spontaneously generated by the participants who perform the dual tasks of composing and enacting their parts as the drama progresses. This form of unrehearsed drama is a process of guided discovery led by the teacher for the benefit of the participants."

A "must-read" is Miriam Martinez, "Motivating Dramatic Story Reenactments," *The Reading Teacher*, 46 (May 1993), 682–688. Martinez describes "spontaneous, child-initiated, child-directed" dramatic activity in early primary classrooms.

An easy introduction is the repetitive story. To begin, children decide how key words should be spoken and take turns playing the lines over and over. For example, in dramatizing "The Little Red Hen," children decide how the hen must have gone about her tasks and how she would have spoken her important line, "Very well then, I will do it myself!" The teacher asks, "How do you think the hen worked when she planted the field? Reaped the wheat? Took it to the mill?" Youngsters answer by showing. They repeat the recurring hen line and the lines of the other animals, each time varying their voices to show differences in meaning. Then, guided by the teacher, they improvise the words and actions of the Little Red Hen when she is faced by three other animals who want to take her bread away.

Dorothy Heathcote (1983), noted for her work with creative drama, goes beyond stories to organize dramatic activity around historical periods and events. Heathcote describes how she uses drama to help older children get a sense of the events relative to General Wolfe's siege of Quebec. Children do not look at Wolfe from "over there" or "outside." They become Wolfe, who must decide what to do when faced with the imperative "Give us your orders." Children must draw on their relevant knowledge about Wolfe, the military and political situation at Quebec, the weather, and the soldiers to make a response.

THE FORUM · On Creative Oral Expression

1. Pamela Nelson describes the importance of drama within the language arts: "Improvisational drama integrates and incorporates all the components of the language arts. Students read, write, listen, speak, and move in order to communicate with other participants. Attention is currently being directed toward the relationship of drama to increased growth in language and cognition" ("Drama, Doorway to the Past," *Language Arts*, 65 [January 1988], 20–25).

2. June Cottrell writes about the purpose of creative drama: "Through movement and pantomime, improvisation, role-playing and characterization, and more, children explore what it means to be a human being. Whether the content of the drama is based in reality or pure fantasy, children engaged in drama make discoveries about themselves and the world."

   Cottrell emphasizes the importance of drama in upper elementary grades as a "vehicle for integrating and applying language arts concepts and skills to the teaching of history, geography, and the natural sciences." She elaborates on the uses of drama in the study of history: "The chronological nature of history is a perfect match for . . . creative drama activities, particularly sequential pantomime and listening games and add-on scenes. History deals with actions, so almost any event can be translated into a sequential pantomime activity. A few possible topics for later elementary classes are these: the Great Explorations, the events that led to the Revolutionary War, the defense of the Alamo, the trek west to California or the adventures along the Oregon Trail, the Lewis and Clark Expedition, the exploration of the poles, the use of the 'underground railroad'" (*Creative Drama in the Classroom: Grades 4–6* [Lincolnwood, Ill.: National Textbook, 1987], 1, 6, 186).

3. Lynne Putnam recommends dramatizing nonfiction with very young children: "When given the opportunity, young children can 'become' anything their teacher is reading about. The possibilities are endless. . . : bears hibernating in their dens, dinosaurs moving through swamps, thunderstorms brewing, volcanoes erupting, the earth rotating on its axis. . . . Invariably, the children appear to be thoroughly absorbed and enjoying themselves, as if at play. They also appear to retain more of the information presented" ("Dramatizing Nonfiction with Emerging Readers," *Language Arts*, 68 [October 1991], 463–469).

Questions to Consider

What are the purposes of creative oral expression in the elementary language arts? What specific strategies did Karin Topping use to involve her students in dramatization during storytelling? What other strategies are available to you? What learnings might result?

See Heathcote's book *Drama as Context* (Aberdeen: National Association for the Teaching of English, 1980). Read also June Cottrell, *Creative Drama in the Classroom: Grades 4–6* (Lincolnwood, Ill.: National Textbook, 1987), for descriptions of lessons integrating drama into content-area study.

As Heathcote explains, now "there is a sudden pressure on the learners: 'These guys are expecting me to tell them what to do.'" Responding to this pressure, participants in a drama "unpack" previously held conclusions; they actively use information encountered and make new and different connections. Here the teacher's role is that of "journeymaker"—to take students on a "journey of learning." The teacher must press and ask if participants are to discover the meaning behind the material they are studying. Often it is the teacher who must pose the problem situation that begins the drama—the what-if question that gets participants thinking.

Readers' Theatre

For an example of Readers' Theatre in a third-grade class, see James Flood et al., "Am I Allowed to Group Using Flexible Patterns for Effective Instruction?" *The Reading Teacher*, 45 (April 1992), 608–625. For an example using nonfiction, see Terrell Young and Sylvia Vardell, "Weaving Readers' Theatre and Nonfiction into the Curriculum," *The Reading Teacher*, 46 (February 1993), 396–405.

Students can also write Readers' Theatre scripts based on wordless or near-wordless books. An example is David Wiesner's Caldecott-winning *Tuesday* (New York: Clarion, 1991), a far-out flight of the imagination.

Another exciting form classroom drama can take is Readers' Theatre. Using Readers' Theatre, students read a story aloud, with different students reading the parts of various story characters and using variations in intonation, pitch, and reading rate to bring the story alive. Typically, one child reads each character's part. Linda Hoyt (1992) suggests variations on this format: Children read parts chorally or read in small groups. This lets every child participate, helps slower readers "experience reading at a rate that approximates oral speech," and "encourages repeated readings for fluency."

Children can dramatically read directly from a text, using the quotation marks to tell them when the narrator is speaking and when each character comes in. At times, children read dramatically from scripts on which individual roles have been specially marked. But as Hoyt believes, the most effective scripts for Readers' Theatre are those designed by students. Students can list the main characters and then choose portions of the story to read aloud dramatically. The teacher's role here is to prepare for dramatic oral reading by modeling for the students ways to use the voice to express thoughts, feelings, and mood.

Pantomime

As youngsters perform dramatically, they must at times call upon the art of pantomime. In pantomime, the gesture, the glance, the grin, and the gait are the media of communication as hands, face, and body work together to send a message.

Pantomime is important in language programs. First, through pantomime children can loosen any inhibitions about expressing themselves nonverbally. Second, they gain control over their nonverbal expressions, which are as significant in face-to-face communication and in creative drama as they are in pantomime. Third, they begin to realize the importance of body language in communication and become aware of the nonverbal messages that others send.

Class Pantomimes   Pantomime should start as a class activity, with all children interpreting an action or feeling. Children express more freely when everyone, including the teacher, is involved. A beginning for the very young is Let's Pretend play. Children pretend they are

- Rubber bands stretching or masses of clay being flattened;
- Balls rolling, bouncing, and hurtling through the air;
- Kites flying on the breeze;
- Animals such as snakes, horses, kangaroos, sea gulls, tigers;
- Machines such as helicopters with propellers, windmills on a breezy day, jackhammers tearing up the street;
- Natural phenomena such as waves rolling shoreward, winds gusting, snowflakes floating earthward, clouds bouncing.

Kindergartners and preschoolers can interpret these actions to music. With desks pushed back, they stretch, roll, spin, and wiggle as the music inspires them.

Middle-graders enjoy pantomimes in which everyone performs. Let's Pretend play for the middle grades includes pretending to swim, ride a bike, bounce a ball, jump a rope—of course, without water, bicycle, ball, or rope. They move on to more sophisticated actions that require synchronization among participants. For example, youngsters toss an imaginary ball in circle groups of five or six. The teacher serves as choreographer, calling out changes in the ball: "Now the ball is a large beach ball! Now it is a bowling ball, very heavy to throw! Now it has become a ping-pong ball!" As the size and weight of the imaginary ball change, children must interpret the differences in the way they toss it. Pantomimes of this sort make excellent warm-up exercises for older students who have had little experience with creative drama in lower grades.

Performance Pantomimes   Many types of stories lend themselves to pantomimed telling:

- *Nursery rhymes.* Several youngsters pantomime rhymes such as "Little Miss Muffet," "Little Jack Horner," "Jack and Jill" as watchers try to guess the rhyme.
- *Fables.* Several children pantomime the actions of fables such as "The Wind and the Sun," "The Reed and the Oak," and "The Miller, the Boy, and the Donkey," while a narrator reads the fable.
- *Talking-beast tales.* Children pantomime the actions of tales such as "The Three Little Pigs" while a narrator reads. Then they pantomime the story, trying to tell it totally through actions.

Upper-graders who have seen comedians perform humorous pantomimes on TV can make up original skits to share wordlessly. Humor is achieved in pantomime through exaggeration, so children should select topics that can be exaggerated—catching a mosquito or scratching an itch when one's arms are full.

Learning Through Pantomime   Pantomime serves two purposes in language programs. First, through it students learn to handle nonverbal communication, and for this reason alone pantomime deserves a place in the elementary curriculum. In addition, through pantomime children come to better understand their language. There are several ways children can learn about language through pantomime:

More verbs to pantomime: *whistled, tapped, pounded, shoved, lifted, bounced, threw, turned, rubbed, leaped, pulled, laughed, brushed, twisted, stared, cried, smiled, frowned, kicked, hammered, sawed, picked, crushed*

✦ Children can pantomime verbs, such as *stalked, sauntered, strutted, wavered,* and in the process increase their vocabulary.
✦ Children can see the contribution of adverbs and adjectives to sentences by nonverbally showing the differences in meaning suggested by modifiers, as in these examples:
    The lazy boy walked in.
    The eager boy walked in.
    The tired girl walked in.
    The determined girl walked in.

Objects to use as the basis for creative and spontaneous pantomimes might include a hammer, a long piece of rope, a rake, a banana, a cooking pot

✦ Children can play with metaphors and similes by pretending an object is something else and using it to pantomime the pretended one. Then they write sentences with metaphors and similes that express the creative relationship. For example, in pantomime a mop can become a witch's broomstick or a dancing partner as children pantomime and compose: "Mopping the floor, he looked like a witch riding a broomstick" or "Mopping the floor, he looked like a dancer waltzing his partner across the room."
✦ Children can demonstrate their comprehension of a reading passage by interpreting it nonverbally. They show how one character walked, another felt, another looked. Or children can pantomime a scene they have read.
✦ Children can demonstrate processes and actions in discussions. Teachers must look for points in talk time to ask, "Will you show us?" For example, a youngster talking about how she navigates on a skateboard can demonstrate techniques while talking.

As these examples indicate, pantomime fits naturally into a variety of classroom experiences. It is an integral part of storytelling and creative drama.

Drama Festivals and Formal Drama

Teachers must guide children as they begin to function, circulating among collaborative teams, making suggestions, and helping children prepare by trying out words and gestures.

Children who have experienced participatory storytelling, spontaneous drama, and pantomime can go on to tell and dramatize stories, grouped in "little theater companies." At times, all the members of the class can contribute to a story festival, or an extravaganza that focuses on tales from a particular country, by one author, on one topic, or of one kind (myths, fables, tall tales). More often, only a few students contribute to a briefer sharing time. Those who wish to share sign up, indicating their story title, their medium (puppet, pictures, filmstrip), their name, and their little theater company (see Figure 6.1).

To get things started, one teacher assembles a collection of books; in each book, she slips a card. Students who read a particular book sign its card. When several signatures appear, the teacher forms those students into a performing company to share the book with others. Some books in the collection are word-

A Visit with Hans Christian Andersen

The Life of Hans Christian Andersen: a presentation by the Andersen Reporters—Tom, Kev, Jake, and Marcia.
"The Steadfast Tin Soldier": a puppet show by the Danish Puppeteers—Ruth, Karen, Moose, Gil, Mary, and Bob.
"The Ugly Duckling": a dramatization by the Playing Five—Martin, Max, Janey, Jill, and Brenda.
"The Little Mermaid": a shadow play by the Four Keys—Nate, Herb, Kathie, and Sallie.
"The Emperor's New Clothes": a filmstrip-telling by the Script Writers—Fran, Phyllis, Frank, and Joe.
Talking with Andersen: an interview with the Star Interviewers—Angela, Jose, and Marie—and with Hans Christian Andersen, played by Milt.
Some Andersen Riddles: all participants.

Today's Announcer—Rose

Figure 6.1 Example of an Upper-Grade Drama Festival Program

less. Students with reading problems can select these books to translate into verbal stories to share orally.

For ideas see Daniel Sklar, *Playmaking: Children Writing and Performing Their Own Plays* (New York: Teachers and Writers Collaborative, 1991).

Fairy tales are particularly useful in this context. A classroom Dramaland Book Shelf should hold collections of Grimm, Andersen, Asbjornsen, and Moe; adaptations of French tales by Perrault; modern tales like E. B. White's *Charlotte's Web*, P. L. Travers's *Mary Poppins*, and Astrid Lindgren's *Pippi Longstocking*; collections of myths; storybooks that tell just one fable, such as Brian Wildsmith's version of LaFontaine's "The Rich Man and the Shoe Maker"; and books that relate one old fairy tale or tall tale.

Children working cooperatively in little theater companies need ways to avoid extensive memorization of stories they tell and dramatize. They can experiment with

- A narrator who reads long descriptive passages, simulating the wandering storyteller of yore;
- Cue cards held up and changed by a "stagehand";
- Notes written behind scenery objects;
- Scrolls containing the lines that players hold and unroll as the playlet progresses, reading their lines from the scrolls;
- Spontaneous adaptations of the lines; children know "about" what they are going to say but make up specific lines as they go along.

At times youngsters enjoy dramatizing plays they themselves have written. Students who have collaborated in the writing of a short play share it dramatically with the class. Acting out is followed by conversation in which listeners tell which actions or words in the story they liked. At other times individual youngsters who have written short stories convert them into playlets or pantomimes for group dramatizing.

During actual sharing sessions, informality is the key. Although the sharing may be dramatic, it is not a magnificent production with elaborate props and scenery, nor do children practice extensively or memorize lines. Rather, emphasis is on enjoying language and literature. The only audience is classmates and teacher; contributions are not graded, and children feel no pressure to produce perfect performances. Upper-graders generally add to the fun by hamming it up—a positive addition, for relaxed players enjoy performing.

Materials to Support Creative Oral Expression

References to assist in story sharing are Ramon Ross, *Storyteller*, 2d ed. (Columbus, Ohio: Merrill, 1980), and Pamela Cooper and Rives Collins, *Look What Happened to Frog: Storytelling in Education* (Scottsdale, AZ: Gorsuch-Scarisbuck, 1991).

Teachers begin oral communication by sharing stories with children. Shortly, however, children assume the role of storyteller; they tell stories or parts of stories they have read. In their storytelling children use the same materials teachers use to extend story meanings: pictures, puppets, flannel pieces. Let us next consider some of the techniques children can learn to use as they share stories.

Using Pictures to Tell Stories

Pictures add a visual dimension to story sharing. Here are some ideas for using story lines and boxes, story rolls, transparencies, and filmstrips to enhance an oral message.

Story Lines and Boxes   Flat pictures add impact to story sharing. Several children who have written or read a story can render key scenes in picture form. These can be hung sequentially on a story line as the children share their story with the class. Or, if only two or three children share a story, they can mount key story scenes they have reproduced on each of the six faces of a good-size box. As they share the story, they display appropriate pictures. Children who do not enjoy drawing can snip pictures from magazines to mount on their story boxes or on construction paper to hang on the story line during sharing.

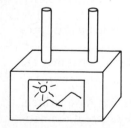

Story Rolls   The story roll is a related device for sharing. Individually or in groups, children draw story scenes on a roll of paper. They attach the short ends of their completed story rolls to cardboard tubes, slip them into circles cut into a viewing box, and rotate them to pull the roll through the box so that the pictures are visible through a large rectangular cut in one side. Displaying their pictures sequentially, students relate the story happenings. A variation of the story role is to mount pictures on a window shade, which is pulled down to reveal pictures as a story unwinds.

Transparencies   If facilities for making transparencies are available, children can use them for sharing stories. Each child in a listening group selects a picture from the storybook. With the aid of a thermofax machine, the teacher makes a transparency of the selected pictures; then each child colors his or her selection. Later, in story sequence, each child places the transparency on the "stage" of the overhead projector to tell about that part of the story.

Students can produce original, single transparencies based on an exciting incident in a book read. Projecting their transparencies, students tell about the incidents in question, not revealing the outcome but relating the exciting build-up. This sharing format can turn into a book sale, with a speaker enticing listeners to read the whole story.

Filmstrips   If a filmstrip of a story is available, that strip—without the audiotape that may accompany it—can serve as the medium for sharing by youngsters who have read the original book version. A small group follows up a reading or listening experience with a viewing of the silent strip. Then they use their memory of story events to devise their own version, which they share with others while showing the strip.

Advantages of Pictures   Children who use visuals in storytelling enjoy several advantages:

+ They learn the importance of supplementing words with visuals that enhance a message.
+ In many cases, the visuals become the outline for presenting, providing a mental reminder of thoughts to be presented.
+ Some children feel more comfortable and secure if they have visuals to help them in presenting.

Using Puppets in Drama and Storytelling

Few youngsters or oldsters can resist the appeal of puppets.

Ways to Make Puppets   Students can make hand puppets from

+ Paper bags to which features have been added with flo-pens, crayons, construction paper, or yarn;
+ Socks, stockings, or work gloves to which features have been added with buttons, yarn, or scraps of material;
+ The hand by marking features directly on the fist or fingers;
+ Styrofoam or ping-pong balls stuck on the fingers or on ice cream bar sticks; glitter, buttons, and yarn form the features.

Students can make head puppets that they hold directly over their faces from

+ Paper plates, with features drawn with crayon and flo-pen and eyes cut through the plates;
+ Full-size paper bags in which eye, nose, and mouth openings have been cut.

They can make body puppets that completely cover the puppeteer from

✦ Large cartons from which one side has been removed and through which a head hole has been cut in the opposite side; the cartons can be painted colorfully;

✦ People-shaped and -size cutouts; youngsters stretch out on a piece of heavy-grade cardboard and their classmates trace their body outline; the youngsters cut out the outline, color themselves in, and hold their puppets in front of them during sharing time.

Most of these puppets require little time to assemble and little artistic talent to produce—and the results can be striking.

Some teachers who include puppet play among the options from which children can choose as they share stories keep a Stuff Sack in the classroom with ribbons, bows, twine, scraps of fabric, lengths of old yarn, paper bags, worn-out but clean socks and gloves, paper plates, buttons, and other odds and ends. Children contribute to the Stuff Sack and draw materials from it as they assemble puppets for story sharing. Sometimes children will be creative

Informal dramatic performances should emphasize the pleasure of sharing stories and should involve children in a variety of creative storytelling strategies. (© 1993 Elizabeth Crews)

in the design of their puppets, choosing materials not in the bag or not attempted before.

The overhead projector can also be used to flash puppet shadows on a screen.

Shadow puppets, which are part of the culture of Indonesia, can become a lively part of creative classroom dramatics as well. In Indonesia, puppets are made from hard leather in which tiny holes are punched to outline facial and body features. The puppets are held up behind a thin curtain, and a strong beam of light is shone from behind the puppets through the curtain. In a room that is otherwise darkened, the puppets appear as silhouettes that walk, lean over, and even raise their arms, since arms are attached to the body with clips and each arm is connected to a separate stick that is moved up and down to operate it. Upper elementary pupils can construct a shadow puppet from heavy-grade cardboard, punch tiny light-passage holes in the manner of the traditional Indonesian puppet, and mount the puppet shape—which can be anything from a person to a tree or house—on a stick. For a stage, a good-size piece of thin sheeting is suspended vertically. The light source is an overhead or slide projector.

Suggestions for Puppetry   Here are some general suggestions for handling puppets:

+ Don't involve too many puppets in a show; three or four are about all elementary students can manage.
+ Suggest that young children audiotape the storyline that accompanies puppet movement. Generally children have trouble speaking lines and manipulating puppets simultaneously.
+ Help children in upper grades arrange cue cards so that they do not have to memorize lines. Cue cards can be taped to the back edge of the table behind which puppeteers are performing or down the sides of a box or regular puppet stage. Remind students that notes on unattached pages will get disarranged during telling and cause confusion. Or designate a narrator who reads most of the lines; performers interject the words said by the puppets they are manipulating.
+ Suggest that each child manipulate only one puppet so that he or she can effectively interpret the action through puppet motion. Talk about the messages sent through a nod and a shake of the head, the slump of the body, the tilt of the head, the way people walk. At some point, have all children take a puppet in hand to express feelings like tiredness, happiness, sadness, wide-awakeness, anger, and friendliness.
+ Help children play with their voices to express feelings vocally. Children can experiment with expressing fear, pleasure, fatigue, warmth, dislike. They can make their voices sound young or old, far away or nearby, high or low pitched, loud or soft. They can produce story noises like growls, snarls, hoots, chuckles, groans. Sound is fundamental in puppet plays, so do some preparatory work in which students hold a similar puppet head they have made and experiment with different ways to vary voice pitch and loudness.

✦ Devise an original way for upper elementary graders to share books they have read with other students.

✦ To get a feel for pantomime, share a story nonverbally, drawing on facial and body expressions to communicate.

Choral Speaking

The story-sharing and dramatic techniques just described can be adapted for sharing poems. Some stories are actually verses, especially picture storybooks such as those by Dr. Seuss. Dr. Seuss's *Green Eggs and Ham* and *The King's Stilts* are particularly suitable for class pantomime while a narrator reads the lines.

Choral speaking is another way to interpret poems. It is a group approach through which people gain a feel for poetic sounds and relate oral interpretation techniques to the communication of meaning. Although most choral speaking is used with poetry, the techniques can be applied to prose selections.

Introducing Children to Choral Speaking

For ideas on doing poems with children, read Nancy Larrick, *Let's Do a Poem* (New York: Delacorte, 1991). For recent poems to chorus, use Jeanne Harms and Lucille Lettow, "Recent Poetry for Children," *The Reading Teacher*, 45 (December 1991), 274–279.

In choral speaking, children, led by a conductor, recite together or in turn, the lines of a poem. In the lower grades, the piece is usually a short one that the teacher first recites to the class. Having heard the teacher recite it several times, the children join in. In the lower and middle grades, the piece may be printed as a chart that is sometimes called a Poetry Broadside. Still, the teacher must orally introduce the piece, perhaps pointing to the words while speaking. In the upper grades, the piece may be on a duplicated sheet or in a book that children have.

Choral-Speaking Roles Because a class chorus resembles an orchestra, the role of conductor is pivotal. The conductor is responsible for establishing the rhythm, indicating when groups will contribute their parts, and keeping everyone together. Therefore, at first it is vital that the teacher speak clearly and lead the chorus with hand or arm. A drum helps maintain the beat; the conductor beats the drum with one hand and leads the chorus with the other.

After a time, a youngster assumes the role of Keeper of the Rhythm, striking the drum as the class choruses to the beat. With some groups, it is helpful to convert a rhythm band stick into a baton and conduct with it. To choristers, a flick of the stick means "halt" and a point of the stick means "join in." After a time, some children will want to assume the role of Conductor of Chorus: The volunteer takes baton in hand to lead the class.

Another role that adds to the pleasure of choral speaking is Title Giver. Rather than having the entire class chorus the title and author of the piece, one chorister does it. Responding to a point of the stick, the Title Giver recites title and author. This is fine to do when the piece is by a class member; the young poet is reinforced by hearing not only the selection recited but his or her name as well.

Choral Speaking and Writing   Choral speaking can grow out of children's writing. Often a piece that children have cooperatively composed can be used for choral speaking. Children follow a class writing experience by standing and reciting their pieces together. In reciting they may find rough spots that need changing, so before reciting it again, they add, delete, or change words. Children who have written poems by themselves or in small groups may volunteer their pieces for class interpretation. In this case, they print Poetry Broadsides and conduct the class chorus themselves.

Children as Orchestrators of Choral Speaking   Children should participate in the orchestration of choral-speaking selections. While working on a piece, students decide how they will chorus it—which lines to recite loudly or softly, smoothly or haltingly, for greater or lesser emphasis.

By participating in these orchestrational decisions, children encounter fundamental elements of oral communication. They relate elements such as loudness/softness, short pause/long pause, high pitch/low pitch to meanings being communicated. They interpret punctuation vocally, pausing longer at a period stop than at a comma stop and longer at a semicolon stop than at a comma stop. In this respect, students acquire fundamental understandings of language as well as enjoy the "music" of poetry.

A popular piece for children to orchestrate together is Rose Fyleman's "Goblin," for its meaning is evident and the punctuation and italics are easy to translate vocally:

Rose Fyleman, *Picture Rhymes from Foreign Lands* (New York: J.B. Lippincott, 1935, 1963). Children can compose original versions by substituting sets of rhyming verbs, as in

He flips
And he dips
And he clips
And he slips.
He calls
And he falls
And he wanders in
the halls.

> **A Goblin**
>
> A goblin lives in *our* house, in *our* house, in *our* house
> A goblin lives in *our* house all the year round.
> He bumps
> And he jumps
> And he thumps
> And he stumps.
> He knocks
> And he rocks
> And he rattles at the locks.
> A goblin lives in *our* house, in *our* house, in *our* house.
> A goblin lives in *our* house all the year round.

One group decided to speak the beginning and ending sections in unison, stressing the italicized *our*. They decided too that it would be most effective if they spoke the first "all the year round" in a staccato whisper. They made the second reading of the refrain louder and louder to suggest that the goblin was getting closer and closer. This contrasted with the quiet of the last four words, "all the year round," which they again whispered.

The class decided that the short lines in the middle should be recited by individuals. The lines should be spoken quickly, with each child in the chain contributing promptly. To help the children do their parts, the conductor pointed from one to the next to keep the action going.

Different Ways to Chorus a Piece

As the previous example implies, it is possible to arrange a selection and choristers in a variety of ways. Here are six formats for class chorusing:

Refrain Poems with repetitive refrains lend themselves to choral speaking. The teacher reads or recites the main verse, and the children join in on the repetitive refrain. A piece that lends itself to the refrain format is David McCord's "Song of the Train." The narrator recites the initial four lines of each stanza, and the class joins in on the repetitive lines.

Other poems for refrain chorusing are Laura Richards, "The Umbrella Brigade" and "The Baby Goes to Boston" (children speak the repetitive lines); Walter de la Mare, "Quack!"; Kate Greenaway, "Jump—jump—jump"; Mother Goose, "The Mischievous Raven"; Margaret Wise Brown, "Little Black Bug."

David McCord, "Song of the Train," *Far and Few: Rhymes of Never Was and Always Is* (Boston: Little, Brown, 1952). Using the same pattern, upper-graders can write lines about a jet, a motorboat, or a blender.

Song of the Train

Clickety-clack
Wheels on the track,
This is the way
They begin the attack:
} lines to be spoken by a narrator

Click-ety-clack,
Click-ety-clack,
Click-ety, click-ety,
Click-ety
Clack
} lines to be spoken by the choral group

Clickety-clack,
Over the crack,
Faster and faster
The song of the track:
} lines to be spoken by a narrator

Clickety-clack,
Clickety-clack,
Clickety, clackety,
Clackety
Clack.
} lines to be spoken by the choral group

Riding in front,
Riding in back,
Everyone hears
The song of the track:
} lines to be spoken by a narrator

Clickety-clack,
Clickety-clack,
Clickety, clickety,
Clackety
Clack.
} lines to be spoken by a choral group

A teacher can use the choral speaking of a poem such as "Song of the Train" during content-area study. In this case, children chorus the poem as the anticipatory set of a lesson within a transportation unit.

For unison chorusing:
Spring is showery,
    flowery, bowery;
Summer is hoppy,
    croppy, poppy;
Autumn is wheezy,
    sneezy, freezy;
Winter is slippy,
    drippy, nippy.
—Mother Goose

Unison   A conductor can lead an entire class in chorusing a piece. Especially with children in lower primary grades, the selection initially should be short, probably no longer than the four lines of the refrains they have been contributing as part of refrain chorusing. Also, because children have trouble coordinating their voices, it helps to begin with a rhythmic selection. Kindergarten and first-grade teachers recommend nursery rhymes like "Pat-a-Cake" and "Pease Porridge Hot." Little rhymes like Robert Louis Stevenson's "Rain" and "Time to Rise" are also recommended. With older children, humorous poems such as Ogden Nash's "The Hippopotamus" are appropriate:

> ### The Hippopotamus
>
> Behold the Hippopotamus!
> We laugh at how he looks to us,
> And yet in moments dank and grim
> I wonder how we look to him.
>
> Peace, peace, thou hippopotamus!
> We really look all right to us,
> As you no doubt delight the eye
> Of other hippopotami.

Choral speaking a piece like "The Hippopotamus" is fun. It also adds much to ongoing study, in this case to an upper-grade study of cultural diversity. The poem has an important underlying theme: We should not judge others by appearance alone, and cultural differences are what make the world fascinating.

For line-a-child chorusing, use John Ciardi, "The River is a Piece of Sky"; Eve Merriam, "A Lazy Thought," "Mean Song," and "Conversation," in *There Is No Rhyme for Silver* (New York: Atheneum, 1962); Vachel Lindsay, "The Potatoes' Dance," *Collected Poems* (New York: Macmillan, 1925).

Line-a-Child or Line-a-Group   A series of children or groups can, in turn, speak a line or two of poetry. Verse with short lines and distinct line endings lends itself to line-a-child chorusing. A fine piece for line-a-child interpretation is Shel Silverstein's "Helping":

> ### Helping
>
> Agatha Fry, she made a pie,
> And Christopher John helped bake it.
> Christopher John, he mowed the lawn,
> And Agatha Fry helped rake it.
> Zachary Zugg took out the rug,
> And Jennifer Joy helped shake it.
> And Jennifer Joy, she made a toy,
> And Zachary Zugg helped break it.

One student says the lines about Agatha Fry; a second says the lines about Christopher John.
One student says the lines about Zachary Zugg; another says the lines about Jennifer Joy.

And some kind of help
Is the kind of help
That helping's all about.
And some kind of help
Is the kind of help
We all can do without.

} All students join in on the
refrain.

This piece is excellent for chorusing because the repetitive structure is striking and the content lends itself easily to integration into a social studies unit. To introduce a unit on community helpers, a teacher could recite the poem as students follow along on a chart. Students join in and then brainstorm about people who help them. See Chapter 9 for more ideas for using the Silverstein poem.

For the older voice choir, less rhythmic, more sophisticated pieces are preferred. For example, junior and senior high school students often read "Cuccu Song" as part of their study of early English literature. Composed about 1250, the song goes like this:

Cuccu Song

Sumer is icumen in;
*   Lhude sing cuccu!*
Groweth sed, and bloweth med,
*   And springeth the wude nu.*
Sing Cuccu!

Cuccu, cuccu, well singest thu, cuccu:
*   Ne Swike thu naver nu;*
Sing cuccu, nu, sing cuccu,
*   Sing cuccu, sing cuccu, nu!*

For sound-group chorusing, use the following:
Whisky, frisky,
Hippity hop!
Up he goes
To the treetop!
Whirly, twirly,
round and round!
Down he scampers
To the ground.
Furly, curly,
What a tail!
Tall as a feather,
Broad as a sail!
Where's his supper?
In the shell,
Snap, cracky,
Out it fell.
—Anonymous

Groups of choristers can recite lines that communicate meaning: "Sumer is icumen in," "Groweth sed, and bloweth med," "And springeth the wude nu." Another group recites lines that incorporate "Sing cuccu." As they chorus, upper-graders acquire a feel for the piece and an increased understanding of the meaning that the Anglo-Saxon poet was trying to communicate. At this stage too, students consider the punctuation and make their pause patterns reflect it.

Sound Groups   Dividing a class into students with high-pitched and low-pitched voices and having the contrasting groups speak different sections of a poem is a form of choral speaking sometimes termed *antiphonal*. For this, poems with segments that can be distinguished according to meaning and/or mood are appropriate.

One piece for two-voice interpretation is "If You Ever" (author unknown): One group choruses the lines that repeat "ever, ever, ever" and the other the lines that repeat "never, never, never."

If You Ever

If you ever ever ever ever ever
  If you ever ever ever meet a whale   } *first group*
You must never never never never never
  You must never never never touch its tail   } *second group*
For if you ever ever ever ever ever
  If you ever ever ever touch its tail   } *first group*
You will never never never never never
  You will never never never meet another whale.   } *second group*

Some of the poems of A. A. Milne can be chorused pleasurably in sound groups. "If I Were King" is good for two-sound interpretation, while "The Four Friends" works effectively with four sound groups, each group speaking the lines about one of the four friends. Both poems are in the classic *When We Were Very Young*.

Simultaneous Voices, or Rounds   A variation on the group format is to have two groups speak different words at the same time. Paul Fleischman's *Joyful Noises: Poems for Two Voices* contains poems set up to be chorused in this way, as does his earlier *I Am Phoenix: Poems for Two Voices*. After chorusing Fleischman's poems about insects and birds, children can create and chorus poems for two, three, or even four voices.

Similarly, a main group can chorus the words of a poem while other groups simultaneously contribute repetitive chanting sounds. If each group joins the chorusing several seconds after the preceding group, the result is roundlike. To make rounds from poems, the teacher should select pieces with a steady rhythm, such as nursery rhymes. Starting with one like "Hey Diddle Diddle," teacher and students repeat it until all are familiar with the words and rhythm. They keep the beat through an even striking of a drum. Once children know the rhythm, one group repeats a simple but related chant such as "Moo, Moo. Moo, Moo." After the chanting group is in full swing, the rest speak the lines, maintaining the same beat as the chanters. With older children, two or three different chants can go on simultaneously—chants like "Middley Moo. Middley Moo" or "Moo Fiddley. Moo Fiddley."

Body Chants and Finger Plays   Children can add actions to their interpretations of many poems. Verses filled with action words are ideal for body chanting and chorusing. An old favorite is "Hickory, Dickory, Dock!":

Hickory, Dickory, Dock!

Hickory, dickory, dock!
The mouse ran up the clock.
The clock struck one.
The mouse ran down.
Hickory, dickory, dock!

Hey diddle diddle!
The cat and the fiddle!
The cow jumped over the moon.
The little boy laughed to see such sport,
And the dish ran away with the spoon.

Turn a simple verse like this into a poem for three voices by having one group repeat "tick tock" and another "tickety tock" as a third group choruses the rhyme.

As young children chorus the first two lines, they climb their hands upward in steplike increments. When chorusing the third line, they use their arms to strike one o'clock. On the last two lines, they make descending motions with their hands.

Not all students need contribute the same actions to a body chant. A class may identify several actions that fit the meaning and form into sections, with each section contributing a different action. For example, while interpreting "Hickory, Dickory, Dock," one section may decide to move heads left and right, a second to tick index fingers left and right, and a third to swing arms back and forth. Since members of each section must synchronize their motions, it is helpful to designate one member of each section as Concert Master. At a signal from the Conductor, the Concert Master of a section starts the motions; others in that section synchronize with the Conductor.

Very young children in nursery school and kindergarten enjoy the action of finger plays. In finger plays, children speak or sing a short, rhymelike piece, simultaneoulsy interpreting it with fingers and body. Through finger play, children come to enjoy the sounds and rhythms of poetry and increase their control over the fine muscles of their fingers. Also, some rhymes include number and/or directional concepts. As children interpret the numbers and directions with their fingers, they increase their understanding of number sequences, elementary addition and subtraction, and *left/right, up/down,* and *through/into.*

Traditional plays that you may recall from childhood are "Eensy-Weensy Spider," "I'm a Little Teapot," and "Where Is Thumbkin?" A teacher can also convert familiar poems into finger plays with the assistance of children. One young group created this play based on "It's Raining":

It's raining. It's pouring.	*(Move hands up and down as fingers simulate rain.)*
The old man's a-snoring.	*(Make snoring noises.)*
He went to bed	*(Bend head to pretend sleep.)*
And bumped his head	*(Rub head.)*
And couldn't get up in the morning.	*(Bend head again to pretend sleep.)*

Here are a few newer pieces for finger and action play that reinforce understanding of number and spatial concepts (on successive repetitions of the first finger play, children substitute words like *rabbits, children, squirrels* and so forth for fingers):

Climb and Hide

Fingers climb up ladders.	*(Make fingers walk upward.)*
They tumble down the slide.	*(Make fingers slip downward.)*
Fingers run quite quickly	*(Run with the fingers.)*
To find a place to hide.	*(Put both hands behind back.)*

Plop, Plop, Plop

One great, green frog sitting on a rock	*(Stick the thumb of one hand through the fist of the other.)*

A source of finger-play ideas is Sarah Hayes and Toni Goffe, *Clap Your Hands: Finger Rhymes* (New York: Lothrop, Lee & Shepard, 1988).

Read Harp (1988) for a discussion of how to use song charts to teach the natural rhythm of language.

Jumps into the water and
    makes a big plop.
Two great, green frogs
    sitting on a rock
Jump into the water and
    make a bigger plop.
Three great, green frogs
    sitting on a rock
Jump into the water and
    make the biggest plop.

(Dive the thumb off the hand
that simulates the rock.)
(Stick two fingers of one hand
through the fist of the other.)
(Dive the two fingers off the
"rock" hand.)
(Stick three fingers through
fist of other.)
(Dive the three fingers off the
hand that simulates the rock.)

Starlings at Play
Ten chattering starlings fly
    out to play
Sunday morning at the break of
    day.
Nine of the starlings hide
    themselves away.
Now one seeks carefully for
    where they stay.

(Move all fingers in a
flying motion.)

(Make a fist with both hands,
letting one finger protrude.)
(Wiggle the one finger.)

Ten chattering starlings fly
    out to play
Monday morning at the break
    of day.
Eight of the starlings hide
    themselves away.
Now two seek carefully for
    where they stay.

(Move all fingers in a
flying motion.)

(Make a fist with both hands,
letting two fingers protrude.)
(Wiggle two fingers.)

In repeating, children decrease the number of starlings and change the days.

Choral Speaking in the Language Arts

For examples of poems for choral speaking, see Sonja Dunn, *Butterscotch Dreams* (Markham, Ontario: Pembroke, 1987). For a discussion of choral speaking in English as a Second Language programs, see Joyce and Daniel McCauley, "Using Choral Speaking to Promote Language Learning for ESL Students." *The Reading Teacher*, 45 (March 1992), 526–533.

Choral speaking fits into the overall language program in many ways. Children can chorus poems they have read and ones they have written, write pieces that pattern as do poems chorused, expand choral speaking into spontaneous dramatizations—and in the process make discoveries about writing style, punctuation, and sentence patterning. Not only can children interpret poetry through verse choirs; they can also interpret prose selections. In the process, they begin to understand the repetitive patterns of prose. Because choral speaking can lead in so many directions and stimulate children to think creatively as they interpret a piece, teachers must not overlook choral speaking as a component of whole-language sequences.

Choral speaking also has a role in content-area study. As youngsters study different periods, places, and peoples, they can read and chorus related poetry. For example, Native American chants, songs of pioneers, railroaders, and canal builders, and laments for those lost in battle are appropriate for chorusing as part of the study of American history. Translations of Chinese nursery rhymes, African chants, and Old English verses are appropriate as part of the study of history and sociology. Through chorusing poetry, students get a better "feel" for the time, place, and people they are studying.

Should choral speaking be used for assembly programs and presentations? Many language authorities have suggested that to get children to speak a poem in perfect coordination is difficult and requires endless repetition, especially if children are to perform a lengthy piece in unison. Practicing the same selection over and over for a performance, however, causes children to lose interest. Although a short, simple choral-speaking selection may be included at times in an assembly program, chorusing has its value mainly as a learning, rather than performance, activity. It is a way for children to enjoy, interpret, and experience literature and language together.

✎ BUILDING AND REFINING YOUR TEACHING SKILLS

✦ Review the characteristics of unison, refrain, line-a-child, sound group, simultaneous voices, and body chant. Then decide how you and a second-grade group could orchestrate a poem (such as "One Misty, Moisty Morning") from an anthology.
✦ From an anthology select a piece to use as a choral-speaking activity during content-area study with upper-graders. Decide how you would orchestrate it. Write on a copy of it who will do each line and how it will be done. If you are teaching, share the poem with a group.

.... A Summary Thought or Two

CREATIVE ORAL COMMUNICATION

One of the best ways for students to develop the ability to express themselves orally and creatively is to become involved with stories and poems and perform them in a variety of ways. Ways to express and perform stories include participatory storytelling, spontaneous drama, Readers' Theatre, pantomime, formal drama, and choral speaking.

Some teachers consider the activities with stories and poems described in this chapter the "fluff" of the curriculum—something to get to if time permits. Even some experienced educators take this view of creative oral communication. Today, however, with the heightened interest in whole-language philosophy, educators are discovering the importance of creative communication at every level of schooling. In participatory storytelling, spontaneous drama, Readers' Theatre, pantomime, formal drama, and choral speaking, emphasis is on making meaning through language and getting pleasure from involvement with books and stories. This is the same emphasis that permeates whole-language theory.

Educators are also realizing the significance of creative oral activities in content-area studies, especially at the upper elementary level. Drama is a way to make history come alive. Storytelling and choral speaking can both introduce and culminate unit study across the curriculum. In using language in natural, creative ways during content-area study, children become more confident language users even as they develop their understanding of subject matter.

RELATED READINGS

Barton, Bob, and David Booth. *Stories in the Classroom*. Portsmouth, N.H.: Heinemann Educational Books, 1990.

Christie, James. "Dramatic Play: A Context for Meaningful Engagement." *The Reading Teacher*, 43 (April 1990), 542–545.

Cooper, Pamela, and Rives Collins. *Look What Happened to Frog: Storytelling in Education*. Scottsdale, Ariz.: Gorsuch Scarisbrick, 1991.

Cottrell, June. *Creative Drama in the Classroom: Grades 1–3*. Lincolnwood, Ill.: National Textbook, 1987.

———. *Creative Drama in the Classroom: Grades 4–6*. Lincolnwood, Ill: National Textbook, 1987.

Dunn, Sonja. *Crackers and Crumbs: Chants for Whole Language*. Portsmouth, N.H.: Heinemann Educational Books, 1990.

Glazer, Joan, and Linda Lamme. "Poem Picture Books and Their Uses in the Classroom." *The Reading Teacher*, 44 (October 1990), 102–109.

Heathcote, Dorothy. *Drama as Context*. Aberdeen: National Association for the Teaching of English, 1980.

———. "Drama as a Learning Medium." *Language Arts*, 65 (January 1988). This issue focuses on drama and learning.

Heinig, Ruth. *Improvisations with Favorite Tales: Integrating Drama into the Reading/Writing Classroom*. Portsmouth, N.H.: Heinemann Educational Books, 1992.

Manna, Anthony, ed. *Drama and Language*. Urbana, Ill.: National Council of Teachers of English, 1985.

Martinez, Miriam. "Motivating Dramatic Story Reenactments." *The Reading Teacher*, 46 (May 1993), 682–688.

McCaslin, Nellie. *Creative Drama in the Classroom*. 5th ed. White Plains, N.Y.: Longman, 1990.

Morgan, Norah, and Juliana Saxton. *Teaching Drama*. Portsmouth, N.H.: Heinemann Educational Books, 1987.

Pellowski, Anne. *The World of Storytelling*. Rev. Ed. Bronx, N.Y.: H. W. Wilson, 1990.

Tarlington, Carole, and Patrick Verriour. *Role Drama: A Teacher's Handbook*. Portsmouth, N.H.: Heinemann Educational Books, 1991.

CHAPTER 7

Functional Oral Communication

Conversing and Reporting

Reflecting Before Reading

BEFORE reading the chapter, read the title, the headings, and the end-of-chapter summary. Then answer the questions in the margin on this page.

How can the teacher involve children in functional oral communication?

in reporting?

What is important in the assessment of growth in speaking?

Presenting ideas in a clear way

Asking questions to get information

TEACHING IN ACTION   *An Idea Fair*

Mr. Bruce's sixth grade was gathered in the school cafeteria for the Idea Fair that culminated an integrated unit on Machines and Modern Society. Two youngsters were sitting behind each of four tables located in the far corners of the cafeteria. The others were gathered in four listening-reaction groups, each group sitting before an Idea Table.

Illustrated Reporting

At one table, a group was listening to Sylvia and Mike describe the contributions of the steam engine to modern society. As part of their presentation, the two stood up and demonstrated how steam can power a series of blades. They directed a jet of steam onto a pinwheel, which rotated on its axis. They also explained a diagram they had drawn showing how a steam engine works and explained the events leading to the first Atlantic steamboat crossing by referring to a time line posted above their Idea Table. During the presentation, members of the listening group asked questions, especially as the two presenters talked about their model engine.

As Sylvia and Mike described their work, other pairs of students informally presented illustrated reports at other tables. One pair described the contribution of the iron horse and the importance of the golden spike. Another talked about the horseless carriage and the importance of "snake oil" in making the automobile an integral part of modern society. Still another focused on the airplane. The topics came from a section of the social studies book they were using. The information came from a variety of references, including trade books and an encyclopedia. In each case, the presenters referred to diagrams, pictures, and/or models and encouraged "audience participation."

Revolving Groups

Refining oral reporting skills

When each team had reported to its listening group, the groups moved to the next Idea Table. Accordingly, those who had reacted to Sylvia and Mike's presentation on the steam engine moved to the iron horse Idea Table; those who had heard about the iron horse moved to the horseless-carriage table; and so on. This meant that each pair of reporters eventually had to repeat their presentations four times; it also meant that listeners felt freer about contributing questions and ideas, and speakers gradually refined their oral presentations.

Talking Informally Together

Refining skill in discussing

After the four groups had visited each Idea Table, the class convened as a "seminar" to make connections within the data. Guided by teacher questions, the students talked about the ways in which machines changed society, people's initial reaction to the changes, and the problems machines triggered. To facilitate the interchange of ideas, the teacher had prepared a discussion outline as in Figure 7.1. Youngsters recorded points on their outlines as volunteers recorded those points on a transparency displayed with an overhead projector.

Organizing for Talk

See page 225 for an explanation of Idea Fair.

Mr. Bruce's Idea Fair was a clear success, because the sixth-graders knew their topics well. They had begun by reading in their textbooks but had gone far beyond to search library sources for data to render visually and for anecdotes to

MACHINES AND MODERN SOCIETY	
A. Ways machines changed society	1. 2. 3.
B. People's initial reaction to changes	1. 2. 3.
C. Problems brought by machines	1. 2. 3.

Figure 7.1 A Discussion Outline

add interest. They had spent several language arts/social studies/art periods in preparation. Then, too, as the sixth-graders were ferreting out significant points, creating visuals, and organizing their ideas for sharing, Mr. Bruce had been working with them on basic communication and study skills. In their collaborative groups, he was teaching them how to select, organize, and connect ideas. He was helping them think about how to present their findings in a way that would encourage listener participation. In addition, Mr. Bruce had set up his class in a way that facilitated communication—as an Idea Fair that made presenting less stressful and also fostered the natural give-and-take that characterizes general conversation. In such a situation, young people—whether they were gifted, average, or slower in ability—could ask questions without feeling "ready to sink into the earth." They did not feel that they must "hold their tongues" but could actively join in.

Contexts for Speaking

Conversing

Discussing   Reporting

In this chapter, we will consider how to structure conversation and discussion so that students enjoy oral interaction. Then we will consider ways to help children acquire the basic study and presentational skills so important in oral reporting. Finally, we will look at the assessment of oral communication.

Learning to Converse: Speaking with Others

Michael Halliday (1975, 1977) explains that through interaction with people in their immediate environment, young children learn to use language for a variety of purposes and to communicate a variety of meanings. Children learn early to communicate that they want something. This is what Halliday calls the "I want," or the *instrumental*, function of language. Children also learn to use language to mean "do as I tell you." By using language in this way, children control the behavior of particular individuals in their environment; this is the second, or *regulatory*, function of language. Third, children learn to use language to mean "me and you"—an *interactional* function through which youngsters greet and name specific people and manage the social environment.

A fourth function of language, according to Halliday, is the *personal*; at times children use language to express their awareness of self and to express feelings. This is the "here I come" function. The fifth function of language is to mean "tell me why"; children begin to use language to ask all manner of questions about the world around them—the *heuristic* function. Then there is the *imaginative* function, or what Halliday calls the "let's pretend" function. Using this, children create a universe of their own—a universe that at first is just sound plays but ultimately develops into the make-believe of story and poem.

According to Halliday, by the time they are eighteen months old, children have learned to use language to express these six kinds of meanings. Only somewhat later do children begin to use language to serve another purpose: to mean "I've got something to tell you." Halliday writes that "the idea that language can be used as a means of communicating information to someone who does not already possess that information is a very sophisticated one which

Working in groups or pairs, children refine their conversational skills as they build understanding of the content areas. (© 1993 Elizabeth Crews)

depends on the internalization of a whole complex set of linguistic concepts that the young child does not possess." Although it emerges later than the other functions, the *informative* function is a dominant one in the adult's use of language.

It almost goes without saying that children in classrooms should be involved orally in using language to achieve the full range of language functions and in using language to reflect on all kinds of experiences, both direct and vicarious. Unfortunately, however, research indicates that relatively little time is allocated in many classrooms to the natural give-and-take of conversational discussions. A study by Joanna DeStephano, Harold Pepinsky, and Tobie Sanders (1982) indicates that much classroom interaction requires only one-word answers by children, that teachers do most of the explaining and talking, and that little actual dialoguing occurs, especially during group instruction in reading. David Dillon and Dennis Searle (1981) find a similar pattern in their study of oral interaction in a first grade. They note that the functions for which children use language in the classroom are restricted and in no way reflect the diverse functions for which children use language in the home environment. This restriction is serious, especially when we consider that it is through talking out and about that children learn to use language to reflect on experience. For this reason, teachers must consider how to make natural conversation an integral part of their classroom.

Read Kathleen Berry (1985) for a discussion of the importance of talking as part of subject matter learning. For a more comprehensive treatment, see *The Language of School Subjects*, ed. Bruce Gillham (Portsmouth, N.H.: Heinemann Educational Books, 1986).

THE FORUM   On Talk in Whole-Language Classrooms

1. Describing whole-language classrooms, Claire Staab writes, "In whole-language classrooms one can observe children talking. Whole-language teachers do not believe in the old adage, 'A silent classroom is an effective classroom.' This is not to say that whole-language teachers do not have times for quiet and that whole-language teachers have not established routines or classroom rules. It does imply, however, that whole-language teachers believe in the value of talk and structure their classroom activities so that talk can happen productively" ("Talk in Whole-Language Classrooms," in *Whole-Language: Practice and Theory*, ed. Victor Froese [Boston: Allyn and Bacon, 1991], 46).

2. Susan Hepler writes of the importance of talking our way to literacy: "In the past, talk in the classroom has frequently been regarded as 'cheating,' as 'not doing your own work,' or as one teacher put it, 'If your mouth is engaged, your brain is not.' But in the last decades, we have come to see how important talk is to thinking, to writing, and to developing a social structure in the classroom that supports learning" ("Talking Our Way to Literacy in the Classroom Community," *The New Advocate*, 4 [Summer 1991], 179–191).

3. Judith Wells Lindfors outlines three valuable aspects of talk. First, a child has a theory of the world in his or her head. Talk expands and changes the child's theory; it is a way of learning. Second, talk makes understanding more precise; the act of talking about something sharpens a child's understanding of it. Third, talk increases a child's ability to remember over time; a child is more likely to remember things he or she has talked about (*Children's Language and Learning*, 2nd ed. [Englewood Cliffs, N.J.: Prentice-Hall, 1987]).

Questions to Consider

How do you react to Staab's and Hepler's points about a quiet classroom? At what point must quiet prevail? What routines or rules governing talk in classrooms do you believe are imperative?

Conversational Discussion Skills: What Are They?

Conversational discussion skills are of several types. A first type relates to language use. The conversationalist is able to

- ✦ Select the appropriate words to communicate ideas clearly,
- ✦ Use sentence patterns to make his or her ideas easy to follow,
- ✦ Shift from formal to informal language patterns depending on the situation.

A second type relates to thinking patterns. The conversationalist is able to

- ✦ Follow the line of thought of previous speakers and comment and ask questions in terms of what has gone before,
- ✦ Put thoughts together in a logical and clear way,
- ✦ See the relationships between the major ideas being discussed and specific information he or she can contribute,
- ✦ Move the conversation forward by generalizing, summarizing, or hypothesizing.

A third type relates to interpersonal functioning. The conversationalist is able to

- ✦ Wait his or her turn to comment and refrain from monopolizing the conversation,
- ✦ Encourage others to comment or raise questions,
- ✦ Contribute with confidence and poise,
- ✦ Contribute courteously, with control over voice and body.

Conversational Discussion Skills: How Are They Taught?

To achieve these objectives, the teacher should schedule time during which children are encouraged to talk about themselves, report something exciting they did, tell about something they anticipate doing, describe their likes and dislikes, or describe things heard, seen, or read. Many teachers schedule chat times before vacation, after an important event such as the arrival of a new sibling or a new student, after viewing notable films or television programs, and as part of story reading and response.

Conversations occur in a number of places and contexts in classrooms. Some are spontaneous, as when children and teacher chat in the playground and share their feelings about a game just played or when youngsters talk informally as they return from a class outing. Some occur in the classroom when the teacher discovers a child who is bubbling with excitement about something seen, heard, or experienced. At times the teacher draws the child aside and chats with him or her. At other times the teacher gathers a group of youngsters around the excited one so that the child can tell everyone. On still other occasions, when many students have much to talk about, the teacher allows time for chatting mates to talk with one another. Some teachers have found it productive

Enjoy reading "Conversations as Contexts for Poems, Stories, Questions" by Pat Thomas-Mackinnon in *Language Arts*, 69 (December 1992), 588–603. Read Claude Goldenberg, "Instructional Conversations: Promoting Comprehension Through Discussion," *Language Arts*, 46 (December 1992/January 1993), 316–326, for ideas on planning instructional discussions.

to pair off children for conversation. Then, during conversation breaks, chatting mates get together to share. Some have found it productive to identify a corner of the room as a conversation center, where two or three youngsters (with or without the teacher) can gather for informal talk. The activities described on pages 153–154 in Chapter 5 are also useful for encouraging natural conversation.

Task Groups   Of course, classroom oral interaction can be more structured, at which point it warrants the use of the term *discussion*. Especially when a teacher has definite content objectives, he or she may divide a class into discussion groups and give each group a specific talk task. To help students focus on the task, the teacher may provide questions for group consideration. Kathleen Berry (1985) describes a discussion lesson in which students in groups considered economic factors surrounding the early fur trade in Canada using a series of task questions provided by the teacher. Categories of questions based on this lesson are given in Figure 7.2. These categories indicate the kinds of questions a teacher can give task groups so that they learn to communicate as they learn content.

Merging Groups   If group size is small, merging groups for summarizing purposes is feasible. For example, three youngsters who have come to a conclusion as to why the fur trade was so important in Canada and have formulated an opinion about the ethics of using animal skins for clothing merge with a second group. At this point, groups explain their conclusions and opinions and try to convince those in the merged group of the validity of their choices.

Read Donna Alvermann, "The Discussion Web: A Graphic Aid for Learning Across the Curriculum," *The Reading Teacher*, 45 (October 1991), 92–99, for a full description of this approach.

Donna Alvermann (1991) recommends a think-pair-share format for getting children to think about ideas and contribute to a discussion. In Alvermann's format, individuals think about what they want to say and then pair up to discuss their thoughts with a partner. Next, partners merge with another pair of students to work toward consensus. Finally the two sets of partners—a merged group—decide on the ideas to share during general class discussion, with a group spokesperson taking the lead. Given this discussion format, students have multiple opportunities to speak. Alvermann recommends the use of a discussion web (see Figure 7.3) as students work in both pairs and merged pairs and as they share ideas with the class.

Revolving Groups   Sometimes it is challenging to talk about a topic as a member of several groups. Moving into a different group, a youngster may rephrase his or her comments or propose an argument in a different way. At times he or she may restate an idea just presented by another person in a previous group. This activity encourages interaction and exchange of ideas.

Using Groups: Some Problems   Often new teachers shy away from using small groups in their classrooms. Youngsters chatting together independently, even if occupied with a stimulating task, can get noisy, and noise is taboo in some schools. How to control noise level is a significant concern because in turning off noise, teachers can turn off enthusiasm.

- **Definitional Questions**

  What does *exploration* mean? What does *discovery* mean?

- **Background Information Questions**

  Who were the people important in the fur trade? What methods did the fur traders use to get furs? What means did they have to trade their furs? How was the fur trade organized? Where and when in Canada was fur trading important?

- **Hypothetical Questions Requiring Projections and Guesses**

  Why was fur trading especially important in Canada? Do you think that fur trading would have been as important in the American Southwest as it was in Canada? Why? Why not? Why were furs important then? For what were they most likely used? Do you think furs were considered of more value then than they are today? Why? Why not? Why do you think people back then wore fur garments? Why do they wear them today?

- **Relational Questions**

  What is the relationship between the price of furs and the cost of production? What is the relationship between the price of furs and people's desire for them? At what point would you say that prices are too high? What examples from your own life can you relate to the pricing of goods?

- **Ethical Questions**

  Is it morally right to kill animals for their skins to use in making clothing? Why? Why not? Do you think that it was "more right" to do that back in early Canadian days than it is today? Do you think that it is "more right" to do it today? Why? Why not?

Figure 7.2   Kinds of Questions to Encourage In-depth Discussion

Some preliminary attention must be given to noise control. In small-group interaction, one must keep the voice at a moderate level and refrain from speaking when someone else is talking. Before a class breaks into groups, the teacher must set guidelines and indicate ways he or she will ask for the groups' attention when circumstances warrant it. When several groups are to function at the same time, it may help to move into a larger facility, such as the cafeteria or gymnasium, that can better accommodate the sounds of group interaction.

Courteous Communication: The Teacher as Model

Courtesy to others is important in oral interaction. It is also difficult to teach. Displaying a chart with items like "Remember to say thank you," "Do not interrupt a speaker," "Be thoughtful of others," and/or "Wait your turn" results in few

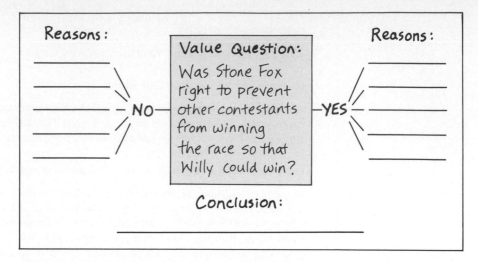

Figure 7.3 A Discussion Web for Critical Thinking
SOURCE: After Alvermann, 1991.

behavioral changes, since behavior is bound up in one's concept of self and one's value system. How, then, does one teach the conventions of courteous communication?

One beginning is for the teacher to serve as a model of courteous communication. As Lorraine Wilkening, a remarkable kindergarten teacher, chats with pupils and guides their interaction, she makes a point of being courteous. When she must stop in midconversation to handle an office communication, she halts with, "Excuse me, please, for just a moment." After youngsters sing a song to her delight, she remarks, "Thank you very much." When she sees that one child does not have space, she thoughtfully suggests, "Tracy doesn't have enough room. Let's all move down to give her room."

More directly, she explains the purposes of social conventions as the need arises, as it often does in kindergarten. "It really is not fair to tell the answers when it isn't your turn. It means that you get more than one turn." Later she comments, "It was good that we all gave Steve a chance to answer. Thank you, class." Through constant reliance on polite forms of communication, Ms. Wilkening is making courtesy an integral part of her classroom environment and controlling discipline at the same time. And her method works. In return, her students pepper their conversation with "thank you," "excuse me," and "you're welcome," modeling their talk and behavior after a teacher whom they respect and who respects them.

Modeling their behavior after the teacher's, youngsters can learn to handle the ordinary social amenities. Many teachers normally take the time to introduce a person dropping in to visit the classroom by saying simply, "Boys and girls, I would like to introduce Mrs. Lovel to you. She is Marcia's mother and has come to enjoy the things we are doing." The children respond with a "Good morning" or "Good afternoon." Upon leaving, the visitor contributes a "Good-bye" and student respond in turn. Once the protocol for introductions has been established through situations like this, children can do the introductions. When a parent drops by, the child can introduce him or her.

Whenever a group is engaged in a presentation, social amenities are part of it, too. One student serves as the announcer, introducing other participants and closing the session with a thank-you. The announcer also begins appropriate applause to end each selection. By the same token, when a speaker visits the class, one student should serve as host and announcer. The host first chats with the speaker to find out some interesting fact to include in the introduction; he or she then introduces the speaker and expresses a thank-you at the end.

BUILDING AND REFINING YOUR TEACHING SKILLS

+ Observe a master teacher as he or she interacts with children. Consider: How does this teacher encourage children to contribute ideas? How does he or she maintain an atmosphere of courteous communication in which children wait their turns and do not interrupt one another?
+ Design a task sheet that could serve as a discussion outline for a small group in upper grades. Use content from the social studies as the basis for your guide.

Learning to Report: Speaking in Front of Others

Conversing is only one dimension of speaking. A second dimension is presenting, or reporting. Children need considerable assistance if they are to learn to present their ideas in front of others in a clear and interesting way, especially when those ideas are based on data that reporters must gather systematically. They need help in (1) defining their purposes as they prepare to report, (2) taking notes to use when they report, (3) organizing and connecting their information, (4) using visuals as part of a presentation, (5) using their voices, their bodies, and space effectively, and (6) reporting in a variety of settings. In this section, we will consider ways to help children acquire these skills, keeping in mind that some of these skills are equally important in developing a written report and that oral reporting can lead naturally into written reporting.

Defining Purposes

Before gathering information for presenting to others, youngsters must have their purposes clearly in mind; they must know the kind of information they need and the type of forum in which they will present it. To this end, teacher and students should discuss the whys, and wherefores, and whats of data gathering before beginning. Without such a preliminary discussion, children are likely to gather all sorts of irrelevant and uninteresting data.

For example, before children build a database on a topic, the teacher should prompt discussion by asking, "What is the main question we want to answer? What are related questions? What information is related to these questions? What information will appeal to our audience?" Children limit their investigation to one main area and devise a series of specific questions to guide their search so that they do not stray from the point.

To teach children to define their purposes, as a culmination of a unit on the Period of Exploration, a teacher may model the process by asking a question such as "Who was the greatest explorer of this period?" In preparation, students discuss their task: to select someone they believe was the greatest explorer and then convince others of the validity of their choice. They identify the kinds of facts they will need to make their choice and then support it—probably a description of what the explorer did and when he did it.

Teachers can develop problems such as this that correlate with unit study in the content areas. In this way, young people learn to gather and share information as a natural part of subject matter investigations. All areas—from art to zoology—are contexts for building information-gathering skills. There are so many opportunities for information gathering within ongoing curriculum activities that there is no need to create topics simply for the purpose of providing experience in gathering information.

Taking Notes to Use in Reporting

To function efficiently as reporters, young researchers must be able to take notes, or to compile a database on a topic. There is no one best approach to note taking. The best way is the way that meets the needs of the situation. Here are some note-taking approaches students can try.

Note Cards   A note card is a simple approach that can be used even by relatively young children. For example, children who will report on a planet within the solar system as part of a study of astronomy can divide a note card into two sections. In the first section, the children list basic information about the planet they have chosen; in the second, they tell why they believe there is or is not life on that planet.

Students can use note cards in a variety of contexts, including interviewing, firsthand observations, and library investigations. For example, students going on a nature walk can carry along a card. During a preliminary talk session, they prestructure their note cards by writing "Observation One" on one side of the card and "Observation Two" on the other side. At the investigation site, each child records his or her observations on a note card. Children can do the same for recording data from a science experiment on which they will later report to the class.

At first, investigative note cards of this kind emerge from preparatory discussions about the purposes of the research activity so that students see the relationship between their purposes and the design of their cards. Eventually, students design their own cards for recording.

Data Webs, or Maps   A second approach to note taking is the data web, or map—a network of interrelated words and phrases connected to a central topic hub and to one another that highlights interrelationships among the data. Children who have used data webs to record their knowledge of a topic before and during listening as described in Chapter 5 can design similar webs to record and display data for reporting. Youngsters generally need step-by-step instruction in setting up a web for data collection. The teacher should model the thought processes for designing a web. He or she might say:

After Bess Stimson, "Thinking Logically," a paper given March 1989, Association for Supervision and Curriculum Development, Orlando, Florida.

> If I were getting ready to collect data for an oral report on Native Americans in North America, I would probably start by identifying the particular tribes I wanted to investigate. It's good to narrow a topic to something manageable. Also, by selecting particular tribes, I can zero in on information that would interest a group to whom I was going to report. I would then make up some questions that I could ask about each tribe: Where did these people live? What were their houses like? What kind of clothing did they wear? What were their primary occupations? What customs were uniquely theirs?
>
> In preparing to take notes, I would put my topic in the center of a data web. I would write the names of the tribes I had selected on lines connected to the central topic. Then I would write words related to the questions I wanted to answer on lines connecting with the tribal names. As I read in reference books, I would write answers directly on my web. When I report my data to others, I would use entries in my web as notes and refer to them as I spoke. I would even use my web later on as notes if I wrote a report on the topic.
>
> Now let's make a data web for collecting data about holidays we celebrate. Let's model this web after mine. What topic would you place at the center? What kind of information would you want to collect and report about each holiday? What items would you place on lines extending from the center?

Computer hint: Students can compile their data charts on desktop computers equipped with a simple database or word processing program. They can also get information from computer databases. See Robert Rickelman, et al., "Electronic Encyclopedias on Compact Disc," *The Reading Teacher*, 44 (February 1991), 432–434, for a description of *Compton's Multimedia Encyclopedia*.

One advantage of a data web such as this is that it is relatively easy to make comparisons once the database has been compiled. Students can be encouraged at the end of a report to tell ways in which items are similar or different and to generalize about the topic they have investigated. See Figure 7.4 for a sample web.

Data Charts   A difficult task for upper-graders is taking notes on a topic from several references. One way to approach this task is to use a data synthesis chart as in Figure 7.5. Before gathering information on a topic, youngsters, guided by the teacher, brainstorm questions that are basically subtopics of their main problem, much the way they devised questions about their topic in designing a data web. For example, in preparing to investigate endangered species, some

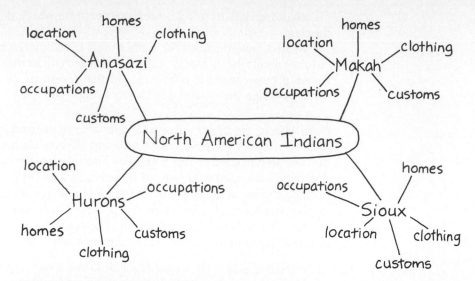

Figure 7.4 A Data Web for Note Taking

sixth-grade science students posed four questions: What is an endangered species? What are some species that are endangered today? Where are these species found? Why are they endangered? These questions became labels that headed columns on a data chart. In the left-hand column, students listed references they would check. They completed the chart by consulting each reference on each question and placing their data in the appropriate rows and columns. They learned that once they had found an answer in one reference and recorded it in their chart, it was not necessary to write the same information when found in another reference.

In reporting on their findings, students integrate information from one or more references and/or computer databases and report conflicting data provided by the different sources. As with data webs, students can use their charts as notes during oral reporting, speaking informally from their charts or displaying them with an overhead projector as they speak. Later they can convert their data charts into writing guides. The directions at the bottom of Figure 7.5 show how to expand a note-taking and oral reporting guide into a writing guide. The directions demonstrate that the tasks performed in oral and written reporting overlap and thus should be taught together.

Outlines Although many youngsters—as well as adults—have trouble taking notes in formal outline form, some attention should be given to outlining because this skill is generally required in high school. Also, outlining helps youngsters to make connections within a set of data.

A teacher can use the same strategy for introducing outlining as that used to introduce webbing and charting. Students brainstorm topics or questions to be answered through an investigation. These questions or topics become first-level headings in a data-collection outline. Students add information beneath

DATA CHART ON ENDANGERED SPECIES

	What we want to know:	What is the Definition of Endangered Species?	What Are Some Endangered Species Today?	Where Are These Species Found?	Why Are Some Species Endangered?
References Used	What our science text says:				
	What our encyclopedia says:				
	What a trade book (name: _____) says:				

WRITING FOLLOW-UP: Write four paragraphs. In each paragraph include points from more than one reference.

Paragraph 1: Explain the meaning of *endangered species.*
Paragraph 2: Describe some endangered species of today.
Paragraph 3: Explain some locations in which endangered species are found today.
Paragraph 4: Explain why some species are endangered.

Figure 7.5   A Data Synthesis Chart

James Hoffman (1992) proposes additions to the data synthesis chart shown in Figure 7.5: a second row labeled "What We Know," in which students answer their questions based on what they know before they read, a final summary row in which students sum up data from all the references, and another column labeled "Other Interesting Facts."

the main headings as they read. In this respect, the outline becomes a reading guide. Figure 7.6 is an example of a data collection outline. Figure 7.7 shows a data chart with the same kinds of headings. Note that in each case, students generalize and conclude based on their findings.

Jotting Books   For informal reporting, students may keep cumulative Jotting Books—small, bound Idea Books in which they record notes on classroom activities, readings, and interviews. In addition, students jot down miscellaneous thoughts for sharing—an observation made on the way to school, a fact heard on TV, or a joke or poem—all thoughts "too great to be forgotten." Jotting Books can be made by stapling oak tag covers to several sheets of paper.

By recording in Jotting Books, young people discover how helpful it is to note important thoughts before those ideas escape the mind. Students can also learn how to subdivide the Jotting Book into sections, recording different kinds of thoughts in different sections. Jotting books have "carry-along capacity": Books can be carried to assembly programs and class outings.

Students can use their Jotting Books to record details about school events and become Town Criers, announcing findings to the rest of the class. They can use their Jotting Books to record the progress of a classroom pet, the weather, the results of a science experiment, or their thoughts while reading. Talking from their notes rather than reading word for word, students orally report their findings. Similarly, students jot down details from television or radio news reports and share what they have learned during a Reports-on-the-State-of-the-World Time. Data collected in Jotting Books can be used for writing as well as for oral sharing.

Organizing and Connecting Information

If oral reports are to communicate more than a series of related facts, children need to develop skill in organizing and connecting their data for presenting to others (Spivey, 1991). If students have selected their data systematically using note cards, webs, charts, and outlines, they probably have already developed an organization, or design for reporting. The framework they have used to collect data is the framework they will use to present it. As suggested in the previous sections, students can be encouraged to speak informally from their cards, webs,

ANIMALS WE WANT TO MEET

I. Koala

    A. Where the koala lives

        1. Kind of habitat

        2. Countries

    B. What it looks like (physical characteristics)

    C. What it does (behavioral characteristics)

II. Panda

    A. Where the panda lives

        1. Kind of habitat

        2. Countries

    B. What it looks like (physical characteristics)

    C. What it does (behavioral characteristics)

III. Kodiak bear

    A. Where the Kodiak bear lives

        1. Kind of habitat

        2. Countries

    B. What it looks like (physical characteristics)

    C. What it does (behavioral characteristics)

Connecting: How are these animals similar? How are they different?

Figure 7.6 An Outline for Selecting, Organizing, and Connecting Data
NOTE: Create outlines for note taking by brainstorming and organizing points cooperatively.

CHART FOR REPORTING ON CULTURE GROUPS

Organizing: Complete our chart by reading in at least two reference books from the Reading Nook.

What we want to know:	Kind of Home in Which They Live	Kind of Clothing They Wear	Kinds of Food They Eat	Where They Live	Climate of the Area
The Laplanders					
The Masai					
The Thais					

Making connections: How does the climate of the region where the group lives affect the kinds of homes, clothing, and food they use?

Writing:

Paragraph 1
Describe the Laplanders and how they live.

Paragraph 2
Describe the Masai and how they live.

Paragraph 3
Describe the Thais and how they live.

Paragraph 4
Explain the relationship between climate and food, homes, and clothing of a people.
Use examples from your data chart.

Figure 7.7   Data Synthesis Chart for Reporting

NOTE: Teachers should not provide the data synthesis chart; rather, teacher and children cooperatively create the chart through brainstorming and talking aloud together.

charts, and outlines. They can print completed data-gathering devices on charts or chalkboard or make overhead transparencies of their charts and webs to project as they present.

As children prepare to report, however, they may need help in identifying more fundamental relationships within their data. The teacher may have to encourage students to ask these questions:

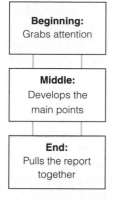

Beginning:
Grabs attention

Middle:
Develops the main points

End:
Pulls the report together

◆ Which facts and ideas are the main ones? Which are the subordinate ones? Which facts and ideas should we emphasize? Which ones should we not present? (See Chapter 5 for a discussion of main and subordinate ideas.)
◆ Which points should we present first? Last?
◆ Which points should we present together?
◆ How can we sum up at the end? (See Chapter 5 for a discussion of how to make a summary.)

Children also may need some help in organizing their reports so that there is an introduction that grabs attention, a middle that develops the major points, and an ending that pulls the report together. To help students see the importance of this kind of organization for reporting, the teacher can model the

Talking about their social studies projects, children develop their ability to present their ideas to others. (© 1993 Jean-Claude Lejeune)

process of speechmaking, presenting a speech, and having students analyze how the teacher began and how he or she ended.

Using Visuals in Reporting

Visuals such as time lines, homemade maps, globes, flowcharts, graphs, tables, and actual objects add interest to a presentation. The teacher who presents a model speech to the class should model how to use visuals to highlight ideas. He or she should also help children make and choose visuals as they prepare to report.

Teaching for Visual Literacy   As students prepare to report, the teacher should circulate among groups and encourage them to think in visual terms about the facts and ideas they have collected for presentation. In some instances, students can make large charts to display and refer to during sharing or use a computer to create graphic displays. In other instances, they can draw and print their visuals on strips of paper to display progressively on a flannelboard or the chalkboard. Or they can draw their visuals on acetate to display with an overhead projector. In a similar way, they can use an opaque projector to project flat maps, charts, and graphs during their reports. Through this kind of activity, young people are learning the importance of visuals in forceful communication; at the same time, they are becoming visually literate.

Using Realia in Reporting   An object, model, and/or picture can aid in communicating a message. These kinds of presentations lend themselves to the use of firsthand materials:

Read Rita Roth, "Practical Use of Language in School," *Language Arts*, 63 (February 1986), 134–142, for an excellent discussion of show-and-tell.

✦ *Show-and-tell.* Primary children bring in an object to tell about as they show. Generally, youngsters are eager to participate in this kind of sharing, which can be included as part of a Daily Reporting Time. On other occasions, schedule an I Was There Time: Children report on things that they have observed or that have happened to them.

✦ *Demonstrate and elaborate.* According to Dorothy Nelson (1976), the traditional show-and-tell of primary grades can become a more sophisticated enterprise called "D. and E." (Demonstrate-and-elaborate), which is applicable through junior high school. Emphasis is on demonstrating rather than on displaying, with young people electing to demonstrate activities such as how to hold a ski pole and turn on skis, how to hold a ping-pong paddle, how to do magic tricks. Some children bring in photographs they or their parents have taken, food samples they have prepared, or musical instruments they play. Others bring in games, marionettes, or lucky coins to tell about.

✦ *Explaining how it works.* A specific D. and E. task is to find out how a particular object is made or how it functions and to explain the process using an actual part to demonstrate. Objects to explain include a light bulb, automobile piston, bottle opener, jack, faucet, or lid remover.

✦ *The world in our hands.* A globe that can be removed from its cradle is a fine visual for sharing geographical information. As children explain, they hold the "world in their hands," pointing to specific locations. Commercial wall maps can be used in a similar fashion.

✦ *Picturing it.* In describing social and natural phenomena, a picture is often worth a thousand words. Ask young children to share pictures as they talk about unusual plants and animals, occupations, people of different lands, and geographical features. Speakers hold up pictures from encyclopedias, atlases, and magazines such as *National Geographic*, or they distribute sketches they have made as in Figure 7.8. Invite youngsters preparing for informational sharing to search the school's filmstrip collection for possible strips to show. Rather than your selecting and showing the filmstrip, encourage students to take the initiative.

Figure 7.8   Children's Art: A Means of Recording and Sharing Data
SOURCE: Courtesy of Ndungu Muthegu, age 11, Nairobi, Kenya.

Using Voice, Body, and Space Effectively

A speaker may have gathered considerable data, organized those data in a logical or even creative way, and prepared numerous visuals to share, but if that speaker does not use his or her voice, body, and space effectively, the result can be a deadly boring presentation.

Activities to develop vocal expressiveness: (1) Recite the dictionary with great feeling; (2) recite the sports page as though you were a sports reporter; (3) deliver the spelling words as though you were a gossip reporter on TV.

Using the Voice Effectively The voice plays a major role in holding listeners' attention. Good speakers change the speed of their voices, vary loudness, pitch their voices attractively, and avoid mannerisms that may affect listeners negatively.

Young people need to experiment with variations in speed, pitch, loudness, and tone. Probably the best way to experiment is to record an oral report on tape. This technique is especially good if the presentation is a team endeavor, for group members can listen to themselves in playback, assessing their vocal expression, the overall organization and clarity of their presentation, and their general knowledge of the topic.

Using the Body Effectively Effective communication is as dependent on dynamic use of the body as it is on dynamic use of the voice. The use of visuals is one way to encourage gesturing and movement of the body in oral reporting. The student who uses a time line to show relationships will point to each entry on the line as he or she talks; the student who works from a map will point to locations on it. Pointing, moving toward, and holding up are all nonverbal communication devices necessary when using a visual. These gestures add action and force to a presentation.

If the school or community owns a camcorder, it can be used to videotape presentations for eventual self-study. Each student views his or her contribution to a program and evaluates it in terms of such questions as: Did I make eye contact with my audience? Did I gesture automatically? Did I change my facial expressions as required? In viewing a videotape, young people often can spot their own problems and without prompting improve on them during future reporting sessions.

Using Space as Part of the Message Arranging a classroom to facilitate communication invites forceful student presentations. This means that a presenter need not share by standing alone in front of the class; rather he or she selects a comfortable position that fits the message. Perching on a high stool, sitting on a swivel chair, standing next to a projector are possible positions. Listeners may sit in groups or in a circle, on the floor or in chairs as the situation requires.

Reporting in a Variety of Settings

Major formats for reporting include the small feedback group, the panel, and the individual report. By functioning in a variety of settings in a relaxed classroom environment, children anticipate sharing rather than fear it and gain poise in reporting to others.

The Small Feedback Group   Too often teachers think of oral reporting as a whole-class activity in which one or two youngsters speak to the class. This setting, however, may be the least productive. A much more productive setting is a small feedback group in which listeners can more easily ask questions.

One way to organize the class for reporting is the Idea Fair described earlier in this chapter. Here one or two reporters share with a group of between four and ten students. In this organizational pattern, several reporters function simultaneously and must repeat their presentations as listening groups revolve through the Idea Fair. A variation of the Idea Fair is to have a team of reporters set up in a corner of the classroom. As two or three students complete an assignment, they visit the Idea Corner to listen to the team describe its findings. Eventually all students hear the presentation.

Three advantages accrue from this organizational pattern:

+ Students must repeat their reports, and in so doing they refine their presentations.
+ Listeners in small groups are more willing to render verbal feedback. Similarly, reporters are more at ease when presenting to smaller groups.
+ Because each group may have heard a slightly different presentation, the whole-class discussion that follows revolving-group reports is more likely to serve a summarizing function.

The panel presentation format works especially well in content-area studies.

The Panel Presentation   During a panel presentation, each reporter presents information on one aspect of a larger topic. In some instances, after reporting, panelists discuss points developed during the reporting phase, and listeners pose questions and offer opinions.

One advantage of the investigative-reporting-team approach is that young people must work together to select information and organize their reports. Through cooperating, they acquire small-group interaction as well as search skills. A second advantage is that several students investigating a topic must subdivide it into smaller segments so that each member can focus his or her attention on one segment. In so doing, young people learn to identify manageable subdivisions. Third, students have an opportunity to try out on their classmates, ideas about content and ways of presenting that content visually. Others supply feedback, so that final presentations are forceful and interesting. Fourth, students presenting as part of a panel support one another; no one has the feeling of standing alone.

Younger students serving on a panel can share books they have read. Each panelist simply retells an episode, and the audience contributes questions. Similarly, younger students can sit as a panel to share their impressions of a common experience—an exciting event witnessed, a TV program viewed, a trip taken together. At first, a teacher moderates panel presentations in primary classes so that children develop an understanding of the moderator's role in introducing the topic and the panelists, calling on questioners, and thanking panelists.

Shortly, students assume the role of moderator, modeling their activity after the teacher's.

Topics for reporting include "Personalities in the News," "It Happened 100 (50, 25, 10) Years Ago Today," "Election Update," "And the Winner Was!", "Personalities from the Past," "I Met ____ !", "I Visited ____ !", "Now My Opinion Is ____," "A Discovery That Changed the World," "An Event That Changed History."

The Individual Report As a format for sharing, the individual report has wide applicability at all grade levels. One form of reporting is the announcement, in which a child very briefly, and with little preparation, tells about a coming event. At the opposite end of the continuum is the investigative report, in which a student shares information acquired through considerable study. Show-and-Tell and Demonstrate-and-Elaborate, described previously, are other forms of individual reporting, as is the monologue, in which a youngster assumes the identity of a personality of the past, the present, or fiction and explains happenings from that person's point of view. Children doing monologues may don simple costumes to get a feel for the people whose identity they are assuming. For example, a pair of glasses pulled down on the nose can turn a reporter into a Benjamin Franklin who shares his thoughts on the Revolutionary War. An old oil lamp held in hand transforms another monologist into a Florence Nightingale who tells of the Crimean War.

✎ *BUILDING AND REFINING YOUR TEACHING SKILLS*

✦ Devise a format for reporting that would be successful in primary classrooms. Then design a variation that would be workable in intermediate classrooms. If possible, test your formats with students.

✦ Experiment with making transparencies to use with an overhead projector. Find an easy way for students to use transparencies as visuals during panel presentations or individual reporting.

Assessing Growth in Oral Communication

Oral communication skills are among the most important skills to be developed through language arts programs. Youngsters who can define the purposes of their investigations and take notes in a functional way have acquired lifelong learning skills. Similarly, youngsters who can report on and converse about their ideas have acquired the ability to influence others. For these reasons, there is need for continuing assessment of children's growth in these areas.

Guidelines for Building an Assessment Program

In assessing children's growth in oral communication, teachers should design evaluation programs with three major characteristics:

1. Children should be involved in the assessment. They should apply clearly stated criteria to their own activities and later discuss their self-assessments with the teacher.
2. Fear of failure should be minimized. A teacher should put youngsters at ease by establishing an informal, nonevaluative atmosphere. External evaluation should be avoided. Asking listeners to criticize a presentation takes the pleasure out of reporting and introduces fear. Keeping a marking book open and writing down a grade at the close of a report adds uneasiness. Self-analysis should take the place of external evaluation.
3. Assessment should be in terms of a number of behaviors. Teachers can identify specific learnings to be acquired and help children assess themselves in reference to those learnings. In this way, youngsters can identify strengths as well as weaknesses.

Using Performance Checklists to Assess Growth

Performance checklists are lists of basic learnings to be acquired. Because learnings are stated rather precisely as observable behaviors, they make self-analysis a relatively easy process. For example, a learning that might appear on a performance checklist of oral language skills is "I comment in terms of what others have said."

In assessing their progress in reference to such a statement, students may use categories such as Very Often, Often, Sometimes, Never; or Very Easy Task for Me, Easy Task for Me, Hard Task for Me. For each learning, the self-evaluator checks the appropriate category. Or students may rank order a number of learnings from one requiring the most improvement to one requiring the least. This forces youngsters who tend to evaluate themselves positively in all areas of their performance to identify areas that need work.

Figure 7.9 provides a checklist for upper elementary students and summarizes the learnings in this chapter. Of course, a teacher must modify the list to meet the needs of his or her students and the curriculum. Students who complete a series of checklists over time can keep them in their showcase portfolios along with work products that indicate growth. At the end of a marking period, teacher and student talk about the checklists and work products and set goals for the coming months.

.........A Summary Thought or Two

FUNCTIONAL ORAL COMMUNICATION

The major theme of this chapter is that conversational and oral reporting activities should be a part of the elementary curriculum. Through activities that encourage youngsters to express their ideas orally, students refine their ability to contribute to

A SELF-EVALUATION CHECKLIST FOR ORAL COMMUNICATION

Specific Learnings	The Rating Scale		
	Always	Some-times	Never
A. SPEAKING WITH OTHERS			
1. I speak clearly when I converse.			
2. I use appropriate words to communicate my ideas.			
3. I comment in terms of what others have said.			
4. I contribute ideas that interest others.			
5. I wait my turn and do not interrupt.			
6. I do not monopolize the discussion.			
7. I contribute with confidence.			
8. I am courteous in speaking with others.			
B. SPEAKING IN FRONT OF OTHERS			
1. I know my topic.			
2. I keep my points on the topic.			
3. I make notes in preparation that help me when I present.			
4. I organize my speech with a beginning, a middle, and an end.			
5. I sum up the main idea at the end.			
6. I speak clearly when I report.			
7. I make eye contact with my listeners.			
8. I gesture and move smoothly.			
9. I use visuals effectively.			

WHAT I CAN DO TO BECOME A BETTER SPEAKER:

Name of student _____   Date of self-evaluation _____

Date of teacher/student conference _____

Figure 7.9 A Self-Evaluation Checklist for Assessing Oral Communication

the give-and-take of conversational discussions and to report ideas to others. They learn to use both body and voice to heighten the impact of a message and to share their knowledge in diverse settings.

Simultaneously, students should be taught how to prepare ideas for sharing; to make both discussions and reports worthwhile, speakers must know what they are talking about. These skills include defining the purposes of an investigation; taking notes from references; organizing and connecting information; using visuals in reporting; and using voice, body, and space effectively.

The skills important in selecting and organizing ideas for oral reporting are equally significant in preparing ideas for written reporting. These skills, however, have been described here as components of oral rather than written reporting because of the fundamental nature of oral communication and because oral reporting can lead to writing. Far too often, teachers reverse the natural oral-to-written language sequence; they ask students to research a topic, write a paper on that topic, and then give an oral report on it. What may happen as a result is that students read their written reports aloud. In so doing, they have little or no opportunity to develop oral presentation skills. On the other hand, if report writing follows oral reporting or discussion, the preliminary speaking can help students crystallize their thinking and make written reporting easier in the long run. At the same time, students learn to speak from notes rather than simply to read aloud.

A second theme of the chapter is that conversational and presentational skills can be developed through content-area study. Children must talk about something. This "something" can be meaningful ideas from science, social studies, health, music, art, or mathematics.

RELATED READINGS

Adams, Dennis, and Mary Hamm. *Cooperative Learning: Critical Thinking and Collaboration Across the Curriculum*. Springfield, Ill.: Charles C. Thomas, 1990.

Atwell, Nancie. *Coming to Know: Writing to Learn in the Intermediate Grades*. Portsmouth, N.H.: Heinemann Educational Books, 1989.

Booth, David, and Carol Thornley-Hall, eds. *The Talk Curriculum*. Portsmouth, N.H.: Heinemann Educational Books, 1992.

Cazden, Courtney. *Classroom Discourse: The Language of Teaching and Learning*. Portsmouth, N.H.: Heinemann Educational Books, 1988.

Clay, Marie, et al. *Record of Oral Language and Biks and Gutches*. Portsmouth, N.H.: Heinemann Educational Books, 1983.

Cudd, Evelyn. "Research and Report Writing in the Elementary Grades." *The Reading Teacher*, 43 (December 1989), 268–269.

Dalton, Joan. *Creative Thinking and Co-operative Talk in Small Groups*. Portsmouth, N.H.: Heinemann Educational Books, 1992.

Dudley-Marling, Curtis, and Dennis Searle. *When Students Have Time to Talk: Creating Contexts for Learning Language*. Portsmouth, N.H.: Heinemann Educational Books, 1991.

Dwyer, John. *"A Sea of Talk."* Portsmouth, N.H.: Heinemann Educational Books, 1991.

Genishi, Celia, Andrea McCarrier, and Nancy Nussbaum. "Research Currents: Dialogue as a Context for Teaching and Learning." *Language Arts*, 65 (February 1988), 182–191.

Klein, Marvin. *Talk in the Language Arts Classroom*. Urbana, Ill.: National Council of Teachers of English, 1977.

Newkirk, Thomas, and Patricia McLure. *Listening In: Children Talk about Books and Other Things*. Portsmouth, N.H.: Heinemann Educational Books, 1992.

Phelan, Patricia, ed. *Talking to Learn: Classroom Practices in Teaching English*. Urbana, Ill.: National Council of Teachers of English, 1989.

Shuy, Rogers. "Research Currents: Dialogue as the Heart of Learning." *Language Arts*, 64 (December 1987), 890–891.

CHAPTER 8

From Experiencing to Critical Thinking

Reflecting, Writing, and Reading Together

Reflecting Before Reading

BEFORE reading the chapter, read the title, the headings, and the end-of-chapter summary. Then answer the questions in the margin on this page.

Why are experiencing with all the senses and brainstorming important as a base for reflecting, writing, and reading?

_____

_____

What is critical thinking?

_____

How does the teacher teach for critical thinking?

_____

_____

This lesson exemplifies what is known as LEA, the Language Experience Approach. The theory behind LEA is that experience is the best foundation for language development and what children have written (or dictated) is the best material for them to use in learning to read.

TEACHING IN ACTION   Billy Goat: A Language Experience

Karen Donovan's first-graders were learning about farms. As part of an integrated language arts, science, and social studies unit, the class visited a farm. Spying cows, pigs, horses, and goats, the first-graders stopped to talk about the animals. The teacher asked, "What is this animal doing? What words can we use to describe it? What do we like about it?" Pointing and responding, the children exclaimed, "Look at the goat. It's on the roof of the house!" "Look at the chickens. They are fighting!"

Excitement ran high on the bus as the children returned to their city school. Without prompting, the first-graders talked about things they had seen, gave their opinions, and described animals they liked. There was much talk, starting with "Did you see?" as the children asked others if they had noticed this or that.

Experience Charting, Reading, and Rereading

Back in the classroom, Ms. Donovan clustered her first-graders around the recording easel, on which she had mounted a piece of chart paper. "Let's write about the animals we liked best. We'll start by listing the animals we like and the reasons why we liked them."

As the youngsters proposed animal names and reasons for their choices, the teacher recorded their responses as a two-column table on the chart paper.

Next, she asked Chen-li to select the animal he liked best. He chose "The Brown and Black Horse." Other children who also chose the horse raised their hands. The youngsters did this for each animal, in the process registering their preferences for the best-liked animal. The winner was Billy Goat. Most of the children had been fascinated by the way Billy sat on the roof of his house. Furthermore, this was the first time many of these urban youngsters had seen a goat "in the flesh."

Before composing, the children talked about the goat; most contributed an idea to the brief discussion. Then six children volunteered their reasons for choosing Billy. Each child dictated a sentence about the goat, as the teacher recorded it on the chart paper:

> # Billy
>
> The billy goat is cute. He has a long beard. His legs are long and skinny. He has a big belly. He looks funny sitting on the roof of his house. He might get hurt if the roof didn't have those bumps.

When Ms. Donovan had printed the experience-story chart, she read it to the children and asked them for a title that would sum it up. They volunteered suggestions, which she listed; then they gave reasons to support the titles they liked best. After much reflection and discussion, the youngsters chose "Billy."

The teacher encouraged the children to reread the story. The youngsters came to the easel to read aloud each sentence, indicating the left-to-right progression by moving their hand under the words. Almost all the children had a chance to read the chart.

Writing and Dictating Individually

The next day, as the children worked independently, Ms. Donovan and an aide worked with individual children, talking and writing about other animals they had seen. For example, Chen-li, a gifted child who was hesitant about writing down his ideas because his native language was not English, dictated lines about his favorite horse. The aide recorded them on lined paper pasted on one side of a large piece of construction paper, helping him when he ran into trouble finding the English word to express what he wanted to say. Chen-li read his own words back to the aide, again finger pointing the words. Later Chen-li drew the

Expressing an opinion supported with reasons—simple critical thinking

Arriving at group consensus through active listening and voting

Summarizing a judgment

Titling a composition based on the main idea

Making sense of dictated words—reading with meaning

Composing original ideas for writing; recording ideas on paper

Read Sheri Coate and Marrietta Castle, "Integrating LEA and Invented Spelling in Kindergarten," *The Reading Teacher*, 42 (March 1989), 516–519.

See Russell Stauffer, *The Language-Experience Approach to the Teaching of Reading* (New York: Harper & Row, 1980).

brown-and-black horse and read his story to his classmates, who received his offering with applause.

Meanwhile, on their own, other youngsters wrote about their favorite animals, giving reasons for their choices. In writing, these students used invented spelling—a combination of print, numbers, and pictures to get their ideas onto paper. They had been told not to worry about spelling of words but just to get an idea down so that they could share it later. The teacher also conferred with these youngsters, encouraging them to reflect more critically on why they liked the animals chosen for writing.

When each child had completed a page by dictating or writing and had shared his or her work, the teacher published the papers by posting them around the perimeter of a bulletin board captioned "Animals We Saw and Liked." In the center, she mounted the large experience-story chart about Billy Goat, to which the children attached a blue ribbon.

Teaching for Active Thinking

Had you gone along with Ms. Donovan and her class on their visit to the farm and observed in her classroom upon their return, you would have seen a group of children actively engaged in thinking aloud. You would have seen children using oral language as a bridge into and between reading and writing activity. To encourage her first-graders to reflect on and express their ideas, this teacher was relying on the time-proven strategies of the language experience approach and more recently developed techniques associated with whole language. These techniques include

✦ Providing direct experiences as a base for reflecting out loud, dictating to a scribe, writing, and reading;
✦ Encouraging children to use all their senses to gather data for thinking, talking, and writing;
✦ Brainstorming and webbing words, facts, and ideas;
✦ Thinking critically by reflecting together on meaningful content, going from simple to complex, voting, rank ordering and defending choices, and writing and reading.

In the sections that follow, you will read about these techniques—techniques that build upon one another.

Experiencing: A Base for Reflecting, Reading, and Writing Together

In taking her class to a farm, Karen Donovan was recognizing a fundamental principle of language arts instruction: To be able to reflect on ideas and express them orally and in writing, young children must be involved in seeing or doing beforehand or simultaneously. Firsthand experiences provide the content for thinking and sharing.

Experiences in the Out-of-Doors

Outdoor experiences can stimulate ideas for talking and writing. Just a short walk in a nearby park or meadow can summon up impressions such as these dictated by a first-grader:

> ### Fall
>
> *At the park I saw trees.*
> *I saw pebbles, chestnuts, leaves.*
> *I heard birds chirping, boys screaming, and leaves crunching.*
> *I smelled the grass and the flowers.*
> *I felt leaves and water.*
> *I tasted the water. It was cold.*
> *I like this month.*
> *—Dena, age 6 ¹/₂*

As Dena's poem suggests, even simple excursions can spark ideas. For example, on a day when new snow covers the ground, youngsters can build a snowman, make footprint trails in the snow, shake snow from branches, and draw pictures in the snow with a twig. Before venturing forth, a teacher may share a story such as Ezra Jack Keats's *The Snowy Day*. On returning to the warmth of the classroom, children will be eager to talk about things seen and felt. Older students may be able to contrast the cold of the outdoors with the warmth of the indoors and dictate pairs of alternating lines; for instance, a line beginning "Outdoors . . ." alternates with a line beginning "Indoors. . . ."

In areas with open space, children can walk through newly plowed fields, through woods filled with crackly fall leaves, through a grove of bushes or trees heavy with fruit, across desert sands, or by a brook that is home to water striders, mayfly larvae, and a snail or two. They capitalize on whatever nature has to offer. Children may see birds, insects, worms, or perhaps a lizard or a box turtle. On nature walks, the teacher can introduce children to the slimy feel of algal strands, the prickliness of palm fronds, or the lingering smell of pine. Remember the first time you flipped over a rock and saw an earthworm wiggle away? Recall your feelings. Children filled with similar feelings often bubble over with excitement.

In urban areas, the environment offers different experiences for talking and writing. As sidewalk engineers, children can "direct" construction at a local building site, experiencing the thrill of watching a construction worker stride across a beam stretched over empty space. Or children can walk city streets listening for human sounds or looking at different forms of architecture that reflect the historical development of their city. Children can identify examples to talk about later in their classroom.

Firsthand experiences in the out-of-doors can provide the content for thinking, talking, and writing together. (© 1993 James Carroll)

Structured Field Trips

Youngsters can visit a number of places to gather impressions for talking and writing. Here are just a few:

- ✦ Shops in the community, particularly a bakery, bank, pet shop, barber shop. Returning to the classroom, children describe things seen at each stop and build an experience-story chart that summarizes their trip.
- ✦ Civic buildings, such as the local courthouse, police station, firehouse, library. Children describe the place visited and the services provided.
- ✦ Industrial parks and large shopping complexes. On the school bus, youngsters drive by these establishments to find out what kinds of businesses are located there. Later they discuss their findings and summarize them on a chart or map.

Experiences such as these are as appropriate for stimulating thinking and talking among older students as they are in eliciting ideas for experience-chart writing. Older children can learn how their community functions and at the same time gather information for discussion. In short, children of all ages benefit from direct experiences with their world.

Nature in the Classroom

That world includes the classroom. Nature can come to school for children to experience. Fluffy, a well-loved guinea pig, is a popular resident of one kindergarten. Each week, a kindergartner is responsible for feeding Fluffy. Each week, too, children gather to talk about Fluffy's reaction to food, her appearance, and her activity during the week. On Friday, they compile a weekly report: "February 5, 1994: This week Fluffy did not move around much. She just sat in a corner. Fluffy was very tired."

In another classroom resides Yellow Back, a box turtle that roams freely, competing for space with two-legged residents. Periodically, Yellow Back becomes the topic for talking and writing, especially when he crawls into a tight place and requires assistance in squirming free.

Upper-grade teachers who find caring for large animals a time-consuming task can have students observe smaller organisms—ants, hermit crabs, land snails, and goldfish, to name just a few. Upper-graders periodically record data about the organisms' behavior, sharing the data during reporting time. If children record in tabular form, they will simultaneously learn a way to systematize observations. Data can eventually form the content for cooperatively written paragraphs.

Ongoing Projects

Classroom projects, as well as a bit of nature brought to school, can provide the content for talking and writing. Planting evergreen tree seedlings, for example, is a worthwhile endeavor. Upper-graders plant treelets following directions provided by a commercial supplier. Groups of planters set out and study the progress of several seedlings. Later they explain to the whole class the problems encountered. They keep a written log of what they did, how a seedling appeared when first planted, and how it looked after selected intervals. In southern climates, children can plant citrus treelets, palm seedlings, or cacti; force bulbs in flower pots; or raise bean plants from seeds and record data about their development.

Social sciences, art, and music projects have similar potential. Through project activity, children gather data and formulate ideas to talk and write about.

Purposes of Experiencing and Talking Together

For a discussion of oral composition as a basis for reading and writing, see Sylvia Ashton-Warner, *Teacher* (New York: Simon & Schuster, 1963).

The examples just described share a common feature: Experiencing and talking together lead to writing and reading. Youngsters require much direct involvement and talking out before writing and reading. Without this involvement, students may have little to write, and may approach a reading selection with little prior knowledge of the content of the selection to be read. Without the preliminary talk that should accompany direct experiences in schools, children may lack the vocabulary and related conceptual understandings that they need to read with comprehension and compose with clarity. This is especially so for at-risk learners who have had only limited experiences with the world around them and few opportunities within their home environments to use language to reflect on their experiences.

Learning About the Way Print Works   Experiencing, talking, listening, writing, and reading together help children understand the way words work on paper. Interacting socially with children in an environment that encourages them to use language to express their thoughts, the teacher serves as scribe and records their thoughts on paper for them. In doing so, the teacher is introducing children to basic principles of written language: Thought units consist of individual words; words are written from left to right; first letters of beginning words are written in upper case; periods end sentences. Children must master these principles in learning to read and write.

After youngsters have composed together, they move from group talking and writing to individual writing and dictation. A youngster writes alone or works with a scribe, who records the child's ideas on paper; the child adds illustrations. Because children dictate only a few lines at this stage, a scribe can record many ideas in a short period. At the same time, children write independently, using invented spelling to represent their thoughts on paper.

Later children who have written or dictated thoughts read them to the group, displaying their original illustrations and telling about their ideas. They also go to the reading center to reread their friends' compositions, asking for assistance from the child-authors when they run into difficulty. In this situation, children go beyond experience and talk to write and to read; they are becoming literate in the same natural and interactive way that they learned to speak and listen.

Soon first-graders are composing and reading on their own. This does not mean, however, that students can dispense with experiencing and talking together. As explained in previous chapters, throughout elementary school youngsters benefit from discussing their thoughts. Sharing information and ideas with one another, they clarify and expand what they are thinking and at the same time acquire basic oral communication skills. Similarly, students do not dispense with writing together. Throughout elementary school, children benefit from group writing. By cooperatively constructing sentences and paragraphs, upper-graders learn new ways to express and organize their ideas, acquire basic writing skills, and gain security in their ability to formulate ideas.

Building Functional Vocabulary   Experiencing and talking before reading and writing also expand a child's functional vocabulary. As children talk about events experienced, they use words that the teacher has interjected into the discussion. If children are talking about a class trip to a nearby airport, they may describe the way airplanes take off and land on the runways. For them, *runway* may be a new word that they learn to handle through group talk. Other words that could be interjected into this discussion are *taxied, hangar, ramp, check-in counter, metal detector*—all rather sophisticated words for primary-age children but words that become meaningful through experience and talk. Children may wish to make a chart of these words so that when they write and read on the same topic, the words, correctly spelled, are clearly visible. This technique works equally well with older children who encounter words new to them as a result of a common experience and who will meet and use those same words later in reading and writing.

Using All the Senses to Heighten Perceptions

Encouraging children to think about what they taste, touch, smell, see, and hear is a way to heighten their perceptions of an experience. By focusing on impressions received by all their senses, children gain the detail to share through writing and talking and background that serves them in good stead when they read.

Tasting, Touching, Smelling, Seeing, and Hearing: Some Examples

How does the teacher structure experiences to encourage youngsters to use all their senses to gather data for expression? Here are two examples.

An Outing   Thinking together about a recent outing, Anita Toth's fourth-graders dictated lines about what they had seen, heard, smelled, and touched:

> **Our Outing**
>
> We saw a tiny waterfall, a dirty yellow cat, lots of crispy leaves, a fallen tree that was decaying, rocks and stones, green moss, many birds, a rabbit's hole, sand, and dirt.
> We heard noisy car engines, crackling leaves, roaring airplanes in the sky, and a loud fire engine siren.
> We smelled the scent of pine as we walked along. We broke pine needles and the scent got stronger.
> We touched rough bark, brittle leaves, and smooth rocks.

As the fourth-graders contributed specifics, Ms. Toth asked them for greater detail. "What kind of tree did we see? What was happening to it?" she asked a child who had suggested that they had seen a tree. In response, the child described the tree as fallen and decaying. In similar fashion, Ms. Toth prompted another child to describe the leaves as crispy, another to describe the car engines as noisy, and still another to tell what was done to make the pine more fragrant. The teacher herself contributed the word *roaring*. In this instance, the teacher's questions encouraged children to reflect on the impressions they were receiving with all their senses.

Other cooking adventures that lead to talking and writing are making peanut butter, applesauce, pizza, pancakes.

Popcorn   Deborah Battiato also used questions to get her second-graders to be more reflective, but in contrast to Ms. Toth, she structured a literature-cooking experience for impression gathering. She began by sharing Nancy Byrd Turner's rhythmical poem "Popcorn Song." The poem begins, " 'Pop-pop-pop,' said the popcorn in the pan" and contains many repetitions of the *pop-pop-pop* line, which makes it ideal for choral speaking. The children decided how to speak the lines and who should chorus which lines.

Then the teacher plugged in a corn popper and waited. As the kernels burst, the children described their impressions: "The corn is making exploding noises"; "The corn is jumping up and down"; "It is dancing a jig." Removing the finished popcorn, the children thought about what it looked like. They suggested "round balls," "cotton," "a bug," "a flower." They described the corn as "white, yellow, and brown" and as "bumpy, curly, fluffy, and light." They described the smell as "strong and good," the taste as "crunchy, buttery, and good," the feel as "hot when just done and cold sometimes too." In the bowl, the popcorn was "quiet."

As the children contributed ideas, Ms. Battiato recorded them on a data chart as in Figure 8.1. Selecting from the charted words, Mark wrote:

> **Homemade Popcorn**
>
> *White crinkly circles of fluffy cotton,*
> *Popping in the pan, make screeching noises.*
> *They look like bumpy clouds*
> *Quiet among piles of other corns.*

OUR IMPRESSIONS OF POPCORN

What is happening in the popcorn pot?	What does the popcorn look like?	How can we describe our popcorn?	Why do we pop corn?
The popcorn makes exploding noises in the pot. It jumps up and down. It goes in all directions in the pot.	It looks like -- round balls, cotton, flowers, a bug, a cloud, circles.	It -- is white, yellow, and brown; is bumpy, curly, light, and fluffy; feels hot when just done, cold sometimes.	We pop corn because -- we like it; we are having a party; it is delicious; it is tasty to munch.

Figure 8.1   A Chart of Sense Impressions

In this instance, the chart helped Mark move from expressing his impressions orally to expressing them on paper.

The lesson involved these components:

1. An oral encounter with literature;
2. A firsthand experience affecting all the senses—tasting, touching, smelling, seeing, and hearing;
3. Question sequences that forced children to think about their sense impressions;
4. Writing, either teacher guided, small group, or individual.

Activities with the Senses

Here are some relatively easy activities for making children aware of the impressions they receive with their senses and for helping them find words to express their ideas:

◆ *Smell and talk.* Fruits such as lemons, pineapples, and bananas exude a strong aroma when first opened. Schedule a "whiffing" event in which children, in groups, open a sample. Children write down words to describe the aroma. On another occasion, schedule a spice or herb "whiffing" (nutmeg, ginger, cinnamon, curry, thyme, mustard). An obvious time for this activity is within study of plants and their characteristics.

See Lynn Rothwell, "Making a 'What Is It?' Book," in *The Best of Livewire*, selected by Julie Jenson (Urbana, Ill.: National Council of Teachers of English, 1989), for another idea for charting sense impressions.

◆ *Look and talk.* Color, luster, size, shape, weight, and movement are categories for thinking about the appearance of objects like rocks, shells, leaves, and insects. Make a columnar chart with these key words as heads (see Figure 8.2). Children select objects to list and describe on the charts. Later they read their descriptions while others guess the objects. Charted information can be converted into Guess What? paragraphs for others to solve.

◆ *Bubbles are. . . .* A bubble-blowing event focuses attention on clear descriptions of sense impressions. To simplify preparation, buy a bottle of liquid soap intended for bubble making and use the loop that comes with the solution. On a day when the sun sparkles, fill a window area with bubbles. Children describe the appearance and smell as well as the feel of bubbles when touched and broken. They compare the bubbles to other things, as Ryan did after experiencing a bubble-blowing event on a sun-filled day:

> **Bubbles**
>
> *Bubbles are—invisible moons,*
> *transparent lemons,*
> *colored balloons,*
> *floating rainbows,*
> *spinning wheels,*
> *empty snowballs.*

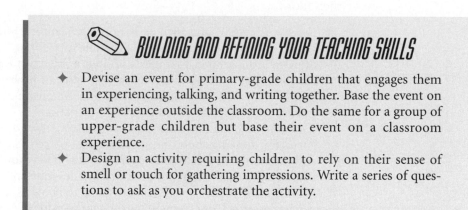

THIS IS THE WAY IT IS				
Object	*Color*	*Size and Shape*	*Weight*	*Movement*
grasshopper	dull brown	about 3 cm, has three pairs of legs, has two pairs of wings, has antennae	very light	moves by hopping
a light bulb	whitish with a silvery end, yellow when in use	round at one end, has a narrower neck at the other end; about 13 cm long	very light	stationary even when in use

Figure 8.2 An Observations Chart

✎ BUILDING AND REFINING YOUR TEACHING SKILLS

✦ Devise an event for primary-grade children that engages them in experiencing, talking, and writing together. Base the event on an experience outside the classroom. Do the same for a group of upper-grade children but base their event on a classroom experience.

✦ Design an activity requiring children to rely on their sense of smell or touch for gathering impressions. Write a series of questions to ask as you orchestrate the activity.

Brainstorming and Webbing as a Base for Reflecting, Writing, and Reading Together

One exciting technique for thinking together is brainstorming. In brainstorming, each participant contributes whatever words or ideas come to mind in reaction to a particular object or event. Whether relevant or not, all contributions are accepted and recorded so that they are available for reflection and composing. At times, brainstormed words are recorded in a web that highlights relationships. Figure 8.3 is an example of an idea web that grew out of pre- and postreading talk.

Brainstorming and webbing need not follow a group "happening," especially when youngsters in upper grades draw from a storehouse of previous experiences. However, teachers find that brainstorming produces an amazing

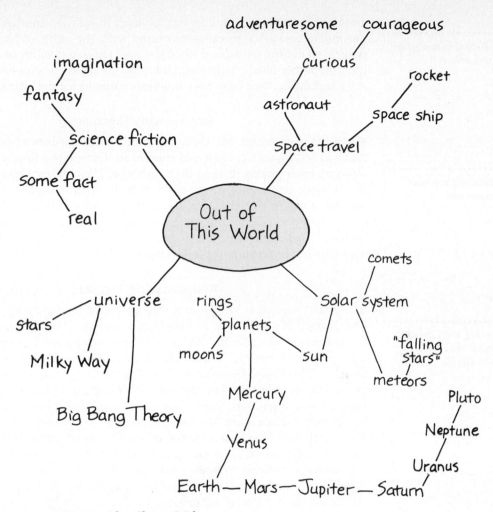

Figure 8.3 An Idea Cluster Web

quantity of material if children first experience together, as the following literature-based vignette demonstrates.

TEACHING IN ACTION   EXPERIENCING AND BRAINSTORMING

Anne Grant opened to the first page of Leo Lionni's *The Biggest House in the World* and read the title. At the same time, she turned on a recording of "Serenade" from the ballet *Les Millions d'Arlequin* by Ricardo Drigo. As Ms. Grant read about the snail whose dissatisfaction with being so little caused him to grow bigger and bigger until he was too large to move to another cabbage head, the music created a mood in harmony with the story. When story action peaked, so did the music, and when the snail realized the folly of his dissatisfaction, the music lilted once more. Listening, the children were entranced by the story and music, their faces reflecting their empathy for the little snail.

Experiencing Together

When the story ended, Ms. Grant said not a word but instead picked up a cup that was resting on a counter and reached in. Out came a tiny brown snail that was tentatively poking its head from its house. The children clustered around to look closely. Some grasped the mollusk by its shell to look even more closely through a magnifying glass. Ms. Grant distributed empty snail shells to youngsters on the perimeter of the group because they were having trouble seeing the live one. These children rubbed their fingers across the snail shells and stuck their smallest fingers into the inner chambers.

Brainstorming Together

Finding and categorizing
words to express
impressions

Excitement reigned as Ms. Grant spread a piece of oak tag on the easel, for on it was a sketch of a shell with an outline of a snail protruding from it. While one student served as scribe, the others called out "snail words," prompted by guiding questions from Ms. Grant. The children proffered snail words they had heard in *The Biggest House in the World*: *light, carry, twisting, twitching, house, small, hidden, cabbage*. They also offered describing words like *brownish, tiny, round, slimy, wiggly, slow, hard*. They contributed words like *coiled, spiral, circular, looped, staircase* when Ms. Grant suggested they outline the internal pattern of the shell. Focusing their attention on the movement of the little brown specimen, the children told how the snail navigated: *slipping, turning, sliding, cruising, gliding, slinking, creeping, crawling*. They brainstormed snail-related expressions like *portable house, mobile home, house on wheels, house without wheels, on the go, moving on, carrying your house with you, don't get too big for your britches*. The class scribe printed all these words on the perimeter of the snail shape as well as along the inner swirls of its spiral. When the children were unsure of a spelling, the Dictionary Sleuth checked it so that the resulting "word thingumajig," as the children called word charts like this, would be accurate. Figure 8.4 illustrates a similar word chart for a tortoise.

Composing Together

Having brainstormed a pool of words and phrases for expressing snail thoughts, the youngsters composed together. They created a *diamanté*, a structured form consisting of seven lines with a contrast. The diamanté follows this pattern:

First line:	A noun that names an object or thought
Second line:	Two adjectives that describe the first noun
Third line:	Three participles (-*ing* or -*ed*) that are associated with the first noun

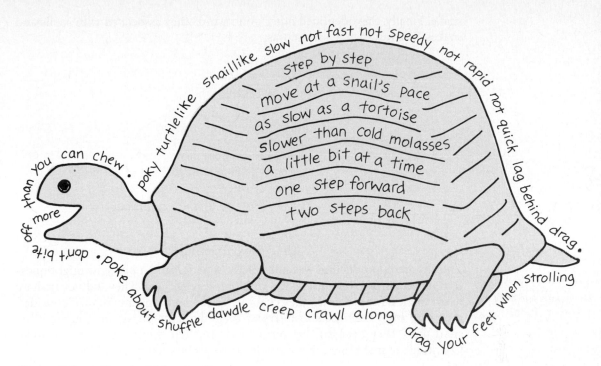

Figure 8.4 A Tortoise Thingumajig

Fourth line:	Four nouns, two referring to the noun in line one, two to the noun in line seven
Fifth line:	Three participles that are associated with the noun in line seven
Sixth line:	Two adjectives that describe the line seven noun
Seventh line:	A noun that names an object or thought that is the opposite of the one in the first line

To begin group writing, Ms. Grant printed *SNAIL* at the top of a large sheet of paper. She asked the youngsters to think of animals that were the opposite of a snail in some way. Children proposed the elephant, which is very big; the rabbit, which is very fleet; the snake, which is stretched out; and the slug, which has no house. Having made a number of proposals that fit into the bigger than, faster than, longer than, and "nakeder" than categories, the children reflected on their proposals and compromised on the snake "because it begins with the same sound as *snail*." The teacher wrote *SNAKE* at the bottom of the paper.

At this point, the children selected adjectives from the words previously brainstormed. They selected two they thought were most descriptive of their snail and suggested two parallel words to describe the snake. Then they selected three *-ing* words about their snail and thought of three parallel words for the

Composing words into
descriptive thought

snake. Finally, they identified other noun words they associated with snails and snakes. The resulting diamanté was:

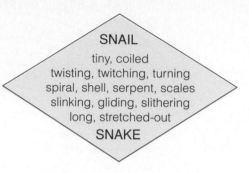

Chorusing Together

The children's production was not exactly "poetic," and a biologist might question its accuracy. Nonetheless, the children were thrilled. They did not hesitate when the teacher suggested they chant it. To the accompaniment of "Serenade," they rose from their seats to interpret their thoughts physically. Chanting the snail lines, they brought their arms close to their bodies to twist and turn. Chanting the snake lines, they extended their arms to slink and slither.

Writing Independently

Designs and Patterns in Nature (Mahwah, N.J.: Troll Associates).

Now the children were ready for something quieter. That "something" was a filmloop called *Designs and Patterns in Nature*, to which the teacher added the music of "Serenade." Viewing the loop, the children identified animals about which they could compose a nature thought.

Composing ideas independently

Filmloop, projector, paper, flo-pens, and other books about animals went into the writing/reading center. There youngsters could review the loop, select an animal, devise word thingumajigs, and/or compose an animal thought, perhaps (but not necessarily) in the pattern of a diamanté. In another corner of the center, the teacher posted the snail thingumajig, the outline for a diamanté, and a list of animals that differ from a snail. Children composing at this station could select one of these contrasting animals to draft into an original snail diamanté. The following week, many youngsters composed in the writing center, printing their finished products on construction paper cut in the shape of their animals.

Brainstorming in a Variety of Contexts

Brainstorming is a dynamic way to assist children who have trouble reflecting on ideas as part of writing. By brainstorming, children discover words and thoughts that might never surface if they were composing on their own. In effect, words and ideas mushroom as creative relationships emerge.

These relationships are the content of written expression. Using the ideas that emerge, children can compose paragraphs of description, stories, and informational explanations, as the following examples demonstrate.

Descriptions   Brainstorming works well as a springboard to descriptive writing. For example, one teacher began a writing sequence by showing the full-color sound filmstrip *The Sea*—part of the narrationless perception series from Educational Dimensions Corporation—which, through music and photographs, develops awareness of the sights and sounds of the sea. After viewing the strip, the children brainstormed sea sights, adding striking adjectives to each sight—not just *fog* but *dense fog*, not just *gulls* but *screeching, squawking gulls*. Based on these phrases, the children, in collaborative teams, wrote brief descriptive paragraphs about the sea.

Stories   A second teacher used brainstorming as part of story writing. Upper-graders in his class listened to Ferde Grofé's "Cloudburst" from the *Grand Canyon Suite*. Listeners contributed naming and describing words and then combined their words into powerfully descriptive sentences:

Other fine selections include Grofé's *Mississippi Suite*, Rimsky-Korsakov's "Flight of the Bumblebee," Grieg's "March of the Dwarfs," Donaldson's *Once Upon a Time Suite*, and Saint-Saëns' "Danse Macabre."

Storm Words

Describing Words
noisy, banging,
crashing, breaking,
streaking, striking,
wet, spattering, dark,
burning, bright,
blowing, bending, tossing

Naming Words
storm, cloudburst,
thunder, bolt, streak,
lightning, rain, wind,
shower, flood, danger,
disaster, warning, alarm,
thunderheads, clouds

Descriptive Sentences
Heavy rain bombarded the
    dry earth.
Blowing, screaming wind swirled
    sand upward.
Lightning bolts fired up the sky.

Children can read storm stories and poems as part of the learning experience.

Next, the children thought up story ideas—things that could happen during a freak storm. For instance, a prospector is caught in a storm and must escape the flash flood filling the canyon. Since these youngsters lived in a region where gentle brooks turn into torrents during storms, the prospector idea appealed immediately. The teacher encouraged students to consider other possibilities. They concocted ideas like these: A car breaks down, stranding a motorist out in the desert in a storm; during a storm a lizard, a miner, and a burro take refuge under an overhanging cliff; two boys disobey their father and get lost in the desert during a storm. After a number of relatively similar ideas had been thrown into the idea pool, the children composed "storm stories," working individually or in coauthoring pairs as they preferred.

Informational Content   A third teacher brainstormed in an informational context. To middle-graders, he read a short informational book that describes the water cycle. He asked half the class to listen to find out the steps in the cycle and the other half to think of related words and ideas. After the reading, the children made a circular chart showing steps in the cycle and added related words such as *shower, snow, hail, cloud, rain, brook, stream, river, lake, pond, ocean, runs down, runs into, rushes by, erodes, evaporates, precipitation*, and *cycle*. When the chart was filled, the children, in four-person teams, composed sentences summarizing the steps in the water cycle. Each group member took a turn writing a sentence by selecting key words from the brainstormed pool.

See the teaching-in-action vignette that opens Chapter 5 for an example of brainstorming and webbing before and during listening.

Brainstorming Before Reading   A fourth teacher used brainstorming to help children get a hold on their existing knowledge of a subject before reading about it. The subject was computers. The teacher began simply by asking students what they thought of when they heard the word *computer*. The youngsters offered myriad associations, which the teacher typed into a computer equipped with a word processing system. When the computer screen was filled with words, teacher and students reordered their list; they grouped together words and sentences about what computers do and put together ideas about how computers came to be. Into a third category, they put words that identify parts of a computer; into a fourth, names of computers; into a fifth, the names of computer languages. Each youngster received a printout of the brainstormed words and categories.

Now the children were ready to read a short article about computers from the weekly current events paper in use in that class. As they read, they jotted onto the printout the new words and ideas they met: They put the new items into the vacant slots in the network of ideas and words that represented the knowledge they already had.

Advantages of Brainstorming   As these examples suggest, brainstorming is a flexible strategy that can be adapted to provide words, sentences, and ideas for different kinds of expression: poemlike thoughts, paragraphs of description, stories, and explanations. It can be used to identify what youngsters already know about a topic before reading on it; in this way, readers bring their prior knowledge to bear in comprehending the selection. Furthermore, brainstorming requires considerable verbal interaction among participants. As youngsters interact, they learn to respect the contributions of others, to verbalize their own ideas, and to function in a group setting. In this respect, brainstorming achieves goals of oracy and literacy.

The Teacher's Role in Brainstorming

The success of brainstorming in eliciting ideas for writing and background for reading depends in large measure on the teacher's ability to question. First, the teacher must ask questions that lead students to reflect on their sense impres-

Similar topics for brain-
storming include sights, tastes,
smells, feelings of Thanksgiving, birthdays, New Year's,
Christmas, Chanukah.

sions. For example, leading a Fourth of July brainstorming, one teacher queried, "What sounds do we associate with the Fourth? What sights? What tastes? What smells?" Remembering that feelings are generally associated with an event, she asked, "How do we feel on the Fourth?" When the children proffered nouns, she asked for companion adjectives and phrases so that a word like *fireworks* mushroomed into "exploding fireworks that filled the sky with color."

Questions to Guide Brainstorming   Other kinds of questions to guide brainstorming include

- ✦ *Objects*. What things do we associated with *X*?
- ✦ *Descriptions*. What words can we use to describe *X*?
- ✦ *Actions*. What actions do we associate with *X*? (Encourage children to identify action words by asking for words ending with -*ing* and -*ed*.)
- ✦ *Reactions*. How do we feel about or react to *X*?
- ✦ *Synonyms*. What are synonyms for *X*?
- ✦ *Antonyms*. What are antonyms for *X*?
- ✦ *Comparisons*. To what other things or events can we compare *X*? In what way(s) are the two things similar?
- ✦ *Contrasts*. What things or events are extremely different from *X*? In what way(s) are they different?
- ✦ *Words beginning with specific letters of the alphabet*. For example, what words beginning with *s* and with *t* do we associate with *X*?

These categories obviously overlap; in this instance, however, the overlap is unimportant because the goal is not to categorize but to provoke an outpouring of ideas.

Books for word brainstorming:
George McDermott, *The
Stonecutter* (New York:
Viking, 1973)—power words;
Leo Lionni, *Swimmy* (New
York: Pantheon, 1963)—fish
and swimming words; Mary
Stolz, *Storm in the Night* (New
York: Harper & Row, 1988)—
storm and night words.

Keeping Ideas Flowing   For a first brainstorming, it is generally easiest to begin with verbal stimuli like a story, film, filmstrip with narration, or series of poems and ask children to listen for key words and phrases. These words get the ball rolling so that a chart of brainstormed words rapidly takes form, and children receive immediate reinforcement. The stimuli words trigger other words, perhaps related in sound as well as in meaning. When suggestions wane, the teacher may contribute a word or ask a question to start children thinking in other directions.

Building Vocabulary Through Brainstorming

A major outgrowth of brainstorming is vocabulary development. As participants suggest words and search references for additional words, they meet new or relatively unfamiliar expressions. Injected into class talk-times and charted, these words become more accessible for writing and speaking and more meaningful when encountered in reading.

Synonyms At times brainstorming can become word play, the goal being growth in word power. Take, for instance, play with the word *fast*. Brainstormers pour out as many *fast* words as they can: describers like *quick, speedy, swift, hasty*; expressions like *quick as a wink, in short order, in no time flat, in the twinkling of an eye, like a house afire*; actions like *dart, sprint, bound, step on it, rush*; things like *cannonball, lightning, rocket, arrow, jet*. This activity can take place on a continuing basis; a youngster cuts a piece of oak tag into a representational shape and mounts it in a word-storming center, where pairs of youngsters go to contribute additional words to the shape. See Figure 8.5 for an example.

Adjectives are fun words for brainstorming because thinkers can travel in endless directions. Particularly workable words include *slow, heavy, dizzy, grouchy, mighty, light, free, clever, terrible, friendly, shy, proud, funny, hot,* and *tired.* Students print an adjective at the top of charting paper. As a group activ-

A word source: W. Cabell Greet, *In Other Words: A Beginning Thesaurus (K–2)* (Glenview, Ill.: Scott, Foresman, 1969), and *In Other Words: A Junior Thesaurus (3–6)* (Glenview, Ill.: Scott, Foresman, 1969).

Figure 8.5 A Sun Thingumajig

ity, they contribute all kinds of related words; or they go in pairs to a word-building center to add their contributions to an expanding chart.

Another kind of play is with overused words like *nice* for which children identify possible substitutes. In the same way they toy with overused verbs, identifying variants of *say, walk, do, make,* or even *fall down.* The resulting charts become original thesaurus pages to which writers refer as they compose. These charts are especially useful because they supply an accurately spelled word pool for writing.

Words for Writing   Brainstorming inevitably offers the opportunity for follow-up writing. Children who have identified *say* synonyms can write conversation stories in which characters do a lot of talking. In composing these stories, youngsters rely on such words as *directed, exclaimed, mentioned*—words brainstormed earlier. Similarly, children who have identified *grouchy* words write stories in which characters are *cranky, glum, grim, sour*—again, words identified through brainstorming.

If youngsters collect their words on colorful thingumajigs or simple charts, these visuals can serve as focal points for learning stations where students write. Having brainstormed words, children propose writing topics, print them on cards, and mount them around the jig or chart. With a pouch of paper and a pouch for completed papers, the writing station is open for business. After several students have visited and written, they share their stories based on the word and topic charts. In this way, youngsters hear charted words in meaningful contexts.

Brainstorming Activities

Here are some additional ideas for brainstorming:

✦ Writing a thank-you note to a speaker or to someone who has helped on a class trip, youngsters brainstorm ideas to include. A group is responsible for writing a draft and selects ideas from those proffered by the class. The writing team shares its draft with the class, listens to suggestions, and prepares a final draft.

✦ After completing a social studies unit, children brainstorm what they consider to be key ideas and record these points randomly on the chalkboard.

✦ Children brainstorm the sights, sounds, and sensations of an odyssey beneath the sea. Guide youngsters to describe what they might see as they explore a coral reef or a sunken Spanish galleon. Do this as part of a science unit.

✦ Foods popular with youngsters can stimulate a flow of words. Good for this purpose are hamburgers, pizza, ice cream cones, and tacos. Brainstormers concoct pizza, hamburger, or hot dog thingumajigs in which words form the boundaries of a large cutout of the food as in Figure 8.6. Then they write descriptive paragraphs or poems using their words. Do this as part of a health unit.

Similarly, children can brainstorm the sights, sounds, and sensations of a space trip. Share Joanna Cole's magic school bus stones in this context.

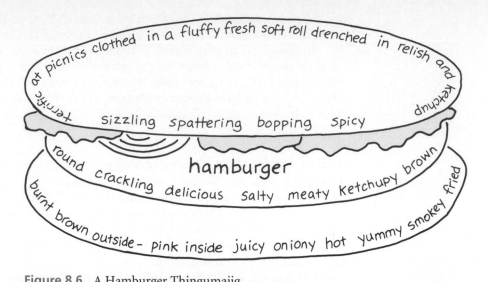

Figure 8.6 A Hamburger Thingumajig

Thinking Critically Together: A Way to Clarify Ideas

Today the language arts are defined in terms of four processes—listening, speaking, reading, and writing—that form an integrated whole: language in action. Thinking is the thread that links the four processes, because to listen, speak, read, or write productively requires thought. Thus, teaching the language arts means stimulating children to use language to reflect on their experiences with life, literature, and language. In this section, we will consider strategies that encourage children to think out loud and heighten their ability to think critically.

What Is Critical Thinking?

Matthew Lipman argues that "critical thinking is skillful, responsible thinking that facilitates good judgment because it (1) relies upon criteria, (2) is self-correcting, and (3) is sensitive to context" ("Critical Thinking—What Can It Be?," *Educational Leadership*, 46 [September 1988], 39). Criteria are "reliable reasons."

The work of Robert Ennis (1987) on critical thinking relates to instruction in the language arts. Ennis broadly defines critical thinking as "a practical reflective activity that has reasonable belief or action as its goal. There are five key ideas here: *practical, reflective, reasonable, belief,* and *action.* They combine into the following working definition: *Critical thinking is reasonable reflective thinking that is focused on deciding what to believe or do.* Note that this definition does not exclude creative thinking. Formulating hypotheses, alternative ways of viewing a problem, questions, possible solutions, and plans for investigating something are creative acts that come under this definition." The National Council of Teachers of English Committee on Critical Thinking in the Language Arts (Bosma, 1987) agrees: "Critical thinking is a process which stresses an attitude of suspended judgment, incorporates logical inquiry and problem solving, and leads to an evaluative decision or action." From this point of view, critical thinking involves problem solving, decision making, and the rendering of judgments.

James Hoffman (1992) believes that problem solving, decision making, and judging are learned behaviors. He contends that some students learn these critical-thinking skills on their own, whereas some never learn them. He hypothesizes that "through good instruction" all students can successfully acquire critical-thinking skills. The Committee on Critical Thinking in the Language Arts proposes that critical thinking be taught in the language arts because thinking and communication are interrelated. The Committee believes this teaching should encourage a state of mind that stimulates children "to wonder, to doubt, to search out meanings, and to evaluate" (Bosma, 1987).

See Chapter 3 for material on children's developing ability to make critical judgments, Chapter 5 for material on critical listening, Chapter 7 for questions that encourage in-depth thinking and a discussion web for critical thinking, and Chapter 13 for material on critical reading.

How does the classroom teacher build critical-thinking skills, especially when critical thinking is conceived as encompassing not only evaluative but decision-making and problem-solving behaviors? The answer lies in discussions about literature and life. Because thinking and "languaging" go hand and hand, children should have endless opportunities to make evaluative judgments as they study literature and the content areas. These opportunities should start orally, for oral language activity can model for students how to use language to think. Students should talk together about literature, especially literature that speaks to injustice, people's inhumanity to one another, and environmental issues. As Bigelow (1992) explains, "Instead of merely absorbing the authors' words, children can begin to argue with them. Significantly, to invite students to question the injustices embedded in text material is implicitly to question the injustices embedded in the society." In talking together about literature, children can also begin to recognize their own biases and gather alternative ideas (Lehman and Haynes, 1985; Smith, 1990).

This section describes a lesson sequence that occurred in one sixth grade. It provides a format for designing a similar sequence of critical-thinking experiences—a sequence called a *talk track.*

On the Nature and Importance of Rational Thought

1. Barry Beyer defines thinking as "the search for meaning. It consists either of finding meaning assumed to exist already or of making meaning out of something that has no readily apparent meaning" (*Practical Strategies for the Teaching of Thinking* [Boston: Allyn and Bacon, 1987], 16).

2. Raymond Nickerson describes reasoning as "the processes we use to form and evaluate beliefs—beliefs about the world, about people, about the truth or falsity of claims we encounter or make." He states that reasoning is "a matter of both attitude and knowledge: one is unlikely to reason well about any subject unless one is deeply desirous of doing so, and one has some knowledge of the subject about which the reasoning is to be done. Neither a closed mind nor an empty one is likely to produce much that would qualify as effective reasoning. On the other hand, an open and reflective mind, coupled with a little knowledge and an eagerness to acquire more, will reason as a matter of course."

   Nickerson continues, "Reasoning also has to do with the careful and critical use of language. Indeed, reasoning and language usage are so tightly intertwined that it is often difficult to tell whether a particular problem should be considered a problem of reasoning or one of language usage" (*Reflections on Reasoning* [Hillsdale, N.J.: Erlbaum, 1986], 1).

3. Nickerson also speaks to the question of why thinking should be taught: "We want students to become good thinkers because thinking is at the heart of what it means to be human; to fail to develop one's potential in this regard is to preclude the full expression of one's humanity. Thinking well is a means to many ends, but it is also an end in itself" ("Why Teach Thinking?" in *Teaching Thinking Skills: Theory and Practice*, ed. Joan Baron and Robert Sternberg [New York: W.H. Freeman, 1987], 32).

Questions to Consider

Why is it important to teach for critical thinking? How are teaching for critical thinking and teaching for oral language development interrelated? How can teachers use literary transactions to heighten children's ability to think critically? Consider your own ability to think rationally: Are you able to formulate and evaluate beliefs about the world in a rational way? Are you able to formulate opinions based on what you hear and read? Do you have a reflective mind? Do you use language carefully and critically?

TEACHING IN ACTION   *Thinking Critically Together*

In 1984, Theodore Seuss Geisel received a special Pulitzer citation "for his contribution over nearly half a century to the education and enjoyment of America's children and their parents" (*The New York Times*, April 17, 1984). Read Elizabeth Moje and Woan-Ru Shyu, "Oh, The Places You've Taken Us," *The Reading Teacher*, 45 (May 1992), 670–676, for a summary of Dr. Seuss's life.

It was after lunch. Returning to their classroom, Henry Dag's sixth-graders spied a marqueelike sign mounted on an easel at the doorway:

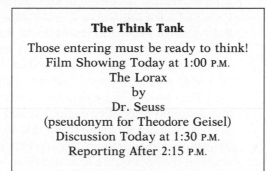

> **The Think Tank**
> Those entering must be ready to think!
> Film Showing Today at 1:00 P.M.
> The Lorax
> by
> Dr. Seuss
> (pseudonym for Theodore Geisel)
> Discussion Today at 1:30 P.M.
> Reporting After 2:15 P.M.

A rotating spotlight flashed colors in sequence across the sign. The classroom was dark, ready for a film showing.

Gathering impressions for expression

With no preliminaries, the teacher flicked on the projector, and the reds, yellows, blues, and greens of *The Lorax* danced across the screen. The students sat entranced watching the Onceler systematically destroy the land as the Lorax warned of impending disaster.

Clarifying Thinking Through Talk

At the film's end, Mr. Dag asked, "How many of you liked the Onceler in the film? Wave your hand if you do." No hands went up. "How many of you liked the Lorax? Wave your hand." There was a flurry of hands, and the teacher continued, "Let's talk about why we all disliked the Onceler. What are some of the specific things the Onceler did that we didn't like?"

Identifying specific examples to support an opinion

At that, children began to contribute. One told of how the Onceler had dumped Gluppity-Glupp and Schloppity-Schlopp into the rivers, a second of how the Onceler had polluted the air with fumes, another of how the Onceler had cut down the Truffla Trees, and still another of how the Onceler had scarred the earth to construct roads. At one point, to jog students' memories, the teacher pantomimed an Onceler act: smoking a big cigar and shaking ashes onto the floor. He asked students if they could pantomime another act. One youngster portrayed nonverbally how the Onceler had peeled a banana and carelessly thrown the peel out the window. During this stage, a student served as scribe, recording examples.

Going beyond stereotyped explanations
(Note: It is important to stress that the Onceler represents all of us—not big business—if we are to avoid an anti-industry bias.)

"Did the Onceler do anything that was good?" queried Mr. Dag. Children pondered. Then one volunteered that the Onceler had supplied jobs, which meant better homes and food for the Onceler people. A second suggested that the Onceler had saved the last Truffla Tree seed so that Truffla Trees could grow again.

Next children pondered why the Onceler had done what he had and who the Onceler really was. Almost unanimously the sixth-graders decided that greed was the motive and that the Onceler was "big business."

"Do you think that the Onceler was really just that?" the teacher pressed. The scribe read an item from the list the class had previously developed—that the Onceler had cut down all the Truffla Trees. "Has anyone here caused a tree to be cut down unnecessarily—just *once?*" To jog ideas, the teacher rolled up a piece of clean paper and tossed it into the basket. At that, many hands went up as the children related times when they had thrown away paper items they could have reused. One youngster described something he had recently read about how used paper is changed back into pulp and converted into new paper products. Item by item the youngsters went through the list recorded by the scribe and described when they themselves had just once acted like the Onceler. Gradually, they began to comprehend that *they were the Onceler* and that greed was too general a reason to explain acts like those in the movie. They began to comprehend the importance of suspending judgment until they had considered the facts of a case.

Perceiving relationships

Contributing ideas to class discussion

Students focused now on the Lorax. "Why did everyone like the Lorax? What did the Lorax do that we liked?" The children supported their earlier vote by describing specific acts of the Lorax. "Whom did the Lorax stand for in real life?" The children decided that the Lorax represented everyone who speaks up even when others take an opposite stand.

Convincing Others

After the class had spent a good deal of time considering "what" and "why," Mr. Dag shifted gears. "So far," he announced, "we have been judging the rightness and wrongness of acts. As we have seen, some acts seem worse than others. Now we are going to rank acts in terms of which ones are worse than others. I have a sheet in which I have described acts very similar to the ones committed by the Onceler. Put a number 1 in the square next to the name of the offender you consider to be the worst one, a number 2 next to the name of the offender you consider to be a little less bad, and so on down the line." The teacher distributed the sheet in Figure 8.7, and the children individually rank ordered the offenders.

Contributing ideas to consensus group

When each student had completed a sheet, the teacher divided the class into five teams. The teams were to arrive at a compromise sheet that to some extent embodied the thinking of each member. Those whose opinion differed from others' with respect to the rank ordering of items had to try to convince others on the team. In so doing, the children became actively involved in trying to change opinions so that the composite ranking would reflect reasons they believed were significant. Mr. Dag waited until the teams had compiled their composite rankings, which they recorded in the second box next to each name on the task sheet. At that point, the Team Secretary recorded the consensus on a

---

A POLLUTION EVILS BOARD

The Litterbug ☐ ☐

A man is driving along an open stretch of a major interstate highway. He decides to have some candy; so he opens a package, pops a piece into his mouth, and tosses the wrapper out the window.

The Smokestack ☐ ☐

A large electrical generating plant produces power by burning a high-sulfur coal. It emits thick gases into the air.

The Hog ☐ ☐

A child asks for an extra big piece of dessert, but finds that he or she is too full to eat the whole thing, so leaves the rest to be thrown out.

The Dumper ☐ ☐

An oil tanker cleans its tanks by dumping what is left offshore. The oil washes ashore, gumming up miles of beach and marshland.

The Puffer ☐ ☐

The sign in the people-filled, unventilated room reads: "No Smoking." A woman lights a cigarette and smokes until the room is smoke filled.

Figure 8.7   A Task Sheet for Rank Ordering Opinions

chart the teacher had outlined on the chalkboard. The team findings are shown in Figure 8.8.

Together the class analyzed the results, considering in what respects team rankings, although different, were similar. They noted that all teams had ranked the Smokestack and the Dumper as very bad, and they gave reasons for those high rankings: the fact that the acts hurt more people and were committed by groups rather than by individuals. Teams ranking the Dumper higher than the Smokestack (and vice versa) gave reasons to support their rankings. In like manner, participants considered acts they had generally ranked as least offensive: littering and puffing. Again, they verbalized the criteria they had used to formulate their judgment.

Defending a position orally

Composing Together

To wrap up the session, Mr. Dag turned to *The Lorax*. He opened to the page toward the end that shows a memorial-like pile of rocks bearing the imprint *UNLESS*. "What significance does the word *unless* have in the story?" he asked.

DATA TABLE					
Team No.	The Litterbug	The Smokestack	The Hog	The Dumper	The Puffer
1	4	2	3	1	5
2	4	1	5	2	3
3	4	2	5	1	3
4	5	1	4	2	3
5	3	2	5	1	4

Figure 8.8 A Data Table for Recording Opinions

Remembering the film, the children explained that unless everyone was more careful, the earth would be no more. The teacher wrote the main clause on the board and followed it with a series of *unlesses* in the following pattern:

The earth will be no more
    unless _____
    unless _____
    unless _____
    unless _____

Summarizing key ideas through oral composition

On the spot, the class composed a string of specific *unless* clauses based on their discussion:

The earth will be no more
    unless we protect the forest from being cut away,
    unless we stop the fouling of the air,
    unless we halt the reckless dumping into our waterways,
    unless we work together to save the land.

That brief summary composition ended the Think Tank Session for the afternoon.

Reading and Composing Alone

The next afternoon, Mr. Dag's sixth-graders saw a sign that said "The Writing Box" spread across the doorway marquee, and they entered the Box to write allegories modeled after *The Lorax*. To introduce the form, the teacher had the children read a second allegory by Dr. Seuss, *The Butter Battle Book*. Then they talked about how the story communicated its message and compared it with *The Lorax*. They quickly perceived that in allegories story characters stand for persons in real life and story acts stand for real-life acts. They saw that by using a representational technique writers send a message to readers. Following the talk-time, the children spent the afternoon composing allegories. Some worked by themselves, others in writing teams. For fun, they signed their stories with pseudonyms.

Composing original stories

Teaching Critical Thinking: Reflecting on Meaningful Content

A first strategy that triggers critical thinking is to provide students with meaningful content about which they can talk. Substance or content is essential if discussions in elementary classrooms are to touch on fundamental problems, issues, and ideas and if students are to participate fully in a discussion. How does the teacher provide children with the background necessary for critical thinking?

Teachers must organize activities based on their understanding of children's cognitive development. See Chapter 3 for a discussion of developmental stages.

Thinking Aloud About Literature   Ideas in books are the warp and woof of discussion and eventually of writing. Talking together about ideas met in stories becomes oral pondering as youngsters identify key strands, note relationships among strands, weave them together into generalizations, and ultimately formulate opinions and judgments. Writing together becomes a means of recording ideas discussed and summarizing and clarifying them.

In the episode just described, an allegorical film supplied the content for thinking, talking, and writing together. Other materials provide content more suited to the cognitive abilities and interests of primary children. A teacher can share a short story or poem, which the children later ponder as a group. Very young children can ponder a feeling book like Judith Viorst's *I'll Fix Anthony*—the internal talking of a little brother as he tells himself what he will do "when he is six" to get back at his big brother. Children decide whether they like Anthony and whether they like the little brother. They identify mean acts and good acts. They think about why the little brother has mean thoughts. They describe times when they felt just like the little brother and said, "I'll fix _____." Children who are six go on to write their own repetitive lines patterned after Viorst's: "When I'm seven, _____."

See Mary McFarland, "Critical Thinking in Elementary Social Studies," *Social Education*, 49 (April 1985), 277–280, for specific ideas for involving youngsters in critical thinking, especially as they study history. Also read Claude Goldenberg, "Instructional Conversations: Promoting Comprehension Through Discussion," *The Reading Teacher*, 46 (December 1992/January 1993), 316–326.

Thinking Aloud About Content-Area Issues   Youngsters can also think out loud about issues related to social studies, science, and current events. For example, a teacher can share a news clipping that describes a controversial current event. Students listen and then, guided by teacher questions, identify key points and formulate opinions. Historical events can be treated in the same fashion. Studying events such as the "treason" of Benedict Arnold, the "civil disobedience" of the Boston Tea Party, and the duel-shooting of Alexander Hamilton, youngsters read several accounts of the events. They identify key factors and note discrepancies. They ponder reasons for actions and try to view an issue from all sides. Ultimately, discussants formulate their own positions, take sides, and support their positions with reasons. The word *positions* in the preceding sentence is significant, for within discussion groups all children need not arrive at the same opinion.

Graphic information can also provide context for thinking aloud. Several political cartoons about the same event, a series of graphs or maps, and data from experimental studies can be examined and discussed in teacher-guided or small groups. The possibilities are endless.

Teaching Critical Thinking: Going from the Simple to the Complex

A second strategy that triggers critical thinking is to lay the foundation for higher-order thinking tasks by starting with lower-order ones. The teacher in *The Lorax* vignette did this when early on he asked students to name the acts committed by the Onceler. Specifying examples is a lower-order task. Higher-order tasks include

1. Describing data,
2. Grouping related items,
3. Labeling groups or categories,
4. Formulating generalizations and inferences,
5. Identifying criteria for judging and developing judgments based on these criteria (Taba, 1964).

Hilda Taba's research (1967) indicates that if children are asked to perform a higher-order, more abstract thinking operation before identifying specific examples, they generally are not able to perform the higher-order task, and discussion founders. It indicates that to involve children in thinking about complex interrelationships, a teacher should sequence questions from less to more abstract, as Mr. Dag did in the model teaching-in-action lesson. See Figure 8.9 for question sequences that lead to critical thinking as a response to literature.

Taba's work verifies that guiding a discussion to involve children in critical thinking is not easy. When planning a discussion (as differentiated from a lower-order conversation), teachers must identify a tentative track of questions through which to guide youngsters in pondering diverse ramifications. Although in the actual discussion teachers will diverge from their plans, it is helpful to consider in advance the sequence of questions. In essence, teachers must have a discussion plan and, as they teach, apply that plan flexibly to involve children in productive thinking and talking.

Teaching Critical Thinking: Voting

A third strategy for involving children in critical thinking is voting. The teacher in *The Lorax* vignette opened the session with a simple vote; listeners indicated by waving their hands whether they liked or disliked a character. Sidney Simon et al. (1972) advocate judgmental voting, especially as an ice breaker. In voting, every participant is involved; no one sits back while others talk, since everyone reacts with a nonverbal signal: hand waving. Simon suggests five nonverbal signals students can make, although one can stick to simple hand waving if preferred:

✦ Thumbs up and waving if reactors are in high agreement,
✦ Thumbs up if reactors like or agree,
✦ Thumbs down if reactors dislike or disagree,

◆ Thumbs down and waving if reactors dislike or disagree violently,

◆ Arms crossed if reactors have no comment.

That the first response is nonverbal and in unison has advantages, according to Simon. A nonverbal response is easier to make than a verbal one. Reactors need not phrase a sentence; rather, they react almost spontaneously. For children fearful of participating orally, a unison response allows immediate participation as their responses blend into the group's. Also, the fact that children are con-

---

I. QUESTIONS THAT ENCOURAGE CHILDREN TO THINK CRITICALLY ABOUT A BOOK OR STORY THEY HAVE READ

Background questions

- Who are the characters? How does the story begin? How does it develop? How does it end? What is the story saying to you? What is its message?

Critical-Thinking Questions

- What part of the story do you like best/least? What makes you like/dislike it?
- What character do you like best/least? What did that character do/not do that makes you like/dislike him or her? Why does that act appeal/not appeal to you? When has anything similar happened to you?
- What picture do you like best/least? What is it about that picture that makes you like/not like it?
- What words or groups of words appeal/do not appeal to you? Why do you like/dislike those words?
- Is the message or the story a valid one? Does it give a truthful picture of what happens in the real world? Why? Why not? Does the message apply to life today? Why? Why not? Does the message mean anything to you personally? Why? Why not?
- Are there stereotypes in the story? Give some examples.

Summary-Evaluating Questions

- Would you like to read this story again? Why? Why not?
- Would you like to share this story with a friend? Why? Why not? What kind of person would like/dislike this story? Why?
- Is this a good story? What evidence do you have to support your judgment?

II. QUESTIONS THAT ENCOURAGE CHILDREN TO THINK CRITICALLY ABOUT STORY AND EVERYDAY ACTS

Background Questions

- What did the character (person) do or say when . . .?
  (Ask children to describe a particular act.)

(continued)

Figure 8.9 A Chart of Teacher Questions That Trigger Critical Thinking

II. QUESTIONS THAT ENCOURAGE CHILDREN TO THINK CRITICALLY ABOUT STORY AND EVERYDAY ACTS (CONT.)

Critical-Thinking Questions

- Was it right (fair, just, smart) for the character (person) to do that? Was it right for the character to say that? Why? Why not?
- What happened as a result? How did that act affect other people?
- What circumstances led him or her to do that?
- What was his or her reason for doing that? Was that reason a good one? What evidence do you have to support your judgment?
- What moral principles, or big ideas about right and wrong, are behind what you are saying?
- What would you have done if you have been the character? Why would you have done that? How would other people have judged your act? Why?

Figure 8.9 *Continued*

tributing even though their contribution is part of a unison response accustoms them to joining in. The initial involvement breeds greater involvement as youngsters get caught up in an issue.

Teaching Critical Thinking: Rank Ordering and Defending

Asking students to rank order and then defend their ordering is a fourth strategy that encourages children to think critically. In ranking, discussants choose among alternatives and explain the reasons for their choices. In so doing, they discover that issues are often more complex than is apparent at first. The teacher in *The Lorax* vignette used this approach when he asked children to rank the five acts on the evils board. Students had to make choices, defend them to their team, develop a group consensus, and defend their consensus before the class.

The value of ranking and defending lies in the fact that students must go beyond the simple labels *good* and *bad* and judge the extent of good and evil. In so doing, youngsters function within a gray area in which there is no absolute right or wrong. Since not all children in a class rank a series of alternatives in the same way, the strategy elicits a difference in opinion, and that difference is a key to involved discussions. Youngsters typically are eager to defend their team's reasoning, and discussion becomes fast and furious.

In the lesson with *The Lorax*, the teacher devised the alternatives that students ranked and presented them in written form. A teacher can vary the technique by delivering the options orally. With this variation, students will refine their listening skills. Using an oral approach in lower grades, a teacher may limit alternatives to three so that youngsters will be able to recall significant details.

Or the teacher can work with a small writing team to compose alternatives related to a social science or current events topic being studied, a story read, or a film viewed. In that case, individuals from the writing team present the alternatives orally to the class for rank ordering. Or if youngsters have pondered an evils board of the teacher's making, individually they can devise a follow-up sheet of related evils for rank ordering and discussion.

Teaching Critical Thinking: Writing and Reading

In teaching thinking, writing and reading are fundamental strategies, especially when used in concert. Writing is a way to make thoughts stand still so that they can be examined. It is a form of communication that forces one to handle relationships and organize ideas logically. At its highest level, reading requires the interpretation of meanings not explicitly stated in the text, the generation of comparisons and contrasts, the classification of ideas, and the formulation of generalizations and judgments. Research by Robert Tierney (1990) indicates that evaluative thinking and perspective shifting increase when reading and writing occur together. Reading and writing foster critical thinking, but when used together, they form a powerful combination.

As the previous literature-based vignette suggests, writing is a natural outgrowth of thinking aloud. To follow discussion with composing is one way to focus on key points and to teach summarizing. At the same time, the teacher discovers whether students have comprehended the major points discussed and can distinguish the significant from the insignificant. This is especially true in teacher-guided group writing, in which children together think through ideas and propose sentences to include in a cooperative composition.

Specific teacher-guided group writing activities to use as follow-up to a discussion are numerous, especially in science and social studies. For example, children who have discussed the meanings expressed in a graph can compose a one-paragraph summary. Children who have talked about a series of pictures can compose a paragraph or two explaining relationships. Children who have orally analyzed a series of maps can organize a paragraph that translates into verbal form the ideas shown visually. In this way, development of thinking and writing skills becomes an objective of content-area teaching. Skills are taught naturally as youngsters work with meaningful content.

Similarly, reading is a natural component of thinking-aloud sessions. Youngsters can read to find related facts and ideas, categorize facts and ideas, contrast one selection with another, generalize, and criticize.

The teacher is the key factor in determining whether reading develops critical thinking prowess. The focus he or she gives to classroom reading determines what levels of thinking children pursue—whether they read only to get the facts explicitly stated, read for ideas implied in the text, and/or rely on their own background information and associations in their interpretation of the text. In the previous teaching-in-action vignette, Mr. Dag asked his sixth-graders to

See P. David Pearson and Dale Johnson, *Teaching Reading Comprehension* (New York: Holt, Rinehart and Winston, 1978), 157–164, for a discussion of what these authors call "text explicit," "text implicit," and "script implicit" reasoning in reading. Read Taffy Raphael's "Question-Answering Strategies for Children," *The Reading Teacher*, 36 (November 1982), 186–190, for a discussion of the Question-Answer Relationship (QAR) strategy. Using QARs, children identify the three ways they find answers to questions. Answers to "Right There" questions are right in the text; answers to "Think and Search" questions must be put together from ideas in the text; answers to "On My Own" questions must be found within children's own knowledge base.

compare Dr. Seuss's *The Butter Battle Book* with *The Lorax*, a selection about which they now had considerable understanding. Thinking through similarities, the children discovered the characteristics of allegory, which they went on to use in their own writing, and also discovered fundamental meanings that they could apply to problems of everyday life. In the process, they were using language to reflect on experience, something Anne Dyson and Celia Genishi (1983) call the "essence of critical verbal thinking." In short, they were learning to think.

Planning for Critical Thinking: Talk Tracks

Oral language involvement is essential in a language arts program that teaches critical thinking. By using oral language to reflect on their experiences, children can try out and refine thinking processes fundamental to reading and listening

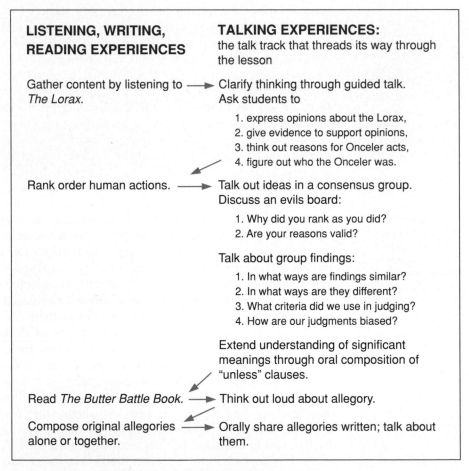

LISTENING, WRITING, READING EXPERIENCES

TALKING EXPERIENCES: the talk track that threads its way through the lesson

Gather content by listening to *The Lorax.* → Clarify thinking through guided talk. Ask students to
  1. express opinions about the Lorax,
  2. give evidence to support opinions,
  3. think out reasons for Onceler acts,
  4. figure out who the Onceler was.

Rank order human actions. → Talk out ideas in a consensus group. Discuss an evils board:
  1. Why did you rank as you did?
  2. Are your reasons valid?

Talk about group findings:
  1. In what ways are findings similar?
  2. In what ways are they different?
  3. What criteria did we use in judging?
  4. How are our judgments biased?

Extend understanding of significant meanings through oral composition of "unless" clauses.

Read *The Butter Battle Book.* → Think out loud about allegory.

Compose original allegories alone or together. → Orally share allegories written; talk about them.

Figure 8.10 A Talk Track for Critical Thinking

See William Teale, "Toward a Theory of How Children Learn to Read and Write Naturally," *Language Arts*, 59 (September 1982), 555–570, for a discussion of the importance of social interaction in learning to read and write.

with comprehension, to writing and speaking with clarity, and to general problem solving.

To this end, the teacher may want to plan in terms of "talk tracks": sequences of oral language activity that tie children's previous experiences to a particular situation at hand—a story to be interpreted, a project to be completed, a question to be resolved. A talk track is simply an oral track that winds its way through children's planned and unplanned classroom activity.

Figure 8.10 diagrams the listening, talking, reading, and writing activities that Mr. Dag used in relation to *The Lorax*. This talk track highlights the oral interactions children will experience. A teacher can design similar talk tracks based on hypothetical problems in social studies (You Are There at the Boston Tea Party—What Will You Do?), current issues (You See a Classmate Copying During a Test—What Do You Do?), a science demonstration (What Happens to Ice Held in Sunshine?). The purpose of a talk track is to get children thinking aloud so that they learn to use language to reflect on experiences—direct experiences in the real world and vicarious experiences from the world of books—and to use language to think critically.

BUILDING AND REFINING YOUR TEACHING SKILLS

This section has set forth a design for sequencing activities so that children think critically as they work with ideas from books and from the content areas. That design can be summarized as follows:

◆ *Contact with content.* Students have access to meaningful facts and ideas that serve as content for thinking aloud.

◆ *Thinking aloud.* Students orally ponder the content. They identify examples, formulate generalizations and inferences, and develop opinions and judgments. As they think aloud, they vote, rank order, hypothesize about what they would do, and defend their positions.

◆ *Composing together.* In teacher-guided and independent group composition, students summarize ideas discussed. The thoughts are charted so that when children write independently, they can review ideas using their charts.

◆ *Reading and composing alone.* Students independently write and/or read material based on what they have talked about and composed together.

Devise a sequence based on a literary selection or on content area material that includes these components. Organize the sequence as a talk track.

.........A Summary Thought or Two

FROM EXPERIENCING TO CRITICAL THINKING

Everyone has experienced the frustration of taking pen in hand to compose a letter, a report, or perhaps a story, only to find that words are hard to come by. Similarly, everyone has experienced the frustration of reading a selection and being unable to comprehend it. In contrast, everyone knows the joy of talking out ideas with a companion and discovering that ideas take new forms and directions. In thinking aloud, a person finds words to express ideas and expands the ideas themselves. Everyone also knows the joy of approaching the reading of a difficult text armed with considerable prior knowledge garnered in talk with friends. The text is not difficult; ideas are easy to grasp as one perceives written ideas in terms of what one already knows. The known comes to the aid of the unknown.

Remembering their own frustrations and joys, teachers should take care to build in successes rather than failures as they design language experiences. As this chapter stresses, teachers need to help children learn to use language to reflect on their experiences to prepare them for independent reading and writing. Teachers can provide this help by engaging children in experiencing, brainstorming, and thinking critically. Through talking, listening, and writing together, children find ideas to communicate and words with which to express ideas on paper. They develop the vocabulary and conceptual background important in reading and listening. Simultaneously they acquire oral language facility through active communication.

RELATED READINGS

Applebee, Arthur, and Judith Langer. "Instructional Scaffolding: Reading and Writing as Natural Language Activities." *Language Arts*, 60 (February 1983). 168–175.

Baron, Joan, and Robert Sternberg, eds. *Teaching Thinking Skills: Theory and Practice*. New York: W.H. Freeman, 1987.

Beyer, Barry. *Practical Strategies for the Teaching of Thinking*. Boston: Allyn and Bacon, 1987.

Booth, David, and Carol Thomley-Hall, eds. *Classroom Talk: Speaking and Listening Activities from Classroom-based Teacher Research.* Portsmouth, N.H.: Heinemann Educational Books, 1992.

Costa, Arthur, ed. *Developing Minds: A Resource Book for Teaching Thinking*. Alexandria, Va.: Association for Supervision and Curriculum Development, 1985.

Heath, S. B. "The Sense of Being Literate: Historical and Cross-Cultural Features." In *Handbook of Reading Research, Vol. II*. Ed. R. Barr et al. New York: Longman, 1991, 3–25.

Hennings, Dorothy Grant. *Beyond the Read Aloud: Learning to Read Through Listening and Reflecting*. Bloomington, Ind.: Phi Delta Kappa, 1992.

Kirby, Dan, and Carol Kuykendall. *Mind Matters: Teaching for Thinking*. Portsmouth, N.H.: Heinemann Educational Books, 1991.

Kolb, David. *Experiential Learning: Experience as the Source of Learning and Development*. Englewood Cliffs, N.J.: Prentice-Hall, 1984.

Marzano, Robert. *Cultivating Thinking in English and Language Arts*. Urbana, Ill.: National Council of Teachers of English, 1991.

———. "Language, the Language Arts, and Thinking." In *Handbook of Research on Teaching the English Language Arts*. Ed. J. Flood et al. New York: Macmillan, 1991, 559–586.

McMillan, Merna, and Lance Gentile. "Children's Literature: Teaching Critical Thinking and Ethics." *The Reading Teacher*, 41 (May 1988), 876–878.

Nielsen, Allan, *Critical Thinking and Reading*. Urbana, Ill.: National Council of Teachers of English, 1989.

Olson, Carol. *Thinking Writing: Fostering Critical Thinking Through Writing*. New York: HarperCollins, 1992.

Presseisen, Barbara. *Thinking Skills: Research and Practice*. Washington, D.C.: National Education Association, 1986.

Raths, Louis, et al. *Teaching for Thinking: Theories, Strategies, and Activities*. 2nd ed. New York: Teachers College Press, 1986.

Silberman, Arlene. *Growing Up Writing: Teaching Our Children to Write, Think, and Learn*. Portsmouth, N.H.: Heinemann Educational Books, 1991.

Sternberg, Robert J. "Critical Thinking: Its Nature, Measurement and Improvement." In *Essays on the Intellect*. Ed. Frances Link. Washington, D.C.: Association for Supervision and Curriculum Development, 1985.

Wilson, Marilyn. "Critical Thinking: Repackaging or Revolution?" *Language Arts*. 65 (October 1988), 543–551.

Lizzy Kushner
Gr. 3 Rm. 22
Lying   The Thanksgiving Tresure By Gail Rock

I think you should only lie in a matter of life or death,
but other wize you should never lie. For example, when Addie
went on the highway when she wasn't sopposed to, that was
lying. When Addie went to Mr. Rehnquist's house for the
Thanksgiving dinner and her dad sad not to, that was lying.
I said it once and I'll say it again, you should only lie
in a matter of life or death.

For example of life or death if my friend was wanted
and if they found my friend my friend would die I would
defenitly lie.

Lizzy thought critically about questions of right and wrong in *The Thanksgiving Treasure* **as she made her journal entry and amended it** (courtesy of Lizzy Kushner and Micki Benjamin).

PART FOUR

WRITTEN COMMUNICATION IN ACTION

"When I use a word," Humpty Dumpty said in a rather scornful tone, "it means just what I choose it to mean. . . ."

"The question is," said Alice, "whether you can make words mean so many different things."

"The question is," said Humpty Dumpty, "which is to be master—that's all."

—Lewis Carroll, *Through the Looking Glass*

How do we help children become masters of words—especially written words? How do we help children to say what they mean as they write and make meaning with words as they read? In answering these questions, we must delve deeply into how writers and readers function, we must think about how children develop as writers and readers, and we must consider the nature, the structures, and the kinds of written communications—stories, poems, and nonfiction—that children write and read.

The chapters in Part Four focus on written communication within an integrated language arts. The basic theses of the chapters are that to learn to write children must function as authors, processing and reprocessing ideas the way real authors do; that to learn to read children must be involved from the start in authentic reading, making their own meanings as they interact with an author's ideas; that reading and writing blend as children use writing to respond to written ideas and as they read to find ideas to express in their own writing; that the conventions of writing and the skills of reading are best learned in meaning-filled contexts when children need the conventions and the skills to make meaning and to communicate.

As you read these chapters, ask yourself: How can I encourage children to function as authors? How can I involve them in authentic reading? How can I guide children to read as they rehearse for writing and write in response to reading? Ask, too, the ultimate question: How can I help children discover the excitement of writing and the joy of reading?

CHAPTER 9

Writing as Idea Making

Creative Thought in Action

Reflecting Before Reading

What is creative thinking?

_____
_____
_____

What is the relationship between thinking and writing?

_____
_____
_____

How do young children emerge as writers?

_____
_____

How does the teacher involve children in creating prose and poetry?

_____
_____
_____

Expanding ideas through writing

BEFORE reading the chapter, read the title, the headings, and the end-of-chapter summary. Then answer the questions in the margin on this page.

TEACHING IN ACTION   Journals, Idea Clusters, and Other Ways to Make Ideas

It was a cold December morning, and snow was in the air. Jennifer Chou's third-graders came into their room, went to their desks, took out their writing journals, read the replies Ms. Chou had written to them based on their prior entries, and without prompting began to write. After greeting her youngsters, Ms. Chou did the same: She went to her desk, took out her journal, and jotted down ideas.

Making Ideas Through Sharing Ideas

When the third-graders began looking up to indicate they had written some first thoughts, Ms. Chou told them to gather around her in the Magic Circle. She asked if any of them wanted to share anything they had written in the past few days—a piece they had worked on during Writing Workshop or even what they had just written in their journals. The children in this class were accustomed to sharing their drafts, and many were eager to read their work aloud. Using her checklist indicating which students had not shared in the past week, Ms. Chou selected three sharers.

Each child in turn sat in the Author's Chair, which was placed in the Magic Circle, and read what he or she had written. Sean shared sentences he had written about a fire in his neighborhood. When he had finished, his classmates received his work by first summing up what he had said and then by asking him

Expanding ideas
through sharing

things about the fire that he had not told them in his writing: How did the fire start? What time had the fire happened? How had he felt? Had anyone been hurt? Sean answered the questions, putting check marks on his paper to remind him of spots where he might add ideas. Then Trudie "celebrated" his writing by telling him, "I liked your story. I liked what you said about the firefighters."

Sean answered, "I'll let you read it when I get it fixed."

Two other youngsters shared what they had written. Their classmates responded as they had with Sean: summing up the main points, asking for more information, and commenting on what they particularly liked.

Making Ideas Through Idea Clustering

After the three youngsters had shared, Ms. Chou distributed construction paper and crayons. She explained to the third-graders, "On my way to school today, I thought about what I would write during journal time. I let my ideas roll around in my head. I made 'mind talk.' By the time I got to school, I was sure I wanted to write about how I felt about winter coming, but I didn't have any specific ideas ready to write, and so this morning I just played with words on paper."

Developing an idea
through clustering

Ms. Chou then went to the board. "Because I did not know where to begin, I drew a circle in the middle of my paper like this, and I wrote *winter* in the circle. Then I began to sort of 'idea doodle.' I drew a line outward from the circle and wrote the word *cold* at the end. I added *snow* to that, and then *ice.* I kept adding words to words as they came to mind." With that, Ms. Chou added the words to her Winter Idea Cluster and asked the students to draw a similar cluster on the construction paper using their crayons. She asked them to think of words that came to their minds. When many hands went up, she told the students to add their words to their own papers. She continued to "doodle," adding more words to the cluster on the board. After a few moments, she stopped to ask the students to give her words from their clusters, which she added to hers. She told the students that if they ran out of words or phrases to add to their clusters, they could help themselves to ideas from her cluster or from a neighbor's.

Read Gabriele Rico, *Writing the Natural Way* (Los Angeles: J. P. Tarcher, 1983), for a thorough discussion of idea clustering and writing.

When the board was filled with a cluster of thoughts (see Figure 9.1), Ms. Chou asked the children to help her write a first sentence that would get her started writing about winter. She suggested that they write the starting sentence by focusing on one group of thoughts within their webs, then write another by focusing on a different group within the webs. Again, when hands went up, she told the students to write their ideas around the edges of their own idea clusters. As the children drafted starting thoughts, she wrote her own ideas on her cluster and then added several offered by the children.

With that, Ms. Chou asked a student to copy the cluster on the board so that she could use it as an idea bank when she wrote in her journal tomorrow. Ms. Chou told the children to fold their idea clusters in half and place them in their active-writing portfolios. She told them that winter thoughts was an option they could select to write about during Writing Workshop time or in their journals sometime during the day if that topic appealed to them. She

Winter is a
happy time

A snow blanket
covers the land

Climb on
our sleigh

Down, down, down

I speed across
the ice into the wind.

Figure 9.1 An Idea Cluster on Winter

suggested that if they ever had trouble getting started in writing, they could always do what she had done that morning: draw an idea cluster and write several possible starting sentences around its edges.

Making Ideas Through Listening, Reading, and Talking

Having modeled the process of idea development through clustering, Ms. Chou dismissed most of the students. These students needed no additional direction at this point; they knew from prior experiences that they were to take out their active-writing portfolios and work on something "in process." Students like Sean could work on revising a piece they had shared with the class. Some could work on a piece they wanted to share. Others could work with their Writing Editor, sharing and getting feedback on a piece already begun. Some could select a topic from the many options they had recorded on the inside of their writing portfolios and start a new piece. Others could read published pieces by other students that hung from the classroom clothesline. Still others could read from a book they had in progress. The one thing they all had to do was keep a log of how they spent the time—a log that Ms. Chou looked over each day.

While most students worked independently on writing or reading or collaborated on editing, Ms. Chou worked in the Conferencing Center with seven

The writing child is a thinking child. (© 1993 Michael Zide)

youngsters who in the past had had trouble getting started in writing. She introduced the poem "Helping" by Shel Silverstein by asking them what thoughts the word *helping* brought to their minds. As the students responded, they recorded the words idea cluster style on paper. Then Ms. Chou read the poem aloud, and the students followed along on their own copies. Next, the students orally chorused the poem and talked about what Silverstein was saying (his main idea), how Silverstein had structured the piece, and what they liked about it. They mentioned the repetitive style and the rhyming names. They talked about times when people had given them good help and times when people had given them help they could have done without. They mapped the structure of the poem to show the flow from supporting details to main idea as in Figure 9.2. They also brainstormed writing possibilities that appealed to them based on "Helping" and recorded those options on the inside of their portfolios for future reference: "What I Like or Don't Like about the Silverstein Poem," "When Someone Gave Me Help I Could Do Without," and a poem structured like "Helping."

See Chapter 6, pages 197–198, for a copy of "Helping."

Making Ideas Through Conferencing

The seven students in the work group returned to their desks. Ms. Chou then called three other youngsters to the Conferencing Center. The night before,

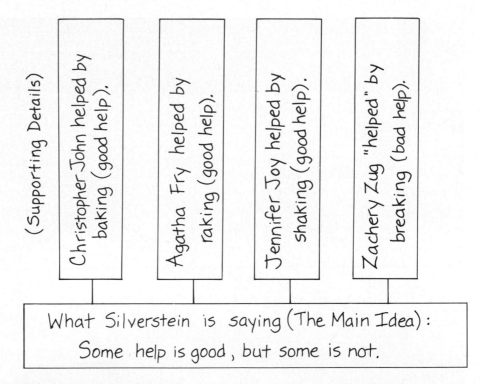

Figure 9.2   A Map of Shel Silverstein's "Helping" Showing the Main Idea and Supporting Details

See Figure 10.8 for a conference guide that identifies problem elements with which a teacher can help a student during a conference.

these children had placed papers that they believed were ready for a prepublication conference in Ms. Chou's Ready for a Conference basket. Ms. Chou had read the papers in preparation for the conference. During the conference, each child read his or her composition aloud, told what he or she thought were its good points, and indicated where help was needed. Both Ms. Chou and the other two children in the group gave help as requested. Ms. Chou also focused each child's attention on two or three sentences that needed revision. In general, these sentences had the same problem element, which Ms. Chou checked off on a conferencing checklist that the student took back to his or her desk to refer to during rewriting. Together teacher and students talked about how to make these sentences "better." Finally, with the children helping and watching, Ms. Chou highlighted misspelled words with a yellow highlighting marker to give the young authors guidance in reworking their compositions for publication in the classroom newsletter.

Following the conference, the students went back to work on their own. Ms. Chou began to circulate from desk to desk for "quickie conferences." Students who had run into difficulty while Ms. Chou was working at the Conferencing Center had written their names on a section of the chalkboard labeled "Must Have a Teacher Conference Today." At this point, Ms. Chou helped these students talk through their ideas and problems.

Idea Making in Action

In Ms. Chou's classroom, idea making—or creative thinking—is what writing is all about. Children in her class make ideas as they write spontaneously in their journals, share what they have drafted, "mind talk" before and during writing, and conference with their teacher. Although Ms. Chou's goal is helping children grow in writing skills, her initial emphasis is on helping them generate the ideas they express through writing—that is, on the higher-order thinking that is the core of the writing process.

Because idea making is the heart of writing, let us consider the nature of creative thought and what it means in terms of writing in the elementary grades.

What Idea Making Is About

In *On Knowing*, a brief volume that is a classic in education, Jerome Bruner (1962) speaks of the creative process: "The act of a person creating is the act of a whole person. . . . it is this rather than the product that makes it good and worthy." To Bruner, a creative act is one that "produces *effective surprise* . . . that strikes [the creator] with wonder or astonishment." Everyone has experienced the surprise that is part of creating—of coming upon a good idea. Often it is this surprise that makes creating a joyous adventure and propels one to complete the physical and mental tasks that are part of bringing a creative idea to fruition.

The word *creative* here does not imply that creativity in writing is restricted to the making of poems and stories. Ronald Cramer (1979) reminds us, "The term *creative* is intended to express the idea that . . . words and sentences are the personal product of the [person's] experience and imagination. The product itself may be a letter, a story, a poem, a report, an observation, or an account." The idea may be an opinion, a generalization, a conclusion, a hypothesis, a unique relationship. To formulate that idea, the writer may have to analyze and evaluate as well as synthesize.

Creating is a paradoxical process, according to Bruner (1962), requiring detachment and commitment, passion and decorum, freedom and domination, deferral and immediacy. To put together fresh combinations, thinkers must detach themselves from existing forms; they must escape the constraints of the expected. But at the same time, creators must care deeply about understanding and discovering. They must be both detached from the available and committed to the novel.

In like manner, people must be both passionate and decorous to create. They must let ideas wing away in the arms of passion, soaring until the mind has explored every ramification. They must thrill to the expansion of ideas, perceiving the beauty of intertwining relationships. But as Bruner explains, "There is a decorum in creative activity: a love of form, an etiquette toward the object of our efforts, a respect for materials." It is decorum that allows the mind to control and shape the random flow of ideas.

In explaining the third paradox, freedom and domination, Bruner describes the point at which a poem in the process of being created takes form. The poem-in-process becomes an entity in its own right, an externalized object, something "out there" that dominates the writer, compelling him or her to complete it. The creating poet begins to serve the poem rather than the poem serving the poet. When that happens, the writer is freed of defenses that prevent him or her from expressing innermost thoughts. Because the piece is "out there," the writer can experiment with style and content without feeling vulnerable.

Deferral and immediacy are paradoxical aspects of creating, too. Creators have a wild flow of ideas that at times cry out to be expressed. They know what they want to say; they rush to record. But as Bruner maintains, only occasionally does the piece "come off lickety-split," finished in first draft in a form the writer likes. Bruner speaks of "precocious completion," suggesting that deferral in producing a finished draft is generally necessary. Writers must stand back; they must "distance" themselves from what they have created and examine it with a fresh eye.

Creating and School Writing

This brief discussion of the paradoxical aspects of creating provides a framework for thinking about writing as it occurs in schools. At some point, children

Meredith Ann Pierce, whose books include *The Darkangel* and *A Gathering of Gargoyles* (Atlantic Monthly/Little, Brown), describes what happens to her as she writes: "When I sit down to write, I enter a state that is very like dreaming. I become still, relaxed. I lose all track of my surroundings and of the passage of time. I'm not easy to rouse from this state by telephones ringing or my housemates shouting up the stairs, but I surface on my own from time to time, and more often than not, it's to find myself speaking: dialogue mostly, or the closing lines of a scene—replaying them endlessly until I get them right. I'm told that I also talk in my sleep" ("The Queen of the Night," *The New Advocate*, 1 [Fall 1988], 221).

Pierce also talks about the way she feels about writing: "'Tyger Tyger! burning bright.' I was in love with that poem when I was little. The ferocity and sensuality of its fevered imagery quickened my imagination deliciously and made me think of dark forests, and wandering, and coming unexpectedly upon that which, all unknowingly, I had been seeking—a great cat, incandescently kindled, its fearful symmetry immortally framed. I am in love with it still.

"To write a novel is to be in love. It is to wander dark forests, encountering tigers. I've been referred to as a writer of fantasy stories that have strong female protagonists. Upon reflection, I suppose this is true. I've written four novels, all of them high fantasy, and in three of the four, the main character is female. Yet when people ask me about my heroines, where they come from, on whom they are modeled, and I respond, '"The Tiger" by William Blake,' I'm looked at as though I haven't answered the question" ("A Lion in the Room," *The Horn Book*, 64 [January/February 1988], 35).

Questions to Consider

How does Meredith Ann Pierce make her ideas? What relationship do you perceive between the writings of Pierce and Bruner? What can teachers do to engage children in the higher-order thinking operations that are at the heart of the writing process? What approaches did Ms. Chou use in the opening vignette to engage children in the creative writing process?

should experience the detachment from what is known and the commitment to know more, the passion to fly with ideas and the decorum ultimately to control them, the freedom to express ideas and the domination by those ideas, the need for immediate expression and the need to defer for review. To this end, school writing *should not*

+ Require students to write without opportunity for prior thought. Ideas are not "made" on a topic on command.
+ Cast the teacher in the role of external evaluator.

- ✦ Emphasize form over ideas. Form follows ideas, and form flows from ideas when the writer recognizes the value of what he or she has created.
- ✦ Take away the joy of creating.

To this end, school writing *should*

- ✦ Provide youngsters with time to create ideas, strategies for expanding ideas, and opportunity to talk out and share ideas.
- ✦ Emphasize idea making in all kinds of contexts—the writing of prose as well as poetry, the writing of critical reports as well as stories. Teachers and students must realize that writing critically is a creative endeavor, for it requires the making of ideas.
- ✦ Encourage youngsters to review their writing, to stand back and look with a "fresh eye."
- ✦ Encourage children to use their peers as sounding boards for idea making.
- ✦ Enable children to experience the "effective surprise" that is what idea making is all about.

Idea Making and Emergent Writing

Making ideas through writing should occur the moment a child sets foot in a classroom. It is not something that must wait until children have learned the alphabet or know how to read. Research indicates that most children are writers before they come to school and are eager to write in nursery school and kindergarten.

Young Children as Writers: What the Research Says

The young child is surrounded by print. Print is on cereal boxes on the kitchen table, everywhere in supermarkets, on signs and billboards, on television, on calendars. Print is in books, magazines, and newspapers that family members read and share. Surrounded by print, young children come naturally to understand that print is used to talk about things around them; in time, they come naturally to use print creatively to express their thoughts.

See also Marcia Baghban, *Our Daughter Learns to Read and Write: A Case Study from Birth to Three* (Newark, Del.: International Reading Association, 1984), for an account of another child's emergence as a writer.

How Young Children Invent Language to Write In *GNYS AT WRK*, Glenda Bissex (1980) chronicles her son Paul's writing development starting when he was about five. Paul's first writing was the production of a welcome-home banner for his mother. The banner was replete with his unique combination of original letters, a combination that language educators have termed *invented spelling*. A viewer of educational television programs depicting letters and sounds and a member of a family in which reading and writing played a significant role, within months Paul was spontaneously writing messages like *RUDF* (Are you deaf?), a message he used to get his busy mother's attention.

Read Dorothy Strickland and Lesley Morrow, "Emerging Readers and Writers: Young Children's Early Writing Development," *The Reading Teacher*, 42 (February 1989), 426–427.

Many researchers have documented that at home, young children willingly plunge into writing ideas on paper with an originality all their own and enthusiastically read back what they have created, in the process adding orally to their written ideas. At this stage and in this context, children's writing departs from conventional letter formation and spelling. Yet, as Diane DeFord and Jerome Harste (1982) maintain, this writing is much more than scribble. The writing of typical three- and four-year-olds already demonstrates an impressive understanding by the children of the nature of written messages and the written form of their language. Children begin to exhibit knowledge of linearity, left-to-right and top-to-bottom directionality, and uniformity of size and shape. In addition, Harste (1982) has found evidence in children's early writing of intention (purpose in writing), invention (creativity of ideas), and organization (logical development of ideas). According to Nigel Hall (1987), by the time children enter school, most know that

✦ Writing is a meaningful language activity;
✦ The purpose of writing is to communicate messages;
✦ Written language is composed of various elements;
✦ Writing takes on certain forms and structures.

Vera Milz (1985) confirms young children's rudimentary understanding of written language. Milz has found that many first-graders are already experimenting with written language to record and request information, to pretend and to build relationships. In short, first-graders are using higher-order thinking as they function as emerging writers.

Stories courtesy of DeeJay Schwartz, a kindergarten teacher. Names of stages are after Charles Temple et al., *The Beginnings of Writing*, 3d ed. (Boston: Allyn and Bacon, 1993).

Stages in Writing Development

Obviously not all children of the same age or grade level write in the same way. This can be seen in the children's writing in Figures 9.3 through 9.6. All the children whose writing appears in these figures were in kindergarten at the time.

Omari's story (Figure 9.3) represents an early developmental stage in making ideas with print: preletter making, or line making. His writing, however, is not scribble. Omari has a clear understanding of left-to-right and top-to-bottom progression. He knows that writing tells a story, for he reads his story. His teacher, DeeJay Schwartz, reports that each reading is the same and is almost a perfect rendition of what the tour guide said when the children visited the dinosaur museum, a visit that provided Omari with the ideas for writing. His teacher further reports that although Omari knows letters and sounds from nursery school, at this stage he does not want to be bothered with them in writing.

Kerry's story (Figure 9.4) represents another developmental stage in writing: random letter making. As Ms. Schwartz reports, Kerry knows that letters exist and can distinguish among sounds, but at this stage words look like bunches of random letters to her, and she has not yet perceived the relationship between sounds and letters. When asked to read what she has written, she says, "Well, I just wrote this, but I don't know what it says because I didn't learn to read yet." But Kerry, too, has a considerable understanding of print; she knows that writing progresses from left to right and from top to bottom.

Figure 9.3 Omari's Story: Preletter Stage of Writing Development
Source: Courtesy of Omari Jefferson.
Note: See Omari's name in the box on the left.

Figure 9.4 Kerry's Story: Random Letter-Making Stage of Writing Development
Source: Courtesy of Kerry Bogert.

Figure 9.5 Raphael's Story: Early Phonemic Stage of Writing Development
Source: Courtesy of Raphael Horowitz.
Note: Raphael's story says, "He has plates like spines."

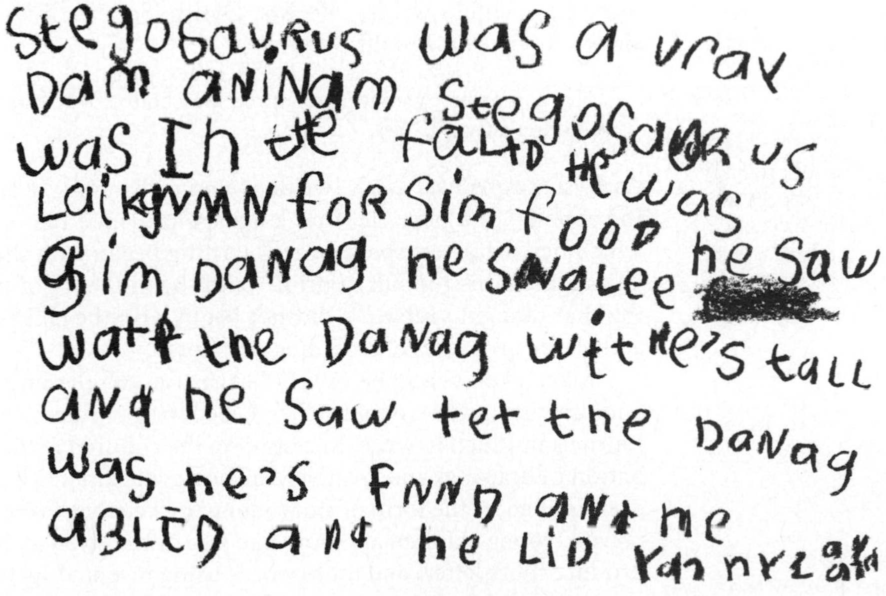

Stegosayrus was a vray
Dam aninam Stegosaurus
was Ih te fauid He was
Laikymn for sim food
Gim Danag he snalee He saw
watt the Danag wit He's tall
and he saw tet the Danag
was he's FNNn ant ne
aBLED ant he LID ran nrzaid

Figure 9.6 Katie's Story: Advanced Phonemic Stage of Writing Development
Source: Courtesy of Katie Burk.

For a review of fifteen years of research on children's emergent writing, read Elizabeth Sulzby, "Research Directions: Transitions from Emergent to Conventional Writing," *Language Arts*, 69 (April 1992), 290–297.

Raphael's paper (Figure 9.5) represents still another stage in writing development: the early phonemic stage. This kindergartner hears and understands the relationship between letters and sounds, especially consonants. He sounds out words he wants to write, estimates how they are spelled, and writes the words that way. He knows there are words and sentences, for he inserts breaks between some words and between sentences. At the early phonemic stage of writing, he is beginning to abide by many conventions of English writing, especially as they apply to the use of consonants.

Katie's paper (Figure 9.6) represents yet another stage: letter name, or advanced phonemic writing. Katie has control over both consonants and vowels. She divides her story into discrete word units. And she tells a great story! As Ms. Schwartz reports, Katie loves writing and reading, and she will try any word. Once she starts either activity, she keeps going until her eyes and/or fingers tire. Katie's enthusiasm and confidence are contagious. She reads her story in this way:

> Stegosaurus was a very dumb animal. Stegosaurus was in the field. He was looking for some food. He saw some danger. He suddenly whacked the danger with his tail and he saw that the danger was his friend and he apologized and he lived happily ever after.

See Anne Dyson and Celia Genishi, "Whatta Ya Tryin' to Write?: Writing as an Interactive Process," *Language Arts*, 59 (February 1982), 126–132; Anne Dyson, "Teachers and Young Children: Missed Connections in Teaching/Learning to Write," *Language Arts*, 59 (October 1982), 674–680; and Anne Dyson, "Reading, Writing, and Language: Young Children Solving the Written Language Puzzle," *Language Arts*, 59 (November/December 1982), 829–839.

Talking, Drawing, and Writing Especially with nursery school, kindergarten, and first-grade children, talking, drawing, and writing blend. Youngsters often use pictures and oral language to flesh out their written stories. Anne Dyson (1981) describes the relationship between the language and visual arts in one young child's writing. To Ms. Dyson, Sara orally told her "Yes Go" story shown in Figure 9.7 in this way:

> Her name's here [pointing to *Sara*]. Somebody yelled "Go." She said "No." Then another girl said, "Yes."

As Dyson explains, "Sara's [written] text is dynamic; it provides the dialogue—the action—of a plot. Her oral language provided the narrative context within which her characters spoke." Sara's writing began with the "selection of an idea, a thought, a thing to put in print—and the discovery of some strategy for making that thought visible." It did not begin with the child's understanding of the alphabetic principles of recording on paper.

Mary Ellen Giacobbe (1981) has also noted the interrelatedness of writing and drawing. A classroom teacher, Giacobbe gave her newly arrived first-graders journals in which to write. In response, the children tended to produce a combination of drawings and creatively spelled print. Interestingly, the tool given children influences the form of storytelling they choose (Woodward, 1984). Given a crayon, young children are more likely to draw; given a pen or a pencil, children produce more letters and more words using invented spellings.

See J. Cook-Gumperz and J. Gumperz, "From Oral to Written Culture: The Transition to Literacy," in *Variations in Writing*, ed. M. Whiteman (Hillsdale, NJ.: Erlbaum, 1981).

Writing and Reading For young children there are no unnatural divisions between writing and reading. Through reading—or through listening to stories

Figure 9.7 Sara's Story
Source: Courtesy of Anne Dyson and the National Council of Teachers of English.

read aloud to them—youngsters begin to perceive relationships between print and speech. For example, picture books that use -*ly* words show young listeners how information conveyed through tone of voice is put down on paper; the writer writes, "'Be quiet,' the teacher said *softly*," to tell how the teacher spoke the words. As Kenneth and Yetta Goodman (1983) summarize so simply and clearly, "Children use in writing what they observe in reading" and in listening to stories. To this end, children must begin to read like writers and notice some of the characteristics of print that are all around them. But ultimately they must write, for it is when children "try to create written language that this observation focuses on how form serves function."

In *What Did I Write?*, Marie Clay (1975) explains why children's early writing has an impact on reading. Children who write—even if they use invented spellings—still manipulate the units of written language: letters, words, and sentences. They must attend to the details of print as they construct words letter by letter; in the process, they become more aware of letter features and sequences. The words children write are the ones they get to know and soon can read on their own.

In summary, the current research on children's early writing emphasizes the following points:

✦ Young children can write creatively before they can spell, before they know the conventions of written language, and before they read.
✦ Teachers must provide young children with opportunities for writing. Children should be encouraged to write, inventing their own way of writing down that meets the needs of the creating they are doing at the moment.

With young children, talking, drawing, and writing blend. (© 1993 Michael Zide)

✦ Children should be encouraged to use talk to expand the ideas they have expressed through drawing and print.

✦ Children need to participate in a host of literacy events—oral encounters with print—so that they have an opportunity to observe the characteristics of print and use them in their writing.

Ways to Help Young Children Emerge as Writers

Involving very young children in writing requires thought on the part of the teacher. As many a nursery school, kindergarten, or first-grade teacher knows, young children are egocentric beings whose worlds revolve around themselves. They are curious about that world—a world close at hand. The attention span of kindergartners and first-graders lengthens each day, but attention still lags quickly. At this stage language expands almost exponentially, with new words entering children's speaking vocabularies daily. Just gaining skill as recorders, young learners find writing down letters a time-consuming task.

These characteristics of young learners determine a teacher's approach to beginning composition. Youngsters at this stage must be personally and actively

THE FORUM   On Children as Emerging Writers

1. James Moffett and Betty Jane Wagner recommend four concurrent activities for becoming literate: "Following a printed text with the eyes while hearing it read. Dictating while watching the words being written down. Writing independently by inventing spelling. Playing word-making and word-recognizing games." As Moffett and Wagner explain, "Read-along takes the reading viewpoint; invented spelling, the writing viewpoint; and dictating, both. Word-making games emphasize writing; word-recognizing games, reading" ("What Works Is Play," *Language Arts*, 70 [January 1993], 32–36).

2. Lesley Mandel Morrow writes, "Adults should take children's early writing seriously as interesting evidence of the kinds of experiments with writing that contribute centrally to their literacy development. Children's early writings are to be enjoyed, valued, and understood. . . .

   "We must realize that what young children write about and how they approach writing is more important than their mechanics of writing (spelling, penmanship, punctuation, and spacing). Mechanical skills *are* related to writing, but not writing as we are concerned with it in early childhood literacy development. Learning to write involves learning to compose texts that convey meaning" (*Literacy Development in the Early Years: Helping Children Read and Write* [Englewood Cliffs, N.J.: Prentice-Hall, 1989], 157).

Questions to Consider

Do you agree with the four concurrent activities Moffett and Wagner recommend? Why or why not? Do you agree that what young children write about is more important than their mechanics of writing? Why or why not?

Lucy Calkins stresses that students become involved in their writing when they write on topics important to them. (*Lessons from a Child: On the Teaching and Learning of Writing* [Portsmouth, N.H.: Heinemann Educational Books, 1983]).

involved in choosing writing topics. Generally, before writing they need to experience and observe, handle, dramatize, and talk out. While writing, they need to talk audibly or subaudibly to themselves.

Because kindergartners and first-graders are only beginning to develop skill in recording ideas on paper, written activity must take into account the level of that skill. Some teachers have found the following activities useful as children start to write.

Drawing and Writing with Invented Spelling   Young children benefit from an approach to writing that does not stress precision in spelling. As children write, they should be encouraged to get their thoughts down on paper in any way they want—drawing, invented spelling, or whatever. The thought is more important than the manner in which it is recorded.

One way of handling invented spelling is to suggest that children think in terms of consonant sounds and provide them with a few consonants to use by teaching those particular sound/symbol correspondences. Donald Graves (Walshe, 1982) has found that youngsters can write using invented spelling "so long as we provide them with six consonants, any six." Children are encouraged to use the consonants they know to "hold the place" of a word or idea. Teachers who allow creative spelling realize that excitement about writing is more important in the early years than precision in recording.

Keeping a Journal   One of the first contexts in which young children should be encouraged to write using their invented spellings and pictures is the journal. At the nursery and kindergarten levels, a journal can be a homemade booklet of pieces of construction paper cut in half and stapled together. Children put an illustration, a title, and their name on the cover. They write whatever they want in the journal, at times prompted by classroom experiences, at other times unprompted—just because they feel like it.

Read and enjoy Barbara Bode, "Dialogue Journal Writing," *The Reading Teacher,* 42 (April 1989), 568–571. Bode states that a dialogue journal is "one way to unlock the literacy puzzle."

After making journal entries, children read them to their teacher or volunteer to share their entries with the class. The teacher also responds to the student by writing back in the journal—creating a written dialogue with the child. In the latter case, the teacher reads what he or she has written to the child, pointing to the words and perhaps asking the child to read along on a second reading. The advantage of this procedure is that it provides the child with a model of letters and words to include in future entries.

Dictating and Publishing   Even as children write using drawings and invented spellings, they participate in experience story writing, with the teacher recording dictated sentences on chart paper or on a computer in language-experience style. Youngsters contribute beginning letters and punctuation marks to the charts as they learn to construct them. At times the teacher talks out how he or she is translating sounds of words into symbols on paper. For example, in recording the teacher says, "I want to write the word *dog. Dog*—the sound that I hear at the beginning of the word *dog* is put down on paper with the letter *d*. I hear the same sound at the beginning of my name—Dorothy. That is why I begin my name with the letter *D*." At the same time, children individually dictate their thoughts to the teacher or to an assistant who records the sentences for them and stops once in awhile to talk out how he or she is translating speech sounds into writing. Used in this way, the language experience approach provides children with a model of how writing relates to the sounds of speech.

If the teacher records a youngster's dictated sentences in pencil, the child can later trace the letters using a brightly colored crayon to provide a publication copy. This helps the child practice letter forms, or penmanship, in a meaningful context and gives him or her a sense of possession of the words recorded on paper. When a child can trace the words he or she has dictated, the teacher records by skipping a line after each line recorded. The youngster publishes by copying each recorded word in the space immediately under it.

Reading Recovery, a first-grade program to help poor readers, was developed in New Zealand by Marie Clay. See "Reading Recovery 1984–1988" (Columbus, Ohio: The Ohio State University, 1988).

Collaborating at Writing   Reading Recovery, an early intervention program geared at helping at-risk six-year-olds emerge as readers, uses a different approach to emergent writing, an approach based on the one-to-one interaction between a teacher and a child (Clay, 1985). In Reading Recovery, the child writes unaided what he or she can while the teacher watches. When the child reaches a word that he or she cannot write, the teacher asks, "What can you hear? What letters would you expect to see?" In a section of paper above the child's composition, the teacher draws the number of boxes that corresponds to the number of phonemes (speech sounds) in the word the child wants to write. The child writes the letters in the boxes that represent each sound to him or her, and the teacher provides help with silent letters and letters that represent difficult sounds or sounds the child has not yet mastered. Having drafted the desired word in this way, the child writes it into the ongoing part of his or her composition. Later, as the child reads, the teacher informally reinforces the same sound-symbol correspondences the child has used in writing.

Brainstorming Words for Writing   Without question, first-graders are thwarted in composing by their limited spelling skills. To encourage children to write despite this limitation, some teachers periodically stand at the board before and while students compose. Children brainstorm words they wish to use, and the teacher writes them on the board. This strategy pays secondary dividends: A word one student identifies may spur others to use it as well.

One first-grade teacher uses a variation on this approach. She posts twenty-six charts around her room under the chalkboard areas and labels each chart with a different letter of the alphabet. When children brainstorm a word before writing or call for one while writing, she records it on the appropriate chart. If the word is already on a chart from a previous day, she directs attention to it. In this way, words children are using begin to decorate the walls of the classroom.

To help children gain skill as recorders, from time to time the teacher may organize a more structured activity. The teacher guides youngsters to brainstorm on a particular topic. For example, Emily Davis had her first-graders brainstorm the months of the year and reasons they liked some months better than others. As the children supplied month names, she listed them in a column on the lefthand side of a chart; as they gave reasons, she listed them on the right side. Then she suggested a structured writing option starting in this way:

> The month I like best is _____ . I like it because _____ .
> I also like it because _____ .

To complete the composition, the children selected words and phrases from the brainstormed chart and used invented spellings to write additional thoughts.

Of course, teachers should provide words children need in writing only sparingly. Youngsters should generally try out spellings on their own and have plenty of opportunities to invent spellings as they compose.

Emergent Writing in the Early Years

A Word Chart:
B b
  1. book
  2. ball
  3. bridge
  4. by
  5. Bill

Researchers have noted differences in the way young children approach writing at home and at school. According to R. K. Moss and John Stansell (1983), children's school writing often reflects a teacher's concern that children make their letters and copy words correctly. In contrast, home writing is more creative, revealing children's belief that the purpose of writing is expression and enjoyment.

DeFord and Harste (1982) have found similar differences between classes in which teachers stress form over meaning and those in which meaning takes precedence over form. In the first kind of classroom, youngsters soon learn that "if you can't spell, you can't write" and that finding the right letters to represent word symbols on paper is what writing is all about. In the second kind, children invent spellings as they experiment with the wonder of language and delight in the process of creation. Here idea making is what writing is about.

Making Ideas with Prose

Donald Graves (1983), Lucy Calkins (1986), Thomas Newkirk and Nancie Atwell (1986), Roy Peter Clark (1987), and other teacher-writers propose that the way to make ideas through writing is to write about things that are personally significant. This means that the teacher does not assign all children to write on a given topic; rather, as Clark explains, children should "explore their lives, schools, and communities for story ideas."

Experienced teachers know that children have difficulty identifying topics for writing. These teachers know they have a responsibility to help children find meaningful writing topics. One way teachers can provide guidance in topic identification is modeling. Earlier in this chapter, we saw Ms. Chou model how she thought about her topic for writing long before it was time to write. Her modeling said to the children, "Authors don't just sit down and write; they think about their writing when they are doing other things—like coming to school." Her modeling also said, "Sometimes authors have to work on idea making; they need a way to make ideas grow. Idea clustering is a way for you to start ideas flowing, and this is how I do it."

Read Joyce Lee, "Topic Selection in Writing: A Precarious But Practical Balancing Act," *The Reading Teacher,* 41 (November 1987), 180–184, for a discussion of ways to balance writer selection of the topic with teacher assignments.

A second way to help children identify writing topics is to talk about writing possibilities at the end of each lesson. Ms. Chou did this when she had her reading group brainstorm writing possibilities based on Silverstein's "Helping" and list them in their writing portfolios. Brainstormed topics became writing options from which the children could help themselves when they began to compose. An advantage of this approach is that writing becomes an integral part of the curriculum. Children identify writing options in social studies, science, mathematics, health, art, and music; they identify options based on their reading of poems and stories. Another advantage is that children have content to develop through writing. Having talked about ideas during a small- or large-group discussion, children start to write with a background of words and thoughts in mind.

A third way to help children select their own topics for writing is to organize group writing activities that demonstrate the forms for writing that are available to authors. No child will decide to write a haiku poem unless he or she knows about haikus. No child will decide to write a tall tale unless he or she is aware of that kind of story. To expand children's writing horizons, teachers must involve children in various forms of written expression. Frances Christie (1986) explains, "When children enter schools and begin learning to read and to write, they are actually engaged in learning the various written genres of their culture. If this is the case, it follows that teachers should have an appreciation of the kinds of genres relevant to school learning. Once they do appreciate the kinds of genres required, they will be able to teach them to children, helping them to identify and adapt appropriate generic models." In this section, we will examine prose forms that children may wish to sample through writing. In the next section, we will consider poetry and language forms.

Journals and Dialogue Journals

In Beverly Cleary's Newbery Award–winning *Dear Mr. Henshaw*, Leigh Botts writes a letter to his favorite author, Mr. Henshaw, asking for answers to questions about writing books. That letter turns into a full-fledged correspondence between reader and author when Henshaw turns the tables and asks Leigh to answer some questions. Mr. Henshaw eventually encourages Leigh to keep a diary. At first Leigh pretends he is writing to Mr. Henshaw, but soon he is consigning to his journal his sad and sometimes funny thoughts about his divorced parents, the theft of goodies from his lunch bag, and his own writing problems.

In the past, diary keeping preoccupied many people, both the great and the ordinary. For example, John Evelyn kept a diary in which he chronicled events in his own life as well as events in the England of his day. An ordinary Revolutionary War foot soldier recorded his day-to-day struggle for survival during that war. These classic diaries, as well as Joan Blos's Newbery Award–winning *A Gathering of Days: A New England Girl's Journal*, are models a teacher can share to introduce children to "journalizing."

To encourage children to write in their journals, some teachers, like Ms. Chou, dedicate time each morning to journal writing and keep their own journals, which they share with their students from time to time. When children see that their teacher is writing and they cannot interrupt her, they are less likely to ask for help in spelling and more likely to rely on invented spellings.

Sometimes too the teacher can suggest that students pretend, as Leigh Botts does in the Cleary book, that they are writing to a pretend person in conversational style; children write as though they were talking to that person. Of course, the pretend person can be the teacher. The teacher suggests, "Just start your entry with Dear Ms. Chou."

See John Evelyn, *Diary of John Evelyn, 1620–1706* (London: Dent, 1907), and Joseph Plumb Martin, *Narrative of the Adventures, Dangers and Sufferings of a Revolutionary Soldier* (Hallowell, Maine: Glazier, Masters and Co., 1830). Both diaries are available in reprinted editions. See also Eleanor Schick, *My Album* (New York: Morrow, 1984), for another story that includes journal writing.

In this context, as Linda Gambrell (1985), Roger Shuy (1987), and Jana Staton (1988) contend, dialogue journals pay dividends. Using dialogue journals, the teacher reads an entry and writes a reply in the child's journal, not identifying writing errors or criticizing but following up on the ideas. When a child has misspelled a word, the teacher might use and underline that word, correctly spelled, in the reply.

Preschool is not too early to begin journals. Preschoolers can keep picture diaries in which they make daily entries; they can record in a combination of script and pictures—whatever meets their needs. Older students can carry the journal format over into storymaking. They can write as though they were a character from the past and respond to events of that period. As classroom teachers attest, journal writing is productive; it gets children into the writing habit.

Letter Writing

Read Donald Graves, *The Reading/Writing Teacher's Companion—Investigate Nonfiction* (Portsmouth, N.H.: Heinemann Educational Books, 1989), for ideas involving children in writing nonfiction.

For students who have written in journals, letter writing is a natural next step. Peggy Heller, a creative teacher in an urban magnet school, introduced her third-graders to letter writing through a pen pal unit. Youngsters first wrote a cooperatively composed letter to a professor at a nearby college, requesting her to ask her undergraduates if they wanted to be pen pals. The group letter served as the model through which the youngsters learned the structure of a friendly letter. Soon youngsters and college students were exchanging letters.

Unfortunately, one youngster did not get a response from her pen pal. Taking matters directly into her own hands, she decided to make the professor her pen pal and wrote the letter shown in Figure 9.8.

As with journal writing, educators generally propose that children be taught to write letters as though carrying on a face-to-face conversation with the person to whom they are writing. They should be taught to appreciate the reader's interests and anticipate the reader's questions.

For a discussion of interactive telecommunication, read Margaret Moore, "Electronic Dialoguing: An Avenue to Literacy," *The Reading Teacher*, 45 (December 1991), 280–286. For a list of children's books helpful in teaching letter writing, see Carolyn Phelan, "Writing the Mail—Letters in the Classroom," *Book Links*, 1 (July 1992), 6–11.

Modeling helps here. In guiding the writing of a cooperative letter to send home to parents to invite them to a class play, the teacher can ask, "If you were talking to your mother or father about our play, what things would you want to tell about? What would your mother or father want to know?" Prompted in this way, children may suggest, "The play is funny. You will laugh a lot," or "I am the clown. I wear a tall hat," or simply "We all get dressed up"—statements that become sentences in the cooperative letter or in children's personalized versions.

The social arena of classroom and community provides innumerable opportunities for conversationally styled but meaningful letters. Friendly notes can be written to classmates who are at home sick, speakers who have visited the class, or parents who have supplied refreshments. In the upper grades, the class Social Committee, which changes its membership monthly, may take care of the class's social obligations, writing letters during independent study times. In lower grades, letter writing can become a group writing experience, with all children suggesting possible lines to include in a cooperative letter and selecting those that say what the class wants to express.

THE FORUM On Journals and Journal Writing

Edward Jenkinson writes, "Journals play a vital role in the development of fluency. Hundreds of elementary school teachers now have their students write in journals every day . . . Teachers do not grade journals. Instead, they collect them periodically, read the entries, and make encouraging comments or ask questions that will prompt students to write more. . . . Journals are places for experimentation. Student writers can explore a variety of subjects; can plumb the depths of their feelings; can solve problems, personal and academic; can try a variety of forms; and can, above all, practice, practice, practice. . . . Journals, class notebooks, course journals, logbooks, writer's notebooks, and student project books serve as vehicles to help students learn to write. They are also excellent places for students to write to learn about school subjects, about experiences, about themselves, and about life" ("Learning to Write, Writing to Learn," *Phi Delta Kappan*, 69 [June 1988], 712–717).

Questions to Consider

1. What relationship do you see between what Jenkinson says and what Ms. Chou did in her classroom?
2. How do you see yourself using journals with early primary youngsters? With upper elementary students? For what purposes would you use journals?
3. Currently some educators are suggesting that when teachers read children's journal entries, they invade children's privacy. What is your reaction to that statement? How could you avoid such a charge in your own teaching?

As models, use Janet Ahlberg and Allan Ahlberg, *The Jolly Postman or Other People's Letters* (Boston: Little, Brown, 1986) and *The Jolly Christmas Postman* (Boston: Little, Brown, 1991). Use Loreen Leedy, *Messages in a Mailbox: How to Write a Letter* (New York: Holiday, 1991), to introduce letter writing to K–4 youngsters.

In the context of writing letters to real people, schools teach not only conversational style but the conventions of letter writing. Some teachers have found that providing models of social and business letter and envelope forms is helpful. Students analyze elements of a form and then model theirs after it. One teacher printed a letter and envelope on the classroom floor with washable shoe polish. By the time the polish had worn off the floor, students no longer needed the crutch it supplied. Figure 9.9 gives a model to use in teaching business letter form; it can be modified to serve as a model for social letters.

Opinion Paragraphs

As a writing option based on the poem "Helping," Ms. Chou's students proposed a paragraph telling their opinions of what was good and bad about the poem. Writing opinion paragraphs is a "natural" in many contexts—after

132 Shelly Avenue

Elizabeth, New Jersey 07083

October 18, 1994

Dear Dockter Hennings,

My name is Debbie. It would be very nice to be a pen-pal. I never tried being a pen-pal. This is my first time.

I am eight years old. I am in third grade. I was bornd at 1986. My birthday is at April 14th. It was on a Saterday 12:00 P.M.

I like my gymnastiks, dancing and playing frizbe. I like gym mostly because it gets me in good shape and keeps me healthy. And I like dancing and frizby because there fun.

I want to become a dockter like you dockter Hennings. And if I can't go for a dockter I might go for a teacher.

Love,

Debbie Vasilopoulos

Figure 9.8 Debbie's Letter to a Pen Pal

Note: For Debbie, writing the letter had a significant purpose: She wanted a pen pal.

```
                    18 River Road                      return address
                    Columbia, South Carolina 29206     date
                    March 4, 19__


River Restoration Foundation                           name and
2000 Atlantic Avenue                                   address of
Cocoa Beach, Florida 32931                             sendee


Dear _____:                              greeting

        _____

        _____

        _____.    body

        _____

        _____.


                Yours truly,                           closing

                Hugh Troy                              signature

                Hugh Troy
```

Figure 9.9   Form for a Business Letter

reading a selection, after viewing a film, following a general discussion in content-area studies as well as in literature studies.

Again, the teacher needs to model the process of opinion writing. Having just discussed the duel between Hamilton and Burr, teacher and students can formulate an opinion about the rightness and wrongness of dueling: "Dueling is a stupid way to settle a dispute." The teacher can write that opinion on the chalkboard as the first, or topic, sentence in an opinion paragraph and ask, "What reasons do we have to support our opinion?" Children divide into three-person writing teams to complete the paragraph, adding sentences that give supporting reasons. Gathering together after team writing, children share their paragraphs and then analyze the structure of what they have written. In this case the structure is deductive, for the paragraph begins with a general point—the opinion—that is followed by specific supporting detail. Upper-graders can graphically map the structure of their deductively organized paragraph and use their map as a guide for writing opinion paragraphs of their own choosing. The map helps students clarify their thinking and leads to the development of a

Idea-making questions for opinion writing: What is important to me? What do I think? How do I feel about it?

Figure 9.10 is helpful in teaching paragraph structure. The teacher models how he or she designs a main idea and supporting detail by plotting them on the main idea/ supporting detail organizer before writing a paragraph.

logical argument. Figure 9.10 shows a graphic organizer for a deductively structured paragraph as well as for an inductively structured one in which the support comes first, followed by the topic sentence that states the opinion. In the same way used to model the writing of a deductive paragraph, the teacher should model the writing of an inductive paragraph and set up a laboratory time in which children, in groups, write opinions using that structure.

Reports

Especially in upper grades, students should write reports as part of content-area units. Reports should include information gathered from references and from interviewing as described in Chapter 7. Note cards, data webs, data synthesis charts, and informal outlines are as helpful in preparing for written reports as they are for oral reports. But as with oral reports, teachers should ask students to go beyond the facts and create ideas when they write reports. They should encourage students to hypothesize, predict, generalize, conclude, and formulate opinions.

See pages 312–314 in Chapter 10. The vignette also demonstrates an approach to teaching paragraph design.

Of course, teachers should not simply assign children reports to write. They must model the whole process of drafting a report just as they model the process of drafting opinion paragraphs. The vignette that opens Chapter 10 describes a way to model report writing.

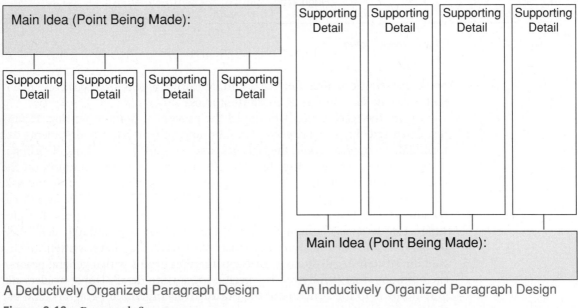

Figure 9.10   Paragraph Structures

Narratives

A narrative tells a story of events, either true or fictitious. As Dan Kirby et al. (1988) remind us, "The effective use of narrative is essential to thinking and to intellectual development. Most other forms of writing seem to be permutations or translations of some sort. . . . Any writing program that short circuits narrative or uses it only for young or developmentally immature children is simply working against the natural development of language. Narrative is the way we make sense of our world and of our experiences in that world."

Figure 9.11 outlines the kinds of narratives to which children should be introduced so that they can use these forms to make their own ideas. To introduce children to one of these forms of narrative, a teacher can take the following steps:

✦ Model the form by oral sharing and/or individual reading of a sample of the form.
✦ Identify key elements of the form and generalize about them.
✦ Engage children in oral storymaking using the form.
✦ Include that kind of story as a writing option from which children can select for individual writing.

Read Ruth Nathan and Charles Temple, "Classroom Environments for Reading and Writing Together," in *Reading and Writing Together*, ed. Timothy Shanahan (Norwood, Mass.: Christopher-Gordon, 1990), for descriptions of classrooms in which writing flows out of reading authentic texts—texts that serve as models.

✎ BUILDING AND REFINING YOUR TEACHING SKILLS

✦ Become a teacher-writer. Start your own journal, and write in it each day. Become accustomed to observing life around you as you seek ideas for writing. Create an idea cluster for writing.
✦ Become a teacher-writer. Read one of the books in the chart in Figure 9.11. Then write a narrative based on the form of that book.

Making Ideas with Poetry

Writing poetry demands that one create word images as powerful as those created on canvas. It requires one to use language in unique ways, make words dance tunefully across the page, and use space creatively. In this section, we will discuss poetic forms children can use to do this.

KIND OF NARRATIVE	CHARACTERISTICS	TITLES FOR READING ALOUD AND ALONE
Account	A retelling of events that actually happened	*Susanna of the Alamo: A True Story* by John Jakes (1986)
Biography	True account of a person's life by another person (Note: when children write biographies suggest they use the first person. This adds freshness.)	*Amos Fortune, Free Man* by Elizabeth Yates (1950); books by Jean Fritz; *Lincoln: A Photobiography* by Russell Freedman (1987); *Anthony Burns: The Defeat and Triumph of a Fugitive Slave* by Virginia Hamilton (1987)
Autobiography	True account of a person's life written by the person	*Little by Little: A Writer's Education* by Jean Little (1988); *Starting from Home: A Writer's Beginnings* by Milton Meltzer (1988); *A Girl from Yamhill: A Memoir* by Beverly Cleary (1988)
Historical fiction	A story based on events that actually took place	*Sarah, Plain and Tall* by Patricia MacLachlan (1985)
Realistic fiction	A story in which a character solves a problem in a realistic way	*Tales of Fourth Grade Nothing* by Judy Blume (1972); *Island of the Blue Dolphin* by Scott O'Dell (1960)
Mystery	A story in which a character unravels a series of clues to solve a mystery; filled with suspense and action	Encyclopedia Brown stories by Donald Sobol; *From the Mixed Up Files of Mrs. Basil E. Frankweiler* by E. L. Konigsburg (1967); *The Westing Game* by Ellen Raskin (1978)
Fantasy	A story in which magical things happen and in which there are magical beings such as wizards and dragons	*Cinderella* and similar fairy tales; *Wizard of Oz; Alice in Wonderland;* recent tales such as Richard Egielski's *Hey, Al* (1986)
Talking-beast tale	A fantasy in which animals are personified; they talk and act as people do	*Charlotte's Web* by E. B. White (1952); old tales such as *The Little Red Hen* and *The Three Little Pigs*
Fable	A tale told with an acknowledged moral	Old fables by Aesop and La Fontaine; modern fables by Arnold Lobel, *Fables*
Pourquoi tale	A story that creatively explains a custom, a natural phenomenon, or an animal characteristic	*Why Mosquitoes Buzz in People's Ears* retold by Verna Aardema (1975); the *Just So Stories* by Rudyard Kipling
Tall tale	A story in which a main character can do impossible deeds; a tale filled with superlatives	Old stories about Pecos Bill, John Henry, Paul Bunyan; *McBroom* tales by Sid Fleischman

Figure 9.11 Kinds of Written Narratives

Note: Read literature like this to students as models of kinds of writings they can pursue.

Creating the Images of Poetry

For a case study of poetry writing in fifth grade, read Mary Comstock, "Poetry and Process," *Language Arts*, 69 (April 1992), 261–267. For a case study at the primary level, enjoy Lisa Lenz, "Crossroads of Literacy and Orality: Reading Poetry Aloud," *Language Arts*, 69 (December 1992), 597–603.

Through poetry, writers create some of the clearest images. Through poetry, too, teachers can help children appreciate the beauty of word pictures and help them create vivid images of their own. Children, however, should not begin by analyzing poetic images to the bone, dissecting metaphors and similes, or defining words. The analytic approach, carried to extremes, may account for many students' aversion to poetry.

A more productive beginning is to ask children to listen to a poem with eyes closed and visualize in their mind's eye the picture the poet is painting with words. As a starter, poems like Lewis Carroll's "The Crocodile," in which the image is easy to picture, will appeal:

> **The Crocodile**
>
> How doth the little crocodile
>   Improve his shining tail,
> And pour the waters of the Nile
>   On every shining scale!
>
> How cheerfully he seems to grin,
>   How neatly spreads his claws,
> And welcomes little fishes in
>   With gently smiling jaws.

Having visualized a poem, middle-graders can put their "visions" on paper through an art medium they select. Listeners to "The Crocodile" may pick the bright greens and blues of tempera paint to translate Carroll's compact verbal image into picture.

A raindrop falls in a puddle and is gone.—*A second-grader's thought.*

Free Thoughts   Perhaps the easiest form for creating word pictures is the unstructured line or two—a *free thought*. Here is a free thought by a fourth-grader, who closed her eyes and described as clearly as she could a picture she saw only in her mind's eye. It was recorded for her by a scribe so that she could keep her eyes tightly closed and her picture clearly in mind.

> **Karen's Thought**
>
> I see Musty Diano.
> She has long black hair to the floor.
> She has silver in her hair and uses it to mop.
> She has long eyelashes, and uses them for paintbrushes.
> Her fingernails are like swords one mile long.
> Musty Diano sweeps the floor with her hair and sings a song.

When Karen opened her eyes, she painted her word picture on paper. Next to her picture of Musty Diano, she wrote the thought she had just spoken, changing it somewhat in the process.

Many teachers have found that art is a natural bridge into free verse. Students can begin with art forms that relax them: finger painting, molding clay, sculpting soap. Through the chosen art medium, young artists express a thought or feeling, which they then put into words.

The Haiku   In recent years, elementary teachers have been inviting students to compose *haiku*, three-line verses that in the hands of Japanese poet masters of the seventeenth century became delicate instruments for expressing feelings and pictures about nature, especially seasonal variations. Through their haikus, the early poet masters grasped the "essential quality or essence of reality" and achieved "direct and lucid expression" of this reality. Edward Putzar, a historian of Japanese literature, explains, "The power to reach this goal of understanding lies within a child." The fact that children speak with directness and see the essence of things probably accounts for the success many youngsters have in creating haiku moments. Success relates also to the brevity of the form—just seventeen syllables that pattern in three lines: five, seven, five.

To inspire her sixth-graders to look for the essential quality within nature and express it with directness, one teacher snipped Japanese prints from a book purchased for this purpose. Each child who felt inspired selected a print. Lynn selected a delicate lotus and created this haiku:

> *The pink swamp flower*
> *Has a beauty of its own—*
> *A heavy fragrance.*

Judi selected a vibrant print of a wild horse and composed:

> *Horse runs endlessly:*
> *Searching through the golden hills,*
> *He looks for the herd.*

Because a haiku is comparable to a single image captured on film, colored pictures can evoke the word pictures that are the stuff of haiku, particularly nature shots glorifying the beauty of the earth.

The Tanka   The *tanka* (or *waka*, as it is called in Japanese poetry circles) is more popular in Japan than the haiku and is also much older, dating to the fourth century. Like the haiku, the tanka achieves its poetic flavor through the musical quality of the words and the beauty of the images. The topic is nature and the seasons; the form is short, five lines of thirty-one syllables, distributed according to the pattern five, seven, five, seven, seven, as seen in Figure 9.12.

See William J. Higginson; ed., *Wind in the Long Grass: A Collection of Haiku* (New York: Simon and Schuster, 1992), for a collection of haiku from many parts of the world.

Use firsthand experiences with nature to stimulate haiku making as well. For an example, see the discussion of the tanka that follows.

A delightful book of tankas is Virginia Olsen Baron, ed., *The Seasons of Time* (New York: Dial, 1968). A book of modern tankas is Lucille Nixon, trans., *Sounds from the Unknown* (Athens, Ohio: Swallow, 1963).

Figure 9.12   A Tanka Drawn in Response to an Original Ink Blowing

Because the tanka is longer than the haiku, it permits an expanded word picture, just as a camera equipped with a wide-angle lens permits photographs that encompass a larger view. Here is a sample that abides by one of the original traditions of Japanese poetry; it names a season:

> *Crystal ice daggers*
> *Glisten in the winter trees—*
> *   Bending branches down.*
> *I listen for gusting wind:*
> *I hear sharp icicles fall.*

Because traditional tankas express seasonal thoughts, it is possible to combine firsthand seasonal observations with the writing of the Japanese characters and words for the seasons. To introduce the form, one teacher takes youngsters outdoors to see and feel striking moments in nature—a wildflower breaking into bloom, a bird's nest hidden in a remote corner, a clear puddle that reflects the sky, colored leaves falling, snow sitting on fence posts after a storm. As a

spring

summer

autumn

winter

class, they capture the moment first on film and then in a tanka. As the children compose, the teacher encourages use of the seasonal word—*autumn, winter, spring, summer*—as a describing word, or adjective, in the manner of the early Japanese poet masters.

When students have composed a seasonal tanka together, the teacher introduces the Japanese character and word for the season through a chart as in the margin. As children individually discover other nature moments and capture them in original tankas, they enscribe the tankas on long scrolls no wider than ten centimeters. On their scrolls, off-center at top and bottom, they paint in black the Japanese character and the word for the season they are describing. The children mount each end of their scrolls on a dowel so that the scrolls can be rolled up as Japanese scrolls commonly are.

The Senryu   The *senryu* is a Japanese poem that is structurally similar to the haiku but concerned with human rather than physical nature. Often it is humorous, and sometimes it does not follow the syllable pattern of the haiku. Working within the senryu form, students can choose topics for writing that appeal to them: surfing, baseball, bicycling. If they apply the syllable requirements of the haiku loosely, they have in senryu a form that requires directness and clarity but allows considerable freedom:

> *Skiing down the mountain:*
> *I cut myself in half*
> *To avoid a tree.*

An English/Japanese dictionary will captivate young poets. A pocket-size version gives Japanese equivalents in both script and characters for terms like *baseball, bicycle, circus*—any one of which could be the subject of a senryu. Students can search an English/Japanese dictionary for words that are the topics of their senryus and paint the Japanese equivalents in both script and characters on their poetry pages.

The Cinquain   Although not of Japanese origin, the *cinquain* is associated with haiku and tanka because of its brevity. As developed by Adelaide Crapsey, cinquains consist of five lines with a two-four-six-eight-two syllable pattern for a total of twenty-two syllables:

> *The gull*
> *effortlessly*
> *glides on the downward breeze*
> *to land on the soft, sandy beach:*
> *Quiet.*

Some teachers simplify the cinquain so that the number of words rather than syllables per line is the major requirement:

```
 first line  =  one word
second line  =  two words
 third line  =  three words
fourth line  =  four words
 fifth line  =  one word
```

Whichever way teachers introduce the cinquain—in terms of syllables or numbers of words—they should stress the importance of painting a clear, direct picture and allow variation rather than demanding strict adherence to the structural elements.

In "The World Outside My Skin," Eve Merriam writes, "Connections to be sure, are what poetry thrives on, whether through simile or metaphor. This is like *That*. This is so much like *That* it can merge and become the other. My love *IS* a red, red rose." In *Fanfare*, No. 1, Norwood, MA: Christopher-Gordon, 1993.

The Simile   The nineteenth-century English poet Alfred, Lord Tennyson, wrote this poem:

> **The Eagle**
>
> *He clasps the crag with crooked hands:*
> *Close to the sun in lonely lands,*
> *Ringed with the azure world, he stands.*
>
> *The wrinkled sea beneath him crawls;*
> *He watches from his mountain walls,*
> *And like a thunderbolt he falls.*

Visualize the scene in your mind's eye. You can do this easily because Tennyson painted a vibrant word picture. Can you picture the eagle poised on the mountain crag and then falling "like a thunderbolt" from the blue?

When Tennyson described the eagle as falling like a thunderbolt, he was making an idea through simile. A *simile* is a creative comparison between two things people tend not to associate, in this case between the fall of an eagle and a thunderbolt. A simile relies on the word *like* or *as* to make the connection. Tennyson's simile is effective because he went beyond ordinary associations to create a unique relationship.

A teacher can introduce children to the simile by orally sharing pieces such as that by Tennyson, having children chorus the pieces, and including the writing of a simile series as a writing option (see Figure 9.13). Later, as children read, they keep alert for similes to share from the Author's Chair.

The Metaphor   In composing, one young student called a wasp's nest "an insect condominium." A second called a bare branch "a grasping hand." A third called a computer "a boxed mind." A fourth wrote:

> *The sun was a pat of butter*
> *Melting on a hot potato.*
> *It was juicy and tasty,*
> *And we ate it at night.*

Figure 9.13 Simile Series by a Second-Grader
Source: Courtesy of G. Franzblau.

In making these ideas, these young writers were relying on *metaphors*, creative comparisons that assert an unordinary relationship without the assistance of *like* or *as*. The metaphor and the simile are examples of the figurative, as opposed to the literal, use of language.

Students can write metaphors as last lines in haikus, as parts of free verses, and as lines within stories. To this end, as teacher and children make idea clusters before writing, the teacher should include metaphorical relationships to encourage children to do the same. Review Ms. Chou's idea cluster in Figure 9.1 on page 272 to find a metaphor ready for writing.

As with the simile, students should look for metaphors in their reading and share those they find. They should do this as they read informational prose as well as stories and poems, for metaphors are common in the sciences (the heart as a pump, the computer as a brain).

Playing with the Sounds of Poetry and Language

See Lee Galda, "Read Me a Poem, Sing Me a Song," *The Reading Teacher*, 45 (October 1991), 144–151, for a discussion of sound in poetry. For examples of poems to share, see Stephen Dunning, Edward Lueders, and Hugh Smith, comps., *Reflections on a Gift of Watermelon Pickle . . . and Other Modern Verse* and *Some Haystacks Don't Even Have Any Needles and Other Modern Verse* (Glenview, Ill.: Scott, Foresman, 1967, 1969).

Sound is an integral element of fine poetry. Listen to the sounds of Edward Lear, whose nonsense verse provides numerous examples to sharpen students' perception of sounds in writing:

> *A was once an apple-pie,*
>   *Pidy,*
>   *Widy,*
>   *Tidy,*
>   *Pidy,*
> *Nice insidy,*
>   *Apple-pie!*

Having listened to such repeating sounds, to onomatopoeia, rhyme, and rhythm, children can create poems with sounds that tease both ear and mind.

Repeating Sounds Modern-day poets supply many sound plays to start children on the road to sound-filled composing. Eve Merriam's *It Doesn't Always Have to Rhyme* belongs on every classroom "poet tree"—a table on which poetry books stand to form the shape of a fir tree. Merriam contributes a delightful piece called "A Jamboree for *J*" that is a fun-laden medium for introducing children to alliterative sounds: "It japes, it jibes, it jingles, / it jitterbugs, it jets." As the Merriam lines demonstrate, *alliteration* is the repetition of the same first sound or letter in a group of words or a line of poetry.

Students can do alliteratively nonsensical things with other letters of the alphabet. For example, after one group heard Merriam's piece, they wrote "A Laugh on *L*," which began similarly: "It's hard to make an *L* sound anything but laughing. / *L* leaps, it leans, it leaks, / it likes, it loves." Titles with which students can play alliteratively in this way include "A Fair for *F*," "A Troubled *T*," "A Play with *P*," "Everywhere with *E*." Children can invent original titles and verses based on the beginning sounds of words, and when they get stuck for a word, they can "pull a Lear": invent one that sounds just right.

Use Eve Merriam's "Will You?" and David McCord's "The Pickety Fence" to introduce children to onomatopoeia. They can be found in Lee Bennett Hopkins, *Side by Side* (New York: Simon & Shuster, 1988).

Onomatopoeia Onomatopoeia is the use of words that imitate the sound associated with an object, as in *slap, buzz,* and *crash*. The very young love making the sounds of a rooster, cow, lamb, and other barnyard animals, so sound-making time can blend with poetry making as children contribute favorite sounds and add a few descriptive words to make a line of poetry. Oral composition of a series of structured lines—guided by the teacher—provides an easy introduction to onomatopoeia for the kindergartner. Later, the child dictates lines he or she has invented independently—lines that contain different sounds but are structured after lines written together.

Slightly older students enjoy alternating lines of sound with lines of words. Joey did this, writing bee sound effects into his word picture:

> *Bzzzzzzzzzzzzzzzzzzzzzz*
> *The bumblebee buzzes around me!*
> *Bzzzzzzzzzzzzzzzzzzzzzz*
> *He stings me!*
> *OUCH! OUCH! OUCH! OUCH!*

Children can build all sorts of sounds into word pictures: jackhammers, garbage trucks, lions, kittens, fire engines, the pounding of their hearts, the roar of the "ocean" in a seashell. Obviously this is the time to integrate writing and listening, with children listening to the sounds around them to translate into sound thoughts and listening to poems and stories in which sounds are expressed phonetically.

Rhyming Plays, Couplets, and Limericks The Japanese forms of unrhymed verse developed because the Japanese language is filled with similar vowel sounds and does not lend itself to creative rhyming effects. Not so with English. Rhyme as well as rhythm accounts for the enduring popularity of such old-time favorites as "One, Two, Buckle Your Shoe."

Some of these favorites can become the means by which youngsters first attempt simple rhymes of their own. For example, teacher and primary pupils can create original versions of "One, Two, Buckle Your Shoe" after they hear the sounds as the teacher shares the poem and after they brainstorm words that end with the same sounds as the words *two, four, six, eight, ten*. The teacher writes rhyming words for each of these number words in five columns on the board and tapes cards already lettered with the alternate lines of the poem—"One, two," "Three, four," "Five, six," "Seven, eight," and "Nine, ten"—on a second board, leaving room beneath each line for suggested rhyming lines. Drawing from their brainstormed pool of rhyming words, children put together original second lines to go with each number line, proposing several possible lines for each. Later children independently select the lines they prefer to go with the number lines and publish them as their original versions of the "Rhyming Number Book." Results may resemble the following, written by a young group at Halloween:

One, two,
The witch went boo!

Five, six,
She was in a fix.

Three, four,
She fell through the floor.

Seven, eight,
That was her fate.

One pattern to use for follow-up puts the number sequence in threes rather than twos, as in "One, two, three / I broke my knee! / Four, five, six / . . . "

Children who have played with pairs of rhyming words in this way are composing *couplets*, two lines that rhyme together and are approximately the same length. Again, it is fun to start as a class with a given line and dream up several possible rhyming second lines. Some of the first lines of less familiar nursery rhymes are easy to build into couplets: "Once I saw a little bird," "Barber, barber, shave a pig," "Fishy-fishy in the brook," "Little Robin Redbreast sat upon a tree." Of course, youngsters are not told the familiar second lines, at least until they have put together their own pairs.

With older students, there is fun in limericks, especially if the introduction is an oral interpretation session in which each youngster shares a limerick by the nonsense master Edward Lear. Because Lear's nonsense is old, a teacher is free to duplicate his limericks and distribute them to students. A delightful limerick is

There was an Old Man with a beard,
Who said, "It is just as I feared!—
Two Owls and a Hen,
Four Larks and a Wren,
Have all built their nests in my beard!"

Children will quickly pick out the five-line pattern of the limerick as well as discover the *aabba* rhyming pattern. Children tap the rhythm of a limerick, perhaps on rhythm instruments, so that they feel the stress on the second, fifth, and eighth syllables of each line. Only after considerable oral work with limericks should youngsters try to compose their own.

The Sounds of Prose   Sound is equally important in prose. Sometimes, when faced with two ways to structure a sentence, a writer selects one rather than the other simply because it sounds better. Work with sound/meaning relationships prepares children to make such decisions as they gain sophistication as creative writers. A primary purpose of play with sounds of poetry, therefore, is to develop heightened awareness of the significance of word music in communication.

* Devise an activity in which young students express feelings through both words and pictures. Try it with a group.
* Become a teacher-writer. Write an original free thought, a haiku, a tanka, and a cinquain. Experiment with metaphor.
* Compose an original couplet, quatrain, and limerick. If you are teaching, share your poems with children so that they see you are writing just as you are asking them to do.
* Design an activity that involves children in the fun of alliteration. Try the activity with a child or a group.

Creating with the Architecture of Poetry

Concrete poetry, or figured verse, has a long history. Such poet masters as Robert Herrick, George Herbert, Lewis Carroll, and more recently e.e. cummings have given us figured verse—poems written so that their printed shape communicates a meaning related to the subject. Children delight in seeing and composing poems in which words and visual images interrelate. Young children especially find the concrete more meaningful than the abstract, as the studies of Piaget confirm.

Lewis Carroll, *The Annotated Alice* (New York: Clarkson Potter, 1960).

Visualizing Words   An easy introduction to writing figured verse is to print a word or phrase so that the design relates to the meaning. Some words lend themselves readily to this picture-word play: *tall, thin, short, narrow, up, down, around, north, above, below, scared, shivery, dark, smile*. Others take more imagination; the margin samples can be used as an invitation to children to play with words in similar fashion.

As Martin Gardner points out in his notes to *The Annotated Alice*, this kind of creating is more significant than it may first appear. Advertisements, book jackets, magazine mastheads, and signboards frequently heighten meanings through the design of words on a page. Students should be able to clip examples from magazines and newspapers to add to a bulletin board collection that includes samples they have devised and proceed to write their own advertisements that include words made visual.

Once children have done some visualizing of words, they incorporate the technique in thoughts they write. They may decide to take just one word and express it visually whenever it occurs in a piece, as a first-grader creatively did in

his story entitled "A Vine," or in visual language: " 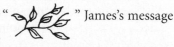 " James's message

Figure 9.14 A Composition About a Vine That Grows

says, "A vine grew and grew and grew and grew and grew." He made the vine taller and taller to communicate growth (Figure 9.14).

Squiggling and Shaping   Squiggling is another device for introducing children to the fun of building words into concrete pictures. A squiggle is a series of lines drawn in a design so nonrepresentational that children can read their own impressions into it. One teacher begins the activity by giving children a scrics of lines on a duplicated sheet. She asks youngsters to hold the sheet in each of the four directions and to brainstorm what the lines could represent in each case. Then together they choose one direction and idea and write a thought about that idea, printing the thought along the squiggle lines. Later, on their own, they choose a different direction and write a thought based on their impression of what the squiggle represents when so viewed. Figure 9.15 is an example that works well because children can see in it not only fireworks but also waves, snakes, water dripping down a windowpane, jet trails in the sky, anchors dropping from boats, Spanish moss hanging from trees—depending, of course, on the direction from which they view it. Students can create any number of other squiggles that will be equally productive. A few examples are shown in the margin.

The outline of an object like a car, a pair of spectacles, a pair of scissors, a hand, or a shoe also stimulates youngsters to create original word-picture

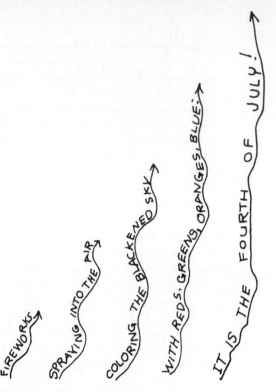

Figure 9.15 Squiggles

relationships and sometimes motivates the child who has little interest in written expression. Youngsters compose a story or poemlike piece and write the lines along the perimeter of the shape drawn on paper or in lines that actually form the shape. One example to demonstrate shaping is the wave in Figure 9.16.

Acrostics

Balloons				
Blow up and tie up				
A big balloon.				
Let it fly free.				
Let it dance.				
Open up the string!				
Out comes the air and				
Now the balloon				
Spins in crazy, arching zooms.				

Wind Thought			
W	I	N	D
h	c	o	r
i	y	i	a
s		s	f
t		y	t
l			y
i			
n			
g			
wind:			

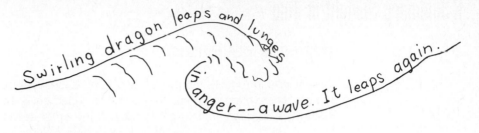

Figure 9.16 A Concrete Poem
Note: The writing of a concrete poem can be a response to literature or to content-area ideas.

"Balloons" and "Wind Thought" are acrostics, or ABC poems. They have a visual dimension in that the letters of the subject word are written in bold print and form the beginning letters of the lines. Even very young children who have just learned to differentiate among beginning sounds of words can write or patch together simple acrostics. The very young write only one word or phrase next to each letter of a word listed downward on their page.

Summary: Visual and Verbal Communication   Generally, if a class is engaged in an art activity, enthusiasm reigns as students work on projects. An advantage of involving youngsters in written expression that has a visual component is that enthusiasm for art may be transferred to expressing with words. Also, there is a security factor. Some youngsters feel more comfortable communicating visually. When a writing activity has a visual component, these students are more secure than they might have been if the writing were strictly verbal. Especially with younger children and those who have problems expressing themselves verbally on paper, a teacher should search out ways to correlate written expression with other forms of creative communication.

> ✎ *BUILDING AND REFINING YOUR TEACHING SKILLS*
>
> ✦ Devise an original squiggle. With a class, brainstorm ideas as to what it could represent. Engage the class in writing based on one interpretation of the squiggle.
> ✦ Become a teacher-writer. Write your own figure poem to share with a group of students. Also, try writing the following words so that their meanings are communicated through their visual arrangement on paper: *revised, scrambled, head over heels, rain, patchwork quilt.*

.... A Summary Thought or Two

WRITING AS IDEA MAKING

This chapter introduces the thesis that writing is idea making—that creating ideas is what fine writing is all about and that an open environment that encourages creativity is essential if ideas are to flow. The chapter describes how idea making through writing begins in nursery school, where children write even before they understand alphabetic principles and invent their own ways of recording. It describes ways to integrate writing with reading, drawing, and talking.

A basic principle underlying the chapter is that the teacher must model idea making in writing. The teacher models thinking by writing with the children, demonstrating ways to develop ideas, and structuring experiences so that young-sters learn the multitude of writing options available to them. These options include journals and dialogue journals, letters, opinion paragraphs, investigative reports, narratives, and poems of all kinds.

When teachers view themselves as authors, initiate writing activities that stim-ulate children to take off in a multitude of directions, are enthusiastic and filled with ideas of their own, children develop a positive view of writing. Children begin by focusing on ideas as they write. They know they have a story to tell and begin to enjoy writing their stories for others to read.

RELATED READINGS

Baghban, M. *Our Daughter Learns to Read and Write: A Case Study from Birth to Three*. Newark, Del.: International Reading Association, 1984.

Calkins, Lucy. *The Art of Teaching Writing*. Portsmouth, N.H.: Heinemann Educa-tional Books, 1986.

Carey, Michael. *Poetry Starting from Scratch*. Urbana, Ill.: National Council of Teachers of English, 1989.

Clark, Roy Peter. *Free to Write: A Journalist Teaches Young Writers*. Portsmouth, N.H.: Heinemann Educational Books, 1987.

Crowhurst, Marion. "The Effects of Correspondence with an Older Audience." *Language Arts*, 69 (April 1992), 268–273.

Danielson, Kathy. "Learning about Early Writing from Response to Literature." *Language Arts*, 69 (April 1992), 274–280.

Denman, Gregory. *Sit Tight and I'll Swing You a Tail: Using and Writing Stories with Young People*. Portsmouth, N.H.: Heinemann Educational Books, 1991.

Dyson, Anne. "Individual Differences in Emerging Writing." In *Children's Early Writing Development*. Ed. M. Farr. Norwood, N.J.: Ablex Publishing, 1985.

Fletcher, Ralph. *What a Writer Needs*. Portsmouth, N.H.: Heinemann Educational Books, 1992.

Graves, Donald. *Experiment with Fiction*. Portsmouth, N.H.: Heinemann Educa-tional Books, 1989.

———. *Explore Poetry*. Portsmouth, N.H.: Heinemann Educational Books, 1992.

———. *Investigate Nonfiction*. Portsmouth, N.H.: Heinemann Educational Books, 1989.

———. *Writing: Teachers and Children at Work*. Portsmouth, N.H.: Heinemann Educational Books, 1983.

Grossman, Florence. *Listening to the Bells: Learning to Read Poetry by Writing Poetry*. Portsmouth, N.H.: Heinemann Educational Books, 1991.

Hall, Nigel, Anne Robinson, and Leslie Crawford. *"Some Day You Will No All About Me": Young Children's Explorations in the World of Letters*. Portsmouth, N.H.: Heinemann Educational Books, 1991.

Hansen, Jane. *When Writers Read*. Portsmouth, N.H.: Heinemann Educational Books, 1987.

McClure, Amy. *Sunrises and Songs: Reading and Writing Poetry in Elementary Classrooms*. Portsmouth, N.H.: Heinemann Educational Books, 1990.

Noyce, Ruth, and James Christie. *Integrating Reading and Writing Instruction in Grades K–8*. Boston: Allyn and Bacon, 1989.

Olson, Janet. *Envisioning Writing: Toward an Integration of Drawing and Writing*. Portsmouth, N.H.: Heinemann Educational Books, 1992.

Rico, Gabriele. *Writing the Natural Way*. Los Angeles: J. P. Tarcher, 1983.

Shanahan, Timothy, ed. *Reading and Writing Together*. Norwood, Mass.: Christopher-Gordon, 1990.

Stewart-Dore, Nea. *Writing and Reading to Learn*. Rozelle, Australia: Primary English Teaching Association, 1986.

Temple, Charles A., Ruth Nathan, and Nancy Burris. *The Beginnings of Writing*. 3d ed. Boston: Allyn and Bacon, 1993.

Traxel, Joel, ed. *Fan Fare: The Christopher-Gordon Children's Literature Annual*. No. 1: Poetry. Norwood, Mass.: Christopher-Gordon, 1993.

Watts, Irene. *Making Stories*. Portsmouth, N.H.: Heinemann Educational Books, 1992.

CHAPTER 10

Writing Processes
The Child Writer as Author

Reflecting Before Reading

What processes comprise the act of writing?

How can the teacher involve children in these processes?

How can the teacher assess children's growth as writers?

BEFORE reading the chapter, read the title, the headings, and the end-of-chapter summary. Then answer the questions in the margin on this page.

TEACHING IN ACTION   *The Desert*

The youngsters in Brad Kamolsky's fourth grade were gathered around three pieces of chart paper posted on the classroom bulletin board. This was the final week of their integrated focus unit on desert regions of the world, and today they were summarizing what they had learned.

Factstorming and Categorizing: Rehearsing for Writing

Searching their learning logs for hints recorded earlier, the students called out words or facts about deserts as three scribes listed on the charts the points mentioned. When the charts were filled with words and phrases, students and teacher contemplated what they had recorded. Circling in red the word *Sahara*, Mr. Kamolsky asked, "What does the word *Sahara* tell us?" After students had responded, he prompted, "What other words also name desert regions?" At that point, students came forward to circle in red the names of deserts found on their charts. Later, responding to a similar question sequence posed by the teacher, they circled in orange items dealing with topographical features of deserts, in green items pertaining to desert plant life, in blue items related to animal life, and in purple items dealing with human adaptations. They categorized as miscellaneous those items that did not fit any of these categories.

Having helped the students organize their data, Mr. Kamolsky focused on one category: points circled in red. "Let's review," he said, "where all these deserts are located." With that, the children made a chart in their learning logs

In this episode, children are learning through writing as well as learning to write.

Seeing relationships within data

with the name of each major desert and next to each name the geographic location.

Drafting Ideas

When everyone had made a chart, the teacher continued, "Now we are going to translate the information from our chart into a paragraph. What is the big idea that this chart communicates? What are all the facts telling us?"

············
Getting ideas down

Dead silence descended on the class for this was a hard, main-idea question. Then Barbara suggested, "There are really lots of deserts." Ramon volunteered, "They are found all over."

"OK," answered Mr. Kamolsky. "Both of your ideas are good ones. If we were writing a paragraph about where major deserts are located, we could begin with those ideas. Who can convert Barbara's idea into a sentence to begin a paragraph?"

On the chalkboard, Kamel recorded "Deserts are all over." Erica recorded, "There are many deserts in the world." In this way, the children added sentence after sentence until the paragraph in Figure 10.1 emerged.

Revising

Where discipline is a problem, this lesson can be structured as a teacher-guided, small-group session. In small groups, even less interested students can join in.

At this point, Mr. Kamolsky guided the fourth-graders in reviewing what they had drafted. "How can we take the thoughts in our first two sentences and expand and combine them into one sentence?" he asked. Orally, students played with the opening sentences, finally settling on "There are many deserts all over the world." In turn, they reworked the other sentences they had drafted. Prompted by the teacher's questions, they clarified their thoughts by adding or deleting words, combining sentences, revising punctuation and capitalization, and changing word order. Figure 10.2 shows their revised draft.

Collaborative Writing and Publishing

The following morning, the fourth-graders collaborated in writing teams. Each team focused on a set of points circled in a particular color after the factstorm-

Deserts are all over. There are many deserts in the world. We have the Mohave Desert and the Imperial Valley Desert in the United States. The largest desert is the Sahara. The Sahara Desert is in Africa. There is another desert in South America and there are some deserts in Chile and a desert in Argentina. There is a big desert in Australia.

Figure 10.1 First Draft of a Cooperative Composition

Deserts of the World

There are many deserts all over the world. The largest deserts are the Sahara, found in Africa, and the desert in central Australia. South America has deserts in Chile and in Argentina. North American deserts are the Mohave Desert and the Imperial Valley Desert.

Figure 10.2 Revised and Edited Draft of a Cooperative Composition

ing of the previous afternoon. Concentrating on those facts, the teams first made a chart that highlighted relationships within their data. Then they decided what main idea held those facts together and drafted a paragraph that stated it along with supporting points, just as they had done during the teacher-guided group rehearsal for writing on the previous day. As follow-up, they were to revise and edit their paragraphs and produce a clean copy on chart paper.

The next day, the writing teams mounted their paragraphs around the room in preparation for a class revising/editing workshop. Now the entire class studied the paragraphs, reworked them, and decided on the best order for grouping the paragraphs into a cohesive composition. When the fourth-graders were satisfied with what they had done, one student volunteered to type the final draft into the computer and run off copies to send to the other fourth grades.

See pages 327–336 for a detailed discussion of revising and editing. See the checklist on pages 342–343 for a guide for assessing children's growth as editors.

Writing Processes

See the vignette that opens Chapter 9 for another example of the writing processes.

What were Brad Kamolsky's fourth-graders learning from their unit of study about deserts? Obviously the students were learning about desert regions, but obviously too they were learning ways to organize paragraphs around a main idea, to combine ideas into complex sentences, and to vary sentences for effect. In addition, they were learning something about writing processes: the importance of rehearsing ideas before writing (in this case by factstorming, categorizing, and charting ideas), the malleability of first drafts, the steps to take in revision, the pleasure of sharing ideas through writing. In short, they were learning to write by writing.

Teaching Writing Processes

Studies conducted during the 1970s and 1980s by the National Assessment of Educational Progress (NAEP) confirm the need for ongoing programs through which children learn to write. Between 1969 and 1974, the NAEP (1975) found "increases in awkwardness, run-on sentences, and incoherent paragraphs." Students expressed themselves in only the simplest sentence patterns and with a limited vocabulary. In 1986, the NAEP further reported that tests of writing showed that young people lacked the ability to use writing to analyze and evaluate what they read (LaPointe, 1986). In sum, many students appear to lack the ability to write.

Writing Instruction: Approaches That Have Not Worked

For a similar review of the literature, see George Hillocks, "Synthesis of Research on Teaching Writing," *Educational Leadership*, 44 (May 1987), 71–82.

Granted that the need to teach writing exists, how do teachers go about this task? Elizabeth Haynes (1978) summarizes much of the research on the teaching of writing: "Historically, if there has been any consistency in the teaching of writing in this country, it lies in the fact that most of the approaches used have been negative." One major approach is to teach grammar. Research studies reviewed by the Curriculum Commission of the National Council of Teachers of

English in 1935 and more recently by Ingrid Strom (summarized in Haynes, 1978) show that knowledge of traditional grammar has almost no relationship to the ability to speak or write clearly. To teach grammar is *not* to teach writing.

A second approach is to encourage children to write frequently by assigning topics and then correcting student errors. This technique often is begun in the elementary years and continues through secondary schooling. Although the evidence is hazy, most studies, according to Haynes, indicate that "mere writing does not improve writing. Further, although more research is needed to determine the most effective kinds of marking and teacher comments, it seems safe to conclude that from the studies to date, intensive correction of errors [by the teacher] is futile."

Involvement in Writing Processes

Read also Donald Murray, *Expecting the Unexpected: Teaching Myself—and Others—to Read and Write* (Portsmouth, N.H.: Boynton/Cook, 1989) and Ralph Fletcher, *What a Writer Needs* (Portsmouth, N.H.: Heinemann Educational Books, 1992).

Today another approach to teaching writing is evolving: to view writing as a series of interrelated processes and involve children in all aspects of those processes so that they develop a sense of personal authorship and of ownership over what they write. According to Donald Murray (1982), Roy Peter Clark (1987), and others who have analyzed what successful writers and writer-journalists do when they compose, writers generally write for a specific audience on topics about which they feel strongly and have something to say. They go through a rehearsal period in which they try out their ideas pictorially, verbally, and even physically, in the process expanding on and changing what they want to say. At some point, writers put ideas on paper in a rough draft, realizing full well that what they are creating is only a beginning that will change as they gain better control over what they are trying to say to their readers and how they are saying it. After putting something down on paper, most writers revise: They rework ideas, add, delete, change. They edit spelling, punctuation, capitalization, and other aspects of language usage. After some time has passed, they look at what they have written with a fresh eye. They ask others within their writing community for advice and make changes in response. They contemplate, they criticize their own writing, and eventually they say, "Enough!" They go to press: They share what they have authored. And as most writers write, they read. In so doing, they see how other authors handle ideas on paper.

Viewing writing from a process perspective, theorists propose that a writing program should develop in children a sense of functioning as an author within a community of fellow authors. Such a program should involve children in

✦ Independent reading and listening to reading;
✦ Rehearsing ideas before and during writing;
✦ Drafting on topics they choose themselves, with the clear understanding that what they write is only a beginning;
✦ Revising and editing that is not simply copying teacher corrections but includes reworking ideas and speculating on areas that can be improved on;
✦ Publishing what they have written for others—their audience—to read.

In this chapter, we will consider these components of a writing program, remembering that writing is a continuous act in which there are no divisions among reading, rehearsal, drafting, revising, and sharing—that in writing in action, these processes meld and flow together.

Reading and Writing

Children acquire writing skill by reading content written in different styles and modes of discourse. As David Dickinson (1987) states, "Exposure to books influences language and writing. Poor readers often have less control of varied aspects of language structure." (See also Squire, 1983; Stotsky, 1983; Tierney and Pearson, 1983.)

Jane Hansen (1987) explains this relationship between writing ability and time spent in reading by describing the reading-writing behavior of a fourth-grader named Jenny. Having composed a story in which the parts melded beautifully, Jenny remarked during a conference, "I've never written anything before where the parts fit together so well." When the teacher asked her how she had done it, Jenny was unsure at first. She paused to consider. Then she answered, "It must be because I'm reading *Tom's Midnight Garden*. . . . When you read famous authors like Philippa Pearce, you notice how their words fit together." With that, she paged through *Tom's Midnight Garden* to find an example of how Pearce had made her words fit together. As Hansen summarizes, reading fine literature can help children learn to write: "The more children listen, talk, write, and read good books, the more they enjoy the music of language."

Independent Reading: A Component of a Writing Program

Some schools immerse children in literature and make free reading an important part of the school day. In one school, quiet reigns for twenty minutes a day as students, teachers, principals, secretaries, and custodians settle down with a book they have chosen. In another school, each classroom has a nook reserved for independent reading. The first-grade book nook has a table and a carpet beneath it on which youngsters can stretch out to read. The third-grade nook is an area partitioned off with waist-high pegboard behind which are a few child-size rocking chairs. The fourth-grade nook is an industrial-size carton into which a window has been cut so there is light for the youngster who crawls in to read. The children make weekly excursions to the school library to select books for independent reading in the classroom nook and at home in the evenings and on weekends. Parents are encouraged to talk with children about books the youngsters are reading.

Teachers can motivate children to read. To do this, one teacher strings a wire high across her classroom. At one end, students attach a wormlike head cut from green construction paper. As they complete books, children cut paper

Barney the Bookworm

strips, print the book title and author on a strip, and loop it around the wire, pasting the two ends together. Each green book loop becomes a segment of Barney the Bookworm's body.

Another teacher prompts children to write brief comments about books read, print the comments on cards, and place the cards on a "Books for Sale" bulletin board. Between other activities, a child takes a card he or she has written and auctions it off to the class: "I have one adventure story with a wolf dog named Jim Ugly, a fake funeral, a bounty hunter, and a wild ending. What am I bid?" Bidders bid books they have read, with the auctioneer accepting a bid for a book he or she wishes to read.

Listening to Reading

Donald Graves writes, "Surround the children with literature: Children who hear good literature . . . pick up voices, stimulate intentions, feel language, try new narratives" ("Teacher Intervention in Children's Writing," *Language Arts*, 60 [October 1983], 845).

The surest way to bring children and books together is for the teacher to read aloud, something that primary children savor (Trelease, 1989; Hansen, 1987). As Frank Smith (1992) explains, reading to children not only puts children in the "company of people who read" but also puts them in the "company of authors." Reading aloud, the teacher shares the pictures, changes vocal and facial expressions to reflect mood and dialogue, and maintains eye contact with listeners. To make the reading-writing connection, the teacher encourages children to listen for words and sentences that are particularly striking by suggesting, "As I reread this sentence, think what makes it so good."

Upper-graders also enjoy listening while a teacher reads aloud. Especially good at this level are informational books from which a teacher extracts a section relevant to thematic-unit study. After reading a portion, the teacher places the book in the reading nook, where children help themselves to other parts. Or the teacher can share an audio- or videotape of a first segment of a book, placing the tape in the listening nook, where youngsters can continue to listen.

Then too, children enjoy listening to unique volumes such as the *Guinness Book of World Records*. They are intrigued to hear about the tallest, the longest, the biggest, the smallest. They return again and again to this fascinating book and eagerly write and publish their own book of class records, styling it after the original.

Rehearsing for Writing: Pictorializing, Talking About, and Thinking Through

Studies suggest that *rehearsal,* or prewriting, activities that involve children in thinking about ideas have a powerful impact on children's writing. Widvey (Haynes, 1978) finds that a process of problem solving that takes place before actual writing improves the writing that follows. Similarly, Radcliffe (Haynes, 1978) reports that writing is facilitated by a talk-write sequence. More recently, Donald Graves (Walshe, 1982) concludes that young writers benefit from an extended "rehearsal" period before and while they write. Roy Clark (1987) reports on the use of note taking, listening and interviewing, observation, and brainstorming in getting ready to write.

Rehearsing by Pictorializing

Read R. D. Walshe (1982), p. 10.

Donald Graves and his associates at the University of New Hampshire describe some of the rehearsal activities of young children. One activity is pictorializing—drawing a picture as part of the thinking that precedes writing. Describing Sarah, a first-grader, one member of Graves's research team notes, "Before Sarah writes, she draws a scene and explains it to the researcher or another young writer who is usually drawing and talking, too. Then she writes about the scene she drew. Sarah finishes the page and begins the same sequence for her next episode" (Graves and Sowers, 1979). Because pictorializing appears to be a natural way in which young children plan ahead as they write, teachers should encourage this activity and help children refine their use of drawing as they rehearse for writing.

See Chapter 9 for ways to encourage very young children to write.

Young children can use pictorializing to rehearse before writing about events of which they were a part. They draw a series of pictures to tell their readers what happened and then translate their drawings into sentences. Children can use a similar pictorial series to rehearse before storymaking. Reports and stories based on a picture series tend to be more organized than those based on memory, for the pictures help young writers keep the sequence of events in mind. This suggests one of the major contributions of pictorializing to writing: Through pictorializing, young writers learn to organize their thoughts.

Rehearsing by Talking

Even as young writers pictorialize, they use words to think through what they want to say on paper. Rehearsal speech can take these forms:

1. Youngsters talk to themselves in their heads or aloud as they select topics for writing, before they write, and as they write. "Mind talk," discussed in Chapter 3 (See pages 84–87), is a powerful rehearsal tool.
2. Youngsters talk informally to classmates, describing pictures they are drawing and telling what they are writing before and while they write. Peer talk should be encouraged, not discouraged; writing is not a silent activity.

See Lucy Calkins, *Lessons from a Child* (Portsmouth, N.H.: Heinemann Educational Books, 1983), pp. 27–28.

3. In a peer rehearsal interview, one youngster asks questions of another to get him or her to think through details to include in a piece he or she has chosen to write. A group of writers may also gather together to talk out ideas prior to or during writing. In this context, children ask one another questions to start ideas flowing. Both the peer rehearsal interview and the talk group reinforce for young writers the fact that they are writing for an audience—in this case, their peers.
4. Youngsters talk informally to the teacher, who circulates among them as

they write. The teacher encourages rehearsal talk by asking questions that help young writers grasp their topic, identify the details necessary to develop their ideas fully, and devise an overall structure for expressing ideas.

5. Youngsters talk in teacher-guided groups as part of a precomposition activity. Teacher-guided group talk helps children identify topics for writing and think through relationships within data. It can help them focus on ways to design paragraphs to highlight relationships. During teacher-guided group talk before writing, children can also compose orally together, modeling their oral compositions on pieces they have heard or read and thereby gaining an understanding of how to structure stories when they write on their own. In the following sections, we will consider ways to use teacher-guided group talk to help children think through and plot out their ideas before writing.

Rehearsing by Thinking Through Relationships

At some point, young writers must learn strategies for thinking through relationships before writing. Because different kinds of thinking go into the development of different kinds of writing, children must have opportunities to think through all manner of content so that they know how to rehearse for informational as well as for story writing. A productive context for acquiring thinking strategies is a teacher-guided writing group. By orally playing with relationships in material, students learn to analyze ideas in ways they could not before. In this section, we will consider interactive approaches to teaching children how to think through ideas as they prepare to write stories and informational prices.

Planning for Story Writing: Plotting Out Story Elements   Stories have a structure (Glenn and Stein, 1979). To write a story is not to record a random series of events. It is to design a setting, characters, a problem or conflict, actions through which the conflict is resolved, and an emotionally satisfying ending that reinforces the theme of the story. Reading stories, children begin to grasp story structure, especially if teachers help them play with these elements.

A teacher can model how to use a plot plan (see Figure 10.3) to rehearse a story for writing. Together, using the guide, students identify the characters and the setting of their story. They decide on the problem and the steps they are going to build into their story to resolve it. When children write stories on their own, they follow the same strategy, making several different plot plans before beginning to draft. Also before drafting, children can orally share their plans; in so doing, they talk out (or orally rehearse) their stories.

In like manner, the teacher can model how to use story lines and story staircases for storymaking by engaging youngsters in talk about a story they will make together. As the class talks out the events they want to include in a class story, students and teacher plot them chronologically on a straight or undulating line, incorporating sketches above and below the line. Story lines can be rel-

PLOT PLAN
Main character(s)
Setting (time and place)
The problem (or source of conflict) in the story

The steps through which the problem is resolved
  1.
  2.
  3.

The way the problem is finally resolved
The big idea told through the story
The title of the story

Figure 10.3 A Plot Plan for Storymaking

atively complex even in lower grades and include words as children learn to handle them. If students are writing a step-by-step tale in which each event builds on preceding ones, plotting events on a story staircase helps young authors think through the complexities of their tale. On each step, children make a sketch and plot key words that suggest what will happen next in their stories. On the landing, they plot out the climax. As children rehearse by plotting stories on a staircase, they should think and talk out alternative ways to reach the landing so that story events flow together smoothly and the ending develops out of prior events. Figure 10.4 presents a model of a story staircase based on Eric Carle's *The Rooster Who Set Out to See the World*. A teacher may wish to share that story with a class, model how to make a staircase that maps out major events, and then engage children in oral storymaking using a staircase as a rehearsal strategy. Later, during writing workshop, children may decide to create their own step-by-step stories using a similar rehearsal strategy.

A variation of the story staircase is the flowchart, in which arrows connect sketches or verbal descriptions to show direction of story events. Flowcharts (see Figure 10.5) are especially useful as children rehearse circular tales—stories in which a main character leaves home to find adventure but returns at the end. Students plan ahead why the character leaves home, what adventures the char-

Richard Bach's *Jonathan Livingston Seagull* (New York.: Macmillan, 1970, and Walker & Co., 1985, paper) is a classic that can be used in upper grades as a model for this kind of story.

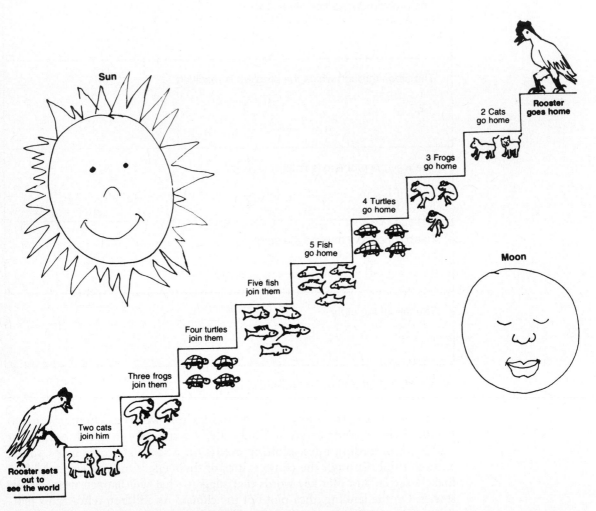

Figure 10.4 A Story Staircase: A Plan for Plotting a Step-by-Step Story
Source: Based on a Story by Eric Carle, *The Rooster Who Set Out to See the World* (Franklin Watts 1972).

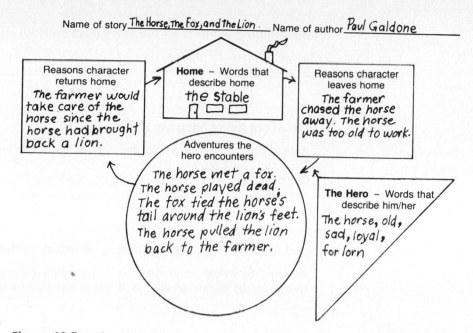

Name of story The Horse, The Fox, and the Lion . Name of author Paul Galdone

Reasons character returns home
The farmer would take care of the horse since the horse had brought back a lion.

Home – Words that describe home
the Stable

Reasons character leaves home
The farmer chased the horse away. The horse was too old to work.

Adventures the hero encounters
The horse met a fox. The horse played dead. The fox tied the horse's tail around the lion's feet. The horse pulled the lion back to the farmer.

The Hero – Words that describe him/her
The horse, old, sad, loyal, for lorn

Figure 10.5 A Flowchart for Plotting a Circular Story

acter experiences, and why the character returns home. In early primary grades, a rehearsal flowchart can be a series of drawings tied together with arrows; in upper grades, students make a story flowchart with words. In either case, the teacher should model how to create a flowchart based on a story read and how to design one in rehearsing for storymaking. Students who have used flowcharts to rehearse stories during teacher-guided group writing can use the same type of chart as an independent writing, listening, or reading guide.

Story flowcharting is a useful rehearsal strategy when children create stories in which the action keeps repeating, each time with a slightly different twist. The model in Figure 10.6 is for the Caldecott Honor book *Mice Twice* by Joseph Low. It shows the three repetitive events in the tale:

1. Cat invites Mouse to supper. Realizing what Cat plans for her, Mouse brings Dog with her for a six o'clock supper consisting of two bits of cheese.
2. Before leaving, Dog invites Cat to supper the next evening. Cat and Wolf show up for the seven o'clock supper, planning that Cat will get Mouse and Wolf will get Dog. But they are foiled when they find Dog and Crocodile at Dog's house.
3. Before leaving, Cat invites Mouse and Dog to supper at eight o'clock the next evening. Cat has Lion there. But Mouse and Dog bring along Wasp, who chases Lion away while Dog chases Cat.

The final line is a satisfying conclusion to the repetitive tale: "If Cat did escape, you may be sure he never bothered Mouse again." A teacher can share this

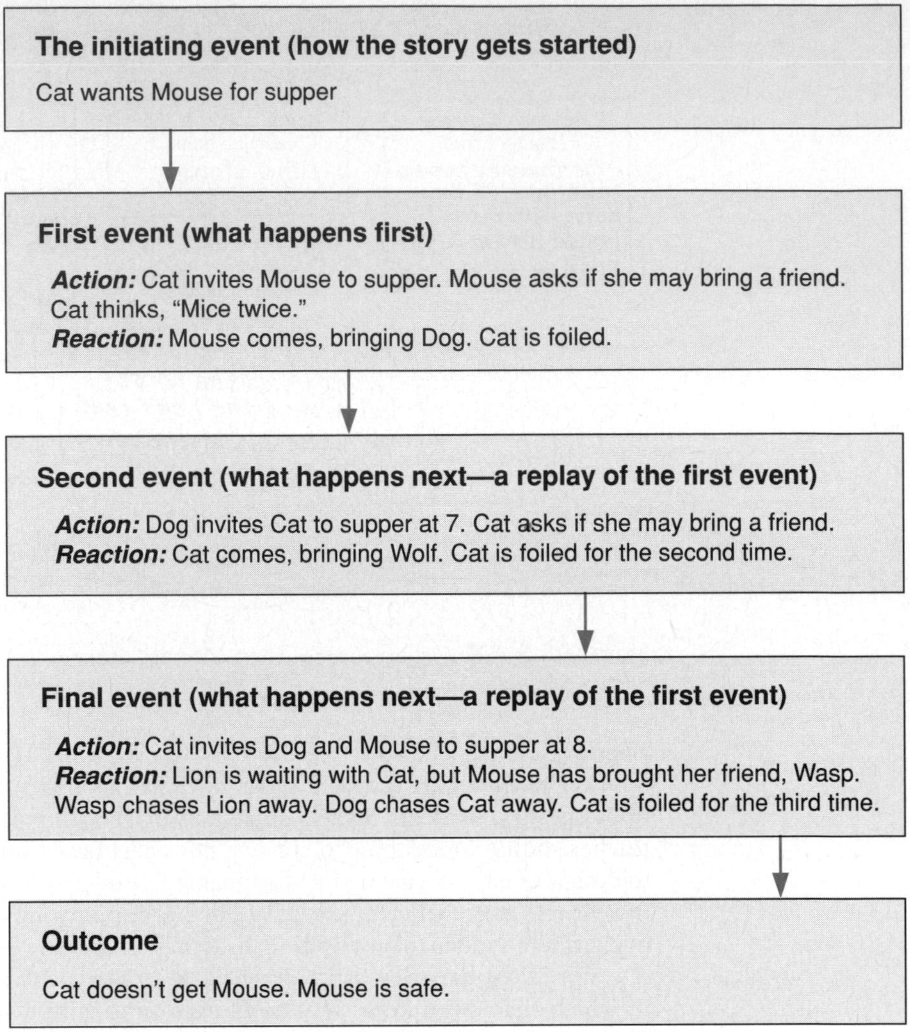

The initiating event (how the story gets started)
Cat wants Mouse for supper

↓

First event (what happens first)
Action: Cat invites Mouse to supper. Mouse asks if she may bring a friend. Cat thinks, "Mice twice."   *Reaction:* Mouse comes, bringing Dog. Cat is foiled.

↓

Second event (what happens next—a replay of the first event)
Action: Dog invites Cat to supper at 7. Cat asks if she may bring a friend.   *Reaction:* Cat comes, bringing Wolf. Cat is foiled for the second time.

↓

Final event (what happens next—a replay of the first event)
Action: Cat invites Dog and Mouse to supper at 8.   *Reaction:* Lion is waiting with Cat, but Mouse has brought her friend, Wasp. Wasp chases Lion away. Dog chases Cat away. Cat is foiled for the third time.

↓

Outcome
Cat doesn't get Mouse. Mouse is safe.

Figure 10.6 A Plot Plan for a Repetitive Tale: *Mice Twice* by Joseph Low

humorous story and then model how to make a flowchart to highlight the repetitive nature of the tale. As a follow-up activity, students and teacher talk through their own repetitive story, plotting events on a similar flowchart. Following the class story analysis and storymaking time, students can add repetitive stories to the list of writing options from which they choose during writing workshop.

Planning for Informational Writing   In the teaching-in-action vignette that opens this chapter, students were learning to rehearse as they planned and wrote an informational report on deserts. Children factstormed, categorized their facts, and then organized their data as a chart, which they used to write a series of paragraphs, each focusing on one main idea. The instructional sequence included these steps:

1. *Factfinding.* Students located data about which they wanted to write.
2. *Factstorming and categorizing.* Students brainstormed what they knew and grouped these data based on shared relationships.
3. *Charting.* Students studied their data, identified relationships, and made a chart highlighting the relationships.
4. *Teacher-guided group writing and rewriting.* Students cooperatively drafted a model paragraph based on their chart; together they revised and edited what they had drafted.
5. *Independent writing and rewriting.* In small groups, students made other charts from the data and drafted paragraphs based on their charts.

In this instance, through teacher modeling, the students were learning a rehearsal strategy: factfinding, factstorming and categorizing, and charting.

See Shirley Haley-James, "Helping Students Learn Through Writing," *Language Arts*, 59 (October 1982), 726–731, for a discussion of webbing as it relates to writing.

A teacher can also model how to use a combination of factstorming, categorizing, and webbing as children rehearse for informational writing. For example, Florence Amos's fifth-graders went on an elephant-factfinding mission. They searched references and found fascinating elephant facts for factstorming. When they had filled the board with their facts, the children organized items into a *web*, or map, that highlighted relationships. Guided by the teacher's questions, they categorized the facts—facts that pertain to physical characteristics, to habitat, to habits, and to the importance of elephants. Working from these main categories, they plotted a fact web on the board as in Figure 10.7 and cooperatively wrote a first paragraph.

The factfinders then divided into collaborative teams. Each team wrote a short paragraph containing only one category of fact. Later, guided by Ms. Amos, the class sequenced and organized the individual paragraphs into a report on elephants.

The instructional sequence in this case included these steps:

1. *Factfinding.* Students located data for writing.
2. *Factstorming.* Students set out their data where they could analyze it for relationships.
3. *Webbing.* Students searched the data for relationships and organized those data based on relationships perceived.
4. *Teacher-guided group writing and rewriting.* Students cooperatively composed a model paragraph based on one category of data.
5. *Independent writing and rewriting.* Students wrote similar paragraphs, drawing on data from their webs.

• • • • • • • • • • • • • • • • • • •
Finding related facts and organizing data for writing

Through this series of activities, Ms. Amos's fifth-graders were learning how to gather data and sequence and organize them for writing. They were learning a rehearsal strategy—webbing—that helps writers draft cohesive, logically sequenced paragraphs. Once children have experienced webbing as part of a

Figure 10.7 A Web of Elephant Relationships

teacher-guided group writing experience, they can use webs to plot out reports before drafting them.

Some educators call these graphic organizers *webs* to emphasize that what is important is the relationships, or meanings, clarified by the arrangement of data on the page. Others call such graphic organizers *semantic* or *idea maps*. Regardless of what they are called, these devices function as writing outlines. Karen Bromley (1991) claims, however, that webs have a distinct advantage over a traditional outline:

A web is a nonlinear representation of information, whereas an outline is linear. If an idea is omitted in the creation of an outline, it must be squeezed into the outline later or an arrow used to identify where it fits. With a web, an idea or piece of information can be recorded on each strand without attention to order. . . . Before writing, the writer can number each strand in the order in which it is to be included in the written piece. In this way, webbing allows the writer to think and record ideas in random order but sequence in a logical way (pp. 7–8).

In addition, students seem to enjoy making webs, perhaps because there is no one best way to design them and the format is not overwhelming.

Rehearsing: What Is It All About?

As this section has implied, rehearsing for writing can assume a variety of forms. Young authors can pictorialize and/or talk out ideas as they choose topics for writing and before and during writing. Rehearsing before oral storymaking, they can plot out, or map, stories, basing their rehearsal on their understanding of story structure. They can create stories individually, rehearsing by using story staircases and flowcharts. During content-area studies, they can factstorm, categorize, chart, and/or web before drafting together and before pursuing a similar writing activity on their own.

Involved in these ways, young authors are learning how to select and expand on a topic for writing and get themselves ready to write stories or expository paragraphs on a topic they have chosen. Graves (1983) emphasizes the importance of children's selecting their own writing topics; selecting topics, young authors gain a sense of ownership over their writing that makes them want to write. Teachers, of course, propose writing options based on children's reading, content-area studies, current events, personal interests, and group writing activities. But the ultimate decision about what a particular child writes on a particular day is the child's.

Drafting

Theorists use the term *drafting* to describe what happens when writers start recording ideas on paper. Most agree that what is important at this stage is how writers view what they are doing. Successful drafters know that getting ideas down is crucial in a first draft and that the words they record are only a jumping-off point. Successful drafters know that they can go back later to fill in holes, check spelling, and smooth out expression. Lucy Calkins (1986) compares the writer at this point to an artist: "Like an artist with a sketch pad, [the writer] begins to find the contours of [the] subject. [The writer] makes light, quick lines; nothing is permanent. Each writer has his or her own style. Some bolt quickly down the page, their momentum building, their pencil leading in unexpected directions. Others work in smaller units, toying with their beginnings, trying a line one way and then another, drawing in to write, then pushing away to see what they have said." Clearly, successful writing requires a mindset about processing words on paper.

First Drafts as Tentative

As children draft, they should start with the assumption that what they are doing is tentative; they will change and shape their writing as they go along. For this reason, youngsters should be encouraged to cross out, insert new ideas, and draw arrows; invent spellings; use lines, letters, or drawings as placeholders when words and spellings are out of reach; keep concerns about neatness and good penmanship to a minimum; cut apart sections and staple in additions; and use Post-its™ for lengthy insertions. According to Donald Graves (1979), children who no longer erase but handle words in these ways know that words are "temporary, malleable, or clay like. The words can be changed until they evolve toward the right meaning."

Some young writers find Graves's idea of multiple starts helpful. Children who are having trouble getting started with a composition or part of one draft a beginning sentence knowing full well that they probably will not use that opening. They then write several more beginnings and choose the one they think will do the trick. Use of multiple starts hammers in the fact that what is written on paper is tentative—that changes are the norm, not the exception.

To emphasize the significance of first drafts, the teacher can suggest that children select some of their first drafts for posting on a section of the bulletin board titled "Writing in Process—Our First Drafts." This is important for slower children who may have fewer revised versions for posting; they, too, get a chance to share their written ideas—which is what writing is all about.

Probably the single most significant determinant of how children view the process of drafting ideas is the teacher. The teacher who introduces writing by reminding children to use their best penmanship, keep papers neat, and never erase builds an erroneous picture of first drafting. The teacher must view first drafts as beginnings if young writers are to acquire this more productive view of drafting. Cambourne and Turbill (1987) explain that teachers who are most successful in helping children make meaning with writing "do not expect children's first attempts to be perfect first time around." They understand that "children need to know they can try out their hypotheses and make mistakes, and that their approximations will be accepted, for only then will they be prepared to take risks and experiment in their learning."

Writing Workshops and Writing Portfolios

Teachers have found that organizing the class as a *writing workshop* helps children realize that first drafts are simply beginnings. A writing workshop is a time when students function as active writers within a community of authors. During a writing workshop, some authors rehearse, some draft, some edit and revise, and some design a publication copy. Throughout emphasis is on getting ideas on paper without concern for neatness and the mechanics of writing and later going back to revise and edit pieces chosen for publication. In a workshop environment, although students are drafting individual compositions, a sense of community develops as everyone writes. At times the community of writers includes the teacher, who writes individually at his or her desk or models the process of drafting by talking out his or her thoughts and recording them on a chalkboard or on an overhead transparency while the children listen, watch, and sometimes contribute suggestions.

Teachers have also found that the use of *active-writing portfolios* affects children's view of writing, especially their view of first drafts. Children place drafts-in-process into their personal writing portfolios, or folders, so that they can keep track of them and have continued access to them. During writing workshops and independent study times, students can

✦ Rehearse ideas, begin drafting, and add the first drafts to their active-writing portfolios;
✦ Work on a first-draft-in-process already in the portfolio;
✦ Edit and revise pieces chosen for publication from those in the portfolio;
✦ Cull from the portfolio pieces they have begun but lost interest in.

Reworking successive drafts in their portfolios, young authors come to understand that first drafts are exactly that—first, or embryonic, ideas that they will ultimately refine into published writing.

Although students can make their own active-writing portfolios simply by folding a large piece of construction paper, a folder with pockets works especially well. The pockets enable students to organize their work. Children keep first drafts in the lefthand pocket, choosing from them pieces to carry through editing, revision, and publication. They keep pieces they have chosen to publish in the righthand pocket, stapling together the successive drafts of each composition stored there.

Children also write on the surfaces of their active-writing portfolios. On the front cover, they list topics and ideas for future writing; on the back cover, they list topics on which they have written or are currently writing, with a notation about the stage to which a piece-in-process has advanced. On an inside surface, children write points to look for during editing. Graves (1983) suggests other uses to which portfolio surfaces can be put: to list skills a student has mastered or wants to master, topics a student knows much about, and books a student already has written.

Revising and Editing

Rewriting, which includes revising and editing, is an integral part of most writing. In *revising*, authors reread what they have written to see where their ideas need restating, expanding, and/or reorganizing. In *editing*, writers check spelling, capitalization, punctuation, usage, and related elements. Donald Graves (1983) has studied the revision behavior of beginning writers. He reports that even beginning writers can make changes in their writing. However,

Knowledge of these copy-editing marks is helpful to student authors:

Common editing marks:
/ make lower case
≡ capitalize
∧ add something
⊙ put a period
⋏ put a comma
⌐ take away
¶ make a paragraph
reverse order

"Teachers can play a significant role in releasing a child's potential for revision." What the teacher emphasizes in revising is what child-editors tend to do. The teacher who stresses neatness and handwriting will find that children emphasize those factors in their revisions. In contrast, the teacher who stresses reorganization of text and the addition and deletion of ideas will find that children focus on those elements.

Some teachers do not give students the opportunity to revise and edit. Instead, they correct children's writing "errors" and ask students to copy the changes. In many instances, students copy unthinkingly and even introduce new "errors" in the process. Teachers who use the correction/copy sequence may wonder how to engage children in the active higher-order thinking implicit in the revision process. In the following sections, we will consider ways to make revising and editing an integral part of classroom writing.

The Teacher Conference

See also Barry Lane, After "THE END": Teaching and Learning Creative Revision (Portsmouth, N.H.: Heinemann Educational Books, 1992) for a discussion of revision processes.

The *individual conference* used in conjunction with children's active-writing portfolios is the cornerstone of a writing program in which young authors revise and edit their work. In *Writing: Teachers and Children at Work* (1983), the definitive reference on writing conferences, Graves notes that the personalized conference between teacher and young writer offers the student an opportunity to develop self-critical powers and learn what to do in reworking a paper.

The basis of a conference is a piece that the young author selects from among his or her early drafts and has collected in his or her active-writing portfolio. Graves (1976) suggests that a teacher begin by asking a child to go through the portfolio of writings-in-process: "Look at the papers in your folder and choose the one you think is best and next best . . . and then the next best. What makes this the best?" Once a piece has been chosen for review, the teacher's task is to elicit information rather than tell the child what to do. The teacher proposes, "Read me your most exciting part." If the teacher senses a need for more detail here, he or she continues, "You say he had an accident in the race. What happened to the car? What did the front fender and headlight look like after it hit the guardrail?" Or "What will happen next?" "Why was he scared?" "Tell me more about this bit." The purpose of these early conference questions is to get children to volunteer ideas that will strengthen their writing.

Graves maintains that teacher interest in what a child writer is saying determines the success of a conference. The teacher is asking the child to teach him or her about the topic; in Graves's words, the aim here is to "foster a burning desire to inform."

In "When All the Right Parts Don't Run the Engine," Language Arts, 70 (January 1993), 12–13, Cynthia Bury says, "Create a setting that nurtures the writer. 'Enabling' writing occurs one student at a time." This is why conferencing is such a powerful tool for changing children's perceptions of writing and revision.

During a conference, the initial focus is on the purpose of the child's writing, the content, and the style. But eventually attention also focuses on editing and on the surface mechanics. The teacher may ask, "You have two thoughts in this sentence. Read it aloud and tell me where the first one ends." Or "What kind of punctuation do we need to reflect the excitement of the story here?" At this stage, the teacher teaches a point of usage to the child, who needs it to clarify his or her writing. Working with third-graders, researcher Lucy Calkins (1982) has discovered that when children write, they "reach" for the skills they need. They ask for instruction on how to handle their writing problems and in the process learn to use commas, periods, and quotation marks. In Calkins's words, "They find punctuation everywhere and make it their own."

Because intonation and punctuation are related, students should be encouraged to read parts of their compositions aloud during an editing conference. In so doing, young authors begin to equate a relatively lengthy pause with a period, a shorter pause with a comma, and an upward rise of the voice with a question mark. Reading aloud also helps them identify awkwardness of expression, missing word endings, and sometimes even misspellings. Later, as students edit independently, they read their compositions to themselves to identify similar spots where changes in punctuation are needed.

Some teachers—like Ms. Chou, whom we met in Chapter 9—end a conference by listing areas for rewriting on a writing conference guide, which students place in their active-writing portfolios and take back to their desks to refer to during rewriting (see Figure 10.8). In using such a guide, however, teachers do not touch on every problem in a particular composition; rather they note the one or two major problems on which students should focus as they rework their papers.

Graves (1983) suggests that teachers schedule a final teacher-student conference before a student makes a publication draft of a composition. According to Graves, the student should prepare for the conference by taking these three speculative editing steps:

1. Circling potential spelling errors,
2. Putting a box around potential punctuation errors,
3. Drawing lines under spots where the language doesn't sound right.

Graves recommends that the teacher say to a child who has trouble locating his or her own errors. "There are five words misspelled here. I want you to circle which of these may be those five." Graves suggests that speculating in this manner gives students practice in estimating where they will have to edit for spelling, punctuation, and language usage.

The Peer Collaborative Conference

Graves writes, "Peer audiences have an effect on children's revision, and their use of new approaches to the writing process" (R. D. Walshe, 1982, p. 63).

To encourage oral reading of compositions-in-process and talking out of ideas, some teachers pair students for collaborative revising and editing. Pairs work together, reading aloud first a piece composed by one, then a piece by the other member of the pair. If children are familiar with teacher conferences, the teacher may suggest that they ask each other the same questions he or she has asked them. At an initial conference, the peer asks his or her partner, "What is the most exciting part? What more do you want to say about this? What

TEACHER CONFERENCE NOTES

Name of author: _____

Title of piece: _____

Date of conference with teacher: _____

What we like about this piece:

Tell me more about:

Revise (one or two of these items):

The setting: _____   The characters: _____

Story beginning:_____   Story middle: _____

Story ending: _____   Order of events: _____

Connecting words: _____   Title: _____

Edit (one or two of these items):

Rework paragraph breaks: _____

Rewrite incomplete sentences: _____

Rewrite run-on sentences: _____

Combine sentences: _____

Edit capitalization at highlighted points: _____

Edit punctuation at highlight points: _____

Check spelling of highlighted words _____

Figure 10.8 A Writing Conference Guide for Upper Grades

happened next? After that? At the end?" During a later conference, students listen for punctuation "spots," check words in the dictionary, and discuss points of usage. Collaborative editing of this kind is a good way to get students talking about their writing as they prepare it for sharing. Figure 10.9 is a guide students can use as a framework for a peer conference. After conferring with a peer, students rework their compositions, staple the peer conference guide to their papers, and place their papers in the Ready-for-a-Teacher-Conference basket.

SELF-CONFERENCE NOTES

Name of author: ______________________________

Title of piece: ______________________________

Date of review: ________________

What I like best about what I wrote:

What I want to make better:

Figure 10.9 A Peer Conference Guide

The Revising/Editing Workshop

Enjoy Nancy Knipping, "Let Drama Help Young Authors 'Re-See' Their Stories," *Language Arts*, 70 (January 1993), 45–50, for a different approach to story revision—acting out stories to decide how to make them better.

The *revising/editing workshop* is a group approach to revision and editing. In preparation for this special kind of writing workshop, several students choose a first draft from their active-writing portfolios to share with the class or a collaborative team. They make transparencies of their papers. During the workshop, the students take turns serving as the presenter, displaying their papers, explaining why they used certain words and phrases, and asking for feedback. Workshop members respond by first paraphrasing what they think the authors are trying to say and then identifying the words and phrases in the papers they think are the most effective. Next, the presenters ask for help with some aspect of their compositions—the aspect that probably led them to select the piece for presentation. The emphasis here is on helping authors strengthen their writing. Workshop members offer suggestions that authors only consider in revising their papers; they do not necessarily take them. After all, they are the authors and must decide what they want to say and how to say it.

At times, at the end of a workshop the teacher makes a suggestion about a presenter's first draft based on problems he or she has noted in several students' writings, making it very clear that this is a generic problem present within the community of writers. After the presenter has reacted to the suggestion, the teacher asks the workshop members to locate a first draft of their own in their writing portfolios and decide whether to revise in terms of the suggestion.

Sentences from several students' papers can serve as the content for a workshop. In preparation for this kind of workshop, the teacher reads students' first drafts and "lifts" sentences from several papers that embody the same writing problem, for example, a run-on sentence or a lack of sufficient detail. The teacher records these sentences on a transparency or a ditto master. During a workshop, students edit the problem sentences. In follow-up individual editing, they edit their own first drafts, focusing on the problem they have been considering during the workshop. The clue in this type of workshop is to select sentences that highlight a writing problem that a number of students are encountering.

The Teacher-Guided Group Review

See pages 2–9 and 312–314.

Teacher-guided group review is another way to involve youngsters in talking about their writing and revising and editing it. Children who have collaborated to compose a piece, as in the vignettes that open Chapters 1 and 10, follow writing together with reviewing together. Guided by teacher questions that help them pinpoint ideas, sentences, or words to revise, children reconsider what they have drafted. In this context, a teacher may find it necessary to focus on one particular revision problem. For example, in one first grade, students dictated the following series of sentences to the teacher, giving the sentences not in any logical sequence but in the order in which the thoughts came to mind.

> I like to build a snowman. We like snow. Snowflakes fall on the ground. Frosty the snowman could be alive. Snowflakes are white.

In reworking their first draft, the children decided that not all the sentences were about the same topic; there were actually two topics. With that idea in mind, the children ordered the sentences that related to the first topic; these became the first paragraph in their revised experience report. In like manner, they ordered the remaining sentences to form a second paragraph and made changes in words and capitalization. The revised draft was printed by a student volunteer and reread several times during the day:

Snow

We like snow. Snowflakes fall to the ground. They are white.

We like to build a snowman. Frosty the Snowman could be alive.

In teacher-guided group review, the teacher should ask questions that focus children's attention on possibilities for change. Where might we add a word or sentence? Where might we take one out? How could we reorder our sentences to make better sense? Where might we combine two sentences? What title could we add to sum up what we have said? In this way, young writers learn what to do in reviewing—what things to think about. In this way, too, children develop the habit of revision and begin to view it as an integral part of writing.

Word Processing with a Computer

This edition of *Communication in Action* was written on a Macintosh computer using the word processing system *Microsoft Word*. This writer finds the system exceptionally good for authoring.

Technology now provides word processing equipment to facilitate revising and editing. Personal computers equipped with word processing systems allow a writer to type a first draft of a composition on a keyboard and simultaneously display it on a televisionlike monitor. With knowledge of a few computer commands, the writer can delete unwanted words and add others, combine sentences, change word and paragraph order, add punctuation and capitalization, run a spell checker, and tell the printer to print a paper copy. The writer can also use software that checks usage and provides an on-screen thesaurus. Similarly, he or she can use databases that provide content for writing.

Some students with physical disabilities find that they are better able to enter words into a computer than onto paper. Voice-driven computers are especially helpful.

Today simple word processing systems are available for the beginner. They provide an easy introduction to word processing; given a users' manual, a computer, a disk drive, and a printer, teachers with no particular mechanical apti-

Children can edit and revise their first drafts with the help of a computer. (© 1990 Jeffery W. Myers/Stock Boston)

tude can teach themselves how to use a personal computer for word processing. With a little practice, teachers can learn to use word processing as part of teacher-guided group writing, revising, and editing and soon have youngsters using it for independent writing.

Researchers have investigated the use of word processing programs in children's writing. Juanita Avinger (1984) compared stories that children dictated to teachers who recorded them for the youngsters on paper with dictated stories that the teacher recorded on a computer. She reports that students whose work was recorded via computer dictated more sentences than those whose work was recorded on paper. Also, their sentences were more complex and their stories contained more description. Virginia Bradley (1982) reports a similar finding in cases where children dictated in groups. Stories recorded on word processors tended to be longer, perhaps because of the speed with which dictation can be typed into a computer and the size limitations imposed by a piece of chart paper.

Bill Barber (1982) also reports positive results from using word processing programs with first-graders. In his study, Barber had youngsters first write their own versions of an experience using invented spellings. Then he had youngsters dictate sentences from their papers as contributions to a class story—an excellent teaching technique, by the way. Barber notes that "the processes of editing and revising seemed to occur naturally as they (the children) read from the monitor. They quickly noted the difference between my standard spelling on the monitor and their own invented spellings." The outcome was an in-context spelling lesson on the relationships between sounds and the ways those sounds are recorded on paper.

The use of word processing programs in writing, however, does not teach children what revising and editing are all about. Often upper-graders who are taught how to type stories into a computer and use the editing commands to produce another draft simply make cosmetic changes; they do not expand thoughts, clarify ideas, or reorganize even though the computer program would let them make these changes with ease. Teachers cannot expect that use of the computer will teach children what is important in revising and editing. Teacher conferences, peer conferences, active-writing portfolios, teacher-guided group writing and rewriting, workshop periods when everyone revises his or her writing and some children share drafts with which they have been struggling are the ways to get children revising and editing naturally. Figure 10.10 depicts these dimensions of classroom rewriting activity; it also summarizes key writing processes.

Sharing and Publishing: The Child Writer as Author

In Ellen Blackburn's first-grade classroom (as in Jennifer Chou's third grade), there is an Author's Chair. Each day, children take turns sitting in the chair to read aloud what they or another child or adult author has written. Listeners

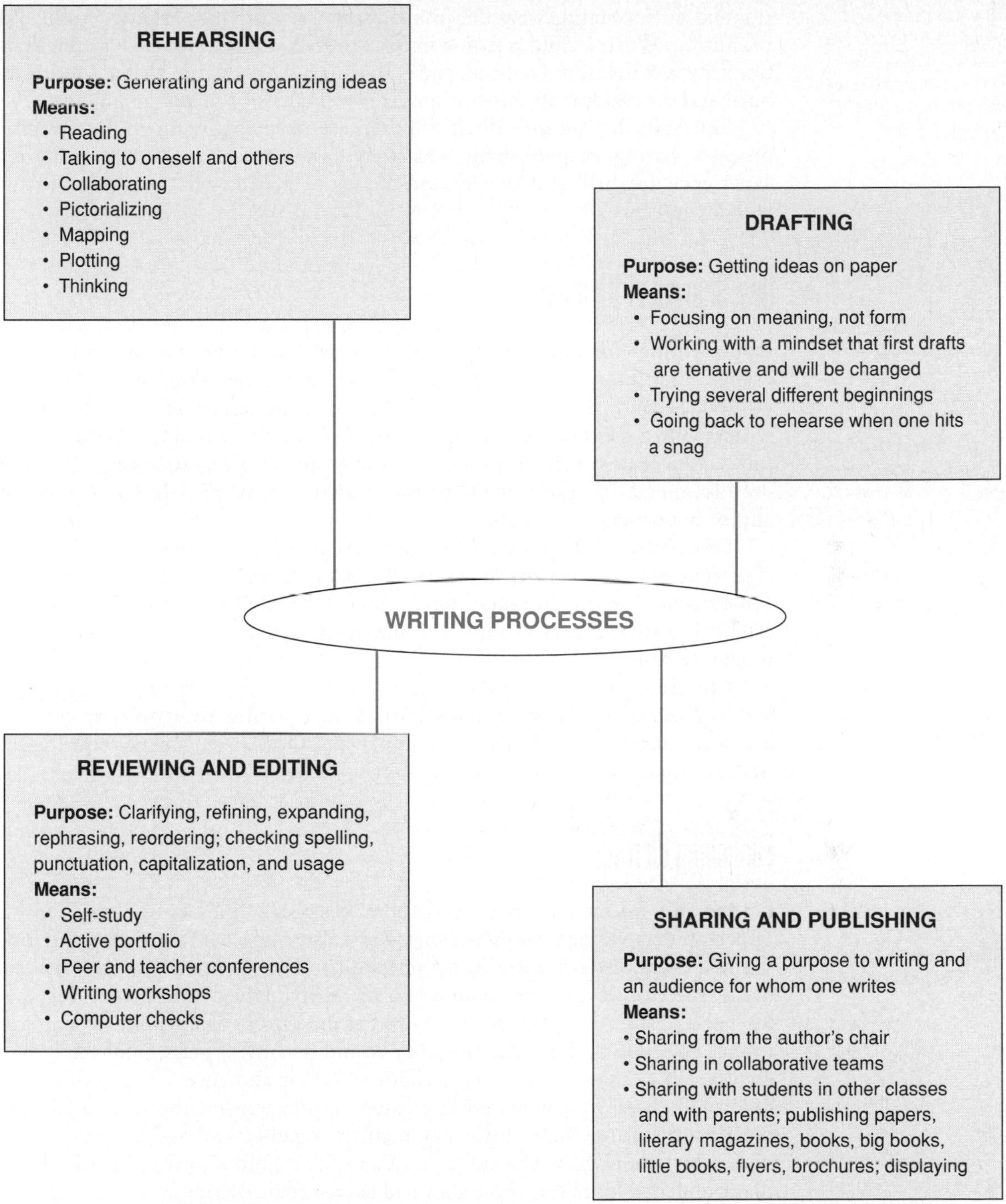

REHEARSING

Purpose: Generating and organizing ideas
Means:
- Reading
- Talking to oneself and others
- Collaborating
- Pictorializing
- Mapping
- Plotting
- Thinking

DRAFTING

Purpose: Getting ideas on paper
Means:
- Focusing on meaning, not form
- Working with a mindset that first drafts are tenative and will be changed
- Trying several different beginnings
- Going back to rehearse when one hits a snag

WRITING PROCESSES

REVIEWING AND EDITING

Purpose: Clarifying, refining, expanding, rephrasing, reordering; checking spelling, punctuation, capitalization, and usage
Means:
- Self-study
- Active portfolio
- Peer and teacher conferences
- Writing workshops
- Computer checks

SHARING AND PUBLISHING

Purpose: Giving a purpose to writing and an audience for whom one writes
Means:
- Sharing from the author's chair
- Sharing in collaborative teams
- Sharing with students in other classes and with parents; publishing papers, literary magazines, books, big books, little books, flyers, brochures; displaying

Figure 10.10 Writing Processes: Purposes and Means

respond by first stating what they think a story says and then asking questions of the author. When a child is sitting in for a professional author such as Bill Martin, Ezra Jack Keats, or Dr. Seuss and is sharing a story by that writer, Ms. Blackburn and the children together propose answers the storymaker might give.

Sitting in the Author's Chair, children are participating in another writing process: sharing, or publishing, what they have written. In so doing, children experience the thrill of authoring and the joy of sharing what they have written with an audience.

The Author's Chair is described in Donald Graves and Jane Hansen, "The Author's Chair," *Language Arts*, 60 (February 1983), 176–183.

Oral Sharing of Writing

See Gene Maeroff, "Author's Day at P.S. 11: A Celebration of Books," *New York Times*, June 19, 1984, C1. This article describes the writing program in the Highbridge section of the Bronx in New York City. The program was developed by Lucy Calkins.

Opportunities for oral sharing of writing need to be built into writing programs. First, most youngsters take pleasure in reading aloud what they have written. Second, the fact that they will share with classmates provides young writers with a purpose for writing and an audience for whom they write. Sometimes, too, oral sharing can substitute for more laborious rewriting. The final draft is an oral one, presented to classmates from an original draft on which the author has penciled changes.

Of course, children should be free to decide when not to share. Some ideas are too personal—too close to the heart—to let others hear. Youngsters can keep some of their writing in a Keep Out! folder that only they see. The teacher can establish a special drawer into which writers tuck pieces they want only the teacher to read.

Children can also use other means for sharing their writing. Young poets can lead classmates in choral renditions of their poems. Young playwrights can lead a company in productions of their playlets. Oral sharing blends equally well with art, dance, and music.

Publishing Writing

Share Joan Nixon, *If You Were a Writer* (New York: Four Winds, 1988), to show children what it means to be a writer.

On the door of one sixth-grade classroom was a sign "Pine Brook Press." Inside upper-graders worked on their own or in authoring/illustrating teams writing original picture storybooks. To interest students in book writing, their teacher had earlier rolled into the room a cart of newly arrived storybooks. Together teacher and students had read and looked at the variety of story and art patterns in the collection and decided that they would become a press, publishing their own books to share with younger children—their audience—and to distribute to local libraries. Now they were engrossed in story writing; they would go on to illustrate the stories, bind stories and pictures together, and design covers. Eventually they would go to the kindergarten and first grades to read their books to the younger children for whom they had geared their writing.

Young authors' conferences in some areas of the country provide opportunities for students to share their writings with others.

Young authors take pleasure and pride in making books. Cut-out books like Eric Carle's *The Very Hungry Caterpillar* can inspire young writers to dream up stories that they illustrate graphically as the masters of storybook writing have done. Tiny books like Maurice Sendak's *Nutshell Library* invite children to "think small" and create their own hand-size books about little things like mice, mites, nuts, or even prunes. ABC books, counting books, and day books—in which each page tells a happening for each day of the week—make easy beginnings for young authors/illustrators. Nonverbal stories in which pictures carry the story line and there are few or no words are helpful in developing understanding of story sequence and structure.

Bookmaking need not be as sophisticated an activity as it was in this sixth-grade class. Very young children can compose simple books made up of a series of illustrated pages, written with invented spellings. Slightly older children can select a piece they have written, revise and edit it, and publish it as a book. Books of these kinds can be placed in the classroom reading nook where children go to browse and read. See Figure 10.11 for a way to make a bound book.

Children can also publish literary magazines and newspapers to which each youngster contributes one or more pieces. A mimeographed or computer-printed magazine can simply be a collection of children's writing or can feature

✎ BUILDING AND REFINING YOUR TEACHING SKILLS

+ Become an author. Think about something you want to say. Sketch a picture sequence that communicates your message, or rehearse your ideas in your head. As you rehearse, begin to draft ideas, realizing that you will change the words you are recording. Get as many ideas down as you can; do not worry about spelling or writing mechanics. Then revise. Start by elaborating on ideas that are unclear in retrospect. Delete unnecessary words. Reorganize where necessary. Edit by checking spelling, punctuation, and capitalization. Enter your changes on your first draft. Share your writing orally, reading from the first draft but including your changes.

+ Participate in a revising/editing workshop with peers who have also drafted a piece. Use a copier to make copies of your paper. Have peers summarize the message they get from your paper. Have them question you to help you clarify your thinking. Then make another draft, including changes made in response to peer suggestions.

+ Working with a youngster, talk out an idea he or she has for writing. Encourage the child to use pictures to rehearse for writing. Then ask the youngster to draft some ideas without worrying about spelling and writing mechanics. Later, confer with the youngster and help him or her identify strong points and a place or two for revising.

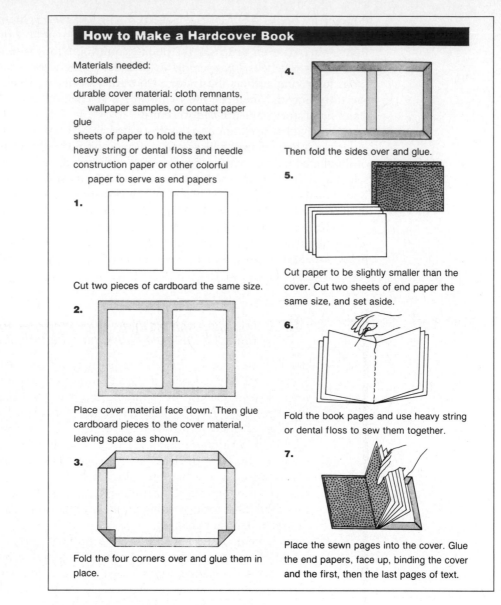

How to Make a Hardcover Book

Materials needed:
cardboard
durable cover material: cloth remnants,
    wallpaper samples, or contact paper
glue
sheets of paper to hold the text
heavy string or dental floss and needle
construction paper or other colorful
    paper to serve as end papers

1.

Cut two pieces of cardboard the same size.

2.

Place cover material face down. Then glue cardboard pieces to the cover material, leaving space as shown.

3.

Fold the four corners over and glue them in place.

4.

Then fold the sides over and glue.

5.

Cut paper to be slightly smaller than the cover. Cut two sheets of end paper the same size, and set aside.

6.

Fold the book pages and use heavy string or dental floss to sew them together.

7.

Place the sewn pages into the cover. Glue the end papers, face up, binding the cover and the first, then the last pages of text.

Figure 10.11 Steps in Making a Bound Book

Source: Reprinted by permission of the Riverside Publishing Company.

Note: Publishing children's stories as bound books provides a purpose for children to revise and edit what they have drafted. However, teachers must be careful not to overemphasize bookmaking to avoid children's spending an undue amount of time decorating their books—time better spent in writing. See Kirby's warning in the Forum on page 315.

Poetry Pages, Laugh Lines (jokes, riddles), Story Spots, Opinion Notes (book, film, and TV reviews), Puzzle Pages, and Advertisements. A newspaper can feature editorials, news stories, letters to the editor, political cartoons, comics, sports, social events, classified advertisements, advice to the lovelorn, and cooking hints. Using desktop-publishing software that enables the writer to print in columns, set visuals in conjunction with print, and use a variety of fonts, students can create rather professional-looking publications, especially if they study real magazines and newspapers for styling ideas.

Publishing in classrooms can take other forms. An obvious approach is bulletin board posting in the classroom, the hall, or neighboring classrooms where others outside the class group have the opportunity to read the publication. Important here is the fact that children have a purpose for writing and rewriting; they are getting material ready for publication—for reading by others. When children—all children in a class—know that a piece they have drafted will be published in some form, they are more likely to polish it carefully. Now they have an audience. Now they are authors.

Observing and Assessing Children's Development as Authors

To teach writing is to engage children in an array of writing processes. Given this premise, a teacher cannot simply read students' papers to correct the "errors" and think that he or she has assessed children's progress as writers. Obviously, at some point a teacher reads students' papers, but in a process approach to writing instruction, the focus in assessment is rather different from that in an assign/correct approach.

Observing and Assessing Children as Writers

In a process approach to writing instruction, the teacher studies children's behavior *as they write* to determine how they are developing as authors and to identify the kind of instructional assistance needed (Bunce-Crim, 1992). The teacher studies the successive drafts of children's writing in their active-writing portfolios to note the kinds of changes children are making as they develop their ideas from one draft to the next. The teacher also notes the topics children choose, specific skills that need attention, and the overall progress of children as writers. Here the focus is on children as rehearsers, drafters, revisers, editors, and sharers. Figure 10.12 is a checklist of concerns the teacher may consider in assessing an upper elementary child's development as an author.

In addition, today more and more teachers are asking students to create what Tierney, Carter, and Desai (1991) call *showcase portfolios* to use for assessing progress. To compile a showcase portfolio, students periodically cull from their active-writing portfolios a representative sample of their writings-in-process and their published writings that showcase their development as

AN OBSERVATIONAL CHECKLIST OF WRITING BEHAVIORS				
	Always	Generally	Sometimes	Never
A. The child as rehearser				
1. uses pictures to rehearse				
2. uses mind talk before drafting				
3. talks to others before drafting				
4. participates in group rehearsal activities				
5. uses graphic organizers during rehearsal				
6. uses story maps to plot out stories				
B. The child as drafter				
1. views first drafts as beginnings				
2. uses copyediting symbols				
3. crosses out, circles, adds on freely during drafting				
4. goes back for more rehearsing when hitting a snag in drafting				
C. The child as reviser and editor				
1. changes the focus of the composition				
2. revises by adding information				
3. revises to achieve well-organized paragraphs				

Figure 10.12 An Observational Checklist of Writing Behaviors

writers. The use of showcase portfolios for assessment arises out of the belief that assessment should focus on "what students are actively doing" and out of a commitment "to student involvement in self-evaluation and helping students to become aware of their own development as . . . writers."

Recently the state of Vermont (Vermont Assessment Program, 1991) opted for an assessment of students' writing achievement based on the showcase portfolio model. Fourth- and eighth-graders in Vermont now compile portfolios that include

See Marna Bunce-Crim, "Evaluation: Picture of a Portfolio," *Instructor*, 101 (March 1992), 28–29, for a description of one Vermont fourth-grader's portfolio.

1. A table of contents.
2. A dated "best piece," chosen with the teacher's help. A best piece is one "the student feels represents his/her best achievement as a writer."
3. A dated letter from the student to the assessors, explaining the choice of the "best piece" and the process of its composition.
4. A dated poem, short story, play, or personal narration.

C. The child as revisor and editor (cont.)	Always	Generally	Sometimes	Never
4. revises to achieve a logical sequence				
5. revises to include transitional words for clarity (*first, however, also*)				
6. revises to avoid awkwardness				
7. substitutes more effective words				
8. deletes unnecessary words				
9. edits nonstandard expressions, such as *ain't*				
10. edits for punctuation and capitalization				
11. edits spelling				
12. rewrites for motor aesthetics				
D. The child as sharer				
1. enjoys sharing his/her papers orally				
2. takes pride in compiling a publication copy				

Name of child: _____ Date of observation: _____

Child's comments: _____

_____

Figure 10.12 Continued

5. A dated personal response to a cultural media or sports exhibit or event or to a book, current issue, math problem, or scientific phenomenon.
6. At the fourth-grade level, a dated prose piece from any curriculum area that is not "English"; at the eighth-grade level, three dated prose pieces from any curriculum area that is not "English" or "Language Arts."

Teacher reviewers use the pieces in children's showcase portfolios to analyze whether children maintain a clear purpose in their writing, develop a coherent organization, provide details that support their main points, develop a personal voice or tone, and demonstrate ability to use language (usage, spelling, capitalization, punctuation, and sentence forms) correctly. Classroom teachers in other states and at other grade levels can employ a similar approach, asking their students to select specific kinds of pieces from their active-writing portfolios to include in their showcases.

Obviously, standardized tests of writing do not provide the depth of information about children's writing progress that portfolios do. Sheila Valencia (1990) explains, "No single test, single observation, or single piece of student

"Parents need to be made aware that assessment is based on different kinds of data. Often they do not understand, or agree with, portfolio assessment" (Anita Baker, Baylor University, in a letter to the author, 1992). "Parent education is needed to help build respect for the writing program. The teacher should send an explanation of the program to parents so that they understand the school's philosophy regarding standard usage and spelling" (Edward Plank, Millersville University, in a letter to the author, 1992).

work could possibly capture the authentic, continuous, multi-dimensional, interactive requirement" of portfolio assessment. Showcase portfolios pay secondary dividends as a means of communicating this view of assessment to parents. "Portfolios can help parents understand the ongoing development of their children. . . . With this kind of frame, parents are less likely to put undue value on the results of test scores. They come to realize that numerical scores provide only limited information about their children's abilities" (Siu-Runyan, 1991, p. 124).

Using Rating Scales to Judge Writing Competency

At some point, a teacher or school may want to make holistic, or general, judgments about the overall competency of child writers. Useful here are evaluative criteria, or competency scales, that describe levels of writing achievement at specific grade levels. A number of such scales are available today. A few school districts are even developing their own scales to judge the efficacy of the writing program within the district. The Grosse Pointe, Michigan, school district, for example, has devised a scale for assessing writing performance from grades 1 to 10. The emphasis in the Grosse Pointe scale is on whether the writing communicates a clear message. Level 4 on each scale represents the achievement expected of students in that grade in Grosse Pointe. Figures 10.13 and 10.14 show the levels of competency in the Grosse Pointe scale for grades 1 and 2 and for grade 6, respectively. These scales give a general idea of what holistic, evaluative criteria are all about.

For grades one and two, the levels represent stages of development based entirely upon the child's ability to communicate meaning in writing. The ability to use the conventions of written expression (correct spelling, punctuation, capitalization, etc.) is not evaluated until grade three.

Beginning Writing

Level 1   The writing does not contain at least three complete thoughts that can be readily understood and are about the same topic.

Level 2   The child can organize some complete thoughts and express them in writing. Some passages may not readily be understood. The ideas tend to be restatements of the same thought or to be a "list of sentences" with only one word different in each sentence.

Level 3   The child can express a number of related ideas about a topic so that each idea after the first says something else about the topic or tells what happens next. Taken as a whole, however, the topic does not have a sense of completeness.

Competent Writing

Level 4   The child can compose a completed series of ideas which are readily understood. The writing, however, consists entirely of basic sentence patterns.

Highly Competent Writing

Level 5   The child can compose a completed series of ideas about a topic, some of which are expressed in non-basic sentence patterns or contain a connecting word to join two main ideas. The ideas, however, tend to be expressed one at a time in simple sentences. The writing does not contain sentences packed with information and ideas.

Superior Writing

Level 6   The child can compose a completed series of ideas about a topic and can compose complicated sentences, each with enough content to have been expressed in three or four simple sentences. The writing, however, does not contain insights or creativity.

Level 7   The child can compose a completed series of ideas about a topic with some complicated sentences and can compose with insight and creativity.

Figure 10.13 Evaluative Criteria for Grades 1 and 2

Not Competent

Level 1 The writing does not contain an understandable message. It either contains passages that cannot be readily understood or contains an insufficient number of related thoughts to comprise a message.

Level 2 The student can express a message that can be readily understood although the writing contains numerous deficiencies in wording, spelling, punctuation, or capitalization, judged by standards appropriate for the grade.

Marginally Competent

Level 3 The student can express a message that can be readily understood and does not contain numerous gross deficiencies in wording, spelling, punctuation, and capitalization. The writing, however, is not competent in at least one of the following skills:

Completeness of content   Use of several non-basic sentence patterns
Sentence sense   Use of connecting words to join sentences
Spelling   Some use of subordination
Punctuation and capitalization

Competent

Level 4 The student can compose a completed series of ideas about a topic with the basic skills, listed above at a level appropriate for the grade. The writing does not, however, demonstrate the use of good vocabulary, good sentence structure, a controlling idea, and some interpretation.

Highly Competent

Level 5 The student can compose a completed series of ideas about a topic with basic skills at a level appropriate for the grade and with good vocabulary, good sentence structure, a controlling idea, and some interpretation. The writing does not, however, contain passages of superior writing with characteristics such as insight, creativity, or vitality of expression.

Superior

Level 6 The student can compose a completed series of ideas about a topic with excellent skills appropriate for the grade, with good vocabulary and sentence structure, with a controlling idea, and with a passage of superior writing. Superior writing contains characteristics such as insight, creativity, or vitality of expression.

Level 7 The student can compose a completed series of ideas about a topic with excellent basic skills appropriate for the grade, with good vocabulary and sentence structure, with a controlling idea, and with a sustained excellence of expression. The student can compose with insight, creativity, or vitality and richness of expression.

Figure 10.14 Evaluative Criteria for Grade 6

...........A Summary Thought or Two

WRITING PROCESSES

The major thesis developed in this chapter is that elementary-grade students should participate directly in the processes that comprise the act of writing. They should rehearse before and during writing, draft with the mindset that what they record is simply a beginning, revise and edit their drafts, and eventually share their writings with others so that they experience the thrill of authorship and of being a member of a community of writers. Simultaneously, youngsters should read all kinds of printed materials; through reading, students begin to comprehend the nature of print.

The chapter also describes strategies for involving children in writing processes: pictorializing, talking about, and thinking through; factstorming, categorizing, and charting or webbing; story plotting out; teacher and peer conferences; teacher-guided group writing and rewriting; the revising/editing workshop; the active-writing portfolio; the Author's Chair, oral sharing, and bookmaking; and the showcase portfolio. Through activities such as these, young writers learn not only what is involved in writing but they learn how to organize and sequence their thoughts for writing and they develop the skills of writing. In essence, they become young authors.

RELATED READINGS

Atwell, Nancie. *Side by Side: Essays on Teaching to Learn*. Portsmouth, N.H.: Heinemann Educational Books, 1991.

Balajthy, Ernest. *Microcomputers in Reading and Language Arts*. Englewood Cliffs, N.J.: Prentice-Hall, 1986.

Belanoff, Pat, and Marcia Dickson. *Portfolios: Process and Product*. Portsmouth, N.H.: Heinemann Educational Books, 1991.

Calkins, Lucy. *The Art of Teaching Writing*. Portsmouth, N.H.: Heinemann Educational Books, 1986.

———. *Living Between the Lines*. Portsmouth, N.H.: Heinemann Educational Books, 1991.

Cambourne, Brian, and Jan Turbill. *Coping with Chaos*. Rozelle, Australia: Primary English Teaching Association, 1987.

Clark, Roy Peter. *Free to Write*. Portsmouth, N.H.: Heinemann Educational Books, 1987.

Glazer, Susan, and Carol Brown. *Portfolios and Beyond: Collaborative Assessment in Reading and Writing*. Norwood, Mass.: Christopher-Gordon, 1992.

Graves, Donald. *Writing: Teachers and Children at Work*. Exeter, N.H.: Heinemann Educational Books, 1983.

Hall, Nigel. "The Emergent Writer, Chapter 4." In *The Emergence of Literacy*. Portsmouth, N.H.: Heinemann Educational Books, 1987.

Hansen, Jane. *When Writers Read*. Portsmouth, N.H.: Heinemann Educational Books, 1987.

Harp, Bill, ed. *Assessment and Evaluation in Whole Language Programs*. Norwood, Mass.: Christopher-Gordon, 1991.

Jenkinson, Edward. "Learning to Write/Writing to Learn." *Phi Delta Kappan*, 69 (June 1986), 712–717.

Johnson, Paul. *A Book of One's Own: Developing Literacy Through Making Books*. Portsmouth, N.H.: Heinemann Educational Books, 1992.

Karelitz, Ellen Blackburn. *The Author's Chair and Beyond: Language and Literacy in a Primary Classroom*. Portsmouth, N.H.: Heinemann Educational Books, 1993.

Moore, David et al. *Developing Readers and Writers in the Content Areas*. New York: Longman, 1986.

Murray, Donald. *Shoptalk: Learning to Write with Writers*. Portsmouth, N.H.: Heinemann Educational Books, 1990.

Nathan, Ruth et al. *Classroom Strategies That Work*. Portsmouth, N.H.: Heinemann Educational Books, 1988.

National Assessment of Educational Progress. *Write/Rewrite: An Assessment of Revision Skills*. Denver, Colo.: National Assessment of Educational Progress, 1977.

————. *Writing Mechanics, 1969–1974*. Denver, Colo.: National Assessment of Educational Progress, 1975.

————. *Writing Trends Across the Decade, 1974–1985*. Princeton, N.J.: National Assessment of Educational Progress, 1986.

Parsons, Les. *Writing in the Real Classroom*. Portsmouth, N.H.: Heinemann Educational Books, 1991.

Proett, Jackie, and Kent Gill. *The Writing Process in Action: A Handbook for Teachers*. Urbana, Ill: National Council of Teachers of English, 1986.

Silvers, Penny. "Process Writing and the Reading Connection." *The Reading Teacher*, 39 (March 1986), 684–688.

Spandel, Vicki, and Richard Stiggins. *Creating Writers: Linking Assessment and Writing Instruction*. New York: Longman, 1990.

Tierney, Robert, Mark Carter, and Laura Desai. *Portfolio Assessment in the Reading-Writing Classroom*. Norwood, Mass.: Christopher-Gordon, 1991.

Wilde, Jack. *A Door Opens: Writing in Fifth Grade*. Portsmouth, N.H.: Heinemann Educational Books, 1993.

CHAPTER 11

Language Patterns, Usage, and Grammar

Managing Ideas

BEFORE reading the chapter, read the title, the headings, and the end-of-chapter summary. Then answer the questions in the margin on this page.

TEACHING IN ACTION   *Punctuating Direct Quotations*

Fourth-graders in Jeanne Smith's class were studying fables. During their genre-type unit, they were both reading and writing fables—a literary form that generally includes dialogue. One day, after the youngsters had read "The Rooster and the Pearl," Ms. Smith gathered the children in the Magic Circle to play with the way dialogue is handled on paper. To this end, she had composed cards that when put together summarized "The Rooster and the Pearl." The cards were

| A rooster | Aha | He | A farmer's wife | She | Well |

| He | To each his own | he said | pecked happily at his corn |

| said the rooster | I | snatched it up with delight | saw the pearl |

| picked up the pearl | and | he said | came upon a pearl |

| here is something to eat | discovered it was not corn |

| would rather have food than pearls |

See Deborah Abbot, "Aesop's Fables," *Book Links*, 2 (September 1992), 56–60, for ideas for teaching fables and a bibliography of children's books.

To form these phrases, the teacher had cut up eight sentences, dividing each sentence or clause between subject and predicate but maintaining as units conversational indicators such as "said the rooster."

Reconstructing the Story

Building words and phrases into logically sequenced sentences

Ms. Smith distributed the cards and directed, "Hold up your cards so everyone can see." Then she asked, "Who has the card that begins the fable?" Working from that question and cooperating orally, the youngsters reconstructed the story from the cards. In so doing, they juggled pieces so that the story would flow logically.

When the cards were in order, Ms. Smith had the children read the lines aloud, expressing meaning vocally and pausing where necessary. After the choral reading, one student remarked that the sentences did not have punctuation to signal the pauses needed when reading. These youngsters had been working on punctuation and were developing a conception of the relationship between punctuation and meaning. At that point, Ms. Smith took out her punctuation blocks, small rectangular pieces of wood on which she had drawn commas, periods, question marks, exclamation marks, and quotation marks. Each block held two marks, one on each of the two opposite faces. She distributed the blocks to the students.

Discovering how to punctuate units of direct conversation

One by one the children added the marks to the sentences they had reconstructed. Because this was their first structured experience with punctuation of direct quotations, the teacher had to assist. She referred the children to the story in the book to discover how to place the comma or period in relation to the quotation mark at the end of a group of spoken words. Youngsters modeled their punctuation after the way it was done in the book. Because this was also the first time the class had functioned in this way, Ms. Smith had to stop twice to review with students the rules of behavior they had previously agreed on.

Discovering and Generalizing About Conventional Usage Patterns

When the sentences had been punctuated according to conventional usage patterns, the teacher guided youngsters to state generalizations about the punctuation of direct quotations, based on the specific instances in their reconstructed story. Her first question was "What words do we place within quotation marks?"

Generalizing about punctuation conventions

Sherie answered, "Words that are said." On a piece of chart paper, Ms. Smith recorded Sherie's generalization. The teacher continued, "Where do we put the comma or period in relation to the quotation mark at the end of a group of spoken words?" Herb answered this time: "In front of the end quotation mark." This became the second point on the chart.

"One more generalization, please!" urged the teacher. "Let's consider how we handle an exclamation point when the words spoken are an exclamation." Sylvia generalized this time: "When words spoken are an exclamation, we put the exclamation point in front of the end quotation mark."

This is the discovery approach—a way for students inductively to put relationships together.

"Look now at the quotation mark at the beginning of a group of spoken words," prompted Ms. Smith. "How do we handle that?" Tim was quick to respond: "A beginning quotation mark comes right before the words spoken." Tim's point became a generalization on the language chart.

Applying the Generalizations

Relating specific problems to generalizations

At that point, Ms. Smith gathered up and redistributed the punctuation blocks. The students again added the marks to the story, but this time they told which generalizations on the chart were guiding their action. Having reset the punctuation, the students expanded the fable by first adding adjectives, then adverbs, and finally prepositional phrases.

Writing stories with direct conversation

Since "The Rooster and the Pearl" was one of a series of fables the youngsters had been reading, they knew the characteristics of a fable and added fables to their list of writing options that they kept at the front of their active-writing portfolios. Ms. Smith mounted the language chart on the bulletin board and suggested that students edit for punctuation after writing their fables. One fourth-grader wrote:

The Rainbow

Once there was a hunter who wanted to catch a rainbow. The rainbow hung over a cliff. One rainy day the hunter was out hunting animals. When the rain stopped, he saw the rainbow and said, "I will catch it so my life will always be warm." He tried to reach it, and he fell off the cliff!

Moral: Don't reach for something for yourself that belongs to everyone.

—*KIM LECHNER*

Reviewing to reinforce understanding

At a learning station, the teacher placed the punctuation blocks and the sentence strips for "The Rooster and the Pearl." Students could go there to reconstruct and punctuate the story again. And they did, for building and punctuating sentences in this literature-based context had puzzlelike qualities that these fourth-graders enjoyed.

What was Jeanne Smith's intent in structuring this lesson as she did? What learning goals was she seeking? One of her goals was related to sentence building—putting words together in typical sentence patterns. Through the reconstruction activity, she hoped the fourth-graders would gain a heightened sense of what a sentence is. A second goal related to punctuation and capitalization conventions. Specifically, the lesson allowed her to review the way to handle direct quotations at a point when students were using direct quotations in their writing. In sum, she was introducing the children to the conventions of written language.

Usage, Grammar, and Writing

How does a teacher help children use written language in a standard way? As Dan Kirby et al. (1988) remind us, the way to help youngsters is not by asking them to study traditional, prescriptive grammar, do grammar worksheets, and take punctuation quizzes. *The hours children spend learning grammatical terminology and filling in blanks and circling words in grammar exercises have no positive impact on children's writing.* Numerous research studies and analyses of those studies (Elley et al., 1976; Petrosky, 1977; Haynes, 1978; Newkirk, 1978; Hillocks, 1986, 1987) support that conclusion. What does have an effect is an integrated language arts program with the following characteristics:

Some big books print conversation in color within quotation marks, which make them useful in considering punctuation conventions relative to direct quotations.

1. Children spend much time listening to and reading written language. Helpful here are texts that children read along as teachers read aloud, especially big books—those giant-size books that are popular today and can be used in so many different ways. Reading a big book to a class, the teacher runs his or her hand under the lines of print, pausing briefly to show sentence beginnings and endings. Children read the big books together, making their voices show meanings signaled by punctuation. Later they generalize about how punctuation signals help an author communicate meaning. Helpful, too, are story listening and choral speaking. Such activities are much more than fun; they are pivotal, for they help children hear "book talk" and distinguish it from speech.

2. Children spend much time writing on their own and in teacher-guided groups. When recording children's writing for them on experience story charts, the teacher asks youngsters to contribute by making the capital letters that begin sentences and the punctuation marks that end them. She or he uses the word *sentence* to refer to the units of written text children are drafting cooperatively and alone. Writing on their own, children become active users of language. As Lucy Calkins (1986) explains, "The infrequency with which students write is a major reason for their problems with mechanics and spelling. . . . The single most important thing we can do for students' syntax, spelling, penmanship, and use of mechanics is to have them write often and with confidence."

3. Children spend much time editing what they have written. In an editing conference, the teacher listens to the children read their writings aloud. She or he helps them to translate the oral sounds of language into the punctuation marks of written language and to think about standard usage of language (such as agreement of subject and verb) as writers prepare a publication draft. Providing such instruction at the point when it is needed (when children are getting ready to publish pieces), the teacher gathers several youngsters for a cooperative editing-instructional session. Teacher and children consider a piece or two by members of the collaborative group; together, based on instruction from the teacher, they rework sentences, fix punctuation so that it communicates their meaning, or edit for an aspect of standard usage. Most teachers have found that, at any one time, it pays to focus on one major usage problem rather than on several problems. Youngsters who have worked together in such a group become their own instructional team; working independently, they read and edit one another's papers in terms of what they have just learned in the teacher-guided editing-instructional session. Roy Peter Clark (1987) elaborates, "Every teacher knows that a class of fifth graders will exhibit certain kinds of usage problems. They will misuse the comma, write in fragments, and mix up homonyms. But not every class will exhibit the same problems in the same order. *Teachers can teach lessons on the problems that are revealed in their students' writing.*" In the same vein, Clark reminds us, "Teach grammar, usage, and mechanics as tools, not rules."

See Chapter 10 for more on the editing process and ways to use conferences and writing workshops so that children refine their ability to handle the conventions of written language even as they need those conventions to write with clarity.

4. Children spend some time playing actively with aspects of written language.

Because language play is a topic we have not yet considered in this book, in Chapter 11 we will focus on ways to involve children in it, especially as language play relates to children's own writing and editing. We will first consider ways to involve children in sentence building so that they develop a sense of what a sentence is and use their understanding to write complete and clear sentences. We will also consider ways to involve children with punctuation and capitalization conventions at the point when they need them to write. Finally, we will talk about the place of formal grammar in the language arts. The reader, however, should keep in mind two underlying assumptions as he or she thinks about the chapter:

✦ Usage and grammar are best taught in the context of students' purposeful reading and writing.
✦ Usage and grammar are only small parts of a language arts program in which communication is in action.

Learning to Control the Sentence

To write effectively, one must be able to manipulate sentences. John Harris (1986) maintains that there is a fundamental difference in the syntactic features of speech and writing. Speech is formed from loosely coordinated chains of clauses, not all of which are sentences. Harris uses this oral exchange as an example of loosely coordinated groups of words that, other than the first, are not sentences in the strict sense of the word:

Are you going to the theater tonight?
No. Tomorrow.

In contrast, sentences are a structure of main, subordinated, and embedded clauses.

Study this unedited composition by a second-grader named John:

Snow

Snow it is snowing today everywhere there is snow it is fun to play and you can play snow ball fights and we throw snowballs at each other and berry our selfs and make angals in the snow.

Obviously John has exciting ideas, and he has a rather clear concept of a paragraph. He writes of snowball fights and snow angels in a paragraph that focuses on one major idea: having fun in the snow. Obviously, too, John does not have a concept of written sentences as linguistic units; he does not know where one sentence ends and the next begins; he does not use the signals that indicate sentence beginnings and endings. In short, he has not yet conceived that there is a difference between speaking and writing (Harris, 1986).

Sentence Making: What the Research Says

Researchers have amassed considerable evidence on children's developing ability to handle sentences in writing. According to Kellogg Hunt and Roy O'Donnell (1970), young children have trouble building several related ideas into one sentence. They rely on *and* to string thoughts together, as in "I saw a dog and he was big and he was with a boy." More mature writers are more likely to combine the thoughts: "I saw the big dog that was with the boy."

Jack Perron (1978) believes young writers gain control over the sentence, and over sentence-combining strategies, through "a glacially slow process, currently without much help from teachers." His research indicates that direct experience with sentence-combining can help children more rapidly control sentence writing patterns. Perron writes:

> The six-month study demonstrated that a grammar-free program of sentence combining (SC) lessons backed by games, activities, and experiential exercises in SC manipulation, does encourage syntactic growth in the writing of fourth graders. It also demonstrated that games and activities do provide a valuable supplement to the language arts curriculum.

Other studies affirm Perron's findings. John Mellon (1969) notes a gain in seventh-graders' writing skills through a program in which students systematically combine sentences based on symbolic clues for sentence building. Frank O'Hare (1973) finds a similar gain among seventh-graders who combine sentences based on word clues. Studies by Hunt and O'Donnell (1970) and Barbara Miller and James Ney (1968) demonstrate similar gains at the fourth-grade level. A study by Elizabeth Stoddard (1982) using SC activities with fifth- and sixth-graders shows gains in syntactic fluency and overall writing quality.

Playing with Sentence Parts

Millions of students have memorized the definition "A sentence is a group of words that expresses a complete thought." However, a sentence is not the only way to express a complete thought. As the example on page 353 shows, people at times express complete thoughts through single words and phrases when speaking. Today linguists propose that a better approach to building sentence sense is to have children manipulate sentence parts and gradually acquire a fun-

See William Strong, *Creative Approaches to Sentence Combining*, and George Hillocks, "Grammar and the Manipulation of Syntax," *Research on Written Composition* (Urbana, Ill.: ERIC Clearinghouse on Reading and Communication Skills, 1986), for reviews of SC studies.

damental understanding of the two-partedness of a sentence and the way writers use capital letters to signal sentence beginnings and punctuation marks to signal sentence ends.

Sentence reconstruction, as we saw it in the opening vignette, is one way to play with sentence parts. The teacher distributes phrase cards to students reserving one card for himself or herself. Some phrases (such as *a girl in my class*) can function as subjects of sentences, others (such as *made a home run*) as predicates. Students build sentences from the parts, reading them aloud to hear the sound each sentence makes. They add end punctuation and beginning capitalization. Figure 11.1 shows the layout of sentences resulting from this kind of sentence reconstruction.

Students who have built sentences from subject and predicate parts can create their own subject and predicate cards. Using their cards, they can locate a friend who has created a subject or predicate part that can go with one of theirs to form a sentence. Finding an agreeable mate, children read their resulting sentences aloud, testing them to see whether they have the sound of a sentence. Similarly, in editing their own writing, they read their sentences aloud, testing them to see whether they have "the sentence sound."

Playing with Sentence Patterns

This section is based on transformational-generative grammar principles. See Chapter 3, pages 92–93, and page 380 in this chapter for a discussion of t-g grammar.

Linguists have identified basic, or *kernel*, sentence patterns through which people communicate. Although research has not shown a connection between chil-

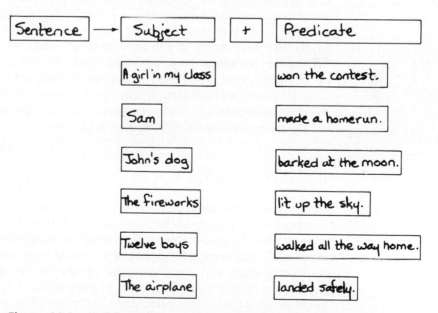

Figure 11.1   Building Sentences from Subject and Predicate Parts

dren's understanding of these patterns and their ability to write, a plausible hypothesis is that children who have had considerable practice reading and writing in many patterns may begin to sense the essence of a sentence. Figure 11.2 outlines kernel sentence patterns.

Teams can compete to see who can compose the largest number of sentences adhering to a particular pattern within a given time period. Later the class judges sentences as each team displays its sentences with labels so that the structure is apparent. At some point, too, young writers should look at their own writings to identify patterns they overuse and rewrite to achieve variety.

Expanding Sentences

Students can use a pyramid as a form in which to expand sentences.

Dogs run.
Red dogs run.
Red dogs also run.

Children can expand sentences or, as one language series puts it, they can make sentences "grow." A fun way is to clip just two words on the sentence clothesline—words such as *alligators* and *swim*—in reverse sentence order: *swim alligators*. Young children can order the pair and then add adjectives, adverbs, and prepositional phrases by writing them on cards and clipping the cards to the line. Then they shift to other kernel patterns, such as "The monkey spied a tiger." "The monkey was afraid." A teacher should keep punctuation cards and capitalization markers ready so that pupils include the appropriate signals. Children who have expanded sentences in this way expand their own sentences as part of revising editing workshops.

Edward Plank (1992) reports that upper-graders, especially those who learn best when they are physically involved, enjoy "becoming" words in sentences they are expanding. To start what Plank calls a "human-sentence game," three students become the three words in a kernel sentence such as *The dog ran*. Saying their words, they stand in order before the class. Other students decide what words they will become to join the sentence, encouraged by teacher prompts: "Where do you belong in our sentence? Where else could you fit? What do you do in the sentence? Who names something? Who describes something?" As the sentence grows, other children become punctuation marks. Plank suggests that this physically involved activity reinforces not only children's concept of a sentence but also their understanding of punctuation.

Transforming Sentences

Phrase cards: *run away, walk slowly, jump the cracks, raise your hand, walk, open the door, get the clock, turn off the radio.*

To encourage sentence building with transformations of the basic patterns, Mr. Lombard, a third-grade teacher, converts his classroom floor into a composing stage, where children construct sentences. He distributes phrase cards and a number of cards bearing the word *you*. He retains one *you* card, places it on the composing stage, and asks, "Who has a predicate part to complete this sentence?" Mr. Lombard gets half a class of possibilities, which are laid beneath a predicate label card. Other participants contribute their *you* cards under a sub-

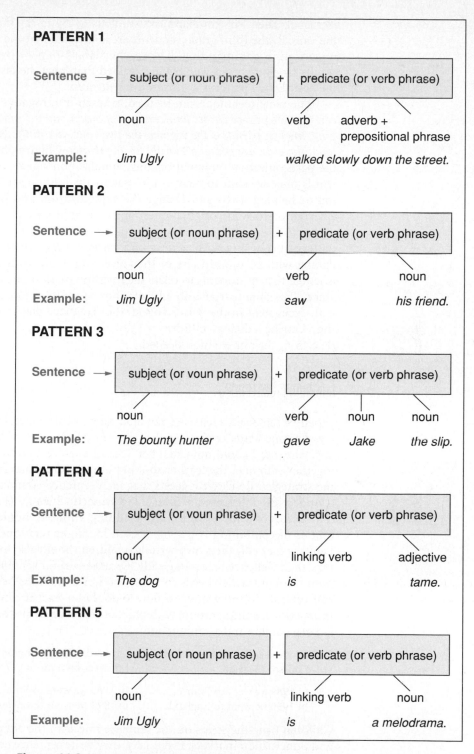

PATTERN 1

Sentence → subject (or noun phrase) + predicate (or verb phrase)

noun

verb   adverb +
        prepositional phrase

Example: *Jim Ugly*   *walked slowly down the street.*

PATTERN 2

Sentence → subject (or noun phrase) + predicate (or verb phrase)

noun

verb   noun

Example: *Jim Ugly*   *saw*   *his friend.*

PATTERN 3

Sentence → subject (or voun phrase) + predicate (or verb phrase)

noun

verb   noun   noun

Example: *The bounty hunter*   *gave*   *Jake*   *the slip.*

PATTERN 4

Sentence → subject (or voun phrase) + predicate (or verb phrase)

noun

linking verb   adjective

Example: *The dog*   *is*   *tame.*

PATTERN 5

Sentence → subject (or noun phrase) + predicate (or verb phrase)

noun

linking verb   noun

Example: *Jim Ugly*   *is*   *a melodrama.*

Figure 11.2   Sentence Patterns for Writing

ject label. Then Mr. Lombard asks students to try to say the sentences without the *yous*. By the third grade, students are able to see that the subject parts can be unspoken in commanding. The teacher labels *Imperative* the grouping that results by eliminating *you*; having applied that label, he also begins to refer to the basic kernel patterns as *declarative sentences.*

The same technique can be used to teach interrogative patterns. A teacher can provide phrase cards: *John, has come, Susan and my mother, have gone shopping, my best friend, is the winner, the two cows, are in the barn, the radio, is too loud, the girls, are going to Florida for the winter.* Children build sentences from the parts, injecting punctuation and capitalization signals. When asked, "What words must we shift to convert our statements into questions?" they shift linking or helping verbs and change the capitalization and punctuation signals. They go on to write original questions with appropriate punctuation. Eventually, a teacher can introduce other patterns that require a question mark—patterns beginning with *which, what, where, who, whom, when,* and *how* or ending with an upward rise of the voice. Oral work with question patterns is essential to help students to relate the question mark to the upward inflection of voice. The same is true with exclamations, since they, too, have a vocal equivalent: excitement in the voice. This kind of language play relates directly to editing. During editing, children orally read sentences they have written to determine the punctuation needed.

Combining Sentences

A pair of sentences such as "I ran after Sue. I could not catch her" can be organized as one sentence to show the inherent relationship between the two: "I ran after Sue, but I could not catch her." Because children typically string sentences together with *and*, the teacher should put some emphasis on sentence-combining strategies. Research suggests that such sentence-combining activity without a lot of stress on grammar "is an aid to syntactic fluency" (Haynes, 1978).

As part of teacher-guided group editing, children should consider the possibilities of combining two sentences to highlight relationships between ideas. Later, as they edit their own writing, children should also look for ways to organize their sentences more logically. Because run-on sentences are such a common error, a teacher needs to stress ways of combining sentences to avoid the run-on trap. To show students how to do this, a teacher can provide them, in an instructional editing group, with pairs of sentence strips that they join with the aid of a comma and a conjunction:

Read Virginia Bradley, "Improving Students' Writing with Microcomputers," *Language Arts,* 59 (October 1982), 738–741, for a description of sentence-combining activities using a personal computer.

I arrived at the station on time. I missed the train.	I arrived at the station on time, but I missed the train.
In 1989 we went to France. In 1990 we went to England.	In 1989 we went to France, whereas in 1990 we went to England.

Children hang the strips on the sentence line with the aid of conjunction cards and punctuation markers. Eventually, they write sentence equations:

Combined Sentence = Subject + predicate, conjunction
                               subject + predicate.

Combined Sentence = Subject + predicate;
                               subject + predicate.

Within the requirements of each equation, youngsters write their own samples. Later, clipping the sentence-combining patterns to the inside cover of their writing portfolios, they use the equations as they combine sentences during editing. The equations serve as guides as children decide whether they have used conjunctions, commas, and/or semicolons accurately.

Embedding Ideas

By the middle grades, youngsters begin to rely on complex sentences to express involved relationships. Most children need some help structuring and punctuating the sophisticated sentences they are now composing. Much of this help occurs on a one-to-one basis during teacher-pupil conferences. In addition, this is the time to try a class activity or two in which children together build longer sentences by inserting one sentence into another.

In preparation, several students write out a series of phrase and punctuation cards such as the following:

Connecting Words, or Subordinators:	although, since, while, when, after, just as, if, as, wherever, because
Verb Phrases:	was predicted, rained, was late, missed the bus, am her best friend, invited me to her party, was in the gym, put the balls away, arrived, climbed on, had been in school ten minutes, dismissed us, trusted me, was getting interesting, is right behind me
Noun Phrases:	she, the school bus, we, the principal, the lesson, my dog, everyone, snow, it, I (and five additional *I* cards)
Commas:	ten comma cards
Periods:	ten period cards
Capitals:	a number of long Cuisenaire rods to mark capitals
Labels:	four SUBJECT labels, four PREDICATE labels, two SUBORDINATOR labels

The principal

dismissed us.

Students distribute all the cards except the noun phrase card *the principal* and the labels. The teacher places the card with *the principal* on the composing floor or tapes it to the board and asks students to contribute a predicate part to complete the sentence. Children place the period and capitalization marker in the sentence. Those who think they have possible SUBJECT parts place or tape their cards beneath *the principal*, which they label SUBJECT. Students next try to pair their predicate parts with subject parts already in place, labeling that column PREDICATE. By juggling cards, youngsters should be able to build fifteen sentences. They add punctuation and capitalization markers to form "law-abiding sentences." Incidentally, since punctuation and capitalization are part of the conventions of writing, the phrase *law-abiding* is helpful to beginners.

When all the parts are in place, children check each sentence to identify non–law-abiding sentences. There will be some, since fifteen sentences will have been composed and only ten period cards provided.

The next step is to rehabilitate the non–law-abiding sentences. With guidance, children can transform two sentences with the aid of the subordinators they still hold by inserting one within another. A result may be "Although snow was predicted, it rained." On board or floor, students add the comma between the parts and add labels so that the pattern is apparent. Students continue to build other sentences by placing word and phrase cards below those in the model sentence:

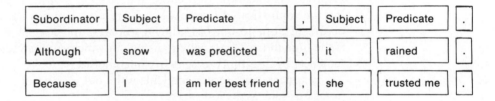

When children have inserted and juggled cards to form seven sentences, they take the next step: shifting a sentence so that the subordinator is between the clauses, as in "It rained although some snow was predicted." Using the remaining labeling cards, children construct the equation for the pattern and shift the other sentences into the new pattern:

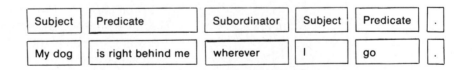

See also Jack Perron, *The Impact of Mode on Written Syntactic Complexity: Parts I, II, and III*, Studies in Language Education Report No. 24, 25, and 27 (Athens, Ga.: University of Georgia, 1976). Also available through ERIC: ED 126 531 and ED 125 511.

The next step is for youngsters to write original sentences that adhere to the pattern. Marion Crowhurst's research (1979) has indicated that one way to encourage the construction of complex sentences is to ask youngsters to compose in the argumentative mode. Writing options in this mode include "Convince your mother to let you look at a particular television program" and "Present an argument about why the afternoon recess break should be extended. Address your argument to the principal." Having written such pieces, youngsters check their sentences against the equation patterns to see whether they have composed any complex sentences and punctuated them correctly.

Composing Sentences: A Summary and a Few Suggestions

One of the most basic skills a person must acquire is the ability to compose sentences. This skill does not come from memorizing a definition. It most probably comes through diverse encounters with sentences, sentence writing, and sentence editing. For this reason, schools must provide children with opportunities to hear, manipulate, write, and edit sentences, engaging them simultaneously in fundamental aspects of sentence design: use of periods, exclamation marks, and question marks at sentence ends; use of commas in complex patterns; and use of capital letters at sentence starts. Here are a few suggestions for additional sentence work:

Reread pages 95–96 of Chapter 3 on the vocal intonation of English sentences.

✦ When children compose fragments, write them on sentence strips. Have children first read the fragments without the rhythm, rises, and falls of a sentence. Then have them generate statements and questions based on the fragments. Stress the sound of the sentences as students chorus their statements and questions aloud. Ask students in editing pairs to locate fragments in their own writing.

✦ When children compose run-ons, write those sentences on strips. Have children chorus them aloud, making the sound of two sentences with a pause between. Encourage children to expand their sentences orally, listening to the sound of the sentences. Ask students to work in editing pairs to locate run-ons in their own writing.

✦ When children compose "drag-on sentences"—a series of sentences strung together with *ands*—try sentence lifting. Write an example on a large piece of construction paper. Have children cut apart each sentence unit. Then guide them in putting the parts together as one sentence with only limited reliance on *and*. For example, one teacher lifted the drag-on sentence "Saturday we went downtown and we saw some friends and we had lunch and we all went to a movie" from a student paper. Youngsters reconstructed it to state, "On Saturday when we went downtown, we had lunch with some friends and went to a movie with them."

✦ Supply a list of possible subjects, such as *a twisting tree, the whistling wind, Joe and Jack, a long and deserted road, a steady rain, a dirt path, a cold little dog, I, one truck, two black automobiles.* Children write sentences that start with the given subject parts. Then they select some sentences to write into a story.

✦ Supply a list of possible predicates, such as *was knocked down, struck the ground, ran as fast as possible, called the police, opened the door slowly, placed a hand on the knob, heard a squeaky noise in the distance, looked out the window into the stormy night.* Children write sentences ending with the given predicates. They then select some of their sentences to include in a story.

✦ Encourage children to manipulate a variety of other patterns, working from models such as Christina Rossetti's "Wind":

> *Who has seen the wind?*
> *Neither I nor you:*
> *But when the leaves hang trembling,*
> *The wind is passing through.*
> *Who has seen the wind?*
> *Neither you nor I:*
> *But when the leaves bow down their heads,*
> *The wind is passing by.*

Children begin their own versions with questions like "Who has heard the snow?" "Who has touched the moon?" "Who has heard the grass?" "Who has held the rain?" Encourage children to create their original Who has _____? first lines.

✦ A pleasurable activity is interpreting fundamental sentence punctuation with sounds. Read a paragraph to the class, stopping at each punctuation marker. Listeners must interject the appropriate punctuation by making a predetermined sound: ding-dong = exclamation; plunk-plunk = period, whooo = question mark, coooo = comma.

✎ BUILDING AND REFINING YOUR TEACHING SKILLS

✦ Locate a poem or story to use in introducing children to a particular sentence pattern. Structure an activity based on the poem or story. To get started, check Eric Carle's *The Mixed-up Chameleon*. With its repetitive if-then pattern, this delightful book is superb for introducing the cause-and-effect sentence structure.

Learning to Manage the Conventions of Writing

Differences of opinion exist about which language generalizations should be taught and whether nonstandard speakers should be asked to add standard patterns to their speaking and writing repertoires.

Hand in hand with the ability to control a variety of sentence patterns in writing is the ability to manage conventions associated with capitalization, punctuation, and usage. By *usage* here we mean ways of using contractions, plurals, tenses, and so forth.

Today most language arts textbook series and school language guides present generalizations about language use that have wide application. Generalizations that are part of most programs include conventional ways to manage sentences, paragraphs, capitalization, punctuation, and nouns and verbs in writing. Figure 11.3 outlines skills typically taught. It can be used as a checklist

A WRITING SKILLS CHECKLIST			
The child is	Never	Sometimes	Always
1. Able to compose sentences; specifically he or she a. writes a variety of sentence patterns and expansions of them			
b. transforms sentence patterns to gain variety and clarity			
c. combines sentences and inserts one sentence into another in writing			
d. writes complete sentences			
e. uses words other than *and* to connect thoughts in writing			
f. writes effective dialogue			
g. writes sentences in which phrases, clauses, and words are placed so meaning is clear			
2. Able to punctuate a. sentence ends			
b. series			
c. dates			
d. addresses			
e. direct address			
f. direct quotations			
g. abbreviations			
h. appositives			
i. parenthetical expressions			
j. yes/no patterns			
k. letter salutations and closings			
l. subordinating and coordinating patterns			
3. Able to capitalize a. sentence beginnings			
b. beginnings of direct quotations			
c. proper nouns			
d. proper adjectives			

Figure 11.3   A Writing Conventions Checklist

	Never	Sometimes	Always
e. important title words			
f. titles of distinction			
4. Able to write in paragraph units; specifically he/she a. starts a new paragraph to show major thought units or units of conversation			
b. sequences ideas logically within and between paragraphs			
c. uses transitional words to indicate relationships among ideas			
d. indents the first word of a paragraph			
5. Able to handle nouns and verbs; specifically he/she a. uses verb tenses and irregular verbs in a standard way			
b. uses helping verbs, or auxiliaries in a standard way			
c. handles pronouns in constructions like "She gave it to Mary and them."			
d. spells contractions correctly			
e. handles negative patterns in a standard way			
f. distinguishes between such word pairs as *teach/learn* in writing			
g. restricts *ain't* to informal speech			

Figure 11.3 Continued

to diagnose children's ability to handle conventions as they write and to assess children's growth as writers.

How to Teach Usage Patterns: Beginning with Oral Language

Having identified usage patterns children need to edit their own writing successfully, how does a teacher structure experiences so that children develop the requisite skills? Because written language reflects the spoken language to a great extent, a teacher will want to begin by planning sessions in which children orally play with and hear standard patterns until those patterns sound natural to them. This is fundamental, especially for children whose native language or dialect is not standard English. In these cases, a teacher may invite students to express an idea first in their own dialect and then translate it into standard English. In this way, they work simultaneously with their *everyday talk* and with *school talk*.

A *dialect* is a regional or social variation of a language. *Nonstandard* refers to dialects that differ from those used within the general population.

Generating and Reconstructing Sentences It is relatively easy to begin with language children generate. For example, if a teacher's goal is to help children feel natural with the sounds of nouns and verbs that agree in number, stu-

This section is derived from the work of transformational-generative linguists. See pages 92–93 and page 380.

dents can generate sentences that adhere to a simple noun verb-noun pattern and in which present-tense verbs agree with subject nouns. Children generate sentences modeled after two sentences the teacher supplies:

Elephants pull logs.   An elephant pulls logs.

Models are printed on sentence strips and taped to the chalkboard. As children generate other sentences following the same pattern, they write them on the board below the appropriate model, depending on the number of "doers." They speak and respeak the sentences generated and gradually become comfortable with the sound of the standard form.

On another day, the teacher displays strips containing the sentences children generated the day before. Now, however, the sentences have been clipped between subject and predicate parts. Children must reconstruct the sentences, mating a subject part with an "agreeable" predicate part. Again, as students put parts together, they read and reread the results so that the language patterns begin to sound natural to them.

Call this the "Agreeable Parts Game." Also, play the Oral Transformation Game, where children make questions and negative statements from their agreeable kernel sentences.

Expanding Sentences   On still another day, students play the Oral Expansion Game. They expand their agreeable kernel sentences, each child orally adding a word or phrase to a base sentence that grows bigger on each respeaking. They can expand silly agreeable sentences such as "An elephant eats pizza" in the same way. This oral activity provides an opportunity for players to hear subject nouns and verbs that agree in number.

Applying Understanding to Writing

Children who have worked orally with sentences that abide by a basic language convention should apply their understanding as they write. Structured writing is useful in this context. For example, children who have played orally with agreeable subjects and predicates write in patterns that force them to generate subjects and verbs that agree in number. Creating orally together, one group produced this piece:

Call pieces with only a one-word subject and a one-word predicate "two-fers." When handling two-fers, children write one line to a page and illustrate it to communicate the number of the subject.

Our People Poem

Anne sings.	_Joey talks._
Debbie springs.	_Mika walks._
Cathy eats.	_Greg races._
Chris treats.	_Alicia traces._
Beth reads.	_Ann pleases._
Amy leads.	_Kristan sneezes._
David teases.	_Diane jots._
Consie freezes.	_Susie plots._

Then they expanded their noun-verb lines to include adjectives and adverbs:

Call pieces with four words to the line "four-fers." Children can also create three-fers—pieces with an adjective, noun, and verb pattern.

Our People Poem

Cheerful Anne softly sings.
Fast Debbie gracefully springs.

Happy Cathy neatly eats.
Kind Chris surely treats.

Silent Beth quietly reads.
Managing Amy guidingly leads.

Joking David playfully teases.
Shivering Consie totally freezes.

Loud Joey always talks.
Jolly Mika happily walks.

Speedy Greg quickly races.
Talented Alicia accurately traces.

Helpful Ann usually pleases.
Sick Kristan loudly sneezes.

Careful Diane leisurely jots.
Mysterious Susie cautiously plots.

See also Merriam's "Spring Fever," in which lines pattern after "Danny dawdles."

Patterns for Writing   It is easy to find patterns for writing that reinforce language conventions. Books like Eve Merriam's *It Doesn't Always Have to Rhyme* and *There Is No Rhyme for Silver* supply numerous patterns. In "The Cat Sat on the Mat," for example, there are lines such as "They frisk, They scramble, They tickle, They tangle." Children can write similar pieces about other animals. In the process, young writers will generate sentences that pattern simply: "They (*verb*)." Later students compose singular animal poems in which lines pattern "My cat snarls" or "My cat purrs."

Other pieces reinforce different conventions. In "Mr. Zoo," Merriam repeatedly substitutes *he's* for *he is*. Students working with contractions can model pieces after it. In "'I,' Says the Poem" she plays with direct quotation. Children who are learning how conversation is written down can select a literary form, an animal, a plant, or an object and speak for it, modeling the piece after Merriam's and in the process apply their understanding of punctuation of quotations.

Motivate children by reading Janice Udry, *What Mary Jo Shared* (Niles, Ill.: Whitman, 1966).

Similarly, teachers can structure group writing so that patterns they want to reinforce are generated. After a listening/show-and-tell time, for instance, one third-grade teacher summarized with the children what was shared during talk-time. She started with an introductory statement: "Here is what we shared today." Then she asked children to itemize what was shared: Mary Jo's father, Sallie's turtle, Stephen's "magic" boots, Jed's sore cut. She wrote down the items, the result being examples in the possessive form. Later she cut up the list so that each item was divided into three parts, as in *Mary Jo*, *'s*, and *father*. Children reconstructed the pieces so that "the objects belong to the right people." Such teacher-guided writing activity plays an important role in building language understanding.

Structured group writing can play a similar role in upper grades as an introduction to more sophisticated language patterns. To introduce appositives, one sixth-grade teacher used structured writing based on a shared story. He read Gerald McDermott's *The Stonecutter* to a group. Then he invited students to summarize on individual sentence strips the main events of the story, with each sentence patterning after one he provided. The teacher's sentence was

Tanaku, the stonecutter, wished to be a prince so that he could have great wealth.

Try having children read their sentences with only one comma just after the name to see how important the commas are in communicating meaning.

Youngsters contributed sentences like

Tanaku, the prince, wished to be the sun so that he could have great power.
Tanaku, the sun, wished to be the cloud so that he could be more powerful.

In summarizing, the students relied, as had the teacher, on appositives. As an independent writing activity, the students later wrote original stories about Obara, the fisherman; Timaro, the teacher; and Nikimo, the painter. In their stories, the character successively became other people or things.

Nonpatterned Writing   Of course, a teacher should encourage spontaneous writing in which children apply the language conventions on which they have worked orally. To do this, the teacher provides a model against which youngsters judge their writing as they prepare a revised draft. That model can be sentences students have generated orally or sentences they have reconstructed based on a story read or heard. The latter was the case in Jeanne Smith's lesson with "The Rooster and the Pearl."

To encourage children to apply their understanding of language conventions as they revise, the teacher must relate writing options to those aspects of usage being stressed. In this respect, Jeanne Smith's selection of "The Rooster and the Pearl" was ideal for teaching conventions related to direct quotations. Fables generally contain much direct conversation. In writing original fables, therefore, students inevitably write dialogue—something they have just handled—and they can review as they edit by referring to the models posted on the bulletin board.

Roy Peter Clark, the journalist-teacher, proposes posting a "Yucky List" of writing problems (Clark, 1987). His list includes such items as *there/their/they're; its/it's; two/to/too; fragments*. Children check the "Yucky List" as they edit.

In this respect, too, the sixth-grade teacher's selection of *The Stonecutter* was ideal for studying appositives, especially since he asked children to write similar sequences involving appositives. Through careful pairing of introductory story material and follow-up writing options, a teacher can ensure some carryover from oral usage sessions to editing activity.

Working from Written Samples of Language

In some instances, as in the case with placement of punctuation marks inside or outside of quotation marks, a language convention is strictly a written one that is more arbitrary than logical. As a result, intonational clues fail to guide the writer in deciding whether to capitalize, how to punctuate, or what form to use. In these cases, a teacher may start with samples from stories children have read. Studying the samples, young language investigators decide what to do in a particular instance—where to place punctuation markers and whether to capitalize.

Think again about the teaching-in-action vignette with "The Rooster and the Pearl." In it, Jeanne Smith asked students to study the fable they had read to see how to manage the comma and quotation marks at the end of a conversational unit. In punctuating a reconstruction of that fable, they modeled their usage after one in a respected source.

Another analytical approach is to collect a sampling of sentences in which the language is handled in a similar way—for instance, a group of sentences in which commas separate items in a series. Youngsters study the models to determine how to manage this problem in editing. A similar approach is to provide children with stories that contain several samples of the same usage convention. Children analyze how the language is handled in those instances and then write stories in which they handle language in the same way. For example, upper-graders studying adjective forms (*big, bigger, biggest; gigantic, more gigantic, most gigantic*) can discover how to handle them by looking at tall tales. Since these tales are often filled with *mosts, -ests, mores*, and *-ers*, youngsters are able to extract any number of sentences to serve as models as they compose original tall tales loaded with comparatives and superlatives.

When upper-graders extract sentences from their reading and compose additional sentences to serve as writing models, they print the sentences on strips, which they lay out on the table or floor. Some teachers provide separate punctuation markers rather than placing the punctuation on the strips with ink. In this way, children can return to the punctuationless sentences and review by resetting the punctuation markers. A teacher can make punctuation markers by cutting narrow pieces of Styrofoam into small squares and painting punctuation marks on each side.

Discovering and Stating Generalizations

A second advantage of laying out sentences and adding punctuation markers is that the markers stand out from the rest of the sentence and prompt the discovery of relationships about the way the written language operates. At some point, children will begin to describe the workings of their language system; they will formulate general statements that explain how people handle certain patterns, especially in writing. Doing this, students of the English language are functioning as descriptive linguists.

Generalizing Based on Samples Generated Youngsters generalize after they have generated numerous sentences that contain the same usage pattern. For example, having generated sentences that tell about actions they performed yesterday, youngsters study their samples to figure out what clues communicate that the action took place in the past. Eventually they generalize that the form of the verb and the word *yesterday* are important clues. To test their generalization, students orally transform their sentences to communicate that the action is occurring today. They compare the verb forms to see how they change as the time relationship changes.

Having generalized, young linguists record their statements on chart paper and organize their individual chart pages together as a big book called "How to Edit It!" that hangs in the classroom. In editing and revising their own compositions, writers flip through the pages to locate a generalization that guides them in handling a particular usage problem. Generally the big book is left open to the page of generalizations most recently recorded by the group.

Writing follows generalizing. Having analyzed the clues that tell readers something occurred in the past, youngsters write stories that happened in the past: "I met George Washington," "I was on the *Titanic*," and "I spoke to Julius Caesar" are topic options requiring the past tense. Writers can develop their own topics by choosing a person, place, or event from the past.

This example suggests how to structure lessons that develop understanding of usage conventions that have some reflection in speech. Lessons should include

1. Generation of many language samples that are similar—to ensure similarity, the teacher provides a pattern for sentence generation;
2. Analysis of sentences generated to discover common features;
3. Verbalization and recording of generalizations to serve as guides for revising and rewriting;
4. Writing in response to topic options structured so that students apply the generalizations.

Generalizing from Samples in Reading Materials

In like manner, students generalize from sentences extracted from their reading. For example, encountering the difference in the written form between *it's* and *its*, youngsters can generalize from silly homophone stories like this:

Is It *It's* or Is It *Its*?

"It's a nice day today," said the oak tree to the weeping willow.

The willow shook its branches at the oak and bent its trunk down. "I don't think it's so nice. It looks as if it's about to rain."

The oak waved its highest branches in the air and answered, "It's all in your roots how you view the weather. It's a fine day if you think it is. It's a bit cloudy, but it's spring. Now it's time to wave and toss about." The oak turned its bark upon the weeping willow and waved and tossed its branches higher into the air. "Poor willow," the oak said to itself. "It's just unfortunate that it cannot forget its troubles and enjoy this fresh spring day."

To guide discovery of generalizations, a teacher asks, "What is the meaning of *it's* in the first sentence? Of *its* in the second sentence?" As is true with homophones, the difference lies in the meaning being communicated, a difference that youngsters can figure out for themselves. Having generalized that *it's* is used whenever the meaning is *it is* and *its* is used whenever the meaning is ownership, children write their own silly *its/it's* stories in which they repeatedly use these words.

The structure of this lesson serves as a model for classroom study of many language conventions that have no reflection in speech:

1. Study of written samples that focus on a particular usage problem,
2. Generalization based on the samples,
3. Writing and editing that require application of the generalization.

Encourage children to write similar fun stories in which they repeat sets of homophones: bear/bare, they're/their/there, pair/pear/pare.

An inductive teaching model:
specific
↓
general
↓
application

Specific Activities for Teaching Language Conventions

Because of heightened interest in what has been called "the basics," some schools require direct attention to the conventions of writing. As outlined in Figure 11.3, these conventions relate to beginning and ending sentences and paragraphs, handling capitalization and punctuation conventions, and managing noun and verb usage patterns. In this section, we consider meaning-based activities for teaching these aspects of usage.

Basic Punctuation and Capitalization

Especially with young children, some stress should be placed on how to begin and end sentences. This subject can be introduced as children dictate group experience stories. After children have composed, the teacher goes back and notes with the children the sentence beginnings, asking participants how the sentence beginnings are similar. If youngsters have had prior work distinguishing between upper- and lowercase letters, they will be able to explain that sentence beginnings are capitalized. Now as the teacher records, children who know how to write capital letters print on the story chart the beginning capital letter of each sentence.

Simultaneously, young children work with sentence endings. As suggested earlier in this chapter, children composing together add the marks that signal sentence endings and reread what they have cooperatively composed to express the sentence signals with vocal inflections. Later, as the teacher orally reads the story, stopping at sentence ends, the children hold up period, question mark, or exclamation mark cards at appropriate points.

Children can prepare for eventual writing of sentence beginnings and endings by doing much the same with big book stories. Children express ending punctuation through vocal intonation and point out other sentence beginnings using punctuation and capitalization clues. Similarly, children identify paragraph beginnings in the big books they are reading and generalize about paragraphing clues.

In the same way, when children reconstruct sentences from word cards, they add the marks that signal sentence beginnings and endings. Punctuation and capitalization markers are on standby so that children can add the markers to their sentences. For this purpose, the teacher should not capitalize words on cards used for sentence building so that participants can capitalize as part of group sentence building. Big capital letters can be superimposed on the first letters of words to indicate the uppercase form.

Children should apply their growing understanding of sentence signals as they edit. After children have written short compositions, they check whether they have put in the markers signaling sentence beginnings and endings. Because of the relationship between vocal intonation and punctuation, editing at first should be a collaborative activity, with two youngsters working together

Some Victor Borge recordings are based on this technique. Check your local video dealer for videotapes.

For a discussion of research on teaching punctuation through writing-editing conferences, read Patricia Cordeiro, Mary Ellen Giacobbe, and Courtney Cazden, "Apostrophes, Quotation Marks, and Periods: Learning Punctuation in the First Grade," *Language Arts*, 60 (March 1983), 323–332.

Skills can be taught on a one-on-one basis to meet individual needs. (© 1990 Suzanne Szasz/Photo Researchers, Inc.)

first on one person's composition and then on the other's. Such focused self-editing is particularly necessary at about second grade, when children write more extensively and need to check back on the sentences they write.

One caution before going on. Teachers of second- and third-graders sometimes complain that it is very difficult to teach children to write down sentences in ongoing paragraph form. Some children write sentences in lists. Perhaps the reason is that primary teachers may have recorded experience stories in this way. Even in early recording, teachers should beware of that practice and instead record sentences in paragraph fashion, leaving considerable space between sentences to show the breaks. Similarly, children who are reconstructing a story from individual word cards should be encouraged to lay out the sentences in paragraphs rather than in lists.

Capitalization in Writing

Capitalization can be taught through a wide variety of activities that occur naturally across the curriculum. Here are a few ideas:

✦ *Capital word searches.* Children search for words that are not sentence beginners but start with capital letters. Searchers clip those words and mount them collage fashion on colored construction paper. Later they analyze the words to develop generalizations about the kinds of words writers capitalize. Generalizations become guide charts used in editing and revising.

✦ *A class directory.* Middle-graders compile a directory that includes their names, addresses, and telephone numbers. In so doing, they work with capitalization of names, streets, towns, and states, as well as with the punctuation of addresses. The directory is organized alphabetically so that youngsters practice alphabetizing.

✦ *A class calendar.* Early primary-graders make a large calendar chart for each month as it arrives and place the name of the month at the top, with the days of the week above each column. They indicate important monthly events in the calendar blocks, using capitalization where necessary.

✦ *Books in circulation.* Children compile running lists of books they have read. These should include title, author, and publisher for each entry, with capitalization as needed and underscoring of titles. Each time a youngster completes a book not previously read by someone else in the class, he or she adds an entry to a class list or bibliography.

✦ *Mapping our town.* Children make large-scale maps of their area and label them to indicate rivers, schools, churches, municipal buildings, shopping centers, stores, and banks, as well as the names of streets and adjacent towns. Labels are added to show country and state. All proper names are printed with first letters capitalized.

Punctuation in Writing

Oral activity, modeling, and analytical approaches are probably the most useful ways to introduce punctuation patterns to children who need them in writing. The teacher provides models that contain a particular usage, and children generate sentences that pattern similarly. For example, when introducing date punctuation, a teacher might lay out sentences like these, stripped of punctuation:

> July 4 1776 was an important day in the history of our nation.
> She was born on May 10 1980 in Virginia.

Young authors enjoy Nora Gallagher, *How to Stop a Sentence and Other Methods of Managing Words* (Reading, Mass.: Addison-Wesley, 1982). Gallagher explains, "Some punctuation marks mean 'stop.' Others are signals for things to come. Many punctuation marks are like ballet directors: they tell you how a sentence should be danced." What a good idea—dancing to sentences!

Drawing on knowledge garnered through observant reading and using punctuation blocks or strips, students add the punctuation. Children generate other sentences that, like the models, include dates. These are recorded on sentence strips without punctuation; participants add punctuation markers by referring to the models. This kind of study with date punctuation is repeated on several occasions. Then youngsters generalize about date punctuation usage and record generalizations on a language chart, "How We Write It."

At this point, the teacher should suggest writing options that require dates.

THE FORUM On Teaching Writing Skills Through Writing

1. Because of the renewed interest in basic skills, some teachers are turning to drills and workbook exercises to teach children how to capitalize, punctuate, and use conventional language usage patterns. But, as Lucy Calkins writes, when children invent and use punctuation for their own purposes—to communicate their feelings and thoughts—"they learn more effectively than if they were doing drills, workbook exercises, and language lessons." Not only do they learn but they come to like punctuation marks. Calkins explains, "The urge to tell leads children to struggle with punctuation and language mechanics. 'I want to publish my mini-bike report. Will you help me make it perfect?' 'How can I make the wicked robot groan and yell?' When children write, they reach for the skills they need. . . . Young writers need time to run into their own problems, to ask their own questions. Only then can skills be learned in context—for the context is not the subject matter, but the child's question, the child's need" ("When Children Want to Punctuate: Basic Skills Belong in Context," *Language Arts*, 57 [May 1980], 567–573).

2. Roy Peter Clark takes a similar tack in *Free to Write:* "The work of your students will teach you what they need to learn and what you need to teach. Grammar taught straight out of a book may be boring to students who have already mastered a skill and impenetrable to students not ready to learn it. Teachers should read the writing of their students to make decisions about how and when to teach. Students may be using quotation marks correctly but may be having trouble with 'who' and 'whom.' *Instead of using canned material, teachers can use examples from student work for lessons*" [Emphasis added]. ([Portsmouth, N.H.: Heinemann Educational Books, 1987], 137).

Questions to Consider

Lucy Calkins' and Roy Clark's theory of skills instruction is that skills should be taught as children need them to write. How would you explain and validate this approach to parents who want their children to learn the basics? What strategies can you use to teach usage skills as children write? What strategies did Ms. Smith in the opening vignette use to teach skills? At what point might you teach language conventions out of the context of writing? How might you organize such instruction so that there is carryover to writing and editing? How might you develop understanding of and ability to apply language conventions during content area studies and as part of authentic reading of literature?

The Lion's Roar
The Lion's roar
is like a cry in the
wind. Sometimes it is because
of pain or anger. He is the king
of the jungle and roars
at his subjects. This
lion is a pussycat deep
inside. He is more gener-
ous than any other
beast in the jungle.
This is the lion:
Generous at heart.

Figure 11.4 Punctuation (the Colon) Learned Through Writing

This would be equally true in lessons designed to teach children other written language conventions (see Figure 11.4). Here are some ideas for punctuation activities:

✦ *Letter writing.* Children write letters to students in other schools asking to exchange materials needed for science or social studies such as leaf, soil, or water samples. They write letters to pen pals, industries, travel bureaus, governmental agencies. Letter-writing integrates nicely with the study of punctuation of dates and addresses. Student letter writers also will need to know how to punctuate the salutation and complimentary closing of a letter.

✦ *Everything we saw.* Children returning from a field trip enumerate everything they saw on the trip: "We saw _____ , _____ , _____ , and _____ "; "We liked _____ , _____ , _____ , and _____ ." Lower-graders can dictate their experience summaries.

✦ *Things we do.* Children enumerate games they play, places they go in the community, activities they carry out in school, and so forth. The result will be series patterns to be punctuated.

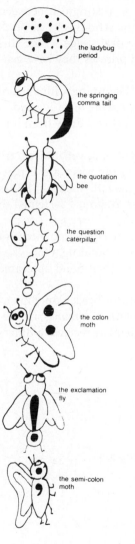

the ladybug period

the springing comma tail

the quotation bee

the question caterpillar

the colon moth

the exclamation fly

the semi-colon moth

◆ *Pausing and punctuating.* The teacher prints on a card a sentence like "Susan my sister slipped on a banana peel," and asks children to read it aloud to show meaning vocally. Then the teacher asks them to read it again to communicate a different meaning. Students add punctuation markers to show the different meanings expressed through various pause patterns and follow up with oral interpretation of similar sentences: "Ms. Martin my math teacher is sick today"; "Timothy her friend owns the candy store." Upper-graders will delight in composing confusing sentences that can be interpreted in two ways in the manner of the model sentences. Groups compose sentences and present them to the class by pantomiming the two different meanings while one member of the group displays the punctuationless sentences. Listeners decide how the pantomimed interpretations are punctuated and add markers to two copies of the sentence written on strips. Sentence strips with commas in place can be mounted on the bulletin board to serve as references during the editing of stories entitled "Jane Doe, the Doctor," "William Wilkes, the Wild Wolf," and so forth.

◆ *Playing yes/no.* The pause in speaking and the comma in writing also communicate differences in some *yes* or *no* patterns. Children orally interpret sentences like "No people are allowed there" and "Yes men are eager to get ahead," reading from sentence strips without punctuation. In groups, children write their own confusing *yes* and *no* sentences stripped of punctuation and later share specimens with the class through pantomime. Classmates add the punctuation that fits the pantomimed meanings.

◆ *Without the signals.* The teacher gives upper-graders paragraphs with all sentence signals removed; those signals include punctuation and capitalization markers as well as spaces between words. Children who have just received such stripped-down paragraphs try to read them aloud on the spot. Children will see the importance of conventional signals and enjoy adding them to the paragraph puzzles.

◆ *The war of the insects.* Youngsters meet the Punctuation Bugs depicted in the margin. Upper-graders enjoy writing original stories about "The War of the Insects," in which all the Punctuation Bugs fight for sentence supremacy. Youngsters can write similarly creative versions describing the origin of the punctuation marks at a point when writing had no periods, commas, quotation marks, and so forth. Later students check their concocted explanations against the etymological entries.

Noun and Verb Usage

Oral activity, modeling, and analytical approaches are as useful an introduction to noun and verb usage patterns as they are to punctuation patterns. Of course, the teacher emphasizes the application to editing. Here are some specific activities that offer practice with nouns and verbs:

◆ *Plural stories.* Begin a list of plural subjects with items like *many frogs, some knights, a king and a queen, five oranges and one pear, thousands of lily pads, two large lakes, high mountains, the sun and the moon.* Ask children to contribute additional plural subjects to the embryonic list by going to a chart during independent-work times to add more plural subjects. With children who speak a form of Black English, you may have to distinguish between the everyday way of indicating more than one and the school way; in Black English, utterances like *three orange* are acceptable oral usage. Once students have a lengthy list, they use some of the noun phrases they have generated as subjects in their stories.

◆ *Singular stories.* Do the same with singular subjects, beginning with a list of items like *a red hot sun, the looking glass, the strange-looking man, a wandering minstrel.* Children add their contributions to the list and draw from it in writing singular stories.

◆ *It happened yesterday.* To get children writing conventional verb forms, try stories set in the past. When youngsters are studying the westward expansion, provide writing options that center on that period, such as "I Was There at Sutter's Creek," "I Went West in a Covered Wagon," "I Helped to Settle California."

◆ *A sentence building.* As shown in Figure 11.5, students tape large pieces of colored construction paper together to form a sentence building. Once they have filled in each piece with the appropriate words, they build agreeable sentences by selecting words from their buildings.

◆ *The elephant's trunk.* Write sets of four related noun phrases on slips of paper: *the elephant's trunk, the elephants' trunk, the elephant's trunks, the elephants' trunks.* Make enough slips so that each participant receives a differ-

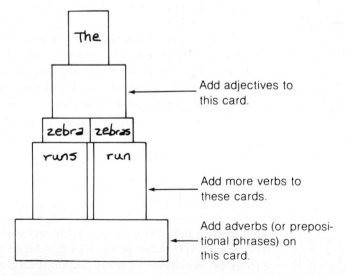

Figure 11.5 A Sentence Building

ent one. Each child draws a picture to depict the meaning of the phrase. Some pictures will be outlandish, such as one showing an elephant with several trunks and one showing several elephants sharing one trunk.

✦ *Finding the negative markers.* Middle-graders search sentences for negative-meaning words. As youngsters find the words, they write on slips of paper the sentences containing them. Paper a bulletin board with the slips, and ask children to generalize from their data about how we say *no* in English. Eventually, ask children to search their papered bulletin board for written instances of double negatives, such as "I didn't get no noodles." Ask them to listen for this usage in conversation, noting examples in their Jotting Books. Help children discover that today this form is employed in very informal conversation and is generally not found in written communication.

✦ *Contracting speech.* Contractions are fine material to teach children about the shortening that occurs as language is spoken and about how this changes language. On a card, letter a pair of words that has a contraction form. On the reverse side, letter the contracted ending so that when the right end of the card is folded over the end of the word, the contraction results.

> Ask youngsters to consider the advantage of word shortenings in conversation. Working from a list that you supply, children make a class set of Shortening Cards, with each youngster producing a different contraction to share.

✦ *Writing conversation tales.* Conversations written down often contain contractions. Suggest a writing option in which students write "Corny Conversations" and include sentences like these:

"I can't," said the ant.	"I'll do it," offered the kangaroo.
"I won't," hooted the owl.	"The asp isn't," hissed the adder.
"I'm a brain," claimed the ape.	"You'll fall," called the fawn.
"The mouse couldn't," whined the wolf.	

cannot

't

can	't

✦ *Ain't not allowed on paper.* Upper-graders conduct an *ain't* search. They keep ears alert for *ain't* on TV, in movies, in their own conversation, in school; they keep eyes alert for *ain't* in books, magazines, papers. Based on their findings, youngsters generalize about situations in which the contraction *ain't* is not used and when it may be socially acceptable.

A Warning About Teaching Usage Patterns

When involving elementary children with conventional language patterns, teachers should remember that the objective is appropriate usage depending on the communication situation: formal writing, informal writing, formal speaking, informal speaking. Learning appropriate usage does not come through memorization of rules; rather, it comes through considerable oral involvement with forms of language in different communication situations. It comes through experiences in writing that elicit those forms.

Teachers must therefore take care that stating generalizations does not become the focus of language activity. Verbalizing generalizations should simply be a means of summing up what is becoming second nature and of describing the way the language is used. Accordingly, teachers should avoid such assignments as "Memorize the seven uses of the comma" and tests that ask children to recall those usages. Language work of this type wastes time better spent in listening to, speaking, reading, and writing a variety of patterns.

Similarly, teachers must take care that usage study starts orally. Having students work in solitary fashion through a series of textbook or workbook exercises after a brief explanation does not result in improved usage. The textbook should serve as an adjunct to teacher-guided sessions in which children actively play with their language. The teacher can use the book as a source of sentence material for students to manipulate together, as a reinforcement to provide additional practice after considerable oral manipulation, and as a source of ideas to modify to meet individual needs.

✎ BUILDING AND REFINING YOUR TEACHING SKILLS

✦ Summarize a short reading selection on sentence strips. Cut the strips into noun and verb phrase units. In a talking-together session, involve children in reconstructing the story by laying out the strips on the composing stage area of your classroom floor. Invite participants to reset the punctuation.

Grammar: Describing the Language

Not only do language arts programs emphasize teaching conventional usage patterns, but they also give some attention to introducing youngsters to ways of describing the operations of their language—in other words, *grammar*. A grammar describes the syntax of a language—the patterns of sentence and phrase formation in that language.

Robert Hillerich (1985) clarifies the distinction between grammar and usage. He explains that "grammar has to do with the way words are strung together in order to make intelligible (or 'legal') sentences in the language. 'I brung the pencil' is grammatical; 'I the brung pencil' is not." In contrast, usage is a "matter of language habit" and social acceptability. Hillerich further explains, " 'I don't have a pencil' is socially acceptable usage in school, but 'I ain't got no pencil' is unacceptable."

Traditional Grammar

For many years, most English grammar was prescriptive rather than descriptive. Early language investigators studied Latin grammar and prescribed how English should be used based on the Latin model. In the 1700s, when a formalized English grammar began to emerge, Latin was believed to be the most eloquent language. Consequently, it became the source of precise rules that even today serve in some programs as the content of school grammar.

See Chapter 3, pages 101 and 103, for a tree and a chart showing that English is a Germanic, *not* a Romance or Latin-based, language.

The problem with this approach to school grammar study is twofold. First, Latin grammar is a poor model for English grammar. Latin is a highly inflectional language. This means that word endings are significant in communicating meaning. In contrast, English depends more on word order than on inflectional endings to communicate meaning. Order of words in sentences, not inflectional endings, allows a listener to distinguish the difference in meaning between "The man killed the tiger" and "The tiger killed the man."

Second, the precise rules devised in the 1700s to describe the language can hardly describe the English of today. Modern linguists accept the fact that language continually changes—as new words appear, old words acquire new meanings, and words drop from everyday use. It also changes in syntax—the patterns in which speakers put words together. An English grammar must reflect these changes if it is to be accurate. Traditional Latin-based grammar does not.

Twentieth-Century Linguistics

The twentieth century has seen the emergence of the scientific study of language: linguistics. Using systematic analysis, *structural linguists* have been able to describe rather precisely the structures through which speakers communicate meaning in English. As we saw in Chapter 3, they have described the importance of intonation in communication. They have also described how we communicate meaning through

+ *Sentence patterns:* the order of words in sentences, or the syntax of English;
+ *Class words:* nouns, verbs, adjectives, and adverbs;
+ *Function words:* words like noun markers, verb markers, phrase markers, clause markers, and question markers that communicate relationships among the four major word classes;
+ *Inflectional endings:* endings like the *-s* through which we form a plural noun or the *-ed* we use to show past time;
+ *Affixes through which we change words from one class to another:* for example, *govern,* a verb, becomes *government,* a noun, with the addition of the affix *-ment,* while *courage,* a noun, becomes *courageous,* an adjective, with the addition of the affix *-ous.*

To describe English using these features, the structural linguists devised a vocabulary for talking about the language. Instead of talking about only eight parts of speech, linguists recognize four major *word classes*—nouns, verbs, adjectives, and adverbs—and *function words*—prepositions, determiners, pronouns or noun substitutes, auxiliaries, intensifiers, and conjunctions.

Structural linguists also approach the definitions of parts of speech from a different perspective. No longer is a noun defined simply in terms of the name of a person, place, or thing. The structuralists prefer to talk about clues that help distinguish among words as those words work or pattern in sentences—clues such as affixes and inflections associated with a particular part of speech, the characteristic positions in a sentence occupied by a part of speech, and the function words that pattern with a particular part of speech.

More recently, language study has assumed another orientation. Using some of the terminology of the structuralists as well as their analytical approach, *transformational-generative linguists* have described the way speakers use language to generate, or produce, sentences. These linguists have identified basic, or kernel, sentence patterns to describe English syntax. They have gone on to describe the ways speakers expand the basic patterns and the ways speakers transform sentences into questions, commands, and negative statements. They have explained how people insert or embed one sentence into another to produce more complex sentences. The ideas on pages 355–360 of this chapter are derived from transformational-generative linguistics.

Classroom Applications

Unquestionably, the work of the structural and transformational-generative linguists is carrying educators closer to an accurate description of how the English language works and how people generate sentences. Unquestionably, too, the linguists are supplying simple and analytical approaches and clearer definitions based on syntax with which youngsters can begin to understand the workings of their language.

Limitations to Consider   In some instances, however, teachers are turning the work of the linguists into new content to be memorized. In some classrooms, students are memorizing the new parts of speech and formulas for sentence generation, expansion, and transformation. When this occurs, the work of the linguists is subverted.

Second, in some language programs, youngsters in elementary grades construct intricate language tree diagrams based on the linguists' conceptualizations. These techniques are advanced tools of language scholars that contribute little to elementary language understanding and make language investigation tedious for the beginner. The same can be said of some terminology devised by scholars to describe the intricacies of language. Too much terminology too quickly encountered frustrates even the brightest youngsters.

Linguistics in the Elementary Grades   Which aspects of linguistics should be taught and learned in the elementary grades? To answer this question, the

A kernel sentence adheres to a NP & VP pattern—a noun phrase followed by a verb phrase. See Figure 11.2 for a list of NP and VP patterns

A good teacher reference is Constance Weaver, *Grammar for Teachers: Perspectives and Definitions* (Urbana, Ill.: National Council of Teachers of English, 1979).

reader must consider why children learn formal grammar in the first place. Most research indicates that knowing about nouns, verbs, and so forth makes little difference in one's ability to speak, read, write, or listen. No, schools do not involve children in grammar study to help them communicate more effectively; rather, such study provides youngsters with a vocabulary to use when talking about language, helps them intellectually understand and appreciate the way their language communicates meanings, and helps them gain skill in analyzing language. Just as in science classes, a major goal is to have children learn the methods through which scientists discover new knowledge, so a goal of language study is to have children learn the ways of language investigation. This learning is part of general education.

From this point of view, the aspects of linguistics that contribute to a very general understanding of the structure of the English language are what need to be emphasized. Educators can draw content from the work of the structuralists and the transformationalists, selecting aspects that lend themselves most easily to firsthand involvement with language. Teachers should limit linguistic vocabulary to terms essential to communicating about language at an elementary level: names of parts of speech and words describing basic sentence components, such as noun and verb phrases.

The Parts of Speech

Here is a description of the four classes of words and the function words. Teachers may find that the terminology in their school texts varies from that given here. To prevent confusion, teachers should adhere to the terminology in the school's language curriculum.

The Four Major Classes of Words

1. *Nouns*
    ✦ Nouns have a plural form, achieved through addition of -s or -es and sometimes through internal changes, as in *child/children*.
    ✦ Nouns have a possessive form, achieved through addition of 's and sometimes of just '.
    ✦ Nouns can be signaled by a determiner, as in *a girl, those apes, my gift, five robins*.
    ✦ Nouns can pattern with prepositions and can have their places taken by pronouns.
    ✦ Nouns pattern in certain ways, as shown in the following test frames in which each blank represents a possible noun slot:
       The _____ ran into the _____ .
       Some _____ bought a/an _____ at the _____ .
       I sent the _____ some _____ .
       She is the _____ .
    ✦ Noun affixes include -*ness, -ment, -age, -hood, -er, -ence, -ance, -ity, -tion*.

2. *Verbs*
   - ✦ A verb form changes to indicate time relationships.
   - ✦ A verb form changes to agree in number with its subject noun.
   - ✦ Verbs may pattern with auxiliaries, in which case it is the auxiliary that changes form to show time or number relationships.
   - ✦ Verbs pattern as shown in the following test frames in which each blank represents a possible verb slot:
   The horse should _____ . Should the horse _____ ?
   The boy _____ the dog.
   The girl _____ my friend. The story _____ long.
   The farm _____ in Nebraska.
   - ✦ Verbs have an *-ing* form.
   - ✦ Verb affixes include *-ate, -ize, -ify,* and *-en,* as well as prefixes such as *be-, dis-, re-,* and *en-*.

3. *Adjectives*
   - ✦ Adjectives pattern with intensifiers, as in *very happy, terribly sick, too damp, most pleased.*
   - ✦ Adjectives have two favored positions, as shown by the following test frame in which each blank represents a possible adjective slot: The _____ car seems very _____ .
   - ✦ Most adjectives have a comparative and a superlative form, achieved by the addition or *-er* and *-est* or by placement of the words *more* or *most* before long adjectives, as in *more wonderful, most brilliant.*
   - ✦ Adjective affixes include *-ful, -less, -able, -ive, -y, -ous, -en.*

4. *Adverbs*
   - ✦ Adverbs pattern with intensifiers, as in *very slowly.*
   - ✦ Adverbs tend to be movable and, therefore, can be found in many spots in a sentence; they are best recognized in the terminal position, as shown in the test frame:
   The man ran _____ . The baby cried _____ .
   - ✦ Some adverbs have a comparative and a superlative form, achieved by the addition of the words *more* or *most* before the adverb, as in *more rapidly, most assuredly.*
   - ✦ Adverb affixes include *-ly, -where, -ward,* and *-wards.*

The Function Words

1. *Determiners, or noun markers*
   - ✦ Determiners are found in noun phrases and signal that a noun is coming.
   - ✦ The determiner position is before the noun, as in the following test frames:
   _____ man won _____ race.
   _____ horses pull _____ logs.
   - ✦ There are different kinds of determiners, as shown by this sampling: *a, an, the; his, your; one, eighteen; this, these, that; many, some, all.*

On Playing with Language Structure
The Why and How

1. Citing research evidence that indicates that students' conscious under-standing of grammar has no effect on the quality of their oral and written compositions, Patrick Groff raises a pertinent question: "Why cannot modern grammar be defended in the same manner as is other science instruction? We would not dismiss teaching about the circulatory system, for example, because of a complaint that such instruction does not make students' blood flow more properly. Accordingly, one may legitimately argue that a body of scientific knowledge as intrinsically human as is the understanding of how people form intelligible sentences surely is worthy of inclusion in the school curriculum at some level" ("Is Grammar Teaching Worthwhile?", *Practical Applications of Research*, 2 [March 1980], 4).

2. Barbara Hutson writes, "Children can learn a great deal about language structure by using it, handling it, manipulating it, playing with the 'mater-ial' of language to find out what it will and won't do, and what happens when you change some piece." Manipulations students can perform on a sentence include adding, deleting, rearranging, and substituting words; they can join sentences together and embed one sentence within another. For helping children develop concepts about language structure, "Writing is an even more powerful approach. . . . Feedback and rewriting can help students become sensitized to spelling patterns, the functions of punctuation in representing intonation patterns and intensity, and the effects of choice of words or rearrangement of sections of a story or report" ("Moving Language Around: Helping Students Become Aware of Language Structure," *Language Arts*, 57 [September 1980], 614–620).

Questions to Consider

Is the teaching of grammar in schools as important as the teaching of communication? Why or why not? What is the function of grammar in the elementary language arts curriculum? How should teachers involve children in their language? What specific strategies can you use to get students "handling," "manipulating," and "playing with" language so that they understand and appreciate the wonder of words? Do you remember your own early experiences with formal grammar? Were they positive or negative experiences to you? Why? How broad is your own understanding of how the English language functions? What is the function of grammar in the elemen-tary language arts curriculum? How should teachers involve children in their language?

2. *Prepositions, or phrase markers*
    ✦ Prepositions pattern in phrases with nouns, as shown in the following test frames:
    The cat crawled _____ the tree.
    The house _____ the corner is red.
    The bell rang _____ noon.

3. *Pronouns*
    ✦ Pronouns substitute for nouns in a special way; they provide information about sex, number, and definiteness.
    ✦ Pronouns change form depending on their function in the sentence.
    ✦ Pronouns can serve as a noun phrase in a sentence and occur in any of the characteristic positions occupied by noun phrases.

4. *Auxiliaries, or verb markers*
    ✦ Auxiliaries pattern with verbs and signal that a verb is coming.
    ✦ Auxiliaries change form to show changes in tense and in number.

5. *Intensifiers*
    ✦ Intensifiers pattern with adjectives and adverbs.
    ✦ The word *very* functions as an intensifier. Therefore, a test for an intensifier is to substitute other words in the *very* slot in the sentence "The girl is very sad."

6. *Coordinating conjunctions*
    ✦ Coordinating conjunctions connect two sentences, generally assisted by commas when the sentences are long. Words that may function as coordinators include *and, but, yet, or, so, for.* (Note: These words may have other functions in a sentence.)
    ✦ Coordinating conjunctions connect sentence parts of equal weight. The result may be a compound subject, a compound predicate, a compound adjective, a compound prepositional phrase, and so forth.

7. *Subordinating conjunctions*
    ✦ Subordinating conjunctions are used to insert one sentence into another. Words that can function as subordinators include *although, after, since, when, because* in the slot " _____ he came, I was happy"; and *who, that* in "The one _____ came in first was the winner." These structures clarify relationships among sentence ideas by indicating time, cause, purpose, and so forth.

Ways to Teach the Parts of Speech

How does the teacher involve children in grammar, especially parts of speech, without diminishing children's delight in language and expression? The answer lies in oral language play: generating language samples, cooperatively analyzing the samples, and generalizing about the way the language works. The answer also lies in referring naturally during editing and reading to the way words function in sentences.

Teaching with Test Frames   An easy oral introduction to parts of speech is to structure sentence-generating activities around the test frames that linguists have devised to show how particular parts of speech pattern. Phyllis Bartkus introduces "nounness" to her second-grade class by displaying three word cards and a period card in the chalk trough so that they look like this:

Then she distributes individual word cards, some bearing words that can function as nouns, others bearing possible adjectives. Children place their words in the sentence slots. At first, the sentence-building rule is only one word to a slot, and some children find their words do not work in either slot. Shortly the rule changes, and children can place two words in a slot. Youngsters who previously found their words could not work alone in a slot are now able to place them. The adjective holders discover that their place is just before the word cards—the nouns—previously placed in the sentence slots and just after *The* and *a*. Since this is an introduction to nouns and adjectives, Ms. Bartkus does not introduce terminology or definitions at first; this comes later, after the children have built nouns and adjectives into a number of test frames. At that point, Ms. Bartkus begins to call one group of words *nouns* and the other *adjectives*, and children describe how nouns and adjectives work and pattern in sentences.

Phyllis Bartkus's approach is a model for lessons with other parts of speech. For instance, youngsters who are learning about verbs play with a frame such as "The man _____ ." From adverb and verb cards, children select words that can work alone in the slot to form a sentence. Later they generate other words that can function there and then introduce into the test frame cards with words that can function as adverbs. They try the adverbs in several sentence locations to see the distinctive quality of adverbs; the adverbs have no preferred spot in a sentence but are movable. In each case, children are playing orally and together with language, they are having fun discovering the way their language works.

Teaching with Sentence Ladders   For follow-up, youngsters can play with sentence ladders. Each ladder is a test frame for a part of speech or of a phrase. Figure 11.6 shows two ladders, one highlighting nouns and the other prepositional phrases. Children orally generate words to attach to the steps on the sentence ladders. Having generated words, they build sentences choosing from words on the ladders.

When introducing parts of speech, teachers should discuss related parts together. For example, determiners, which signal that nouns are coming, should be handled with nouns. The teacher might focus on a noun phrase such as *The*

A noun ladder:

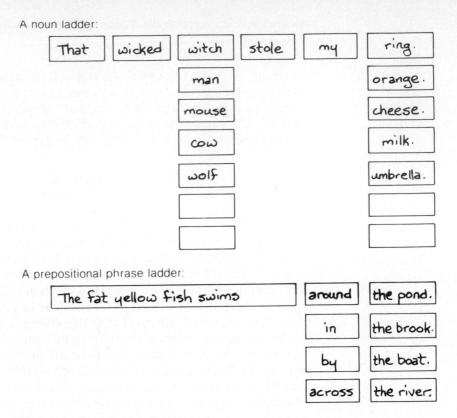

A prepositional phrase ladder:

Figure 11.6 Sentence Ladders

shoes in the sentence "The shoes are on the table." Quickly and orally, children substitute words for the noun *shoes* and then words for the determiner *The*.

Teaching Grammar Through Writing and Editing Once children have some idea of the parts of speech, their growing conceptions can be the base for patterned writing. For example, children, working in teams, write chain sentences by folding back strips of paper and writing down in succession words that can function as the parts of speech announced. The teacher starts by announcing, "Determiner." Each child writes a possible determiner on the top of his or her paper strip, folds the strip back, and passes it to a team member. Next, the teacher calls, "Adjective." Children respond by writing at the new top of the strip a possible adjective, without looking at the determiner. Again the paper strip is folded back and passed to another team member as the teacher calls, "Singular noun," then "Verb," and so forth. The result should be grammatically sound sentences, though doubtless a bit nonsensical. Students can share their sentences, talking about why the sentences still sound like sentences. Much the same can be done by calling out successive parts of speech in a sentence pattern and having teams cooperatively build sentences on the board that conform to the directions given.

A similar activity is to ask teams to construct sentences that tell *what, what happened, how, where,* and *when.* To facilitate construction, students make labeling cards with those words and tape the cards to the chalkboard. The teacher may provide a model sentence as given here:

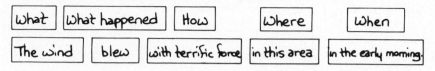

Teams generate additional sentences, write them on paper strips, and mount the strips beneath the appropriate labels. Later they shift the *how, where,* and *when* units around in the sentences, in the process seeing the impact of their moves on sentence meaning. Later still, they write original paragraphs that include *how, where,* and *when* information. In doing this, students are playing with prepositional phrases and adverbs, which lend considerable detail to sentences. Even as students play with language in this way, they can be using the appropriate terminology naturally to talk about what they are doing.

A more involved activity is patterned writing. One of the best examples was shared by a second-grade teacher, Eileen Hoernlein, who discovered the poem "Beans, Beans, Beans," by Lucia and James Hymes in *Hooray for Chocolate.* Ms. Hoernlein orally shared the poem with second-graders who had had considerable previous experience with nouns and adjectives. Her follow-up was a challenge to them: Write a poem using adjectives and nouns like the Hymeses have done:

Read "Verb Poetry" by Patricia Morton, in *The Best of Livewire,* selected by Julie Jensen (Urbana, Ill.: National Council of Teachers of English, 1989), for a way to encourage children to brainstorm verbs and use them to write action-filled poems.

> Beans,
> Beans,
> Beans.
> Baked beans,
> Butter beans,
> Big fat lima beans,
> Long thin string beans—
> Those are just a few.
> Green beans,
> Black beans,
> Big fat kidney beans,
> Red hot chili beans,
> Jumping beans too.
> Pea beans,
> Pinto beans,
> Don't forget shelly beans.
> Last of all, best of all,
> I like jelly beans!

To help the youngsters along, the teacher outlined the pattern for writing shown in Figure 11.7. She also involved the youngsters in oral composition. Together they composed a similar poem in which the repeated word was *sandwiches.*

```
_____noun_____,

_____noun_____,

_____noun_____.

_____  _____noun_____,

_____  _____noun_____,

_____  _____  _____  _____noun_____,

_____  _____  _____  _____noun_____ -

Those are just a few.

_____  _____noun_____,

_____  _____noun_____,

_____  _____  _____  _____noun_____,

_____  _____  _____  _____noun_____,

_____  _____noun_____ too.

_____  _____noun_____

_____  _____

Don't forget _____  _____noun_____.

Last of all, best of all.

I like _____  _____noun_____.
```

Figure 11.7   A Writing Pattern

Each youngster then selected one noun word and described that object in the manner of "Beans, Beans, Beans." Children were encouraged to use words other than adjectives to communicate a clearer message if they wished. In other words, the pattern was applied loosely. Here is an example.

Bugs,
Bugs,
Bugs.
Bad bugs,
Spider bugs,
Daddy long leg bugs,
Dead, smushed up bugs—
Those are just a few.

> *Cockroach bugs,*
> *Green bugs,*
> *Brown, yellow, black bugs,*
> *Lightning bugs too.*
> *Don't forget ant bugs.*
> *Last of all, best of all,*
> *I like ladybugs!*
> —*MICHAEL ROBINSON*

The diamanté provides a similar pattern for writing, also based on parts of speech. Figure 11.8 is an example of a diamanté. As made clear in the following sample, the diamanté is a study in contrasts: The last word of the poem, a noun, represents an opposite of the first word, also a noun, and the adjectives, participles, and nouns in the first half refer to the first noun while the words in the second half refer to the last noun.

King	*noun*
Rich, Powerful	*adjective, adjective*
Demanding, Commanding, Ruling	*-ing, -ing, -ing*
Leader, Royalty, Low, Peasant	*noun, noun, noun, noun*
Working, Obeying, Despairing	*-ing, -ing, -ing*
Poor, Powerless	*adjective, adjective*
Slave	*noun*
—*JOSEPH BORES*	

A truncated diamanté centering on just one object works equally well, especially with younger children. Such a form can also introduce youngsters to the metaphor, for in putting together a last line, they must dream up a creative comparison.

A truncated diamanté by Carol O'Hare's second grade:
Snow—
Sparkling, cold, soft,
Blowing, twinkling, melting
on the rooftops:
Nature's ice cream.

A truncated diamanté by Jody Donahue's fifth grade:
Raccoon—
Furry, mysterious, black-lined,
Scrambling, scolding, raging,
Like a thief in the night.

Icicle—	*noun—*
Cold, hard, glassy,	*adjective, adjective, adjective,*
Shining, dripping, breaking:	*participle, participle, participle:*
Winter's sword.	*creative comparison.*

Of course, the best context for enriching children's growing concepts of basic class words is during an editing and revising workshop or conference. Once students have a rudimentary understanding of the parts of speech, during editing the teacher can ask children, "Can you substitute a more exciting or precise verb for this one?" and then suggest, "Try editing your first draft by substituting more exciting or precise verbs." At the same time, children make word charts of powerful verbs to substitute for weaker ones: for the word *ran*, children chart words like *hustled, bolted, streaked*, and *sped*; for a verb like *looked*,

Immigrants
Poor, Frightened
Packing, Traveling, Wishing
Newcomers, Dreamers, Citizens, Voters
Working, Playing, Learning
Happy, Safe
Americans

East St.
School

Figure 11.8 A Group Diamanté
Source: Courtesy of Louise Patterson.

they chart words like *stared*, *glared*, and *peeked*. At the same time, children can pantomime meanings of interesting action verbs like *hobbled*, *bowed*, and *swayed*.

In like manner, a teacher can help students revise their first drafts by adding descriptive adjectives, moving adverbs, and checking the agreement of subject nouns and predicate verbs. In making these editorial suggestions, the teacher should use the terms *noun*, *verb*, *adjective*, and *adverb* naturally so that children begin to "pick up the lingo" and use those terms naturally as well.

Teaching Grammar Through Reading Another natural context for reinforcing children's growing concepts of the parts of speech is during the literary

After reading a short story or a chapter of a novel, upper-graders refine their understanding of parts of speech by considering the author's style—his or her use of descriptive adjectives, intensifying adverbs, and expansive prepositional phrases. (© 1993 Michael Zide)

conversation that follows the reading of a short story or, in upper elementary grades, a chapter of a novel. Some teachers ask students after reading to identify several words that are interesting or new to them and to jot down the page locations of those words. During follow-up discussion, students orally share with the class the sentences containing the unfamiliar words. The class uses the context to figure out the meaning of each word and identifies how it functions in the sentence—as a noun, adjective, verb, or adverb. Together students formulate a dictionary definition, including the part of speech. The teacher records the complete definition on a cumulative vocabulary chart, which is exhibited in the classroom as an aid to vocabulary development. See Figure 11.9 for an example of a word chart based on a chapter from *Maniac Magee*.

Also, after reading a chapter of a book, upper-graders in teams identify powerful verbs that make the chapter exciting, colorful adjectives that create vivid pictures in the mind, and/or phrases that "strike the heart." Then too, literature study teams can make lists of adjectives the author uses to describe the characters and the setting. They can use the terms *noun, verb, adjective, adverb,* and *prepositional phrase* in talking about the author's writing style.

For example, in reading *Sarah, Plain and Tall* by Patricia MacLachlan, a literature study team compared the author's use of color-designating adjectives in

> Maniac Magee   Chapter 9
> runt (noun)   a very small animal
> skirted (verb)   went along the edge of,
>   avoided
> miniature (adjective) very small, tiny
> scraggly (adjective)   ragged, worn looking,
>   tattered

Figure 11.9 A Word Chart Based on a Chapter from *Maniac Magee*

the first and third chapters and made a list of those words in each chapter. They discovered that MacLachlan used color-designating adjectives only sparingly in the first chapter but lavishly in the third. "Why did she do this?" the literature study team asked. The students hypothesized that Sarah came in the third chapter, and when she arrived, she brought color into the children's lives. Another team searched the entire book for the noun *sea* and discovered that the author used that noun in every chapter. "Why did the author do this?" the team asked. The students hypothesized that the author was trying to make a connection between the "ocean" sea of Maine and the sea of grass of the prairie; the sea is important in the novel. Another team searched for the names of flowers (all nouns), another titled each chapter with a single determiner and noun that summed up the chapter, another titled each chapter with a verb, and another titled each chapter with a prepositional phrase. These examples demonstrate a literature-based approach to grammar. As children read fine literature, they expand their understanding of the way their language works by using grammatical terminology to study a writer's style and to make meaning with the story.

Teaching with Workbooks and Computers: A Questionable Practice

In the past—and, unfortunately, in some cases today—much language study has been a solitary pursuit, with children completing worksheets and textbook exercises after a brief explanation by the teacher. Now the same thing is beginning to happen with computer-assisted instructional programs that teach parts of speech and usage conventions. Very often, however, such programs are nothing more than workbook pages on a screen—drill and practice whose only advantage over a workbook is immediate feedback as to whether responses are right or wrong. Educators must evaluate carefully those computer programs that purport to teach grammar and/or usage. They must ask, "What is this program teaching? Do I want to teach that? Can I teach more effectively and naturally through oral language interaction, writing, and reading so that children develop an appreciation of their language and use terminology as an aid to editing and interpreting literature?"

✦ Locate a piece of writing to convert into a parts-of-speech pattern for structured writing. Decide the grade level for which the pattern is appropriate. Try the pattern with children.

✦ Devise an inductive lesson to involve children orally in the study of a particular grammatical relationship. Prepare the materials you will need. Try the lesson with a group.

✦ Analyze several language arts textbooks published in the last three years to determine

1. How the sentence and the parts of speech are defined;
2. What specific aspects of usage are being taught and which approach is advocated;
3. The amount of space dedicated to formal language study compared to speaking, writing, listening, and literature-related activity;
4. The nature of the activities and the opportunity given students to discover relationships for themselves.

.........A Summary Thought or Two:

LANGUAGE PATTERNS, USAGE, AND GRAMMAR

The major thesis of this chapter is that usage and grammar are best taught in the context of students' own reading and writing. Children learn to use the conventions of written language by listening to and reading written text, and by spending a lot of time writing and editing their writing. Research indicates that study of formal grammar does not improve writing, but some work with sentence building has a positive effect on it. To this end, children should have opportunities to play actively with sentence making in challenging ways. This is essential if the objective of language study—heightened appreciation and understanding of the beauty and power of language—is to be realized.

As the chapter points out, language study should begin with children orally generating sentences, expanding them, transforming them, and combining and embedding them. In an interactive context, children learn ways to talk about and describe their language; they learn the grammar of their language. Through such playful manipulation of language, students discover fundamental language relationships, which they apply in writing.

Teachers must find creative ways to make language study exciting. In making language study challenging, they teach children that language is a wondrous tool through which to communicate thought.

RELATED READINGS

Calkins, Lucy. "When Children Want to Punctuate." In *David Graves in Australia*. Ed. R. D. Walshe. Portsmouth, N.H.: Heinemann Educational Books, 1982.

Clark, Roy Peter. "Editing." In *Free to Write*. Portsmouth, N.H.: Heinemann Educational Books, 1987.

Daiker, Donald, et al., eds. *Sentence Combining: A Rhetorical Perspective*. Carbondale, Ill.: Southern Illinois University Press, 1984.

Hillerich, Robert. "Dealing with Grammar." In *Teaching Children to Write, K–8*. Englewood Cliffs, N.J.: Prentice-Hall, 1985.

Hillocks, George. *Research on Written Composition: New Directions for Teaching*. Urbana, Ill.: ERIC Clearinghouse on Reading and Communication Skills and the National Conference on Research in English, 1986.

————. "Synthesis of Research on Teaching Writing." *Educational Leadership*, 44 (May 1987), 71–82.

Kirby, Dan, et al. "Beyond Interior Decorating: Using Writing to Make Meaning in the Elementary School." *Phi Delta Kappan*, 69 (June 1988), 718–724.

Noguchi, Rei. *Grammar and the Teaching of Writing: Limits and Possibilities*. Urbana, Ill.: National Council of Teachers of English, 1991.

Strong, William. *Creative Approaches to Sentence Combining*. Urbana, Ill.: National Council of Teachers of English, 1986.

Weaver, Constance. *Grammar for Teachers: Perspectives and Definitions*. Urbana, Ill.: National Council of Teachers of English, 1979.

Wilde, Sandra. *You Kan Red This! Spelling and Punctuation for Whole Language Classrooms, K–6*. Portsmouth, N.H.: Heinemann Educational Books, 1991.

CHAPTER 12

Spelling, Dictionary Use, and Handwriting

Tools of the Editor's Craft

BEFORE reading the chapter, read the title, the headings, and the end-of-chapter summary. Then answer the questions in the margin on this page.

How do children develop as spellers? How can the teacher facilitate this development?

_____

_____

How can the teacher encourage dictionary use?

_____

_____

What is important in teaching manuscript writing? cursive writing?

_____

_____

TEACHING IN ACTION   *Spelling Patterns and Writing*

Monday morning! Fred Bronsky's third-graders had entered their room a bit tired and quiet, but by ten-thirty they had come to life so Mr. Bronsky called a group of nine youngsters to the spelling table. To start, he asked two students to read aloud pieces they had been writing and explain how they had figured out the spelling of words during editing. He asked several others to share words from their writing that they were unsure of; other students in the group suggested spellings for dictionary checking.

Sorting

Recognizing words with structural similarities

Then Mr. Bronsky spread a series of cards face down and said, "Let's play a round of Word Sorts. Do you recall the rules?" One student explained that in playing they took turns turning over word cards. When they had figured out how the words on the cards were the same, they took a number to show when they had figured it out and turned their backs so they didn't see any more clues.

For a discussion of playing spelling games, read James Moffett and Betty Jane Wagner, "What Works Is Play," *Language Arts,* 70 (January 1993), 32–36.

At that point, the game began. Tom turned over *dark*. Marcia turned over *star*. Bruce uncovered *porch*. Jack turned over *born*. Pete turned up *door*. Suddenly Marcia's hand shot out to take number one from the pack of cards; then she turned her back. As *Mars, floor, start, lark,* and *story* appeared, other children took numbers and turned away so that they could not see additional clues. They had to figure out the shared feature based on the cards seen at the point when they took a number.

"O.K. Write the word *hypothesis* on a slip of paper, figuring out the spelling using any clues you can think of. Then record your hypothesis, or best guess, about how the words are the same." The children speculated about the spelling of *hypothesis* and wrote their hypotheses regarding the shared feature on strips to which they added their order number. Strips went down on the table and students compared them. They had all figured it out: The words contained a vowel-*r* spelling. "Great!" rewarded Mr. Bronsky, who declared the youngster with the lowest number card the winner.

"Now let's sort the words into related piles." On the desk he placed *star*. "Pick a word that goes with *star*." Five hands shot across the desk to add *dark*, *start*, *chart*, *short*, and *bark*. "All but one!" One hand snaked out to pull *short* from the group. "Explain why." Bruce explained that *short* did not have an *ar*. Ronald added that the word did not have the same sound as the others. With the word *short*, Ronald began a second pile, words that contained *or*. On the spot, the third-graders made labeling cards (*ar* words /är/, *or* words /ôr/) and added them to the piles to which they applied (see Figure 12.1).

Mr. Bronsky gathered the word cards and handed them to Pete to read without showing the cards to the others. As Pete read, the eight other students pointed to either the *ar* or *or* label. Pete checked to see whether the letters on the word card corresponded to the letters on the labeling card before placing it in the pile indicated by the pointers. Because a few children pointed incorrectly, the group repeated the activity.

Generalizing About Sound-Symbol Relationships

"Before we take a pretest on these words," Mr. Bronsky continued, "we'll talk about how in writing we spell words that have the sound as in *bar* and *car* or the

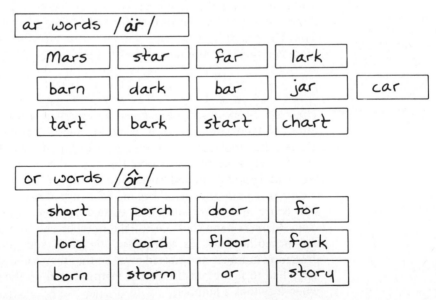

Figure 12.1 Sorted Word Cards

Sorting activities teach that words are objects that can be examined (Henderson, 1990).

Identifying groups of words that contain the same sound

sound as in *for* and *door*. When we hear the final sound in *bar*, what letters do we use to represent the sound on paper?"

Pete volunteered, "*Ar.*"

Mr. Bronsky replied, "Give that idea in a sentence, Pete, and put a couple of examples in the sentence." When Pete gave his sentence, Marcia recorded it as Pete's Generalization in the spelling book the group was writing. Because this was a publication copy, she used her best handwriting:

> **Pete's Generalization:**
>
> We use the letters <u>ar</u> to spell /är/ in words like <u>bar</u> and <u>car</u>.

Robin contributed the next generalization without prompting, modeling hers after Pete's:

> **Robin's Generalization:**
>
> We use the letters <u>or</u> to spell /ôr/ in words like <u>for</u> and <u>door</u>.

Mr. Bronsky urged, "Look at all our /ôr/ words; in some cases, the symbol is not just *or.*"

Bruce saw the point and amended Robin's generalization by adding "and sometimes *oor.*" He added the generalization to the group's spelling book.

Then the youngsters took a pretest as the teacher dictated the list of structurally related words they had been analyzing: *star, start, dark, fork, floor,* and so forth. Students corrected their papers by checking their spellings against those on the game cards and writing the correct spellings next to any incorrect ones.

Mr. Bronsky then distributed a puzzle sheet on which he had listed definitions of words containing -*ark*. Later working independently, youngsters were to figure out what the words were and write them on the sheet—a further practice in spelling words with the /är/ sound.

At that point, Mr. Bronsky had the children compare their spellings of *hypothesis.* Because there were several spellings, the children explained the reasoning behind their inventions. Finally, the Dictionary Sleuth for the day conducted a dictionary search, guided by the other children's suggestions to look first under *highpo-*, then *hipo-*, and finally *hypo-*. Mr. Bronsky summarized, "When I draft my ideas during writing, I give a word my best shot. Often I know that I don't have it right, but that I will get back to the word during

Discovering generalizations about the relationship between phonemes and graphemes

Identifying individual spelling problems

Refining the ability to work with -ar and -or

Using invented spellings to make a dictionary check

editing. During editing, I circle the words I think might be misspelled and check them one by one in the dictionary. In doing this, I identify the various ways a speech sound is recorded on paper. I say to myself, 'That sound could be spelled this way, this way, or even this way. I will have to look up each possible spelling until I find the dictionary spelling.' I think through possible spellings in this way when I edit. I don't do it while I am drafting because it breaks my train of thought." With that, the third-graders went to their places to write and/or read independently, resort the /är/ and /ôr/ words into related groups, and dictate those words to one another.

Steps in the Lesson Sequence

Fred Bronsky's small-group spelling lesson focusing on a within-word spelling pattern took no more than twenty minutes. During that short time, he

1. Helped children edit spellings of words from their writing,
2. Presented children with words that share a relationship,
3. Helped them to sort those words based on similarities and differences,
4. Asked children to state generalizations discovered through analysis of the word sorts,
5. Dictated a pretest of words related to the generalizations and had children correct their pretests,
6. Provided for follow-up practice,
7. Modeled how students could use their understanding of sound-symbol relationships to invent spellings while drafting and check their inventions against the dictionary during editing.

A teacher can use these steps to structure spelling lessons in which children develop an understanding of word patterns and relationships and the ability to invent spellings as a basis for dictionary checking during editing. Mr. Bronsky uses these steps because he believes that there is a logic to English spelling, which—if understood—can help children spell well. He also believes that spelling is for writing and it is his job to help children apply their understanding as they write.

What We Know About Spelling

The steps for designing spelling lessons just outlined are founded on current research and theory on how English words are spelled and how children develop the ability to spell. During the last twenty years, researchers have discovered much about how children develop as spellers. Through their studies of children's invented spellings, researchers such as Edmund Henderson (1990), Charles Read (1971), Darrell Morris (1983), Shane Templeton (1979), Charles Temple et al. (1988), and Marie Clay (1975) have identified stages through which children generally progress as they master the spelling of words. Henderson (1990) has categorized these stages as (1) preliterate spelling, (2) letter name

Figure 12.2 A Child's Early Writing with Words He Said as He Read It
SOURCE: Courtesy of Eric Ransom.

spelling, (3) within-word pattern spelling, (4) syllable juncture spelling, and (5) derivational and meaning-based spelling. In this section, we will examine this growing body of knowledge.

Preliterate Spelling

As we noted in Chapter 9, if very young children are given a pencil, they "write." At first, they make random markings that are more like drawings than writing (Gill, 1992; see Figure 12.2). But at some point children begin to handle the pencil in a way different from that used in drawing (Henderson, 1990). They begin to make markings that go from left to right, write in left-to-right waves, and incorporate letter- and numberlike forms. They ask for letters to write their names; and, in turn, if someone asks them to write a word, they record a letter—the initial consonant of that word or what they hear as the initial consonant. For example, they write *monster* as *m, dressing* as *jr, bottom* as *b.* Henderson and his associates describe children who perform in this manner as preliterate spellers. Children at this stage "know what writing is and what it does." They know the difference between writing and pictures and imitate writing in creative ways. They do not yet, however, write words with beginnings and endings; in short, they do not have a concept of what a word is (see Figure 12.3).

By *finger pointing*, Morris means tracing under words with the hand while reading.

Until children have developed an awareness of word units, are able to map spoken to written words, and are able to "read the spaces" that occur on the printed page, they are "seldom able to represent more than the beginning consonant letter in their invented spelling." Morris (1983) uses finger pointing during oral reading as a test of children's concept of word. He reads a poem to children, pointing to each word as he reads. Children join in to chorus the poem; later they take turns finger pointing as they repeat the poem aloud, trying to synchronize the words they speak with the words they point to.

Morris finds that first-graders fall into three groups based on this simple diagnostic test. Some youngsters cannot connect spoken with written words as they finger point; these youngsters generally represent only beginning consonants in their invented spellings and are clearly preliterate spellers. Others can finger point as they read but only to a degree; when they mismatch written and spoken words, they exhibit only a limited ability to correct their slip-ups. Interestingly, these children demonstrate some ability to include both beginning and ending consonants—syllable barriers—in their invented spellings. On the other hand, youngsters in this group have only limited ability to represent vowels in their spellings. At this stage, children are likely to spell *monster* as *mst, dressing* as *jrsn, bottom* as *bdm* (Henderson, 1990).

Letter Name Spelling

Still other first-graders have a functional concept of a word. They can finger point as they read with a high degree of accuracy. They can identify individual

STAGE	CHARACTERISTICS	HOW TO HELP CHILDREN AT THIS STAGE
Pre-literate spellers	Children show interest in making marks on paper; they create meaningful scribble by enscribing random lines and waves, letterlike shapes and random letters. Children cannot finger point precisely; they do not have a concept of a word.	*As Part of Reading and Writing:* Read poetry charts and big books aloud, following the words you read with your hand. Ask children to chorus the charts and books. Ask individuals to finger point and lead the chorus as the class joins in. Take dictation from children, saying words as you write them on the chart. Reread the charts, following words and lines as you read them with your hand. Ask children to do the same.
Letter name spellers	Children can finger point; they have a concept of word. In their invented spellings they begin to represent a consonant sound with the consonant as they say and hear it in the alphabet; they represent a vowel sound with the vowel from the alphabet with the closest sound to what they hear.	*As Part of Writing:* Give children hints as they write as to the way to represent language sounds in their writing. Celebrate the sound/symbol correspondences that children demonstrate in their writing to encourage children to use their emerging understanding. *As Part of Formal Spelling Activity:* Involve children in word sorts (e.g., let's put all the words in our story that begin with the same sound as *boy* in this pile of words; they all begin with the letter *b*).
Within-word pattern spellers	Writers begin to vary spellings based on where the sound occurs in a word or how it is used in a word—on the within word patterns of the English language. They honor short and long vowel markers in their invented spellings.	*As Part of Writing:* Focus children's attention on within-word patterns as they edit their invented spellings. As part of editing, hint as to how certain patterns are spelled, especially vowel patterns. Encourage generalizing based on several words with the same pattern. *As Part of Formal Spelling Activity:* Involve children in word sorts to discover some of the within-word patterns of English. Start with words that include a particular pattern. Encourage analysis and generalizing about when a sound is spelled in a particular way.
Syllable juncture spellers	Writers hear the syllables in words and begin to control the spelling at the syllable breaks in multisyllable words. Writers control the roots and affixes of the language and use their understanding of word building characteristics of English (such as compound words) in their invented spellings. They begin to manage the schwa in their invented spellings.	*As Part of Writing:* Focus children's attention on the word-building characteristics of English as they edit their invented spellings. Give hints as part of the editing process as to how certain roots, prefixes, and suffixes are spelled. Help children to generalize. *As Part of Formal Spelling Activity:* Involve children in word sorts so they discover some of the word-building characteristics of English. Start with a series of words that include a particular word-building problem, such as words that double a final consonant when a suffix is added. Encourage analysis and generalizing about how to handle similar words in editing.
Derivational spellers	Writers use their understanding of word origins and related meanings in their invented spellings.	*As Part of Writing:* Focus attention on words that are related because of a common origin or meaning during editing. Give hints during editing as to why words are spelled as they are. Help children to generalize about how origin affects spelling. *As Part of Formal Spelling Activity:* Involve children in word sorts so that they begin to relate words that share a common origin or meaning. Start with some words that have a common origin, such as words that spell a final long *a* as *et*. Encourage analysis and generalizing.

Figure 12.3 Stages in Spelling Development

For ways to use students' errors to assess their spelling development, see Robert Gable et al., "Assessing Spelling Errors of Special Needs Students," *The Reading Teacher*, 42 (November 1988), 112–117.

words in a poem they have finger pointed. They can "sound their way through words," representing both consonants and vowels rather accurately. These youngsters are *letter name* spellers; they spell *monster* as *moth, mostr,* or *monstr*; *bottom* as *bodm, bodu, bdim,* or *bdm*; and *dressing* as *gasin, jesin,* or *gesg*. Their misspellings reflect the ordered nature of their thinking and the stage of spelling at which they are functioning.

Read (1971) describes how letter name spellers operate. These youngsters start by using the alphabet names of letters to encode. Using this system, children have little difficulty writing down a representation of a sound that equates easily with an alphabetic pronunciation, as is the case with many consonant sounds and the long vowel sounds. Short vowels and blends such as *dr*, however, are a different matter. In working with short vowels, children generally substitute the long vowel that is closest to the sound of the short vowel they want to use; for example, they substitute the letter *a* for the short *e* in *pen*; the letter *i* for the short *o* in *got*. The results are invented spellings like *pan* and *git*. In the case of a blend such as *dr*, they tend to disregard the *d* and write what they hear as *jr*.

See Hanna, Hodges, and Hanna (1971) for a description of this and other regularities.

That this letter name spelling strategy works to some extent is a result of the rather consistent way speech sounds are represented on paper. Although in the past some educators stressed the inconsistencies in the English spelling system, linguists today highlight the regularities. Take, for example, the way the letter *t* is used to represent the speech sound /t/. According to Paul Hanna, Richard Hodges, and Jean Hanna (1971), *t* is used 96 percent of the time to represent /t/. Linguists call the smallest unit of speech sound a *phoneme* and the written representation of a speech sound a *grapheme*. Thus we can say that the grapheme *t* is used overwhelmingly to represent the phoneme /t/.

Other graphemes serve with equal consistency. Hanna, Hodges, and Hanna (1971) report that *d* represents /d/ in almost 98 percent of the cases in which the speech sound occurs. *B* represents /b/ about 97 percent of the time, and the same is true of the use of *n* and *r* to represent /n/ and /r/. Similarly, the /a/ as in *pan* and *at* is represented by *a* more than 96 percent of the time.

Even some of the spelling demons are more regular than is at first apparent. Hanna, Hodges, and Hanna explain that only parts of a demon depart from expected sound-symbol relationships. For example, *women* is regular except for the /i/ in the first syllable; all the other phonemes are represented by graphemes as expected. According to Hanna et al., the number of spelling demons is small—only 3 percent of the core vocabulary. In sum, we can say that English is an alphabetic language that has important phonetic characteristics. The phonetic characteristics are what young children use as spelling clues as they become letter name spellers. They are also one kind of clue that older children use in checking spellings in a dictionary.

Within-Word Pattern Spelling

Read Henderson (1990) for a comprehensive discussion of children's spelling development.

But as we all know, English is not strictly phonetic, primarily because it contains words borrowed from other languages and incorporates changes that have occurred over the years. Children must begin to perceive what Henderson (1990) calls the "patterns that exist within words" to master English spelling. One pattern is the presence of two vowels in words in which the long vowel sound occurs (e.g., *cake* and *team*). As children become *within-word pattern* spellers, they tend to spell *cake* as *caek* or perhaps *kake*. They may spell *team* as *teem* or *teme*. These spellings are logical for youngsters at this stage of development. Rather than showing disappointment with primary youngsters who produce them, teachers should recognize the spellings as evidence that youngsters are beginning to perceive the patterns within words.

Syllable Juncture Spelling

Now too, youngsters show evidence of their growing ability to work with common inflectional endings (*-ed, -ing, -s*), compound words, suffixes and prefixes, and syllable units in their invented spellings. For example, beginning word pattern spellers tend to spell words such as *better* as *betir* or *beter* and *picked* as *pickd* or *pickid*.

Invented spellings such as these represent a natural next stage in children's spelling development. They reflect a growing ability to handle the word-building characteristics of English. Linguists tell us that many English words are built by the addition of inflectional endings: the plural endings on nouns, tense-changing endings on verbs, endings like *-er* and *-est* on adjectives. Through the addition of inflectional endings, *dog* becomes *dogs*, *walk* becomes *walked*, and *slow* becomes *slower*. Children who have learned to handle these aspects of language have become *syllable juncture* spellers.

In English, other words are built by adding suffixes and prefixes to roots. Adding affixes, a writer may change how a word functions in a sentence. For example, the word *loose* can function as an adjective; with the addition of *-ly* it becomes *loosely*, which can function as an adverb; with *-ness* it becomes *looseness*, which functions as a noun; with *-en* it becomes *loosen*, which serves as a verb. Still other words are products of compounding, the combining of two short words to form one, as in *anywhere*, *anthill*, and *sidewalk*. To master English spelling, children must master these problems involving syllable junctures.

Youngsters must also grasp the way units are joined to form multisyllable words. Henderson (1990) finds that as children struggle with syllable joinings, invented spellings such as *inocent* for *innocent* and *accomodate* for *accommodate* are common.

Derivational and Meaning-Based Spelling

As they mature as spellers, children perceive the role of meaning in English spelling and begin to function as *derivational* and *meaning-based* spellers. For example, the spelling of *muscle*, with its so-called silent *c* in the middle, makes sense when considered along with the meaning-related *muscular*. The spelling of *bomb,* with its silent *b,* is completely logical when considered in relation to *bombard.* As Templeton (1979) explains, when children begin to handle words in which meaning and/or derivational relationships are significant, "teachers can point out these regularities, and students can subsequently be on the lookout for similar patterns."

Based on Templeton (1979).

In the same way, spellers think in terms of meaning when considering homophone pairs (e.g., *sewing* and *sowing*). These spellings make sense if one considers the confusion that could result if the orthography system did not clarify different meanings communicated by similar-sounding words. Templeton gives as examples two sets of sentences: "I *herd* the cows" and "I *heard* the cows"; "I run a *sowing* machine" and "I run a *sewing* machine." In each case, spelling differences clarify meaning.

As they mature as spellers, too, children perceive the role of origin, or derivation, in English spelling, for the past history of words is an important determinant of how we spell words today. In some instances, linguists can explain current spellings in terms of the way words were pronounced in the past. For example, linguists explain the silent *k* in *knight* in terms of the past, when speakers pronounced the *k.* They explain the *et* spelling of /ā/ in *ballet,* *buffet,* and *croquet* in terms of a common French origin. Only through mastery of what Henderson (1990) calls "derivational constancy" do children become proficient spellers. The fine spellers—the spelling bee champions—draw on a wide range of semantic (meaning), derivational, and word-building clues, resorting to letter name spelling only when other means fail. These spellers know that there is a multifaceted logic to our spelling system and use all the clues at their command (Hodges, 1982).

Introducing Children to the Logic of English Spelling

Today many spelling authorities advocate that children be given opportunities to investigate the multifaceted logic of English spelling so that they develop a growing awareness of the principles underlying spelling and need not rely on memorization for learning new words (Schlagal and Schlagal, 1992; Teale, 1992).

There are several ways to organize children's activity to achieve this goal, including a systematic, formal approach; a systematic approach that relies on grouping, cycles, and individual contracts; and an individualized approach based on personal writing needs.

A Systematic, Formal Approach

Spelling instruction often occurs as part of a systematic study of the way the English language works. In most formal spelling programs in use today, learners work with the basic relationships within the English spelling system. Spelling lists are composed of structurally related words—words that exemplify a partic-

THE FORUM On Spelling and Writing

1. Kristine Anderson writes, "First and foremost, effective spelling instruction must be embedded in whole-language experiences, with meaningful practice and experimentation in both speech and writing. Since learning to spell, like learning to speak, is a developmental process, children must be encouraged to explore the ways in which spoken language relates to written language. They need opportunities to formulate and test hypotheses about the writing system in a supportive environment where errors are considered a natural part of learning to spell" ("The Development of Spelling Ability and Linguistic Strategies," *The Reading Teacher,* 39 [November 1985], 145).

2. In answer to the question "What method for teaching spelling works best?", J. Richard Gentry replies, "Allowing children the freedom to take risks in their own writing is the best technique I know of. . . . To teach kids to spell, get them to write. Break down the inhibitions and unpleasantness surrounding spelling and allow kids the chance to be wrong. This technique isn't simple. Nor does it suggest that spelling is learned exclusively in an informal manner—that is, incidentally through experiences in writing" (*Spel . . . Is a Four-Letter Word* [Portsmouth, N.H.: Heinemann Educational Books, 1987], 27–28).

3. Bill Teale suggests an eclectic view toward spelling instruction: "The field is struggling with finding a coherent approach to spelling. Such an approach would emphasize integrated, functional, holistic language arts instruction, while at the same time it would draw children's attention to the orthographic patterns of words in ways that help them learn principles and strategies they use in writing and reading. Memorizing spellings is not useful; learning how words work and seeing the application of these insights for writing and reading is" ("Dear Readers," *Language Arts,* 69 [October 1992], 401–402).

Questions to Consider

What is the function of invented spelling in writing? How should teachers handle children's invented spelling? Is incidental teaching of spelling as part of writing activity enough? What aspects of spelling should be highlighted in a formal spelling program? In what ways does Mr. Bronsky's lesson in the opening vignette reflect elements important in learning to spell? How can the teacher organize writing activity so that children develop as spellers as they use their growing understanding of English spelling to draft and edit what they have composed?

ular phoneme-grapheme correspondence, within-word pattern, word-building principle, meaning relationship, or derivation. Children analyze related words, sort them according to similarities and differences in spelling, and generalize based on relationships they perceive. This is an inductive, or discovery, approach.

Teaching Related Words Through Discovery Most systematic spelling programs introduce first-graders to the graphemes (letters or groups of letters) through which particular phonemes (speech sounds) are represented. For example, one week first-graders wrestle with words such as *boy, ball,* and *bat* to help them make the connection between the sound /b/ and the letter *b*. By fourth grade, students handle more sophisticated sound-symbol relationships. One week, they sort and generalize about such words as *riddle, muscle, whistle, wrestle, puzzle* and *nickel, chapel, label, model, cancel*; another week, they discover relationships among *wagon, gallon, cotton, common,* and *lesson,* as well as *cabin, cousin, satin,* and *ruin.*

In most systematic spelling programs, emphasis in upper elementary grades is on word-building characteristics and word origins. Note that the fourth-grade lists just given include two-syllable words, so youngsters are generalizing about syllable joinings. In later lessons, children add affixes to roots and form multisyllable words. Here, too, weekly word lists contain structurally related words to allow learners to perceive how words are put together in English. One week, they build words by adding *-ed* and *-ing* to roots ending with the letter *y.* Another week, they build words using a prefix, a root, and a suffix. Still another week, they sort and generalize about words that have a common origin.

In each instance, lessons are organized so that children discover basic relationships for themselves by looking at words that share a feature but also differ in some way. They sort the words into groups according to the differences, as we saw in the vignette that opens this chapter. Sortings can be based on symbols used to represent a speech sound, on the way a particular affix is added, or on a common origin. Reasoning from the groupings they have formed, students propose generalizations about the spelling of their language, which they apply to other words spelled according to the same principles.

In inductive, or discovery, learning, students do not memorize generalizations; rather, they put together pieces of a generalization so that it is meaningful to them. Most specialists agree that memorizing generalizations has little effect on ability to spell. Students must work actively with generalizations to make them useful in drafting and editing.

This approach applies especially to generalizations about word building. Ernest Horn (1960), whose name continues to be associated with spelling instruction after many years, identifies three generalizations that children should discover and use:

✦ Words ending with a silent *e* usually retain the *e* before suffixes beginning with a consonant (*lone* → *lonely* and *lonesome*). Words ending with a silent *e* usually drop the *e* before suffixes beginning with a vowel (*hike* → *hiking*).

Robert Hillerich (1978) suggests that students search for words with a particular sound, such as /ē/. After doing this, students sort their words into groups based on the spelling of the sound, for example, *e: even, she, begin; ea: eat, team, meat; ee: see, feet, keep; eo: people.* Later students search for more words, perhaps sorting out words that spell /ē/ as *y, e-e,* or *ie.*

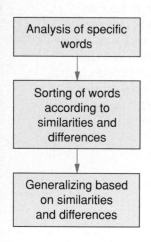

Paraphrased after Horn (1960).

See pages 368–369 for a description of a discovery, or inductive, learning approach in which children generalize about language usage conventions. See the chapter-opening vignette for an example of inductive teaching.

✦ In words ending with a consonant and a *y*, the *y* is changed to *i* when suffixes—except those beginning with *i*—are added (*lady* → *ladies, cry* → *crying*). In words ending with a vowel and a *y*, the *y* is not changed to *i* when suffixes are added (*lay* → *laying*).

✦ In words of one syllable and words accented on the last syllable, ending in a single consonant preceded by a single vowel, the final consonant is doubled when a suffix beginning with a vowel is added (*tug* → *tugging, begin* → *beginning*).

To teach these rules using the discovery approach, the teacher presents a series of words that adhere to a rule, asks questions that help children sort the words into groups, and guides children in figuring out the generalization and its limitations.

Teaching Irregular Words   Of course, not all words follow predictable sound-symbol relationships, within-word patterns, or word-building principles. William Kottmeyer calls irregularly spelled words *snurks*. He tells his students that to conquer a snurk, they must identify the snurky part to see where it departs from an expected spelling. For example, children identify *key* as a snurk because "we expect to spell /ē/ with *e, ee*, or *ea* at the end of one-syllable words like *me, see*, and *tea*." In this case, /ē/ is spelled *ey*. Figure 12.4 shows a spelling ladder that identifies a snurk.

Hanna, Hodges, and Hanna (1971) propose that irregular words may have to be learned through repeated use, with students using visual and kinesthetic clues as aids. This is especially true of the demons among the one hundred words used most frequently in writing. Figure 12.5 lists those words as identified in Ernest Horn's classic study. According to Horn (1926), they account for 65 percent of the words written by adults. A word like *the*, second on the list, is an example of an irregular word that must be learned through repeated use.

Some teachers encourage students to print or write irregular words they have misspelled in large letters on individual cards. Students tack the cards higgledy-piggledy around the room as visual reminders of the spellings. Other teachers encourage students to make and post collages or creative fingerpaintings that include irregular words they are having trouble spelling. Because students have the visual images constantly before them, they use those words in writing and get control over the spellings. Still other teachers use computer programs that provide repetitive practice with irregular words. Ernest Balajthy (1986) suggests that teachers must pick and choose carefully from among computer programs, avoiding those that ask a child to select a correctly spelled word from among incorrect versions that reinforce incorrect visual images.

An article that claims spelling is not a thinking activity but a function of visual memory is "Spelling: Tyranny of the Irrelevant," *Phi Delta Kappan*, 73 (April 1992), 638–640.

Teaching Children How to Study a Word   Most systematic spelling programs teach students a way to study difficult words. Spellers are taught first to look closely at a word they have misspelled, for visual elements are important in spelling. They look at the shape of the word and the letters of it and try to visualize the word in their mind's eye. According to Tom Nicholson and Sumner

Second-graders can learn inductively by adding words to word ladders, which consist of words containing the same sound, even though the sound is represented by different letter patterns. By studying the ladders, children draw conclusions about the spelling of the sound. In Figure 12.4, they conclude that *ay* is a common spelling of /ā/ when the sound occurs at the end of the word and *ai* and *a-e* are spellings when the /ā/ occurs in the middle of the word. They can add the Kottmeyer symbol for snurk next to words on the ladder that have unexpected spellings.

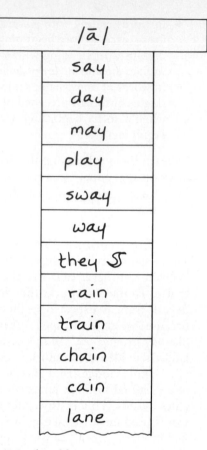

Figure 12.4 A Spelling Word Ladder

Schachter (1979), a kind of "knowledge used in spelling is what seems to be a visual dictionary in our heads of words and their graphic forms. Many of these words have unpredictable spellings and are usually learned as unique structures of graphemes, or as small 'associative sets' of words which have the same irregular spelling." Nicholson and Schachter give as an example of an associative set the words *fight, light,* and *night.* As examples of words with unique structures of graphemes, they cite *the, was, laugh,* and *ancient.*

Spellers are taught next to check meaning and pronunciation in a dictionary if they are uncertain about how to use or say the word and then to say the word aloud. They are taught to listen to the sounds of the word and think about relationships between letters and sounds, identify prefixes and suffixes, or relate words to other words they already know how to spell. They are taught to cover the image of the word and try to write it several times.

The last step relies on kinesthetic learning, which is especially important with children who have certain learning disabilities, such as hearing problems. To practice the spelling of words they have misspelled, these youngsters can

BASIC SPELLING WORD LIST

1. I	21. at	41. do	61. up	81. think
2. the	22. this	42. been	62. day	82. say
3. and	23. with	43. letter	63. much	83. please
4. to	24. but	44. can	64. out	84. him
5. a	25. on	45. would	65. her	85. his
6. you	26. if	46. she	66. order	86. got
7. of	27. all	47. when	67. yours	87. over
8. in	28. so	48. about	68. now	88. make
9. we	29. me	49. they	69. well	89. may
10. for	30. was	50. any	70. an	90. received
11. it	31. very	51. which	71. here	91. before
12. that	32. my	52. some	72. them	92. two
13. is	33. had	53. has	73. see	93. send
14. your	34. our	54. or	74. go	94. after
15. have	35. from	55. there	75. what	95. work
16. will	36. am	56. us	76. come	96. could
17. be	37. one	57. good	77. were	97. dear
18. are	38. time	58. know	78. no	98. made
19. not	39. he	59. just	79. how	99. glad
20. as	40. get	60. by	80. did	100. like

Figure 12.5   The One Hundred Most Frequently Used Words

write the words in sand, on a magic slate, on the chalkboard with a wet brush, or with tempera paint on large sheets of newspaper. The idea is to provide practice that is pleasurable.

A Systematic Approach That Relies on Grouping, Contracts, and Cycles

For a discussion of the rise of ability-grouping, read Nancy-Jo Hereford, "Making Sense of Ability Grouping," *Instructor,* 102 (May/June 1993), 50–52. The article summarizes Robert Slavin's six strategies for effective instructional grouping.

Many elementary teachers find it difficult to introduce children systematically to the logic of English spelling through an approach in which all youngsters work with the same generalizations. In any class, there are children who are functioning at different developmental levels: Some are functioning as letter name spellers, some have control over within-word patterns, and others are able to handle word-building principles and words that are related as a result of a common origin. Similarly, some children are facile problem solvers; they can look at a group of words and identify features common to that group. Some have extensive dictionaries-in-the-head where they have stored numerous word relationships. In contrast, other children have severe weaknesses in these areas.

Organizing Study Groups   To meet the diverse spelling levels and needs within a class, some teachers divide students into spelling groups according to the children's development as spellers and use contracts to further individualize work within the groups. Here is how Fred Bronsky—using a weekly spelling cycle—manages the three spelling groups that operate in his third-grade class.

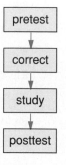

Day 1   On the first day of a spelling cycle, Mr. Bronsky meets with one group for a discovery-type lesson. Children sort words and generalize about them as in the opening vignette. After that, the teacher pretests students on a list of words related to the generalization they are learning. Children correct their own pretests by referring to the correct spelling on the word cards they have sorted. Most research indicates that the *pretest-correct-study-posttest* sequence is productive for increasing spelling skill (T. Horn, 1947).

Then Mr. Bronsky explains related practice options that students will complete on their own during successive spelling periods. To meet individual needs, he gives each youngster a spelling contract (see Figure 12.6). The contract specifies a few activities that all children in the group are to complete. Youngsters add to their contracts spelling activities that help them with their special spelling problems—options such as resorting the words being highlighted during that particular cycle, retesting on the words with a spelling mate, making a collage of highlighted words, writing a composition containing some of the highlighted words, concocting an original crossword puzzle, and studying words they have misspelled in writing.

Day 2   Students work independently on activities listed in their contracts. They usually begin with required tasks.

Day 3   Students continue to work independently. They may pair with a spelling pal for retesting on words, join with others in the group to play a spelling game, practice by using a related computer program, or edit a draft in their active-writing portfolios. They use their word study plan to master personal words incorporated into their contracts.

Day 4   Students continue as on Day 3. More students turn to actual writing and begin to draft, revise, and edit stories in their portfolios.

Day 5   Students work on revising and editing a piece they have drafted. They take a posttest on the words highlighted during the cycle.

INDEPENDENT STUDY GUIDE: SPELLING

Spelling agenda for week of _____

Name _____

Mark the time and date when you begin an activity in column 1 and when you complete an activity in column 2. You may add original activities at the bottom of the chart. You must complete activities that follow bullets.

1	2	Activity
		• Complete the duplicated puzzle game sheet no. 2
		• Resort the highlighted words. Brainstorm other words with the same pattern.
		• Run a self-test of the words, using the tape at the spelling table.
		• Analyze and study your personal words. Run a self-test.
		• Play one of the spelling games at the spelling table with your partner.
		• Original activity:
		• Original activity:

Figure 12.6　A Spelling Contract

Managing the Cycles　Mr. Bronsky has three groups operational in his class. The M Group begins a cycle on Monday and completes it on Friday. The W Group begins on Wednesday and ends on Tuesday. The F Group begins on Friday and ends on Thursday. This cycling of three groups frees the teacher on Tuesday and Thursday to work with students who need special attention as a result of misunderstanding or absence and those who are such good or weak spellers that they cannot gain from activity with any of the groups. Mr. Bronsky reserves a few minutes during the week to return to a group to dictate words on the final day of a cycle, but this is really unnecessary. If words and sentences have been tape-recorded, children can take a mid-cycle or end-of-cycle test monitored by a student from another group.

By grouping for instruction, teachers can "place [students] in instructionally appropriate materials," highlighting different words and generalizations with students who are functioning at different developmental levels (Morris, 1987; Bloodgood, 1991; Schlagal and Schlagal, 1992). Emphasis with one group may be on within-word patterns, with another group on word-building principles. By grouping, too, teachers can allot more time to a set of words with youngsters who need more reinforcement of spelling generalizations. In addition, individual students can work on words they have misspelled in writing. Children include these words in their contracts.

An Individualized Approach Based on Personal Writing Needs

A must-read is Joan Novelli, "Strategies for Spelling Success," *Instructor,* 102 (May/June 1993), 41–42, 47 for a description of how one first-grade teacher organizes an individualized program.

Another approach to spelling instruction is individualized, based on children's need to spell words in their writing. Within the context of a writing conference, the teacher builds a spelling program personalized for each student. In conferring with a primary-grade student about a draft of a composition the child intends to publish, the teacher helps him or her identify five or six words that the student has misspelled. An upper-grader may identify about ten words. Teacher and student talk briefly about the "hard" spots in the misspelled words, relating the errors to generalizations about English spelling. For example, with a child who has spelled *babies* as *babys,* the teacher explains how to form the plural of words that end in *y.* Having focused on such "hard" spots, the child writes the five or six chosen words at the back of his or her learning log.

Working collaboratively with a spelling pal, the student now rewrites the words as the pal dictates them. Pals take turns dictating and being tested on their words. They correct their words cooperatively, using the spellings of the words in their learning logs as guides. Spelling pals collaborate on several occasions until each child thinks he or she has gained ownership over his or her words. At some point, the teacher asks all students to meet with their spelling pals to dictate and be tested. Words correctly spelled are starred in the student's learning log, at which point teacher and student, during another writing conference, add other words to the student's learning log list, choosing from those the child has misspelled in writing.

An obvious advantage of this approach over one in which children learn words from a formal spelling program is that students learn to spell words that they use in speaking and writing; these words, therefore, are meaningful to them. A second advantage is that students often learn not only their own words but their pal's words. A disadvantage is that it is relatively difficult to teach children the underlying generalizations that control the spelling of words in English when they are working with individual words rather than with groups of linguistically related words. Children are more or less learning to spell by memorizing individual words rather than by identifying relationships within a group of words.

Some teachers modify the personalized spelling approach to overcome this disadvantage. In conferring over a paper to be published, student and teacher select only one or two misspelled words to add to the student's personalized spelling list. For each word chosen, the child brainstorms other words having the same pattern. For example, with a very young child who has misspelled *my* as *mi*, the teacher might suggest, "I know that when you write the word *I* you spell the long *i* sound with the letter *i*, just as in the alphabet. But in the word *my*, you write the long *i* sound with the letter *y*. Let's think of other words in which we hear the long *i* sound at the end." As the child suggests such possibilities as *by, fly, why, cry*, the teacher helps the child record these four words under the word *my* in his or her log. Once the child has done this, the teacher asks, "When we hear the long sound of *i* at the end of a word, what is a very common way in which we write it down?" Having generalized, student and teacher talk about a second word that the child has misspelled in the prepublication draft. In this way, the child develops a personalized spelling study list of related words based on one or two words that he or she has misspelled.

Later, collaborating together, spelling pals explain their generalizations to each other before they dictate their words. With this approach, children become spelling teachers as well as learners; each explains the generalizations being learned to his or her spelling pal. Again, pals correct their words cooperatively, checking against the models in their logs. Again, too, teachers who use this approach have found that children learn not only their own words and the generalizations that explain them but each learns his or her pal's words as well.

Although the example just cited is at the early primary level, the same approach is possible with older students. If, for example, a third-grade boy spells the word *blew* as *blue* in the sentence "The wind blew through the trees," during a prepublication writing conference the teacher might brainstorm with him words in which this vowel sound is spelled *ew* and words in which it is spelled *ue*, in the process talking about the problem of English homophones. The student brainstorms words such as *flew, knew, dew,* and *chew* and *clue, true,* and *due* and lists them in his log for later study and testing with a spelling pal. In the same way, a sixth-grade girl who has spelled *clarify* as *clarafy* brainstorms other words that end as does *clarify—modify, gratify, signify*. She generalizes that when words end with the same sounds as *clarify,* they are spelled with an *-ify*, not an *-afy*; she may also generalize that all these words function as verbs in sentences.

Regie Routman (1993) writes: "A classroom that encourages children to be good spellers provides, . . . lots of mini-lessons to see word patterns, develop rules, notice unusual features of words (these lessons arise from what the teacher notices the children need) . . ."

Some teachers further modify the personal spelling approach by scheduling mini-lessons with groups of youngsters who exhibit a similar spelling problem (Bartch, 1992). These teachers examine children's papers for common spelling errors such as the spelling of *are/our, their/they're*, contractions, *-ed* endings, silent letters, *qu* spellings, *wr* spellings, possessive forms, and *ie/ei*. When they find that several youngsters exhibit the same difficulty, they gather them together for a discovery-type lesson that focuses on the problem. They then encourage children to edit their writing based on what they have learned in the mini-lesson. At the same time, these teachers encourage students to keep individual spelling-word banks to use as personal dictionaries during editing and post often-used words on a word wall that students also refer to during editing. Teacher Judie Barch reports that this approach has had the greatest impact "during writer's workshop. As the children write, they use their strategies for spelling their words." They often stop, too, to talk about words and are more aware of words and the relationships among them. The children "are becoming independent spellers."

Making Spelling Speculation a Meaningful Part of Writing

The term *invented spelling* is commonly used by language arts educators. The teacher may prefer to use the term *developmental spelling* when explaining the spelling program to parents. Because the idea of encouraging children to write by celebrating their early attempts may be new to parents, the teacher must explain the approach to them and at times to administrators.

See the Teacher-as-Researcher Forum on pages 437–441 for a description of how one kindergarten teacher is experimenting with invented spelling. Also read Susan Sowers, "Six Questions Teachers Ask about Invented Spelling," in *The Heinemann Reader,* ed. Brenda Power and Ruth Hubbard (Portsmouth, N.H.: Heinemann Educational Books, 1991).

Read Sheri Coate and Marrietta Castle, "Integrating LEA and Invented Spelling in Kindergarten," *The Reading Teacher,* 42 (March 1989), 316–319.

The goal of spelling instruction is for children to use their growing understanding of the logic of English spelling as they draft their ideas, edit what they have written, and later check their spelling inventions in a dictionary. Spelling, after all, is for writing. Therefore, regardless of the approach teachers use to involve children in the logic of English spelling, they must make the writing connection.

Drafting and Invented, or Speculative, Spelling

Teachers should encourage children from the moment they enter school to speculate about the spellings of words as they make first drafts and to use words they know they are unable to spell. Mr. Bronsky did this in the opening vignette when he asked children to predict the spelling of *hypothesis*—a word they probably had never before tried to spell—and explained to them how he uses invented, or speculative, spelling during drafting.

Philip DiStefano and Patricia Hagerty (1985) explain, "The first step in teaching spelling is to let the students experiment with language while writing and not worry about their spelling. . . . students must become risk takers when they use language." By systematically inventing spellings as part of writing, children make the transition from being letter name spellers to using within-word patterns, syllable-joining patterns, and derivational and meaning-based relationships to guide their predictions. Summarizing the research on children's development as spellers (Read, 1971; Bissex, 1980; Ferreiro and Teberosky, 1982; Bouffler, 1984), Brian Cambourne and Jan Turbill (1987) note: "As children continue to write using their temporary or invented spellings, they gradually proceed through a series of approximations to the conventional forms of spelling, experimenting with different unconventional versions of the same word." Cambourne and Turbill give Simon's development as an example: Simon's attempts to write *saw* over a six-month period proceeded from *s* to *sor*, to *swa*, and finally to *saw*.

Editing and Spelling

During editing for publication, writers need to focus on spelling. Roy Peter Clark (1987) provides a series of ideas for helping children improve their work during the final stages of composition:

Or have students use a computerized spelling checker.

1. During final editing, encourage students to circle words they speculate they may have misspelled. Students who cannot speculate about and identify possible misspellings cannot correct them.
2. Ask students to run a dictionary check on words they have identified as possible misspellings and have approximated rather closely but not exactly.
3. Provide students with the correct spellings of words they have written with a spelling far removed from the correct one, such as *numonya* for *pneumonia*. Ask students to record the correct spellings of the words in the backs of their learning logs.
4. When students have not identified the possibility of a misspelling where one exists, put a dot in the margin next to the line in which the word appears.
5. If a student has made many spelling errors, pair that student with a good speller. The good speller can help the poorer one identify possible misspellings and help him or her run a dictionary check based on speculative spellings.
6. Make a final check of spelling yourself before students publish their work.
7. "Publish the work with the mistakes corrected. This final step sends an important message to the writer: that publication is so important the editor will not tolerate errors in spelling." Publication tells students, "Here is why these things are important to learn. Now everyone can read what you have to say."

In classrooms that have a computer equipped with a word processing program and a spelling checker, children can use the spelling checker during the final phase of editing. A spelling checker highlights words that do not conform to any words in its dictionary. Students using a checker have to decide whether their spelling of highlighted words is really wrong or whether the highlighted words are simply not in the spelling checker dictionary. As Ruth Betza (1987) explains, the negative aspect of this procedure is that "a spelling checker has limitations in knowing whether all words are correctly spelled or not." A positive aspect is that upper elementary children hypothesize about language and take control of decision making as they edit. They have to decide whether to accept what the checker says or to check on the checker by using a dictionary.

Spelling Across the Curriculum

The kinds of activities just described should occur across the curriculum. In every area of study, elementary teachers should encourage youngsters to identify relationships among words as they read and apply their growing understanding of English spellings as they edit their writing.

To this end, teachers should write key words such as these on the chalkboard during content-area study and help children see relationships.

For example, children who meet the phrase "Declaration of Independence" can relate the word *declaration* to the word *declare*. By making this relationship, children are less likely to write about the "Decoration of Independence," as one adult of this author's acquaintance still does. In like manner, students of geology identify the word-building units in the word *geology, geo-* and -*ology;* they talk about the meanings of these units as they use the word in writing and go back to edit. Similarly, they look at how the vowel sounds are encoded in the word *sedimentary* and talk about the origins of the word *igneous,* which comes from the Latin word meaning "of fire."

Only by applying their understanding as they meet words in diverse contexts do children develop functional spelling ability. The ultimate success of spelling study is children's ability to edit their own writing as they write across the curriculum, not their ability to spell correctly on a weekly spelling test. In that respect, the very act of writing on a variety of topics provides opportunity for growth in spelling.

✎ *Building and Refining Your Teaching Skills*

✦ Design a discovery-type spelling lesson modeled after Mr. Bronsky's. In your lesson, do not start with a spelling book; rather, use the book for follow-up and reinforcement.
✦ Analyze several spelling programs. Decide which programs best lend themselves to discovery of fundamental spelling relationships.

Using the Dictionary

A basic tool for the speller is the dictionary. There are three kinds of dictionary-related learnings important at the elementary level. First are abilities related to locating and interpreting entries: the abilities to alphabetize, use guide words, find a word of uncertain spelling, interpret definitions to determine how a word should be used, pronounce words based on their phonetic spellings, and interpret etymological notations. Second is appreciation of the value of the dictionary as a reference and writing tool. All the skill in the world matters little unless the writer takes dictionary in hand as the need arises. The third kind of learning, important in the upper grades, is the ability to handle other, dictionarylike tools: the thesaurus, a dictionary of synonyms, a rhyming dictionary, and indexes.

Wanting to Use the Dictionary

Perhaps the most effective way to get children to value the dictionary is to make it the most important book in the classroom. Each day a student serves as Dictionary Sleuth; the sleuth's job is to check the spelling of difficult words recorded on chalkboard or charts. As students brainstorm words and record them on the board, the sleuth keeps the dictionary on standby alert. When writing on the board and encountering a tricky word, the teacher nods toward the sleuth to run a dictionary check. When conferring with children who are editing written work, the teacher keeps a dictionary close at hand. Instead of marking a misspelled word, the teacher comments, "Steve, I'm not sure about this word. Let's check it," and hands the dictionary to Steve, who looks it up on the spot.

Although a picture dictionary with large print is perfect for young children, large, thick dictionaries serve particularly well in upper elementary classrooms. Fifth- and sixth-graders, of course, must practice working with the book, but once skill in locating and interpreting entries has developed, checking a word is a real challenge. The Dictionary Sleuth glories in the role of custodian of a book that is almost as big as he or she is.

Alphabetizing

ABC books and picture dictionaries are contexts for younger children to learn to alphabetize. On a page a youngster writes a word, perhaps with the teacher's help, and draws a picture about it. If each child works with a word beginning with a different letter, youngsters bind the pages in alphabetical order to form an original ABC book. Slightly older children produce a picture dictionary, each child preparing one page that includes a word, the word used in a sentence, and a descriptive picture.

Children can make shoe-box dictionaries by filing individual word cards alphabetically. On the cards are words the child commonly misspells. Looking for a word in his or her file, the child must rely on growing ability to work with alphabetical order. As files expand, primary children create markers to divide cards into alphabetical groupings.

Primary-grade teachers have found that this is a time to put their story clotheslines into service as youngsters play Hang the Alphabet. This activity requires twenty-six clothespins and a stack of index cards, each card inscribed with one letter of the alphabet in its lowercase form. The cards are dealt to youngsters in the group, who clip their cards to the line in alphabetical order. During the first few playings, an alphabet is posted around the room so that young children can check their growing alphabet line against a line already in correct order. Later the posted alphabet is taken down. Now as children rehang the alphabet, they must complete the task on their own. Later children hang the alphabet printed in uppercase letters.

Older students can work in the same way with word cards. A first set comprises twenty-six words, each beginning with a different letter. A second set of cards consists of words beginning with the same letter. More complex sets are made of words starting with the same first two letters or even the same first three letters. Older students clip their cards alphabetically on the clothesline, which now can be suspended from a light fixture so it hangs downward and words are placed beneath one another as in a dictionary column. The activity

Caution: If your cards are lightweight, tape your line against a wall surface to prevent them from flipping over.

can be converted into a learning station, where one or two students order words on their own.

Using Guide Words

Ability to handle guide words is essential if students are to use the dictionary efficiently. To introduce students to guide words, some teachers have found the following sequence useful. They

1. Make word cards, each containing a guide word from a dictionary page. They use guide words from three successive pages of a dictionary, such as *leaf* and *leasing, least* and *leg, legacy* and *leisure*;
2. Make word cards of entries found on those three dictionary pages;
3. Lay out the guide words on the floor;
4. Deal the word cards to students, who place their words in alphabetical order between the appropriate guide words.

Later all the cards are gathered at a learning station, where youngsters who need additional practice go to group words within appropriate guide words. Other sets of cards can be placed at the station so that students handle words from different sections of the dictionary.

Locating Words of Uncertain Spelling

See Marvin Morrison, *Word City: A New Language Tool* (Stone Mountain, Ga.: Pilot Light Books, 1982), for a unique solution to the problem of looking up words one does not know how to spell.

A major strength of a spelling program that encourages invented spelling and develops understanding of sound-symbol relationships is that the child has somewhere to begin when looking up a word he or she does not know how to spell. How often does a teacher hear "How can I look it up if I don't know how to spell it in the first place?" The child who has some understanding of the graphemes through which a particular phoneme can be represented has a starting point. The searcher begins with the most common graphemes used to represent the phoneme and systematically checks out possibilities.

Of course, young children will become disheartened if they look too long and are unsuccessful. When checking a paper for possible spelling errors, the child who has looked up three or four invented spellings to no avail may turn to a spelling pal for a consultation. The two search together and, if still unsuccessful, may ask for searching assistance from the general editor—the teacher.

To avoid failure, at times the teacher supplies words in the form of an editing guide. Hanna Walsh, a first-grade teacher, encourages her children to use invented spellings as they draft their ideas in pencil. Later she places a different number above each word that needs to be rewritten. She keys the numbers to a slip of paper that she staples to the corner of the page. By each number on the slip, she writes the word correctly spelled. Children erase their own spellings and replace them with the teacher's. One advantage of this technique is that edited papers are available for bulletin board mounting. A more important advantage is that in drafting, youngsters draw on their understanding of sound-symbol relationships—the same thing they do when looking up a word of uncertain spelling in the dictionary.

Interpreting Dictionary Entries

As students enter the upper elementary grades, the dictionaries they use contain some entries that are relatively complex. Children can grapple with these complexities in small-group work sessions. The teacher begins by printing a dictionary entry on a transparency that is projected for group viewing. Children start with a simple entry, such as this one from *Webster's II Riverside Beginning Dictionary:*

> **can o py** *noun* (kan' ə pē), a covering that is usually made of fabric and hangs over a bed, entrance, or throne.

Students draw their conceptions of *canopy* based on the information given. Since the dictionary supplies a picture, children can compare drawings. If one youngster holds the dictionary from which the entry came, that person checks the pronunciation by referring to the model words at the bottom of the page or at the beginning of the dictionary. Once meaning and pronunciation have been clarified, students consider the way the word functions in sentences. In this case the word is a noun, one of the easiest to start with because the word has a concrete referent.

In the upper grades, dictionary entries are more complex and often include information about word relationships. Again children can compare drawings based on verbal definitions to pictures in the dictionary. They check the beginning section of the dictionary to discover how to interpret the etymological information. In some entries, children will encounter information on synonyms, special usages, and frequently confused words. Again, an overhead transparency that all can see turns dictionary study into a discussion time in which youngsters cooperatively solve dictionary puzzles.

Much dictionary work should occur as part of content-area study. As children encounter words of uncertain meaning or pronunciation, they run an immediate dictionary check. At that point, teacher and students puzzle out the notations in an entry. By placing dictionary work in a meaningful context, the teacher helps children see what a helpful tool a dictionary is.

Meeting Other, Dictionarylike References

Most people overuse certain words, and as a result these words have lost communicative power; *funny, cute, like, put,* and *make* are examples. Children can construct cards inscribed with alternates or synonyms that have nearly the same

As a July 12, 1992, AP release reports, "Dictionaries are hardly snuggle-up-with kinds of books, but each new edition tells a story. . . ." The press release also reports that the third edition of the *American Heritage Dictionary* (Boston: Houghton Mifflin, 1992) contains 16,000 words added since the 1982 edition. New entries include "chemical dependency," "ombudsperson," and "junk bonds." Students can predict words that are not in the 1992 edition but will be in a future one.

meaning as the original but communicate the idea more fully. They print a word such as *funny* on a small strip of paper attached to a rope hanging in the classroom. As students discover plausible substitutes—*amusing, entertaining, humorous, laughable*—they print those words on other strips that they clip to the same rope. Eventually, students turn the bulletin board into an original thesaurus by hanging several lengths of rope on it, each containing alternates for an overworked word.

The thesaurus is a gold mine for word searchers. The synonyms for *funny* given above are from *In Other Words: A Beginning Thesaurus* by Greet, Jenkins, and Schiller—a splendid volume that should be found in every lower elementary classroom. *In Other Words* provides synonyms for tired and overused words, defines substitutes, and supplies sentences to explain word functioning. It also gives antonyms. Students who can locate words in this beginning thesaurus may decide to create an original thesaurus containing the most overworked words they know, plus viable substitutes. Each study team contributes a page to "Our Classroom Thesaurus."

Upper-graders enjoy *In Other Words: A Junior Thesaurus* by Greet et al. (Glenview, Ill.: Scott Foresman, 1969), and Scholastic Books, *Synonym and Antonym Dictionary*.

Teaching Manuscript Letter Forms to Active Young Writers

Generally, children are introduced to manuscript writing, or structured printing, when they come to school. Some specialists advocate a manuscript for young children composed of letters formed from discrete and unslanted lines, circles, and humps. The rationale is that it is easier for youngsters to distinguish letter parts and form the letters in manuscript than in regular handwriting, where the letters slant and flow into one another. Then, too, most books are written in print; by learning to print, children transfer learnings from one language art—reading—into another—writing down. Of course, manuscript writing is not something learned and eventually forgotten; manuscript writing is a lifelong skill. Adults must print signs, charts, and posters and complete forms that require printing rather than writing.

See Marie Ice, "It's D'Nealian. It's Delightful," *School and Community*, 66 (May 1980), 19, and ERIC Document Ed 169 533 by Donald Thurber.

D'Nealian manuscript, developed by Donald Thurber, offers a continuous approach to beginning handwriting. In addition, D'Nealian manuscript letters slant in the same manner as in cursive; letter forms in manuscript and cursive writing are more similar than in other handwriting programs. As a result, the rationale states, "the basic patterns are there when the time comes to learn cursive." See Figure 12.7 for the letters and numbers from the D'Nealian program.

In this section, we will look at ways to introduce children to manuscript and to provide meaningful practice. We will begin by visiting Ms. Robinson's kindergarten, remembering that young children should be encouraged to compose in any form they choose and to invent letter forms as well as spellings to express their ideas. We recall, too, that Ms. Robinson provides her students with many opportunities simply to write—for writing is when handwriting is in action.

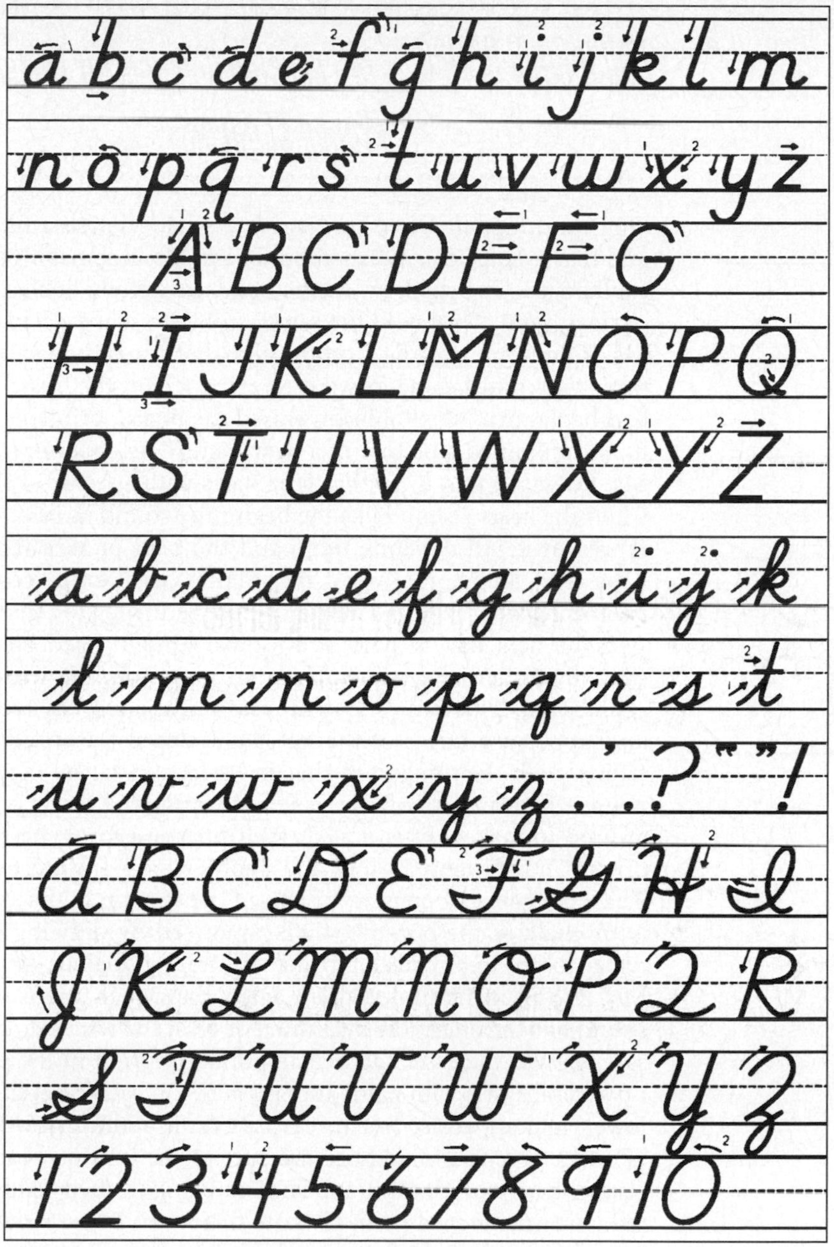

Figure 12.7 D'Nealian Letter and Number Forms

SOURCE: D'Nealian is a registered trademark of Donald Neal Thurber. Copyright © 1987 by Scott, Foresman and Company.

TEACHING IN ACTION *Introducing Manuscript Letter Forms to Young Children*

In a line, circle, and hump system;

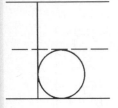

In a slanted manuscript (D'Nealian)

Use Bobbye Goldstein, *Bear in Mind: A Book of Bear Poems* (Viking, 1989) as a source of read-aloud poems during this kind of unit.

One morning, after her kindergartners had viewed a filmstrip on black bears and had listened to a poem about bears, Ms. Robinson printed a large *b* on the chalkboard. The children watched as she carefully drew a line down and then a circle around. They used the same strokes to make a *b* in the air and compared Ms. Robinson's *b* to the *b* on the alphabet cards pinned below the board. Then three youngsters came forward to print a *b* on the board. When most children had had a turn, Ms. Robinson erased the board, printed another lowercase *b* on it, and mounted a picture of a bear there. The children said the word *bear*, and Ms. Robinson told them that *bear* starts with a *b*. She explained that in writing, when she hears a sound like the beginning sound in *bear*, she writes down a *b* to represent it. All day long the *b* and the bear picture remained on the board. After completing other work, the children went to the board to practice writing *b*s, erasing what they had written before returning to their seats.

The next day, as part of a topical unit focused on bears, Ms. Robinson shared another bear poem. That morning, too, she wrote a *b* and a *B* on the chalkboard. This time she demonstrated the strokes used to make the lower- and uppercase forms of the letter and asked the students to make the letter strokes with their fingers in the air. In each instance, she presented the component strokes in a rhythmic way and repeated, "Draw a line down, and circle around to make a little *b*." For the uppercase form she repeated, "Draw a line down. Draw a loop around and another loop around to make the capital *B*." The left-handed youngsters practiced the rhythm of the strokes by making them with chalk at the board. Others practiced by drawing with crayon on plain paper folded to provide a top and a bottom guideline. As the children practiced, Ms. Robinson reminded them again that when she is writing and hears the sound like the one at the beginning of *bear*, she writes down a *b*.

Because the easel had been a popular option in the past, Ms. Robinson set up several easels with paint and brushes. On each easel she mounted a model of lower- and uppercase *b*s. The easels became additional writing stations for independent practice. In addition, as part of the unit on bears, Ms. Robinson read several bear stories, asked students to bring in their teddy bears for show-and-tell, and encouraged them to write their own bear stories and publish them as "My Own Bear Book." As the children wrote their stories, they used the *b* to hold the place of words starting with /b/.

Early Handwriting

Building manual dexterity

In active kindergarten classrooms, children use their invented spellings to write from the moment they arrive. Their teachers also provide a variety of meaningful activities that increase children's ability to control the fine muscles of the hand and to differentiate among shapes. These activities include

- ◆ Drawing with brush and paint at easels in the art area,
- ◆ Drawing on large sheets of paper with husky crayons,
- ◆ Working with modeling clay, sometimes molding the material into letterlike shapes,
- ◆ Manipulating interlocking puzzle blocks,
- ◆ Plugging colored sticks into the holes of a board to form designs.

As youngsters paint, draw, and handle materials, experienced teachers watch to determine which children tend to use the left hand. Of course, there is nothing wrong with being left-handed, and children should be allowed to use the hand with which they feel more comfortable. The purpose of early identification is to meet the special needs of left-handed youngsters.

Structured Activities   Most kindergarten teachers also engage children in more structured handwriting-related activities. One day, for example, Ms. Robinson shared Tana Hoban's *Circles, Triangles, and Squares,* a book of photographs incorporating geometric shapes. In preparation, she had cut a circle, a square, and a triangle from colored construction paper and mounted them on her magnetic chalkboard. As the children studied the photographs in the book, they located these shapes and talked about them. As follow-up, the kindergartners traced the shapes with crayon, cut them out, and pasted them on construction paper in a creative pattern.

On another day, Ms. Robinson presented a more difficult task for the students, who until now had been writing on unlined paper. She duplicated a sheet with four well-spaced, parallel lines, as shown in the margin. Between the first two lines she drew a circle, between the second and third a triangle, and between the last two a square. On their copies, the children were to draw more shapes within each space.

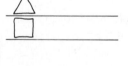

·········
Forming the letters of one's name

Visual Experiences with Words   At the same time, Ms. Robinson provided many visual experiences with words. Before children arrived on the first day of school, she had affixed a nameplate to each desk. Each plate was colored oak tag inscribed with a child's name, starting with an uppercase first letter and followed by lowercase letters. When a youngster completed a drawing or a story with invented spellings, Ms. Robinson wrote the child's name lightly in pencil in the upper right-hand corner, modeling the way to make the component strokes of each letter. With dark crayon, the child then made the letters of her or his own name, following the teacher's model. Because the children produced several papers each day, they had many opportunities to write the letters of their names. Very soon, the children were writing their names on their papers, using correct letter forms, on their own initiative.

Each day, too, Ms. Robinson engaged the kindergartners in experience chart writing. As she printed words the children dictated, she was careful to make her letters similar to the models posted on the children's desks as well as below the chalkboard. She formed the letters as outlined in the program used in the school district. Not all handwriting programs rely on the same letter shapes or sizes. In some, the letters are straight up and down; in others, the manuscript letters are slanted.

At the same time, the children were developing a heightened familiarity with letter shapes. They built skyscrapers from alphabet blocks. They played with alphabet noodles, forming them into collagelike designs by gluing them to small oak tag squares. They matched blocks and noodles to the letters on the guides mounted in the classroom and placed their alphabet pieces in the same order.

These activities achieve many objectives. They help children perceive differences in shapes, recognize letter shapes, relate speech sounds to letters, and appreciate the value of recording ideas on paper.

More Early Handwriting-Related Activities   Working with preschool or kindergarten youngsters, teachers can experiment with some of Ms. Robinson's letter-forming activities. Here are two other ideas:

✦ *Giant Letters.* Cut child-size upper- and lowercase letters from corrugated cardboard. Children paint the letters bright colors. Throw the large letters on the floor, then the small ones. Children order the letters by picking them up and matching shapes with those on the classroom wall. They also match lower- with uppercase equivalents. For even more fun, young children pick up lowercase letters and dance to music with their uppercase partners. When the music stops, children exchange letters and start again when it resumes. On another occasion, organize the activity as a musical-chairs-type of game, placing one less letter on the floor than the number of dancing children. When the music stops, each child picks up a letter. A child who does not find a letter is eliminated from that round. He or she selects a letter from those replaced on the floor by still active participants—perhaps a letter from her or his name—to take out of the game.

✦ *Letter Verses.* One kindergarten teacher composed a little verse to go with each letter and set the verse to music. Her verse for capital *B* is

> *I can make the letter B,*
> *And this is the way I do it.*
> *A line down and around and around,*
> *And that is the capital B.*

Her verse for lowercase *b* is almost the same:

> *I can make the letter b,*
> *And this is the way I do it.*
> *A line down and just once around,*
> *And that is the little b.*

On the playground, this teacher chalks giant upper- and lowercase *b*'s. The children play follow-the-leader as they skip around the outline of a letter and sing the appropriate verse. Teachers can compose original third lines for each of the other letters.

Individual Differences Not all children need equal attention to handwriting-related skills. Some can control a pencil at an early age; others have more difficulty controlling the fine muscles of the fingers and perceiving the distinctions in the way letters are made. As a result, the teacher must study the behavior of individual children to determine who needs more practice in this regard.

Designing Structured Handwriting Lessons

Pamela Farris (1991) writes, "Teachers in early childhood education should teach handwriting through direct instruction, for it is a basic and important skill for writing."

As children enter first grade, they may need help in refining the way they form their letters, especially when they begin to use lined paper. At this point, the teacher takes advantage of paper with a lighter guideline between two darker ones and an open area at the top for drawing. He or she structures a practice lesson in this way:

Goal: The children form clear renditions of the letters *l* and *i*. They form a word with *l* and *i*, neatly spacing the letters within the word and allowing sufficient space between words.

According to a line, circle, and hump system

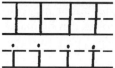

According to D'Nealian

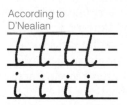

Sequence for the teacher:

1. Within the first double space on your model sheet, write a lowercase *l*. Demonstrate precisely where the top of the letter begins and where it ends. Children print a row of *l*s across the page.
2. Within the second double space on your sheet, print a lowercase *i*. Again, demonstrate where the top of the letter begins and where the bottom sits. Demonstrate where the dot is placed. Children print a row of *i*s across the page.
3. Within the third space on your paper, print first an *l*, and then an *i*. Children alternate *l* and *i* across their pages. Encourage them to repeat a rhythmic verse as they print.
4. Talk about how it feels to be sick. Explain to the children that sometimes they say they are "ill" when they are sick. Encourage them to describe times when they were ill. Then print the word *ill* within the fourth double space. Allow time for children to print the word on their papers. Then demonstrate how they can use the width of their pointing finger to figure out how much space to leave between words: "Just one finger width from the end of the word *ill*; let's begin the word again." Children continue to write the word *ill* across the page, separating each instance with a finger width, or with an ice cream stick if they are left-handed.
5. After children have filled the remainder of their papers with copies of *ill*, suggest that they fold their papers in thirds. Children draw three pictures in the open area at the top to tell a story about when they were sick—a story

with a beginning, a middle, and an end. They include letters and words as well, using invented spelling.

On succeeding days, a teacher starts handwriting lessons with a brief review and then introduces the form of the lowercase *t,* the upper-case *L,* and the uppercase *I.* Children practice forming and spacing words such as *it, It, Ill, Lit, lit.*

Basic Guidelines for Teaching Manuscript Letter Forms

The structure of the lesson just described suggests five guidelines for introducing first-graders to clear forms of manuscript letters:

✦ *Introduce letters with a similar form together.* Some penmanship programs group the *i, l,* and *t* for instruction, since they are formed from a basic downward stroke. They are taught as a unit, perhaps with the capital letters formed in a similar way: *L I T H F E.*

✦ *As soon as children have a small repertoire of letters they can form clearly, have them combine letters into words.* This adds the element of spacing, which makes children gauge distance within and between words. Children can use an index finger or ice cream stick to estimate distance—one finger's width between words, two between sentences, two for indenting.

✦ *Make sure that what children print is meaningful.* As children gain control of letters, ask them to print short sentences with their practice letters. Younger children can practice forming a letter beneath a picture of an object whose name begins with it, or they can sketch and write stories about practice words in the space above the practice lines. Children's stories can be made to have two, three, or four episodes by folding the drawing space into the appropriate number of segments.

✦ *Provide letter models.* There are two types of models. First are letters the teacher makes when demonstrating how to form a letter. When demonstrating, the teacher draws attention to where to begin a stroke, where to terminate it, what direction to move to make circles, and how many strokes to use to form the letter. Second are the models displayed around the room. Most commonly used are the letter strips placed below or above the chalkboard. To be most effective, models should be placed at eye level, where they can be touched and traced. Also available are alphabet guide charts illustrating steps in letter formation, as shown in Figure 12.8. Another aid is a small card of upper- and lowercase letters. Many teachers tape a card to an upper corner of each student's desk.

✦ *Include instruction on how to get ready to write.* The teacher must show youngsters how to sit and how to position the paper. For manuscript writing with no letter slant, the paper is generally held perpendicular to the body and parallel to the edge of the desk for both right- and left-handed writers. If left-handed children find this position awkward, they can experi-

Figure 12.8   Working with Alphabet Charts
SOURCE: Courtesy of Zaner Bloser.

ment with a second position, advocated by the Zaner-Bloser handwriting program (see Figure 12.9).

Children also need instruction in how to hold their pencils. Observe any group of people—whether first-graders or college students—as they write, and you will find any number holding their pencils in all sorts of weird ways. These "self-learned ways" may impede writing and, therefore, should be diagnosed and remediated by an alert teacher, who guides children in a more efficient way to hold their pencils.

Providing Meaningful Practice

Meaningful handwriting practice should be part of publication activity. Once children have mastered basic letter forms, they print the cards and charts needed for instruction. Children can take turns producing

✦ *Cards* to display weekly spelling words; to study subjects and predicates, parts of speech, synonyms, homonyms, antonyms, contractions, alphabetical order, and so forth;

✦ *Charts* of words to substitute for worn-out words, of spelling generalizations, of poetry selections, and of procedures used in the classroom during science investigations;

✦ *Labels* to affix to objects in the classroom, to desks naming who sits there, and to cabinets identifying what is kept there;

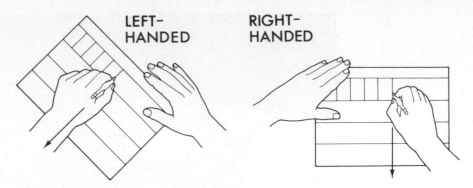

LEFT-HANDED **RIGHT-HANDED**

Figure 12.9 Zaner-Bloser Method Writing Positions

✦ *Duplicating masters* of selections for body chants and choral speaking, of material for a class newspaper or magazine, of discussion topics, and of summaries resulting from social science investigations.

See Chapter 10 for ideas for publications that provide handwriting practice as part of the writing process.

Children can also select some of their own writings to revise and publish. Each child contributes a piece to a class book of stories; each renders in his or her very best handwriting the revised piece chosen for inclusion. Bound together, contributions are placed in the reading center or the library for others to enjoy. Students can make a similar collection of hand-printed poems; they print their contributions on large-size, heavy-grade paper and add colorful drawings. The final product is a "big book" that must be read by sprawling on the floor.

Work that children enjoy rendering in their publication manuscript includes

✦ *Original greeting cards* to give to family members or classmates;
✦ *Invitations* to parents to a class performance, to other classes to share a party or performance, and to speakers requesting that they visit the class;
✦ *Letters* to pen pals and to editors of local papers;
✦ *Thank-you notes* to those who have helped the class.

Upper-graders can use the same activities to practice their cursive letter forms.

Since handwriting is a tool for recording thoughts on paper, repeated use in real-life situations and in preparation of written content provides the best practice. Children practice as they prepare final drafts of stories, poems, and reports. They practice as they write memoranda to teacher and classmates. If children are continuously involved in composing and publishing, they will by necessity be involved in handwriting. After sessions in which letter shapes are introduced and the steps important in forming the shapes are stressed, there is a decreasing need for systematic lessons as children use handwriting on a daily basis and the teacher works with individual children to overcome their special problems.

Diagnosing Children's Handwriting Problems

Six elements result in legible manuscript: shape, size and proportion, slant, spacing, steadiness of line, and styling—the six Ss of manuscript. As youngsters build skills, weaknesses are diagnosed in terms of the six Ss so that additional instruction can be provided to meet individual needs. In addition, watching children as they write may bring to light problems associated with positioning of paper and pencil. How do children grasp the pencil? Some children may grip it tightly, others may hold it at the point, and still others may hold it between the middle and pointing fingers.

Discovering problems common to several children, a teacher can schedule time for small-group remedial instruction. For example, youngsters having difficulty with alignment, or getting letters to rest on the base line, gather together and focus directly on their problem. At other times, a teacher helps an individual child with a special problem.

Children should be a part of the diagnostic process. At first, the teacher supplies youngsters with a simple self-assessment checklist. Later children devise checklists geared to recognized weaknesses. Periodically they select a paper to analyze. It should be a publication draft done for bulletin board mounting or taking home. If the assessment is recorded on the same checklist on several occasions, youngsters can identify areas requiring more practice. Figure 12.10 provides an example of a self-assessment checklist.

🖉 BUILDING AND REFINING YOUR TEACHING SKILLS

✦ Assume your first-graders have received instruction in writing *l*, *i*, and *t* in both lower- and uppercase forms, as well as in writing the uppercase forms of *H*, *F*, and *E*. Now you wish to introduce the *h*. Outline the steps in the lesson.

✦ Compare the form of the letters in two different handwriting programs. In what ways do the programs differ in their approach to manuscript writing?

LOOKING AT MY OWN HANDWRITING		NAME: _____											
Letters I have trouble making:	Jan 1		Jan 15		Feb 1		Feb 15		Mar 1		Mar 15		
	Yes	No	Yes	No	Yes	No	Yes	No	Yes	No	Yes	No
Do I keep my letters parallel?												
Do my letters stand on the base line?												
Are my upper-case and large lower-case letters filling the space?												
Are my little lower-case letters half-sized?												
Do I space my letters clearly?												
Do I space my words evenly across the page?												
Are my letter lines even and steady?												
Is my paper neat?												

Figure 12.10 A Self-Assessment Handwriting Checklist

Moving from Manuscript Letter Forms into Cursive Forms

Transition cursive:

Adult cursive:

Generally, children are introduced to cursive forms, or script, at the end of second grade or the beginning of third grade. The cursive children use initially differs to some extent from adult cursive. Because it differs, it is sometimes called *transition cursive*. In some penmanship systems, transition cursive is larger in size than adult cursive and retains the two-to-one proportion characteristic of manuscript: the small lowercase letters are half the size of uppercase and tall lowercase letters. In adult cursive, the small letters are approximately one-third the height of full-size letters. Transition cursive is commonly used through fourth grade; by fifth grade, youngsters write in adult cursive on paper without central guidelines.

In this section, we will look at ways to help children move from manuscript to cursive letter forms. We will begin by again visiting Fred Bronsky's third grade.

....

TEACHING IN ACTION   *Introducing Cursive Letter Forms*

....

When Fred Bronsky's third-graders entered their classroom late in September, they noticed a change. Above the manuscript letter strips mounted around the room was a second set of letters—cursive. On their desks, below the letter guides in the right-hand corner, was a second letter guide—cursive. On the board was a series of guidelines.

Mr. Bronsky, a teacher who took little time with preliminaries, jumped into his lesson as soon as the children had settled down. "Watch me," he directed. "I'm going to write something twice. You will have to tell me how each writing differs." He picked up chalk, broke it in two to prevent squeaking, and wrote within the first guidelines:

$$A \ cat \ can't \ dance.$$

Then he wrote within a second set of guidelines below the first:

$$A \ cat \ can't \ dance.$$

In D'Nealian, letters would be slanted.

....

Perceiving differences between manuscript and cursive letter forms

"Differences now?" he queried, and the children volunteered explanations: The first was manuscript, the second adult writing; the first was straight up and down, the second slanted; the first had separated letters, the second joined letters; when writing the first, Mr. Bronsky had stopped between letters, while in the second he had kept on going.

"Exactly right," Mr. Bronsky commended. Then he went to a second series of lines he had prepared on the board. Between the first two, he wrote the word *cat* in manuscript. Between the next two, he wrote *cat* again in manuscript. Between the last two, he wrote *cat* in cursive. Then he demonstrated, using dotted lines added to the middle version (see diagram), how the letters in manuscript relate to the letters in cursive.

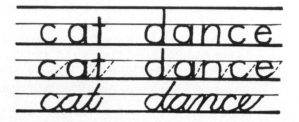

....
Practicing letters that
begin with undercurve
He made a similar connection between the manuscript and cursive letters in the remaining words of his model sentence.

Mr. Bronsky distributed practice paper. The paper was ruled with a heavy base line at half-inch intervals and a lighter midguideline. As he distributed the paper, he visited among the children, showing how to position it on the desk, how to grasp the pencil, and how to position the body for writing. Mr. Bronsky then went to the board to introduce the letters with an undercurve beginning:

$$\mathscr{i}\ \mathscr{i}\ \mathscr{u}\ \mathscr{s}\ \mathscr{t}$$

He demonstrated the *i*—starting on the base line, moving upward with an undercurve, moving downward toward the base line, moving upward with a second undercurve, and dotting in the space above. The children took pen in hand and, as Mr. Bronsky rhythmically repeated, "Curve up, move down, curve up with a tail, dot the *i*" and wrote a row of *i*s on the ruled board, they did the same on their papers. A few left-handed children wrote on guidelines on the board next to the teacher's.

....
Feeling the rhythm of
cursive writing
Mr. Bronsky demonstrated other letters with an undercurve beginning—*u* and *s*—and rhythmically described the component strokes as he formed them: "Curve up, bring it down, curve up again, bring it down, and up with the tail— the little *u*." "Curve up, bring it down, tie it around, curve up with the tail—the little *s*." He encouraged the children to repeat the jingles to themselves while practicing the letters. In short order, the third-graders were joining undercurve letters into words—*it, sit, us*—which they practiced on their sheets.

On successive days, the teacher introduced other letters with undercurve beginnings—*w, e, r*—and letters with undercurve beginnings and large loops—

l, f, b, h, k, p—essentially following the letter groupings in the handwriting program in use in his school. Soon he was introducing other lower-case groups:

1. Those beginning with an overcurve ($\nearrow$), the hump letters like *m n x y z;*

2. Those beginning with a downward curve ($\mathcal{C}$), the small oval letters like *a d g q o c;*

3. Those containing a lower loop like *j g p y z q f.*

Later the third-graders studied the uppercase letter groups, again working concurrently on letters sharing a structural feature.

If Mr. Bronsky had been using a different handwriting program, such as D'Nealian, Palmer, or Noble and Noble, he would have followed a similar sequence. He would have provided instruction in how to hold pencil and paper; taught structurally related letters together; provided classroom models of each letter; introduced letter strokes to a rhythm; and moved quickly from individual letters to words and sentences to develop spacing skills. There would have been a difference, however, in the final letter shapes, depending on the particular program in use. Before beginning instruction, a teacher should check letter shapes and overall letter heights to be consistent with what children have learned in previous grades.

Preparing for Cursive Writing

Practicing curves and circles

Just as Ms. Robinson readied her students for manuscript writing, so did Mr. Bronsky prepare his third-graders for cursive. As with the introduction to manuscript, this preparatory work can take several forms.

First, for several weeks before the formal introduction of cursive, Mr. Bronsky began to write in cursive on the chalkboard and on the duplicated sheets he distributed to accustom the children to reading words written in cursive. In addition, he changed his handwriting center. He sectioned off a corner portion of the chalkboard and each day affixed a series of guidelines with masking tape. Each day, too, at the top of the board, he drew a flowing, repetitive pattern—a series of connected and slanted lines, connected and overlapping backward circles, connecting undercurves, connecting overcurves. Individual students could go to the center to spend five minutes or so forming and erasing their reproductions.

Helping Left-Handed Children

Identifying left-handed writers

During this time, Mr. Bronsky checked to make sure children were at ease with the hand they had chosen for manuscript writing. He wanted to be certain which children were right-handed and which were left-handed so that he could help them with the writing position of hands and paper and provide extra time for left-handed students to work at the board.

The recommended position for right-handed writers is to hold the paper so that the bottom forms a thirty-degree angle with the table edge and the left hand is placed in the upper left-hand corner of the paper to steady it. Most handwriting specialists recommend that left-handed writers place the paper so that it is in a position that is the mirror image of the one recommended for righties: the right bottom corner pointing toward the writer, the right hand in the right top corner to steady the paper, and the left hand guiding the pencil from left to right, as shown in Figure 12.11.

Although one left-hander, John Ramsey (1988), has described his own successful use of the rightward-slanting paper position, some left-handed writers find that if they use the position shown in Figure 12.11, they cover with their writing hand the letters and words they have just written. Because of this, lefties cannot look back on their writing. One left-handed person resolved this dilemma by inventing his own system. He pulls his paper down by the left-hand bottom corner so that the bottom edge forms at least a fifty-degree angle with the table edge. Without hooking his wrist, he writes uphill, making it possible for him to write most legibly and at the same time see the letters coming from beneath his pen without arching his hand in the upside-down position many left-handed writers adopt. Given the uncertain state of knowledge about left-

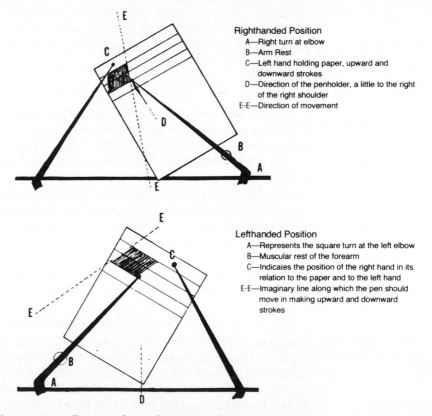

Righthanded Position
A—Right turn at elbow
B—Arm Rest
C—Left hand holding paper, upward and downward strokes
D—Direction of the penholder, a little to the right of the right shoulder
E-E—Direction of movement

Lefthanded Position
A—Represents the square turn at the left elbow
B—Muscular rest of the forearm
C—Indicates the position of the right hand in its relation to the paper and to the left hand
E-E—Imaginary line along which the pen should move in making upward and downward strokes

Figure 12.11 Paper and Hand Positions for Cursive Writing

handed writing, perhaps the logical course to follow is to show left-handed youngsters the traditional position. If that proves unwieldy, children should be encouraged to experiment to find a position that serves them best.

Providing Meaningful Practice

Read Thomas Wasylyk, "Teaching Left Handers the Write Stuff," *The Reading Teacher,* 42 (February 1989), 446–447.

Having systematically introduced the lower- and uppercase letter forms, a teacher will want to provide continued and meaningful practice with cursive writing first in the transitional and then in the adult style. Many of the activities described in the manuscript section apply equally to cursive: Upper-graders prepare observational charts, word cards, labels, and so forth. They write letters, invitations, and greeting cards. In addition, they experiment with some of the following publication activities:

✦ Youngsters write and send notes to one another. From half-gallon cardboard milk containers, the teacher fashions a series of pigeonholes, one for each student. Students label their pigeonholes, into which others, including the teacher, tuck notes, papers being returned, or special assignments.

✦ Upper-graders compose nature haiku and cinquains, which they copy in their best cursive onto pieces of brown paper bag, ripped to form jagged edges. The poems are taken outside, attached with twine to trees and shrubs, and left to weather. They truly become "nature poems." The weathered poems are collected and mounted on a bulletin board captioned "Nature's Handiwork."

✦ Obtain old wallpaper sample books from a wallpaper store. A student who has written a poem selects a page from the sample book that evokes the same mood as the poem, cuts a rectangle from the page, writes the poem on it, and mounts the piece on a larger sheet of dark construction paper to which he or she adds designs cut from the remainder of the sample page.

✦ Scrolls are fun to write, correlate nicely with social science content, and provide meaningful handwriting practice. Children studying colonial America write pseudo-proclamations, such as those that might have been written the day after the Boston Tea Party or those that announced the Stamp Tax Act. Children studying ancient Greece and Rome write proclamations that might have been read before the governing councils. Proclamations are written in cursive on the unwaxed side of shelf paper, the ends of the paper are attached to dowels, and the proclamations are delivered as part of a class "We Are There" happening. In this activity, as in the others described here, children use their handwriting skill as a tool for clear communication.

✦ Preparing an illustrated story "movie" is a pleasant way to practice cursive. A student who has written a short story divides it into five or six episodes. The writer inscribes each episode on a separate piece of white lined paper, mounts the paper off center on a sheet of construction paper, and draws an illustration on the construction paper. The writer-illustrator then tapes all the pages produced in this manner into a strip that he or she feeds through the opaque projector to share with classmates.

Most of these activities provide practice either as part of ongoing classroom activity or as follow-up to written expression and science or social studies. As in the lower grades, the best practice is repeated use in publishing writing.

In addition, there may be call for more direct practice, especially as fifth-graders change to adult cursive. To facilitate the transition to adult cursive, youngsters use paper without a central guideline and with lines about 3/8" apart, the same as the legal-size yellow tablets in common use. Students systematically practice lowercase letters from each letter group, working on the letters with undercurve beginnings, downward curve beginnings, upper loops, and lower loops; they work on the uppercase letters as well.

In similar fashion, youngsters work on special weaknesses identified by studying samples of their own cursive. Students can check the legibility of indi-

Chalkboard work can provide meaningful handwriting practice. (© 1990 Paul Fotin/Stock Boston)

vidual letters by punching a hole about one centimeter in diameter in a card. They place the hole on top of a sample of each letter as it appears in their writing. By masking all the other letters, the evaluator can get a better idea of the clarity of individual letters. Failing to close up letters like *a, o,* and *d* is a common problem that can cause confusion and that students can identify by close checking through a masking hole.

The ultimate criterion in judging handwriting is whether the writing is legible. At all levels, but particularly in the middle and junior high schools, students express their individuality through their handwriting. To insist that youngsters practice to the point where letters are perfect duplicates of the models in a handwriting system is often to ask the impossible and generally to ask the unnecessary. Students above grade five will need to refine skills periodically to ensure continued legibility, but after a point individual styling should be a factor in handwriting.

Keyboarding

Although keyboarding is a skill area separate from handwriting, its growing importance should be acknowledged. The ability to produce typed copy has been required primarily by those entering the secretarial professions and those doing a great deal of writing in advanced high school and college programs or in their work. Today, however, the need for keyboarding skill is increasing with the widespread use of computers with typewriterlike terminals, especially inexpensive, tabletop microcomputers. As a result, schools need to reconsider their decision about the point at which they make keyboarding instruction available to students. The upper elementary grades is not too early to begin.

.... A Summary Thought or Two

SPELLING, DICTIONARY USE, AND HANDWRITING

To write effectively, people must create the ideas that are the substance of expression. Without ideas to be expressed, writing serves little purpose. For this reason, most writing programs have rightly stressed idea making.

But to make ideas is not enough. To write effectively, people must be able to manipulate language on paper, especially if thoughts are to receive more than passing attention. Others judge ideas by the words selected to express them, by the way those words are spelled, and even by the appearance of the paper.

Accordingly, spelling, dictionary skills, and handwriting are basic tools that children should acquire in language arts programs. As this chapter explains, schools should be concerned about developing children's ability to

- Handle regular sound-symbol relationships and spell words that do not adhere to expectations;
- Spell multisyllabic words made up of suffixes, prefixes, and roots; spell compound words; and handle homonyms;
- Arrange words in alphabetical order and locate words ordered alphabetically;
- Use the dictionary to check spelling, find a substitute for an overworked word, check word meaning, and determine pronunciation;
- Produce clear manuscript in which letters generally conform to conventions regarding size, slant, shape, spacing, line strength, and styling;
- Produce a legible form of cursive, starting in third grade.

As this chapter has also emphasized, children acquire and refine these skills through lessons that focus on particular learnings and through drafting and editing as part of subject content and ongoing class activity.

A final caveat is in order. Because ideas are basic in writing, the process of recording ideas should not block expression. Stopping in midthought to check spelling or word meaning in the dictionary and writing painstakingly so that *o*s, *a*s, and *d*s are tightly closed to prevent misinterpretation may cause writers to lose the thoughts they are trying to express. The time for concern about dictionary checking, spelling, and handwriting is not in midthought; it is afterthought, as writers return to dress up what they have written.

Accordingly, as children compose stories, poems, and reports, teachers should not remind them to watch their spelling and write in their best penmanship. Editing is the point for checking spelling. Publishing is the point for well-styled handwriting as children select pieces to share. To turn a creative writing experience into a handwriting or spelling test is to take the creativity out of the experience.

· ·

THE FORUM   The Teacher as Researcher

See *Language Arts,* 65 (December 1988). The theme of the issue is the role of research in language arts. Also read Eleanor Kutz, "Teacher Research: Myths and Realities," *Language Arts,* 69 (March 1992), 193–197.

Deejay Schwartz, a kindergarten teacher, perceives herself as a teacher-researcher. Several years ago, she began to experiment with invented spelling, and now she asks her kindergartners to write daily from the time they arrive at school in the fall. Here she explains how she began to investigate her students' early writing development.

The Journey

I teach kindergarten in a suburban elementary school. In a typical class, although a few youngsters come to school able to break their thoughts into word units, most have not yet developed a concept of a word; they tend to write in strings of letters without word breaks. Most also come to school knowing that there is a "right" spelling regardless of how open and encouraging of their invented spellings I am. I asked myself: "How can I help the children learn more about words even as they use their invented spellings to write?"

To begin, I hypothesized ways in which spelling "lessons" and eventually handwriting "lessons" were an integral part of the writing process. I kept trying out these ways, modifying what I was doing as I went along, and discovered two approaches with which I am now experimenting.

Sometimes—though not always, for I have my children writing daily in many different formats, including journals—I ask children to divide construction paper into three parts. I suggest that they rehearse by drawing whatever story they are planning to write in the first section of the paper as they "mind talk" their stories. Having rehearsed, the children use the second section to draft using their invented spellings.

After children have drafted, I confer with each one, asking each child to read his or her story. As the child reads, very lightly in pencil I record the piece in "dictionary spelling" beneath the child's first draft. The child now reads the revised draft and finger points the words as he or she reads. Then together, we find correspondences between the child's invented spelling and the dictionary spelling. In every case there are correspondences, because I include some oral work with sound-symbol relationships (especially with beginning consonants) as part of experience story chart writing and the repeated reading of big books. As the child finds the correspondences, I "celebrate," making him or her feel good about the writing. In Andrew's case (see Figure 12.12), I said, "Look, Andrew! You can write the beginning of *my* and *men*. You know how to use the letter *m* to represent the sound you hear there. Can you find another place where you have a letter that is part of dictionary spelling?"

Having celebrated their writing in this way, children return to their places elated with themselves and with writing; at their table and independently, they trace over the letters I have inscribed for them in dictionary spelling. For me, this last step comprises a handwriting practice at a point in the writing process where it counts—in the production of a publication draft for bulletin board posting.

To emphasize words as units of communication and help children develop a concept of word, I vary my approach periodically. As before, children draw as they rehearse their stories through mind talk. But instead of having children record their stories immediately in invented spelling, I have them further rehearse by telling me what they intend to write. As children tell me, I draw word-length lines in paragraph style on the children's papers. Then children draft their stories, putting each word on a separate line, an activity that stresses word units within thought units (see Figure 12.13). The after-drafting activities are the same as in my prior treatment: The child orally reads what he or she has written, while I record beneath in dictionary spelling; we identify and "celebrate" correspondences between the two drafts; the child practices handwriting by tracing over to make a publication copy.

Figure 12.12 Andrew's Early Writing: "If I was president I would fight for my men."
SOURCE: Courtesy of Andrew Levinson.

For a description of how teacher-researchers publish their findings, read Marilyn D'Alessandro et al., "Writing for Publication: Voices from the Classroom," *The Reading Teacher,* 45 (February 1992), 408–414. See also Karin Dahl, ed., *Teacher as Writer: Entering the Professional Conversation* (Urbana, Ill.: National Council of Teachers of English, 1992).

THE FORUM **The Teacher as Researcher** *Continued*

Reflecting Back

I have found that when children truly "celebrate" correspondences between their invented spelling and dictionary spelling, they are not at all miffed. They actually are encouraged in future writing to express themselves in invented spelling, because they know we will celebrate the correspondences as signs of their growth as writers. As I continue to experiment with these approaches, I find that children keep writing more and are daily adding more dictionary spellings to their repertoire of invented ones. But best of all, they seem to enjoy functioning as authors.

Are my approaches valid teaching practices? Only more experimentation will tell.

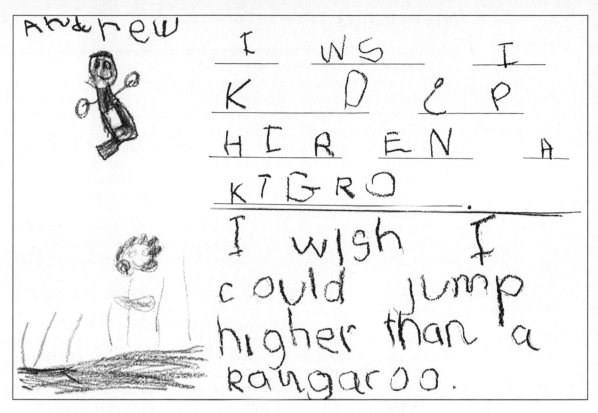

Figure 12.13 Andrew Moves to Standard Writing: "I wish I could jump higher than a kangaroo."
SOURCE: Courtesy of Andrew Levinson.

RELATED READINGS

Bean, Wendy, and Chrystine Bouffler. *Spell by Writing*. Rozelle, Australia: Primary English Teaching Association, 1987.

Farris, Patricia. "Views and Other Views." *Language Arts,* 68 (April 1991), 312–314.

Gentry, J. Richard. *Spel . . . Is a Four-Letter Word*. Portsmouth, N.H.: Heinemann Educational Books, 1987.

Gentry, J. Richard, and Jean Wallace Gillet. *Teaching Kids to Spell*. Portsmouth, N.H.: Heinemann Educational Books, 1992.

Henderson, Edmund. *Teaching Spelling*. 2nd ed. Boston: Houghton Mifflin, 1990.

———. *Learning to Read and Spell: The Child's Knowledge of Words*. DeKalb, Ill.: Northern Illinois University Press, 1981.

Henderson, Edmund, and James Beer. *Developmental and Cognitive Aspects of Learning to Spell*. Newark, Del.: International Reading Association, 1980.

Hillerich, Robert. "Reading Central: Dictionary Skills." *Early Years,* 16 (1986), 14–15.

Hodges, Richard. *Learn to Spell*. Urbana, Ill.: National Council of Teachers of English, 1966.

Horn, Thomas. *Research on Handwriting and Spelling*. Urbana, Ill.: National Council of Teachers of English, 1966.

Koenke, Karl. "Handwriting Instruction: What Do We Know?" *The Reading Teacher,* 40 (November 1986), 214–216.

Language Arts, 69 (October 1992). The theme of the issue is "But What About Spelling?"

McAlexander, Patricia, Ann Dobie, and Noel Gregg. *Beyond the "Sp" Label: Improving the Spelling of Learning Disabled and Basic Writers*. Urbana, Ill.: National Council of Teachers of English, 1992.

Moffett, James, and Betty Jane Wagner. "What Works Is Play." *Language Arts,* 70 (January 1993), 32–36.

Phenix, Jo, and Doreen Scott-Dunn. *Spelling Instruction That Makes Sense*. Lewiston, N.Y.: Pembroke Publishers, 1991.

Ramsey, John. "Why Is Left Handed Writing Still a Problem in the Last 7th of the 20th Century?" *The Reading Teacher,* 41 (February 1988), 504–506.

Read, Charles. *Children's Categorization of Speech Sounds in English*. Urbana, Ill.: National Council of Teachers of English, 1972.

Routman, Regie. "The Uses and Abuses of Invented Spelling." *Instructor*, 102 (May/June 1993), 36–39.

Spann, Mary Beth. "When Spelling Is Thinking." *Instructor,* 101 (March 1992), 500.

Temple, Charles et al. *The Beginnings of Writing*. 3rd ed. Boston: Allyn and Bacon, 1992.

Wilde, Sandra. *You Kan Red This! Spelling and Punctuation for the Whole Language Classroom, K–6*. Portsmouth, N.H.: Heinemann Educational Books, 1991.

CHAPTER 13

Reading for Meaning

Learning to Read and Reading to Learn

Reflecting Before Reading

How do young children emerge as readers?

What is interactive-constructive reading?

How can the teacher encourage children to respond before, while, and after reading?

What is text structure?

How is it useful in making meaning with prose and poetry selections?

How does the teacher encourage library use?

BEFORE reading the chapter, read the title, the headings, and the end-of-chapter summary. Then answer the questions in the margin on this page.

TEACHING IN ACTION   In the Communication Circle

It was a crisp Monday morning. As was their daily custom, the sixteen kindergartners gathered along the perimeter of the bright red rug that set off the Communication Circle within their large classroom.

Attendance checking followed the flag salute and the introductory song. Pointing, the kindergartners counted heads around the circle. Reaching sixteen and knowing eighteen were in the class, they decided two were absent and identified missing classmates. Then their teacher, Lorraine Wilkening, recorded the date in the corner of the chalkboard—a date the children read aloud with her. At that point, the teacher gestured toward a bulletin board chart that contained six words: *milk, paper, blinds, Fluffy, plants, chairs*. "Let's decide who will help with tasks this week," she suggested. Boys and girls volunteered to feed Fluffy, the class pet, to help water the plants, and so forth. Next to the appropriate word on the chart, Ms. Wilkening listed the names of two volunteers, and the entire class "read" back the completed chart so that all would remember their tasks.

Listening and Talking Together

Several books in hand, the teacher settled in a rocking chair at the front of the red rug. "Boys and girls," she announced, "during reading workshop this morning, we are going to read a story about two animals, a hippopotamus and a rhinoceros. Let's look first in the encyclopedia to see what these animals are like."

Recognizing written words

For a discussion of the importance of reading aloud to children and its relationship to comprehension, read Carl Smith, "Reading Aloud: An Experience for Sharing," *The Reading Teacher*, 42 (January 1989), 320.

Developing meaningful concepts before reading

She opened a volume to display a picture of a hippopotamus. Prompted by a question or two, the children described the animal and pantomimed the way the hippo was wallowing in the mud. Then they examined a large picture of a rhinoceros, again describing it, especially the two horns on its nose. Encouraged by their teacher, they compared the rhino's nose with the hippo's. They talked about the rhino's horns and considered possible uses.

Predicting to develop a framework for reading

Then the teacher read the title and displayed the cover of the picture storybook *"You Look Ridiculous," Said the Rhinoceros to the Hippopotamus* by Bernard Waber. She asked the children to think about the meaning of *ridiculous* and to guess why the author had used that word rather than *silly*. She asked them to predict why the rhino might have said that to the hippo. In response to the first question, the children proposed that the word *ridiculous* started the same way as *rhinoceros* and sounded better with it. Responding to the second question, the kindergartners suggested that maybe the rhino might think that the hippo looked ridiculous because it was all covered with mud or because it didn't have horns on its nose.

Building an understanding of story structure

Ms. Wilkening now began the story. Each time before the hippo repeated the question "Do I look ridiculous?" the teacher looked at the class, particularly at those children whose attention was wandering. Anticipating the story question, the students joined in the repetition. When the story ended, the teacher asked the class a series of questions that highlighted the story structure:

- ✦ Who is the main animal in the story? Who is the troublemaker?
- ✦ What did the rhino do to make trouble? Why did he do this?
- ✦ How did this make the hippo feel? Why did she feel this way?
- ✦ What did she decide to do? Why?
- ✦ Whom did she ask first for advice? What answer did she get?
- ✦ Whom did she ask next? Then next? Then next?
- ✦ How did she feel as she went from one animal to the next?
- ✦ How did she finally solve her problem?
- ✦ How did the hippo feel at the end? Why did she feel better?
- ✦ Has anyone ever made you feel the way the rhino made the hippo feel? When?
- ✦ Did you like this story? What was good about it? Bad?

Increasing speaking vocabulary

As the children talked about the characters, sequence of events, and feeling changes in the story, they used the vocabulary of the story. Soon *ridiculous, rhinoceros, hippopotamus*—big words for kindergartners—were tripping off their tongues.

Responding to literature by drawing and writing

Going back through the story, Ms. Wilkening asked the children if they would like to draw pictures of the story animals and write about them with their invented spellings. Children volunteered to draw and write about the hippo, the rhino, the lion, the giraffe, the other animals in the story, and the hippo bedecked with the parts she wished she had. Ms. Wilkening told the youngsters they would use their drawings and writings to review the story action and feelings the next day.

Pantomiming Meanings

Interpreting story meanings

Because the children had been listening and interacting for about fifteen minutes, and the class contained several attention-deficit children, Ms. Wilkening now scheduled a physically active animal time. The children stood up and, to a recording of Saint-Saëns's *Carnival of the Animals,* pantomimed the way the animals in the story moved. To prompt the activity, Ms. Wilkening had pasted photocopied story pictures on cardboard. As she held up the elephant, children became elephants; seeing the monkey, they moved like monkeys.

Listening for Similar Sounds

Distinguishing the sound represented by *r;* auditory discrimination —the ability to distinguish speech sounds— is important in reading

This active time merged into a thinking and listening time. At the top of a strip of chart paper, the teacher wrote the word *ridiculous.* "Now," she announced, "we're going to think about words that begin with the same sound as *ridiculous.* Let's pull on our thinking caps." The children put their hands to their heads and pretended to pull on thinking caps. As they did so, under a lowercase *r* written on the chart, Ms. Wilkening recorded *rain* as she said it. The children repeated *rain* and *ridiculous* and contributed words with the same beginning sound: *red, rabbit, road,* and *right.* When they could not think of another word, the teacher presented a riddle: "I'm thinking of an animal, a little bigger than a mouse. It eats cheese." With this clue, the children produced *rat.* She encouraged, "Who in our class has a name that begins just as *rabbit* does?" With this, they produced *Ruth* and *Rod,* which she recorded under an uppercase *R.* She stapled the strip to a hanger, which she hung from a light fixture. At that point, Ms. Wilkening told the children that when she heard the sound like that at the beginning of *rat,* she used the letter *r* to write it down. This was a "secret" of writing that they might wish to use, too.

ridiculous
rain
red
rabbit
road

Extending story meanings through writing

When they had produced a list of words, the children cooperatively composed a rabbit story, with individual children contributing sentences from the brainstormed word chart. Their story went like this:

The Ridiculous Rat

The rabbit saw a red rat. The rat was sitting by the road. The rabbit said to the red rat, "You look ridiculous. You are red and you look ridiculous."

As children contributed sentences, Ms. Wilkening recorded them on chart paper. Whenever the teacher ended a sentence, one child added the period. Once the story was written, the children read it with their teacher, who moved her hand under the lines from left to right as they read. They read it several times, working on speaking the words in "chunks" of meaning. In so doing, they read the last line with so much feeling that Ms. Wilkening substituted an exclamation mark for the period "to show how to read it." Then individual children came to the chart to read lines as the teacher's moving hand indicated clusters of words to read as units.

Reading from left to right, reading in chunks of meaning, associating meaning with punctuation marks

Reading Writing

Quickly Ms. Wilkening took scissors and cut the story chart into punctuation marks and clusters of words read as units. She clipped the first sentence between *The rabbit saw* and *a red rat,* the second between *The rabbit was sitting* and *by the road.* Then she distributed the pieces. "Let's see if we can find story words that are the same as the ones on our chart list. Who has a piece that has *rat* on it?" Those holding a piece with *rat* came forward to hold their pieces next to that word on the list as others checked to see if the two words were visually the same.

When they had discovered all possible matings, the children—with much teacher guidance—reconstructed the story from the cards. Ms. Wilkening called forward the two holding parts of the first sentence. The children decided which of the two parts went first and which second, laying the parts side by side on the rug and reading the sentence. Youngsters holding parts of successive sentences did the same until the story was together again. During the activity, Ms. Wilkening kept two children closely beside her; these two were youngsters whose attention had been wandering.

Discriminating visually among words; visual discrimination—the ability to distinguish one letter from another—is important in reading

Reconstructing story sentences

Listening for and Spelling More Sounds

At that point, the teacher distributed to each kindergartner a card inscribed with *r*. She announced, "Boys and girls, I'm going to call out words. Some will begin with the same sound as *rabbit, rat,* and *ridiculous*; some will not. When you hear a word that begins with the same sound, hold up your card. What letter is on the card?"

The unison response was "*r*."

"Yes," continued the teacher, "the letter *r*. We use the letter *r* to write the sound we hear at the beginning of *rat* and *rabbit*. Point to another word on our chart that has the letter *r* at the beginning." Children hopped up to point out words.

When all were back in their seats, Ms. Wilkening began a fast word call. Hearing words like *rabbit* and *rat*, the youngsters held up their *r* cards. Hearing words not beginning in the same way, they lowered their cards.

Developing phonemic awareness; distinguishing the sound represented by *r*; reinforcing what has been learned

Developing Number Concepts

A fast finger play came next, sequenced in especially for youngsters who had trouble attending and needed a lot of physical involvement: "There were ten little _____ in the bed, and the little one said, 'Roll over! Roll over!' They

Developing meaningful concepts as a base for reading and thinking all rolled over and then there were nine and the little one said. . . ." On previous occasions children had done the play with kittens, lions, and bunnies. Now they did it with rabbits. The youngsters stood up, sang together, held up fingers to show the decreasing number of rabbits in the bed, and rolled their arms to show rabbit motion. "Did anyone hear any other words in the song," the teacher asked, "that begin with the same sound as *rabbit*?" The children knew the answer and called out *"Roll over"* in the same rhythm they had used in singing.

Emerging as Readers and Writers

Teachers call this activity time a *Reading/Writing Workshop.* See Kathleen Swift, "Try Reading Workshops in Your Classroom," *The Reading Teacher,* 46 (February 1993), 366–371, for a description of Reading Workshop in a sixth grade.

The kindergartners and their teacher had been engrossed for almost forty minutes—a long time, given the short attention spans of these young learners. Action had been fast, with numerous changes in activity to keep attention. Now Ms. Wilkening explained what the children would do when they dispersed. Some would go immediately to the writing center, where they would draw pictures of a rhino, a hippo, or another animal selected from the story *"You Look Ridiculous"* and write about the animal. Others would pair off with their reading partners to take turns reading aloud to each other from books the teacher had shared with the class they had chosen to read. Here reading meant telling the story based on the pictures, the words they could read, and their memory of the story. Still others would draw on the reverse sides of their *r* cards a picture of something beginning with the same sound as *rabbit* and *rat.* The cards would be shared during the languaging-together session on Tuesday morning, with other children guessing the objects and words represented.

At the same time, children met individually with Ms. Wilkening. Some met with her to dictate stories (as in Figure 13.1) or to read stories they had written on their own using invented spellings. For example, Jo dictated an original ridiculous story, reread the story to her teacher, illustrated it, and then read it to a group of working classmates.

Ruth, a gifted kindergartner, read aloud to Ms. Wilkening from a storybook that she had been reading on her own and explained why she liked the story. After reading to Ms. Wilkening, Ruth shared the story with those at the writing table. In this setting, Ruth, Jo, and the others were emerging naturally as readers and writers in ways that met their unique learning needs.

Seeing Structure in Stories

Understanding the structure of the story

Tuesday morning saw this class of young children gathered again in the Communication Circle. Completing the opening exercises and attendance taking, they began this time by sharing their animal drawings and writings and using them to retell the story of the hippopotamus and rhinoceros. As the children retold the story—at times referring back to the book "to get it right"—Ms. Wilkening had them glue their pictures to a large piece of brown paper stretched out on the floor. The children glued their pictures in "story order," starting with the hippo in the mud, continuing with the rhino coming along, and including in sequence each animal the hippo met. The last picture they glued down was the hippo wallowing happily in the mud.

"The lion lives in a cage. He lived in a forest, but a man who worked for a zoo grabbed the lion and put him in a cage. The lion is sad. He would like to get out, but he can't."

Figure 13.1 A Kindergartner's Original Dictation and Art

Comprehending changes in story mood, recognizing the function of certain characters in a story

With that accomplished, Ms. Wilkening asked the children to decide when in the story the hippo was happy and when she was sad. As the children decided, volunteers hopped up and drew happy or sad faces above the glued-down animal pictures on the storymap they were developing together. They noticed that in this story the hippo started out happy and ended up happy as well. They starred the rhino as the troublemaker. Then they retold the story together, using their storymap as a guide.

Extending story meanings through creative thinking

Later that day, children wrote their own troublemaker stories by drawing pictures that showed story action with words spelled as children wished. They had an opportunity to share their stories with Ms. Wilkening and another student in the kindergarten. They posted their stories in the corridor to be "read" and "reread" as children waited in line to go outside or to the auditorium.

Emergent Reading: Decoding Sight and Sound with Meaning

Perhaps the most exciting teaching task of all is the one Ms. Wilkening is performing as part of a reading/writing workshop: helping young children gain control over the written symbols of language so that they can use those symbols to comprehend and enjoy reading. To read, children must learn to distinguish among visual symbols (for example, *d* and *b*) and acquire a sight word vocabulary—a repertoire of words that they recognize and find meaningful on sight without involved analysis.

Important, too, in beginning reading are the abilities to distinguish among the speech sounds and to associate speech sounds with the printed symbols of written language. A good reader does this with little conscious thought, but research indicates that young children can profit from some attention to speech sounds and the ways they are represented on paper (Anderson, 1985). This attention can be a natural part of a language experience, as when Ms. Wilkening asked children, after reading, to supply other words that start the same way as *ridiculous* and to use those words in further writing and reading.

A good reader also perceives the melody of sentence sounds and appreciates the relationships between melody and meaning. In the elementary grades, children gain appreciation of the cadence of written words at the intuitive level by hearing tuneful sentence sounds in stories read aloud, rhythmically chorusing lines together, hearing word music in their mind's ear as they read to themselves, and creating word magic as they compose stories and poems. In a whole-language approach to reading, the ability to work with and appreciate language sounds exists not in isolation but in conjunction with listening and language production.

Teachers who believe in a whole-language approach to early reading create a classroom environment in which children are immersed in meaning-filled print. Children learn to read by reading; they learn to write by writing. Enter Ms. Wilkening's kindergarten, and you see labels everywhere. Children's desks are labeled with their names, the door is labeled *door,* and windows, chairs, and walls also bear labeling cards. Sometimes number words hang from the ceiling next to the numbers themselves; at other times, color words hang next to color samples. As children and teacher talk together, they refer to the labels; children locate letters and labels that apply to what they are talking about. They use the words that fill their classroom as they dictate story charts and as they write independently. And when they need a word that is not around, they invent spellings. Later they read their writings to classmates and read what other children have written.

In Ms. Wilkening's classroom, books are everywhere, for this teacher has "set up the environment to invite participation" (Holdaway, 1986). Ms. Wilkening uses books creatively to help children find pleasure in reading and learn decoding skills "within the context of reading for meaning, rather than in separate exercises" (Somerfield, 1985). She teaches decoding skills as part of actual reading. These skills include left-to-right progression (the ability to follow text from left to right across a page), visual discrimination (the ability to see differences among letters and words), auditory discrimination (the ability to distinguish language sounds one from another), recognition of sight words (the ability to decode specific words on sight), application of simple phoneme-grapheme correspondences (the ability to associate language sounds with letters and combinations of letters), and facility with context clues (the ability to use the surrounding words in a sentence to unlock the meaning of an unfamiliar word).

Attention to ways speech sounds are represented on paper is what we mean by *phonics.* Read Gerald Duffy, "Let's Free Teachers to Be Inspired," *Phi Delta Kappan,* 73 (February 1992), 442–447, for a discussion of the need for some direct instruction as a natural part of language learning.

Research affirms the importance of environmental print in beginning reading. See Harste, Woodward, and Burke (1984).

THE FORUM On Environmental Print and Early Reading

1. Jerome Harste clarifies the importance of environmental print as children learn to read: "Most children as young as 3 can read *Stop* on a stop sign, *McDonald's* when shown the golden arches, and *Crest* when shown a Crest toothpaste carton. By 6, all children can read these and other items of environmental print they frequently encounter. . . . [This] means that we do not have to teach young children to read, but rather we need to support and expand their continued understanding of reading" ("Jerry Harste Speaks on Reading and Writing," *The Reading Teacher,* 43 [January 1990], 316–318).

2. Denny Taylor has studied children's early experiences with print. Describing the children in her study, Taylor writes, "They learned of print through a whole language process; while learning to talk, they learned of the social significance of such signs as 'Two Guys' and 'Exit,' played with reinvention of letters and words, and experimented with 'reading' stories. . . . In the home the label on the shampoo bottle, the recipe for carrot bread, and the neon signs in the street were not constructed specifically to teach reading; they were part of the child's world, and the child learned of their purpose as well as of their meaning" (*Family Literacy: Young Children Learning to Read and Write* [Portsmouth, N.H.: Heinemann Educational Books, 1983], 91, 20).

Questions to Consider

What experiences with environmental print could you build into preschool and primary school programs? How could you organize a preschool classroom to make use of environmental print? Why would this be important?

Read Barbara Park, "The Big Book Trend—A Discussion with Don Holdaway," *Language Arts,* 59 (November/December 1982), 815–821; B. Gail Heald-Taylor, "Big Books," *Ideas with Insights: Language Arts K–6,* ed. Dorothy Watson (Urbana, Ill.: National Council of Teachers of English, 1987); and Phyllis Trachtenburg and Ann Ferruggia, "Big Books from Little Voices," *The Reading Teacher,* 42 (January 1989), 284–289.

This section provides ideas for shared book experiences that teach these skills in a program where emphasis is on meaning and skills are taught through reading.

Shared Book Experiences

Reading skills develop naturally through shared book experiences. This is especially true when well-loved storybooks have been enlarged so that all participants can see text and pictures. Don Holdaway (1982) describes a group of young children gathered around and listening to a big book. The story is *The Teeny Tiny Woman.* When the teacher gets to the repeating line "Give me my bone!" the children spontaneously join in, correctly decoding the words *me* and *my.* When children's attention is drawn to the distinction between the two words, they show no confusion; in a natural reading situation such as this, children have no trouble visually distinguishing the two words. They rather quickly add those words, plus others in the big book, to their sight vocabularies.

Teaching Beginning Reading Skills in Context   Holdaway explains ways to use a big book to help children decode, or figure out, written language as part of a shared book experience. One way is to put flaps over some words or parts of words and ask children to volunteer what is beneath the flaps. Here readers use context naturally to generate meaning from print; they predict and test their predictions by deciding whether the words volunteered make sense in context.

A second way is to prepare word and sentence cards to accompany the text of a big book. Volunteers match the cards with words and sentences in the text. A teacher can also prepare a cutup version of the text as Ms. Wilkening did; he or she cuts apart key story sentences to highlight chunks of meaning, or the natural phrasal units people use in speaking their language. Based on their understanding of sight, sound, and meaning, readers reconstruct the story; they

As children listen to their teacher share a big book, they can see the illustrations and follow the enlarged lines of print. (© 1993 Thomas A. Hoebbel)

juggle sentence pieces around, striving for a synthesis that retells the story with style. They add punctuation marks and then reread the story, reading in chunks of meaning rather than word by word and testing their final arrangement for "word music."

Related Teaching Strategies   By replicating texts on chart paper, teachers can make their own big books of favorite stories to introduce young children to reading. They can also display portions of books with transparencies and overhead projectors. Using this equipment, teachers expose sections of text progressively and draw children's attention to punctuation marks, to repeating words, and to repeating graphemes. They move their hands from left to right beneath lines of print as children follow along or ask a child to finger point as the whole class rereads aloud.

A large-screen computer monitor also can be used if someone has previously typed the necessary text into the computer. An advantage of the computer is that teacher and children can follow words along on the screen with the flashing placekeeper of the computer (the cursor) as they read aloud, reinforcing the left-to-right progression of the text. Similarly, teacher and students can use the cursor to indicate beginnings of words as students read aloud, reinforcing word units for those children who have only begun to develop a concept of word. A second advantage is that the teacher can use the search-and-replace function of the computer to substitute one word for another in the story, for example, *small* for *tiny* wherever *tiny* appears in the story.

Predictable Stories and Poems

Particularly useful in developing young children's sight vocabularies are predictable stories in which words and actions repeat to carry the action forward. After hearing a story once, children join in, "reading along" based on their predictions of what will happen. They read, reread, and then read chorally the repetitive tales from big books or charts on which the stories have been printed; again they match word and sentence cards to words and sentences in the story. In so doing, children become familiar with the shapes and letter sequences of the repeated words and add them to their sight vocabularies. To help children recognize these words, the teacher can ask youngsters to look for distinctive qualities of the words: overall shape, beginning letter, repeated letters.

As Connie Bridge, Peter Winograd, and Darliene Haley (1983) point out, predictable literature has other uses as well. Rhyming stories and poems can help children learn word families containing common phonograms or syllables. Take, for example, this simple nursery rhyme that a teacher prepares as a poetry chart:

> *Good night. Sleep tight.*
> *Wake up bright in the morning light.*
> *To do what's right with all your might.*

Read LaDonna Wicklund, "Shared Poetry: A Whole Language Experience Adapted for Remedial Readers," *The Reading Teacher,* 42 (March 1989), 478–481, and Phyllis Trachtenburg, "Using Children's Literature to Enhance Phonics Instruction," *The Reading Teacher,* 43 (May 1990), 648–654, for a bibliography of trade books that contain repeating phonic elements.

Enjoying this piece during a shared poetry experience, children chorus it after their teacher has shared it with them. After listening and speaking, youngsters listen for words that end with the same rhyming sound as *night: tight, bright, light, right, might.* Studying these words on the poetry chart, youngsters discover the shared letters used to represent the sound *ight,* brainstorm other words with the same sound to record at the bottom of the poetry chart, and create simple rhyming lines that include *ight.*

In the same way, books in which many words begin with the same sounds and symbols can help children build basic phoneme-grapheme relationships. Children search the stories for words that begin with the same consonant sound or blend. They make charts of these words and later use the listed words in their own story and poem making. This would be true of a story such as *The Three Billy Goats Gruff.* Children listen for story words that begin with the same sound as *troll—trip* and *trap.* They suggest others from their speaking vocabulary. Based on the words they discover, youngsters generalize about the way this consonant sound combination, or blend, is written on paper.

Since some predictable books repeat letters of the alphabet, numbers, seasons, days of the week, and months of the year, in reading them children also add to their sight vocabularies words that relate to these concepts.

See Chapter 8 for a discussion of experience story charting with beginning readers.

Of course, the pieces that children individually or cooperatively compose and dictate to their teacher are excellent material for beginning reading; the stories include words that are a meaningful part of children's speaking vocabulary. All of the strategies described so far in reference to big books and predictable stories apply here: joining in while listening; rereading and choral reading; matching words and sentences; masking words; story reconstruction; and searching for similar beginning consonant, vowel, or rhyming sounds.

Meaningful Oral Reading

Another strategy for teaching beginning reading is meaningful oral reading—if used purposefully and with discretion. One useful approach to oral reading that is applicable with older as well as younger students is reading along while listening. In this approach, the teacher reads a story to students, who follow along on written copies. The teacher reads as expressively as possible, clustering words in meaningful chunks and vocally expressing meanings of words and punctuation signals. Listeners volunteer to reread individually and in chorus, modeling their renditions on the teacher's.

Read Sarah Dowhower, "Repeated Reading," *The Reading Teacher,* 42 (March 1989), 502–507.

The teacher then divides the group into two-somes to reread the story to each other. During collaborative reading, two children may curl up under a desk to reread the story orally together. Two others may find a quiet corner. Another two may decide to reread a big book posted on an easel. In the same way, during this kind of collaborative-reading workshop, children may pair off to read trade books—which they have chosen and which are at their independent reading level—orally to each other.

Oral reading can take other forms. One is paired or assisted reading, in which two or more students, chosen at random, read aloud a passage that they have already read silently or that one student and the teacher have read orally together. This activity gives young readers a sense of security and enables the better reader to assist the weaker one with difficult words. A variation of assisted reading, of course, is choral reading in which all group members orally interpret a passage using their voices to clarify meanings. In choral reading, considerable stress can be put on interpreting punctuation marks.

Readers' Theatre is another strategy for developing oral reading skills. Youngsters practice reading from a script and then share their renditions with classmates. See Chapter 6, page 186, for more detail.

At times some teachers rely on oral reading to determine children's comprehension. Needless to say, the ability to decode words in sequence does not necessarily indicate understanding of what is read. On the other hand, oral reading can be the start of a discussion about content, form, and style. Working on literal comprehension of content, a teacher tells a group that has read a passage silently, "Find and read aloud the sentence that describes little Willy's feeling toward his grandfather." Working on comprehension of form, the teacher suggests, "Read aloud a sentence that the author uses to sum up what she is saying." Tapping children's feelings for the sounds of language, the teacher proposes, "Read aloud a sentence that sounds like music." As children volunteer, the teacher helps them read rhythmically, suggesting that a group reread the lines with flair and feeling, phrasing words in chunks of meaning, and reflecting the punctuation signals. In this context, oral reading is a time for appreciating the rhythm of written language. It is a time for working with the "whole" language.

One-to-One Reading for Teaching and Diagnosis of Reading Problems

With children who read on a sound-by-sound basis or have trouble decoding the sounds of their language, the teacher is wise to schedule time for individual oral reading. During a reading conference held while others are reading to themselves or to classmates, the teacher takes these steps:

1. Asks the child to read a short passage at his or her instructional level and talk about his or her reaction to it.
2. Praises the child for something done well, particularly the self-corrections the child has made in decoding.
3. Discusses one or two miscues, or decoding errors, the child did not self-correct.
4. Provides the child with decoding instruction relative to a specific miscue the child has shown. This last step can occur in a small group that the teacher has organized based on a common miscue problem.

Barbara Taylor and Linda Nosbush (1983), who have researched one-to-one oral reading that includes these four steps, report that through its use, poorer readers improve their self-correcting behavior and their overall ability to read for meaning.

One-to-one reading is also a fine setting for diagnosing a child's ability to

See Ken Goodman, *Miscue Analysis: Applications to Reading Instruction* (Urbana, Ill.: National Council of Teachers of English, 1973).

decode, or crack the written code and turn it into meaningful units of thought. In an individual conference, as the child reads aloud, the teacher interprets his or her pattern of miscues, or decoding errors. *Miscue analysis* provides valuable clues to a reader's interaction with a text (Goodman and Burke, 1972).

Summarizing ideas about miscue analysis, Burns, Roe, and Ross (1992) suggest five kinds of questions the teacher should raise in reference to a child's decoding errors:

1. Is the miscue a result of the reader's dialect? If he says *foe* for *four*, he may be simply using a familiar pronunciation that does not affect meaning.
2. Does the miscue change the meaning? If he says *dismal* for *dismiss*, the meaning is likely changed and the substitution would not make sense.
3. Does the reader self-correct? If she says a word that does not make sense but self-corrects, she is trying to make sense of reading.
4. Is he using syntactic cues? If he says *run* for *chase*, he still shows some use of syntactic cues, but if he says *boy* for *beautiful*, he is probably losing the syntactic pattern.
5. Is she using graphic cues? Comparing the sounds and spellings of miscues and expected words in substitutions will reveal how a reader is using graphic cues. Examples of such miscues include *house* for *horse, running* for *run, is* for *it*, and *dogs* for *dog*.

Analyzing a child's miscues in this way provides the teacher with information on what to emphasize with a child: phoneme-grapheme relationships, use of context clues, or use of prediction based on what the child knows about language.

✎ BUILDING AND REFINING YOUR TEACHING SKILLS

✦ This section has presented strategies for helping children build beginning reading skills (e.g., visual discrimination, left-to-right progression, auditory discrimination, sight word vocabulary, sound-symbol decoding skills, use of contextual clues). These strategies include writing and reading stories in which particular speech sounds repeat, masking words with tape, matching words, reconstruction of stories, joining in while listening to repetitive stories, reading along while listening, choral reading, collaborative reading, paired reading, and one-to-one reading. These strategies can be used in reference to big books, charted stories that children have dictated, and/or stories that children are reading from a regular book. Devise a meaning-based lesson that employs one or more of these strategies.

✦ Create a set of materials to help children build early reading skills as part of a shared book experience.

Comprehension: Interacting and Constructing Meaning with Text

Kurt selected a book. He had read other books by the same author, and the cover and title of this one struck his fancy. He read the jacket blurb and then flipped through, looking at the black-and-white line drawings and the chapter titles. The book appeared to be an adventure story—a chase, and he was in the mood for some exciting reading, so he decided to try it.

Sprawling on the floor, Kurt began to read. In the first chapter, he met Jake, the main character, and learned what Jake's problem was; his father had died, leaving Jake and his dog—Jim Ugly—alone. Reading between the lines, Kurt figured out that Jake must be about his own age. He made a fast judgment, too: He decided that he was going to like this book. It was about someone to whom he could relate. Shortly, he was totally immersed in the story, so engrossed in it that he visualized himself as part of the action. Later, having read several chapters, Kurt heard his mother call and had to put down the book, but in doing so he took Jake with him. Now, in his imagination, he spun a tale of his own, of meeting Jake and of the adventure the two would have together.

An Interactive-Constructive (I-C) Model of Reading

Good readers like Kurt interact with texts they are reading. They have personal expectations about what they will get from a selection, and they bring those expectations to bear as they read by predicting and testing their predictions. They actively create meaning by constructing, or generating, relationships between what is within the text and what they already know. This view of reading is called *interactive-constructive*. Proponents of an interactive-constructive (I-C) model of reading believe that the meanings a reader makes depend on what both the reader and the author bring to the text, as shown in Figure 13.2. In contrast, a bottom-up, or text-driven, view of reading sees meaning as residing in the text: The reader's job is to "get at" that meaning by working from the parts (the sounds, letters, individual words) to the whole (the story meanings). An interactive model contrasts, too, with a top-down, or reader-based, view, which sees meaning residing entirely in the reader: According to top-down theory, what the reader makes of a text is what that text is all about (Miller, 1988).

World Knowledge and Reading   In constructing meaning, good readers draw on their prior knowledge of the subject—their "world knowledge." Readers have networks of prior understanding about a topic, what theorists call *schemata*. A schema is a set of expectations, or what George Miller (1988) calls "an abstract knowledge structure stored in long-term memory." In reading, readers modify and add to their existing schemata. From this perspective, the prior knowledge readers have about a subject has as much to do with their comprehension of a passage as the actual words written in it.

Jerome Harste (1989) defines reading as the "process of constructing meaning through a dynamic interaction between the reader's existing knowledge, the information suggested by the written text, and the context of the reading situation."

For a practical discussion of prior experiences in reading, see Cathy Wilson, "Teaching Reading Comprehension by Connecting the Known to the New," *The Reading Teacher*, 36 (January 1983), 382–391.

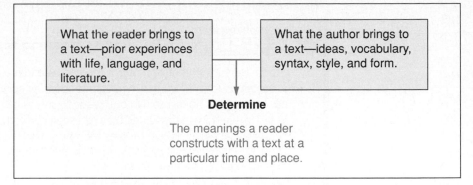

Figure 13.2 An Interactive-Constructive Model of Reading

NOTE: An I-C model suggests that each child's interaction with a particular text differs and that each child constructs meanings that are uniquely his or her own. Instruction based on an I-C model includes considerable individualization.

Researchers have investigated the effect of prior knowledge on comprehension. In one study (Miller, 1988) sixth-graders were asked to read two passages—one about the game of horseshoes, which was familiar to them, and one about an unfamiliar game. The children's comprehension of the passage about the familiar game of horseshoes was greater than their comprehension of the passage about the unfamiliar game. As Miller (1988) explains, the children's existing "horseshoe schema" helped them to "organize and remember the information in the text about the game of horseshoes."

Some theorists (Hirsch, 1987; Ravitch and Finn, 1987) suggest that educators have not given enough attention to the development of children's world knowledge. They contend that young people lack the network of information necessary to read news magazines and newspapers with any degree of comprehension. For example, some high school seniors cannot identify the country on the southern border of the United States and cannot name the New England states. To help children learn to read, these theorists propose, the school must provide a curriculum that requires them to read significant content.

Linguistic Knowledge and Reading   As Figure 13.2 shows, in making meaning good readers simultaneously draw on their knowledge of how language works—their "linguistic knowledge." They apply their understanding of how written symbols are used to represent speech sounds, how sentences are structured (word order), and how ideas are linked into a cohesive message. Look, for example, at this paragraph:

> The monkey swung from tree to tree. When she found a ripe banana, she would stop and pick it, peel it, and eat it. Then she would continue her trip through the trees.

1. Jerome Harste summarizes current reading research and theory: "Linguists tell us that meaning is what language is all about. Without meaning, language is nonsense. No one reads to sound out words; no one writes to see how many words they can spell correctly. Reading and writing are social events which have as their purposes communication and learning" (*New Policy Guidelines for Reading* [Urbana, Ill.: National Council of Teachers of English, 1989], 15).

2. Margaret Meeks describes what happens when a reader reads: "[The reader] recreates the meaning by processing the text at his own speed and in his own way. As he brings the text to life, he casts back and forth in his head for connections between what he is reading and what he already knows. His eyes scan forward or jump backwards. He pauses, rushes on, selects from his memory whatever relates the meaning to his experience or his earlier reading, in a rich and complex system of to-ing and fro-ing in his head, storing, reworking, understanding or being puzzled. Some successful readers say that they feel they are helping to create the work *with* the author. Children talk about being *in* a book, as if that were a place. We know we can possess a book in our heads after the actual volume has been returned to the library. Sometimes we carry phrases and characters about with us for the rest of our lives. . . . This is what the learner has to learn to do, and what we expect teachers to teach" (*Learning to Read* [Portsmouth, N.H.: Heinemann Educational Books, 1982], 21).

Questions to Consider

What do you do when you read? In what way is your mental activity similar to that described by Meeks? In what way does your reading differ? When have you read a book or an article and carried it around in your head for days and weeks? Why did you read that book? How can you help children become to-ing and fro-ing, interactive readers.

To understand this paragraph, readers obviously must be able to decode the words. But equally important, readers must understand word relationships within sentences. They must link the pronoun *it* with its antecedent, *a ripe banana.* They must recognize the time relationships implied by *when* and *then.* They must link the *trip through the trees* in the last sentence to the monkey swinging from tree to tree in the first. Today reading specialists suggest that an important aspect of comprehension is being able to make the linkages suggested by linguistic clues such as these, which give coherence to a selection (Moe and Irwin, 1986).

Knowledge of Text Structure and Reading   The knowledge of text structure that readers bring to a selection also affects comprehension. A story has a structure that includes setting and characters, problem, action and reaction sequences leading to a resolution of the problem, and a theme that binds the story together. An informational passage develops logically, often starting with an introduction that sets forth the thesis, or main idea, and the points that are to come. Headings indicate major sections of the text, and a summary reviews main points. A poem may have a repeating pattern. Writing is by design, not by chance. Being able to perceive and use this design while reading aids comprehension.

Metacognitive Knowledge and Reading   A reader's metacognitive knowledge also determines the meanings that a reader makes with a text. *Metacognition* refers to people's awareness of how they learn, know, and read; it refers to their awareness of how they go about making meaning and how they monitor their own comprehension during reading. Good readers monitor their comprehension knowingly as they read. They raise and answer questions in their heads, they visualize, they predict, they correct their predictions as they go along, they summarize to themselves, and they reread when they know they do not understand. In short, good readers have reading know-how: They know how they approach reading, and they vary their strategies depending on their purpose and the material they are reading. According to Ann Brown et al. (1986), metacognitive control is highly important in reading success.

In sum, readers bring four kinds of knowledge and awareness to reading that affect comprehension: world knowledge, linguistic knowledge, text-structure knowledge, and metacognitive knowledge. In the remainder of this section and in the next section, we will think about ways to help children activate what they know about life, language, and literature as they make meaning with text. We will begin by talking about before-reading activities that heighten comprehension, move to consideration of things to do while reading, and then consider after-reading possibilities.

For a discussion of metacognition and its importance for poorer readers, check Annemarie Palincsar and Kathryn Ransom, "From the Mystery Spot to the Thoughtful Spot: The Instruction of Metacognitive Strategies," *The Reading Teacher,* 41 (April 1988), 784–789. Palincsar and Ransom define *metacognition* as "knowledge of the factors that affect learning activity, including reading, as well as control of these factors."

Before Reading: Activating a Framework for Comprehending

Effective teachers teach young readers strategies for activating what they know on a topic and for increasing their knowledge before reading.

Before-Reading Experiences with Content   As we saw in the vignette that opens this chapter, Ms. Wilkening involved her kindergartners in before-reading talk—talk that prepared them for interactive-constructive reading. Using the encyclopedia pictures, Ms. Wilkening first sparked children's talk about the hippopotamus and how the hippo wallows in the mud, using the word *wallows* in the before-reading talk time and pantomiming the action. Next, Ms. Wilkening shared the encyclopedia pictures of the rhinoceros and got children to talk about the rhinoceros's horns, knowledge important to comprehension in that the hippo's lack of a horn is the problem that starts the story action. Then she involved them in a discussion of the word *ridiculous*. This made it possible for children to predict reasons for the rhino's saying to the hippo, "You look ridiculous."

Teachers need to teach children to predict what they think will happen in a reading selection before reading; prediction gives readers a purpose for reading and a framework for understanding what they read. Children read to test their predictions, or hypotheses. This instructional sequence—predicting before reading, reading to test predictions, and clarifying ideas through discussion after reading—is essentially the sequence of a Directed Reading-Thinking Activity (Stauffer, 1980).

Predictive questions teachers can ask young readers as part of before-reading talk include these:

1. Read the title, study the cover, look at the pictures, and then predict: Who is this about? What is this going to be about? What do you already know about this topic?
2. Look at the way the words are put on the paper and how the lines are organized. Predict: Is it a story? Is it a poem? Is it about facts?
3. Set your purpose: What do you want to get out of this? Fun? Facts? Feeling?
4. Decide: How should you read this? Fast? Carefully?

Teachers can ask upper elementary readers more advanced questions:

1. Read the title. Study the cover, the pictures, charts, graphs, and tables. Scan the passage and read the words in italics and boldface. Read headings and subheadings, if any. Scan the first paragraph and the last. Predict: What is this going to be about? What do you already know about this topic and about this form of writing? Do you need to get more information from another source before you begin?
2. Decide: What kind of piece is this? Story? Poem? Factual article? Very detailed informational piece? Humorous piece?
3. Decide: How is the selection organized? Is there an introduction? A summary at the end? Study questions at the beginning or end? What kind of material is up front? At the end? How are the headings and subheadings laid out? Will the graphics be useful? How?
4. Decide: What do you want to get out of this? Fun? Fantasy? Feelings? Facts?
5. Decide: How will you read this? Just skim for big ideas? Read fast? Read for details? Take notes?

These questions are the same ones youngsters should raise as they prepare for independent reading, especially the reading they do as part of content-area study. By asking these predictive questions during classroom discussion before reading, teachers are modeling the strategies students should use as they read and study on their own.

Before-Reading Experiences with Vocabulary Teachers can also prepare children for reading by working informally with some of the vocabulary

For a discussion of predictive-type questions, read Denise Nessel, "The New Face of Comprehension Instruction: A Closer Look at Questions," *The Reading Teacher*, 40 (March 1987), 604–607.

Read Camille Blachowicz and John Lee, "Vocabulary Development in the Whole Literacy Classroom," *The Reading Teacher*, 45 (November 1991), 188–195.

from the selection. Ms. Wilkening did this by using the words *rhinoceros, hippopotamus,* and *ridiculous* before reading and by having children recall that *ridiculous* means "silly." During the reading, she did it, too, by having the children chorus the repeating line "Do you think I look ridiculous?"

Using the words of a selection during before-reading discussion is perhaps the most natural way to introduce vocabulary essential in comprehending a selection, but there are other ways to do it. One way is brainstorming, followed by webbing. Using this approach, the teacher asks children to call out words, phrases, or ideas that come to mind when they think of the topic of a selection they are about to read. The teacher contributes more difficult words from the selection. The teacher or student scribes record brainstormed items on the board. Guided by teacher questions, participants organize the items in a web that highlights relationships; in other words, youngsters put items together based on relationships they perceive. They may even leave blanks in their web, which they fill as they read. Figure 13.3 depicts a word web that a fourth-grade class might develop based both on what they already know about the Statue of Liberty before reading an informational selection about Miss Liberty and on what they learn by reading the selection. For other ideas to use in structuring before-reading activity, see Appendix A.

Responding While Reading

As was explained in Chapter 3, much of young children's speech is egocentric, meaning that they talk aloud to themselves. With maturity comes the ability to

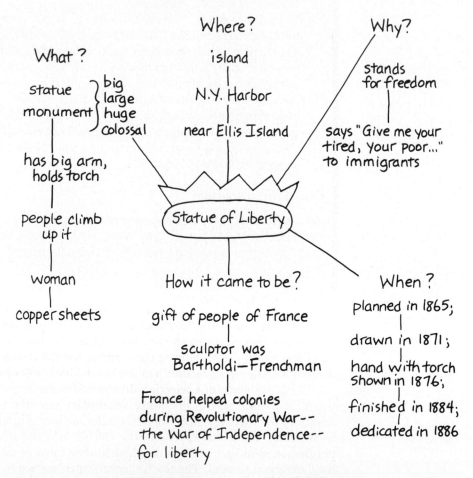

Figure 13.3 A Reading Web Plotted Before and While Reading

direct thoughts to others and the diminution of egocentric speech. Lev Vygotsky (1962) believes that as children mature, egocentric speech is internalized; instead of speaking aloud to themselves, children learn to talk to themselves in their heads. This is inner speech, or mind talk, which is directly related to thought in older children and adults.

Mind talk is what good readers do as they read. They continuously respond to what they read by talking to themselves in their heads (Davey, 1983). They respond by

+ Forming pictures in their minds of what they are reading (visualizing),
+ Linking what they are reading to what they already know,
+ Predicting what is going to happen,
+ Clarifying confusing points,
+ Raising and answering questions about the text and its structure,
+ Evaluating and criticizing what they are reading,
+ Correcting errors in comprehension.

Responding Through Mind Talk Beth Davey (1983), Roger Farr (1987), and Allan Collins, John Seely Brown, and Ann Holum (1991) recommend that the teacher orally model the process of mind talking while reading. Here *modeling* means reading aloud and describing the thoughts that come to mind before, during, and after reading a particular selection. Essentially, what the teacher does is show students how to talk to themselves as part of reading—how to respond by generating their own text and how to monitor their own comprehension. As Collins, Brown, and Holum (1991) explain, "One needs to deliberately bring the thinking to the surface, to make it visible."

How does a think aloud sound in action? Here is an example with the teacher's mind talk, or think-aloud comments, in italics and the text by the author in regular print:

The Bridge They Said Couldn't Be Built
I can tell from the pictures that this is going to be about the Brooklyn Bridge. That's near New York City. It's probably going to tell about how the bridge was built. I wonder why they said it couldn't be built. I'll see as I read.

New York in the Winter of 1866–1867
The winter of 1866–67 *That was just after the Civil War* was one of the worst ever recorded in the history of New York. Snow covered most of the area, and great blocks of ice clogged the East River between Manhattan and Brooklyn. *The East River must separate Manhattan and Brooklyn.* Often the Fulton Street ferryboat was unable to cross the East River. *That was because the ice blocked the river.* So people trying to get to work in Manhattan or return home to Brooklyn were jammed up at each river bank. *I guess the Brooklyn Bridge hadn't yet been built.* What's more, with no electricity and no telephones, there was no way of communicating across the river except by boat. *The telephone and electricity must have been invented after 1867.*

John A. Roebling
One person who didn't think a bridge was impossible was an engineer named John A. Roebling. Roebling was known throughout the world as the expert bridge

This selection is from Lee Sheridan, "The Bridge They Said Couldn't Be Built," in *In Concert* by Leo Fay et al. (Chicago: Riverside Publishing, 1989).

builder of the day. *I guess he had made a lot of bridges.* Suspension bridges were his specialty. *The Golden Gate Bridge is a suspension bridge.* A suspension bridge is a bridge suspended by wire cables hung over towers and fastened on the land at both ends. *That's the definition of a suspension bridge—suspended by wire cables hung over towers and fastened on the land at both ends. I can picture that in my head.*

Roebling had founded his own Wire Rope Company to manufacture the cables for suspension bridges. *I guess he called it wire rope because he was making wire cables.* In 1866 he had just completed the longest suspension bridge ever built—a bridge in Cincinnati over the Ohio River. If anyone could build a suspension bridge over the East River—a length of half a mile—John A. Roebling was the one to do it. *The East River Bridge is half a mile long. That's long.*

Several years earlier, Roebling had submitted a plan for a suspension bridge connecting Manhattan and Brooklyn. No other kind of bridge could be built across an area as wide as the East River and also allow ships to pass underneath. *The East River must have been an important shipping route—many ships because of New York City.* Still, the officials of both New York and Brooklyn had doubts. They rejected Roebling's first plan as impossible. *It says first plan, so he must have kept trying. He must have believed it could be done.*

Suspension Bridges of the Time

Of course, New Yorkers were not exactly wrong to be suspicious of suspension bridges. *Why?* As a rule, suspension bridges in the first half of the nineteenth century *That means the early 1800s* did not seem to have much staying power. *Staying power means the ability to stand up.* The Dryburgh Abbey Bridge in Scotland and several great bridges in England had all been wrecked by high winds. *I guess the winds would be strong across expanses of water.* The world-famous Menai Strait Bridge in Wales would often twist and bounce as high as sixteen feet! *That's three times the height of a person.* It snapped in strong winds and broke three different times, the last in 1839. *But that was 25 years before.*

Tales of disaster on suspension bridges continued. The Roche-Bernard Bridge in France broke down, dropping a railroad train into the river. In the United States, two suspension bridges had broken in storms. *In a storm because that was when the winds were strong.* One of them, the Wheeling Bridge, completely overturned before it plunged into the Ohio River. *I guess that people said the Brooklyn Bridge couldn't be built because of all these disasters. That was pretty scary.*

Farr (1987) suggests that children who have followed a text while listening to a teacher read and orally mind talk identify the strategies the teacher used to think about the selection. Students can record strategies brainstorm fashion on the chalkboard. In this case, they identify the teacher's before-reading predicting based on the title and the pictures, reading to test predictions, visualizing, questioning and answering, relating content to facts already known, correcting of interpretations, clarifying relationships in the text, inferring, restating key information (the definition), and figuring out the meaning of words from context clues. Children volunteer to read successive passages aloud and tell what they are thinking as they read, using some of the same strategies. They pair off to practice mind talk while reading. Eventually children practice the strategies while reading to themselves.

Davey (1983) recommends using self-assessment checklists to monitor thinking-while-reading behavior. An example is given in Figure 13.4. During follow-up discussion, youngsters describe the thoughts that went through their heads as they read.

Responding by Thinking at Progressively Higher Levels   Simple question-and-answer sequences also can help children become interactive-constructive readers. The teacher asks questions that require children to construct meaning from print. In responding aloud, children talk through their thoughts—something they do in their heads when they read independently. After such a discussion, the teacher asks students to identify the kinds, or levels, of questions he or she asked during the discussion and records them on the chalkboard. The teacher explains that these are the same kinds, or levels, of questions they can ask themselves when reading independently. Children can carry on a similar dialogue with themselves as they read on their own. Later children practice asking themselves questions during reading.

    Levels of questions the teacher should model are literal, interpretive, critical, and creative (Burns, Roe, and Ross, 1992). *Literal comprehension* involves the reader with information stated in a selection. That information may be facts, sequences of events, main ideas and generalizations, or causes and effects. In literal comprehension the key element is that the information is spelled out in "black and white." As Burns, Roe, and Ross explain, literal comprehension is fundamental; it requires a thorough understanding of word, sentence, and paragraph meanings and is necessary for higher levels of comprehension.

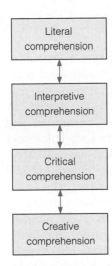

MY THOUGHTS WHILE READING			
	Never	**Some**	**A Lot**
1. I made predictions.			
2. I made pictures in my mind.			
3. I asked myself questions and answered them.			
4. I thought about things I already knew.			
5. I corrected my predictions as I read.			
6. I explained things to myself in my head.			
7. I figured out word meanings by the context of the sentence.			
8. I reread when I knew I did not understand.			

Figure 13.4   A Checklist of Thinking-While-Reading Behaviors

NOTE: Students complete the list after reading a selection, checking items that apply to that particular reading, and explaining how they used each strategy.

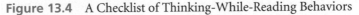

Examples of literal comprehension questions to ask when reading a story include the following:

+ Who are the main characters in the story?
+ Where and when does the story take place?
+ What is the problem, or conflict, in the story?
+ What are the major events?
+ How is the problem resolved?

Literal questions to ask when reading nonfiction start similarly with *who, where, when, what,* and *how.*

Reading at the *interpretive level* means reading between the lines, generating information and ideas not directly stated. In doing this, the reader must make an inference. He or she may have to infer time relationships, such as the year, time of day, or season; geographical relationships; cause-and-effect relationships; the ages, feelings, family relationships of characters; and main ideas and generalizations if these points are not stated explicitly in the text. The reader must study the facts given and put two and two together to make the inference.

Interpretive reading also involves ferreting out meanings communicated through idioms, literary allusions, and figures of speech. The author who writes of a character, "He had no heart," does not mean this literally but is relying on an idiom. The author who describes a man with a Midas touch is communicating something special, too, something meaningful only to the reader who recognizes the allusion to the king who wanted everything he touched to turn to gold. When poet Alfred, Lord Tennyson, wrote of "crossing the bar," he was referring metaphorically to death, not speaking literally of crossing a sand bar. One of the most difficult interpretations readers must make relates to these kinds of references. Readers must bring to bear their previous experiences with language, literature, and life in constructing meanings.

For a discussion of ways to involve children in inferential thinking, read Kathryn Carr, "The Importance of Inference Skills in the Primary Grades," *The Reading Teacher,* 36 (February 1983), 518–520.

Why and *how* questions are inferential if the answers are not given directly in the text. Here are some examples: Why did the man help the driver of the cart? Why did the driver of the cart offer the woman a ride? Why did the woman offer the boy some bread and preserves? How are the stories similar? Different? How are the incidents in the story related to the title "One Good Turn"? What does *preserve* mean in "May heaven preserve you" and in "I believe I smell my favorite peach preserves"? How bad is a "bad" accident?

Teachers can ask for physical and visual as well as verbal responses as they model interpretive thinking: "Show me how the woman moved down the road. Read the driver's statement using your voice the way the driver must have used his. Show on your face the expression that must have been on the boy's face at the end of the story." To help children with figurative meanings, teachers can propose that children draw pictures depicting literal and figurative meanings of phrases in a selection. This is particularly useful with idioms and hyperboles; children enjoy drawing the literal meanings communicated by such phrases as "She wore her heart on her sleeve" and "He was so thin he could fit through a keyhole."

Critical reading requires making judgments. Readers may judge the accuracy of facts, the validity of conclusions drawn, the author's style and competence. They may decide whether they like the way the author began the piece, developed it, ended it, used examples to illustrate the main point, clarified difficult ideas, put words and sentences together, and used figurative language. At its best, critical reading requires suspension of judgment until all the evidence is in, giving reasons for the judgment, and stating the criteria used in making it.

Questions that lead to critical thinking include: Which act in the story was the kindest? Tell why. Which person acted most honestly? Give a reason for selecting him or her. Why was the boy's act a good one? Tell why. What about the story did you like? Dislike? Tell why. At what point in the story were you most surprised? Pleased? Tell why. Which story did you like better? Tell why.

Creative reading calls for the generation of new ideas, insights, applications, and approaches. It requires invention, prediction, and use of the imagination. Proposing an original conclusion or generalization, suggesting related examples and orally composing, drawing, and writing stories with the same pattern or the same words as one read are exercises in creative reading.

Examples of probes that involve readers in creative thinking are: Predict what will happen when the driver of the cart comes upon a woman walking alone. Describe a situation in your life when the moral "One good turn deserves another" applied. Describe someone to whom you could apply the label *generous*. Describe an act you have seen that was as generous as those in the fable. Probes such as these that ask children to predict story outcomes and make applications to their own lives are particularly good for triggering creative reading and for encouring children to mind talk as they read.

One problem often perceived in reading instruction is a predominance of questions and activities that require literal thinking. Without a doubt, readers ask themselves these kinds of questions to get the facts straight. However, fine readers go beyond to think at higher levels as they read.

Responding Through Writing   Writing while reading is another strategy that leads to interactive-constructive reading. One way to encourage writing is the literature response journal. Students record in their journals as they get ready to read, while they read, and after reading. Figure 13.5 shows a form upper-graders can use to guide them as they write and read. Younger children can respond by drawing pictures or writing with invented spellings.

Some teachers give students a prompt or two to think and write about while reading. For example, as her third-graders read a chapter of *Thanksgiving Treasure* by Gail Rock, Ms. Benjamin asked them to consider whether it was ever right to lie or to do something underhanded as the story character did in the chapter read. Children responded to the prompt by writing in their literature response journals. Later they enthusiastically shared their written responses and talked about them. Good prompts for triggering active responses while reading are those such as Ms. Benjamin's that ask for inferential, critical, or creative thinking.

Patricia Kelly (1990) suggests three prompts for triggering a response to literature: (1) What did you notice in the story? (2) How did the story make you

Review the chart of critical-thinking questions in Chapter 8 on page 261. Also check Martha Haggard, "Developing Critical Thinking with the Directed Reading-Thinking Activity," *The Reading Teacher,* 41 (February 1988), 526–533; M. Gail Hickey, "Developing Critical Reading Readiness in Primary Grades," *The Reading Teacher,* 42 (December 1988), 192–193; and Linda Flynn, "Developing Critical Reading Skills Through Cooperative Problem Solving," *The Reading Teacher,* 42 (May 1989), 664–668.

Read D. Barone, "The Written Responses of Young Children," *The New Advocate,* 3 (1990), 49–56, and L. Galda, "Readers, Texts, and Contexts: A Response-based View of Literature in the Classroom," *The New Advocate,* 1 (1988), 92–102.

Read Joanne Hindley, "Books in the Classroom," *The Horn Book* (September/October 1990), 579–586, for one teacher's account of how she and her fourth-graders spent a year together reading and responding to literature. See also Julie Wollman-Bonilla, "Reading Journals: Invitations to Participate in Literature," *The Reading Teacher,* 43 (November 1989), 112–120, for ways to use journals.

MY RESPONSE RECORD

My response to the selection ______________________________

by ______________________________

Date and time when I began to read the book or selection:

MY THOUGHTS AND PREDICTIONS BEFORE READING (record what you think the book or selection is going to be about and what you already know about that topic; make the outline of a story map, a web, a time line, a flow chart, or a data chart to use to take notes when you read):

MY NOTES WHILE READING (make doodles or drawings, jot down ideas that stick in your mind, and/or complete your idea web, time line, flow chart, or data chart as you read):

DATE AND TIME WHEN I FINISHED READING THE BOOK OR SELECTION:

MY NOTES AFTER READING (what you liked or disliked, what you agreed with or disagreed with, how you felt, what this reminded you of, what you learned):

SHARING RECORD:

Date	Students with whom I shared

Figure 13.5 A Reader's Response Record

feel? (3) What does this story remind you of in your own life? In using these prompts with third-graders, Kelly provided a five-minute writing time and an opportunity for students to share their responses with the class. This teacher found that one-line responses dominated initial attempts, but as students became familiar with responding to literature in this way, their responses became more detailed and went beyond literal retelling. Students were increasingly able to put their feelings into words and actually displayed fewer errors in sentence structure.

Some teachers, like Marjorie Hancock (1992), ask children to respond without providing prompts. These teachers encourage students to record "the thoughts going on in their heads." They stress "honesty and trust" in writing responses, downplay correct spelling and writing mechanics, and reply to students' entries with encouraging, nonevaluative comments. As an example of this kind of freewheeling written response, Hancock (1992) provides this series by a sixth-grader:

> Poor Brian you had a great idea but alas, it did not work Well if at first you don't succeed, try and try again (a response while reading Gary Paulsen's *Hatchet* [1987]).

> Reaching out, don't you understand it's just trying to grab a hold and not let go, search until you find your answer. I know you can understand, Dicey. Just try, you can. I know you. I know you can (a response while reading Cynthia Voigt's *Dicey's Song* [1982]).

> Was there really a face in the window? Was someone watching you Ned? What if dad was watching you or mom or Mrs. S. Are you in trouble could you have shot an animal? Listen to your conscience (a response while reading Paula Fox's *One-Eyed Cat* [1984]).

Carole Cox and Joyce Many (1992) provide an example of an eleven-year-old's response to *A Proud Taste for Scarlet and Miniver* (Konigsburg, 1973). Winke's first responses were simply retellings of the book. Then she made a connection with another book and began a story of her own based on it. Finally, she came "face to face with her own beliefs as a result of reading":

> I wonder about life. That lots of people change, even when they are older. Which disagrees with a thought I had—it was harder to change when you are older. Maybe you couldn't change at all. This book makes me disagree with that.

Cox and Many suggest that as Winke wrote, she began to construct her own meaning, her own reality. Her response became aesthetic and centered on her own images, feelings, sensations, moods, and ideas. She began to picture the story in her mind, to extend it by hypothesizing how it could be different, and to relate associations to her own life. For this kind of aesthetic response to happen, Cox and Many propose that students must be free to choose how they will "organize their evocation of a text"—as a poem, a vignette, or whatever. The open-ended prompt these authors suggest is simply "Write anything you want about the story you just read." These authors also stress the importance of providing time for children to respond, opportunities to respond over time, and opportunities for students to talk to themselves, to one another, and to the teacher.

Responding after Reading: Talking, Acting, Drawing, and Writing

There are numerous ways teachers can help children think in depth about what they have read. These include talking about, acting, drawing, and writing.

Talking About   Discussion is a logical follow-up to reading in classrooms. Talking about ideas helps readers to see relationships and to expand their thinking on a topic.

See Chapter 1, page 31, for a discussion of ways to plan literature-based lessons in situations where the teacher is required to use a basal reading series.

One approach to discussion after children have read a selection is the *Literature Group* (Peterson, 1987; Watson, 1988), in which a group of children choose a book to read and discuss. They read that book independently and respond to it by writing in their literature response journals.

When children gather in their Literature Group for discussion with their teacher, their purpose is to reflect and to exchange ideas in a dialogue. As Dorothy Watson (1988) explains, teachers begin a dialogue by asking children to read from their journals or by asking a question that is "an invitation to dialogue":

> What do you think? How are you different now from when you started this book? What do you know or think about now that you didn't know or think about before you started this book? Would you like to share something with us? What would you like to ask the author, or someone in the group, about the book? Does this book remind you of any other literature you know? How did the author get you to think? How did the author get you to feel happy, scared, sad? Do you see any patterns in the pictures or in the story?

Notice that none of Watson's invitations to dialogue are literal questions; rather, they are higher-level, personal-reaction probes. After students have reflected together on a selection, the teacher can review with members of the Literature Group the kinds of questions they used in their dialogue. Children can ask themselves the same kinds of questions during reading and after reading when writing in their journals.

For a description of response groups, read Judith Gold et al., "Whole Language and Teacher/Librarian Partnerships," *Phi Delta Kappan,* 73 (March 1992), 536–537.

Taffy Raphael (1992) proposes a related approach that she calls a Book Club. A Book Club is a group of three to six students who read books, keep literature response journals, participate in Book Club discussions as well as "Community Shares," and learn from their teacher what and how to share. In contrast to a Literature-Group discussion, Book-Club discussions are student led; such roles as facilitator emerge as the group functions as a unit. In their club meetings, students begin by sharing their written responses and then react to them. Community Shares are large-group discussions used to raise students' awareness of what they are going to read and to provide a place for Book Club members to share their findings.

Anthony Manzo (1975, 1985) suggests a more structured discussion approach for dealing with content-area passages—a Guided Reading Procedure (GRP) in which the teacher prepares students for reading by first activating what they know about the content and then setting a purpose for reading. Students read with this purpose in mind. Having read, they brainstorm the facts and ideas they remember as a scribe records those data—whether correct or incorrect—on the board. Children then reread to find data they forgot and to make corrections in what they have recorded.

To help children perceive relationships, the teacher encourages them to manipulate the data, grouping them to clarify relationships such as cause-effect and sequence. At times students group data into charts, grids, webs, or time lines. When students have experienced the Guided Reading Procedure on several occasions, the teacher verbally reviews the steps in the strategy, for students can use the same steps as a comprehension strategy when reading on their own. In doing this, the teacher is helping children develop metacognitive awareness.

In "The Mind's Journey from Novice to Expert," *American Educator,* 17 (Summer 1993), 6–15, 38–46, John Bruer summarizes the research evidence behind reciprocal teaching. This is a "must-read" article.

Annemarie Palincsar and Ann Brown (1985) recommend reciprocal teaching as a discussion strategy after students have read nonfiction. The teacher begins the after-reading discussion by asking a question based on a paragraph, summarizing the material, and making a prediction or a clarification of any difficult parts. Having modeled the comprehension strategy, the teacher asks readers to do the same with another paragraph. The approach is called *reciprocal* because teacher and students take turns being the teacher and asking the questions. Here again, students are building a comprehension strategy of their own and are developing metacognitive understanding. Students are being taught "to monitor their reading to ensure that they are understanding." According to Palincsar and Brown (1986), "Reciprocal teaching has been effectively implemented in both small and large group settings, in a peer tutoring situation, in content area instruction, and most recently in listening comprehension instruction." It also has potential for use with narratives.

Diagnosis of learning problems is an ongoing part of teacher-student dialogue of the kinds just described. Even as children contribute to a discussion, the teacher is observing and assessing their reading-response behaviors. During any one discussion period, the teacher focuses on the behavior of one or two students, using an anecdotal record form as in Figures 13.6 and 13.7 as a guide. After the discussion, the teacher takes a moment to write brief comments about the student or students observed. Or the teacher can use such a form during a teacher-student conference that focuses on a child's independent reading. The teacher asks questions based on the items on the form and notes the student's response on the guide.

Acting and Drawing   Drama, pantomime, and choral speaking are other oral activities that are effective after reading. Having read a story or having read about an event from the past, children can dramatize it. Having read a poem, they can chorus it. Such activities encourage children to think creatively about what they have read.

Just as youngsters use drawing to rehearse for writing, so can they draw pictures after reading. Pictures can take any number of related forms: free art, story

TEACHER OBSERVATION AND EVALUATION GUIDE FOR A LITERATURE SHARING TIME — FICTION	

Student _____ Date _____

Book/Author _____

Reading behaviors	Comments
1. Told the main events of the story.	
2. Identified the big idea of the story.	
3. Used a graphic organizer to map story relationships.	
4. Told how he or she felt as a result of reading the story.	
5. Related the story to his or her personal experiences.	
6. Identified parts he or she liked or disliked and told why.	
7. Compared this story to other stories he or she had read.	
8. Wrote and shared a story of his or her own based on a story read.	

Figure 13.6 An Anecdotal Record Form for Observing Reading Behaviors: Story Contexts

staircases, picture flowcharts, maps, and illustrated time lines. Drawing flows back into talking as children share their drawings; in so doing, children expand on the topic to make new meanings.

Read Evelyn Cudd and Leslie Roberts, "Using Writing to Enhance Content Area Learning in the Primary Grades," *The Reading Teacher,* 42 (February 1989), 392–404.

Writing   Writing, as we have already seen, is a natural follow-up to reading and can take place before and during reading as well. Reflecting on the importance of writing within reading programs, James Squire (1983) states, "Composing is critical to thought processes because it is a process which actively engages the learner in constructing meaning, in developing ideas, in relating ideas, in expressing ideas. . . . To possess an idea that one is reading about

TEACHER OBSERVATION AND EVALUATION GUIDE FOR A CONTENT-AREA READING/SHARING TIME — NONFICTION	
Student _____ Date _____	
Book/Author _____	
Reading behaviors	**Comments**
1. Identified the main topic of the selection.	
2. Identified major ideas.	
3. Used new terminology in talking about the selection.	
4. Organized data graphically.	
5. Drew pictures to highlight relationships.	
6. Wrote a summary of major points.	
7. Related ideas to his or her prior experiences.	
8. Proposed related examples.	
9. Told points with which he/she agreed/ disagreed and gave reasons.	

Figure 13.7 An Anecdotal Record Form for Observing Reading Behaviors: Content-Area Contexts

requires competence in regenerating the idea, competence in learning how to write the ideas of another." Today the prevailing opinion is that the teaching of reading cannot be divorced from the teaching of writing.

Writing is a means of reflecting on what one has read. As noted in Chapter 10, research by the National Assessment of Educational Progress indicates that high school students have little ability to write paragraphs that analyze and evaluate passages they have read. This research suggests that in the past we have failed to link reading and writing activities and to use writing to encourage young readers to generate ideas in response to what they have read.

M. C. Wittrock's research on generative reading (1983) suggests that asking students to generate a summary sentence for each paragraph they read "significantly increased their retention and comprehension of the text." Students who also were given paragraph headings to use in their summary sentences doubled their retention and comprehension.

Enjoy Donald Graves and Jane Hansen, "The Author's Chair," *Language Arts,* 60 (February 1983), 176–183, and Jane Hansen, "Authors Respond to Authors," *Language Arts,* 60 (November/December 1983), 970–976.

In the same vein, Frank Smith (1988) talks of teaching children to read like writers. To read like writers, youngsters anticipate what authors are going to say; they collaborate with authors in constructing meaning as they read. But to acquire this skill, readers must write; they must join what Smith calls the literacy club (1992).

The teacher's role here is many-faceted: to help children see purpose in writing, make available reading materials related to the writing children are doing, read aloud to children, encourage recording reactions in journals after reading, record their thoughts for them at times, and encourage children to share their writing with friends. Children should be encouraged to climb into the Author's Chair and read their writing to classmates; they should be given time to read the writings of classmates—writings such as the piece in Figure 13.8, which a third-grader composed after reading articles about Rosa Parks and the book *Journey to Jo'burg* as part of a unit on freedom.

And, of course, talk is part of the reading-writing environment. Children react orally to what they have heard and read, describing parts they liked best and telling why. The result is better readers and better writers—a blend of reading, writing, listening, and speaking as young learners interact naturally with text, with teacher, and with one another.

✎ BUILDING AND REFINING YOUR TEACHING SKILLS

✦ Locate a book to use with a kindergarten or first-grade class. Design questions to ask as part of before-reading talk time to lay a foundation for children's comprehension of the story.

✦ Find an informational selection that fourth-graders can read silently on their own. Lead a group of youngsters in brainstorming and webbing key background information before reading. If you do not have a group of children to work with, brainstorm what you know about the content of the selection and design a web that highlights relationships so that you better understand what is involved in webbing.

✦ Locate a story or informational selection. Read the selection, paying particular attention to the kind of mind talk you do. After reading, use the checklist on page 000 to assess your mind talk.

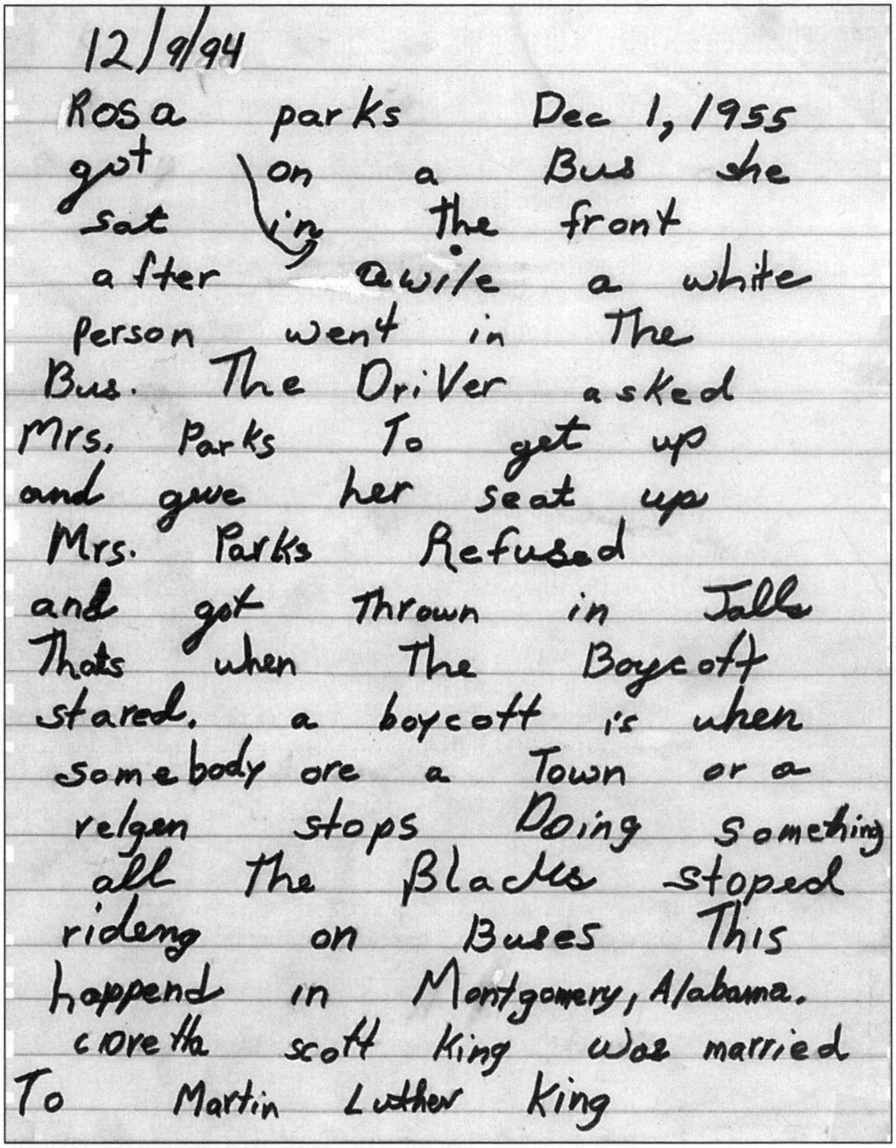

> 12/9/94
>
> Rosa   parks   Dec 1, 1955
> got   on   a   Bus   she
> sat   in   the   front
> after   awile   a   white
> person   went   in   The
> Bus. The DriVer   asked
> Mrs. Parks   To   get   up
> and give   her   seat   up
> Mrs.   Parks   Refused
> and   got   Thrown   in   Jalle
> Thats   when   The   Boycott
> stared.   a   boycott   is   when
> somebody   ore   a   Town   or a
> relgen   stops   Doing   something
> all   The   Blacks   stoped
> rideing   on   Buses   This
> happend   in   Montgomery, Alabama.
> coretta   scott   King   was   married
> To   Martin   Luther   King

Figure 13.8   An Entry from a Third-Grader's Social Studies Log

SOURCE: Courtesy of Helen Spiliotis.

NOTE: Writing about a topic helps students gain ownership over content they are studying. See the paragraph on generative reading on page 474 that indicates the importance of connecting reading and writing in content-area studies.

Comprehending Structure in Stories, Poetry, and Nonfiction

Bill Martin (1974) describes a group of children listening to a selection containing repetitive lines that pattern "Brown bear, brown bear, what do you see?" In successive lines, brown bear becomes red bird and then yellow duck. Hearing the lines, children readily pick up the pattern; when their teacher reads the third repetition, "Yellow duck, yellow duck," without prompting, they join in on the repeating question, "what do you see?"

As Martin explains, children who do this "have figured out how the author put his [or her] story together and they are using this information to help them read pages not even read to them yet." They can anticipate actively because they have learned how the text works. They have figured out the structure and are using it to increase their comprehension.

Comprehending Story Structure

Read M. Dianne Bergenske, "The Missing Link in Narrative Story Mapping," *The Reading Teacher,* 41 (December 1987), 333–335.

Today theorists emphasize the importance of understanding the structure, or overall development, of a story. They contend that children who have within their heads a map, or schema, that embodies how stories develop are better able to comprehend stories they read. According to C. Glenn and N. Stein (1979), stories communicate major pieces of information: a setting, an initiating event, a response, an attempt to satisfy a goal, a consequence, and a reaction. In comprehending a story, students pick up and interpret this key information.

How does the teacher teach so that children perceive story structure? Susan Church (1985) answers that question with a succinct "Not directly." She proposes that children need "many experiences with a variety of genres to allow for the natural development of schemas for text." Here are some ideas for such natural experiences that blend reading stories with listening, speaking, and writing.

See Figure 4.3 for a review of story designs. See also page 123 for a guide to use in plotting out stories before writing. This guide can also be used to map stories read. See Appendix A for ways that children can respond cognitively to a story.

Listening to, Joining in, and Mapping Stories   As Martin (1974) suggests, stories with repeating lines involve young children in story structure. Listeners anticipate the recurring lines and contribute them almost without prompting. Hundreds of storybooks incorporate this feature, especially those based on our folktale heritage: "The Little Red Hen," "The Gingerbread Boy," and "The Three Little Pigs" all have repeating lines that can prompt joining in while listening. Some of these repeating stories are available as big books so that children can follow the lines with their eyes as they anticipate and join in.

Stories in which the action ends where it began and repetition is part of plot development are also good for helping children to perceive the structure of stories. Having listened to these kinds of stories, children can draw a storymap that visually depicts how the story began, how the action developed sequentially, and how the story ended. These maps can take many forms, such as the pie chart in Figure 13.9, the staircase in Figure 10.4, and the flowcharts in Figures 10.5 and 10.6.

Amos and Boris

by William Steig

Amos a mouse is building a boat.
Amos is pushing the boat in
the water. He is sailing when
a head comes out of the water.
Amos is riding on Borises
back. Then Boris took Amos home.
Amos came back with big
elephants and saved Boris.

Figure 13.9   A First-Grader's Circle Pie Chart of *Amos and Boris* by William Steig

Caroll Fisher (1993) writes: "Just as in a good marriage there is more to the couple than two individuals, so in sharing literature by pairs there is more impact than reading two pieces independently."

Older children can also read as a unit stories that rely on a similar plot motif. For example, some stories depict one or more characters as idling while others work—"The Little Red Hen," *Frederick* by Leo Lionni, and *A Treeful of Pigs* by Arnold Lobel. Similarly, some stories depict one or more characters being granted a series of wishes, others are structured around the giving of advice by a wise person, and still others are developed around impossible tasks to be accomplished.

The teacher can assist in making story connections by posing interpretational questions as part of follow-up discussion: How is this story similar to the story we read yesterday? How is it different?

Retelling the Story Lesley Morrow (1985) and Patricia Koskinen (1988) propose that children retell stories they have read. Contributing to a retelling that perhaps takes place as part of a Storytelling Literature Group, children tell and retell stories, each time adding something left out of previous tellings—the setting, a character, a problem, events, or a concluding event. For retelling, the teacher provides cutouts with key transitional words (*Once, Every morning, One morning, All of a sudden, Quickly, When, After that, Then, Because, At last, Finally*) that give structure to the story. As children retell a story, they use these transitional words and hang the appropriate cutouts on the classroom "story line," as in Figure 13.10.

Retelling can also take the form of story reconstruction, as we saw in Chapter 11. In this case, the teacher provides larger blocks of text (individual paragraphs) replete with key transitional words that students put together to form a story. As Dorothy Watson (1988) explains, children use clue phrases, such as *Once upon a time, The first little pig,* and *The second little pig,* to reconstruct the story. In doing this, they demonstrate their growing understanding of story structure. Schema stories, as Watson calls the approach, can be equally useful in teaching the structure of expository prose.

Figure 13.10 A Clothesline Story

Writing for Comprehension Children who have listened to, retold, and reconstructed a story can cooperatively compose stories with a similar structure, guided by questions from the teacher. After composing stories together, students draft stories of their own with a similar pattern, using pictures as the basis for storymaking if they are very young.

One sixth-grade teacher shared Hans Christian Andersen's "The Ugly Duckling" with her class. Independently, they read Leo Lionni's *Tico and the Golden Wings* and then talked about similarities between the two tales. They characterized both as "ugly duckling stories." Before long, the children were creating original ugly duckling stories based on the same motif. One student wrote:

The sequence of an "ugly duckling story" is (1) a character is not accepted by others; (2) the unaccepted one changes in some way; and (3) he or she is accepted.

Teddy, the Porcupine with No Quills

Once upon a time there was a very small porcupine called Teddy who lived in a large, green forest. Teddy was a sad little porcupine. He was sad, because he had no quills like all the other porcupines.

All the other animals in the forest laughed at him because he looked so strange. The bunny rabbits laughed at him. The chattering squirrels laughed at him. The wise old owl laughed at him. Worst of all, his brothers and sisters laughed at him.

Teddy was so unhappy, he hid behind the bushes and cried big pools of tears. He felt very sorry for himself. He was ashamed of his looks and hid behind the bushes whenever the other animals came along.

One day he was awakened by the cries of a bunny rabbit who was being attacked by a fox. Without thinking, he went to help the rabbit even though he had no quills. Rushing to help, he felt wonderful, because quills were growing on his back. He shot the fox full of quills and saved the bunny rabbit.

From then on, Teddy had lots of friends and lived happily ever after.

Comprehending Poetry Structures

Read Leland Jacobs, "Don't Neglect Poetry," in *Teaching K–8,* 22 (March 1992), 88–90. Dr. Jacobs wrote this article shortly before his death on April 4, 1992. He said, "To neglect poetry in the education of children is to neglect an important part of their literature program."

Understanding and appreciation of poetry structures come through similar experiences. This is a fine time for integrating listening, choral speaking, and reading, for students begin by listening and then joining in to chorus a poem such as this one by Langston Hughes:

> *City*
>
> *In the morning the city*
> *Spreads its wings,*
> *Making a song*
> *In stone that sings.*
>
> *In the evening the city*
> *Goes to bed,*
> *Hanging lights*
> *About its head.*

This is an easy poem for students to chorus together after hearing it one or two times as the teacher recites. First, they join in on the lines that open the stanzas, for those lines pattern and repeat: "In the morning the city . . ."; "In the evening the city. . . ." With a few more repetitions, students and teacher are chorusing the entire piece.

When students play orally with a poem, they readily see its design. In this case, they see that the stanzas are structurally the same line by line: The first line of each stanza patterns "In the _____ the city"; the next line tells what the city does; the next starts with an -*ing* action word. Personification threads through both stanzas.

Following that pattern, youngsters write pieces structured after Hughes— poems about the country, the ocean, the mountain. They use repetitive patterns as Hughes does. In so doing, they develop a concept of text structure that helps them make meaning and pleasure with poetry as they read independently.

Young children can do much the same. They begin by listening to and chorusing a perennial favorite, such as "To Market, To Market":

To market, to market, *To buy a fat pig,* *Home again, home again,* *Jiggety-jig.*	*To market, to market,* *To buy a fat hog,* *Home again, home again,* *Jiggety-jog.*

Comprehension of structure at this level comes not through analysis but through repeated chorusing of the piece. It comes, too, through creating stanzas that pattern in the same way. The teacher asks, "What else could we buy at the market?" Youngsters' responses are inserted into the second line as participants rechorus the piece; they substitute a rhyming word at the end:

To market, to market, *To buy a lamb chop,* *Home again, home again,* *Hippity-hop.*	*To market, to market,* *To buy a red hat,* *Home again, home again* *Clickity-clat.*

For an excellent treatment of the importance of teaching reading during the study of science, see Bonnie Armbruster, "Science and Reading," *The Reading Teacher,* 46 (December 1992/January 1993), 346–347. Armbruster writes, "Reading and doing science are similar processes drawing on the same cognitive base. Both are interactive-constructive processes that require critical thinking and reasoning."

Using Structure to Make Meaning with Nonfiction: Study Strategies for Content-Area Reading

Squire (1983) writes, "Reading for sequence in a short story . . . is very different from reading for historical sequence, or reading for sequence in a process article. Direct attention to skill applications in reading (and writing, too) appears to be mandatory and is one reason why content area selections must be introduced in basic reading programs."

There is a structure to nonfiction that students must be able to handle to be successful readers. They must learn to use titles and subheadings to predict what a selection is about. They must learn to use subheadings to figure out the organization, or design, of a passage. Most authors of informational prose build clues into their texts to facilitate comprehension: lines such as "There are three major points. . . . This section explains those points"; introductions that give an overview; conclusions that sum up; highlighted terms through italics; questions at the end; and/or illustrations to accompany each subsection. Most authors also use linguistic clues such as *first, second,* and *finally* to give structure to ideas. To teach for structure in content reading is to model for readers how to use these clues to build a framework for reading.

SQ3R A study scheme called *SQ3R* is helpful in clarifying the structure of an expository piece. SQ3R is a five-step strategy for studying a passage; the steps are Survey, Question, Read, Recite, and Review (Robinson, 1961).

✦ *Surveying.* Talking through a passage before reading is an effective strategy for teaching SQ3R and informational text structure simultaneously. The teacher asks students to read the title first and predict what the passage is about, study the headings to figure out the organization, read introductory and concluding sections, look at the pictures, and note any distinctive aspects. Having *surveyed* the text, students describe what they have done to get ready to read and what they already know about the topic. Talking their way through a passage in this way clarifies its structure and models how readers can use surveying as they study on their own. See Figure 13.11 for a checklist upper-graders can use to guide their study survey.

BEFORE-READING CHECKLIST OF KEY ELEMENTS OF TEXT

Put a check on the line when you have previewed that item. Put a 0 on the line when you preview and do not find the item.

1. Title   _____

2. Key vocabulary listed at the beginning   _____

3. Introductory paragraphs that tell what the selection is about   _____

4. Headings and subheadings   _____

5. Illustrations   _____

6. Italicized or boldfaced terms   _____

7. Summary paragraph at the end   _____

8. Questions at the beginning or end   _____

Figure 13.11 A Checklist for Identifying Key Elements of Expository Text Structure

- *Questioning.* The second step in preparing to read informational texts is *questioning.* Students devise questions to answer through reading by rephrasing the subheadings as questions. These questions give purpose to reading; students read to find answers.
- *Reading.* The next step in SQ3R is *reading.* Students read to find answers to their before-reading questions.
- *Reciting.* Having read a major section of text, students pause to monitor their comprehension by *reciting.* In reciting students mind talk, telling themselves answers to the questions devised during the preview survey or retelling points from the selection. If the students find this impossible, they reread the segment and try again to recite.
- *Reviewing.* Finishing the selection, readers *review* what they have read by talking through the main points of the entire selection, again guided by the questions devised before reading. Reviewing is not a one-time endeavor; students must review on several occasions to remember what they have read.

The SQ3R study sequence just described includes a survey of the material to discover the topic and the organization, devising study questions based on the subheadings, reading, reciting based on the questions, and a follow-up review. This sequence is powerful because the surveying and questioning steps help readers perceive the structure of a selection, which in turn facilitates comprehension by providing a framework for reading.

Expanding on SQ3R   SQ3R has proven a useful study system over the years. One weakness, however, is the limited use of writing; students may write their questions, but that is the extent of the writing activity. Another weakness is that the only before-reading organizational tool is the development of questions to guide the reading. Today reading specialists suggest other strategies a student can use based on a survey of the text: webbing, data charting, and feature matrix charting. Here is a brief description of these strategies:

- *Webbing, or semantic mapping.* Readers preview a selection to identify the topic. They record the topic in the center of the web and then draw lines radiating from that hub, recording at the ends of the lines the subtopics indicated by the subheadings. While studying the text in depth, readers record ideas, plotting them outward from the subtopics. This approach to webbing draws attention to the structure communicated by the headings. The web serves as a graphic organizer that visually displays and highlights the structure of the selection (Church, 1985).

See Chapter 7 for an example of data charts used in this way (Figures 7.4, and 7.5).

- *Data charting.* Earlier in this book, we referred to data synthesis charts as tools for organizing information. These charts can also be used to teach informational text structure. Children create a chart based on the major headings. To be useful in highlighting the structure of the text under consideration, the structure of the chart should parallel that of the text.
- *Feature matrix charting.* Another way to organize for reading is the matrix chart (Stieglitz, 1981; Cunningham, 1987). Before reading, teacher and

students cooperatively brainstorm and list the main categories of data to be investigated through reading. In some cases, the subheadings of a selection to be read supply those categories; for example, if a selection deals with animals, the categories of data are types of animals (i.e., mammals, birds, reptiles, amphibians, and fish). These categories become the labels on the columns of a feature matrix chart. Now students and teacher brainstorm information about animals in general, such as "has hair," "hatches from eggs," "has gills," "has lungs," "has wings," and so on. These become the labels on the rows. Figure 13.12 is an example.

Using the resulting matrix before reading, students make predictions about each group. If they predict that a particular kind of animal has lungs, they place a plus sign (+) in that box in the matrix; if they believe that an animal does not have lungs, they put a minus sign (−) there. If they have no idea, they leave the box empty. As they read, students correct their original predictions. In this case, as with data charts and webs, the feature matrix chart becomes a note-taking guide during reading and a guide for sharing after reading.

How does the teacher encourage students to use these strategies as part of content-area reading? The answer is modeling. The teacher orally "walks children through" content-area selections. Teacher and students cooperatively devise webs and charts based on selections and then use their graphic organizers to guide their reading, their recitation, and their review.

Read Karen Wood, "Guiding Students Through Informational Text," *The Reading Teacher,* 41 (May 1988), 912–920; Jo Anne Piccolo, "Expository Text Structures: Teaching and Learning Strategies," *The Reading Teacher,* 40 (May 1987), 838–847; and George Manolakes, "Comprehension: A Personal Experience in Content Area Reading," *The Reading Teacher,* 42 (December 1988), 200–202.

✎ BUILDING AND REFINING YOUR TEACHING SKILLS

✦ Locate a story or poem with a clear structure. Plan a lesson in which you involve children orally in the piece so that they begin to understand that writing has structure.

✦ Study a chapter of a college text you are reading using SQ3R. Devise a web to clarify the structure of the chapter.

Sustained Silent Reading and Library Visits

Children must have a wide variety of experiences with all kinds of texts to become skillful readers. Children learn to construct meanings and interpret text structure related to stories by reading stories; they learn to read poems by reading poems; they learn to read nonfiction by reading informational articles.

To achieve this breadth of skill, many teachers use Sustained Silent Reading (SSR) or Drop Everything and Read (DEAR). Children spend a portion of each day reading independently in material they select, the only prohibition on

A MATRIX CHART

Directions: Before reading, predict the characteristics of each kind of vertebrate. Put a + in the box if you predict that this kind of vertebrate has that characteristic. Put a – in the box if you predict it does not. If you have no idea, leave the box empty. Read to test your predictions. Add characteristics to the matrix as you read. Generalize after you read.

	Mammals	Birds	Reptiles	Amphibians	Fish
Items identified before reading					
1. has a backbone					
2. has lungs					
3. has gills					
4. lays eggs					
5. gives birth to live young					
6. has wings					
7. has hair					
8. has blood					
Items identified while reading					
1.					
2.					

Generalizations formed after reading:

1. Vertebrates are animals that

2. Mammals are animals that

3. Birds are animals that

4. Reptiles are animals that

5. Amphibians are animals that

6. Fish are animals that

Figure 13.12 A Matrix Chart for Organizing and Predicting Before-Reading Expository Material

choice being that they must eventually make selections from key categories: story, biography, science, history, poetry, humor, and so forth. During reading workshops, as a follow-up to SSR, children confer with their teacher, who asks them to retell, rephrase, and summarize; interpret relationships; evaluate content and style; and create fresh insights. A truly effective school reading program must include both guided and independent reading.

Visiting the Library Media Center

See the March 1992 issue of *Phi Delta Kappan.* The theme is "The School Library for the Nineties."

Children should always have in their desks a book or two that they have chosen for sustained silent reading. To this end, the class should visit the library so that each child can make a selection. Kindergarten is not too early to start these visits. Youngsters squat at their leisure on the floor before the "houses," or shelves, where the picture books are kept and pick books to carry back to the classroom and/or home for reading. The teacher must guide young children as they select books, helping them find books that fit their reading and interest levels; otherwise, a child may return from the library without a book to enjoy. The teacher should send a note home suggesting that the caregiver read the take-home books aloud to the child. To encourage home reading, kindergarten teacher Denise Addona gives an "assignment" to caregivers in her urban school district. They must complete a weekly book report, indicating the name of the book read that week to the child, the number of times they went through the book with the child, and the topics they talked about before and after reading. Ms. Addona has had an amazingly good response to this "assignment."

Teaching Library Skills in the Primary Grades

As primary children visit the library, they should begin to build alphabetizing skills and learn to alphabetize storybooks. Having read a book, a youngster constructs a large spine from construction paper, printing on it the author's last name and the book title. On the bulletin board, students mount their spines alphabetically according to the authors' last names. The result is a mockup of a library shelf that houses fiction.

In the upper grades, children differentiate between fiction and nonfiction. At this point, they take time to browse in specific areas of the library: science, history, sports, biography, poetry.

Teaching Investigative Skills in the Upper Elementary Grades

More complex library skills should be taught as early as second grade. These skills include the ability to differentiate among basic library references (encyclopedias, atlases, almanacs, informational books, magazines, newspapers) and the ability to use indexes, tables of contents, topical headings, guide words, the card catalogue, and computerized book-search lists.

Topics of lessons include using the card catalogue, locating books on the library shelf, locating videocassettes, and finding oversized picture-filled books. Basic references include the *Guinness Book of World Records,* atlases, special dictionaries, and encyclopedias.

Basic References   What type of information does an encyclopedia provide? How does this information differ from that in an informational book? Teachers can structure activities to answer these kinds of questions and to familiarize young researchers with basic references. Here are a few ideas:

✦ *The encyclopedia.* Introduce the organization of encyclopedias by rolling in a set and distributing volumes to small groups of youngsters. Working from front to back of the volumes, students discover the organization. They look up particular items in the index of a volume and locate relevant pages. On the spot, students use the volumes to locate information on a unit being studied, brainstorming possible subtopics related to the unit, locating them, scanning the sections, and sharing ideas. Teachers of young children can introduce the encyclopedia by sharing pictures from *Child Craft, World Book Encyclopedia,* and *Compton's Pictured Encyclopedia* as part of discussion or by reading a very short selection aloud as the foundation for unit study.

✦ *Magazines.* Schedule comparison times when youngsters compare the content and organization of such magazines as *Ranger Rick, Cricket, Newsweek, Consumer Reports,* and *National Geographic World.* This makes a good group activity, with each group studying a sample of each magazine and writing a summary that begins, "*Consumer Reports* contains articles on. . . ."

✦ *Almanacs, atlases, and encyclopedias.* Divide the class into small groups, each to receive copies of an almanac, an atlas, and an encyclopedia volume. Students analyze the volumes and write summary cards for each reference: "An almanac contains . . ."; "An atlas contains . . ."; "An encyclopedia contains. . . ."

✦ *Newspapers.* Collect newspapers over several weeks so that each student has one in hand. Ask children to go through their papers page by page, listing the features found in sequence. Later, in groups, students compare their lists and generalize about how newspapers are organized and the kind of information they contain.

Also have children compare a local newspaper to a regional and a national newspaper. Ask "What kinds of news does each report? What kinds of features does each contain? How do they differ?"

✦ *Informational books.* Distribute a number of informational books on a topic (for example, the American Revolution) and encyclopedia volumes on the same topic. Students scan both to find out how the two types of materials differ. Ask, "Under what conditions would you use an encyclopedia article? Informational books? Both?"

Locational and Library Skills   Youngsters need guidance in using indexes and library-search tools. Here are ideas for organizing the activity:

✦ *Indexes.* Using the index in their social studies or science book, students locate information on a topic. Provide topics during unit study that can be located in several ways, for example, the automobile, which can be traced by looking under *automobile, car, horseless carriage,* or *gasoline.*

✦ *The card catalogue.* Label a series of shoe boxes with the same letter labels found on the drawers of the school card catalogue: *A–C, D–E, F–H,* and so on. After a visit to the library, when all children have brought back a book, each child writes on a card the author's name, last name first. The class decides which "drawer" should contain a card and orders the cards alphabetically within each "drawer."

♦ *Subject, author, and title cards.* Using actual cards from the card catalogue, print up the three cards that exist for each informational book: a subject, an author, and a title card. Do this for five different books, making giant-size cards. Display each set of three cards, guiding children to discover the differences among the cards. Display all fifteen cards at once, encouraging students to group them into three categories: subject, title, author. On a later library visit, children can browse through the card catalogue to see if they can locate samples of the three kinds of cards.

♦ *The numbers have it!* Introduce upper-graders to the Dewey decimal system if the school library is organized that way. Start by making a chart showing the numbers used to catalogue nonfiction. Then gather a pile of books. Children decide how to order the books on the library shelves. To aid in teaching the Dewey decimal system, borrow an idea from Eleanor Schwartz, a librarian who has made numerous book spines imprinted with book title, author, and Dewey decimal number copied from library books. Each youngster in the group holds a spine; cooperatively, children decide how to order the books on a shelf. When youngsters visit the library, they use the major Dewey divisions to locate books they need.

♦ *In the computer.* Where possible, demonstrate how to locate a book in a library having a computerized catalogue.

The major units of the Dewey system are:

000	generalities
100	philosophy
200	religion
300	social sciences
400	language
500	pure sciences
600	technology (applied sciences)
700	the arts
800	literature
900	geography and history

✎ *BUILDING AND REFINING YOUR TEACHING SKILLS*

♦ Prepare a lesson to introduce upper-graders to a reference such as an atlas or the *Guinness Book of World Records*. Through your lesson, help students discover the organization of the volume and provide an opportunity for its meaningful use.

A Summary Thought or Two:

READING FOR MEANING

This chapter develops these major ideas:

1. Reading is an interactive-constructive process of making meaning with a written text. Activities that increase awareness of meanings and encourage children to explore and clarify meanings support reading comprehension.

2. What readers bring to reading—their world knowledge, linguistic knowledge, text structure knowledge, and metacognitive knowledge—is important in comprehension. Accordingly, teachers should structure before-reading activities that help young readers prepare for full comprehension. Many of these activities are oral.

3. Full comprehension involves the generation of literal, interpretive, critical, and creative meanings. Accordingly, teachers should ask questions and develop activities before reading, during reading, and after reading that help children construct these meanings.

4. Children must be able to grasp the structure of a piece—a story, a poem, or an informational text—to construct meanings in relation to it. To this end, teachers should help children perceive the structure of a piece.

5. Specific reading skills and strategies should be developed as part of ongoing purposeful reading activity rather than in isolation.

6. Just as oral activity is an integral part of classroom reading, so is writing. Writing provides students with the opportunity to retell, summarize, analyze, apply, invent, and criticize. It is an ideal way to react to reading, for it forces students to organize thought. The result—given oral activity as well—is an integrated, natural approach to reading instruction.

7. Children should have considerable opportunity to read for pleasure and information. To find books for Sustained Silent Reading, children should go to the library and be assisted in using it productively.

RELATED READINGS

Anderson, Richard et al. *Becoming a Nation of Readers: The Report of the Commission on Reading.* Washington, D.C.: National Institute of Education, 1985.

Clay, Marie. *Becoming Literate.* Portsmouth, N.H.: Heinemann Educational Books, 1991.

Cullinan, Bernice, ed. *Invitation to Read: More Children's Literature in the Reading Program.* Newark, Del.: International Reading Association, 1992.

Duffy, Gerald. "Let's Free Teachers to Be Inspired." *Phi Delta Kappan,* 73 (February 1992), 442–447.

Freeman, Evelyn, and Duane Person, eds. *Using Nonfiction Trade Books in the Elementary Classroom.* Urbana, Ill.: National Council of Teachers of English, 1992.

Hall, Nigel. *The Emergence of Literacy.* Portsmouth, N.H.: Heinemann Educational Books, 1987.

Hart-Hewins, Linda, and Jan Wells. *Real Books for Reading: Learning to Read with Children's Literature.* Portsmouth, N.H.: Heinemann Educational Books, 1990.

Heimlich, Joan, and Susan Pittelman. *Semantic Mapping: Classroom Applications.* Newark, Del.: International Reading Association, 1986.

Holdaway, Don. *Independence in Reading.* 3rd ed. Portsmouth, N.H.: Heinemann Educational Books, 1991.

Irwin, Judith, ed. *Understanding and Teaching Cohesion Comprehension.* Newark, Del.: International Reading Association, 1986.

Language Arts, 70 (October 1993). The theme of the issue is "Reading Instruction Today."

Lynch, Priscilla. *Using Big Books and Predictable Books.* Richmond Hill, Ontario: Scholastic–TAB, 1986.

MacGinitie, Walter. "Reading Instruction: Plus Ça Change. . . ." *Educational Leadership* (March 1991).

Macon, James, Diane Bewell, and MaryEllen Vogt. *Responses to Literature, Grades K–8.* Newark, Del.: International Reading Association, 1990.

Meier, Daniel. "Books in the Classroom." *The Horn Book,* 67 (March/April 1991), 241–244.

Miller, Heidi, Timothy O'Keefe, and Diane Stephens. *Looking Closely: Exploring the Role of Phonics in One Whole Language Classroom.* Urbana, Ill.: National Council of Teachers of English, 1991.

Newkirk, Thomas, with Patricia McLure. *Listening In: Children Talk About Books (and other things).* Portsmouth, N.H.: Heinemann Educational Books, 1992.

Parsons, Les. *Response Journals.* Portsmouth, N.H.: Heinemann Educational Books, 1989.

Power, Brenda, and Ruth Hubbard, eds. *The Heinemann Reader: Literacy in Process.* Portsmouth, N.H.: Heinemann Educational Books, 1991.

Arian Phillips
Gr.3 Rm.22   Jefferson School
You should lie if for a good reason.

It is ok because it is inportant. About
the food. sistuation. The family worked
hard on the food. They spent money. for
the food. that family's worst enimy
is Mr.Rehnquist if they wanted to give
Mr.Rehnquist food they would of don
it them selfs. You saw how mad Addie's
father got when she first menchined
his name and when she said "
Lets inite him for thanksgiving?"
He blewen his top off. Mr.Rehnquist
came out with his shot gun He could
of allmost pull the triger you never
know. I think Carla Mae is smart.
You can tell she is doing something rong
because she didn't tell anyone exsept
her best friend Carla Mae. And she
backed out of it because she knows
Addie's father.

Responding to an event in *The Thanksgiving Treasure*, Arian thought critically about when it was right to lie but came to a different opinion from Lizzy. See page 268 (courtesy of Arian Phillips and Micki Benjamin).

LANGUAGING WITH A "PORPOISE"

"Will you walk a little faster," said a whiting to a snail.
"There's a porpoise close behind us, and he's treading on my tail.
See how eagerly the lobsters and turtles all advance!
They are waiting on the shingle—will you come and join the dance?
Will you, won't you, will you, won't you, will you join the dance?
Will you, won't you, will you, won't you, won't you join the dance?"

—Lewis Carroll, *Alice's Adventures in Wonderland*

Readers who remember these wondrous lines—which are among this author's favorites—know that Alice was muchly concerned for the whiting who was being tailed by a porpoise. She said, "I'd have said to the porpoise, 'Keep back, please! We don't want you with us!'"

But the Mock Turtle, to whom Alice was speaking, explained that they were obliged to have the porpoise with them. In the Mock Turtle's words, "No wise fish would go anywhere without a porpoise."

To this Alice replied with great surprise, "Wouldn't it, really?"

"Of course not," said the Mock Turtle. "Why if a fish came to me, and told me he was going on a journey, I should say 'With what porpoise?'"

"Don't you mean 'purpose'?" said Alice—probably in a very timid voice.

We in language arts instruction have a "porpoise" treading on our tail. Our "porpoise" is that children acquire the ability to communicate effectively, develop a love of reading and of books, and come to understand the power and limitations of their language system. To achieve our "porpoise," communication in all its dimensions must be an integral part of language arts. To this end, we must

1. Involve children naturally and productively in thinking and communicating;
2. Integrate listening, speaking, writing, and reading into communication-centered experiences that are based on the finest literature, meaningful content from the subject areas, and direct contact with the world around;
3. Use a variety of instructional strategies that combine whole class with independent and collaborative learning;
4. Plan ongoing units of instruction to meet the diverse needs of children learning together in multicultural, mainstreamed classrooms.

Most surely, success in achieving our "porpoise" depends on our skill and personality as teachers. Language arts teachers must be searchers, creators, experimenters—searching for new ways to do things, putting ideas together that were never put together before, and willing to experiment and learn from successes and mistakes. Only by doing this, will we as teachers achieve our "porpoise" and bring *Communication in Action* into our classrooms.

Appendices

Integrated Language Arts Activities for Before Reading, During Reading, and After Reading

In a literature-based, whole language approach, teachers are empowered to make decisions about how to help children connect with literature. Teachers must decide the things children will do before they read a piece of fine literature, the way children will read it, and the ways they will respond after reading. Often in making these decisions, teachers integrate the reading of stories with the reading of poetry and nonfiction, blend writing and reading, weave in art and music, and integrate language arts and the content areas. Here is a list of activities, reading options, and responses from which to choose in making instructional decisions.

See unit on Appalachia on the back end papers for an example of this kind of integrational decision-making.

Before-Reading Activities to Encourage an Active Response

1. Children think about vocabulary (in context) that they will need to read the selection with comprehension.
2. Children use title, illustrations, introductory matter, headings and subheadings, and summary matter to predict the main topic or focus of the selection (i.e., what it is about) and the kind of selection it is (poem, story, informational piece, biography, autobiography). They record their predictions in their learning logs or literature response journals.
3. Children think about and organize what they already know about the topic.
   a. Ask children to brainstorm thoughts relative to the topic. List these thoughts on board, chart, or paper as students record in logs or journals.
   b. Ask children to brainstorm thoughts relative to the topic. As they propose items, organize them as a web in which related points are grouped together. Students develop their own webs in their learning logs or literature response journals so that they can add to their webs later as they read.

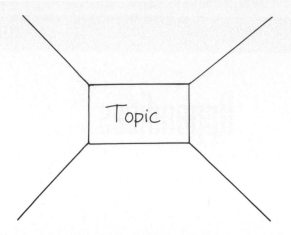

c. Ask children to brainstorm thoughts relative to the topic. As they propose items, ask them to organize them under the terms *who, what, when, where, why*, and *how* in their logs or journals.

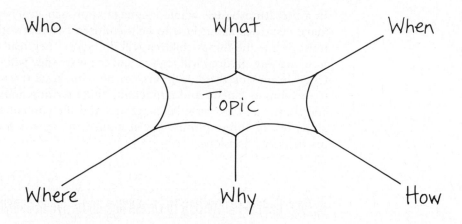

d. Talk together about one or two pictures, charts, maps, or time lines that are included in the selection. Have children tell what they already know about the content of these illustrations.
e. Record on the board the main subheadings; have students tell about what they already know on these topics and what they want to learn.

	SUBHEADINGS	WHAT WE ALREADY KNOW	WHAT WE WANT TO LEARN
1.			
2.			
3.			

f. Using the subheadings, help children make a data chart in their learning logs for recording data during reading.

	EGYPT	IRAN	JAPAN	CHILE	FIJI
Location					
Climate					
Major physical features					
Natural resources					
Primary occupations					

g. Help children write questions in their learning logs based on the sub-headings and predict answers to those questions.

SUBHEADINGS	QUESTIONS	PREDICTED ANSWERS
1.		
2.		
3.		
4.		

h. Help children create a feature matrix chart. Have them predict answers before reading (+ if you predict *yes*; – if you predict *no*; 0 if you have no idea).

FEATURES	PLANT CELL	ANIMAL CELL
has a nucleus		
has a cell wall		
has protoplasm		
has chloroplasts		

i. Read the questions at the end of a selection if there are any. Predict answers together before reading.
j. Have children run their eyes over the selection (scan) before reading. Select words that seem important. Using those words, have children write predictive sentences about the content.
k. Have children scan the selection that is chronologically organized and contains dates. Help them write those dates as a time line in their learning logs before reading.

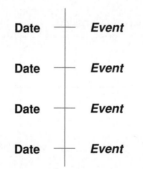

Date —— *Event*

Date —— *Event*

Date —— *Event*

Date —— *Event*

l. Demonstrate something relative to the content of the selection: melting ice, magnets, making a mobile, playing with an optical illusion. Talk and/or write about the demonstration using key words.
m. Talk about elements of story structure: setting, characters, conflict, and so on. Help children make a grid in their literature response journals for

recording elements of the story they are to read based on a survey of the title, pictures, and introductory paragraph.

A STORY MAP
The Main Characters:
The Setting:
The Problem:
The Steps Taken to Solve the Problem:
The Final Solution to the Story:

Working also with stories, students survey pictures and title, as well as the cover, to get some clues to the theme of the story. They record the projected theme in a rectangular box in their journals. As they read, they add events from the story that support the theme and revise their theme based on reading the story.

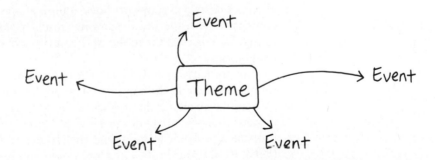

Working with stories, students survey the title, the pictures, and the cover to get some clues to the conflict in the story. They record the projected conflict in a diamond-shaped box in their journals. As they read, they add events from the story that relate to the conflict and revise the projected conflict as they read the story.

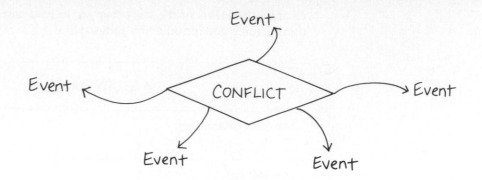

n. Tell about an experience you have had relative to the content. Ask students to relate similar experiences.

o. Read the beginning section to students if it contains a good description of places, persons, or things. Ask students to close their eyes and visualize the place, person, or thing in their mind's eye.

p. Orally share the beginning section if it contains sharp descriptive matter. Ask each student to draw a picture in his or her journal of what is described and then describe it to another student.

q. Share a short related passage orally. The passage can be a poem, a story, an expository piece from an encyclopedia, or a news article that relates to the content to be read. Talk about the passage together.

r. Display a related visual such as a graph, a time line, or a chart that relates to the content to be read. Ask children to tell what the visual says and propose the significance of what is being said.

s. Share a wordless book (such as one by Mitsumasa Anno) that relates to the content to be read. Talk about the book.

t. Hold up a picture or a piece of fine art that relates to the content or story to be read. Talk together about it, describing, inferring, and relating.

u. Share a filmstrip, a series of slides, a film, a tape, or a videotape on the content to be read, and discuss it. Similarly share a piece of classical music that relates to the mood or theme of a story to be read. Discuss the relationships.

v. Involve students in a Readers' Theatre rendition, a role-playing, or a spontaneous dramatization that relates to the content to be read.

w. Pantomime an action that relates to the content to be read. Ask children to guess what you are pantomiming, and talk about it.

x. Propose a problem to be solved that relates to the content to be read (What would you do if . . . ? How would you react if . . . ? How would you feel if . . . ?). Have children postulate solutions and reactions.

y. Provide children with sentence strips that relate to the content of the selection. Ask them to order the strips to make meaning out of them. When put together, the strips should state the main idea or theme of the selection to be read. Then discuss the idea or theme before reading.

z. Provide children with a consumable copy of the selection to be read. Talk through the selection, discussing title, headings, and illustrations. Help children put before-reading notes directly on the copy to organize thinking before reading.

4. Children set a purpose for reading based on their before-reading survey and before-reading organizing-for-reading activity. The purpose for reading may be to

- ✦ Find out more on the topic,
- ✦ Test predictions,
- ✦ Answer questions,
- ✦ Find out how to do something,
- ✦ Find out what happens when . . . ,
- ✦ Relate the selection to something that happened in their own lives,
- ✦ Find out why . . . ,
- ✦ Compare, contrast, categorize . . . ,
- ✦ Solve a problem posed before reading,
- ✦ Decide whether the piece is well written,
- ✦ Formulate a judgment about events recounted in the selection.

During-Reading Activities

1. Children read silently to themselves, keeping their purpose(s) in mind. Often they record in their learning logs or literature journals as they read. They add items to their data charts, cross out erroneous predictions, add items to brainstormed lists, add items to their time lines, write answers to questions proposed before reading, enter data in matrix charts, record key vocabulary in their logs or journals, underscore main ideas, and/or put numbers in front of significant points if working with consumable material.

2. Modeling fluent reading, the teacher reads aloud to the children as they follow along in their texts.

3. The teacher reads aloud to the children as they follow along, stopping periodically to tell what thoughts are going through his or her mind. Here the teacher is modeling thinking-while-reading.

For a description of modeling mind talk, see Beth Ann Herrmann, "Teaching and Assessing Strategic Reasoning," *The Reading Teacher,* 45 (February 1992), 428–433.

4. Children read silently to themselves. Then they reread the selection chorally, with emphasis being on fluent reading.

5. In pairs, children read orally to one another (collaborative reading).

6. Children read silently to themselves. Then they pair off to reread the selection orally with a reading mate. Mates read orally together.

7. Individual children are asked to prepare a paragraph or two for oral sharing. These students read to the class, modeling fluent reading.

8. Children in teams read a section of a text, prepare it for Readers' Theatre, and share it dramatically with the whole class.

After-Reading Responses

Help students organize their written responses by encouraging them to keep an ongoing learning log as part of content-area study and a literature response journal as they read short stories, novels, and poems.

1. Children brainstorm points they remember from their reading. A scribe records these on the board. Students then go back to reread to get more information to add to the board. They organize their data in the form of a web or chart in their logs or journals.
2. Children write in their logs or journals on topics of their own choosing or in response to such questions as these:
   a. What is the main idea or theme?
   b. How does this idea develop in the selection?
   c. What does this idea mean to you personally?
   d. When have you ever experienced something similar?
3. Children orally share their learning log notes and their literature response journal entries. They talk about their notes and entries.
4. Children orally read sentences and paragraphs from the selection to support their written responses.
5. Children share their notes and entries as they participate in Literature Group dialogues.
6. Teacher and students take turns asking questions of one another regarding the content of the selection. The teacher models good question-asking strategies by asking questions that seek contrasts, comparisons, generalizations, inferences, original ideas, and opinions.
7. Children write answers to questions raised before reading and then talk about questions and answers.
8. Children write summaries of the content read. They share their summaries from the Author's Chair.
9. Children write based on some element in the selection: story theme, selection thesis, story structure, selection structure, point of view, author's purpose, and so on. They share their writings from the Author's Chair.
10. From among their writings, children select a piece to publish.
11. Children paint or draw pictures based on their readings. They make an illustration to accompany the selection. Illustrations may be maps, charts, graphs, or tables, as well as artistic renderings. Students orally share their illustrations in a talk-time.
12. Children construct something based on their readings—a diorama, a model, a bulletin board. They orally share their work products.
13. Children respond to the reading with a form of drama, such as monologue, dialogue, role playing, choral reading or speaking, or Readers' Theatre.
14. Children solve a problem based on information uncovered in reading. They share their solutions.
15. Children investigate a topic related to what they have read by reading in a reference book. They share their findings.
16. Children read (or listen to) another passage similar to the one they just read. They compare, contrast, and generalize.
17. Children form into talk/listening teams to share findings from reading. In teams they question one another.

18. Children demonstrate ideas they have read; do experiments based on content read; make things based on directions read.
19. Teacher and students discuss strategies they have been using to make meaning while reading. They verbalize steps in their reading strategies.

APPENDIX B:
Caldecott and Newbery Award-Winning Books

Caldecott Award-Winning Books, 1961-1993

Since 1938, the American Library Association has awarded the Caldecott Medal to the most distinguished picture book for children. The illustrators receiving the award since 1961 are shown in bold type. Use the names of these illustrators to guide your search for striking picture books, for these illustrators are among the finest in the United States.

1993   *Mirette on the High Wire.* **Emily McCully.** New York: Putnam's, 1992.
1992   *Tuesday.* **David Wiesner.** New York: Clarion, 1991.
1991   *Black and White.* **David Macaulay.** Boston: Houghton Mifflin, 1990.
1990   *Lin Po Po.* **Ed Young.** New York: Philomel, 1989.
1989   *Song and Dance Man.* Jane Ackerman. Ill. by **Stephen Gammell.** New York: Knopf, 1988.
1988   *Owl Moon.* Jane Yolen. Ill. by **John Schoenherr.** New York: Philomel, 1987.
1987   *Hey, Al.* Arthur Yorinks. Ill. by **Richard Egielski.** New York: Farrar, Straus and Giroux, 1986.
1986   *The Polar Express.* **Chris Van Allsburg.** Boston: Houghton Mifflin, 1985.
1985   *Saint George and the Dragon.* Retold by Margaret Hodges. Ill. by **Tina Schart Hyman.** Boston: Little, Brown, 1984.
1984   *The Glorious Flight: Across the Channel with Louis Bleriot.* **Alice and Martin Provensen.** New York: Viking, 1983.
1983   *Shadow.* Blaise Cendrars. Ill. by **Marcia Brown.** New York: Scribner, 1982.
1982   *Jumanji.* **Chris Van Allsburg.** Boston: Houghton Mifflin, 1981.
1981   *Fables.* **Arnold Lobel.** New York: Harper & Row, 1980.
1980   *Ox-Cart Man.* Donald Hall. Ill. by **Barbara Cooney.** New York: Viking, 1979.
1979   *The Girl Who Loved Wild Horses.* **Paul Goble.** New York: Bradbury, 1978.
1978   *Noah's Ark.* **Peter Spier.** New York: Doubleday, 1977.
1977   *Ashanti to Zulu.* Margaret Musgrove, Ill. by **Leo and Diane Dillon.** New York: Dial, 1976.

1976 *Why Mosquitoes Buzz in People's Ears.* Verna Aardema. Ill. by **Leo and Diane Dillon.** New York: Dial, 1975.

1975 *Arrow to the Sun.* **Gerald McDermott.** New York: Viking, 1974.

1974 *Duffy and the Devil.* Retold by Harve Zemach. Ill. by **Margot Zemach.** New York: Farrar, Straus and Giroux, 1973.

1973 *The Funny Little Woman.* Retold by Arlene Mosel. Ill. by **Blair Lent.** New York: Dutton, 1972.

1972 *One Fine Day.* **Nonny Hogrogian.** New York: Macmillan, 1971.

1971 *A Story A Story.* **Gail Haley.** New York: Atheneum, 1970.

1970 *Sylvester and the Magic Pebble.* **William Steig.** New York: Windmill Books, 1969.

1969 *The Fool of the World and the Flying Machine.* Retold by Arthur Ransome. Ill. by **Uri Shulevitz.** New York: Farrar, Straus and Giroux, 1968.

1968 *Drummer Hoff.* Adapted by Barbara Emberley. Ill. by **Ed Emberley.** Englewood Cliffs, N.J.: Prentice-Hall, 1967.

1967 *Sam, Bangs, and Moonshine.* **Evaline Ness.** New York: Holt, Rinehart and Winston, 1966.

1966 *Always Room for One More.* Sorche Nic Leodhas. Ill. by **Nonny Hogrogian.** New York: Holt, Rinehart and Winston, 1965.

1965 *May I Bring a Friend?* Beatrice Schenk de Regniers. Ill. by **Beni Montresor.** New York: Atheneum, 1964.

1964 *Where the Wild Things Are.* **Maurice Sendak.** New York: Harper & Row, 1963.

1963 *The Snowy Day.* **Ezra Jack Keats.** New York: Viking, 1962.

1962 *Once a Mouse.* **Marcia Brown.** New York: Scribner, 1961.

1961 *Baboushka and the Three Kings.* Ruth Robbins. Ill. by **Nicolas Sidjakov.** Orleans, Mass.: Parnassus, 1960.

Newbery Award-Winning Books, 1961-1993

Since 1922, the American Library Association has awarded the Newbery Medal to the most distinguished contribution to children's literature. The writers receiving the award since 1961 are shown in bold type. Use the names of these writers to guide your search for books to recommend to intermediate-level children, for these writers are among the finest in the United States.

1993 *Missing May.* **Cynthia Rylant.** New York: Orchard, 1992.

1992 *Shiloh.* **Phyllis Reynolds Naylor.** New York: Atheneum, 1991.

1991 *Maniac Magee.* **Jerry Spinelli.** Boston: Little, Brown, 1990.

1990 *Number the Stars.* **Lois Lowry.** Boston: Houghton Mifflin, 1989.

1989 *Joyful Noise: Poems for Two Voices.* **Paul Fleischman.** New York: Harper & Row, 1988.

1988 *Abraham Lincoln: A Photobiography.* **Russell Freedman.** Boston: Houghton Mifflin, 1987.

1987 *The Whipping Boy.* **Sid Fleischman.** New York: Greenwillow, 1986.

1986   *Sarah, Plain and Tall.* **Patricia MacLachlan.** New York: Harper & Row, 1985.

1985   *The Hero and the Crown.* **Robin McKinley.** New York: Greenwillow, 1984.

1984   *Dear Mr. Henshaw.* **Beverly Cleary.** New York: William Morrow, 1983.

1983   *Dicey's Song.* **Cynthia Voight.** New York: Atheneum, 1982.

1982   *A Visit to William Blake's Inn: Poems for Innocent and Experienced Travelers.* **Nancy Willard.** San Diego: Harcourt Brace Jovanovich, 1981.

1981   *Jacob Have I Loved.* **Katherine Paterson.** New York: Crowell, 1980.

1980   *A Gathering of Days.* **Joan Blos.** New York: Scribner, 1979.

1979   *The Westing Game.* **Ellen Raskin.** New York: Dutton, 1978.

1978   *Bridge to Terabithia.* **Katherine Paterson.** New York: Crowell, 1977.

1977   *Roll of Thunder, Hear My Cry.* **Mildred Taylor.** New York: Dial, 1976.

1976   *The Grey Kind.* **Susan Cooper.** New York: Atheneum, 1975.

1975   *M. C. Higgins, the Great.* **Virginia Hamilton.** New York: Macmillan, 1974.

1974   *The Slave Dancer.* **Paula Fox.** New York: Bradbury, 1973.

1973   *Julie of the Wolves.* **Jean Craighead George.** New York: Harper & Row, 1972.

1972   *Mrs. Frisby and the Rats of NIMH.* **Robert O'Brien.** New York: Atheneum, 1971.

1971   *Summer of the Swans.* **Betsy Byars.** New York: Viking, 1970.

1970   *Sounder.* **William H. Armstrong.** New York: Harper & Row, 1969.

1969   *The High King.* **Lloyd Alexander.** New York: Holt, Rinehart and Winston, 1968.

1968   *From the Mixed-up Files of Mrs. Basil E. Frankweiler.* **E. L. Konigsburg.** New York: Atheneum, 1967.

1967   *Up a Road Slowly.* **Irene Hunt.** Chicago: Follett, 1966.

1966   *I, Juan de Pareja.* **Elizabeth Borton de Trevino.** New York: Farrar, Straus and Giroux, 1965.

1965   *Shadow of a Bull.* **Maia Wojciechowska.** New York: Atheneum, 1964.

1964   *It's Like This, Cat.* **Emily Neville.** New York: Harper & Row, 1963.

1963   *A Wrinkle in Time.* **Madeleine L'Engle.** New York: Farrar, Straus and Giroux, 1962.

1962   *The Bronze Bow.* **Elizabeth George Speare.** Boston: Houghton Mifflin, 1961.

1961   *Island of the Blue Dolphin.* **Scott O'Dell.** Boston: Houghton Mifflin, 1960.

APPENDIX C:
A Bibliography of Subject Indexes of Children's Books Useful in Building Literature-Based, Cross-Curricular Units

Barstow, Barbara, and Judith Riggle. *Beyond Picture Books: A Guide to First Readers.* Ann Arbor, Mich.: R. R. Bowker, 1989.

Booklinks. Chicago: American Library Association. A periodical published six times a year.

Brewton, John, et al. *Index to Poetry for Children and Young People: 1970–1975.* New York: H. W. Wilson, 1978.

————. *Index to Poetry for Children and Young People: 1976–1981.* New York: H. W. Wilson, 1984 (See also more recent supplements.)

Cummins, Julie, and Blair Cummins, eds. *Choices: A Core Collection for Young Reluctant Readers.* Evanston, Ill.: John Gordon Burke Publisher, 1990.

Dreyer, Sharon. *The Book Finder When Kids Need Books—Books Published 1979–1982.* Circle Pines, Minn.: American Guidance Services, 1985.

Freeman, Judy. *Books Kids Will Sit Still For.* 2nd ed. Ann Arbor, Mich.: R. R. Bowker, 1990.

Gillespie, John T., and Corinne Naden. *Best Books for Children, Preschool Through Grade 6.* 4th ed. Ann Arbor, Mich.: R. R. Bowker, 1990.

Lima, Carolyn, and John Lima. *A to Zoo: Subject Access to Children's Picture Books.* Ann Arbor, Mich.: R. R. Bowker, 1989.

Subject Guide to Children's Books in Print. Ann Arbor, Mich.: R. R. Bowker, annual.

APPENDIX D:
Checklist to Evaluate Educational Software

Questions to Ask

1. What does the program teach?
   - ✦ Is its primary objective to teach facts? Vocabulary? Basic skills and concepts?
   - ✦ Does it involve students in problem solving? Decision making? Evaluative judgments?
   - ✦ For what level of student is it intended?
2. Do I want to teach what the program teaches?
3. Do I want to use the computer to teach what the program teaches?
4. Is the content of the program up to date and accurate?
5. Is the content presented appropriate for use in an instructional setting?
6. Are the length and pace of the program appropriate for students of the intended age and/or ability level?
7. Are the directions simple and clear? Do they require interpretation by an adult?
8. Is the textual material readable?
9. What role do graphics play in the program?
10. How effective is the system of rewards and corrections?
11. Does the program allow students who have made an error to try a question or program again? Is there opportunity for students to request more practice with the skill or content being studied?

12. Does the program keep track of student progress?
13. Is the program "user-friendly," addressing the student by name or allowing slight variations in answering, e.g., "y" for yes?
14. Is the program free of "glitches," or computer hangups?
15. How is the program protected from accidental wipeouts?
16. What memory is required to run the program?
17. What additional hardware is required?
18. How much does the program disk cost?

CHILDREN'S REFERENCES

Aardema, Verna. *Why Mosquitoes Buzz in People's Ears.* New York: Dial, 1975.

Anno, Mitsumasa et al. *All in a Day.* New York: Philomel, 1986.

———. *Anno's U.S.A.* New York: Philomel, 1983.

———. *The Sundial.* New York: Philomel, 1987.

Asimov, Isaac. *Words from History.* Boston: Houghton Mifflin, 1968.

———. *Words of Science.* Boston: Houghton Mifflin, 1962.

———. *Words on the Map.* Boston: Houghton Mifflin, 1962.

Avi. *Nothing But the Truth.* New York: Orchard, 1991.

Bach, Richard. *Jonathan Livingston Seagull.* New York: Macmillan, 1970.

Bang, Molly. *The Grey Lady and the Strawberry Snatcher.* New York: Four Winds, 1980.

Baylor, Byrd, *Hawk, I'm Your Brother.* New York: Scribner, 1976.

———. *The Way to Start a Day.* New York: Scribner, 1978.

Beim, Lorraine, and Jerold Beim. *Two Is a Team.* New York: Harcourt, Brace, 1945.

Blos, Joan. *A Gathering of Days: A New England Girl's Journal.* New York: Macmillan, 1979.

Blume, Judy. *Blubber.* Scarsdale, N.Y.: Bradbury, 1974.

———. *Forever.* Scarsdale, N.Y.: Bradbury, 1975.

———. *Tales of a Fourth Grade Nothing.* New York: Dell, 1972.

Brown, Marcia. *Shadow.* New York: Macmillan, 1986.

Carle, Eric. *The Mixed-Up Chameleon.* New York: Harper & Row, 1975.

———. *The Rooster Who Set Out to See the World.* New York: Franklin Watts, 1972.

———. *The Very Hungry Caterpillar.* New York: World, 1969.

Carrick, Carol. *The Accident.* New York: Seabury, 1976.

Cleary, Beverly. *Dear Mr. Henshaw.* New York: William Morrow, 1983.

Clifford, Eth. *A Bear Before Breakfast.* New York: G. P. Putnam, 1962.

Cole, Joanna. Books in the *Magic School Bus Series.* New York: Scholastic, various dates.

Coombs, Patricia. *The Magic Pot.* New York: Lothrop, Lee, & Shepard, 1977.

Cooney, Barbara. *Chanticleer and the Fox.* New York: Crowell, 1958.

Davis, Daniel. *Behind Barbed Wire.* New York: Dutton, 1983.

Ets, Marie Hall. *Play with Me.* New York: Viking, 1955.

Flack, Marjorie. *Ask Mister Bear.* New York: Macmillan, 1986.

Fleischman, Paul. *I Am Phoenix: Poems for Two Voices.* New York: Harper & Row, 1985.

———. *Joyful Noises: Poems for Two Voices.* New York: Harper & Row, 1988.

Fleischman, Sid. *Jim Ugly.* New York: Greenwillow, 1992.

Fox, Paula. *One-Eyed Cat.* New York: Bradbury, 1984; New York: Dell, 1985.

———. *The Slave Dancer.* Scarsdale, N.Y.: Bradbury, 1973.

Freedman, Russell. *Indian Chiefs.* New York: Holiday House, 1987.

———. *Lincoln: A Photobiography.* Boston: Houghton Mifflin, 1987.

———. *The Wright Brothers: How They Invented the Airplane.* New York: Holiday House, 1991.

Galdone, Paul. *The Horse, the Fox, and the Lion.* Boston: Houghton Mifflin, 1968.

———. *The Teeny-Tiny Woman*. Boston: Clarion, 1986.

Gardiner, John. *Stone Fox*. New York: Crowell, 1980.

Giff, Patricia. Books in the *Polk Street School Series*. New York: Dell, various dates.

Goble, Paul. *Death of the Iron Horse*. Scarsdale, N.Y.: Bradbury, 1987.

———. *The Girl Who Loved Wild Horses*. Scarsdale, N.Y.: Bradbury, 1978.

———. *Iktomi and the Boulder*. New York: Orchard, 1988.

Grahame, Kenneth. *Wind in the Willows*. New York: Scribner, 1908, 1940.

Greet, W. Cabell, William Jenkins, and Andrew Schiller. *In Other Words: A Beginning Thesaurus (K–2)*. Glenview, Ill.: Scott, Foresman, 1969.

———. *In Other Words: A Junior Thesaurus*. Glenview, Ill.: Scott, Foresman, 1969.

Grifalconi, Ann. *The Village of Round and Square Houses*. Boston: Little, Brown, 1986.

Hader, Berta, and Elmer Hader. *The Big Snow*. New York: Macmillan, 1972.

Haley, Gail. *A Story A Story*. New York: Atheneum, 1970.

Hall, Donald. *Ox-Cart Man*. New York: Viking, 1979.

Hendershot, Judith. *In Coal Country*. New York: Knopf, 1987.

Hoban, Tana. *Circles, Triangles, and Squares*. New York: Macmillan, 1974.

Hogrogian, Nonny. *One Fine Day*. New York: Macmillan, 1971.

Hutchins, Pat. *Rosie's Walk*. New York: Macmillan, 1968.

Hymes, Lucia, and James Hymes. *Hooray for Chocolate*. Reading, Mass.: Addison-Wesley, 1960.

Kalan, Robert. *Jump, Frog, Jump*. New York: Greenwillow, 1981.

Keats, Ezra Jack. *Apt. 3*. New York: Macmillan, 1983.

———. *The Snowy Day*. New York: Viking, 1962.

Kimel, Eric. *Four Dollars and Fifty Cents*. New York: Holiday House, 1990.

Klein, Norma. *Mom, the Wolf Man, and Me*. New York: Pantheon, 1972.

Konigsburg, E. L. *Jennifer, Hecate, Macbeth, William McKinley, and Me, Elizabeth*. New York: Atheneum, 1967.

———. *A Proud Taste for Scarlet and Miniver*. New York: Atheneum/Macmillan, 1973; New York: Dell, 1985.

Lear, Edward. *Complete Nonsense Book*. New York: Dodd, Mead, 1912.

Levinson, Nancy. *I Lift My Lamp: Emma Lazarus and the Statue of Liberty*. New York: Dutton, 1986.

Levinson, Riki. *Watch the Stars Come Out*. New York: Dutton, 1985.

Lindgren, Astrid. *Pippi Longstocking*. New York: Viking, 1969.

Lionni, Leo. *The Biggest House in the World*. New York: Pantheon, 1968.

———. *Frederick*. New York: Pantheon, 1966.

———. *Swimmy*. New York: Pantheon, 1968.

———. *Tico and the Golden Wings*. New York: Pantheon, 1964.

Lobel, Arnold. *Treeful of Pigs*. New York: Greenwillow, 1979.

Low, Joseph. *Mice Twice*. New York: Atheneum, 1981.

Lowry, Lois. *Number the Stars*. Boston: Houghton Mifflin, 1989.

MacLachlan, Patricia. *Sarah, Plain and Tall*. New York: Harper & Row, 1985.

Maestro, Betsy. *The Story of the Statue of Libery*. New York: Lothrop, 1986.

Martin, Bill. *Brown Bear, Brown Bear*. New York: Holt, 1983.

McCloskey, Robert. *Homer Price*. New York: Viking, 1943; Penguin, 1976.

———. *Make Way for Ducklings*. New York: Viking, 1941.

———. *One Morning in Maine*. New York: Viking, 1952.

———. *Time of Wonder*. New York: Viking, 1957.

McDermott, George. *The Stonecutter*. New York: Viking, 1973.

Meltzer, Milton. *Never to Forget: The Jews of the Holocaust*. New York: Harper & Row, 1976.

Merriam, Eve. *It Doesn't Always Have to Rhyme*. New York: Atheneum, 1964.

———. *There Is No Rhyme for Silver*. New York: Atheneum, 1962.

Milne, A. A. *When We Were Very Young.* New York: Dutton, 1961.

Mosel, Arlene. *The Funny Little Woman.* New York: Dutton, 1972.

Naidoo, Beverley. *Journey to Jo'burg.* New York: HarperCollins, 1986.

Naylor, Phyllis Reynolds. *Shiloh.* New York: Atheneum, 1991.

Ness, Evaline. *Sam, Bangs, and Moonshine.* New York: Holt, Rinehart and Winston, 1966.

Parnall, Peter. *Apple Tree.* New York: Macmillan, 1988.

Paterson, Katherine. *Bridge to Terabithia.* New York: Harper & Row, 1977.

———. *The Great Gilly Hopkins.* New York: Crowell, 1978.

———. *Jacob Have I Loved.* New York: Crowell, 1980.

Paulsen, Gary. *Hatchet.* New York: Bradbury, 1987; Puffin, 1988.

Pierce, Meredith Ann. *The Darkangel.* New York: Warner, 1984.

———. *A Gathering of Gargoyles.* New York: Warner, 1985.

Pierce, Philippa. *Tom's Midnight Garden.* New York: Lippincott, 1984.

Provensen, Alice, and Martin Provensen. *The Glorious Flight Across the Channel with Lois Bleriot.* New York: Viking, 1983.

Raskin, Ellen. *The Westing Game.* New York: Dutton, 1978.

Rawls, Wilson. *Where the Red Fern Grows: The Story of Two Dogs and a Boy.* Garden City, N.Y.: Doubleday, 1961.

Rock, Gail. *Thanksgiving Treasure.* New York: Knopf, 1974; New York: Dell, 1986.

Roy, Ron. *Three Ducks Went Wandering.* Ill. by Paul Galdone. New York: Clarion, 1979.

Rylant, Cynthia. *Missing May.* New York: Orchard, 1992.

Schenk de Regniers, Beatrice. *May I Bring a Friend?* New York: Atheneum, 1964.

Schenk de Regniers, Beatrice, et al. *Sing a Song of Popcorn.* New York: Scholastic, 1988.

Seligson, Susan, and Howie Schneider. *Amos: The Story of an Old Dog and His Couch.* Boston: Little, Brown, 1987.

Sendak, Maurice. *Nutshell Library.* New York: Harper Junior Books, 1962.

———. *Where the Wild Things Are.* New York: Harper & Row, 1963, 1988.

Seuss, Dr. *The Butter Battle Book.* New York: Random House, 1984.

———. *Green Eggs and Ham.* New York: Random House, 1960.

———. *Horton Hatches the Egg.* New York: Random House, 1940.

———. *The King's Stilts.* New York: Random House, 1939.

———. *The Lorax.* New York: Random House, 1971.

———. *And To Think That I Saw It on Mulberry Street.* New York: Vanguard, 1937.

Sewall, Marcia. *The Pilgrims of Plimoth.* New York: Atheneum, 1986.

Sharmat, Majorie. *Frizzy the Fearful.* New York: Holiday, 1983.

———. *Nate the Great.* New York: Dell, 1977.

Smith, Doris Buchanan. *A Taste of Blackberries.* New York: Crowell, 1973.

Smith, Judith, and Brenda Parkes. *The Three Billy Goats Gruff.* Crystal Lake, Ill.: Rigby, 1986.

Sparks, Beatrice. *Go Ask Alice.* Englewood Cliffs, N.J.: Prentice-Hall, 1971.

Spier, Peter. *We the People: The Constitution of the United States of America.* New York: Doubleday, 1987.

Spinelli, Jerry. *Maniac Magee.* Boston: Little, Brown, 1990.

Stockton, Frank Richard. *The Lady, or the Tiger? and Other Stories.* New York: Scribner, 1914.

Stolz, Mary. *Storm in the Night.* New York: Harper & Row, 1988.

Taylor, Mildred. *The Friendship.* New York: Dial, 1987.

———. *Let the Circle Be Unbroken.* New York: Dial, 1981.

———. *Roll of Thunder, Hear My Cry.* New York: Dial, 1976.

Travers, Pamela. *Mary Poppins.* New York: Harcourt, Brace, 1934.

Tworkov, Jack. *The Camel Who Took a Walk.* New York: Dutton, 1951.

Vagin, Vladimir, and Frank Asch. *Here Comes the Cat!* New York: Scholastic, 1989.

Van Allsburg, Chris. *The Garden of Abdul Gasazi.* Boston: Houghton Mifflin, 1979.

———. *Jumanji.* Boston: Houghton Mifflin, 1983.

———. *The Polar Express.* Boston: Houghton Mifflin, 1985.

———. *The Z Was Zapped.* Boston: Houghton Mifflin, 1987.

Viorst, Judith. *Alexander and the Terrible, Horrible, No Good, Very Bad Day.* New York: Atheneum, 1972.

———. *I'll Fix Anthony.* New York: Macmillan, 1983, paperback ed.

Voight, Cynthia. *Dicey's Song.* New York: Atheneum/ Macmillan, 1982; New York: Fawcett, 1987.

Waber, Bernard. *"You Look Ridiculous," Said the Rhinoceros to the Hippopotamus.* Boston: Houghton Mifflin, 1966.

Webster's II Riverside Beginning Dictionary. Chicago: Riverside Publishing, 1984.

White, E. B. *Charlotte's Web.* New York: Harper & Row, 1952.

Withers, Carl. *The Tale of a Black Cat.* New York: Holt, Rinehart and Winston, 1966.

REFERENCES

Alvermann, Donna. 1991. "The Discussion Web: A Graphic Aid for Learning Across the Curriculum." *The Reading Teacher*, 45 (October), 92–99.

Anderson, Richard, et al. 1985. *Becoming a Nation of Readers: The Report of the Commission on Reading.* Washington, D.C.: National Institute of Education.

Anderson, William, and Patrick Goff. 1972. *A New Look at Children's Literature.* Belmont, Calif.: Wadsworth.

Au, Kathryn, and Judith Scheu. 1989. "Guiding Students to Interpret a Novel." *The Reading Teacher*, 43 (November), 104–110.

Aulls, Mark W. 1986. "Actively Teaching Main Idea Skills." In *Teaching Main Idea Comprehension.* Ed. James F. Baumann. Newark, Del.: International Reading Association, 108–115.

Avinger, Juanita. 1984. "Word Processors and Language Experience Stories." *Baylor Educator*, 9 (Spring), 26–28.

Balajthy, Ernest. 1986. "Using Microcomputers to Teach Spelling." *The Reading Teacher*, 39 (January), 438–443.

Baratz, Joan. 1969. "Language and Cognitive Assessment of Negro Children: Assumptions and Research Needs." *American Speech and Hearing Association Journal*, 11, 88.

Barber, Bill. 1982. "Creating BYTES of Language." *Language Arts*, 59 (May), 472–475.

Bartch, Julie. 1992. "An Alternative to Spelling: An Integrated Approach." *Language Arts*, 69 (October), 404–408.

Berghoff, Beth, and Kathryn Egawa. 1991. "No More "Rocks": Grouping to Give Students Control of Their Learning." *The Reading Teacher*, 44 (April), 536–541.

Berko, Jean. 1958. "The Child's Learning of English Morphology." *Word*, 14, 150–177.

Berry, Kathleen. 1985. "Talking to Learn Subject Matter/Learning Subject Matter Talk." *Language Arts*, 62 (January), 34–42.

Betza, Ruth. 1987. "Online: Computerized Spelling Checkers: Friends or Foes?" *Language Arts*, 64 (April), 438–443.

Bigelow, William. 1992. "Once Upon a Genocide: Christopher Columbus in Children's Literature." *Language Arts*, 69 (February), 112–120.

Bissex, Glenda. 1980. *GNYS AT WRK: A Child Learns to Read and Write.* Cambridge, Mass.: Harvard University Press.

———. 1981. "Growing Writers in Classrooms." *Language Arts*, 58 (October), 787.

Bloodgood, J. 1991. "A New Approach to Spelling in Language Arts Programs." *The Elementary School Journal*, 92, 203–211.

Bosma, Bette. 1987. "The Nature of Critical Thinking: Its Base and Boundary." Paper presented at the National Council of Teachers of English Conference, Los Angeles, November.

Bouffler, C. 1984. "Spelling as a Language Process." In L. Unsworth, ed., *Reading, Writing, and Spelling: Proceedings of the Fifth Macarthur Reading/Language Symposium.* Sydney, Australia.

Bradley, Virginia. 1982. "Improving Students' Writing with Microcomputers." *Language Arts*, 59 (October), 732–743.

Bridge, Connie, Peter Winograd, and Darliene Haley. 1983. "Using Predictable Materials vs. Preprimers to Teach Beginning Sight Words." *The Reading Teacher*, 36 (May), 884–891.

Bromley, Karen D. 1991. *Webbing and Literature: Creating Story Maps with Children's Books.* Boston: Allyn and Bacon.

Brown, Ann, et al. 1986. In *Reading Comprehension: From Research to Practice.* Ed. J. Orasanu. Hillsdale, N.J.: Erlbaum, 49.

Brown, Hazel, and Brian Cambourne. 1989. *Read and Retell: A Strategy for the Whole Language/Natural Learning Classroom.* Portsmouth, N.H.: Heinemann Educational Books.

Brown, Roger. 1958. *Words and Things.* New York: Free Press.

Brown, Roger, and Ursula Bellugi. 1966. "Three Processes in the Child's Acquisition of Syntax." In *Language Learning.* Ed. Janet Emig. New York: Harcourt Brace Jovanovich.

Bruner, Jerome. 1962. *On Knowing.* Cambridge, Mass.: Harvard University Press.

Bunce-Crim, Marna. 1992. "Evaluation: Tracking Daily Progress." *Instructor,* 101 (March), 24–26.

Burns, Paul, Betty Roe, and Elinor Ross. 1992. *Teaching Reading in Today's Elementary Schools.* 5th ed. Boston: Houghton Mifflin.

Calkins, Lucy. 1982. "When Children Want to Punctuate." In *Donald Graves in Australia.* Ed. R. D. Walshe, Portsmouth, N.H.: Heinemann Educational Books, 89–96.

———. 1986. *The Art of Teaching Writing.* Portsmouth, N.H.: Heinemann Educational Books.

Cambourne, Brian, and Jan Turbill. 1987. *Coping with Chaos.* Rozelle, Australia: Primary English Teaching Association.

Choate, Joyce, and Thomas Rakes. 1988. "The Structured Listening Activity: A Model for Improving Listening Comprehension." *The Reading Teacher,* 41 (November), 194–200.

Chomsky, Noam. 1968. *Language and Mind.* New York: Harcourt and World.

Christie, Frances. 1986. "Learning to Mean in Writing." In *Writing and Reading to Learn.* Ed. Nea Stewart-Dore. Rozelle, Australia: Primary English Teaching Association.

Church, Susan. 1985. "Text Organization: Its Value for Literacy Development." In *Whole Language: Theory in Use.* Ed. Judith Newman. Portsmouth, N.H.: Heinemann Educational Books.

Clark, Roy Peter. 1987. *Free to Write: A Journalist Teaches Young Writers.* Portsmouth, N.H.: Heinemann Educational Books.

Clay, Marie. 1975. *What Did I Write?* Portsmouth, N.H.: Heinemann Educational Books.

———. 1985. *The Early Detection of Reading Difficulties.* Portsmouth, N.H.: Heinemann Educational Books.

Collins, Allan, John Seely Brown, and Ann Holum. 1991. "Cognitive Apprenticeship: Making Thinking Visible." *American Educator,* 15 (Winter), 6–11, 38–46.

Commission on Reading. 1985. *Becoming a Nation of Readers.* Washington, D.C.: National Academy of Education, The National Institute of Education, The Center for the Study of Reading, 91.

Congress of the United States. 1975. *Education for All Handicapped Children Act, Public Law 94–142.* Washington, D.C.: U.S. Government Printing Office.

Cook-Gumperz, J., and J. Gumperz. 1981. "From Oral to Written Culture: The Transition to Literacy." In *Variations in Writing.* Ed. M. Whiteman. Hillsdale, N.J.: Erlbaum.

Cooper, Pamela, and Rives Collins. 1991. *Look What Happened to Frog: Storytelling in Education.* Scottsdale, Ariz.: Gorsuch Scarisbrick.

Cooter, Robert. 1989. "Assessment." *The Reading Teacher,* 43 (December), 256–258.

Cosgrove, Maryellen. 1987. "Reading Aloud to Children: The Effect of Listening on the Reading Comprehension and Attitudes of Fourth and Sixth Graders in Six Communities in Connecticut." Unpublished doctoral dissertation, University of Connecticut.

Cox, Carole, and Joyce Many. 1992. "Toward an Understanding of the Aesthetic Response to Literature." *Language Arts,* 69 (January), 28–33.

Cramer, Ronald. 1979. *Children's Writing and Language Growth.* Columbus, Ohio: Merrill.

Crowhurst, Marion. 1979. "Developing Syntactic Skill: Doing What Comes Naturally." *Language Arts,* 56 (May), 522–525.

Cunningham, Patricia, and James Cunningham. 1987. "Context Area Reading-Writing Lessons." *The Reading Teacher,* 40 (February), 506–512.

Dale, Philip. 1976. *Language Development: Structure and Function.* 2d ed. New York: Holt, Rinehart and Winston, 18.

D'Alessandro, Marilyn. 1990. "Accommodating Emotionally Handicapped Chidlren Through a Literature-Based Reading Program." *The Reading Teacher,* 44 (December), 288–293.

Davey, Beth. 1983. "Think Aloud—Modeling the Cognitive Processes of Reading Comprehension." *Journal of Reading,* 27 (October), 44–47.

DeFord, Diane, and Jerome Harste. 1982. "Child Language Research and Curriculum." *Language Arts,* 59 (September), 590–600.

DeStephano, Joanna, Harold Pepinsky, and Tobie Sanders. 1982. "Discourse Rules and Literacy Learning in a Classroom." In *Communicating in the Classroom.* Ed. L. Wilkinson. New York: Academic Press.

Dickinson, David. 1987. "Oral Language, Literacy Skills, and Response to Literature." In *Dynamics of Language Learning.* Ed. James Squire. Urbana, Ill.: National Council of Teachers of English.

Dillon, David, and Dennis Searle. 1981. "The Role of Language in One First Grade Classroom." *Research in the Teaching of English,* 15 (December), 311–328.

DiStefano, Philip, and Patricia Hagerty. 1985. "Teaching Spelling at the Elementary Level." *The Reading Teacher,* 38 (January), 373–377.

Durkin, Dolores. 1981. "What Is the Value of the New Interest in Reading Comprehension?" *Language Arts,* 58 (January), 24–25.

Dyson, Anne. 1981. "Oral Language: The Rooting System for Learning to Write." *Language Arts,* 58 (October), 776–784.

Dyson, Anne, and Celia Genishi. 1983. "Research Currents: Children's Language for Learning." *Language Arts,* 60 (September), 751–757.

Elley, W. B., et al. 1976. "The Role of Grammar in the Secondary School English Curriculum." In *Research in the Teaching of Writing,* 10, 5–21. ED 112 410.

Ennis, Robert. 1987. "A Taxonomy of Critical Thinking Dispositions and Abilities." *Teaching Thinking Skills: Theory and Practice.* Ed. Joan Baron and Robert Sternberg. New York: W. H. Freeman, 1987.

Ernst, Franklin. 1968. *Who's Listening?* Addresso Set.

Faix, Thomas. 1975. "Listening as a Human Relations Art." *Elementary English.* 52 (March), 409–413.

Farr, Roger. 1987. Paper presented at the Great Lakes Regional Conference, International Reading Association, October 1987.

Farris, Pamela. 1991. "Views and Other Views: Handwriting Instruction Should Not Become Extinct." *Language Arts,* 68 (April), 312–314.

Ferreiro, E., and A. Teberosky. 1982. *Literacy before Schooling.* Portsmouth, N.H.: Heinemann Educational Books.

Fisher, Carol. 1993. "Pick a Pair for More than Twice the Impact." *The New Advocate* (Spring), xiii–xiv.

Flood, James, and Diane Lapp. 1986. "Getting the Main Idea of the Main Idea: A Writing/Reading Process." In *Teaching Main Idea Comprehension.* Ed. James F. Baumann. Newark, Del.: International Reading Association, 227–237.

———. 1987. "Reading and Writing Relations: Assumptions and Directions." In *Dynamics of Language Learning.* Ed. James Squire. Urbana, Ill.: National Council of Teachers of English.

Ford, Michael, and Marilyn Ohlhausen. 1988. "Tips from Reading Clinicians for Coping with Disabled Readers in Regular Classrooms." *The Reading Teacher,* 42 (October), 18–22.

Fredericks, Anthony, and Timothy Rasinski. 1990. "Involving Parents in the Assessment Process." *The Reading Teacher,* 44 (December), 346–349.

Funk, Hal, and Gary Funk. 1989. "Guidelines for Developing Listening Skills." *The Reading Teacher,* 42 (May), 660–663.

Gallagher, James. 1975. "The Culturally Different Gifted." In *Teaching the Gifted Child,* 2nd ed. Boston: Allyn and Bacon, 367–387.

Gambrell, Linda. 1985. "Dialogue Journals: Reading-Writing Interaction." *The Reading Teacher,* 38 (February), 512–515.

Gambrell, Linda, Patricia Koskinen, and Barbara Kapinus. 1985. "A Comparison of Retelling and Questioning on Reading Comprehension." Paper presented at the National Reading Conference, San Diego, December 1985.

Gambrell, Linda, Warren Pfeiffer, and Robert Wilson. 1985. "The Effects of Retelling on Reading Comprehension." *Journal of Educational Research,* 78 (July/August), 216–220.

Gentry, J. Richard. 1987. *Spel Is a Four-Letter Word.* Portsmouth, N.H.: Heinemann Educational Books.

Giacobbe, Mary Ellen. 1981. "Kids Can Write the First Week of School." *Learning,* 9 (September), 130–132.

Gill, J. Thomas. 1992. "Focus on Research: Development of Word Knowledge as It Relates to Reading, Spelling, and Instruction." *Language Arts,* 69 (October), 444–453.

Glasser, William. 1986. *Control Theory in the Classroom.* New York: HarperCollins.

Glenn, C., and N. Stein. 1979. "An Analysis of Story Comprehension in Elementary School Children." In *New Directions in Discourse Processing,* Vol. 2. Ed. R. Freedle. Hillsdale, N.J.: Erlbaum.

Goodman, Kenneth, and Yetta Goodman. 1983. "Reading and Writing Relationships: Pragmatic Functions." *Language Arts,* 60 (May), 590–591.

Goodman, Yetta, and Carolyn Burke. 1972. *Reading Miscue Inventory: Manual Procedures for Diagnosis and Evaluation.* New York: Macmillan.

Graves, Donald. 1976. "Let's Get Rid of the Welfare Mess in the Teaching of Writing." *Language Arts,* 53 (September), 645–651.

———. 1979. "What Children Show Us about Revision." *Language Arts,* 56 (March), 318–319.

———. 1983. *Writing: Teachers and Children at Work.* Portsmouth, N.H.: Heinemann Educational Books.

———. Donald. 1991. "Trust the Shadows." *The Reading Teacher,* 45 (September), 18–24.

Graves, Donald, and Susan Sowers. 1979. "Research Update—A Six-Year-Old's Writing Process, The First Half of First Grade." *Language Arts,* 56 (October), 831.

Hall, Nigel. 1987. *The Emergence of Literacy.* Portsmouth, N.H.: Heinemann Educational Books.

Hall, Robert. 1960. *Linguistics and Your Language.* New York: Anchor Books.

Halliday, Michael. 1975. *Explorations in the Functions of Language.* New York: Elsevier.

———. 1977. *Learning How to Mean: Explorations in the Development of Language.* New York: Elsevier.

Hancock, Marjorie. 1992. "Literature Response Journals: Insights Beyond the Printed Page." *Language Arts,* 69 (January), 36–42.

Hanna, Paul, Richard Hodges, and Jean Hanna. 1971. *Spelling: Structure and Strategies.* Boston: Houghton Mifflin.

Hansen, Jane. 1987. *When Writers Read.* Portsmouth, N.H.: Heinemann Educational Books.

Harp, Bill. 1987. "What Are Your Kids Writing During Reading Time?" *The Reading Teacher,* 41 (October), 88–89.

———. 1988. "Why Are Your Kids Singing During Reading Time?" *The Reading Teacher,* 41 (January), 454–456.

Harris, John. 1986. "Children as Writers." In *Literacy.* Ed. Asher Cashdan. Oxford, England: Basil Blackwell Ltd., 82–111.

Harste, Jerome. 1982. "What's in a Scribble?" Speech given at the 7th Annual Lester Smith Conference on Educational Research, February 1982, as quoted in DeFord and Harste.

———. 1989. *New Policy Guidelines for Reading: Connecting Research and Practice.* Urbana, Ill.: National Council of Teachers of English.

Harste, Jerome, Virginia Woodward, and Carolyn Burke. 1984. *Language Stories and Literacy Lessons.* Portsmouth, N.H.: Heinemann Educational Books.

Hayakawa, S. I. 1964. *Language in Thought and Action.* 2nd ed. New York: Harcourt Brace Jovanovich.

Haynes, Elizabeth. 1978. "Using Research in Preparing to Teach Writing." *English Journal* (January), 82–88.

Heald-Taylor, B. Gail. 1987. "Big Books." *Ideas with Insights: Language Arts K–6.* Ed. Dorothy Watson. Urbana, Ill.: National Council of Teachers of English.

Heathcote, Dorothy. 1983. "Learning, Knowing, and Languaging in Drama." *Language Arts,* 60 (September), 695–696.

Henderson, Edmund. 1981. *Learning to Read and Spell: The Child's Knowledge of Words.* DeKalb, Ill.: Northern Illinois University Press.

———. 1990. *Teaching Spelling,* 2nd ed. Boston: Houghton Mifflin.

Hildreth, Gertrude. 1966. *Introduction to the Gifted.* New York: McGraw-Hill.

Hillerich, Robert. 1985. "Dealing with Grammar." In *Teaching Children to Write, K–8.* Englewood Cliffs, N.J.: Prentice-Hall.

Hillocks, George. 1986. *Research on Written Composition: New Directions for Teaching.* Urbana, Ill.: ERIC Clearinghouse on Reading and Communication Skills and the National Conference on Research in English.

———. 1987. "Synthesis of Research on Teaching Writing." *Educational Leadership,* 44 (May), 71–82.

Hirsch, E. D. 1987. *Cultural Literacy.* Boston: Houghton Mifflin.

Hodges, Richard. 1982. "On the Development of Spelling Ability." *Language Arts,* 59 (March), 284–290.

Hoffman, James. 1992. "Critical Reading/Thinking Across the Curriculum: Using I-Charts to Support Learning." *Language Arts,* 69 (February), 121–127.

Holdaway, Don. 1982. "The Big Book—A Discussion with Don Holdaway." *Language Arts,* 59 (November/December), 815–821.

———. 1986. "Guiding a Natural Process." *Roles in Literacy Learning.* Newark, Del.: International Reading Association.

Holowinsky, Ivan. 1983. *Psychology and Education of Exceptional Children and Adolescents.* Princeton, N.J.: Princeton Books.

Horn, Ernest. 1926. *A Basic Writing Vocabulary—10,000 Words Most Commonly Used in Writing.* University of Iowa Monographs in Education, First Series, No. 41. Iowa City: University of Iowa Press.

———. 1960. "Spelling." In *Encyclopedia of Educational Research.* 3rd ed. American Educational Association.

Horn, Thomas. 1947. "The Effect of the Corrected Test on Learning to Spell." *Elementary School Journal,* 47 (January), 277–285.

Howard, Robert. 1987. *Concepts and Schemata: An Introduction.* London: Cassell.

Hoyt, Linda. 1992. "Many Ways of Knowing: Using Drama, Oral Interactions, and the Visual Arts to Enhance Reading Comprehension." *The Reading Teacher,* 45 (April), 580–584.

Huck, Charlotte, et al. 1993. *Children's Literature in the Elementary School.* 5th ed. New York: Holt, Rinehart and Winston.

Hunt, Kellogg, and Roy O'Donnell. 1970. "An Elementary School Curriculum to Develop Better Writing Skills." U.S. Office of Education Grant. Florida State University.

Hunter, Madeline. 1982. *Mastery Teaching.* El Segundo, Calif.: TIP Publications.

Joint Committee of the National Council of Teachers of English and Children's Theatre Association. 1983. "Forum: Informal Classroom Drama." *Language Arts,* 60 (March), 370–372.

Kellogg, W. N., and L. A. Kellogg. 1933. *The Ape and the Child.* New York: McGraw-Hill.

Kelly, Patricia. 1990. "Guiding Young Students' Response to Literature." *The Reading Teacher,* 43 (March), 464–470.

Kirby, Dan, et al. 1988. "Beyond Interior Decorating: Using Writing to Make Meaning in the Elementary School." *Phi Delta Kappan,* 69 (June), 718–724.

Kirk, Samuel, James Gallagher, and Nicholas Anastasiow, 1993. *Educating Exceptional Children.* 7th ed. Boston: Houghton Mifflin.

Kolata, Gina. 1987. "Associations or Rules in Language Learning?" *Science,* 237 (July), 133–134.

Koskinen, Patricia, Linda Gambrell, Barbara Kapinus, and Betty Heathington. 1988. "Retelling: A Strategy for Enhancing Students' Reading Comprehension." *The Reading Teacher,* 41 (May), 892–896.

Kucer, Stephen, and Lynn Rhodes. 1986. "Counterpart Strategies: Fine Tuning Language with Language." *Reading Teacher,* 40 (November), 186–193.

Kuhl, Patricia, et al. 1992. "Linguistic Experience Alters Phonetic Perception in Infants by 6 Months of Age." *Science,* January 31, 606–608.

Lange, Bob. 1981. "Directing Classroom Communication." *Language Arts,* 58 (September), 729–733.

———. 1982. "Questioning Techniques." *Language Arts,* 59 (February), 180–185.

LaPointe, Archie. 1986. "The State of Instruction in Reading and Writing in U.S. Elementary Schools." *Phi Delta Kappan,* 68 (October), 838–847.

Lefevre, Carl. 1973. *Linguistics, English, and the Language Arts.* New York: Teachers College Press.

Lehman, B., and D. Hayes. 1985. "Advancing Critical Reading Through Historical Fiction and Biography." *Social Studies,* 76, 165–169.

Lindfors, Judith. 1987. *Children's Language and Learning.* Englewood Cliffs, N.J.: Prentice-Hall.

Loban, Walter. 1963. *The Language of Elementary School Children.* Urbana, Ill.: National Council of Teachers of English.

———. 1976. *Language Development: Kindergarten Through Grade 12.* Urbana, Ill.: National Council of Teachers of English.

Lukens, Rebecca J. 1991. *A Critical Handbook of Children's Literature.* 4th ed. Glenview, Ill.: Scott, Foresman.

Lundsteen, Sara. 1979. *Listening: Its Impact at All Levels on Reading and the Other Language Arts.* Urbana, Ill.: National Council of Teachers of English.

Manzo, Anthony. 1975. "Guided Reading Procedure." *Journal of Reading,* 18, 287–291.

———. 1985. "Expansion Modules for the ReQuest, CAT, GRP, and REAP Reading/Study Procedures." *Journal of Reading,* 28, 498–502.

Maria, Katherine. 1989. "Developing Disadvantaged Children's Background Knowledge Interactively." *The Reading Teacher,* 42 (January), 296–300.

Martin, Bill. 1974. *Sounds of Language Series.* New York: Holt, Rinehart and Winston.

Martin, Samuel. 1964. "Review of Greenberg's Universals of Language." *Harvard Review,* 34, 353–355.

McCrone, John. 1991. *The Ape That Spoke.* New York: William Morrow.

Mellon, John. 1969. *Transformational Sentence-Combining.* Research Report No. 10. Urbana, Ill.: National Council of Teachers of English.

Miller, Barbara, and James Ney. 1968. "The Effect of Systematic Oral Exercises on the Writing of Fourth-Grade Students." *Research in the Teaching of English* (Fall).

Miller, George. 1988. "The Challenge of Universal Literacy." *Science,* September 9, 1293–1300.

Milz, Vera. 1985. "First Graders' Uses for Writing." In *Observing the Language Learner.* Ed. Angela Jagger and Trica Smith-Burke. Newark, Del.: International Reading Association.

Moe, Alden, and Judith Irwin. 1986. "Cohesion, Coherence, and Comprehension." In *Understanding and Teaching Cohesion Comprehension.* Ed. Judith Irwin. Newark, Del.: International Reading Association.

Morris, Darrell. 1983. "Concept of Word and Phoneme Awareness in the Beginning Reader." *Research in the Teaching of English,* 17 (December), 359–373.

———. 1987. "Meeting the Needs of the Poor Speller in the Elementary School." *Illinois Schools Journal* (Spring), 28–41.

Morrow, Lesley. 1985. "Reading and Retelling Stories: Strategies for Emergent Readers." *The Reading Teacher,* 35 (May), 870–875.

———. 1985. "Retelling Stories: A Strategy for Improving Young Children's Comprehension, Concept of Story Structure, and Oral Language Complexity." *Elementary School Journal,* 85, 647–661.

———. 1986. "Effects of Structural Guidance in Story Retelling on Children's Dictation of Original Stories." *Journal of Reading Behavior,* 18 (Spring), 135–151.

Moss, R. K., and John Stansell. 1983. "Wof Stew: A Recipe for Writing Growth and Enjoyment." *Language Arts,* 60 (March), 346–350.

Murray, Donald. 1982. *Learning by Teaching: Selected Articles on Writing and Teaching.* Montclair, N.J.: Boynton-Cook.

National Assessment of Educational Progress. 1975. *Writing Mechanics, 1969–1974: A Capsule Description of Changes in Writing Mechanics.* Washington, D.C.: U.S. Government Printing Office.

Nelson, Dorothy. 1976. "D. and E.: Show and Tell Grows Up." *Language Arts,* 53 (February), 203–205.

"New Dictionary Tells Story of American Life." 1992. A. P. *Newark Star Ledger* (July 12).

Newkirk, Thomas. 1978. *Grammar Instruction and Writing: What Does Research Really Prove?* ERIC Document, ED 153 218.

Newkirk, Thomas, and Nancie Atwell, eds. 1986. *Understanding Writing, Ways of Observing, Learning, and Teaching K–8.* Portsmouth, N.H.: Heinemann Educational Books.

Nicholson, Tom, and Sumner Schachter. 1979. "Spelling Skill and Teaching Practice: Putting Them Back Together Again." *Language Arts,* 56 (October), 804–809.

Nickerson, Raymond. 1986. *Reflections on Reasoning.* Hillsdale, N.J.: Erlbaum.

———. 1987. "Why Teach Thinking?" In *Teaching Thinking Skills: Theory and Practice.* Ed. Joan Baron and Robert Sternberg. New York: W. H. Freeman.

Norwicki, Stephen, and Marshall Duke. 1992. *Helping the Child Who Doesn't Fit In.* Atlanta: Peachtree Press.

O'Hare, Frank. 1973. *Sentence Combining.* Research Report No. 15. Urbana, Ill.: National Council of Teachers of English.

Olson, David. 1983. "Perspectives: Children's Language and Language Teaching." *Language Arts,* 60 (February), 227–229.

Palincsar, Annemarie, and Ann Brown. 1985. In *Reading Education: Foundations for a Literate America.* Ed. J. Osborn et al. Lexington, Mass.: Lexington Books.

———. 1986. "Interactive Teaching to Promote Independent Learning from Text." *The Reading Teacher,* 39 (April), 771–777.

Pardo, Laura, and Taffy Raphael. 1991. "Classroom Organization for Instruction in Content Areas." *The Reading Teacher,* 44 (April), 556–564.

Pearson, David, and Linda Fielding. 1982. "Research Update: Listening Comprehension." *Language Arts,* 59 (September), 617–629.

Perron, Jack. 1978. "Beginning Writing: It's All in the Mind." *Language Arts,* 53 (September), 652–657.

Peterson, Ralph. 1987. "Literature Groups: Intensive and Extensive Reading." In *Ideas with Insights: Language Arts K–6.* Ed. Dorothy Watson. Urbana, Ill.: National Council of Teachers of English.

Petrosky, A. 1977. "Grammar Instruction: What We Know." *English Journal,* 66, 86–88.

Piaget, Jean. 1964. *The Psychology of Intelligence.* Boston: Routledge and Kegan Paul.

———. 1965. *The Language and Thought of the Child.* New York: Meridian Books.

Pinker, S., and A. Prince. 1987. "On Language and Connectionism: Analysis of Parallel Distributed Processing Model of Language Acquisition." Occasional Paper No. 33. Cambridge, Mass.: MIT Press.

Plank, Edward. 1992. Personal communication with author.

Porter, Jane. 1972. "Research Report by James Martin— The Development of Sentence Writing Skills at Grades Three, Four, and Five." *Elementary English,* 49 (October), 867–870.

Purves, Alan. 1975. "Research in the Teaching of Literature." *Language Arts,* 52 (April), 463–466.

Quintero, Elizabeth, and Ana Huerta-Macias. 1990. "All in the Family: Bilingualism and Biliteracy." *The Reading Teacher,* 44 (December), 306–312.

Ramsey, John. 1988. "Why Is Left Handed Writing Still a Problem in the Last 7th of the 20th Century?" *The Reading Teacher,* 41 (February), 504–506.

Raphael, Taffy. 1992. "Research Directions: Literature and Discussion in the Reading Program." *Language Arts,* 69 (January), 54–61.

Raths, Louis. 1978. *Values and Teaching.* Columbus, Ohio: Merrill.

Ravitch, Diane, and Chester Finn. 1987. *What Do Our 17-Year-Olds Know?* New York: Harper & Row.

Read, Charles. 1971. "Pre-school Children's Knowledge of English Phonology." *Harvard Educational Review,* 41, 1–34.

Robinson, Francis. 1961. *Effective Study.* Rev. ed. New York: Harper & Row.

Rodriguez, Richard. 1981. *Hunger of Memory: The Education of Richard Rodriguez.* Boston: David Godine, 60.

Rosenblatt, Louise. 1978. *The Reader, the Text, the Poem.* Carbondale, Ill.: Southern Illinois University Press.

Routman, Regie. 1993. "The Uses and Abuses of Invented Spelling." *Instructor,* 102 (May/June), 36–39.

Rumelhart, D. E., and J. L. McClelland. 1987. "Learning the Past Tenses of English Verbs: Implicit Rules or Parallel Distributed Processing?" In *Mechanism of Language Acquisition.* Ed. B. MacWhinney. Hillsdale, N.J.: Erlbaum.

Samuels, S. Jay, and Alan Farstrup, eds. 1992. *What Research Has to Say about Reading Instruction.* 2nd ed. Newark, Del.: International Reading Association.

Scheflen, Albert. 1972. *Body Language and the Social Order.* Englewood Cliffs, N.J.: Prentice-Hall.

Schlagal, Robert, and Jay Schlagal. 1992. "The Integral Character of Spelling: Teaching Strategies for Multiple Purposes." *Language Arts,* 69 (October), 418–424.

Schreiber, P. A. 1980. "On the Acquisition of Reading Fluency." *Journal of Reading Behavior,* 12, 177–186, as reported by David Pearson and Linda Fielding, "Research Update: Listening Comprehension." *Language Arts,* 59 (September), 617–629.

Shafer, Robert. 1974. "What Teachers Should Know about Children's Language." *Language Arts,* 51 (April), 498–501.

Shuy, Roger. 1987. "Research Currents: Dialogue as the Heart of Learning." *Language Arts,* 64 (December), 890–897.

Simon, Sidney. 1976. *Values, Concepts, and Techniques.* Washington, D.C.: National Education Association.

Simon, Sidney, et al. 1972. *Values Clarification: A Handbook of Practical Strategies for Teachers and Students.* New York: Hart Publishing.

Siu-Runyan, Yvonne. 1991. "Holistic Assessment in Intermediate Classes: Techniques for Informing Our Teachers." In *Assessment and Evaluation in Whole Language Programs.* Ed. Bill Harp. Norwood, Mass.: Christopher-Gordon.

Smith, Carl. 1990. "Two Approaches to Critical Thinking." *The Reading Teacher,* 44 (December), 350–351.

———. 1991. "The Role of Different Literary Genre." *The Reading Teacher,* 44 (February), 440–441.

Smith, Frank. 1983. "Reading Like a Writer." *Language Arts,* 60 (May), 558–567.

———. 1992. "Learning to Read: The Never-Ending Debate." *Phi Delta Kappan,* 73 (February), 432–441.

Snow, C. E. 1977. "The Development of Conversation Between Mothers and Babies." *Journal of Child Language,* 4.

Somerfield, Muriel, et al. 1985. *A Framework for Reading: Creating a Policy in the Elementary School.* North America adaptation by Arlene Pillar. Portsmouth, N.H.: Heinemann Educational Books.

Spivey, Nancy. 1991. "Discourse Synthesis." *The Reading Teacher,* 44 (May), 702–703.

Squire, James. 1983. "Composing and Comprehending: Two Sides of the Same Basic Process." *Language Arts,* 60 (May), 581–589.

Staab, Claire. 1991. "Talk in Whole-Language Classrooms." In *Whole Language: Practice and Theory.* Ed. Victor Froese. Boston: Allyn and Bacon.

Staton, Jana. 1988. "ERIC/RCS Report: Dialogue Journals." *Language Arts,* vol. no. (February), 198–201.

Stauffer, Russell. 1979. "The Language Experience Approach to Reading Instruction for Deaf and Hearing Impaired Children." *The Reading Teacher,* 33 (October), 21–24.

———. 1980. *The Language Experience Approach to the Teaching of Reading.* 2nd ed. New York: Harper & Row.

Stauffer, Russell, and John Pikulski. 1974. "A Comparison and Measure of Oral Language Growth." *Elementary English,* 51 (November/December), 1151–1155.

Sternberg, Robert. 1984. "Testing Intelligence without I.Q. Tests." *Phi Delta Kappan* (June), 694–698.

Stieglitz, Ezra, and Varda Stieglitz. 1981. "SAVOR the Word to Reinforce Vocabulary in the Content Areas." *Journal of Reading,* 25 (October), 46–51.

Stoddard, Elizabeth. 1982. "The Combined Effect of Creative Thinking and Sentence-Combining Activities on the Writing Abilities of Above Average Fifth and Sixth Grade Students." Ph.D. diss., University of Connecticut.

Stotsky, S. 1983. "Types of Lexical Cohesion in Expository Writing." *College Composition and Communication,* 34, 568–580.

Stout, Hilary. 1992. "Many U.S. Children Don't Read Enough, Can't Analyze the Material, Study Finds." *The Wall Street Journal* (May 29).

Strickland, Dorothy. 1973. "A Program for Linguistically Different Black Children." *Research in the Teaching of English,* 7 (Spring), 79–86.

Taba, Hilda, et al. 1964. *Thinking in Elementary School Children.* San Francisco: San Francisco State College.

———. 1967. "Teaching Strategies for Cognitive Growth." In *Conceptual Models in Teacher Education.* Ed. John Verduin. Washington, D.C.: American Association of Colleges for Teacher Education.

Taylor, Barbara, and Linda Nosbush. 1983. "Oral Reading for Meaning: A Technique for Improving Word Identification Skills." *The Reading Teacher,* 37 (December), 234–237.

Taylor, Denny, and Catherine Dorsey-Gaines. 1988. *Growing Up Literate: Learning from Inner-City Families.* Portsmouth, N.H.: Heinemann Educational Books.

Teale, William. 1992. "Dear Readers." *Language Arts,* 69 (October), 401–404.

———. 1982. "Toward a Theory of How Children Learn to Read and Write Naturally." *Language Arts,* 59 (September), 555–570.

Temple, Charles, et al. 1988. *The Beginnings of Writing.* 2nd ed. Boston: Allyn & Bacon.

Templeton, Shane. 1979. "The Circle Game of English Spelling." *Language Arts,* 56 (October), 789–797.

Terman, Lewis, and Maud Merrill. 1960. *Stanford-Binet Intelligence Scale: Manual for the Third Revision Form L-M.* Boston: Houghton Mifflin.

Tierney, Robert J. 1990. "Learning to Connect Reading and Writing: Critical Thinking Through Transactions with One's Own Subjectivity." In *Reading and Writing Together: New Perspectives for the Classroom.* Ed. Timothy Shanahan. Norwood, Mass.: Christopher-Gordon, 131–143.

Tierney, Robert, Mark Carter, and Laura Desai. 1991. *Portfolio Assessment in the Reading-Writing Classroom.* Norwood, Mass.: Christopher-Gordon.

Tierney, Robert, and F. David Pearson. 1983. "Toward a Composing Model of Reading." *Language Arts,* 60 (May), 568–580.

Trelease, Jim. 1989. *The New Read-Aloud Handbook.* Rev. ed. New York: Penguin.

Valencia, Sheila. 1990. "A Portfolio Approach to Classroom Reading Assessment: The Whys, Whats and Hows." *The Reading Teacher,* 43 (January), 338–340.

Vermont Assessment Program. 1991. Montpelier, Vt.: Vermont Department of Education, mimeographed document.

Vygotsky, Lev. 1962, 1986. *Thought and Language.* Cambridge, Mass.: MIT Press.

———. 1962. *Thought and Action.* Cambridge, Mass.: MIT Press.

Walshe, R. D., ed. 1982. *Donald Graves in Australia.* Portsmouth, N.H.: Heinemann Educational Books.

Watson, Dorothy, ed. 1987. *Ideas with Insights: Language Arts K–6.* Urbana, Ill.: National Council of Teachers of English.

Watson, Dorothy. 1988. "What Do We Find in a Whole-Language Program?" In *Reading Process and Practice.* Ed. Constance Weaver. Portsmouth, N.H.: Heinemann Educational Books.

Watson, Jerry. 1991. "An Integral Setting Tells More Than When and Where." *The Reading Teacher,* 44 (May), 638–646.

Weaver, Constance. 1991. *Alternatives in Understanding and Educating Attention-Deficit Students.* Urbana, Ill.: National Council of Teachers of English.

Weaver, Constance, and L. Henke, eds. 1992. *Supporting Whole Language: Stories of Teachers and Instructional Change.* Portsmouth, N.H.: Heinemann Educational Books.

Weiger, Myra. 1976. "Moral Judgment in Children." Ph.D. diss., Rutgers University.

Wells, Gordon. 1979. "Describing Children's Linguistic Development." *British Educational Research Journal,* 5, 75–98.

Wells, Gordon. 1986. *The Meaning Makers.* Portsmouth, N.H.: Heinemann Educational Books.

Wilkinson, Andrew. 1970. "The Concept of Oracy." *English Journal,* 59 (January), 70–77.

Winn, Deanna. 1988. "Develop Listening Skills as a Part of the Curriculum." *The Reading Teacher,* 42 (November), 144–146.

Winograd, Peter, Scott Paris, and Connie Bridge. 1991. "Improving the Assessment of Literacy." *The Reading Teacher,* 45 (October), 108–116.

Wittrock, M. C. 1983. "Writing and the Teaching of Reading." *Language Arts,* 60 (May), 600–605.

Wolf, Maryanne, and David Dickinson. 1985. In *The Development of Language.* Ed. Jean Berko-Gleason. Columbus, Ohio: Merrill.

Woodward, Virginia. 1984. "Redefining Literacy Development: A Social Interactional Perspective." Speech given at the International Reading Association Convention, May 9, 1984, Atlanta.

Zarrillo, James, 1989. "Teachers' Interpretations of Literature-Based Reading." *The Reading Teacher,* 43 (October), 22–28.

INDEX

Fiction, historical and realistic, 296
Field trips
    base for writing and speaking, 44–45, 231, 234–236
    gathering sense impressions, 234–236, 239
Figured verse, 306–309
Figures of speech, 102, 301–303, 466
Fielding, Linda, on listening and reading, 136
Filmstrips, 191
Finger and action plays, 200–201, 446–447
Fisher, Caroll, on literature pairs, 478
Five, Cora Lee, on special voices, 74
Flannel board, 180, 190
Fletcher, Ralph, on writing, 310, 316
Flood, James
    on grouping for classroom instruction, 126
    on oral language and reading ability, 13
    on Readers' Theatre, 186
Flores, Barbara, on myths about learning, 59
Flow diagrams, or charts, 322–324
Flynn, Linda, on critical reading, 467
Focal dimension of a unit, 27
Folders, writing, see portfolios
Ford, Michael, on remedial reading, 60
Forever, 132
Formal operational stage, 81
Four Dollars & Fifty Cents, 119
Fox, Paula, on writing, 141
Fox, Sharon, on oral language development, 106
Fragments (sentence), 361
Frederick , 478
Fredricks, Anthony, on use of checklists by caregivers, 71
Freeman, Evelyn, on using nonfiction trade books, 141, 488
Freeman, Yvonne, on whole language for second language users, 74
Free verse, 240, 297–298
Friendship, The, 113
Frizzy the Fearful , 111
From the Mixed Up Files of Mrs. Basil E. Frankweiler, 296
Frost, Robert, on a sentence, 96
Fuhler, Carol, on learning disabled and literature, 61
Full-class (or whole class) instruction, 22–23
Functions of language, 83–84
Function words, 379–380, 382–384
Funk, Hal and Gary, on listening, 148, 150
Funny Little Woman, The, 121, 174
Fyleman, Rose, "The Goblin," 195

Gable, Robert, on spelling, 402
Galda, Lee
    on multicultural literature, 56
    on the reader's response to story, 109, 467
    on sounds of poetry, 303

Gallagher, James, on gifted children, 66
Gallagher, Nora, on punctuation marks, 372
Gallas, Karen, on sharing time, 182
Gambrell, Linda
    on dialogue journals, 290
    on retelling stories, 183
Games, spelling, 395–397
Garden of Abdul Gasazi, The, 113, 115
Garrett, Jeffrey, on Virginia Hamilton, 116
Gathering of Days: A New England Girl's Journal, 289
Gathering of Gargoyles, A, 277
Geisel, Theodore Seuss, see Dr. Seuss,
Generalizing about
    language usage, 368–369
    spelling patterns, 396–397, 406–407
Generating sentences, 355–360, 474
Generative grammar, 92–93, 380
Generative theory of language acquisition, 92–93
Genishi, Celia
    on early writing, 282
    on the importance of dialogue, 230
    on thinking, 264
Gentry, J. Richard, on teaching spelling, 405, 442
Giacobbe, M. E., on writing and drawing, 282
Gibbons, Pauline, on bilingual learning, 55
Gifted children, 63–66
Gill, J. Thomas, on young children's spelling, 400
Gillet, Jean, on nonstandard English, 60
Gillham, Bruce, on content-area talk, 207
Girl from Yamhill: A Memoir, A, 296
Girl Who Loved Wild Horses, The, 113
Gitelman, Honre, on gifted readers, 64
Glasser, William, on collaborative learning, 23, 50–51
Glazer, Joan, on literature, 203
Glazer, Susan, on portfolios and collaborative assessment, 74, 347
Glenn, C., on story structure, 320, 476
Glittering generalities, 171
Glorious Flight Across the Channel with Louis Bleriot, 129
Go Ask Alice, 132
"Goblin," by Rose Fyleman, 195
Gold, Judith, on literature response groups, 470
Goldenberg, Claude, on conversation, 259
Goldstein, Bobbye, on poetry, 422
Goodman, Kenneth
    on miscues, 455
    on reading and writing, 283
    on whole language approach, 10, 41
Goodman, Yetta
    on miscues, 455
    on reading and writing, 41, 283
Gordon, Dale, on teaching strategies, 40
Grammar
    and reading, 391–392

McCrum, Robert, on story of English, 102
McFarland, Mary, on ideas for encouraging critical thinking, 259
McMillan, Merna, on teaching critical thinking, 267
MacGinitie, Walter, on reading approaches, 489
MacLachlan, Patricia, *Sarah, Plain and Tall,* 32–34, 37–38, 391, end papers
MacNeil, Robert, on story of English, 102
Macon, James, on literary response, 489
Maeroff, Gene, on authors' day, 338
Magazine
    reading, 485–486
    writing by children, 135, 137, 339, 341
Magic Pot, 170
Magic school bus stories, 251
Main ideas, 157–159, 160, 221, 274, 313–314
Mainstreaming, 49
Make Way for Ducklings, 126
Maniac Magee, 53, 110, 391–392
Manna, Anthony, *Drama and Language,* 203
Manolakes, George, on content reading, 483
Manuscript writing, 420–430
Manzo, Anthony, on guided reading procedure, 470–471
Mapping data. See Data webs
Mapping stories, 320–324, A-4, A-5
Maria, Katherine, on learning disadvantaged, 60
Martin, Bill, on comprehension, 476
Martin, James, on sentence skills, 21
Martin, Samuel, on language, 92
Martinez, Miriam, on drama, 184, 203
Mary Poppins, 110, 189
Marzano, Robert, on cultivating thinking, 267
Mathematics and language learning, 157–158
Matrix charts, 482
May I Bring a Friend?, 165
Meaning-based language arts, 11, 15–22
Meeks, Margaret, on what happens during reading, 458
Meier, Donald, on books in the classroom, 489
Mellon, John, on sentencing, 354
Menyuk, Paula, on language development, 106
Merriam, Eve, on poetry, 301, 303–304
Messages in a Mailbox, 291
Metacognition, 147, 459, 471
Metaphor, 188, 301, 389, 466
Mice Twice, 115, 323–324
Microcomputers. See Computers
Migrant children, 57–58
Miller, Barbara, on sentences, 354
Miller, George, on top-down reading, 456, 457
Miller, Heidi, on phonics in whole language, 489
Miller, Howard, on multicultural literature unit, 56
Milz, Vera, on young children's knowledge of print, 279
Mind talk, 84–87, 270, 319, 463–464, 482
Minorities in books, 133–134

Miscues in reading, 454–455
Missing May, end papers
Modeling instruction, 34–35, 149–151, 157–158, 170, 212, 214, 215, 221–222, 320, 463–465, 481–482, 483
Modeling in writing, 16, 288, 310, 329
Model lessons
    brainstorming, 312–314, 361
    content area, 7–9, 44–48, 181–182, 312–314
    critical thinking, 1–7, 255–258
    dramatizing, 180–182
    experiencing and group composition, 2–9, 231–233
    handwriting, 422, 431–435
    language different, 44–48
    language experience, 231–233, 242–246
    listening, 107, 144–147
    literature-centered experiences, 2–7, 107, 135–139, 180–182, 243–246, 255–258
    meeting individual needs, 44–48
    paragraph writing, 312–314
    process writing, 270–275
    punctuation, 349–351
    reading, beginning, 443–448
    report writing, 7–9, 312–314
    sharing stories and information, 180–182, 204–206
    spelling, 395–398
    unit teaching, 2–7, 44–48, 135–139, 312–314
    writing skills, 312–314
    Yellow Ball Afternoon, 76–80
Moffett, James
    on emergent literacy, 285
    on inner speech, 85
    on spelling games, 395, 442
Moje, Elizabeth, on Dr. Seuss, 255
"Molly and Holly," 173–174, 175
Mom, the Wolf Man, and Me, 132
Mood
    in poems, 176
    in stories, 176
Moore, David, on reading/writing in content areas, 348
Moore, Margaret, on telecommunication, 290
Moores, D., on deafness, 67
Moral reasoning, 81–83
Morgan, Norah, *Teaching Drama,* 203
Morphemes, 91
Morris, Darrell, on concept of word, 398, 400, 412
Morrison, Marvin, on dictionaries, 418
Morrow, Lesley
    on story retelling, 183, 478
    on emergent readers, 285
Morton, Patricia, on verb poetry, 387
Moss, R. Kay, on early writing, 95, 288
Motifs of stories, 478, 479
Multicultural classrooms, 22, 49, 54–60
Murray, Donald, on writing 316, 348

Proud Taste for Scarlet and Minerva, 469
Propaganda, 170–172
Public Law 94–142, 49, 60, 66
Publishing children's writing, 20, 135, 137, 286, 336–342,
        428, 435–436
Punctuation marks
    activities for skill development, 331, 370, 372–375
    and choral speaking, 195, 198, 350
    as voice signals, 96, 195, 331, 375, 446
    in questions, 358
    model lesson on quotation marks, 349–351
Puppetry, 181, 192–194
Purpose, in listening and reading, 148–152
Purves, Alan, on reading response, 81–82
Putnam, Lynn, on dramatizing nonfiction, 185
Putzar, Edward, on haiku, 298

QAR strategy, 263
Questioning patterns, 22–23, 162–163, 211, 261–262, 330,
        335
Questioning strategies
    and brainstorming, 248–249
    and listening, 168–170
    as part of writing conference, 330
Questions
    levels of, 465–467
    to encourage discussions, 211, 261–262
    to encourage thinking about stories, 168–170, 261–262,
        444, 460, 465–467
Quintero, Elizabeth, on bilingualism and biliteracy, 54, 71
Quotation marks, 349–351, 366

Ramsey, John, on left handed writing, 434, 442
Rand, Ann, on words, 99
Rank ordering, 262–263
Raphael, Taffy
    on book clubs, 470
    on individualizing, 23
    on QAR strategy, 263
Raths, Louis, on teaching thinking, 172, 267
Ravitch, Diane, on children's knowledge level, 457
Read, Charles, on spelling, 398, 402, 414, 442
Readers' Theatre, 186, 454
Reading along while listening, 274, 285, 453, 464
Reading
    aloud, 2–3, 130, 146–147, 150, 163, 181, 183–184, 318,
        443–444
    and critical thinking, 263–264
    and prediction, 126–127
    and grammar, 390–392
    and talk, 470–471
    and writing, 14–15, 283–284, 317–318, 352, 467–470,
        472–475

assisted, 454
auditory discrimination, 445, 449
choral, 454
collaborative, 453
emergent, 443–448, 448–454
gifted, 63–66
in chunks of meaning, 446, 452
in content areas, 128–134, 318, 460, 461, 470–471,
        472–475, 480–483
interactive-constructive, 456–459
levels, 465–467
miscues, 454–455
model lesson, 443–448
oral, 453–454
pictures, 166, 176
purpose, 470–471
remedial, 61–62
response journal, 2, 3, 122, 169, 467–470
schema theory, 89, 456–457
sustained silent(SSR), 483–484
visual discrimination, 446, 448
whole language approach to, 90–91, 448–455
workshop, 443–448, 453
see also comprehension, vocabulary development
Reading Recovery Program, 61, 287
Reading/writing connection, 14–15, 183–184, 472–473
Reasoning, 254
Reciprocal teaching, 471
*Reflections on a Gift of Watermelon Pickle . . . and Other
        Modern Verse,* 303
Reconstruction of stories, 350, 355, 364–365, 446,
        451–452, 478
Reduction in language learning, 93–94
Rehearsal for writing, 312–313, 318–327
Repetitive stories, 114, 115, 122–123, 184, 323–324
Reporting activities, 78–79, 213–226
Reporting skills
    and creative thinking, 276
    checklist for, 228
    defining purposes of a report, 213–214
    developing and using guides, 205
    gathering information, 214
    news reporting, 78–79
    notetaking, 214–218
    organizing information, 218–222, 324–326
    presenting orally, 224–226
    referencing a topic, 214–222
    responding to, 154–155
    visual aids, 204–205
    writing, 294, 312–314, 324–327
Researching skills. See Reporting skills
Resource room programs, 61–62
Response to literature, 108, 109–110, 137–138, 183
Retarded speech, 69
Retelling, stories, 183–184, 478

Your Opinion of This Book

The author and editors of *Communication in Action: Teaching the Language Arts* would like your opinion of the book after you have read it. Your comments will help us not only in improving the next edition of the text but also in developing other books. We would appreciate your taking a few minutes to respond to the following questions. Please return the form to: College Marketing, Houghton Mifflin Company, 222 Berkeley Street, Boston, MA 02116-3764.

1. We would like to know your reaction to the following features of the text.

	Excellent	*Good*	*Adequate*	*Poor*
a. General interest level of the book compared to other educational texts	_____	_____	_____	_____
b. Writing style and readability	_____	_____	_____	_____
c. Clarity of presentation of ideas	_____	_____	_____	_____
d. Value of the teaching-in-action descriptions at the beginning of chapters	_____	_____	_____	_____
e. Value of specific teaching ideas in each chapter	_____	_____	_____	_____
f. Value of the Forums	_____	_____	_____	_____
g. Usefulness of the sections that give hints for building and refining your teaching skills	_____	_____	_____	_____
h. Value of the points in the margins	_____	_____	_____	_____
i. Helpfulness of the end-of-chapter summaries	_____	_____	_____	_____
j. Your overall evaluation of the book	_____	_____	_____	_____

2. Check one or more of the responses and complete the information requested.

I read *Communication in Action* as part of

_____ an undergraduate course called _____.

_____ a graduate course called _____.

_____ a workshop called _____.

_____ my personal reading _____.

_____ other. Explain: _____

3. Check one or more of the responses.
   I am currently

   _____ a teacher of preschoolers.   _____ a teacher of primary children.

   _____ a teacher of intermediate-school children.   _____ a supervisor.

   _____ an undergraduate in a four-year college.   _____ an administrator.

   _____ a librarian.

   _____ an undergraduate in a two-year college.

   _____ other. Explain _____

   _____

   _____

4. Do you intend to keep the book as part of your professional library?

   Yes ☐   No ☐   Maybe ☐

   Please tell us why. _____

   _____

   _____

5. Please indicate the numbers of the chapters you found most helpful to you as an educator or educator-to-be. _____

   Why did you find these chapters most helpful? _____

   _____

   _____

6. Please indicate the numbers of the chapters you found least helpful to you.

   _____

   Why did you find these chapters least helpful? _____

   _____

   _____

7. What did you like best about this book? _____

   _____

   _____

8. What did you like least about this book? _____

   _____

   _____

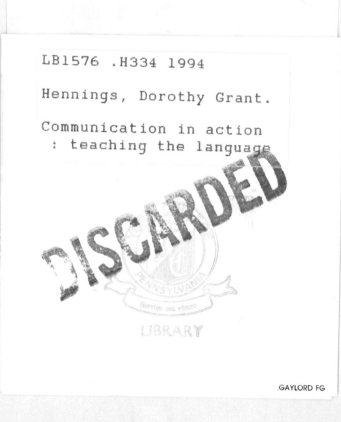

A Literature-Based Unit

FOCAL DIMENSION

Life in Appalachia: Yesterday and Today

The Appalachians of North America extend in a belt from the St. Lawrence valley in Quebec to the Gulf coastal plain in Alabama. It is a region of mountains rich in coal, iron, petroleum, and natural gas. The southern part of this region, where the mountains pass through such states as Tennessee and West Virginia, is the area usually called "Appalachia."

Themes of the Unit

✦ The family group can be a source of love and security; members of a family support each other through pain and hardship; everyone needs something or someone to hang on to; the family is a strong influence in Appalachia.

✦ Our way of life—our socioeconomic level, our religion, our values, our art, our music, our language, our food, our dress, our way of relating to one another—varies depending on the region of the world in which we live. We must all be accepting of the diversity that is all around us.

Objectives of the Unit   Through unit study, children will become more able to

✦ identify the ways geography and natural resources of an area affect people living there and determine to some extent their economic level, the manner in which they make a living, and their everyday life style (dress, food, homes, architecture);

✦ identify interrelationships among the music, art, religion, and language of a region;

✦ accept differences in language, dialects, and religion as a natural aspect of a diverse world; perceive ethnic stereotyping in literature;

✦ build understanding of a region through study of photographs and art that depict the unique way of life of peoples living there;

✦ relate the geography of a region to its geomorphic origins;

✦ plot locations and topography on a map; read locations and topography on a map;

✦ identify characteristics of a family, the ties that bind a family together, and the ways family members can support each other; relate more effectively to members of their own family, be more accepting of the differences that exist within a family, and perceive the needs of others;

✦ bring their own background to bear on the meanings that an author has written into a story and consider the ultimate meaning of a story;

✦ identify uses of figurative language as well as instances of dialect in writing;

✦ use context clues to figure out word meanings and the grammatical use of words;

✦ infer what a character is like by looking at what he or she does or says in a story;

✦ relate setting to plot and characters in a story;

✦ compare and contrast characters in a particular story and in several stories set in the same place; compare how different characters meet similar problems;

✦ compare and contrast events within and between stories set in the same place;

✦ compare and contrast how different authors handle similar content and style their writing;

✦ judge the effectiveness of an author's style and generate opinions of what they themselves like in a story;

✦ compare and contrast the effectiveness of different genre and media in communicating the way of life of a people—art, music, film, photography, poetry, story, nonfiction;

✦ organize data obtained from several sources using a data synthesis chart;

✦ respond in pictorial, written (poetry, story, and nonfiction), and oral form to what they read;

✦ review what they have written in response to what they have read and select a few pieces for revision and for ultimate publication in a class literary magazine.